# introduction to human resource management



second edition

paul banfield
& rebecca kay

OXFORD
UNIVERSITY PRESS

**OXFORD**
**UNIVERSITY PRESS**

Great Clarendon Street, Oxford OX2 6DP

Oxford University Press is a department of the University of Oxford.
It furthers the University's objective of excellence in research, scholarship,
and education by publishing worldwide in

Oxford New York

Auckland Cape Town Dar es Salaam Hong Kong Karachi
Kuala Lumpur Madrid Melbourne Mexico City Nairobi
New Delhi Shanghai Taipei Toronto

With offices in

Argentina Austria Brazil Chile Czech Republic France Greece
Guatemala Hungary Italy Japan Poland Portugal Singapore
South Korea Switzerland Thailand Turkey Ukraine Vietnam

Oxford is a registered trade mark of Oxford University Press
in the UK and in certain other countries

Published in the United States
by Oxford University Press Inc., New York



First Edition 2008



British Library Cataloguing in Publication Data
Data available

Library of Congress Cataloging in Publication Data
Library of Congress Control Number: 2011938964

Typeset by Graphicraft Limited, Hong Kong
Printed in Italy on acid-free paper by L.E.G.O. S.p.A.—Lavis TN

ISBN 978-0-19-958108-5

10 9 8 7 6 5 4 3 2 1

# Introduction to
# Human Resource Management

# Contents in brief

# Contents in full

# List of Case Studies

## Part 3 HRM Processes

## Part 4 Case Studies

# About the Authors

## Paul Banfield

Is recently retired from his full-time career as a lecturer in HR and Programme Director at Newcastle Business School. He is still an active member of the Chartered Institute of Personnel and Development (CIPD) and continues to work as one of their national examiners. In addition to several external examinership roles at UK universities, his primary work is as an EU designated International Expert, working on an EU funded project in Serbia which is designed to build HR capacity and capability in the SME sector.

'To the countless students, who over a wonderfully satisfying and rewarding career, have inspired and challenged me to be a better teacher.'

## Rebecca Kay

Is an HR Consultant based in Sheffield. She is Fellow of the Chartered Institute of Personnel and Development (CIPD) and has a degree in Psychology with the University of Liverpool. She has twelve years' experience in HR managerial roles in the food industry with Northern Foods, including Graduate Development and latterly as HR Manager at Fox's Biscuits. She has nine years' experience at HR Director level in the engineering industry at both Stanley Tools and latterly Cooper Safety.

'I have been fortunate enough to work with many inspirational and talented colleagues and managers, along with a few who have been the opposite. Whilst I have learned from them all, it is the aforementioned who make it all worthwhile.'

# About the Book

Most authors claim that their book is different, and by implication, better, than many others currently in use. Often however, the differences, where they exist, are more superficial than substantial and tend to relate to the choice and range of HRM subject areas rather than the way these areas are treated. We feel that many contemporary introductory HRM books are very similar in terms of style, approach, and coverage and that many are written by academics in an academic style that fails to reflect the realities, uncertainties, and challenges facing those with responsibilities for HRM. This led us to believe that there was a need for a book on HRM that approached the subject in significantly different ways.

What seemed to us to be missing from much of the literature available to tutors and students was a perspective on HRM that combined a strong academic underpinning with a realistic and informed understanding of the challenges faced by HR professionals and line managers in delivering their objectives. We also wanted to adopt a much more critical approach to the relationship between HR activities and their associated outcomes (often taken for granted), and in doing so, question the unproblematical way in which HR contributions to employee behaviour and business performance are often presented.

It is one thing to have a concept of the book that you would like to write—one that aspires to overcome the gap between 'theory' and 'practice'—but quite another to produce one that actually achieves this and provides students with a set of analytical tools and frameworks that are academically rigorous but also offer important insights into the realities, uncertainties, and compromises that HR practitioners and line managers are faced with on an almost daily basis. Only our readers will be able to say whether we have achieved our objective, but we believe that we have reached our goal for the following reasons:

1. It is jointly written by a lecturer in HR and a senior HR practitioner who worked closely together on all the chapters. The result is a fusion of both academic and practical insights which explore how HR is actually practised and experienced in the workplace, and thus overcomes the idealistic and partial insights of many other textbooks.
2. We take a holistic and integrated approach to HRM which avoids presenting HRM as a series of separate activities and as a separate management function detached from wider organizational and business interests and priorities.
3. The text offers an abundance of real-life examples. All chapters offer a range of challenging student activities, mini-cases (insights), and end-of-chapter case studies which cover a range of organizational and business contexts, both in the UK and overseas.
4. The text actively engages students in their own learning and understanding of HRM by presenting them with real-life situations that can be discussed either in a seminar/group context or on a private study basis.
5. The three chapter-long, real-life case studies at the end of the book provide detailed insights into the role of HRM in three different business scenarios: the setting up of an assessment centre; the opening of a new hotel; and the closure of a factory. These chapters draw on the topics covered earlier in the text such as planning, recruitment, selection, redundancy, learning, and training but relate the decisions taken in these areas to the achievement of strategic organizational objectives.
6. The extensive Online Resource Centre provides all the teaching and learning materials needed to support each chapter, removes the need for lecturers to look for additional class and test materials, and gives students the resources they need to build their understanding and to check what actually happened in many of the real-life case studies.

# How to Use This Book

Key Terms

**Hiring or employing** The overall process of taking on new staff from outside the organization.

**External recruitment** The process of identifying and attracting potential employees to an organization to fill current or future vacancies.

**Internal recruitment** The process of identifying current employees who may be suitable for newly created vacancies or for replacing staff who leave.

**Best practi** HR activitie irrespective

**Best fit** Th and how it circumstan It links acti following a

Opportuni

## KEY TERMS

Each chapter begins with clear definitions and explanations of important terms which are explored fully later in the chapter. Understanding these terms from the start makes the ideas and arguments more accessible.

Learning Objectives

As a result of reading this chapter and using the additional web-bas

- identify SHRM as a distinctive approach to and framework for making decisions about how to manage people at work;
- understand what being strategic means and how strategic contribution can be established;
- recognize that implementing chosen HR strategies is problematical and almost always involves changes people b
- understa contribu
- identify consiste culture,

## LEARNING OBJECTIVES

Each chapter establishes the important learning objectives that you can achieve as a result of reading the text, engaging in the different activities, and using the Online Resource Centre.

**STUDENT ACTIVITY 4.1**

1. Test the validity and acceptability of the formula fo organizations for information on how, if at all, they ca amend the formula, in the light of what is found, to in
2. Generate estimated or actual information on financial values for t value for specific recruitment exercises.

## STUDENT ACTIVITIES

All chapters offer several Student Activities that are clearly linked to the preceding text and enable you to learn through practice. They are often research based and problem solving, allowing you to develop your skills through group activities and presentations.

HRM INSIGHT 4.1 **The legal practice that nearly go**

Celia Johnson had been employed by Richard Curtis, ser and Smith, to bring some structure and order to the fir the HR function had effectively been limited to a part-ti after all recruitment and reward matters. In an increasingly compe had been struggling to attract and retain experienced lawyers, some roles, also had to manage different departments within the firm. Ric managerial team, was always on the lookout for new staff.

The firm had no recruitment strategy as such: recruitment was ve external networks, and on following up enquiries and the CVs subm careers. The firm didn't advertise positions and had no formal selectio

## HRM INSIGHTS

Each chapter offers a number of mini case studies that present different scenarios and challenges experienced in the real world of business. They address a varied range of HR problems and requirements to show how HRM operates in practice. They are accompanied by questions.

PRACTITIONER INSIGHT **Francesca Fowler, HR Dir**

At Nottingham Trent University, recruitment is importan opportunity to bring new talent into the organization but to be sure that we are recruiting for the right role. By follo legally compliant and give careful consideration on whether to replac make sure that we use a thorough selection process to bring the best getting it wrong are high and it would be difficult and costly to addr decision.

## PRACTITIONER INSIGHTS

Interviews from practitioners from a variety of organizations ranging from large public and private sector organizations to small companies provide a first-hand reflection on practice from twelve individuals.

RESEARCH INSIGHT 4.1

To take your learning further you might want to read this

**Rioux, S.M. and Bernthal P. (1999), 'Recruitment and S***sions International***

This article looks at the recruitment and selection strategies used by better strategies result in more positive organizational outcomes. T more likely it is that the organization will recruit and retain satisfied importance of the internet for advertising vacancies and discusses w ment practices.

## RESEARCH INSIGHTS

Key papers are summarized at relevant points to help broaden your understanding of the topics covered in each chapter.

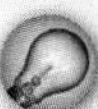

KEY CONCEPT STAGNATION

This term relates to the detrimental effect on creativity, with relying largely, or entirely, on the existing workforce t from outside, which can bring new ideas, challenge, and v to the long-term decline of an organization that is too inward-looking

This importance of integrating recruitment and selection into a w supported by research conducted by Reed Executive, one of t

## KEY CONCEPTS

New concepts are highlighted and explained where they first appear in the text. These key concepts have specific meanings and are part of the language of HRM, and give a strong theoretical and analytical grounding to each chapter.

are used in the assessment process, applicants' ambitions and coaching is used to ensure the rapid integration of new recrui will be much greater than if these requirements were ignore mistakes can be made and the 'wrong' people hired, with unfo for the employee.

Signpost to Chapters 11 and 12: Learning and Deve implications of underperforming staff

Collins (2001) offers an opinion on the importance of being a before making the job offer:

## SIGNPOSTS

Signposts are used throughout the book to indicate where similar HR activities are addressed in other sections in a complementary or a more extensive way.

CASE STUDY

The Midlands Spring Company

The Midlands Spring Company manufactures a wide range of spri industries. It was established by David Wheeler in 1986 and employs in its Peak District factory. David recently passed over management her husband, Alan Johnston. David comes in to work a couple of lie outside the company. Jenny and Alan have been effectively run and, while they have made considerable progress in sorting out so still struggling to deal with all of the issues that are preventing t concentrated his energy on the sales and marketing side of the b

## END-OF-CHAPTER CASE STUDIES

Each chapter finishes with a substantial case study and accompanying discussion questions. These case studies illustrate organizational practice and associated outcomes or create scenarios which present you with problems and challenges. They incorporate many of the key issues and activities covered in the chapter and integrate these in a more holistic way.

REVIEW QUESTIONS

1. Who should be involved in recruiting and selecting staf
2. What are the arguments for fitting the organization organization?
3. What do the concepts 'reliability' and 'validity' mean, ar
4. Making the right selection decision does not guarantee
5. From your own personal experiences of recruitment how do you feel organizations can get the maximur

## REVIEW QUESTIONS

These are designed to reinforce learning by presenting important questions on some of the main themes and issues raised in the chapter. They can also help focus attention on the key learning outcomes and provide guidance for revision.

FURTHER READING

Advisory Conciliation and Arbitration Service (2010) *Deli*

Arnold, D. and Hartman, L. (2005) 'Beyond sweatshops: P *Ethics: A European review*. July, **14**:3, pp. 206–22.

Briscoe, D. and Schuler, R. (2004) 'Global ethics and labo *Human Resource Management*, 2nd ed. Routledge.

Clements, P. and Jones, J. (2005) *The Diversity Training Ha Changing Attitudes*, Kogan Page.

Confederation for British Industry (2008) 'Talent not toke

## FURTHER READING

Additional texts are recommended at the end of each chapter to help you gain deeper subject knowledge as well as learn about alternative ideas and contributions to the mainstream treatment of HRM issues and topics.

# How to Use the Online Resource Centre

## For Lecturers:

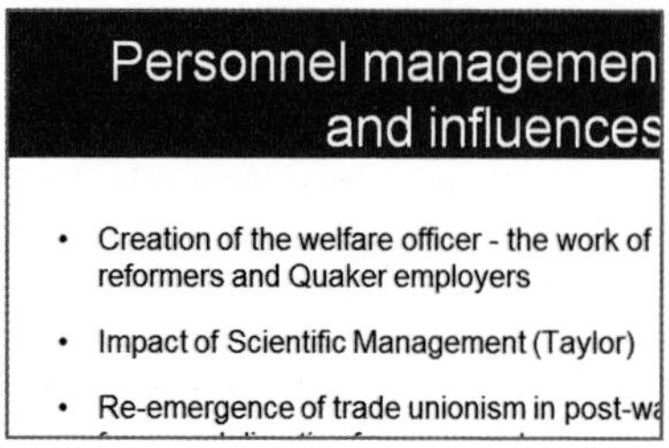

Personnel managemen
and influences

- Creation of the welfare officer - the work of reformers and Quaker employers
- Impact of Scientific Management (Taylor)
- Re-emergence of trade unionism in post-wa

### POWERPOINT LECTURE SLIDES

A suite of chapter-by-chapter PowerPoint slides has been included for use in your lecture presentations. They focus on the key points from each topic to save you time and make a useful class handout. They are fully customizable and can be tailored to match your own presentation style.

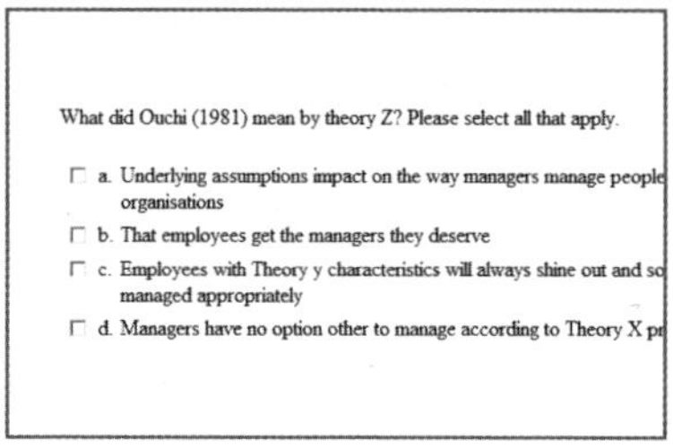

What did Ouchi (1981) mean by theory Z? Please select all that apply.

- a. Underlying assumptions impact on the way managers manage peopl organisations
- b. That employees get the managers they deserve
- c. Employees with Theory y characteristics will always shine out and so managed appropriately
- d. Managers have no option other to manage according to Theory X p

### TEST BANK

The test bank is a ready-made assessment tool that tests student understanding of HRM. Twenty questions per chapter are provided in a variety of question styles which can be imported into testing software and used in your Virtual Learning Environment with automated feedback and grading. This method helps your students understand where they need to improve, as well as informing you of their progress.

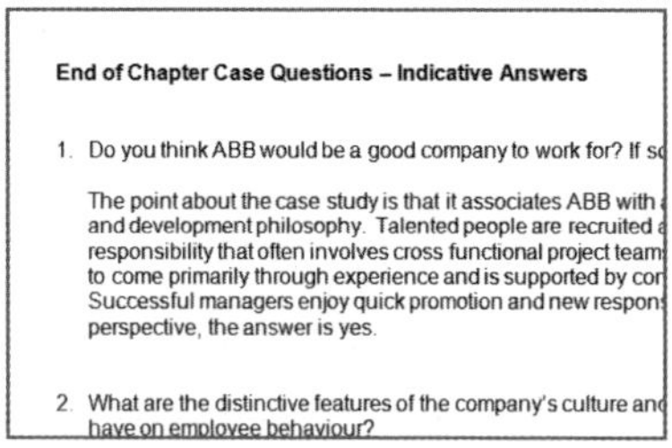

**End of Chapter Case Questions – Indicative Answers**

1. Do you think ABB would be a good company to work for? If s

   The point about the case study is that it associates ABB with and development philosophy. Talented people are recruited responsibility that often involves cross functional project team to come primarily through experience and is supported by co Successful managers enjoy quick promotion and new respon perspective, the answer is yes.

2. What are the distinctive features of the company's culture an have on employee behaviour?

### SUGGESTED ANSWERS TO END-OF-CHAPTER CASE STUDY QUESTIONS

Each chapter ends with a longer case study accompanied by questions. These highlight the key points that students should consider in their answers, to aid seminar preparation.

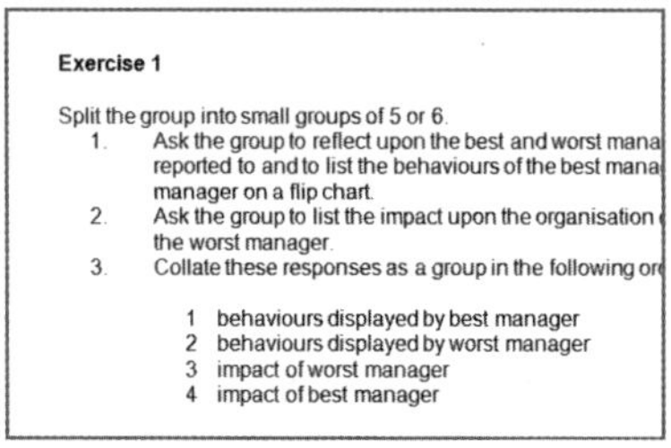

**Exercise 1**

Split the group into small groups of 5 or 6.

1. Ask the group to reflect upon the best and worst mana reported to and to list the behaviours of the best mana manager on a flip chart.
2. Ask the group to list the impact upon the organisation the worst manager.
3. Collate these responses as a group in the following or
   1. behaviours displayed by best manager
   2. behaviours displayed by worst manager
   3. impact of worst manager
   4. impact of best manager

### ADDITIONAL SEMINAR EXERCISES

Finding new and stimulating ways of reinforcing students' understanding of HRM topics can be difficult. These extra ideas for student activities to run in class, linked to key topics and arranged by chapter to fit with your module teaching, provide an additional source to boost your repertoire.

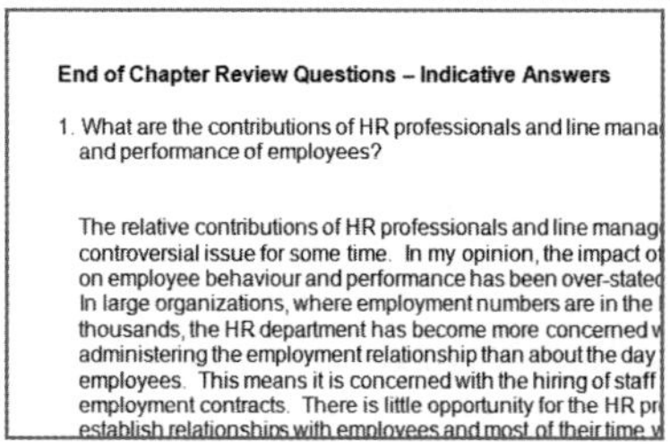

**End of Chapter Review Questions – Indicative Answers**

1. What are the contributions of HR professionals and line mana and performance of employees?

   The relative contributions of HR professionals and line manag controversial issue for some time. In my opinion, the impact o on employee behaviour and performance has been over-state In large organizations, where employment numbers are in the thousands, the HR department has become more concerned administering the employment relationship than about the day employees. This means it is concerned with the hiring of staff employment contracts. There is little opportunity for the HR p establish relationships with employees and most of their time

### DISCUSSION QUESTIONS AND SUGGESTED ANSWERS

Another resource to help seminar planning, these pertinent discussion questions help focus students on the key issues in each chapter and encourage debate of different viewpoints, thus improving their analytical skills. The suggested answers summarize the key points for consideration, and work as a quick reference guide for you to direct your students' discussion.

## For Students:

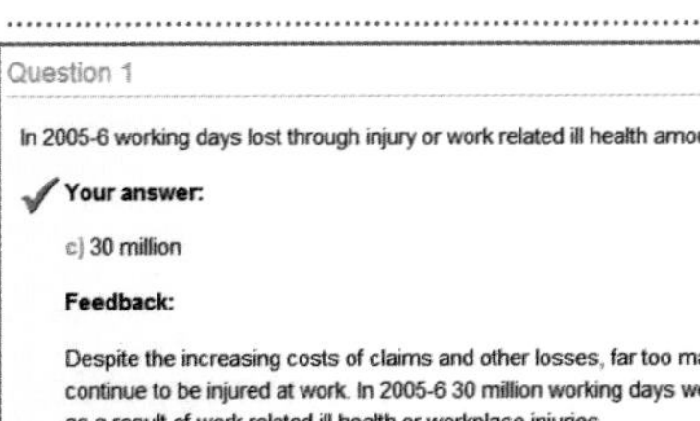


### MULTIPLE CHOICE QUESTIONS

Each chapter is accompanied by ten multiple choice questions that can be completed online to help test your understanding and aid revision. These self-marking questions include instant feedback on your answers and cross-reference to the textbook to assist with your independent study.

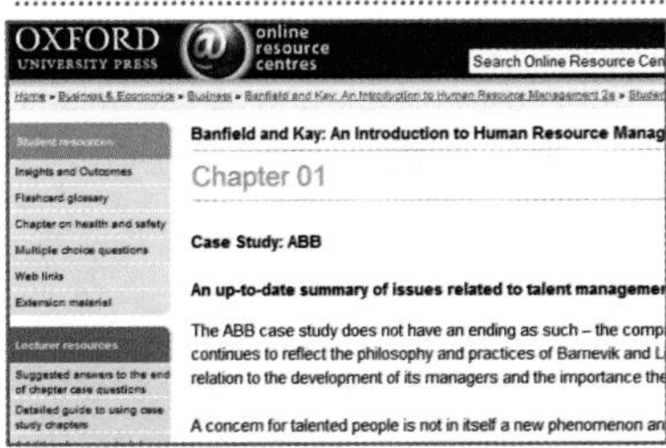


### INSIGHTS AND OUTCOMES

The reality of HRM is complex and far reaching and much can be learned from the outcomes of real-life cases cited in this book. How were these situations actually resolved? What were the developments that followed? How did the company respond? Where indicated in the textbook, HRM Insights and end-of-chapter case studies are followed up online, providing answers to these questions and in-depth analysis of these fascinating examples.

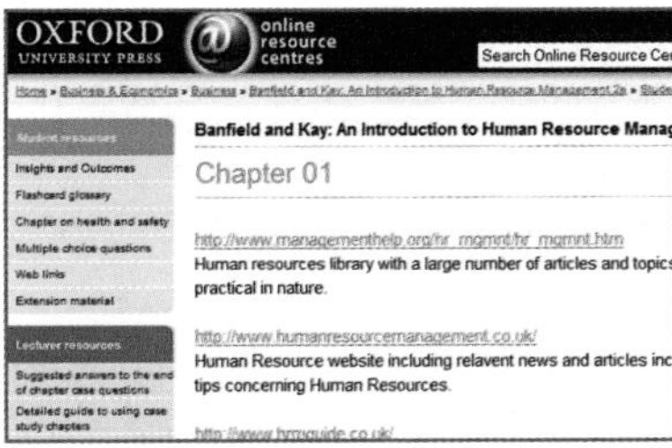


### WEB LINKS

Links to websites relevant to each chapter provide a useful hub from which to start your research project or essay.

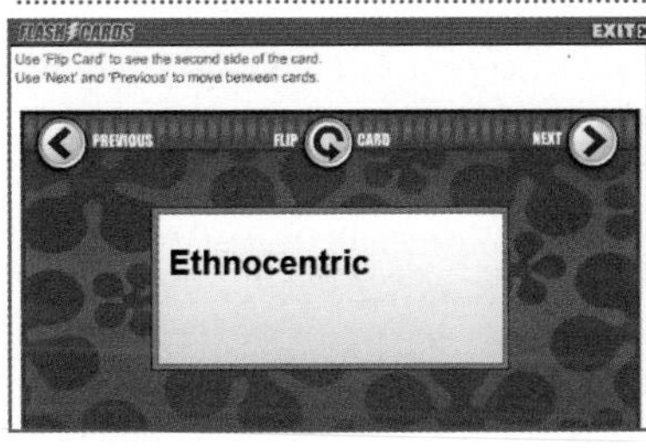


### FLASHCARD GLOSSARY

Learning the jargon associated with HRM can be a challenge, so these online flashcards have been designed to help you memorize the key terms used in the book. Click through the randomized definitions to see if you can identify which key term they are describing!

ORC extension material 2.5

What is the future for HR?

When considering the answer to this question, it is important to understand that it relates pr
HR department and the role of HR professionals, rather than being about human resource
and it is in this context that the debate is continuing. As far as human resource management
there is no equivalent question and debate. As Meisinger (p 189, 2005) asserts:

> The good news is that today the mantra 'people are our most important asset' is not jus
> For most leaders, it's the reality.

Not everyone would agree that each employee has the same value or potential as every othe
that employees are critical to organizational success is now generally accepted. In this sense,
human resource effectively has become even more important in the twenty-first century bec
the resources that organizations utilize, this is the one that is the most difficult to replicate an

### EXTENSION MATERIAL

Additional material of key topics is provided online. This coverage gives you a deeper understanding of interesting aspects of human resource management.

**www.oxfordtextbooks.co.uk/orc/banfield_kay2e/**

# Acknowledgements

I would like to acknowledge the many important contributions made to this book, particularly from Claire Wragg, Mags Healy, Christine Johnson, Yvonne O'Rourke, Dean Royles, Judy Crook, Chris Atkin, Trevor Lincoln, Roger Wilson, Daniel Goulding, Ali Samad, Hillary Collins, and David Lloyd.

Special thanks again goes to William Beckett whose experiences of running a successful business and managing people informs many parts of the book, and to Francesca Griffin and all the production team at OUP for their patience and professionalism.

*P.B.*

I would like to acknowledge the valuable contributions of Leigh Thomasson, Francesca Fowler, Beverley Hodson, and Katy Edmonds to this book. I would also once again like to thank my father Neil Kay, for his pride and encouragement and my brother, Steven Kay, for his guidance.

I would also like to thank the many people who have inspired and encouraged my development, thinking, and values in delivering a professional HR service and business partnership throughout my career, including Leigh Thomasson, Tony McLoughlin, Sally Cabrini, and Francesca Fowler.

*R.K.*

The authors and publisher would like to thank the many reviewers for their helpful comments and suggestions throughout the writing process.

They are grateful to the following for permission to reproduce copyright materials:

Figure 3.2 reprinted by permission of Harvard Business School Press, from *Human Resource Champions* by D. Ulrich, Boston, MA 1997, p. 24, © 1997 by the Harvard Business School Publishing Corporation, all rights reserved; Table 5.1 reproduced from WERS 2004 First Findings © Crown Copyright/ESRC/ACAS/Policy Studies Institute; Table 7.2 reproduced from *Diversity in Business: A Focus for Progress Survey Report* (CIPD, 2007), with the permission of the Chartered Institute of Personnel and Development, London; Figure 8.2 A Competency Model for Overseas Working is taken from *International Recruitment, Selection and Assessment* (P R Sparrow, 2006), with the permission of the publisher, the Chartered Institute of Personnel and Development, London; Table 9.4 Summary of 2004 Absence Surveys reproduced from *Managing Sickness Absence in the Public Sector—A Joint Review by the Ministerial Task Force for Health, Safety and Productivity and the Cabinet Office*, November 2004 © Crown Copyright/CBI; Figure 10.2 reproduced from Kolb, David A., *Experiential Learning: Experience as a Source of Learning*, © 1984, p. 42, Fig. 3.1, adapted with the permission of Pearson Education, Inc., Upper Saddle River, NJ; Figure 10.3 adapted from: Kolb, David A., *Experiential Learning: Experience as a Source of Learning*, and Honey, P and Mumford, A 2006, *The Learning Styles Questionnaire*; HRM Insight 10.3 Paul Kearns' Story of an Unhelpful Director, taken from *Evaluating the ROI from Learning* (P Kearns, 2005), with the permission of the publisher, the Chartered Institute of Personnel and Development, London.

Crown Copyright material is reproduced under Class Licence Number C01P000148 with the permission of OPSI and the Queen's Printer for Scotland.

Every effort has been made to trace and contact copyright holders but this has not been possible in every case. If notified, the publisher will undertake to rectify any errors or omissions at the earliest opportunity.

# Foundations of Human Resource Management

# 1

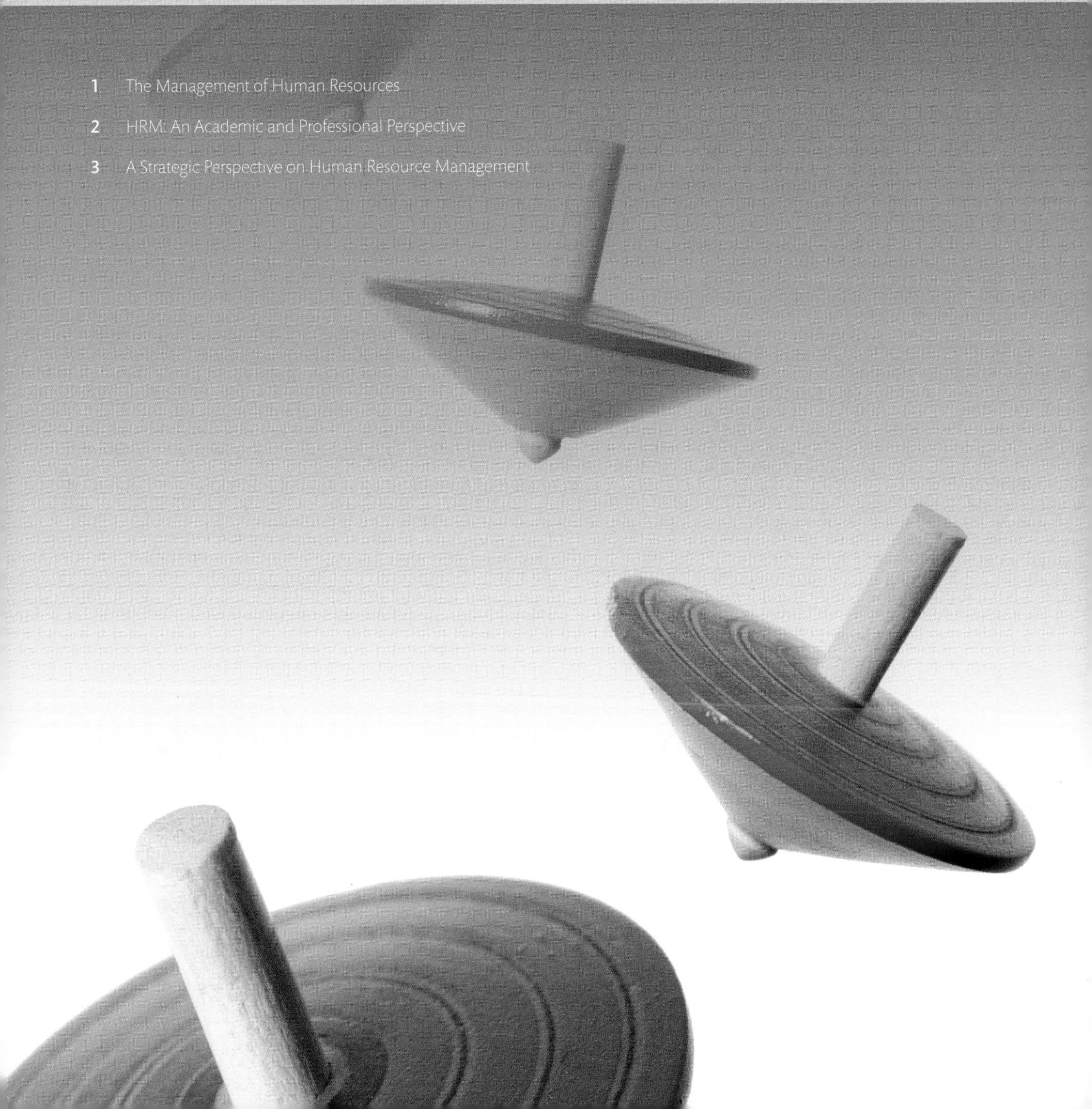

# The Management of Human Resources

# 1

## Key Terms

**Dialectic** The tension that arises between conflicting ideas, interacting forces, or competing interests. The term can also be used to explain the process of reconciling opposing opinions or facts by means of argument and discussion.

**Philosophy** An enduring framework of beliefs, values, and ways of doing things that can exist at the individual and organizational levels. A shared philosophy is a powerful way of creating a common purpose and set of expectations as to how people behave.

## Learning Objectives

As a result of reading this chapter and using the Online Resource Centre, you should be able to:

- understand the challenges faced by management in using people as human resources;
- understand the implications of changing environments for the way people are managed;
- develop effective strategies for managing tension and conflict at work;
- explain why an underpinning philosophy is a necessary part of effective people management;
- understand why the emotional dimension of work is critical to the effective management of people.

# Introduction

## Managing people in the twenty-first century

It might seem strange to begin our analysis of the management of human resources in the twenty-first century by looking back in time, but the reason for this is to do with our ability to learn from the past and to use this understanding to help make sense of the challenges facing management today and in the future. Learning about the way in which people have been, and should be, managed involves using our personal experiences of managing and being managed, and, for the more serious student, it also involves accessing the wealth of ideas, theories, stories, and research outputs contained in the numerous books and journals devoted to this subject. Not all of these are contemporary, and while many of the most influential were first published many years ago these are no less important for that.

Despite peoples' interest in understanding what managing organizations and people involves, and the ever-increasing amount of information and knowledge available to us, the enduring paradox is that many of today's managers still find the challenge difficult and frustrating. Even where seemingly major breakthroughs in our understanding of management occur (Peters and Waterman, 1982), it soon becomes apparent that many of the successful companies and managers identified by the authors have been unable to sustain their success in the face of rapidly changing environments and the contradictions inherent in employing and managing people.

It is still surprising, however, that, despite this ever-growing knowledge base, many of the problems that troubled earlier generations of managers are, broadly speaking, the same as those facing today's managers. Without claiming that the example below represents the situation in which all managers find themselves, it probably captures the experiences and sentiments of many. The quotation is taken from Tony Watson's influential book on management and the organization of work, and reflects the experiences, sense of frustration, and uncertainty articulated by one manager. It is an extract from part of a conversation between the author and a manager.

> **'So the problem is?'**
> **'It's the people management thing. It's handling the people who work for me. They are a constant headache. I've tried to read the books and I've been on people management courses. I didn't miss one of the OB classes on my MBA course. But I still despair at the difficulty I have with managing the people in my function; sorting out who is going to do what, getting them to do things I want, getting them to finish things on time, even getting them to be where I want them. And that's before I get into all the recruiting, training, appraising and all that stuff.'**
> (Watson, 2002)

It is highly probable that this manager's frustrations with his staff and what managing them involved was mirrored by their sense of frustration and dissatisfaction with him as a manager and the way in which he 'practised' management. Of course, there are many other managers who are more confident about what they do and would claim to be 'good at it', pointing to positive feedback from their staff as evidence of their competence and effectiveness. But the real point of the story is that, despite his efforts—and those of others in a similar position—to learn about managing and to become a better manager, he felt that he hadn't succeeded. Why? Was he looking in the wrong place, reading the wrong books, or listening to the wrong lecturers? We don't know why he failed to make progress: like so many others, whether they are students, human resources (HR) specialists, or line managers, although he was committed to becoming better at managing people, he just didn't seem to have made much progress.

So, where can answers to the question 'how do we manage people' be found? First of all, it is important to realize that this question is more rhetorical than literal. There are no answers as such, at least in the sense of universal and permanent solutions to the kinds of problem this manager and many others face. But if we are realistic and do not expect the search to be an easy or straightforward one, the fact that there are those who have found managing less problematic and, by consensus, are considered to be 'good managers' suggests that there is much we can learn. The important question, though, is not only about what managers need to learn about managing people but whether they *are* learning and as a result becoming more effective in their role. Anecdotal evidence about managers tends to be more about 'bad' managers rather than 'good' ones and it would be naïve to believe that the growth in the number of managers with formal qualifications necessarily translates into changed behaviour in the workplace. 'The Making of Managers' (Handy et al., 1987) and 'The Making of British Managers' (Constable and McCormick, 1987).

Robert Sutton in his witty but perceptive book on managers (and other employees) and their behaviours supports the idea that people leave their managers rather than their organization. He believes, using a distinctive American expression, that:

> **Most of us, unfortunately, have to deal with assholes in our workplaces at one time or another. The No Asshole Rule shows how these destructive characters damage their fellow human beings and undermine organisational performance.**
> (Sutton, 2007)

Taking a more positive line and basing their conclusions on extensive research undertaken by the Gallup corporation, Buckingham and Coffman link the quality and effectiveness of managers, and the performance orientated behaviour of their subordinates, to the answers to the following questions:

1. Do I know what is expected of me at work?
2. Do I have the materials and equipment I need to do my work right?
3. At work, do I have the opportunity to do what I do best every day?
4. In the last seven days, have I received recognition or praise for doing good work?
5. Does my supervisor, or someone at work, seem to care about me as a person?
6. Is there someone at work who encourages my development?
7. At work, do my opinions count?
8. Does the mission/purpose of my company make me feel my job is important?
9. Are my co-workers committed to doing quality work?
10. Do I have a best friend at work?
11. In the last six months, has someone at work talked to me about my progress?
12. This last year, have I had opportunities at work to learn and grow?

The more the answers to these questions are in the affirmative, the more likely the employee will value his or her manager, be a high-performing worker, and less likely to be thinking of leaving the organization. Managers are seen as critical to how a person behaves and performs at work. They argue that:

> **The talented employee may join a company because of its charismatic leaders , its generous benefits, and its world class training programs, but how long the employee stays and how productive he is while he is there is determined by his relationship with his immediate supervisor.**
> (Buckingham and Coffman, 2005)

Accepting that many organizations have understood the importance and implications of these questions and have acted accordingly, whilst others still seem to struggle, we need to know what it is that accounts for such variations in the competence of different managers? One explanation might be linked to the possession of different traits and abilities that are more inherent than acquired, and which lead to certain individuals having the potential to be better managers than others. It might also be because they have learnt to be better managers through reflecting on their personal experiences of managing and because of their sensitivity to the effect that their behaviours have on others. Is good people management something that can be learnt, using the right theories, concepts, and practices, or is it, like leadership, a capability that (some argue) you are somehow born with?

On the one hand, this may be too simplistic a proposition because it forces us to choose between one extreme and another, and, more realistically, the answer might lie somewhere in-between. On the other hand, it does have the virtue of forcing us to consider the merits of both explanations before we reach our own conclusions.

Moreover, managing people is not only about the behaviour and approach of individual managers, but also about the way in which organizations, and the team of managers who influence their philosophy and culture, create particular kinds of environments within which both managers and employees work. When people apply for jobs, not only are they interested in the salary, benefits package, and development opportunities, but they also want to know: 'What is it like working here?' The *Sunday Times* carries out an annual survey of the best places to work in the UK and the results provide valuable insights into why the top-ranking companies are voted by their employees as the best companies to work for (www.bestcompanies.co.uk). What do these organizations know and do that sets them apart from those that are less successful, or those that struggle to get even the basics right? Why is it that, if those organizations who appear to be at least successful in the short term are prepared to publicize their achievements and allow their employees to explain why they are such good places to work, other organizations can't try to emulate them? Or is the problem not one of learning from what others do, but rather one of managers either not liking or agreeing with what they see, or having difficulty in applying the lessons to their own organization that others seem to have learnt so well?

Of all the authors who have influenced the contents and approach to managing people adopted in this book, Jeffrey Pfeffer and Robert Sutton stand out for special recognition and many of their articles and books are referred to in subsequent chapters. However, it is one of their most recent works that is relevant at this point, although many of the key arguments they make are explored in further detail in the next chapter. In *Hard Facts, Dangerous Half-Truths and Total Nonsense* (Pfeffer and Sutton, 2006), they caution against the attractive but misleading belief that becoming a better manager is based on knowing what successful managers do and then somehow trying to learn from and copy their behaviours, a practice sometimes known as 'benchmarking'. Citing Toyota as an example they argue that:

> **Toyota's success is not a set of techniques but its philosophy – the mind-set of total quality management and continuous improvement it has embraced.**

They quote a manager who attended one of their classes who realized the danger of an unthinking or casual approach to benchmarking:

> **We have been benchmarking the wrong things. Instead of copying what others do, we ought to copy how they think.**
> (Pfeffer and Sutton, 2006)

Learning how to become a better manager of people isn't quite as easy as some would have us believe!

Of course, the difficulties that contemporary managers appear to face in learning the 'secrets' of managerial success might have a completely different explanation. Could it be the case that the very nature of what managing people involves has changed so much and continues to change at such a rapid pace that what can be learnt from the past and from our contemporaries quickly loses its value and relevance? If this explanation has any merit, it means that today's managers are looking in the wrong place and learning the wrong lessons for the constantly evolving challenges they face now and will face in the future. If the factors that contribute to managerial success are contextually specific and time-limited, as opposed to being universal and enduring, then our knowledge about management quickly becomes redundant and even irrelevant. Alternatively, the challenge may not be one of discovering new answers and creating new knowledge, but rather one of making sense of what we already know and beginning to use this knowledge more effectively.

At the moment, we can only speculate on these questions, and we will return to them later in the chapter, but the point we would make is that much of what needs to be known about managing people already exists: we actually know more than we think we do. The real challenge is to know where to look and what to look for (Pfeffer and Sutton, 2000).

**STUDENT ACTIVITY 1.1 Researching the Latest *Sunday Times* Top 100 Companies to Work For**

1. Split the seminar group into three groups.
2. The task of group 1 is to research the top ten best big companies to work for and present their findings to the whole group in the form of a PowerPoint presentation.
3. Group 2 has the same task but focusing on the top ten best small companies.
4. The task for group 3 is to read and summarize the main points in Sutton's book (Sutton, R.I. (2007) *The No Asshole Rule: Building a Civilized Workplace and Surviving One That Isn't*, Warner Business Books).
5. In open discussion, explore the findings produced by all three groups and draw appropriate inferences and conclusions.

# Connecting the Past to the Present

The idea that the past has an important contribution to make to understanding the challenges contemporary managers face is grounded in the belief that learning about anything is always built upon what is already known, what has already been tried and what has worked, or not, in particular conditions. While the past provides neither neatly packaged answers nor the secrets of good people management (there aren't any, as such), it does offer insights and reference points that help us to make sense of where we are now and to consider whether the challenges managers face now are the same, different in degree, or different in kind, to those faced by earlier generations of managers.

Try to imagine that you are living in the era of the Egyptian Pharaohs and are sitting on the banks of the River Nile watching the Pyramids being built. What would you have seen? Lots of people would have been toiling in rather unpleasant conditions—the temperature would certainly have been quite hot; different kinds of raw materials would have been moving around the site and the skills and energy of many different kinds of people would have been used to complete the project to specification. You might even have witnessed the odd accident or two, and have noticed groups of people wearing different clothes, walking around and looking important, and generally checking up on things. It's also conceivable that, instead of watching from afar, you might actually have been one of the thousands of workers engaged in building the Pyramids or even the Egyptian equivalent of an employment administrator, with responsibility for ensuring that the workers were fed, housed, and paid (interestingly, contemporary opinion suggests that most workers were in some kind of paid employment as opposed to being used as slaves). Depending on your own skills and experience, you might even have been an overseer—the equivalent of a modern-day supervisor—with responsibility for organizing resources and making sure the workers did what was required of them.

If it's difficult to project yourself so far back in time, consider a more recent period—the industrialization of Britain in the nineteenth and twentieth centuries, and specifically the construction of the country's rail and canal networks. Where did all the workers who built these monuments to Victorian Britain come from? How did they learn the skills they needed, and who determined what and how they were paid? When employers today try to overcome labour shortages in, for example, teaching, nursing, and plumbing, by recruiting people from abroad, we should remember that many of the Irish 'navvies', who built the railways and canals, were also brought in because of labour and skill shortages in England. In times of economic expansion, many industries face the same kind of resource problems: where to get the necessary labour resources with the right skills; how to get the most out of those resources; what to do with them when projects are completed or the economic cycle moved in a downward direction. Has anything fundamentally changed?

Whether those who managed people in Egypt in the fourth century BC and nineteenth-century Britain had an easier task than that of managers today is an arguable point, although given that the situation of the twenty-first-century employee has improved beyond all recognition in comparison with that of our historical comparators—the modern-day employee benefiting from a 35-hour week, extensive employment rights, and compensation for being treated unfairly—there might be a few contemporary managers who believe that the task has definitely become more difficult and complicated! There may also be some employees who might look back in time and wonder what life would have been like without workplace stress, but long hours, authoritarian management, and dangerous working conditions represent equally unattractive features of employment and work.

A tentative conclusion that emerges from these brief references to previous eras might be that, despite differences in organizational form, the power of managers, technology, and social relationships, the challenges that managers faced and the experiences of being employed are not fundamentally different today from the experiences of our predecessors. But, while we have suggested that the fundamentals might not have changed much over time (see www.accel-team.com), it is also undeniable that the conditions in which people are employed and managed have changed as our economic, political and social systems have evolved and become more sophisticated and employee-orientated. A direct consequence of this is that the task of managing has become more complicated and problematic, in the sense that success, even when achieved, is never complete or permanent. It is also subject to more constraints and pressures than ever before. If managing people, or rather managing people effectively—there is an important distinction between the two—was never easy, it is certainly more complex and challenging for the manager in the twenty-first century.

Today's managers have to ensure that goods and services are provided profitably and efficiently, while maximizing the productivity of their workforce. They have to do this in an arena of rising expectations from all stakeholders, global competition, and an ever-changing balance of rights, duties, and responsibilities. But the challenge to management goes beyond this, they also have to ensure that the individuals and teams creating these goods and services work in environments that:

- are rewarding;
- provide opportunities for personal growth and development;
- generate commitment to the organization;
- encourage employees to use their capabilities and potential to the full and in the interests of the organization.

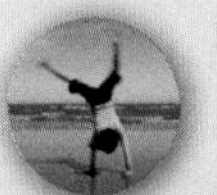

**STUDENT ACTIVITY 1.2 Understanding the Importance of the Working Environment.**

Read the article by Michael West (West, M. (2005) 'Hope springs eternal', *People Management*)

1. On one PowerPoint slide summarize the six main points you think West is making.
2. On a second slide list the changes that an organization could make to create a more positive working environment.
3. On a third slide list the reasons why many organizations find it difficult to build such environments.

It might be argued that those charged with managing organizations have two distinctive, but related, challenges to meet. Firstly, they have to ensure that the interests and objectives of the organization itself are met; secondly, they must understand, and go as far as possible to meet, the legitimate interests and needs of their employees. For the student trying to make sense of whether these two challenges are equally important, it might be worth noting what one successful employer and managing director remarked. In a conversation with one of the authors, William Beckett, head of a small, but successful, plastics manufacturing company in Sheffield commented:

> **the relationship between these is clear: if I don't ensure that the company remains competitive and survives, then my employees' interests don't matter—there won't be any employees, or managers for that matter, to worry about.**

Many other employers (particularly those in the private sector) would probably share this view, but it is also worth noting that one of the most important developments in recent years has been the increasing prominence and importance given to what might be described as the 'people dimension' of management. The reasons for this increasing recognition that 'people matter' are complex and changing, but a consequence, by which managers in earlier times were probably less troubled, is the tension that is created between the interests of the business and those of the people it employs. The squaring of the circle, for managers who are part of this dialectic, is becoming increasingly difficult to achieve.

The basic premise of this book is that, however difficult a challenge managing people represents, some managers and some organizations have been more successful than others who continue to struggle. Why is this? In trying to answer this question, it is worth remembering that, while many organizations claim to be successful, this success is often short-lived and has little to do with developing sustainable people management practices that are effective over the long term. The rise and fall of management 'fads' is also testament to the attraction of 'quick fixes' and easy solutions to requirements and challenges that are anything but superficial and easy to meet. Yet it is possible to identify organizations, as O'Reilly and Pfeffer (2000) have done, which combine profitability and durability through the successful engagement of the emotional and intellectual resources of their people, even though the authors accept that the companies they identify may not be able to sustain their successes forever. What do these companies do that makes them successful and which, at the same time, results in high levels of employee satisfaction? This is the question that this chapter tries to answer.

## Today's Challenges

Before we move on to consider the nature of the challenge that all managers face, it is important to consider the impact of contemporary changes in work and employment that have helped to shape the internal and external environments within which managers have to operate. The changes outlined below represent distinctive and influential characteristics of the postmodern age of employment.

- The rise of self-employment and the independent worker

  Many more people are 'free' to work or not, depending on their particular circumstances, than ever before. Those who want and choose to work also have more choice with regards to who they work for, the kind of work they do, and for how long they are prepared to work. 'Portfolio working' reduces a person's dependency on an individual employer and creates a workforce more able and predisposed to shape its own careers and lifestyles. These people are also able to exercise greater control over levels of 'discretionary effort' and are willing to engage in negotiations over what has become known as the 'psychological contract' (Hiltrop, 1996; Castells, 2000).

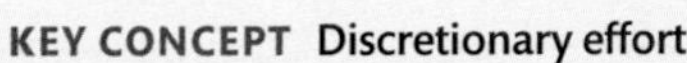

**KEY CONCEPT Discretionary effort**

Effort or performance that is additional to that which the employee is contractually required to deliver. Discretionary effort, by definition, is determined by the individual employee, or by a group of employees, and can represent a significant additional resource if they choose to make this available to management. It can be thought of as the difference between what employees are minimally required to give and what they are capable of giving. One problem with trying to increase the level of discretionary effort is that it is often associated with additional payments and is only made available if it is paid for. This has the potential for increasing the costs of labour, creating the paradox of increased performance but lower productivity. Effective managers are often those that generate higher levels of discretionary from their employees but without having to pay for it!

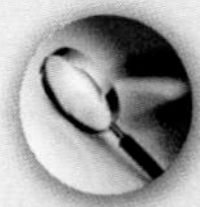

**RESEARCH INSIGHT 1.1**

**Lloyd, R. (2008) 'Discretionary Effort and the Performance Domain', *The Australian and New Zealand Journal of Organisational Psychology*, 1, pp. 22–34.**

The article by Lloyd explores the concept of discretionary effort and links this to employee engagement and work-life balance: and in so doing highlights the issues and conditions that have to be met as employers seek to increase levels of discretionary effort amongst their employees.

Read the article by Lloyd and:

- Explore the link between discretionary effort and the level of employee skills.
- Consider the significance of employee autonomy for discretionary effort.
- Summarize Lloyd's conclusions.

**KEY CONCEPT The psychological contract**

This term is used to describe the unwritten, often unarticulated and not necessarily shared, expectations that exist between employees and managers (as representatives of the organization), which influence the relationship between the two parties and particularly the behaviour of employees (Coyle-Shapiro and Kessler, 2000).

- Changes in the external regulation of employment

  The power of managers to act unilaterally in areas such as hiring and firing, promotion, and payment has been reduced by developments in UK and European legislation that give greater rights to employees and create new responsibilities for employers.

  Particularly important examples of this trend are to be found in the areas of race, gender, and age discrimination; employment protection; the treatment of pregnant women; and trade union membership. One extreme example of the influence of the law on employment decisions can be found when the Swiss giant Nestlé was ordered by a French court to reopen a loss-making plant, employing 427 workers, which had been closed in June 2005 (Evans-Pritchard, 2005). Despite sustained losses over several years, and a commitment either to find the employees jobs in other parts of France or to offer an early retirement package, the judge ordered the company to restart production and re-employ the workers—a decision that was described by Nestlé as 'unbelievable and unprecedented'. While such extreme cases of legal intervention in business and employment are rare, the trend within the European Union to limit management's freedom to take rational business decisions where these threaten the legitimate interests of employees is increasing.

- The emergence of new ideas and ways of managing associated with inward investment and the spread of 'new knowledge'

  Since the days when much of UK industry was regarded as beyond hope, with industries such as motor manufacturing associated with unreliable products, outdated working practices, a strike-prone workforce, and 'macho management', much of the UK's manufacturing sector has been transformed by the influx of new management thinking and practices. Many of these changes can be linked to massive inward investment and the growing influence of Japanese and German companies, which have introduced radically different ideas to the organization of work and the management of employees. The removal of unnecessary and restrictive differences between managers and employees, the harmonization of terms and conditions of employment, the removal of restrictive labour practices, and the emphasis on a new culture of pride and achievement, represent some of the groundbreaking changes that have permeated parts of the manufacturing sector.

Workers who were previously associated with the worst excesses of industrial conflict and inefficiencies have now become the valued employees of some of the most profitable companies in the country. The startling reality is that this transformation has been achieved, with some notable exceptions, with the same labour force (Wickens, 1987).

- **The challenge to, and replacement of, physical power and manual skills by the power of knowledge, creativity, and intellectual capital**

  The increasing importance of knowledge-based industries and the corresponding rise in the number of knowledge workers is creating a different kind of labour force, which has different requirements and expectations of work, and different expectations of how it will be managed. The fact that, in 2005, London's financial heartland was responsible for nearly one-third of the UK's economic output, in comparison with 25 per cent in 1995, shows how important such industries as finance, banking, insurance, consulting, and other parts of the services sector have become. With this growth has come a new kind of employee—the 'knowledge worker' (Swart, Kinnie, and Purcell, 2003). Knowledge workers can be seen to be different from other professional groups because, unlike those who draw upon a distinctive body of knowledge and work from this, the knowledge worker works *with* knowledge—not only their own, but that generated and used by others—generated through such mechanisms as 'communities of practice' and professional networks. The implications of knowledge-based work and the growing numbers of knowledge workers for the way people are managed extend to:
  - the need to align rewards more sensitively with the motivational characteristics of this kind of employee;
  - the nature of supervision and what managing the knowledge worker actually involves;
  - the intrinsic importance of work;
  - work-life balance issues.

  (Scarborough and Carter, 2000; Papadopoulos 2009)

- **A diversified labour force**

  'Globalization' isn't something that only represents what is happening to 'the world outside'. It also expresses the growing richness and diversity that exists within UK organizations, particularly in relation to the workforce. Similarly, 'multiculturalism' is not simply a description of a new society, but of a culturally diverse workplace. New migration patterns are adding to the demographic mix from which the labour force is drawn; labour market activity rates are increasing among ethnic minorities, and increasing numbers of female and older workers have become economically active. These developments are affecting the need for different employment and working arrangements, with flexible and varied contracts, home working, and career breaks becoming well established in certain sectors of the economy.

One of the implications for HR arising from these developments is that a 'one size fits all' approach to rewards, training, communications, and performance management is increasingly unsustainable. Flexibility has been one of the central themes of employment and employee behaviour over the past 20 years, and it is now becoming increasingly significant for the practice of HR (Bishop, 2004).

**STUDENT ACTIVITY 1.3**

**Why are some organizations and certain managers more successful in the way they manage their employees than are others? From a learning perspective, knowing what explains relative failure can be as important as identifying the causes of success.**

1. Think of an organization to which most group members can relate, and which might be considered to have a good reputation for managing people.

2. List the characteristics of this organization in terms of its human resource practices.
3. On a separate sheet, list the practices and behaviours of a manager who stands out as being effective in the way he or she manages. You may even want to organize both lists in terms of the priority or importance of each point.
4. Repeat the exercise, but this time choosing organizations and managers known (or thought) to be less effective and successful in their approach to managing people.
5. Discuss your findings and draw conclusions.

The position adopted throughout this book is that successful HR managers are those who are able to achieve those objectives that are critical to the successful operation of the organization through:

- Ensuring that the supply of human resources is consistent with the changing levels of demand.
- Pursuing strategies that result in improvements in the efficient use of labour and increased levels of labour productivity.
- Maintaining sufficient levels of control of employee behaviour.
- Generating employee commitment and engagement.
- Developing employees as human beings and as economic resources.

And ensuring that, as far as is possible fundamental employee objectives are also met. These include:

- To be treated as a human being first and then as an economic resource.
- To be recognized and valued for what they contribute.
- To be allowed to develop as a person and a resource.
- To be treated and rewarded fairly.

The reality is that often these objectives are not always completely compatible and in certain circumstances they may be in conflict; in fact it is probably more realistic to think of the relationship between the two sets of objectives as being in a state of dynamic tension. The following case study illustrates a situation in which conflict between the two parties developed into a prolonged struggle which has proved costly to both parties.

For information on the respective objectives of employers and employees see the Online Resource Centre extension material 1.1

### HRM INSIGHT 1.1 British Airways

As part of a long running industrial dispute over changes to working conditions, the Unite trade union, representing British Airways (BA) cabin staff, announced on 20 May 2010 a series of rolling strikes designed to disrupt the airline's operations and to put pressure on the company to make concessions over union demands for the restoration of travel concessions withdrawn from those cabin crew staff who participated in earlier industrial action and in regard to the company's decision to discipline union members who had broken their employment contract with the company. It seems as though the original source of the conflict between the union and BA had escalated to include new issues generated as a result of earlier industrial action.

This particular dispute, coming at a time when the company was losing substantial sums of money as a result of the economic recession and disruptions caused by the volcanic eruptions over Iceland, highlights the seemingly intractable differences between the company and its employees. It would be easy to blame the Unite trade union for fermenting the dispute for reasons to do with its own political ideology, but in this case the union has followed legislation governing industrial action and the strikes have been called following large majorities of those who participated in the ballots for industrial action.

Matters are further complicated by the way cabin crew staff are represented and because other trade unions are affected by the dispute. Tension has been reported between Unite, which is a national trade union, and its cabin crew arm, BASSA (British Airlines Stewards and Stewardesses Association), over the conduct of the dispute. The union appears to be trying to contain the dispute and is reported to have reluctantly called the latest round of strikes, having put earlier action 'on hold' in spite of overwhelming votes in favour of action by cabin crew members, but it is those cabin crew members who have been directly affected by reductions in staffing, losses of pay and allowances, the subsequent withdrawals of concessions, and disciplinary action. It seems that the more they feel they have lost, the more determined they are to continue the struggle in order to force the company to back down on its position and make concessions.

The involvement of the union representing BA pilots is a further complicating factor. It was reported that BALPA has written to the newly installed Conservative–Liberal Democrat government, appealing for it to intervene to avert the strike, with its General Secretary calling on the government to use that political momentum to help solve what he called the tired 1970s-style industrial relations (www.wsws.org/articles/2010/may2010/brit-m17.shtml). Clearly, BALPA is not supporting its fellow employees and has been critical of their refusal to take responsibility to make significant concessions to help BA in these difficult times which threaten the company's viability. In addition to the pilots working normally during strikes, they and other airline employees have volunteered to train and work as cabin crew staff to replace those on strike.

The above, brief, description of a potentially damaging industrial dispute is meant to illustrate the difficulties that can be experienced when a highly unionized workforce acts to defend its interests and contractual terms in the face of a determined attempt by an employer to reduce costs and introduce less favourable and more flexible working arrangements. The aim of the following exercise is to try to create some of the feelings experienced by cabin crew staff, the positions taken by the main protagonists and the forces that need to be overcome in order to find ways other than strike action to resolve the dispute. The task:

1. Agree to split your seminar group into three teams, one representing BA management, a second representing union negotiators, and a third acting as impartial observers with a remit to find a solution to the dispute and bring to an end the industrial action.
2. The first two groups should discuss their position and agree on the arguments they intend to make and then come together in a formal meeting chaired by an independent person to formally present their arguments. The impartial team acts as silent observers to this meeting but taking notes of what was said.
3. This impartial group then acts as mediators, meeting with the two other groups to try to reach a compromise between the two sides.
4. All participants come together in open session to discuss what they have learnt from the exercise and why it is sometimes very difficult to reconcile the diverging interests of managers and employees.

# Deconstructing Human Resource Management

Before we can begin fully to understand the challenges facing the HR professional and line managers, it is necessary to look more carefully at the component parts of human resource management and to consider each element separately. Human resource management is not simply a label, an approach to managing people, or a convenient abbreviation. It actually represents something far more complex, the understanding of which is profoundly important to those with managerial responsibilities. We need to extend our understanding beyond the superficial and ask the question: 'What does "human resource management" actually mean'?

## Employees as human beings

Peoples' objectives of work and employment have been briefly touched upon earlier; it is now necessary to explore the nature of what 'being human' means in ways that help to explain how and why, in their role as employees, people behave in the ways that they do. A useful starting point is to examine the assumptions made about people that are used, often unconsciously, to help managers make sense of what managing people involves. Perhaps the most well-known contribution to our understanding of the attitudes and behaviours of employees comes from the work of Douglas McGregor (1960). McGregor presented a dichotomy of the assumptions made about people, which he labelled 'Theory X' and 'Theory Y'.

*Theory X* assumptions are based on a belief that:

- the average human being has an inherent dislike of work and will avoid it if he or she can;
- because of their dislike of work, most people cannot be trusted to do a good job, and therefore need to be controlled and closely supervised;
- people generally prefer to be directed, dislike taking on responsibility, will not change much beyond what they already are and desire a high level of security.

As a result of these assumptions, under Theory X, managers need to develop working environments and organizational controls that reflect the unreliable and problematic nature of their employees.

*Theory Y* assumptions, on the other hand, are based on a different view of people and the way in which they are likely to behave at work. They reflect a view that:

- people enjoy work as a natural and necessary part of the human experience;
- tight control and the use of punishments are not the only, or most effective ways to make people work;
- employees are capable of self-motivation and self-direction, and can, under certain circumstances, show a high level of commitment to management and the organization for which they work;
- the average person is capable of learning and changing, and will be prepared, under certain circumstances, to take and exercise responsibility for his or her and others' actions.

The conclusion reached by McGregor is that, because of the existence of Theory X-based management practices, which he argues are based on a simplistic and partial understanding of people at work, there is a significant gap between what people are doing and giving at work, and what they are capable of. This is a point taken up by O'Reilly and Pfeffer (2000), who argue that, because of Theory X assumptions or the inability and reluctance to create environments that reflect a Theory Y view of their workers, many organizations are failing to unlock the hidden value and potential that their employees offer. They claim that:

> **this 'hidden value' is not scarce or unique, but rather can be found in all companies. It resides in the intellectual and emotional capital of the firm and is in the minds and hearts of its people. Although organisations we describe have used this potential, to achieve great success, most companies squander this resource even as they bemoan its scarcity.**
> (O'Reilly and Pfeffer, 2000)

The significance of this argument can hardly be overstated: it is quite simply that there is, in most organizations, a productive potential that managers are failing to access and utilize because they base their approach to management on mistaken assumptions about the nature of employee motivation. Moreover, because of the assumption that most people fit McGregor's 'Theory X' description, management practice based on this belief also becomes a self-fulfilling hypothesis: employees treated as if they are 'Theory X people' will conform to the stereotype.

McGregor's emphasis on the human side of work is part of a long tradition of management thinking linked to the Human Relations Movement. With its origins in the famous Hawthorne Studies, carried out at the Western Electric Hawthorne Works in Chicago between 1924 and 1927, this movement emphasized the importance of understanding the social and psychological dimensions of employee behaviour. Arising from the work of people such as Andrew Mayo (2001), a set of beliefs emerged that transformed our understanding about work and what people expect from it:

- work is a social activity involving people working together in groups and teams;
- the need for security, sense of belonging, and recognition is more important for morale and performance than the physical working environment;
- an employee is a person whose attitudes and effectiveness are conditioned by social expectations that exist both within and outside the place of work;
- when employees complain, the complaint may have some basis in fact, but can also be seen as a symptom that reflects changes in their status or sense of self-worth.

The so-called 'Hawthorne Effect', which is arguably as relevant today as it was when it was first used, suggests that treating employees as human beings—showing that management has an interest in them and cares about them—will, under most conditions, result in behaviour that is associated with higher levels of production and performance than would have been generated had management failed to demonstrate this concern and consideration. It can be argued, therefore, that the Hawthorne Effect is a consequence of applying Theory Y assumptions to the management of people, and can be seen as representing further evidence to support the belief of Pfeffer and Sutton (2000) that many organizations are failing to access and utilize employee potential (see www.accel-team.com).

William Ouchi's contribution to the debate about how underlying assumptions influence the way in which managers manage people is found in what he terms 'Theory Z' (Ouchi, 1981). In his work, Ouchi takes as his starting point the need to adopt a Theory Y perspective, arguing that workers:

- are capable of demonstrating a strong sense of loyalty;
- will respond positively to working in teams because they are social animals;
- if trusted to work in a demanding, but not coercive, environment, can and will reflect the interests of the organization, as well as their own.

Ouchi's description of the management practices that flow from this conceptualization reflect what can be described as modern Japanese management, which emphasizes:

- personal responsibility and accountability;
- collaborative working;
- devolved decision-making;
- harmonized working conditions.

The debate about whether Theory X or Y accurately reflects the nature of people as employees is often presented in terms of whether people correspond to one or the other sets of characteristics. This is both unhelpful and simplistic. It seems to us much more useful to accept the fact that people have the capacity to be both, and that whether they display the negative characteristics of a Theory X employee or become a more valued and desirable Theory Y employee is driven by their experiences at work, particularly those that relate to how their managers treat them, and the extent to which they see this treatment as reflecting a genuine concern with their social and psychological needs. Whether managers are dealing with Theory X or Theory Y people is not, therefore, a function of any inherent and deep-rooted differences between people, although some are pre-disposed to conform to one or the other profiles, but rather reflects their experiences of being managed and the environment in which they live and work. Put simply, many (although not all) employees behave as Theory X predicts, but do so because of their experiences of work and of being managed in particular ways. It follows, therefore, that these people could become Theory Y employees if the way in which work is organized and the way in which managers control them reflects a different set of assumptions about people and their motivations.

The full richness and insights of McGregor's thinking and writing is often lost to the majority of students who would probably find difficulty in going beyond a set of Theory X and Y statements. In fact these are not theories at all but sets of assumptions that managers hold about their employees! McGregor was fundamentally interested in the human side of enterprise and was part of a humanistic tradition that included people such as Maslow and Herzberg, all of whom believed that contemporary organizations had not come close to optimizing the potential effectiveness of their people. In fact, in a recent book on his contribution to our understanding of human behaviour at work (Heil, G. et al., 2000), the authors believe that McGregor was frustrated by the way management approached organizational improvements. For him, they asked the wrong questions in the wrong places. As an example, he believed that asking the question many managers today ask and are committed to answering is, 'how do you motivate employees?' is misconceived. McGregor's answer is that you don't! He believed that people are naturally motivated and driven by their own set of values and motivations, and that this means they have to be treated as individuals first and foremost. This view may clash with the established orthodoxy, and be rejected by some, but the point about his position is not fundamentally whether people can or cannot be motivated by what others do—there are many different points between these two extremes but how managers choose to frame the problem. In a passage that resonates with references made in Chapter 2 to people's mindsets and how they think, and to the concept of double-loop learning explored in Chapter 10 they say:

> **McGregor recognized the importance of caring about peoples' attitudes, which dictated behavior. He pointed out that we are defined by how we think, and that if we don't change our basic assumptions about people, we will never change what we do.**
> (Heil et al., 2000)

And when they state that McGregor believed that organizations could not be seen as machines, with interchangeable human parts, but as living organizations and communities which both enabled people to grow and develop and contribute to business goals, it shows that for him the way towards organizational success started from this way of thinking rather than one that associated with gimmicks, procedures, or specific programmes. What he offers those interested in change and improvement are not simple prescriptions based on wishful thinking, a sentiment echoed by Herzberg when he said treat me as I am not as you wish me to be, but as a challenge based on understanding human nature and what building successful organizations involves, expressed in his statement that:

> **I will venture the prediction that we will succeed in increasing our utilisation of the human potential in organizational settings only as we succeed in creating conditions that generate a meaningful way of life.**
> ( Heil et al., 2000)

The issues raised by McGregor and developed by Heil et al. are developed in more detail in the section on Management.

**HRM INSIGHT 1.2 The Men's Warehouse**

This case study is based on chapter 4 of O'Reilly and Pfeffer's book, *Hidden Value* (O'Reilly, C.A. and Pfeffer, J. (2000), Harvard Business School Press). It has been chosen because it represents an example of an unfashionable company that achieved success through its distinctive people-orientated business philosophy and, through this, was able to access the full potential of its employees.

The Men's Warehouse is an American clothing retail business founded by George Zimmer in 1973. In a market that faced little or no growth, the company achieved a five-year annual growth rate of 26 per cent in revenues and 29 per cent in net income between 1995 and 1999, a period during which other retail clothing chains closed stores or suffered financial hardship. Why was The Men's Warehouse so successful?

A significant part of the answer can be found in its founder's underpinning humanistic philosophy, which is expressed in the following statement (found on p. 86):

> Our mission . . . is to maximise sales, provide value to our customers, and give quality customer service while still having fun and maintaining our values. These values include nurturing creativity, growing together, admitting to our mistakes, promoting a happy, healthy lifestyle, enhancing our sense of community and striving to become self-actualised people.

O'Reilley and Pfeffer accept that this people philosophy and the need to develop them to be the best they can be is at odds with the prevailing view held by other American retailers and most other industrial companies. It is a philosophy and an approach to managing people that would be difficult to copy, but it is an approach that has worked for this company. In trying to tease out the lessons that can be taken from the case study, O'Reilly and Pfeffer make one powerful statement: in an industry that is not known for the quality of its employees or management concern with their interests, The Men's Warehouse stands out precisely because it didn't treat its people badly! They claim (on p. 97) that:

> By exceeding people's expectations concerning the chances they will be given, the dignity and respect with which they will treated, and the opportunities they will have, the company builds an incredible sense of loyalty and commitment. Doing the unexpected—doing more than is expected—earns the company extraordinary performance from its people. If there is a lesson here, it is the power of treating everyone as if they are important and matter.

Questions

1. Why might this philosophy of managing people be so difficult to copy in other companies?
2. In the light of this philosophy, what do you think the company's approaches to training and compensation are?
3. What is the company's recruitment and selection strategy likely to be? What will it be looking for in new employees?

## *People, pain, and toxicity*

A more recent contribution to our understanding of employees as people and of their behaviour at work comes from Peter J. Frost (2003) and his pioneering study of the emotional dimension of work. Frost accepts that what he describes as 'toxicity' or emotional pain is a normal by-product of organizational life and that the generation of emotional pain is an inevitable part of 'doing business'. He argues that 'normal' levels of toxicity rarely cause long-term damage because of workers' coping strategies, such as the abilities to rationalize, to empathize with each other, and to engage in pressure-releasing behaviours, which, together with the positive effects of 'toxin handlers' means that, more often than not, there is an acceptable level of emotional pain that is time-constrained and is 'fixable'. According to Frost, emotional pain itself is not toxic: what determines whether its long-term effects are positive or negative is how the pain is handled.

Frost, after recounting a story of an employee who had experienced what she considered to be a lack of understanding and compassion from her manager during a difficult period in her life, talks about how unfeeling responses can:

> **undermine peoples' confidence, esteem, dignity and sense of connection to others. It disconnects them from the capacity to respond competently to their painful situation.**
> (Frost, 2003)

The importance of people, as human beings, needing to feel connected and part of something is also central to Harvey's explanation of the Abilene paradox, a seminal book on management and organizational life which we refer to again in Chapter 3 (Harvey, 1996). In the first of the essays called 'The Abilene Paradox',

Harvey suggests that the reason why so many people conform to or do not challenge what others prescribe, knowing either that they disagree or feel such decisions are wrong, is due to their need to remain connected. Paradoxically, he believes that people fear the unknown less than they do the known. He goes on to say:

> **What do we know about that frightens us into such apparently inexplicable organizational behavior? Separation, alienation, and loneliness are things we do know about—and fear. Both research and experience indicate that ostracism is one of the most powerful punishments that can be devised. Solitary confinement does not draw its coercive strength from physical deprivation. The evidence is overwhelming that we have a fundamental need to be connected, engaged, and related and a reciprocal need not to be separated or alone.**
> (Harvey, 1996)

In a presentation (13 May 2010) on the power of positive emotions at work at Newcastle Business School, Professor Michael West made a similar point about the importance of understanding the basic human condition and the way negative experiences affect the individual and undermine their role as worker. He made the following points:

- Relationships are one of the most potent sources of human misery (e.g. death of a spouse).
- Troubled relationships are the most common presenting problem in psychotherapy.
- Chronic conflict and hostility damage the immune system.

Whilst these comments relate to the human experience in general, they have obvious implications for the physical and psychological health of people in their working roles. Firstly, positive working relationships are a critical source of well-being and stability and these relate to managers and fellow workers. Secondly, interpersonal conflict and hostility can have physiological as well as psychological effects and these can manifest themselves in low morale, poor productivity, and absence.

We would argue that the need to be 'connected', and the importance of a person feeling his or her self to be 'part of something' and valued, is fundamental to what being human means. Many employees are motivated to avoid the psychological damaging effects of excessive work-related pressure and the effects of 'organizational toxicity', although we accept that individuals vary in relation to their ability to cope with such pressure and 'toxins'.

While the concepts of organizational toxins and emotional pain are relatively new the same cannot be said for their consequence—stress. While it is undoubtedly the case that certain people seem to prosper in stressful working environments (although for how long is more problematic), and that a certain level of pressure is both necessary and stimulating, stress, when it reaches levels at which people find it difficult to cope, becomes dysfunctional and damaging.

According to the Stress Management Society (www.stress.org.uk) stress can be defined as:

> **a situation where demands on a person exceed that person's resources or ability to cope.**
> (Stress Management Society, 2010)

Interestingly, people may suffer from stress because of too little pressure as well as too much as Figure 1.1 illustrates.

Figure 1.1 suggests that workers who are under-utilized and feel frustrated because of this may also react in ways that are detrimental to the organization, either by simply staying and adjusting to their situation or leaving and seeking alternative and more rewarding employment. But the experience of going beyond what is above described as the optimum position in the relationship between capabilities and work pressures is the one that is closely associated with the conventional understanding of what stress means and what it is linked to. But stress is not simply a function of excessive work pressures; it can also result from how people are treated at work and specifically how they are managed, and this question is addressed in more detail later in the chapter.

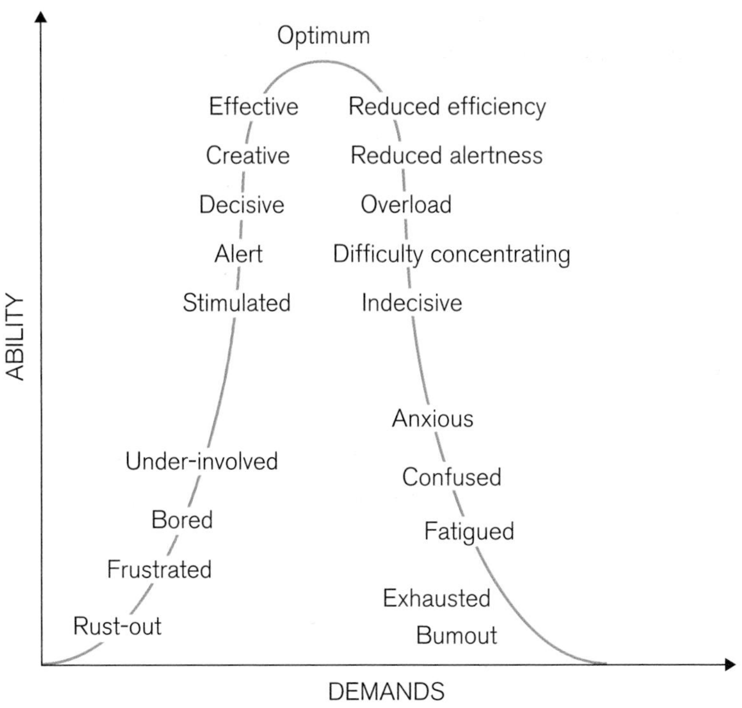


**Figure 1.1** Emotional state linked to relationship between ability and demands of work



According to the Stress Management Society (2010), quoting evidence from the Health and Safety Executive, there is a clear link between stress and ill health. Based on a survey of 700 senior HR practitioners and almost 2,000 employees and reported by *Personnel Today*, the Society claimed that:

- 105 million days are lost to stress each year—costing UK employers £1.24 billion.
- 11 per cent of absence is attributed to stress.
- 52 per cent say stress is increasing.
- 60 per cent claim stress is damaging staff retention.
- 83 per cent think stress is harming productivity.

More recent insights into stress indicate that the situation is becoming progressively more acute. In 2009, NICE (the National Institute for Health and Clinical Excellence), issued guidance aimed at reducing the estimated £24 billion cost to the economy linked to staff absence due to stress at work, with mental health problems in general costing the average company almost £1,000 per employee per year. Interestingly, the guidelines laid particular emphasis for this worrying level of stress and its consequences for both peoples' sense of being able to cope with working life and for lost productivity on the line manager. Professor Cary Cooper who helped draw up the NICE guidelines is reported to have said that:

> **I think central to all of this is your manager. Nobody damages your health more in the workplace, potentially, than your manager.**
> (*Daily Telegraph*, 2009)

In a study for the mental health charity MIND, almost 20 per cent of respondents claimed that they had been ill because they could not cope with pressure in the office, and more than 26 per cent said they felt dread and apprehension the day before they were due to go back to work after a day or weekend off. (McVeigh, 2010.)

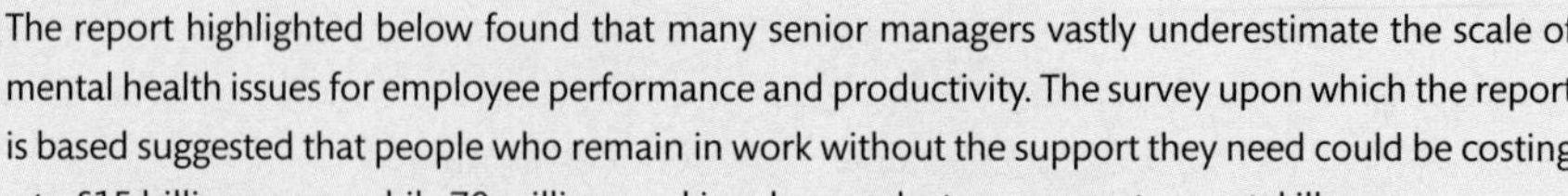

**RESEARCH INSIGHT 1.2 The Costs of Mental Illness at Work**

The report highlighted below found that many senior managers vastly underestimate the scale of mental health issues for employee performance and productivity. The survey upon which the report is based suggested that people who remain in work without the support they need could be costing businesses up to £15 billion a year, while 70 million working days are lost every year to mental illness.

**(Sainsbury Centre for Mental Health, 2007)**

1. Prepare a PowerPoint presentation limited to one slide per task which:
   - Summarizes the key findings of the report.
   - Highlights what realistically can be achieved to address the causes and reduce the costs of mental illness in the workplace.
   - Establishes the link between work-related ill health and sickness absence.

If these statistics and reports are to be believed, a concern with the human consequences of stress and emotional pain, and action to alleviate this, is not only consistent with an organization recognizing its responsibilities to its employees as people, but will also have a beneficial effect on the well-being of the organization. Clearly, the experience of working in contemporary organizations is, for many people, a positive one and provides many important outcomes, both material and intangible. But for others, the pressures of working or working for difficult managers produces very different outcomes, and these can not only result in personal distress and psychological damage but lost productivity, excessive labour costs, and the under-utilization of an organization's human resources.

**STUDENT ACTIVITY 1.4 The Key Role of Managers in Causing and Mediating Stress in the Workplace**

Research and discuss the following questions:

1. How and why does pressure turn into stress, and how do the two states differ?
2. What are managers accused of doing or not doing that creates or increases the level of stress at work?
3. What is the role of 'toxin handlers', and how do they work to reduce the impact of toxic environments and emotional pain?
4. What do managers need to do differently or better to reduce the damaging effects of excessive pressure or anxiety?

## People as a resource

From an economic and business perspective, rather than employees being seen as people, people are seen as productive economic resources, or, to use the language of HR, 'human resources'. From this perspective, employees represent an input to the productive process; they are seen as an economic factor of production with a value and a cost. People are employed not because of employer altruism or because they deserve a job, but because they possess valued physical and intellectual capabilities that are needed in the production of goods and services. People as economic resources become, in one sense, commodities; that is, they have a value that expresses their importance to the productive process, which is reflected in the fact that they have a job and are paid a wage or salary. When their economic value as productive resources falls, they may well lose their jobs or experience pressure for wage/salary reductions. It is more likely that the costs of employees as economic resources become more significant in shaping employers' employment strategies during a recession rather than during periods of economic expansion. But the cost of labour is also a factor in business decisions to off-shore production facilities, where companies move from high- to low-cost economies (http://management.about.com/cs/people/a/offshoring104.htm).

As a commodity, people have no rights as such, although, as human beings in employment, they enjoy varying degrees of protection from the ability or desire of managers to treat them as a commodity. But even these rights do not prevent managers from terminating the employment contract for reasons to do with changes in the need for, or value of, an individual. As the demand for the goods and services falls, or the costs of production become excessive, then the rationale for employing people is removed or is displaced from one location to another.

The current trend towards outsourcing the production of goods and services from the UK and other Western countries to the Far East reflects the economically rational decision of companies to move from employing high-cost workers to employing—at lower cost—workers abroad who may even be more compliant. These economic forces and business imperatives may take time to work through and affect the demand for labour in the UK, and managers may be constrained in how quickly they can respond to them, but only in the most protected of environments can they be ignored for long. However much we want to be treated as people, this underlying dynamic means that we are also a useable and disposable factor of production.

This acceptance that each individual has an economic value commensurate with his or her capabilities partly explains why some people are paid more than others. But does this also mean that some people are more important than others, and does it justify managers treating some differently and more favourably than others whose value to the organization is less obvious? From an economic perspective, the answer must be 'yes'. While we, as employees, all share the same or similar requirements to be treated as human beings, as an economic resource and providers of productive inputs, we do have different values to the organization because the value of our contributions differs. This is an important point because it provides a rationale for the application of differentiated employment policies, under which certain groups or individuals are treated differently with regard to rewards, training and development opportunities, and promotion.

Although not well developed in the UK, the emphasis on the quantitative and financial aspects of employment, under which costs and asset values become key employment criteria, is very much part of mainstream HRM in the USA and is recognized as an academic discipline in its own right, with the titles of 'human resource accounting' and 'personnel economics' (Fitz-Enz, 1990, 2000).

### *People as assets*

The interest in, but difficulty with, 'seeing' people as commodities and treating them in the same way as other tangible assets is that they do not fit the strict definition of an 'asset'. According to Mayo (2001), employees have to be seen as intangible assets because:

- they cannot be transacted—i.e. bought and sold at will;
- their contribution is individual and variable;
- they cannot be valued according to traditional financial principles.

The inability, or reluctance, of many organizations to value their 'human assets' can, however, have important consequences. Firstly, managers who are unable to estimate or calculate an individual's worth or value to the organization are also unable to develop HR practices that reflect these differences in employee performance and contribution. This effectively inhibits the development of an individual or of a differentiated approach to the management of people, with the implication that the 'one size fits all' mindset will continue to be adopted, almost on a default basis. Secondly, returns on investments in training and development will be difficult to calculate because of managerial inability to measure any changes in employee value, through increased competency, that might follow from such an investment.

The re-emergence of this interest in the economic value of people as resources and assets, through the growth in what has been described as the 'expense model' of human resource accounting (Fitz-Enz, 2000; Mayo, 2001), confirms the importance to organizations of finding ways of allocating financial value to employees' asset value, and of being able to calculate the value of employing people through the systematic measurement and evaluation of their costs and the value of their contributions. This is by no means an easy task, but it is nevertheless one that is seen as increasingly important if HR is to engage with, and support, an organization's economic and financial agenda.

The enduring paradox that managers struggle to resolve and which is fundamental to understanding the challenge they face is that employees are both people, with human requirements and sensitivities, *and* economic resources, with differentiated and changing asset values. This dilemma, faced by successive generations of managers, is perfectly captured by Henry Ford, who once asked why he always had to deal with the whole person when he had only hired a 'pair of hands':

> **Hands were what he hired, but troublesome bodies with querulous minds were what he so often got.**
> (Clegg et al., 2005)

## Management

Countless books and articles have been written on, and about, management, to the point at which it can be difficult to identify and to make sense of the myriad of different approaches and traditions. Our advice is that you select a number of authors, whose work is recognized as distinctive, insightful, and original, and become familiar with their ideas and contributions. We have been particularly influenced by such people as Peter Drucker, Tony J Watson, David Ulrich, Jeffrey Pfeffer, and Henry Mintzberg in recent years, but earlier works by Weber, Barnard, Elton Mayo (see references at end of chapter 1 in Hannagan (2002)), and McGregor also stand out for their distinctive contributions to our understanding of how organizations function and how people are, and should be, managed. Consistent with our view that students need to take control of their own learning and development, it is recommended that you agree a personal 'contract' to engage with some of this literature, and to reflect on its relevance and value to your own understanding of what management is about.

As a starting point, consider our earlier references to the building of the Pyramids in Egypt, and of England's canals and railways. Would 'managers' have been found there, doing the same kind of things that today's managers do? Even though the word 'manager' may not have been used, the functions that are generally associated with management—directing and controlling resources—would almost certainly have been understood. As a function, defined as 'what needs to be done' or the 'nature of the contribution required to achieve stated objectives', management, despite its complexities and different traditions, can be understood as being about:

- clarifying objectives;
- planning and organizing;
- directing and controlling.

According to Clegg et al. (2005), this functional and rational approach to management, associated with such people as FW Taylor, Henri Fayol, and Henry Ford, not only identifies key management activities and responsibilities, but also explicitly excludes employees from any meaningful part of what management does. Organizations based on hierarchy, centralized decision-making and a belief that employees were incapable of anything more than following orders produced managers and an approach to management that is associated with Scientific Management and Fordism, significant elements of which are still influential today.

**KEY CONCEPT Scientific Management**

Scientific Management is sometimes called 'Taylorism' after the American employer and writer, Frederick Winslow Taylor, with whom it is closely associated. This theory of management involves the application of precise procedures and approaches to the management and control of work and workers, in contrast to the use of tradition and 'rule-of-thumb' decision-making. Scientific Management seeks to provide a 'one best way' approach to improving labour productivity.

**KEY CONCEPT Fordism**

Fordism was the dominant method of production over the last century and is associated with mass production techniques, extreme forms of the division of labour, and assembly line techniques, reflecting a Taylorist (i.e. Scientific Management) approach to the control of work.

But this historical emphasis on functionality and rationality needs to be put into a more contemporary context, in which:

- as change and increasing complexity become the norm for those organizations exposed to competition and a dynamic external environment, these core functions may, in themselves, be insufficient to deliver all of the required outcomes, and so new management activities may emerge (e.g. the need to communicate, to consult, and to motivate);
- because these functions are essentially technical in nature—they demand specialist knowledge and skills to carry them out to the required standard—who carries them out, i.e. who is seen to or can act managerially, becomes a question of competency rather than of hierarchical position. This conception of management, reflected in the concept of 'empowerment', means that, as the workforce becomes better educated and technically equipped to manage, there is less need for people in formally designated management positions. Such a realization is associated with the notion of self-management, self-direction and self-control;
- challenges emanating from postmodernists raise questions about the effectiveness of traditional approaches to management in delivering sustained economic success in the context of rapidly changing environments. One of the important outcomes of this debate has been the realization that understanding what management involves requires us to accept not one, but several different types of rationality.

What these points actually mean is that the 'old' ideas that management is the province of only those with managerial responsibilities, that it is only done 'to people', and that employees can easily be organized, directed, and controlled, while still retaining some support, are not the only ways of understanding what management involves. For those with responsibility for managing organizations, it is important to consider the limitations of the first conceptualization and also the implications of the second.

As an example of this more 'unconventional' thinking, Cloke and Goldsmith (quoted in Mullins, 2005) claim that 'managers are the dinosaurs of our modern organizational ecology' and that 'the age of management is ending'. They base their argument on the rapid advances in information technology and knowledge growth, increased environmental influences and the continuing search for improvements in productivity, which are forcing organizational leaders to find alternative and more effective ways of controlling activities and regulating behaviour. They believe that organizations which do not understand the need to respond to these dynamic forces, and to share decision-making power and responsibility with their employees, will lose those employees; they also believe that the biggest changes in the history of management are the decline of hierarchy and bureaucracy, autocratic management, and the expansion of collaborative self-management and organizational democracy (see Mullins, 2005).

In his influential books, *In Search of Management* (2001) and *Organising and Managing Work* (2002), Tony Watson reaches similar conclusions to those of Cloke and Goldsmith, but by a different route. In the first chapter of his ethnographical study of a manufacturing company, Watson offers a powerful and persuasive analysis of the meaning and practice of management that is derived from his own observations, from discussions with managers in the company and from his own theoretical insights. One of his more interesting conclusions is that, however much conventional thinking about management is based on the belief that what needs to be managed can, in some mysterious way, be completely captured and appropriated from the working environment and packaged into management jobs, this belief is a fiction.

Support for many of the conclusions reached on the changing nature of management in the twenty-first century is given by the findings of the Tomorrow Project (Moynagh and Worsley, 2001), which reported on conditions of work and employment until 2020. It found that:

- there will be more self-management;
- outsourcing will create these opportunities;
- higher skilled jobs will increase employee discretion;
- managers will develop new ways in which to supervise and delegate work;
- people will want greater responsibility;
- more mundane jobs will be transformed to make employment feel more like self-employment.

To support their conclusions, the authors quote the example of a just-in-time car plant at which many middle-manager jobs have been taken over by assembly workers, who manage day-to-day scheduling, machine set-up, work, discipline, and quality control (Moynagh and Worsley, 2001, p. 96). In a similar vein, Richard Scase (2000) refers to Toyota's Takaoka plant, at which individual workers can stop the assembly line if they see a problem with the production process.

This brief and necessarily limited analysis of the nature of management and its relevance for the management of people at work does, however, allow us to conclude this section with the following observations.

- The traditional divide between those who manage and those who are managed is becoming narrower, increasingly blurred, and, in certain cases, reversed, with the number of managers being reduced and their responsibilities passed to individuals or groups of employees.
- Changes in the nature of work, illustrated by the growing number of knowledge-based jobs, makes traditional ideas of what managing involves increasingly inappropriate. The knowledge owned by such workers cannot be easily appropriated or replicated, and this means that organizations cannot control and motivate the workers as easily as they believed they could when dealing with a less skilled and more dependent workforce.
- Social and technological changes have resulted in much more complex and varied working patterns, with an increasing number of employees working from home or away from the office for long periods.

Inevitably, such changes have resulted in managers and HR specialists having to redefine what managing such staff involves.

But the point made earlier by William Beckett that, without a viable business, any talk of managing people, either well or badly, becomes irrelevant is still fundamental to this introductory exploration of human resource management. It has this status because it locates people in a particular type of relationship with employers and the employing organization. Managing people is not the primary aim of managers; managing the business or organization successfully is what managers will be judged against, and according to Robert Heller (2003) this means:

> **In the final analysis, management comes down to three simple words: revenues, costs and quality.**

A focus on core business outcomes doesn't mean that people are not important—far from it—but it does mean that understanding and addressing the needs of people as human beings is critical to their status as productive economic resources and their ability to contribute to these business goals. However difficult it is for some people to accept, people are not an end in themselves but a means to an end. Although a humanist, psychologist McGregor understood this role and relationship. According to Heil et al. (2000):

> **McGregor believed that organisations would be far more effective when managers offered employees the opportunity to align their individual goals with those of the business. His thinking reinforced the pragmatic message at the core of the famed psychologist Abraham Maslow's work: People are capable of extraordinary accomplishments if they are able to meet their own self-fulfilling needs while pursuing the goals of the organisation.**
> (Heil et al., 2000)

**PRACTITIONER INSIGHT William Beckett, Managing Director of William Beckett Plastics Ltd.**

The following is a description of what the company experienced during the recent economic recession and the action it took to stave off closure. It shows what the company did in order to survive a rapid and steep fall in its orders and highlights the choices management made that ensured its survival.

One of the important things I realised was that previous experience helped in the way I reacted to the 2009 recession. It was also apparent that speed of action was essential to our survival; I know of many other companies whose management delayed taking the necessary action which often came too late to save the businesses. As soon as we realised how badly affected our sales were going to be we immediately started looking at the management accounts to look at cash flow and where we could start reducing costs. Initially that didn't affect our employees. For example we cancelled all our cleaning contracts and took responsibility for cleaning the premises ourselves—the directors shared responsibilities for this—even to cleaning the toilets. We needed to set an example that said we all share the pain of saving the company!

The problem was that this saved only half a job and that wasn't nearly enough: we quickly realised that we had to make cuts in the labour force, but we did this in as fair a way as possible but always having regard for the need to protect and secure key skills. We had to make a 20% cut in shop floor workers and then over 40% in our sales and administration team, but even that wasn't enough. We then instituted cuts in hours and a cut in wages with the Directors taking the biggest cut in remuneration. All over-time and pension contributions were also halted.

This meant that the remaining staff had to do more to cover the work of those who had left, so we had to rely on their willingness and goodwill to keep things going. The decline in sales reached 55% in August 2009 and by that time we had made further redundancies and instituted short-time working. We also made important changes to shift patterns which meant that we were working more efficiently and this also benefitted the operatives who found they had more leisure time to enjoy. Our productivity went up because in the worst of the recession the factory was only open for three days each week and this meant we saved on many of our variable costs.

Although these actions seem extreme they simply reflected a need to reduce costs to reflect a drastic fall in income and cash flow—another month of falling sales would almost certainly have meant that the company went under! And they worked because after August sales increased and we began to bring back those employees who had been temporarily laid off even though we were still losing money. In total we lost £120k in that year. And despite the effect of the cuts on our staff they were incredibly supportive of what we were doing and there was a strong sense of 'being in this together'. No one left for other jobs and we were able to offer those we made redundant their jobs back towards the end of 2009 and into 2010.

The situation now is that the order book is double what it was in 2009. We have increased working hours, re-employed many old staff and are looking to recruit skilled workers again. So, many of the cuts have been reversed as business has improved and the company is on an upward trajectory again.

On reflection, the final point I would make relates to leadership and the importance of understanding the nature and scale of the problem you are faced with. Employees in these circumstances need to feel that the right decisions are being made for the company and that management is doing everything it can to protect all employees in the best way that it can. In these circumstances, when all stakeholders share the cutbacks and additional responsibilities and where management sets a clear example, people will rally together and work towards a common goal.

# A Philosophy of Management

This final section considers more explicitly what has been an underlying theme of the chapter—the role and importance of philosophy for the management of people. It seeks to answer the question: 'Is the existence of a coherent and sustained philosophy of management correlated with effective and successful organizations?' Earlier, we rejected the notion that some special ingredient or single factor might explain why some managers were consistently better than others in managing people as being too simplistic and misleading—but what explanation can be put forward that explains the success of certain organizations while not of others? The contribution of such writers as Pfeffer and Sutton (2000) and Collins (2001) suggests that something to do with philosophy may represent at least part of the answer.

A philosophy of management is far more than a single ingredient—that 'something extra' which explains why some managers seem to be able consistently to outperform their contemporaries—but there is extensive anecdotal and empirical evidence that a particular type of philosophy is associated with managerial effectiveness and organizational success, and that this philosophy is deeply rooted in beliefs about people and their behaviour.

O'Reilly and Pfeffer (2000) emphasize the importance of philosophy and the assumptions managers make about people, and provide detailed accounts of the management styles and practices of eight successful American companies which share a similar approach to managing people, in which managers identify with a distinctive set of values and principles that influence and give consistency to what they do. They quote George Zimmer, founder of the Men's Warehouse, who described how the company's strategy and how it operates comes from a philosophy or world view based on humanistic principles. Zimmer's humanistic philosophy allows him to see the power of untapped human potential, which, when realized, allows win-win outcomes to be achieved, within which the interests of all the key organizational stakeholders can be met.

Collins' 2001 book, *Good to Great*, is also full of references to the values and beliefs held by the leaders and managers of companies he identifies as going beyond being only 'good' and becoming 'great'. Whether these represent a coherent and articulated philosophy of management is less important than the fact that they provide successive managers with a framework for action; within which consistency, rigour and a belief that their way is right for them sustains an environment within which the right kinds of people can prosper, grow, and outperform competitors. Collins and his team of researchers were not interested only in identifying great companies; they wanted to identify the underlying reasons for sustained success, or, as Collins puts it:

> **I think of our work as a search for timeless principles—the enduring physics of great organizations.**
> (Collins, 2001)

**STUDENT ACTIVITY 1.5**

Consider the three examples from *Good to Great* (Collins, J. (2001), Random House Business Books) presented below, and reflect on their application to management decisions and objectives. What do these statements mean for selection, motivation, and people strategy?

1. 'When in doubt, don't hire—keep looking.' (p. 63)
2. 'Spending time trying to motivate people is a waste of effort. The real question is not, "How do we motivate our people?" If you have the right people, they will be self-motivated. The key is to not de-motivate them.' (p. 89)
3. 'The executives who ignited transformations from good to great did not first figure out where to drive the bus and then get people to take it there. No, they first got the right people on the bus (and the wrong ones off the bus) and then figured out where to drive it.' (p. 41)

In one of the most eloquent contributions made on the importance of values and beliefs, Thomas J. Watson Jr (2003), argued that great organizations owed their success not only to the power of their beliefs, but also to the appeal these beliefs had to their employees:

> **I believe if an organization is to meet the challenge of a changing world, it must be prepared to change everything about itself except those beliefs as it moves through corporate life. In other words, the basic philosophy, spirit and drive of an organization have far more to do with its relative achievements than do technological or economic resources, organizational structure, innovation and timing. All these things weigh heavily in success. But they are, I think, transcended by how strongly the people in the organization believe in its basic precepts and how faithfully they carry them out.**
> (Watson, 2003)

Perhaps the most significant conclusion that emerges from this statement is the importance of getting the people that organizations employ to understand and support the values and beliefs espoused by their managers. Too often, managers make the mistake of assuming that simply publicizing mission and value statements is sufficient and that commitment automatically follows. This rarely happens: *living* a philosophy is much more difficult and demanding than articulating and publicizing one!

Reference to the importance of an underpinning and integrating philosophy can also be found in the HR literature. In their important, but largely unrecognized, work on personnel managers, Buckingham and Elliot (1993) argued that simply possessing basic competencies is not a sufficient condition for generating managerial success. This, they suggest, is much more a function of the concepts they use, their values, and how they relate to others. Underpinning their personal characteristics and how they work is what they describe as a conceptual mindset, which they define as:

> **a perspective on their role and its purpose that is significantly different from their less highly rated colleagues.**
> (Buckingham and Elliot, 1993)

They equate this mindset to a philosophy of personnel management that is:

> **strongly rooted in clear perceptions about, and a real commitment to, the value of good employees and of their contribution to the company.**

Buckingham and Elliot found that those personnel managers who were rated more successful than others subscribed to a personal and professional philosophy that helped to shape their thinking and the way in which they discharged their responsibilities. This, combined with an ability to conceptualize and mobilize a range of more effective personal characteristics, was seen as the reason why they were considered to be successful HR managers—a finding that lends further support to the belief that those involved in the management of people need to underpin their behaviour as managers with a clear set of values and beliefs about the employment of people and their relationship to the organization.

## Summary

The purpose of this introductory chapter has been to present our analysis about the employment and management of people within a broader framework of work, organization, and productive activity.

- The chapter also serves as a reference point for those that follow, by which we mean that any particular area of HR—whether recruiting and selecting staff, or training them—needs to be carried out in ways that reflect the interests of the organization and those of the people who constitute its 'human resources'. Recognizing this duality of concerns does not imply that they have to be given equal emphasis, but rather that it is in management's long-term interests to understand and, wherever possible, reflect the things that are important and which matter to employees in the way in which 'the business' is run.

- While it is accepted that external forces influence the degree to which management can act on this requirement, it is also important to recognize that these forces do not determine how people are managed.
- It is clear from references made to those organizations which stand out for being successful 'businesses' *and* which also enjoy enviable reputations for being 'good places to work' that there are choices to be made about how people are managed, and that these choices have consequences for such things as the quality of employee relations, employee satisfaction, and performance and retention rates.
- Treating employees as people and as economic resources is not a mutually exclusive proposition—it is neither one nor the other—but getting the balance right, in the context of each organization's circumstances, represents a fundamental and enduring challenge that not all managers seem capable of meeting.

online resource centre

**Visit the Online Resource Centre that accompanies this book for self-test questions, weblinks, and more information on the topics covered in this chapter.**
**www.oxfordtextbooks.co.uk/orc/banfield_kay2e/**

## REVIEW QUESTIONS

1. To what extent is organizational success a function of the 'human dimension'? What is the evidence that that supports your conclusion?
2. What are the current and future challenges that organizations face with regards to the way in which they manage people?
3. What might happen that will increase the level of conflict between employers and workers? If conflict does increase, is this likely to be because of what employers and managers do, or do not do, or is it likely to be generated by factors outside their control?
4. Why is a philosophy of management important and where can this be found?

***See Online Resource Centre for answers.***

## CASE STUDY
ABB

This case study provides interesting insights into the managerial and personal philosophy of one of Europe's most successful executives, and also demonstrates the fundamental importance of locating the management of people within the wider context of managing the business.

This is a story about the merger, in 1987, of two engineering companies—Brown Boveri from Switzerland and the Swedish firm ASEA—and the role of one of Europe's most well-known and successful chief executives, Percy Barnevik. It is taken from the book *ABB—The Dancing Giant*, by Kevin Bareham and Claudia Heimer (1998, FT/Pitman). ABB was chosen because it represents an example of a company that enjoyed phenomenal growth, financial success, and an international reputation for its ability to operate a highly decentralized international business. It is described by Bareham and Heimer as a 'globally connected corporation operating a loose-tight network of processes, projects and partners that is held together by highly committed people and strongly held principles'. Its approach to business, the way in which it is organized and the approach taken to the management of its employees, certainly in the 1990s, set it apart from many of its contemporaries and brought it to the attention of management writers such as Warren Bennis, who were interested in Barnevik's leadership style and global/local business model (Bennis, 1993).

Always recognizing that further improvements might be made, the company emphasized the crucial role played by its employees, particularly its cadre of managers, and the importance of creating a culture of:

> **continuous learning and change, wherever higher targets and constant transition are seen as normal and positive, not threatening and negative. We will make it happen only by instilling a creative and entrepreneurial attitude in all our employees who welcome change as a challenge.**
> (Bareham and Heimer, 1998)

In addition to his personal qualities and business acumen, Barnevik also had a strong commitment to the company's people, and was able to articulate a distinctive philosophy of management and organization. In chapter 11 of the book, entitled 'Developing ABB's people and corporate glue', Barnevik is quoted as saying:

> **It is fantastic how much business is really about people issues. You never cease to be surprised whether you are a lawyer or an engineer, or if you have a business education, that the question really is: can you communicate, ignite people, be believable, build trust? We talk about having bright strategies. But at the end of the day it comes back to execution. Can you create a culture, leadership, make people buy in, and feel part of it?**
> (p. 317)

Barnevik's successor as CEO, Goran Lindahl, has a similar belief in the importance of the company's human resources, with a particular emphasis on attracting and developing new talent, a role that is seen as being the prime responsibility of line management.

What comes through clearly is the way in which ABB makes strong demands on its people: it is not a company that offers its employees an 'easy ride'. According to Bareham and Heimer, employees—and particularly management—are expected to work extremely hard, perform well, and be technically very good. The existence of internal competition and profit-and-loss centres means that business unit performance is regularly reported, and this has the effect of encouraging people to feel ownership and of meaningful autonomy deep down within the business.

The company also sets high standards in its recruitment of new staff, with all newly appointed professional staff expected to have:

- a good education;
- strong analytical skills;
- good communication skills;
- an interest in, and openness to, other cultures;
- energy, to drive the business.

As far as developing people is concerned, ABB has a very simple approach: after recruiting talented people, give them early responsibility and subject them to a range of informal and formal development strategies. The line drives both sets of activities, with the personnel function supporting the line with leading-edge development strategies rather than with complicated models and elaborate processes. As the head of the corporate management resourcing function, Arne Olssen, is reported to have said:

> **Exposing talented people to demanding assignments and providing feedback and support—this is the key to management development.**
> (p. 326)

Olssen articulates ABB's management development philosophy very clearly, when he states that managers develop:

- 70 per cent on the job;
- 20 per cent by the influence of others;
- 10 per cent as a result of courses and seminars.

Without it being explicitly stated, it is reasonable to assume that the same principles and philosophy also applied to the development of the company's non-management employees.

**Questions**

1. Do you think ABB would be a good company to work for? If so, why?
2. What are the distinctive features of the company's culture and what effect do these have on employee behaviour?
3. What specific examples of management development practices would fit with the company's approach to this activity?

**Insights & Outcomes: visit the Online Resource Centre at www.oxfordtextbooks.co.uk/orc/banfield_kay2e/ for an up-to-date summary of issues related to talent management.**

## FURTHER READING

Covey, S.P. (2004) *The Seven Habits of Highly Effective People*, Simon and Schuster.

Davenport, T.H. (2005) *Thinking for a Living: How to Get Better Performances and Results From Knowledge Workers*, Harvard Business School Press.

Gardener, H. (2007) *Five Minds for the Future*. Harvard Business School Press.

## REFERENCES


Atkinson, J. (1984) 'Manpower strategies for flexible organisations', *Personnel Management*, Aug, pp. 28–32.

Bareham, K. and Heimer, C. (1998) *ABB—The Dancing Giant*, FT/Pitman.

Beardsmore, R. (2006) 'International comparisons of labour disputes in 2004', *Labour Market Trends*, **114**:4, pp. 117–28.

Bennis, W. (1993) *An Invented Life: Reflections on Leadership and Change*, Addison-Wesley Publishing Co.

Bishop, K. (2004) 'Working time patterns in the UK, France, Denmark and Sweden', *Labour Market Trends*, **112**:3, pp. 113–22.

Buckingham, M. and Coffman, C. (2005) *First, Break All The Rules*, Pocket Books.

Buckingham, G. and Elliot, G. (1993) 'Profile of a successful personnel manager', *Personnel Management*, **25**:8, pp. 26–9.

Castells, M. (2000) *The Rise of the Network Society*, Blackwell.

Clegg, S., Kornberger, M. and Pitsis, T. (2005) *Managing and Organisations*, Sage.

Collins, J. (2001) *Good to Great*, Random House Business Books.

Constable, J. and McCormick, R. (1987) *The making of British Managers: a report for the BIM and CBI into management training, education and development*, British Institute of Management.

Coyle-Shapiro, J. and Kessler, I. (2000) 'Consequences of the psychological contract for the employment relationship: A large-scale survey', *Journal of Management Studies*, **37**:7, pp. 903–30.

*Daily Telegraph* (2009), 'Warning: bosses harm your health', 5 November.

Davenport, T.H. (2005) *Thinking for a Living: How to Get Better Performances and Results from Knowledge Workers*, Harvard Business School Press.

Evans-Pritchard, A. (2005) 'Nestlé forced to reopen loss-making coffee factory', *Daily Telegraph*, 27 August, www.telegraph.co.uk.

Fitz-Enz, J. (1990) *Human Value Management: The Value-Adding Human Resource Management for the 1990s*, Jossey-Bass.

Fitz-Enz, J. (2000) *The ROI of Human Capital*, American Management Association.

Frost, P.J. (2003) *Toxic Emotions at Work*, Harvard Business School Press.

Handy, C.B. (1987) *The making of Managers: a report on management education training and development in the USA, West Germany, France, Japan and the UK*, National Economic Development Office.

Hannagan, T. (2002) *Management: Concepts and Practices*, FT/Prentice-Hall.

Harvey, J.B. (1996) *The Abilene Paradox and Other Meditations on Management*, Jossey-Bass.

Heil, G. et al. (2000) *Douglas McGregor Revisited*, John Wiley & Sons.

Heller, R. (2003) 'Management philosophy: Don't be stupid, keep your management philosophy simple', www.thinkingmanagers.com.

Hiltrop, J.M. (1996) 'Managing the changing psychological contract', *Employee Relations*, **18**:1, pp. 36–49.

Hyman, R. (1975) *Industrial Relations: A Marxist Introduction*, Blackwell.

Lloyd, R. (2008) 'Discretionary Effort and the Performance Domain' ,*The Australian and New Zealand Journal of Organisational Psychology*, 1, pp. 22–34.

Mayo, A. (2001) *The Human Value of the Enterprise*, Nicholas Brealey Publishing.

McGregor, D. (1960) *The Human Side of Enterprise*, McGraw-Hill.

McVeigh, T. (2010) 'Workplace stress: Why the Sunday blues are ruining our weekends', *The Observer*, 16 May, www.guardian.co.uk/society/2010/may/16/workplace-stress-sunday-blues

Megginson, D., Banfield, P. and Joy-Mathews, J. (1999) *Human Resource Development*, 2nd ed., Kogan Page.

Moynagh, M. and Worsley, R. (2001) *Tomorrow's Workplace*, The Tomorrow Project.

Mullins, L.J. (2005) *Management and Organisational Behaviour*, Pearson Education.

Office for National Statistics (June 2008) *Economic & Labour Market Review*, **2**:6.

O'Reilly, C.A. and Pfeffer, J. (2000) *Hidden Value*, Harvard Business School Press.

Ouchi, W. (1981) *Theory Z: How American Management Can Meet the Japanese Challenge*, Addison-Wesley.

Papadopoulos, S. (2009) 'Future Knowledge Worker Management—From Work-For-Hire to Intellectual Capital Co-Ownership' http://ezinearticles.com/?Future-Knowledge-Worker-Management---From-Work-For-Hire-to-Intellectual-Capital-Co-Ownership-P1-of-2&id=2657140..

Peters, T.T. and Waterman, R.H. (1982) *In Search of Excellence: Lessons from America's Best-Run Companies*, Harper and Row.

Pfeffer, J. and Sutton R.I. (2000) *The Knowing–Doing Gap*, Harvard Business School Press.

Pfeffer, J. and Sutton, R.I. (2006) *Hard Facts, Dangerous Half-Truths and Total Nonsense*, Harvard Business School Press.

Pink, D.H. (2002) *Free Agent Nation: The Future of Working for Yourself*, Business Plus.

Reilly, P.A. (1998) 'Balancing flexibility—meeting the interests of employer and employee', *European Journal of Work and Organizational Psychology*, **7**:1 pp. 7–22.

Sainsbury Centre for Mental Health (2007) Policy Paper 8: 'Mental health at work: Developing the business case'.

Scarborough, H. and Carter, C. (2000) *Investigating Knowledge Management*, CIPD.

Scase, R. (2000) *Britain Towards 2010: The Changing Business Environment*, ESRC/Foresight.

Shepherd, J.L. and Mathews, B.P. (2000) 'Employee commitment: academic versus practitioner perspectives', *Employee Relations*, **22**:6, pp. 555–75.

Sparrow, P. and Cooper, C.L. (2003) *The Employment Relationship: Key Challenges for HR*, Butterworth-Heinemann.

Stress Management Society (2010) 'Stress at work', www.stress.org.uk/About-stress.aspx.

Sutton, R.I. (2007) *The No Asshole Rule: Building a Civilized Workplace and Surviving One That Isn't*, Warner Business Books.

Swart, J., Kinnie, N. and Purcell, J. (2003) *People and Performance in Knowledge-Intensive Firms*, CIPD.

Watson, T.J. (2001) *In Search of Management*, Thomson Learning.

Watson, T.J. (2002) *Organising and Managing Work*, FT/Prentice Hall.

Watson, T.J. (2003) *A Business and Its Beliefs: The Ideas That Helped Build IBM*, McGraw-Hill Education.

West, M. (2005) 'Hope springs eternal', *People Management*.

Wickens, P. (1987) *The Road to Nissan: Flexibility, Quality, Teamwork*, Macmillan.

# 2 HRM: An Academic and Professional Perspective

## Key Terms

**Personnel Management** The name given to the specialized management function responsible for an organization's employees.

**Human Resource Management (HRM)** A more recent approach to the management of employees, which sees people as a key organizational resource that needs to be developed and utilized to support the organization's operational and strategic objectives.

**Human Resources (HR)** An alternative to 'people' and also the name used by many organizations to describe the specialized department that deals with the administration and management of employees.

**Human Capital** What people are capable of doing, based on the skills and knowledge they posses which is 'owned' by the individual but can grow and increase in value through personal and professional development.

## Learning Objectives

As a result of reading this chapter and using the Online Resource Centre, you should be able to:

- understand the origins and evolution of Human Resource Management;
- explain the reasons for the change in emphasis from Personnel Management to Human Resource Management;
- engage in a critical exploration of HR and its contribution to individual and organizational performance;
- explain why the role of the line manager is critical to the management of human resources.

# Introduction

The aims of the previous chapter were to introduce students to the more general themes and issues that have a bearing on the employment and management of people, and to put these in the context of how organizations function—particularly the way in which their internal and external environments shape and influence the way in which people are managed at work. This chapter continues to explore how organizations have responded to environmental change in the ways in which they manage employees, but with a particular emphasis on the development of the specialist management functions that were established to help organizations deal with the more complex and difficult employment and management issues that began to emerge in the second half of the twentieth century.

One of the key conclusions that emerges from the analysis of how organizations operate is that, while there are choices to be made about how to manage people, and managers enjoy a significant degree of discretion in the selection and application of human resource strategies, very few organizations can escape from the logic of organization, competitive market forces, the importance of efficient production, and the need to achieve and sustain financial stability.

Organizations experience differences in the degree to which these forces impact on the ways in which they function and on how they are managed—differences that reflect size, sector, competitive pressures, and technology, as well the kind of people the organization employs. Almost all, however, experience pressures to use their productive resources efficiently and productively, and to meet financial and performance targets. It would be difficult to argue that, in an increasingly global economy, these pressures are not likely to increase.

Depending on the kind of organization in which they work, the impact of these forces will be experienced differently by the employee. Some will feel protected from external threats and will enjoy relatively stable working lives, but in situations in which change and instability have become the norm rather than the exception, very few are immune to the effects of globalization, legislative and regulatory changes, market upheavals, and financial pressures.

An inevitable outcome of these developments is that management itself has become more complex and demanding, particularly in terms of the responsibilities of managers in managing people. While the 'managers' in charge of building the pyramids and the UK's canal and rail networks were not without their problems, including those relating to the people they employed, it would probably be fair to say that they enjoyed more power and control over their employees, and used these effectively to impose their own will and interests in preference to those of the workforce. In contrast, managers in the twenty-first century are subject to a growing number of regulations and restrictions that limit their freedom to act unilaterally, and are faced with much more volatility and unpredictability in their external environments. This more challenging internal and external environment that organizations face partly explains the development of new ideas and thinking about the management of people and we consider what this involved later in the chapter. However, before we do it is important to re-visit and re-state the nature of the challenges facing managers in the way they manage their employees.

**For an HRM Insight which indicates the difficulties employers face when their operating environment changes, see the Online Resource Centre extension material 2.1.**

# The Challenge in Managing People

There is a wealth of anecdotal evidence to support the view that, while technology, product or service development, and organizational change challenge managers, the challenge with which managers at all levels seem to have the most difficulty is managing people. These are the challenges that can consume a disproportionate amount of management time and energy, and, paradoxically, despite the sustained investment in management education and training, there is little evidence that today's managers feel confident that they have found the answers to the questions and challenges that face them.

But what are these questions and challenges? Without being exhaustive, the following list represents arguably the most common and persistent questions with which managers are struggling.

- 'What makes employees "tick" and how can they be motivated?'
- 'What do people want from work and what is the best way to reward them?'
- 'Where am I going to get well-qualified staff from and what do I have to do to keep them?'
- 'How am I going to get my workers to be more flexible and deliver higher levels of discretionary effort?'
- 'How can I find the right balance between treating my workers fairly and with consideration, but at the same time ensuring that wider organizational interests are not compromised?'
- 'How can I reduce or eliminate the causes of conflict and build a loyal and committed workforce?'

If, as is argued here, these are questions that are relevant and important to *all* 'managers'—from charge-hands and supervisors up to the most senior executives in both public and private sector organizations—how do they relate to Personnel Management and Human Resource Management, as specialized approaches to the management of human resources?

One way of making the connection is to see the emergence of a specialized people management function as an expression of the difficulties and problems 'general' managers faced in the second half of the twentieth century, as the work environment became more volatile and the pace of change began to accelerate. As management, in general, became more differentiated and specialized, the people management aspect began to acquire a distinctive identity, developed more specialist roles, and became increasingly professionalized. Either as a consequence, or as a cause, of these changes, a distinctive, but provisional area of responsibility and set of activities began to be acquired by the new 'personnel managers'. This new domain reflected the specialist expertise and knowledge claimed by this new breed of manager and the ceding of responsibility for people management matters by line managers, who felt unable or unwilling to take the lead in dealing with many of the questions highlighted above.

Figure 2.1 illustrates the shift from the line manager towards the personnel specialist during the latter part of the twentieth century. Interestingly, one of the key changes in the early part of the twenty-first century has been a reversal of this trend and a redefinition of the relationship and responsibilities of the line manager and personnel specialist.

The debate about the respective roles and contributions of line managers and people management specialists has been an enduring feature of the literature on HR, and the work of Hutchinson and Purcell (2003) has been particularly influential in exposing the tensions and contradictions in the relationship between the two. In its extreme form, this late twentieth-century practice of moving responsibility for key aspects of people management away from the line and into centralized personnel departments effectively disenfranchised line managers, and became one of the most important sources of criticism levelled at people management specialists. More recent research (CIPD, 2005, 2010) has found evidence that this loss of responsibility for HR by the line may have had serious consequences because:

> **front line managers played a pivotal role in terms of implementing and enacting HR policies and practices . . . where employees feel positive about their relationship with their front line managers they are more likely to have higher levels of performance or discretionary behaviour.**

The importance of the line to the way in which people are managed and the outcomes that are generated is also recognized by Tyson and Fell (1986), who argue that:

> **All managers of people are 'personnel managers' in the literal sense, that is they have a personnel function to perform.**

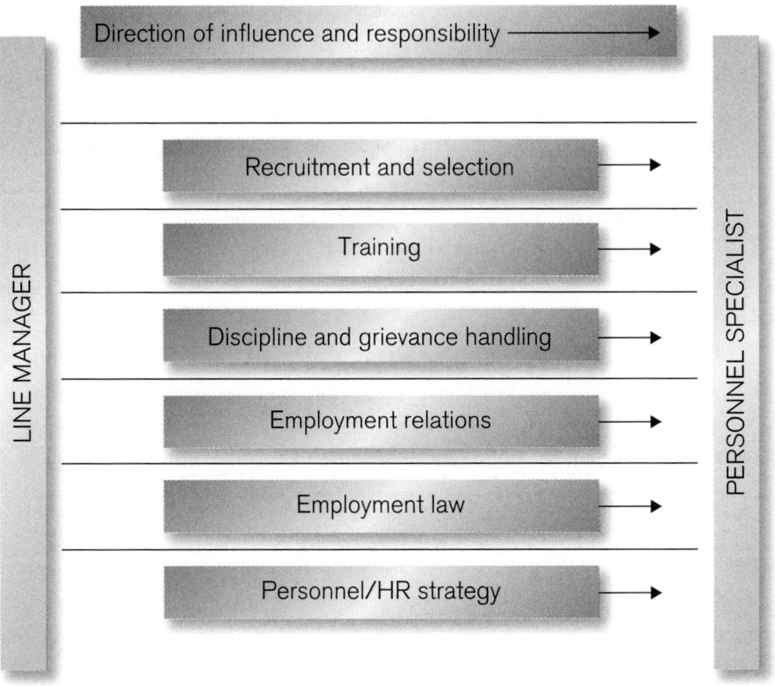


**Figure 2.1** Diagrammatical representation of the shift in responsibility from the line to personnel specialists in the 1970s and 1980s

This means that (using the more contemporary expression) all managers can be seen to be human resource managers because part of their responsibility involves managing resources, of which human resources are a constituent and vital part. Managers who do not, therefore, recognize and fulfil their human resource management role can be said to be failing to meet the full range of their managerial responsibilities.

Confusion surrounding the question of who is responsible and the controversy accompanying the role of centralized HR departments are fundamental problems that still face HR. It is not a problem that can ever entirely be resolved and remains a potential source of tension between line managers and HR professionals. Will the centralized HR department, staffed by HR specialists, prove ultimately to be the preferred model or will its alternative, based on the key role of line managers, come to dominate thinking and practice? In his 1997 article, 'Where is human resources?', Christensen (1997) argues that the future of HR lies in the importance of being able to:

> **differentiate between human resource management and the human resource department.**

He also describes the situation in which, after asking for the HR strategy or plan, senior managers are often presented with a description of current and future activities of the Personnel or HR department, which, he argues, more often than not has little obvious connection to the business. He goes further in this differentiation between the Personnel or HR department and what can only be interpreted as the 'real HR' when he claims that 'the Human Resource Plan doesn't necessarily have anything at all to do with the HR Department', arguing that the HR plan belongs to the business. Accepting that there is a lack of clarity in terms of who is responsible for human resource management, he offers the opinion that:

> **Managers and HR professionals of the future will understand that line managers are the 'people managers' of their organisations and as such, they are ultimately accountable for human resource management.**
> (Christensen, 1997)

The conclusion that can be reached at this point is that the growth of a specialist people management function—the question of what it is called is considered later—has the potential of making major contributions to the way in which people are recruited, selected, trained, and rewarded. While these specialists may have a key role in the design of policies and procedures, however, it is the line managers who have the responsibility *for delivery* and this can never be taken or given away. As a consequence of this realization, the trend over the past ten years or so has been for the line to re-engage more explicitly and directly in the management of its employees, with HR specialists playing a less executive, and more supportive, role.

A consequence of the line re-engaging directly with employees—and one that has major implications for the size of specialist HR departments and for those working in them—is that fewer HR professionals will be needed in this new HR 'architecture'. Reilly and Williams (2006) refer to British Airways halving its HR department in 1989, devolving much of its HR responsibility to line management, and to the BBC, who more recently cut over half of its specialist HR jobs. Clearly, there is an ongoing tension and dynamic between the line and HR specialists, with some organizations abandoning centralized departments altogether in favour of a decentralized and devolved approach to the management of people; others, particularly in the public sector, continue to retain well-resourced HR departments and a key role for the HR specialist.

Arguably the most important question that emerges from the growth of specialist 'people managers' and different approaches to the way in which people are managed is, however, not about differences of definition and conceptual models, but rather about *what* works and *why*. Tyson and Fell (1986) articulate this concern when they pose the question:

**Given that the appointment of these specialists is one answer to the question of how to manage people, how effective is it?**

For a summary of the origins of Personnel Management see the Online Resource Centre extension material 2.2.

# The Rise of Human Resource Management

The term 'Human Resource Management' has its origins not in the UK, but in the USA during the 1980s, and is associated with the work of such writers as Tichy et al. (1982) and Beer et al. (1985). For some, it came to represent a fundamentally different approach to the management of people, based on new assumptions about employees, about the changing nature of work, and about how best to maximize the potential of an organization's human resources. Many UK organizations were quick to embrace this new development and many personnel departments became, almost overnight, departments of human resources (HR); personnel officers were transformed into HR officers and managers. Not all organizations embraced HRM, in that they preferred to retain the 'personnel management' title on the grounds that this avoided the impersonal association with their employees as 'human resources', but, over time, more and more specialized 'people' departments became known as HR departments.

There is, however, still argument and disagreement over what this new development actually represented, although most of the argument and debate has been confined to academics. Those actively involved in the management of people appear to have been less concerned about titles, concerned more with practice and with the effects on employee behaviour and performance of new ideas about commitment, involvement, resource utilization, and the role of the line manager.

The academic debate is, of course, not without interest or relevance for those who practise HR and a number of important contributions to this debate need to be analysed. The key issue—that of whether HRM is, or is not, different to Personnel Management—is considered by Hoque and Noon (2001), who quote both David Guest, arguing that the HRM label *does* represent something new and distinctive, and John Storey, who suggests that there are 27 points of distinction between the two. Yet Karen Legge (1995) begins her chapter on 'Human Resource Management' by quoting a caller on BBC4, who described HRM as:

> **a posh way of describing a personnel manager . . . but it goes a bit further than that.**

In trying to make sense out of what appear to be quite different views, Hoque and Noon argue that:

> **the key issue is whether departments that have adopted the HR title operate differently from those that have retained the personnel title.**
> (Hoque and Noon, 2001, p. 6)

They suggest that, based on numerous anecdotal evidence, the introduction of the HR title has meant little more than a 'change of name on the door'.

Gennard and Kelly (1994) researched the views of personnel directors and came to the conclusion that the debate over differences between Personnel Management and HRM was largely sterile: many of the organizations from which they had gained information displayed evidence of fundamental changes in employment and management practices, but many did not adopt the HR label to indicate or justify these changes. In other words, practitioners were embracing many of the ideas of HRM, but were not necessarily adopting the label or changing the departmental title. Simply looking for evidence of difference by focusing on nominal changes in department titles is not, therefore, likely to be particularly helpful.

In a later telephone-based survey of a wider sample of practitioners, Grant and Oswick (1998) found that 50 per cent of their sample was convinced that HRM was something different to Personnel Management; 37 per cent believed that there was no difference.

A further source of confusion lies in the way in which HRM is split into two forms, with a distinction made between 'hard' and 'soft' types of HRM. The *hard* approach emphasizes the quantitative, strategic aspects of managing people as organizational assets. A *soft* approach instead highlights the importance of communication, motivation, leadership, and the mutual commitment of employees and employers. Unfortunately, using such simplistic terms to represent complex phenomena not only has the effect of trivializing the debate, but also of presenting the practitioner with what appears to be choice between one or the other interpretations. More usefully, it is better to present the challenge as one in which both approaches are incorporated into the practice of HR and of being sensitive to the conditions and circumstances which require an emphasis to be given to the hard or soft versions of HRM.

Despite the differences between, and within, these approaches, it is important to try to capture some of the most important differences between the two, which Figure 2.2 summarizes.

For students coming to this debate for the first time, the attempt to understand the debate about Personnel Management and HRM, and to make sense of the ambiguous language and sometimes inaccessible arguments, can be a frustrating experience. Tony Watson (2002) recorded the story of one student, who was left confused, and an abbreviated version is presented in the following HRM Insight.

### HRM INSIGHT 2.1 The story of Sue Ridgebridge

This story is told in detail by Tony Watson (Watson, T.J. (2002) *Organising and Managing Work*, FT/Prentice Hall). The essence of the story is the confusion and frustration experienced by a student being 'taught' Human Resource Management at a UK university.

The student, Sue Ridgebridge, starts her story by explaining that, when the organization she worked for changed the title of the specialized people management function from 'Personnel' to 'Human Resources', it represented little more than a continuation and development of what had previously been done under the personnel banner. She speculated that the reasons behind the change were more to do with being fashionable and the need to be seen to be moving away from the welfare tradition of Personnel Management towards something more business-orientated.

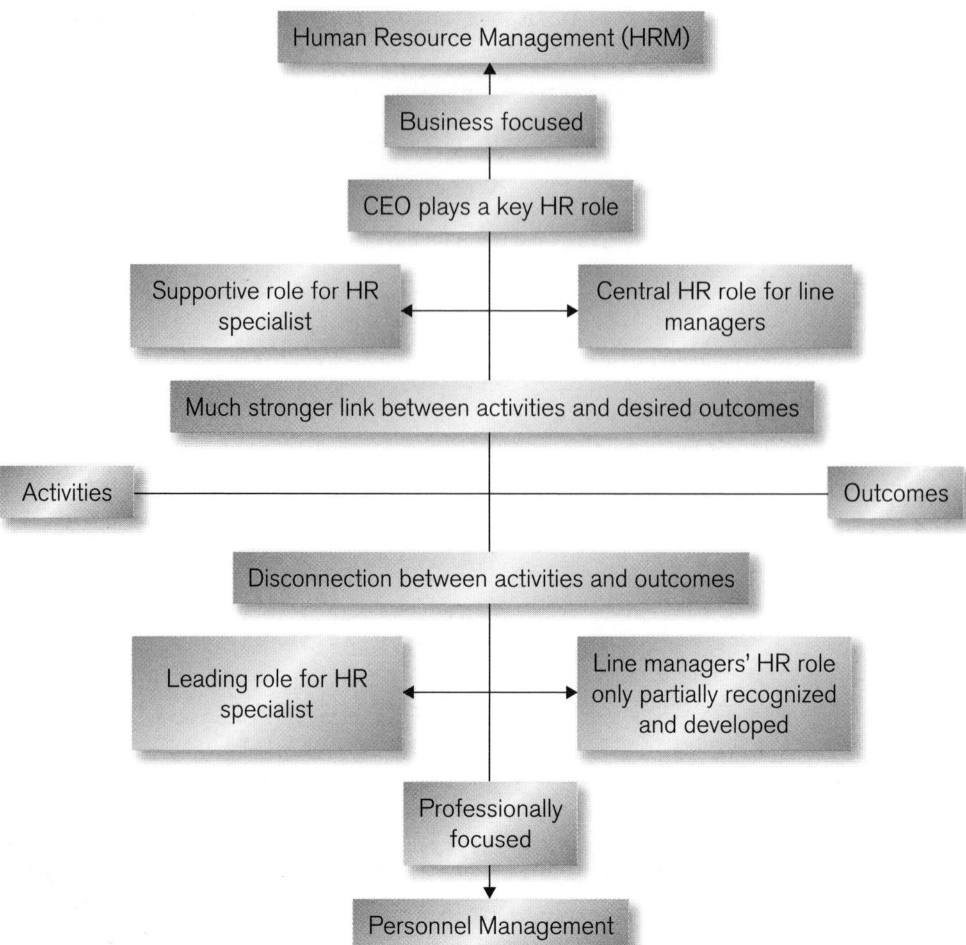


**Figure 2.2** A comparison of Personnel Management and HRM

As far as the experience of being taught HRM was concerned, Sue had a particular problem: she was confused about whether HRM is to do with the general business of managing people or represented a particular approach. She had real difficulty in understanding what one of her tutors meant when he said that 'Human Resource Management is a particular approach to human resource management'! As someone who had spent most of her working life in a personnel department, she also felt aggrieved when her tutors emphasized that the distinctions between Personnel Management and Human Resource Management were to do with the former's:

- short-termism;
- tendency towards a reactive, fire-fighting approach to problems;
- association with collectivism;
- inability to move away from transactional, towards transformational, management;
- lack of a strategic dimension.

When presented with John Storey's list of 27 differences between Personnel Management and Human Resource Management (Storey, 1992), her response was to cross out HRM and re-title the table '27 differences between good personnel management and bad personnel management'. (See also Watson, 2006)

The point about this example is that it highlights the problem that students can experience when being introduced to the subject for the first time, and illustrates the difficulties they have in understanding the terms and labels used by academics, many of which tend to confuse rather than enlighten. It also provides justification for Watson's comment that:

> **these criticisms are well founded and . . . there is a serious ambiguity in the HRM literature about its analytical and prescriptive elements.**
> (Watson, 2002)

What complicates the search for a greater degree of clarity in the characteristics of, and relationship between, these two approaches to the management of people is that academic writers rarely make it known to the reader whether they are offering:

- definitions and descriptions based on *practice*—in other words, whether they are studying these two approaches empirically and making comparisons between the two based on observed or discovered differences; or
- presenting what are known as *analytical or conceptual models*, with each approach associated with certain practices and characteristics based on assumed or conceptualized differences.

What adds to the confusion is, as Storey quite rightly claims, the fact that writers often fail to explain which position they are adopting, and—more worryingly—fail to tell the reader when they switch from one position to another.

Storey also sets out to establish the defining characteristics of HRM, which set it apart from Personnel Management at the philosophical, or belief, level. A more detailed list of 27 different dimensions between the two approaches can be found on page 34 of his book (Storey, 1992). He argues, however, that the following four key elements express the essence of the concept.

- HRM represents the belief that people, or human resources, are the key to organizational successes. The majority of employees, in the way they contribute and work for the organization, can make the critical difference between success and failure, and management needs to understand the employees' value to the organization.
- HRM embodies a much greater understanding and awareness of the strategic importance of the human resource. Its management cannot and should not be delegated to and reserved for human resource professionals, but must involve the direct and ongoing involvement and leadership of senior management.
- HRM, unlike Personnel Management, is central to organizational performance and, as such, must involve all managers with line responsibility. HRM is seen as being delivered primarily by and through line management, who are supported and advised by HR specialists.
- HRM reflects the belief in the importance of integration, both vertical and horizontal, and the use of particular strategies to improve and reward employee performance in pursuit of enhanced organizational performance.

**KEY CONCEPT Vertical integration**

**This relates to the linkage between the policies and practices associated with the management of people, and the wider business or organizational strategies and objectives. Vertical integration can be based on the cascading down of corporate priorities and objectives, which then inform and give direction to HR priorities, policies, and practices. Alternatively, it can be based on representatives of HR informing senior management of the current and future state of human resource capacity and capabilities, which helps to ensure that corporate strategy is grounded in a realistic understanding of what is, or will be, available to deliver the strategy.**

**KEY CONCEPT Horizontal integration**

This relates to the linkage between different HR activities and practices, and emphasizes the importance of looking at what HR does holistically, rather than as separate and disconnected elements. The concept also expresses the need for consistency in the sense that the way in which the activities are carried out reflects understood and agreed strategic objectives. For example, adopting an individualist, rather than a collectivist, approach to the management of people implies the use of individual reward and development practices if consistency in practice is to be achieved.

Whether these defining features of HRM are actually delivered and experienced in practice—that is, whether they become operationalized—is another matter. These differences suggest, at least, that HRM is an approach that is, or should, involve a more systematic and sophisticated engagement with employees and managers as part of the process of adding value to the organization through the efforts and contributions of all of its employees.

Although, in one sense, it matters little what label is used to give an identity to these underlying beliefs, because it is the beliefs themselves that are important, for many practitioners the label *is* important because it symbolizes the departure from one approach to the management of people and the adoption of another. This other approach is considered to be more in tune with changes in the nature of work, the organizational pressures to 'deliver', and the need for a more flexible, committed and productive labour force.

**Table 2.1** A summary of the main analytical differences between Personnel Management and Human Resource Management

| Personnel Management | Human Resource Management |
|---|---|
| Emphasis on collectivity | More emphasis given to individuals |
| Generalized HR solutions | More tailored and bespoke solutions |
| Centralization of HR responsibility | Greater devolution of authority and responsibility for managing people |
| Increasing role for HR specialists | Senior managers and those in line positions seen as key to delivering effective HR 'solutions' |
| Associated with maintaining status quo and stability | Associated with maintaining stability and driving through changes in structures, practices, and capabilities |
| Associated with trade unionism and managing conflict | Associated with capabilities, performance and outcomes |
| 'Can't do' mindset | 'Can do' mindset |
| Thought to be reactive | Associated with a more proactive orientation |
| Associates employees primarily as an economic resource and a cost | Much more emphasis on employees as a source of resourcefulness |
| More operationally orientated | Operates at the strategic and operational levels |
| Lacking in sufficient integration of activities | Strong emphasis on vertical and horizontal integration |

# And then came Strategic Human Resource Management (SHRM)!

One of the questions inevitably asked by students of HR is: 'If Human Resource Management represents, among other things, a more strategic approach to the management of people, what is Strategic Human Resource Management (SHRM) about and how is it different?'

This is a question that has merit and deserves a considered answer. The first thing to say is that SHRM is not a third distinctive and different approach to the management of people, with its own 27 differences that help to establish its separate identity. For many who use this term, it means little more than recognizing the strategic dimension of HRM. In this sense, as Boxall and Purcell (2000) state, when the adjective 'strategic' is applied to HRM, in many cases, it means nothing at all.

Firstly, SHRM, for some academics and practitioners, does represent something more than the strategic dimension of HRM and this 'more' can be explained in three ways. SHRM is concerned with the way in which the management of people is critical to, and contributes towards, organizational effectiveness. It therefore represents a level of thinking and a set of activities that connect the domain of HRM more explicitly to the strategic needs and interests of the organization. Put in a slightly different way, this means that, while HRM is associated with the integration of its activities at the horizontal level, SHRM is more concerned with integrating HRM activities vertically, ensuring that these 'fit' with the strategic direction in which the organization is moving.

The concept of fit and integration is explained in more detail in the next chapter.

For a practical example of the challenges of integrating different HR initiatives together see the Online Resource Centre material 2.3.

Secondly, strategic choice is about making critical decisions in the key areas of managing people, such as rewards, relations, training and development, recruitment and selection, and performance management, and involves management deciding on:

- whether to commit to an individualist approach to employee relations or to recognize and negotiate with trade unions;
- whether to reward employees on merit, performance, and potential, or on the basis of the jobs they do and their length of service;
- whether to employ only talented people or those that are available;
- whether to base the development of employees on learning or training;
- whether to adopt a 'one size fits all' approach to the development of HR practices or to develop more tailored and individualized policies and practices.

SHRM might, in the context of strategic choice, be seen to represent the processes and decisions that shape the organization's philosophy towards its employees and how they are managed in relation to the above strategically important areas.

One final way of making sense of SHRM, and one that is not unconnected to the previous three, is to see it in terms of the development of what Becker et al. (2001) call the 'strategic HR architecture'. This concept expresses the full range of HR activities, interventions, policies, and practices, and links these to the effect they have on the value-creating potential of all employees, and how this added-value potential is actually measured and utilized.

The critical point that emerges from this brief review of key contributions to the meaning of SHRM is that the management of people *must* have a strategic, as well as an operational, direction, but what this actually means and how it is expressed is likely to differ between organizations, which need to express their own unique needs and requirements in determining what SHRM means to them. Whatever their chosen form of expression, one thing that they are all likely to have in common is the need to ensure that what HR does is connected to, rather than disconnected from, the wider organizational context. The strategic dimension of HR is explored more fully in the following chapter, but before we return to this the important relationship between HR and performance needs to be addressed.

## The HRM and Performance Debate

The confusion and lack of consensus over what HRM is, as a distinctive approach to the management of human resources, has been explored earlier in the chapter and the significance of this 'new' thinking about HR in relation to its academic and professional impact has also been alluded to. But the questionable value of this debate is less significant than the much more important question of:

**Does HRM make a difference to organizational performance?**

David Guest's earlier work that linked theories of HRM to theories of organizational performance offered important insights into this critical relationship (Guest, 1997). It resulted in numerous research projects designed to generate hard evidence that would support the claims of those who believed that, not only did HRM have the potential to deliver strategically valuable outcomes, but was actually achieving this, or at least in organizations that embraced this new approach (Neal et al., 2004; Purcell, 2003).

One of the enduring difficulties with HR, both in its departmental and more defused manifestations, is that showing conclusively that what HR does is directly connected to behavioural and organizational outcomes, and this has not only been a problem for HR and its supporters but will continue to remain so because, as Legge argued, it is extremely difficult if not impossible to establish clear cut cause and effect relationships, where what HRM 'does' can be unambiguously connected to particular outcomes.

For a case study that explores the link between HR and performance changes see the Online Resources Centre extension material 2.4

The work of Jaap Paauwe and colleagues in the Netherlands reflects the continuing academic interest in the HRM/Performance relationship. (Paauwe, 2004; Paauwe and Boselie, 2008). After reviewing numerous articles and research papers into the HRM and Performance link, Paauwe and Boselie reach an interesting conclusion. They claim that academics and practitioners need to look beyond the more obvious HR activities such as staffing and human resource planning—and we would suggest others such as appraisal systems and reward schemes. They say:

> **A real contribution to performance . . . will only happen once we approach HRM from a more holistic and balanced perspective, including part of the organizational climate and culture, aimed at bringing about the alignment between individual values, corporate values and societal values. (Paauwe and Boselie, 2008)**

They adopt a conceptual approach, originally developed by Fred Herzberg (2003), arguing that many of the activities undertaken by HR represent hygiene factors which if not done well will result in falling performance, but which in themselves, and even collectively, will not produce the step change improvements that produce sustained competitive advantage.

**RESEARCH INSIGHT 2.1 The HRM and Performance Link**

This exercise is best undertaken in two groups.

One group reads the CIPD report by John Purcell on unlocking the Black Box.

**(Purcell, J. (2003) *Understanding the People and Performance Link: Unlocking the Black Box*, CIPD.)**

The main findings of the report need to be summarized on no more than two PowerPoint slides. On one further slide critically comment on the methodology underpinning the research.

The second group looks at the article by Paauwe and Boselie and again summarizes on two slides the key points they make.

**(Paauwe, J. and Boselie, P. (2008) 'HRM and Performance: What's Next?', *CAHARS Working Papers Series*, Paper 474. http://digitalcommons.ir/cornell.edu/caharsswp/474)**

On a third slide list the so-called HR 'hygiene' activities and compare them with a list of HR 'motivating' activities. Both groups should then present to each other and discuss their findings.

One way of interpreting Paauwe and Boselie's argument is that HR need's to think more holistically in the search for better ways to impact organizational performance, which might be expressed in terms of organizational capability building. This refers to an organization's ability to create, mobilize, and utilize its key resources—in this case its human resources—to maximum effect. The concept emphasizes the key strategic role that HR can, and must, play if the organization is to optimize the contribution from all its employees. The concept is also important because it helps to re-define what HR represents: it is seen less as a series of activities and responsibilities and more in terms of a resource and capability builder and a business function that exercises maximum leverage in the way this resource and its capabilities are used. The debate about HRM, originally expressed as a choice between 'hard' and 'soft' versions is now being defined in relation to two quite different conceptions and levels of organizational engagement. But interestingly, the question again is not about which one to choose but what each actually has the potential to deliver if successfully practiced.

# HR—A Critical Perspective

One of the enduring features of the academic debate on HR is the criticism that has been levelled at HR professionals and the HR function for failing to live up to the expectations of those who were told, or believed, that HR was the key to unlocking the potential of an organization's human resources (Hammonds, 2005). Many of these criticisms are well founded, although it would be wrong to suggest that they apply to all those who work in HR. Equally, many HR departments enjoy a positive reputation and are valued by line managers for the contributions they make to the management of people; others, unfortunately, do not and are more associated with the administration of employment rather than the effective management of people.

Because these criticisms are serious rather than superficial, and are as much to do with the nature of the HR function itself as with those who work in it, it is important that they are properly considered and evaluated and this theme of questioning and critically evaluating HR's role and organizational contributions is further developed in the next chapter. Before this can be done, we must ensure that the meanings of the key terms referred to in this section are clearly understood.

- HR

  This is increasingly used to refer to the human resources department or section that exists in many medium and large organizations. In this sense, 'HR' means the HR department, or the department of human resource management. It doesn't help that the terms HR and HRM are also used interchangeably.

- Personnel departments

  Some organizations have retained the title of 'Personnel', but for our purposes, we can equate the personnel department to that of HR. Organizations such as the BBC use the title People Department as an alternative and less impersonal description.

- The HR function

  This has two meanings. The first is a general one and relates to all of the activities and contributions involved in managing people that are undertaken by managers, and often by employees, throughout the organization. The second meaning is more restrictive and essentially relates to the specialized department, which can be called HR or personnel, within which HR or personnel administrators and professionals are based.

  More recently, the use of the term People Departments has increased, with organizations such as the BBC and Eaga plc adopting these titles. The reason reflects either a pragmatic or philosophical approach to the employment and management of staff, where the word 'people' rather than 'human resources' expresses, for those who prefer people, a real difference in approach and way of working.

The reason for trying to make these differences clear is that, as will be seen later, there are almost 'two' kinds of HR and many of the criticisms made by academics and managers relate to only one of these (Banfield, 2005).

Karen Legge (1978) comments that:

> **On a daily basis personnel managers are confronted by ambiguities that arise out of problems in defining personnel management . . . and which lie at the heart of personnel specialist's perennial concern with the issue of credibility.**

This suggests that many of the criticisms levelled at HR are not to do with lack of professionalism or an inability to operate at a strategic level, although that may well be the case in specific organizations, but reflect deeply rooted issues and problems that may not, in fact, be resolvable. The ambiguities that Legge identifies are:

- The problem of demonstrating unequivocally that HR or personnel, as an organizational activity, can and does make a significant contribution to the behaviour and performance of employees, a point considered earlier in the chapter and one that represents a central theme of the whole book. This is because, as we will see Watson argue later in this chapter, employees, as people rather than resources, are capable of independent thought and action—they are not simply passive 'things to be managed', and behave in ways that reflect their unique individuality and a wide range of influences from within and outside the organization. This means that it is difficult to prove conclusively that either desirable or undesirable employee behaviour—for example, low productivity or high absenteeism—is the *result* of good or bad personnel/HR management. Legge goes on to state that:

  > **Difficulty in demonstrating a direct relationship between personnel management activities and valued organisational outcomes presents particular difficulties for the personnel department.**
  > (Legge, 1978)

- Because all managers, whether specialists in HR or on the line, are in an important sense 'managers of people', that is, human resource or personnel managers (note the significance of the lower case), the contributions that each party makes to desirable and undesirable outcomes is difficult to separate out and measure. This means that it is possible for one party to blame the other when things go wrong and to claim the credit when things go well. Much depends, of course, on the nature of working relationships between specialists and line managers, and the way in which the HR or personnel department operates, but the problem of causal relationship between what one party does and its effects is an enduring one.

- Although nominally offering an advisory service, the HR specialist can be seen by line managers to be taking on executive responsibilities and introducing practices and policies that, although in the interests of the organization as a whole, can be perceived as intrusive, unhelpful and having little relevance to the line manager's priorities and agendas. In seeking to develop their functional expertise and professional identity, those who work in HR can become detached from 'the needs of the business', and, as a consequence, run the risk of being seen as 'marginal' and adding little of value. An example of this tendency might be the increasing emphasis HR give to diversity issues, which, while of social importance, can be perceived by line managers as having little direct relevance to matters of production or to 'bottom-line performance'.

**STUDENT ACTIVITY 2.1 The Business Case for Diversity Training**

1. Research the literature on the business case for managing diversity.
2. Taking the role of a team of HR professionals, prepare a PowerPoint presentation, to be delivered to the CEO of an organization of your choice, which presents your findings and recommendations.
3. Faced with a sceptical and pressurized group of line managers who have responsibility for delivering a product or service—you can pick your own industry or organization—what would you say that would convince them that HR has not jumped on yet another bandwagon and that the investment in learning about diversity issues is justifiable?
4. What desirable or value-added outcomes would you be able to identify from such an investment?

The sense that HR is somehow 'failing to deliver' is a central theme in the writings of a number of influential American writers and is one that is explored further in the following chapter. Jeffrey Pfeffer (1997), for example, writing about the future of HRM, suggests that it would be wrong to conclude that the growing interest in HR and HRM necessarily means that the future of the HR function (in its departmental form) is bright:

> **My advice is to resist the temptation to believe that HR managers and staff in organizations have a rosy future, or a future at all, because there are some profound problems facing human resources as a function within organizations, as contrasted with the study of human resources as a topic area, that makes its viability and continued survival problematical.**
> (Pfeffer, 1997)

Posing the question, 'where is the HR function in the debate about flexibility, contingent working arrangements and the implementation of high performance working practices?', he suggests that the tentative answer is, 'largely absent'. He continues:

> **To the extent it has a presence, HR is frequently an accomplice in a number of trends such as downsizing and contingent work arrangements that promise to actually undo much of the progress made in managing the employment relationship in the past several decades.**
> (Pfeffer, 1997)

Pfeffer is particularly critical of the lack of leadership shown by HR professionals in demonstrating the relationship between HR practices and organizational performance, and he believes that many are unaware of the empirical business case for managing people effectively. Despite these criticisms, he believes that HR professionals do have a future, but only if they change their roles and acquire new skills. Above all, he argues, they need to learn how to add value to the organization.

Dave Ulrich, one of the most influential writers on HR, has levelled similar criticisms at the HR profession. In his 1998 article, 'A new mandate for Human Resources', he asks whether we should do away with HR, justifying this by referring to the serious and widespread doubts about HR's contribution to organizational performance. But before we progress his arguments, it is worth noting that many of the earlier and indeed current definitions of Personnel Management and HRM—he is not distinguishing these from what he means by HR—do not include any explicit reference to organizational performance. In their most recent edition, Torrington et al. (2005) retain, with only slight modifications, the same definition of 'Human Resource Management' as they gave for 'Personnel Management' in 1979:

> **Human Resource Management is a series of activities which: first enables working people and the organisation which uses their skills to agree about the objectives and nature of their working relationships and, secondly, ensures that the agreement is fulfilled.**
> (Torrington et al., 2005)

Nowhere in this definition is there any reference to HR supporting the business, contributing to organizational performance or adding value; whether any of these could be implied in the wording or sentiments expressed in the definition is, at best, arguable. And this is Ulrich's main point: he claims that it is precisely because HR is still associated with traditional activities, rather than with outcomes, and with a concern with consensus, rather than with delivering valued contributions, that many still see HR, as:

> **often ineffective, incompetent, and costly; in a phrase, it is value sapping.**
> (Ulrich, 1998)

On reflection, his answer to these criticisms is not, in fact, to 'do away with HR', but to 'create an entirely new role and agenda for the field', with HR not being 'defined by what it does, but by what it delivers—results that enrich the organisation's value to customers, investors, and employees' (p. 124).

It's interesting to compare the Torrington et al. definition of Human Resource Management with that of a comparable American text. Denisi and Griffin (2001) provide a definition much closer to that with which Ulrich would feel comfortable. They argue that human resource management (the wider function *and* the specialized approach) can be understood as:

> **the comprehensive set of managerial activities and tasks concerned with developing and maintaining a qualified workforce—human resources—in ways that contribute to organisational effectiveness.**

The need for HR—and again it is important to understand that Ulrich uses this to refer to HR professionals and the work of the HR department, not the wider contributions to the management of people that come from senior executives, line managers, and from the employee group itself—to ensure that its activities are connected to the 'real work' of the organization, led him to develop his model of a new HR, which would contribute to organizational competitiveness and performance. This model is summarized in Figure 2.3.

**Figure 2.3** A framework for understanding HR roles and contributions

The four key roles that HR professionals need to play to deliver the contributions outlined in the model are as follows:

- **A partner in strategy execution**

  This doesn't mean that HR should take responsibility for HR and business strategy, which is rightly the domain of the chief executive, but that the head of the HR department should be an equal partner with other senior managers and should 'have a seat at the top table'.

- **An administrative expert**

  This is about getting the basics right and adopting a much more instrumental approach to the use of procedures. The emphasis needs to be on the efficiency of the HR department—reducing its cost base and speeding up its cycle times, without compromising on quality or effectiveness.

- **An employee champion**

  This is about HR recognizing that work intensification and an increased sense of insecurity are becoming the new reality for many people and that this is associated with weakened levels of employee commitment. This, in turn, affects the preparedness of employees to contribute more than their contracted level of effort and performance. The role of HR here is to ensure that employees remain engaged and committed, or become re-engaged, either directly through the activities of HR or by HR working with line managers to ensure that they can create a positive psychological and emotional working environment.

- **A change agent**

  According to Ulrich (1997), this role involves HR in building the organization's capacity to embrace and to capitalize on change. Given that change is the norm for most organizations, the ability to implement and manage the change process is seen as critical to the organization's ability to survive and prosper and to reap the benefits from the changes that have been made. Facilitating change and reducing employee/management resistance is seen as a key HR contribution.

Interestingly, Ulrich is aware of the danger of oversimplifying the roles that HR professionals need to play in order to gain credibility for themselves and the HR function: it isn't simply a question of moving from the operational to the strategic, or from a reactive to a proactive, orientation. The reality is that HR roles are multiple, changing, and complex, involving them in policing *and* partnering, and delivering operational *and* making strategic contributions. He concludes:

> **For HR professionals to add value to their increasingly complex businesses, they must perform increasingly complex and, at times, even paradoxical roles.**
> (Ulrich, 1997)

In a more recent work, Ulrich and Brockbank (2005) refine Ulrich's model of HR roles to reflect a more sophisticated understanding of what HR professionals need to be and to contribute to in the next two decades, compared to the situation in the 1990s. The revised role model emphasizes the importance of the HR professional becoming:

- a developer of human capital;
- an employee advocate;
- a functional expert;
- a strategic partner;
- a leader of the HR function.

The main changes are in the incorporation of the change agent role within that of the strategic partner and the recognition of the importance of leadership in HR.

**STUDENT ACTIVITY 2.2**

In his book, *Human Resource Champions* (1997, Harvard Business School Press), Ulrich compares what he calls the old myths associated with HR with the new realities facing HR professionals. Working in groups, your task is to fill in the 'new realities' part of the table without referring to the book. Only make reference to the original table on completion of the exercise.

| Myths and misconceptions | The 'new realities' |
|---|---|
| People want to work in HR because they like people | *(Complete this part of the table)* |
| Anyone can do HR | |
| HR is woolly and too people-focused | |
| HR is about controlling the line and telling them what to do | |
| HR is about rules and procedures and enforcing these | |
| HR is the conscience of the organization | |
| HR is full of fads and jargon | |
| HR is staffed by nice people | |
| HR is HR's business | |

# Adding Value and Transforming the HR Function

A key theme of Ulrich and Brockbank's 2005 book is that of added value, one that is consistent with the idea that HR, in its departmental form, needs to be known for what it delivers rather than what it does; or put in slightly different way, for outcomes rather than activities. The concept of adding value is in one sense un-problematical, but in another complex and operationally challenging. Part of the difficulties with HR engaged in activities that add value is over what this actually means. Value can be expressed in terms of objective and 'hard' criteria—we can measure added value by volume and value, but it also has a subjective dimension where adding value is linked to individual perception and different stakeholder perspectives rather than unequivocal measurements. Take, for example, the contemporary interest in employee well-being, a development in the work of HR particularly associated with the public sector. Whilst the intentions of an employee well-being policy are difficult to argue with, what do such policies actually achieve, assuming they are successful, and what is the 'value' of any claimed for 'value adding outcomes'? Although there have been developments in HR metrics—see Chapter 11—quantifying the value of such policies is still difficult and any claims made by HR are unlikely to go without challenge. There are, of course, the often ignored costs associated with such policies, and any meaningful attempt to measure added value needs to reflect the balance between costs and outcomes, in other words net added value.

**STUDENT ACTIVITY 2.3**

Read the CIPD Report on well-being at work (Chartered Institute of Personnel and Development (2007) 'What's happening with well-being at work?', www.cipd.co.uk) as part of researching this subject. The activity should be based on groups role playing—with one taking a HR perspective and another representing line managers in the same organization. The organization can be fictitious or based on one known to the participants.

The objective is for the HR group to present a case to the group representing line management in favour of introducing a well-being policy into the organization. They have to present an argued case and identify its added value outcomes.

The second group should read the same report and produce their own presentation which takes a much more critical perspective and reflects a view that such policies are attractive but don't add value to the organization.

Both groups then discuss their respective findings/positions and try to reach a shared position on what well-being policies actually need to deliver to justify their introduction.

One of the most interesting arguments presented by Ulrich and Brockbank is that which supports the increasing use of outsourcing many of HR's administrative functions as a value adding development. HR outsourcing has become popular in the UK as well as in the US, (CIPD, 2005; Lawler et al., 2004), and the position taken by Lawler and his colleagues is that added value is achieved by outsourcing the administrative work of HR, with the value gained from this coming from efficiency savings. This essentially means that more specialized and efficient resources are contracted to do the administrative tasks associated with the 'hiring and firing' of people which in turn reduces the costs of the contracting organization through a reduced HR headcount. A second effect is that, free from time consuming and resource intensive work, the HR department can re-focus its professional staff towards more value-adding activities.

The effect of HR outsourcing is potentially profound in relation to the structure of the HR function. This 'transformation' is highlighted by Lawler et al. when they say:

> **We argue that the field of HR is being split in half. Much of the traditional, administrative, and transactional work of HR–payroll, benefits administration, staffing policies, training logistics, and so forth–must be carried out more efficiently. Most large firms have either built service centres and invested in HR technology or outsourced these transactions. What is left after transactional HR has been automated, centralized eliminated or outsourced forms the heart of this book. The HR Value Proposition.**
> (Lawler et al., 2004)

They define value in terms of the outcome of transactions, which is determined by the recipient rather than the giver. They claim that the HR department adds value when it helps other organizational stakeholders achieve their goals, and as is pointed out in the following chapter, HR has the opportunity to achieve high levels of added value if it can successfully engage with the strategic domain. Lawler et al. also make the point that where organizational resources are becoming increasing scarce and costly, activities that don't add value are not worth pursuing. We would go further, arguing that HR activities that result in negative net added value are not only not worth pursuing but should cease to be part of what HR does.

The theme of transforming HR and making it a relevant, contemporary and value adding business function is continued in the most recent book from the group of US writers associated with David Ulrich (Ulrich et al., 2009). The book offers very little new theoretical content and its central transformation model can be viewed at http://hrtransformationbook.com. What it does represent is a four stage approach to changing the way HR understands the challenges it faces, recognizing the importance of HR becoming integrated with 'the business' and carefully managing its own internal transformation. The four elements/stages in their model are:

- Understanding the external business context and the key requirements and expectations of internal stakeholders and 'customers'.
- Understanding what kind of outcomes the organization needs to be successful now and into the future. These outcomes may differ between organizations and within an organization over time but the essential requirement is that they add value, satisfy customer requirements, and impact on key business metrics.
- Implement an internal transformation of HR. This includes acquiring a new 'mind set' which helps shape and direct thinking and action, develop HR strategies that have a high impact value, achieving efficiencies in the way the HR department operates and building professional and managerial capabilities.

- Understanding the importance of accountability for what is done and what is achieved. This crucially involves bringing the different contributors to the HR function together to share successes and failures. What the HR department needs to do is to accept that much of what it does is 'through the line' rather that in direct contact with employees and this means that failure to recognize mutual responsibilities and accountabilities will only serve to support the displacement of blame.

See the CIPD's latest review of the future of HR to give this debate a stronger UK perspective (CIPD, 2010).

**PRACTITIONER INSIGHT Roger Collins, Director of HR & OD in an NHS Trust Hospital—HR in the NHS: Leading on the pay bill Challenge**

From 2000 until 2008, the role of the HR practitioner in the NHS has been to increase the size of the workforce; the NHS planning framework during that period set out very clear targets for expanding workforce numbers, but now we face a very different situation. Pay makes up approximately 70% of total spend in the NHS and now the focus is very much on pay bill reduction as part of an integrated approach to cost improvement programmes, ensuring that where potential pay bill savings are identified, the impact on the quality of clinical care provided for our patients is not diminished. This is a real challenge. In our organisation, HR is firmly established as a key member of the board team, although this is not uniform across all NHS organisations. However, the workforce agenda is common to all trusts and other NHS bodies.

There is a real need for the HR function to not only look at where pay bill savings can be made, but also how we engage our wider workforce in meeting these financial challenges. Our Trust has just started an open conversation with our workforce regarding potential pay bill savings areas and local staff representatives are aware of the challenge facing the organization. But there is an inherent tension in the need to make savings locally and a fierce desire to maintain national terms and conditions of service on the part of trade union representatives. For our workforce, I feel that saying that we need to save £48 million over the next 4 years really resonates, so we have developed new approaches to getting this message across, breaking down the total figure to the challenge of saving £1 for every £20 we currently spend. As a Trust we have two key campaigns running, Employment Over Earnings and War On Waste. We want to maintain employment for as many of our existing staff as we can, but we also need them to mobilise and join management to identify and drive out waste in all areas of our organisation.

We are very mindful of our corporate and social responsibility. Sixty per cent of our business is in Cumbria and we know that near on 50% of the employed population in Cumbria works in the public sector, so taking posts out of the public sector potentially damages the whole of the Cumbrian economy.

Future supply lines into our organisation have to be maintained too, so we are actively engaging with local schools and colleges to ensure that when we are in a position to recruit, the talent pool out there remains engaged and aware of the rewarding employment opportunities the NHS and the wider public sector has.

In order to manage our organisations successfully now and ensure future sustainability, we need to workforce plan effectively, but this needs to be integrated with our financial and clinical plans and also needs to be mindful of the technological changes which impact upon our clinical delivery. The challenge is huge, but we have to prove that we are an asset to our organisation and not an overhead.

Perhaps the most influential of the contemporary writers on HR is John Boudreau, whose recent book, co-authored with Peter Ramstad, presents an analysis of human resource management that goes 'beyond HR' (Boudreau and Ramstad, 2005, 2007). Their work is both interesting and challenging, but it shares the same theme of HR transformation that characterizes the work of Ulrich and his colleagues. What Boudreau and Ramstad offer is an insight into what we call 'intelligent HR'. They are committed to the development of a new HR paradigm or mind set which they see as key to transforming the function into something that is 'fit for purpose' in a world of increasing globalization, resource constraints, and competitive pressures; they see the evolution of HR as fundamentally involving the use of specialist and superior knowledge to help identify the 'right' kind of HR strategies that will produce competitive advantage. The notion that HR has to be able to do things better or different from its competitors, an argument we develop in the following chapter, is central to their vision of a twenty-first century HR function.

Central to what they offer is what they call a 'decision science' for HR which involves a much more rational and rigorous approach to making decisions that connect human capital to organizational effectiveness and strategic success. They see 'talent' or human capital as the key to competitive advantage but believe that earlier models of HR, based firstly on control and compliance (Personnel Management), followed by the provision of services (HR), whilst not unimportant need to be seen in the context of the new paradigm, central to which is the notion of better decision-making that liberates organizational talent more effectively (Talentship). This interest in promoting better decisions and use of an organization's human resources shares a common foundation with parallel developments in what is called 'evidence-based management', (Pfeffer and Sutton, 2006; Briner et al., 2009). In their book, Pfeffer and Sutton capture the essence of this emphasis on rational and informed decision-making when they say that:

> **management decisions would be based on the best evidence, that managers would systematically learn from experience, and that organisational practices would reflect sound principles of thought and analysis.**

Table 2.2 offers a way of understanding the different paradigms and conceptualizations associated with the HR function in the UK.

**Table 2.2** Ways of conceptualizing the role and purpose of HR

| Requirement | Label | Problems | Consequences | Justifications |
|---|---|---|---|---|
| To care for the physical, psychological, and emotional well-being of employees | The welfare role and function | Can focus too narrowly on employee interests—no explicit recognition of 'business interests' | HR seen as 'soft' and 'woolly'; seen by line managers as of little relevance | Continues to be of fundamental importance in how people are managed and how they behave or perform at work |
| To solve problems and fix things | The fire-fighting role | Largely a reactive role—involves HR dealing with symptoms, rather than addressing underlying causes and problems | HR is often 'busy', but its agenda and focus is limited and misses out on other important areas of contribution | Fixing problems and 'putting out fires' is important: small 'fires' can develop into larger, and more threatening, situations |
| To maintain systems and procedures, with an emphasis on administrative conformity | The conservative and process role | Can focus too narrowly, with little regard for outcomes; HR seen as coercive and reactionary | HR has negative reputation—seen as adding little value and becomes marginalized | Efficient administration is always important and a certain level of procedural regulation is legally prescribed |
| To build capability | HR's strategic contribution and strategic alignment | Can lose sight of the importance of efficient administrative and effective operational interventions | Associated with outsourcing of non-strategic functions and devolvement of many key operational responsibilities to line managers | Easily spoken about and more often than not aspirational; requires different mindsets and skill sets on the part of HR professionals working in this way |
| To support the business and line managers | The 'business partner' role | Requires specialist skills and wider business experience to be effective | Raises questions about the 'professional' dimension of HR | Often ignores tensions between business and professional interests; is 'being good for the business' the only reference point for HR professionals to use to justify their actions? |

**RESEARCH INSIGHT 2.2**

**Griffin, E. et al. (2009) *Maximising the Value of HR Business Partnering*, Roffey Park**

The Roffey Park report on Business Partnering offers insight into how the model works, what the arguments are for this way of delivering HR within the organisation and issues to do with implementation. Read the report and complete the tasks.

- How does a Business Partner approach to HR differ from that based on a centralized HR department?
- What are the expectations of HR professional adopting a business partner role?
- What organizational changes need to be made to facilitate this model of HR?
- What is the evidence on the effectiveness and success of the model?

# Rationality in HR

Ulrich's criticism that HR is over-concerned with activities at the expense of outcomes and value-adding contributions is, in one sense, important because it puts the emphasis on what HR actually achieves. But there remains the question of what HR does or should be doing—that is, its activities—and how these actually produce desired and valued outcomes. Outcomes have to be linked to inputs or activities—they do not happen in isolation!

What has emerged so far in this critical perspective on HR is that many of the activities that HR professionals engage in appear not to be valued by managers and employees. This is because there is either no evidence that the activities actually achieve things that matter or because it is very difficult, as was pointed out earlier, to prove that what HR does actually results in improvements in behaviour and performance. If the latter is the reason, then HR's task is to look carefully at the way in which it measures and evaluates effectiveness; if the problem is more to do with what HR does and how it carries out these activities, then the challenge it faces is more fundamental.

This is something about which Tony Watson (2003) has written extensively and Watson is one of the relatively few writers on HR who confronts the often taken-for-granted assumptions associated with HR activities, and their effects and consequences.

The relationship between what can be understood as the *means* employed by those associated with the HR function (i.e. activities, instruments, and processes) and the *ends* actually achieved, rather than expected, is often seen as unproblematic. But what is too frequently ignored is the existence and effect of powerful mediating factors within the organization that 'interfere' with, and undermine the impact of, many HR interventions. Simply carrying out an activity does not necessarily mean that the intended outcomes are actually achieved; often with HR, the outcomes and consequences that are experienced are more unintended than intended!

To illustrate this point, let us consider one of the most widely used HR practices, the performance appraisal process, which provides an interesting example of how many mainstream writers fail to give sufficient critical attention to what is *actually* achieved from this and many other HR activities.

In her popular textbook *An Introduction to Human Resource Management*, Maund (2001) presents a list of the advantages of an appraisal system, which include the positive nature of formal appraisal meetings between appraiser and appraisee, and the generation of valuable feedback. She is not alone in claiming that performance appraisals offer advantages to the organization; most other mainstream HR textbooks make similar claims. The problem, however, is that there is no recognition that the claimed advantages for performance appraisal *might not* be experienced by those involved in the process or by their organizations.

Taking a more realistic stance, the starting point has to be that many of these claimed advantages are, in fact, potential rather than actual, and—more worryingly—may not, in fact, be experienced by the majority of those involved in the process. This is the basic premise of Coens and Jenkins (2000), who, in their book

*Abolishing Performance Appraisals*, quote numerous writers who claim that performance appraisals, in whatever form, are at best likely to have a limited effect on individual performance, but are actually more likely to result in the *undermining* of employees' morale and performance by their experiences of the performance appraisal processes. They refer to a comment made in the *Wall Street Journal* by T.D. Schellhardt:

> **If less that 10% of your customers judged a product to be effective, and seven out of ten said they were more confused than enlightened by it, you would drop it, right? So, why don't more companies drop their annual job-performance reviews?**
> (Coens and Jenkins, 2000)

The very clear implication is that, in the opinion of this particular commentator at least, one form of performance appraisal was not seen to deliver particularly valued outcomes. But the important point is not only about whether performance appraisal itself is not valued as an activity and fails to deliver improvements in employee performance, but about whether HR is seen to be the driving force behind this activity. As Coens and Jenkins state, as a result of the failure of most performance appraisal schemes, rather than abandon them:

> **HR staff finds itself policing, refereeing, and collecting a lot of paper that doesn't mean much to most people.**
> (Coens and Jenkins, 2000)

This, of course, does little to enhance the credibility of HR.

Yet Maund claims that appraisal, regardless of which system is used and because it is part of the employee development process:

> **has to be perceived, therefore, as useful to everyone concerned.**
> (Maund, 2001)

This is far too simplistic a position to take and is not consistent with the experiences of many people involved in the performance appraisal process, nor is it consistent with the research quoted by Coens and Jenkins. Moreover, it is a position that suggests that there is an unproblematical link between what HR does and what results from its interventions. Using performance appraisal as a specific example helps us to reach the more general conclusion that many HR activities do have an effect on employee and managerial behaviour, but that these effects can be negative as well as positive. However unpalatable it might be to those who are professionally associated with HR, the possibility has to be acknowledged that HR, rather than representing the solution to the challenges of managing people, can, in certain circumstances, be part of the problem.

Watson's analysis of how organizations operate offers an insight into this problem of why what appear to be valued and useful activities do not always deliver desired outcomes. He observed that modern organizations are more or less based on bureaucratic principles, and place a heavy reliance on rational techniques and processes, particularly in the way in which employees are used as resources in the pursuit of organizational goals. Accepting that people, as resources, are also human beings, who have their own interests and can be assertive when they perceive that these interests are being undermined by the activities of the dominant stakeholders, he argues that managers generally—but particularly those involved in the HR function—are subject to what he calls the 'paradox of consequences'. He describes this concept as:

> **The tendency for the means adopted by organisational managers to achieve particular goals to fail to achieve these goals since these 'means' involve human beings who have goals of their own which may not be congruent with those of the managers.**
> (Watson, 2003)

This paradox—which potentially exists in all organizations, although its strength and significance may vary—is closely linked to the Weberian concepts of formal and material rationality. An appreciation of what these two concepts mean for HR is critical to understanding the problematical nature of the means-ends relationship and the experience of unintended consequences.

**KEY CONCEPT Formal rationality**

This refers to the choice and use of planned and sensible techniques and processes to control and manage employees by those in positions of authority. These include workplace rules, processes used in recruitment and selection and performance management, many of the methods used in training, and methods of incentivizing staff. Collectively, these would be defined as 'means'. There is an important sense that these rules, interventions, and activities will work and will have the desired effect because they are theoretically or formally attractive and sensible.

**KEY CONCEPT Material rationality**

This refers to what actually works: results that confirm that the intended consequences following any intervention or action have actually been met. The test of whether any intervention or activity meets the criteria of material rationality is whether it works 'in practice' and generates the desired 'ends' or outcomes.

Because of the effects of the paradox of unintended consequences, the rules and 'ways of doing things' associated with HR, which can often be seen as being formally rational ways of operating and managing, can fail to meet the criterion of material rationality. This helps to explain why many performance appraisal systems, as an example, don't improve performance, but instead undermine it, and don't improve motivation, but instead weaken it. An exclusive reliance on formal rationality also explains why certain types of incentive scheme result in a long-term decline in productivity, and why the use of certain training methods and techniques fail to generate the required learning outcomes.

For insights into the future of HR see the Online Resource Centre extension material 2.5.

# What is the Future for HR?

There is little doubt that HR, as a specialist management function, faces a challenging future: a future that, for some, involves something of a metamorphosis. There also seems to be a general consensus that it has to change before it can meet the requirements and expectations of other organizational stakeholders, and be accorded the status and credibility that the function is seeking. Whether the change, as Rucci (1997) believes, will involve its demise is more problematical and contentious.

What are the changes to which HR needs to commit in order to preserve its future? They can perhaps be expressed in relation to the following:

- Acquiring and applying a much stronger *business orientation* in designing and delivering HR activities and services

  This has major implications for the skills and mindset of HR professionals and in relation to their recruitment and selection. The employment of people from outside of the HR profession to senior HR positions is a trend that is likely to continue.

- Being clearer about the *priorities* they pursue and why certain activities have been prioritized

  This will inevitably mean than the HR agenda and the deployment of HR resources is influenced, if not determined, by the 'users' of HR—i.e. by employees, line managers, and senior executives, as well as HR professionals.

- Developing their *functional expertise*

  This involves developing skills and competences that allow HR to deliver 'solutions' and to offer advice and support to managers that is founded on a body of professional theory that has been tested and refined in countless situations. If line managers retain a degree of dependence on HR experts, then the expertise offered has to deliver the contributions and outcomes that those line managers need.

- Building *personal credibility* and a reputation for reliability and professionalism

  In their article on what distinguishes successful from less successful HR managers, Buckingham and Elliot (1993) found that those rated as 'above average' in performance were associated with:

  - the ability to motivate others;
  - the ability to build relationships;
  - the ability to seek and build commitment;
  - the possession of a conceptual mindset, and a clear perspective on their role and its purpose.

They conclude:

> **This mindset may be defined as a philosophy of Personnel Management and a conceptual ability to define the significant contribution that the personnel professional can make to the organisation. This philosophy is strongly rooted in clear perceptions about, and a real commitment to, the value of good employees and of their contribution to the company.**
> **(Buckingham and Elliot, 2003)**

The future of HR will undoubtedly be influenced by developments in technology, in organizational forms, and in relation to the capability of line managers in taking on much more responsibility for the management of their staff. It might also be argued that its future is in the hands of those who work in HR and whether they can rise to the challenges confronting the profession.

# Summary

- This chapter has deliberately adopted a more questioning and critical approach to the role and contribution of HR in organizations than is found in some other HR textbooks. The reason for this is that HR professionals are under increasing pressure to 'deliver' and those who cannot, or do not, understand what this means will not be considered credible. The departments within which they work are likely to be reorganized and parts of their responsibilities outsourced: this is the new reality.
- HR also operates in an often-unpredictable external environment, which can undermine existing practices and priorities, and transform what the organization expects HR to do. In Chapter 14, the Oliver's case study involving plant closure is an example of what this can involve. The conclusion is, therefore, that HR and those who are associated with it need to become flexible and adaptable, and be comfortable with uncertainty and ambiguity. To be able to do this requires new skills and competences, and the effective recruitment and development of HR staff is becoming increasingly important and challenging.
- Finally, to secure its long-term future as a specialist management function, the evidence from many of the academic contributions on HR suggests that it must become much more 'business-orientated' and deliver value-adding contributions to the business. What this actually means has to be determined within each organization, but it will inevitably involve accepting that the HR agenda has to be more business-led. Those who work in the HR department, meanwhile, must recognize that human resource management has become far more important than Human Resource Management.

**Visit the Online Resource Centre that accompanies this book for self-test questions, weblinks, and more information on the topics covered in this chapter.**
**www.oxfordtextbooks.co.uk/orc/banfield_kay2e/**

## REVIEW QUESTIONS

1. What are the contributions of HR professionals and line managers to the behaviour and performance of employees?
2. What is the difference between human resource management and Human Resource Management?
3. In the context of the knowledge economy, what particular employment and HR practices will be necessary if organizations are going to maximize the performance and contributions of knowledge workers?
4. What will be the issues and pressures affecting HR in ten years' time?

***See Online Resource Centre for answers.***

## CASE STUDY

### Reforming the HR function at the Royal Mail

The material for this case study is taken from a presentation given at the CIPD national conference in 2005.

The Royal Mail, prior to recent changes, employed over 200,000 people and had been a national institution for over 300 years. In the early part of this century, however, it began to suffer serious performance and financial problems. It was known for poor industrial relations and accounted for nearly 50 per cent of working days lost because of strikes. It was a business that was near to insolvency, and was renowned for low pay and long hours, and an overreliance on agency workers. It was, in other words, a business that had failed to adapt its internal structures and culture to a rapidly changing external environment in which increasing competition was the most important development.

The HR function, defined in terms of those who worked in and for the specialized HR department, was costing the business £200 million each year. Approximately 3,700 people were employed in HR, which meant that the ratio of HR staff to total employees was near to 1:55 (i.e. for every 55 employees, there was one member of HR). The primary role of HR was in relation to the trade unions, which defined the state of the company's employee relations. But, increasingly, HR had become associated with numerous policies and procedures covering almost every aspect of the employment and management of people. Unfortunately, the increasing influence of the centralized HR function had led to a de-franchising of line managers, who felt unable to engage directly with their staff.

The need to transform HR as part of changing the culture of the organization was based on a clear understanding of how the 'people' side of the business needed to change. It involved:

- an overall reduction in costs;
- a modernization of employment processes and procedures;
- the professionalization of the HR function;
- a change in the relationship with trade unions;
- adding more strategic value;
- empowering line managers;
- driving change.

The transformation was achieved by creating a new HR architecture, based on a very clear distinction between the different contributions that HR was required to make. The 'new' HR was based on three distinctive domains:

- establishing functional expertise that supported the line;
- creating business partners that worked with the line;
- a shared service capability that delivered administrative efficiency.

The transformation was not achieved without considerable investment in the development of HR staff, supplemented by the injection of new talent to lead the changes. The newly appointed 'Business Partners' were assessed against a demanding competency framework and there was an emphasis away from 'doables to deliverables', with a new focus on how HR could add value to the business.

The results of the transformation were both impressive and challenging. The ratio of HR staff to employees rose to 1:130. A new attitude and relationship with the trade unions resulted in a reduction in industrial disputes and restrictive work practices, and a reduction in headcount of 34,000.

The clear message, however, was that this was the beginning rather than the end of a process. Further competition pressures meant that Royal Mail needed to become more competitive, leading to increasing pressure on jobs and the need to raise productivity levels even higher. For HR, there was 'no hiding place', but its key contributions could only be made as a result of a very different HR architecture and a new relationship with line managers.

**Questions**

1. What particular competencies do the organization's HR 'Business Partners' need to be able to work effectively with line managers?
2. What are shared service centres and how do they operate?
3. What needs to be done to allow line managers to take direct responsibility for managing their staff?
4. What happened to those HR staff that were lost to the company?

## FURTHER READING

Boudreau, J.W. and Lawler, E.E. (2009) *Achieving Excellence in Human Resource Management: An Assessment of Human Resource Functions*, Stanford University Press.

Boudreau, J.W. (2010) *Retooling HR: Using Proven Business Tools to Make Better Decisions about Talent*, Harvard Business School Press.

Chartered Institute of Personnel and Development (2009) 'Human capital'.

Chartered Institute of Personnel and Development (2010) 'HR Business Partnering'.

Mayo, A. (2005) 'Helping HR to understand the strategic value chain', *Strategic HR Review*, **5**:1.

Pfeffer, J. (2005) 'Changing mental models: HR's most important task', *Human Resource Management*, **44**:2, pp. 123–8.

Reddington, M., Williamson, M. and Withers, M. (2005) *Transforming HR*, Elsevier.

Turner, N. (2004) *Achieving Strategic Alignment of Business and Human Resources*, Work Foundation.

Ulrich, D. and Beatty, R.W. (2001) 'From partners to players: extending the HR playing field', *Human Resource Management*, **40**:4, Winter, pp. 293–308.

Ulrich, D., Allen, J., Brockbank, W. and Younger, J. (2009) *HR Transformation*, McGraw-Hill.

## REFERENCES


Banfield, P. (2005) 'Schizophrenia, Inuits and the Holy Grail: A brief reflection on the search for professional identity', *CIPD South Yorkshire Branch Newsletter*, www.cipd.co.uk/branch/syork/newsletter.

Becker, B., Huselid, M.A. and Ulrich, D. (2001) *The HR Scorecard*, Harvard Business School Press.

Beer, M., Spector, B., Lawrence, P., Quinn Mills, D. and Walton, R. (1985) *Human Resource Management: A General Manager's Perspective*, Free Press.

Boudreau, J.W. and Ramstad, P.M. (2005) 'Where's Your Pivotal Talent?', *Harvard Business Review*.

Boudreau, J.W. and Ramstad, P.M. (2007) *Beyond HR: The New Science of Human Capital*, Harvard Business School Press.

Boxall, P. and Purcell, J. (2000) 'Strategic human resource management: Where have we come from and where should we be going?', *International Journal of Management Reviews*, **2**:2, pp. 183–203.

Briner, Rob B., Denyer, D. and Rousseau, D.M. (2009) 'Evidence-based management: concept cleanup time?' *Academy of Management Perspectives*.

Buckingham, G. and Elliot, G. (1993) 'Profile of a successful personnel manager', *Personnel Management*, **25**:8, pp. 26–9.

Chartered Institute of Personnel and Development (2005) 'Outsourcing human resources: A framework for decisions'.

Chartered Institute of Personnel and Development (2005, 2010, 2011) 'The Role of Line Managers in HR', www.cipd.co.uk/hr-resources/factsheets/role-line-managers-hr.aspx.

Chartered Institute of Personnel and Development (2007) 'What's happening with well-being at work?', www.cipd.co.uk.

Christensen, R.N. (1997) 'Where is human resources?', quoted in Ulrich, D., Losey, M.R. and Lake, G. (1997) *Tomorrow's HR Management*, John Wiley and Sons.

Coens, T. and Jenkins, M. (2000) *Abolishing Performance Appraisals*, Berrett-Koehler.

Denisi, A.S. and Griffin, R.W. (2001) *Human Resource Management*, Houghton Mifflin Company.

Gennard, J. and Kelly, J. (1994) 'Human Resource Management: The views of personnel directors', *Human Resource Management*, **5**:1, pp. 15–32.

Grant, D. and Oswick, C. (1998) 'Of believers, atheists and agnostics: practitioner views on HRM', *Industrial Relations Journal*, **29**:3, pp. 178–93.

Griffin, E. et al. (2009) *Maximising the Value of HR Business Partnering*, Roffey Park.

Guest, D.E. (1997) 'Human resource management and performance: a review and research agenda', *The International Journal of Human Resource Management*, **8**, pp. 263–276.

Hammonds, K.H. (2005) 'Why we hate HR', *Fast Company*, August, **98**, p. 40.

Herzberg, F. (2003) 'One more time: how do you motivate employees?', *Harvard Business Review*, January.

Hoque, K. and Noon, M. (2001) 'Counting the angels: a comparison of personnel and HR specialists', *Human Resource Management*, **11**:3, p. 5.

Hutchinson, S. and Purcell, J. (2003) *Bringing Policies to Life: The Vital Role of Front Line Managers in People Management*, CIPD.

Lawler, E.E. III et al. (2004) *Human Resources Business Process Outsourcing: Transforming How HR Gets Its Work Done*, Josey Bass.

Legge, K. (1978) *Power, Innovation and Problem-Solving in Personnel Management*, McGraw-Hill.

Legge, K. (1995) *Human Resource Management: Rhetorics and Reality*, Macmillan Business.

Maund, L. (2001) *An Introduction to Human Resource Management*, Palgrave.

Neal, A., West, M.A. and Patterson, M.C. (2004) 'Do organizational climate and strategic orientation moderate the relationship between Human Resource Management practices and productivity?', Centre for Economic Performance Discussion Paper 624, March.

Paauwe, J. (2004) *HRM and Performance: Unique Approaches For Achieving Long Term Viability*, Oxford University Press.

Paauwe, J. and Boselie, P. (2008) 'HRM and Performance: What's Next?', *CAHARS Working Papers Series*, Paper 474. http://digitalcommons.ir/cornell.edu/caharsswp/474.

Pfeffer, J. (1997) 'Does Human Resource Management have a future?' in Ulrich, D., Losey, M.R., and Lake, G. (eds) (1997) *Tomorrow's HR Management*, John Wiley and Sons.

Pfeffer, J. and Sutton, R.I. (2006) *Hard Facts, Dangerous Half-Truths and Total Nonsense*, Harvard Business Review Press.

Purcell, J. (2003) *Understanding the People and Performance Link: Unlocking the Black Box*, CIPD.

Reilly, P. and Williams, T. (2006) *Strategic HR: Building the Capability to Deliver*, Gower.

Rucci, A.J. (1997) 'Should Human Resources survive? A profession at the crossroads', in Ulrich, D., Losey, M.R. and Lake, G. (eds) (1997) *Tomorrow's HR Management*, John Wiley and Sons.

Storey, J. (1992) *Developments in the Management of Human Resources*, Blackwell.

Tichy, N., Fombrun, C. and Devanna, M.A. (1982) 'Strategic human resource management', *Sloan Management Review*, **23**:2, Winter, pp. 47–64.

Torrington, D., Hall, L. and Taylor, S. (2005) *Human Resource Management*, FT/Prentice Hall.

Tyson, S. and Fell, A. (1986) *Evaluating the Personnel Function*, Hutchinson Education.

Ulrich, D. (1997) *Human Resource Champions*, Harvard Business School Press.

Ulrich, D. (1998) 'A new mandate for Human Resources', *Harvard Business Review*, **76**:1, pp. 124–34.

Ulrich, D. and Brockbank, W. (2005) *The HR Value Proposition*, Harvard Business School Press.

Watson, T.J. (2002) *Organising and Managing Work*, FT/Prentice Hall.

Watson, T.J. (2003) *Sociology, Work and Industry*, Routledge.

Watson, T.J. (2006) *Organising and Managing Work*, 2nd Ed., FT/Prentice Hall.

# 3 A Strategic Perspective on Human Resource Management

## KEY TERMS

**Integration** A preferred relationship between different parts of an organization and 'the whole' and between different functional strategies and the corporate strategy.

**Strategic** A particular mindset and approach defined by a more integrated and holistic view of the world of business and management.

**Strategy** A way of doing things that is intended to produce required outcomes and results.

## Learning Objectives

As a result of reading this chapter and using the Online Resource Centre, you should be able to:

- identify SHRM as a distinctive approach to and framework for making decisions about how to manage people at work;
- understand what being strategic means and how strategic contribution can be established;
- recognize that implementing chosen HR strategies is problematical and almost always involves changes in 'the way things are done' and how people behave;
- understand the concepts of fit and integration and contribute to achieving these objectives;
- identify and deliver HR strategies that are consistent with an organisation's structure, culture, and corporate strategies.

# Introduction

In the previous chapter, reference was made to the way in which thinking and practice around the management of people has evolved and become more sophisticated over time, although whether this also means it has become effective is a quite different question, and one for which there is no straightforward answer. The criticisms of HR that were explored in Chapter 2, and are developed here, still represent real and undeniable challenges to those with responsibility for managing people. The position taken in this book is that many of these criticisms are directed at those who work as professional practitioners in HR and reflect concerns over the way they 'see' their role, the priorities they identify with and the agendas they promote. Such criticisms reflect the frustrations experienced by line managers and senior executives in translating HR's potential and promise into valued and strategically important contributions.

The frequently made claim that 'People are an organisation's most important asset' (Bassi and McMurrer, 2004) whilst rhetorically attractive and frequently stated represents a serious challenge to those working in HR. The challenge is to explain what this actually means for the way the human resource is used in organizations and how its potential is going to be realized. We would argue that this challenge has not always been effectively addressed by HR professionals and the absence of an adequate explanation continues to fuel the doubts of those who view HR as an underachieving management function.

On the other hand, it would be far too easy but unjustifiable to lay the blame for the continuing concerns expressed about HR in terms of individual and professional limitations and deficiencies. The ambiguities and structural difficulties outlined by writers such as Legge (1978, 2005) which were explored in the previous chapter represent important mediating factors that influence how HR can operate and what it can realistically do to change the performance related behaviour of people at work. These limitations, by their very nature, are enduring and cannot be fully resolved or eliminated; they are inherent within all organizations.

The continuing search by those associated with HR for an identity that reflects the importance of the human resource to organizational success, and a recognition of their contribution in delivering this, represents a paradox for which there appears to be no single or obvious answer. There are many paradoxes that exist within the HR function, and in the relationship between HR and the wider organization, but this is arguably the one for which answers and explanations are still being sought. In the Abilene Paradox, Harvey (1996) refers to the work of Robert Rapaport in trying to make sense of what paradoxes are and why certain situations remain paradoxical; from our perspective, why, if people are supposedly the key to competitive advantage and organizational success does the function closely associated with the management of people suffer from persistent criticisms over its value and contribution?

In a general sense, Harvey believes that all paradoxes deal with absurdity, or at least involve behaviour that doesn't make sense, although it does to those directly involved! From an HR perspective, this might be expressed by asking why some HR departments spend most of their time and resources engaged in activities that fail to deliver outcomes that are important to other stakeholders, and in an extreme case, why HR is as much a part of the problem as it is a part of the solution to an organization's underperforming human resources. According to Harvey:

> **paradoxes are generally paradoxes only because they are based on a logic or rationale different from what we understand or expect. Discovering that different logic not only destroys the paradoxical quality but also offers alternative ways for coping with similar situations. Therefore, part of the dilemma facing an Abilene-bound organization may be the lack of a map—a theory or model—that provides rationality to the paradox.**
> (Harvey, 1996)

This chapter is specifically concerned with offering an explanation to some of the key paradoxes associated with HR. We argue that only when these paradoxes are actually acknowledged by practitioners and senior management, as Harvey says, a new logic will emerge that helps those committed to improving the standing and contribution of HR and to address the failings and unrealized potential of the function.

Examples of what we mean by paradox in HR can be found in the writings of Paul Mooney (2001). At the beginning of chapter 6 of his book, Mooney quotes an experienced HR practitioner who says:

> **Our people are too important, too valuable and too capable of doing important work to waste on routine and repetition.**

The paradox in this case is that valuable and talented people are not being fully utilized at work. And the question that needs to be asked is why organizations continue to under-utilize costly and valuable human resources, often forcing staff to restrict their efforts and suppress their desire to do more? Later in the chapter Mooney argues that the relationship between the cost of delivering administrative, operational, and strategic value-added activities is in inverse proportion to the value they generate. In other words, whilst the administrative work of a 'typical' HR department costs 50 per cent of its total budget/resource base it adds something in the region of 15 per cent in added value. Conversely, HR's strategic contribution, he argues, costs around 15 per cent of the budget but generates 50 per cent of total added value. Whilst there are of course issues over how costs and added value are conceptualized and measured, the basic point seems to be fairly obvious and allows us to ask the question:

> **Why is so much of HR's resources, intellectual and financial, spent on activities that produce relatively little added value?**
> (Mooney, 2001)

This is another paradox frequently associated with HR.

**STUDENT ACTIVITY 3.1 Understanding paradox**

This task can be undertaken on an individual basis or as part of a group activity. The objective is to understand the concept of paradox and apply this to HR.

Task 1. Using the two examples given by Mooney, think about the reasons why many organizations under-utilize their staff and why many HR departments spend so much of their resources on administration.

Task 2. Try to identify what the hidden logic is that leads to these kinds of situations.

In this introduction to a strategic perspective on HR, the references to the work of Harvey and Mooney and the importance of the concept of paradox, might itself be considered paradoxical, and readers may be wondering what the connection is between the issues raised by these writers and HR strategy? Put simply, the resolution of the kind of paradoxical situations we and others have identified lies in it embracing a much more strategic role and putting much more emphasis on its strategic contribution to the organization as a whole. It is argued that HR can rid itself of the negative associations with welfare, administration, and procedural regulation, and occupy a place 'at the top table' by adopting a more strategic mind set and operate in a more strategic way. Simply stating an intention to be 'more strategic' is not in itself a sufficient condition to make the transition from its administrative and operational roots to a more elevated and strategic role within the organization. The reason why we believe it is important to understand the nature of paradox and those that relate to HR is that without understanding the hidden logic that explains these paradoxes, its ability to transform itself will be severely compromised.

But what does being strategic actually mean and how can an HR function shift its centre of gravity away from administration and procedural regulation towards a more strategically focused and high value-adding contribution? We try to address these and related questions by:

- Presenting and evaluating some of the key literature contributions from strategic management and Strategic Human Resource Management.
- Considering the link between HR practices and organizational performance as evidenced by the results of contemporary research projects.

- Explaining what being strategic does and can mean for HR and the changes this implies in the HR mind set and the way it makes sense of the challenges and opportunities it faces.
- Providing examples of how different organizations have tried to apply a stronger strategic perspective in the way they develop and implement HR policies and practices.



## Why is Being Strategic So Important and What Does it Mean?

Bassi and McMurrer (2004) provide an answer to the first question that links the importance of a strategic dimension to the impact of globalization and increasing competition on UK businesses, both public and private. They state that:

> **The relentless force of globalization has left only one sustainable path to profitability for firms operating in high-wage, developed nations—to compete based on superior human capital capabilities and strategies. Any benefits that were historically associated with superior technology and access to capital (both physical and financial) are now far too short-lived to provide a sustainable advantage.**

Two points emerge from this statement. Firstly, it goes beyond the simple statement that people are an organization's most important asset by emphasizing that need to gain competitive advantage through the contributions that they make, and secondly, it links the acquisition and development of key human resource capabilities to strategies that harness and apply these to strategically important organizational objectives. Being strategic in HR doesn't just mean creating capabilities but using them. This means that:



> **people not only need to be connected to their job but to each other and their organization.**
> Bassi and McMurrer (2004)

The link between people their attitudes, competences, and behaviour, and how these impact on the organization is a theme that characterizes the report of the Government's Accounting For People Task Force (2003).[1] In the report, one of the task force members commented that:

> **An organisation's success is the product of its people competence. That link between people and performance should be made visible, and available to all stakeholders.**
> John Sunderland, Executive Chairman, Cadbury Schweppes

What is being emphasized here is that through the knowledge and skills of its employees an organization can enhance their performance, but that this link needs to be known and understood by key stakeholders. However, the challenge goes beyond recognizing this link; strategies need to be devised that realise untapped potential and through this deliver the improvements in performance that are increasingly necessary to stay competitive.

Unfortunately, performance improvements that are strategically important are by no means inevitable, and performance can fall as well as increase. The critical question is:

> **under what conditions and as a result of what HR strategies does individual and organisational performance increase?**

This is an important point because it offers an insight into what HR's strategic role needs to be. The position taken here is that this strategic role lies in creating an environment and meeting the conditions that lead to changing mind sets and higher levels of employee engagement—a view that is central not simply to this

[1] A successor to the original Task Force For People, Accounting For People 2.0, was established in October 2010. See *Human Capital Handbook* (2010) HubCap (http://alpha.hubcapdigital.com) in December 2010.

chapter but to the book as a whole. There is no one single 'lever' that can be pulled to elicit the required response; rather we have to consider the nature of the emotional, psychological, and physical environments as having a much more enduring and significant effect on what people think and do at work.

According to Sullivan (2005) the term 'strategic' is one of the most commonly used words in business and management, and is sometimes over-used. He argues that this over-usage is part of the problem—it confuses the 'real' meaning of the term. In support of this position, he provides an interesting insight into why so many people associate themselves and their contributions with being strategic when he states that:

> **The word is just as likely to be uttered by senior executives as it is by people that feel that they need to be 'more strategic' in order to be recognized or successful.**
> (Sullivan, 2005)

Sullivan's comment suggests that there is a certain status or cachet associated with being seen to be acting in a strategic way or engaging in a strategic discourse but which may not necessarily translate into strategic effect or impact. For him:

> **being strategic means having an impact on the things that are most important to an organization—the corporate goals and objectives.**

Talking strategically does not necessarily mean that HR is engaged strategically or has acquired a strategic mind set, and the illusion that the language of strategy implies strategic action, although attractive, is dangerous and is one that not only Sullivan is warning against. In his seminal article for the *Harvard Business Review* Whickam Skinner said:

> **Since Hawthorne, successive waves of people-problem solutions and programs have washed and tumbled through industry. In some desperation, managers have steadily invested in supervisory training, organizational behavior, interpersonal behavior, T-groups, sensitivity training, employee attitude surveys, job enrichment, flexible benefits, and expanded fringe benefits-bigger pensions, subsidized insurance, more holidays, shorter work days, four-day weeks, and canned communications packages—and now companies are attempting to revive the 'work ethic' with human resources departments. Big programs, but where are the payoffs?**
> (Skinner, 1981)[2]

One of the reasons he gives for HR talking big but failing to deliver is to do with what he calls critical problems in the corporate management of personnel, such as the place of human resources management (HRM) in corporate decision-making, the role and priorities of those who work in HR departments, and a lack of human resources management expertise within senior executives. In other words, Skinner was identifying a lack of strategic focus and an inability to implement high impact policies and practices that could have made a difference to organizational measures of performance.

Similar questions about the extent to which, despite much talk and new ideas, little in HR seems to have moved on have been posed by other writers. Kearns for example some 25 years after Skinner's article was published expressed the same concerns when he asked 'How much has HR changed?' (Kearns, 2004).

His rather depressing answer is that despite the increasing specialization and evolution of human resource management (he refers to the emergence of Strategic HRM and Human Capital Management as examples):

> **Any independent observer could be forgiven for asking whether all the name changes have just been cosmetic or if they signify any real, substantive differences.**
> (Kearns, 2004)

Despite the growing evidence that many organizations have built strategically orientated HR functions, (Huselid, 1994; Birdi et al., 2008) a sense that many changes are still at the superficial level and often limited to participation in a strategic discourse, persists. In his critical but widely read article referred to in Chapter 2, Hammonds (2005) tells the story of the HR Director, Julie Muckler, who gave a talk to fellow professionals

[2] Skinner is referring to the Hawthorne experiments carried out in Chicago in the 1920s.

on the subject of 'How to Transform Your Staff into Strategic Business Partners'. As a member of the audience, he recalls after the talk that he had:

> **no idea what she's talking about. There is mention of 'internal action learning' and 'being more planful in my approach'. PowerPoint slides outline Wells Fargo's Home Mortgage's initiatives in performance management, organization design, and horizontal-solutions teams. Muckler describes leveraging internal resources and involving external resources—and she leaves her audience dazed. That evening, even the human-resources pros confide they didn't understand much of it, either.**

Hammonds asks the question about what is driving the strategy disconnect; between what HR professionals seem to be saying and doing and the reality of a much more muted strategic impact. Referring to the work of Linda Gratton (1999) he makes two important points:

1. The majority of HR professionals, although they often possess strong technical expertise and are professionally qualified, struggle to offer a vision of the future and how the organization, as a whole, works and needs to change.
2. There is real difficulty in trying to successfully align HR strategy to business strategy for the simple reason that business strategy can change quickly and arguably is in a constant state of flux, and it is very difficult, if not unrealistic, to constantly adapt aspects of HR such as its recruitment, compensation, and employment policies to maintain this notional alignment.

One final contribution to the on-going debate about HR's strategic role and what HR needs to do to be properly recognized within the corporate world, provides an interesting insight into how the CIPD see the issue. According to a speaker who gave an unscripted talk at the 2009 CIPD Centres' Conference there is real frustration amongst HR professionals because they feel they are not being taken seriously enough and that their contributions are not being recognized by line managers and senior executives. His proposed solution—and way of resolving the paradox—was to argue that HR should adopt a language that these stakeholders could understand and engage in a narrative with them to get the message across. The point he was making was that HR *is* engaged in making strategic contributions; the problem is that this is not recognized by people 'outside' the HR department because they don't really understand what HR is doing. To paraphrase, HR is acting strategically but other people don't recognize this and to overcome this disconnect HR needs to communicate better.

There may well be some merit in this view and undoubtedly a clash of discourses can make it difficult for people to relate to how different management functions and contributions operate. But on the other hand, it also has to be accepted that the problem may not be that managers do not understand HR's contribution and as a result fail to recognize its strategic contribution, but rather that they are very much aware of what HR does and are justifiably critical of its policies and practices as lacking strategic significance and impact. Are we dealing with a problem of communication, perception, or substance?

## Criteria For Determining Strategic Contribution and Outcomes

Despite the differences in the way academics, HR professionals, and senior managers define strategic in relation to HR, and what this means in practice, it seems reasonably clear that 'being strategic' is associated with the following features:

- Having an impact on the organization as a whole, through influencing such things as:
  - its financial performance and/or its economic strength;
  - the characteristics of its working environment which impact on the level of employee satisfaction and engagement and through this the creation of the conditions for high performance working;
  - the organization's competitive advantage over others by developing unique talents and competences.

- Creating organization wide (strategically valuable) capabilities within the workforce as a whole, such as functional flexibility, creativity, learning, and the willingness to engage in discretionary effort.
- Possessing a vision of how the HR function needs to operate and being able to convince other stakeholders of what that vision means in practice.
- Acquiring, nurturing, and retaining talented people.
- However difficult, consistently working to develop specific HR strategies that reflect the strategic needs of the organization.
- Provide leadership and exercise influence at all levels within the HR function and the wider organization.
- The possession of a strategic mind set—the ability to see and think in a strategic way, being forward looking and future orientated.

Figure 3.1 takes this attempt to define what being strategic involves a step further by linking strategic outcomes to key enabling factors.[3]

Being strategic is not a 'tick-box' exercise and it does not equate to engaging in all the above activities. Nor is there an end state at which point HR can claim to have finally become strategic; in a dynamic and

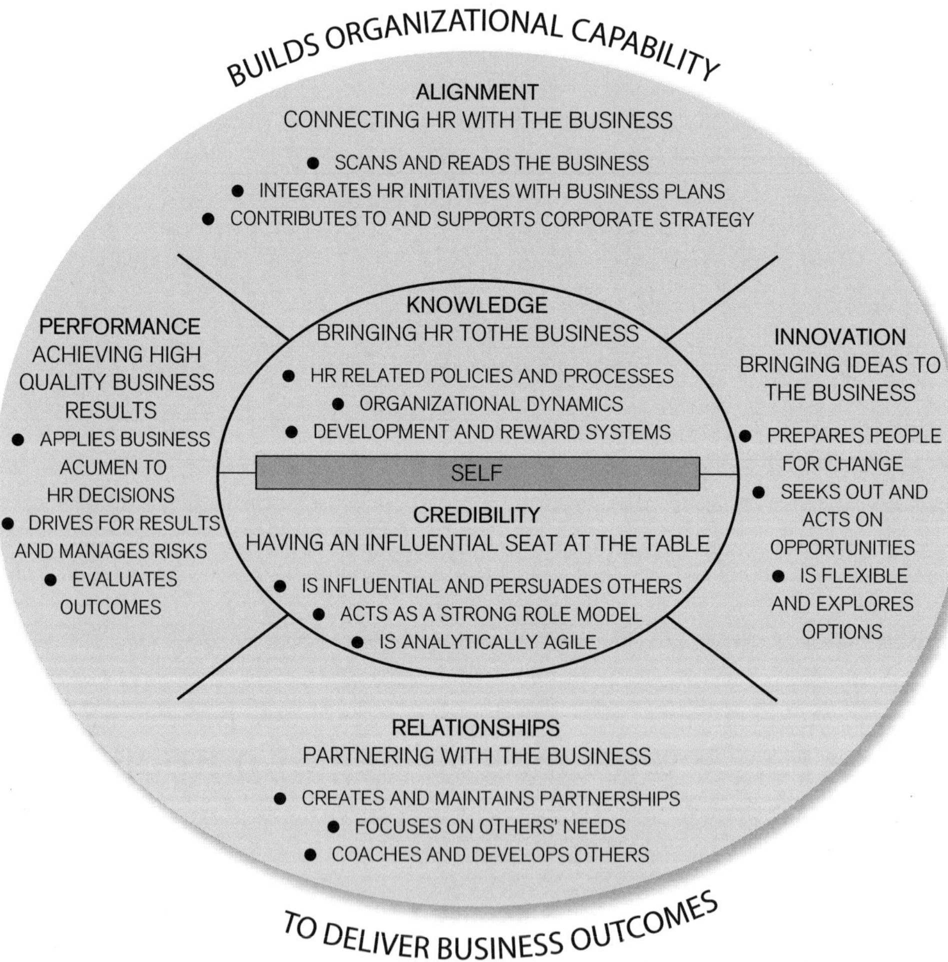


**Figure 3.1** A diagrammatical representation of what a strategic HR function involves

[3] See the CIPD Professional Map for a similar representation of how HR can deliver strategic contributions, http://www.cipd.co.uk/hr-profession-map/explore-the-map.htm.

changing environment the nature of the strategic challenge is constantly changing and priorities become redefined. Despite these necessary caveats, at this point in the analysis we would suggest that being strategic does involve HR in delivering against two key requirements:

1. Building human resource capabilities that can help to meet short- and long-term organizational requirements.
2. Ensuring that these capabilities are used and applied to generate strategically valuable outcomes.

It is also important to note that HR in its departmental form is not solely responsible for these strategic contributions. In the previous chapter we addressed the difficulties and ambiguities associated with defining HR and the different ways it can be conceptualized. Notwithstanding the implications of how we conceptualize HR, the notion that strategic contributions are often the product of strategic partnerships between HR professionals, line managers, and senior managers needs to considered. It is also important to recognize that the nature of HR's strategic contributions is not always the result of rational planning activities but emerges as unexpected situations develop which require speedy action at the strategic level. (Think of the William Beckett insight in Chapter 2.) And finally, the nature of strategic contributions is likely to change in relation to the stage in the development of the organization and its location on the organizational life cycle. HR's strategic contribution will inevitably change as the organization moves from its early, formative stage to a period of growth, maturity, decline, and either re-birth or extinction.

**STUDENT ACTIVITY 3.2 The Concept of the Organizational Life Cycle**

1. Working individually or in teams, research the literature on this concept and construct a diagram that illustrates the shape of the life cycle of a typical organization.
2. At each critical stage in the life cycle identify the different kinds of HR activities and contributions you would expect to be made to support the organization at each stage.
3. Indicate which of these contributions could be considered to have strategic importance, giving reasons for your decisions.

(Lester, Parnell, and Carragher, 2003)

# The Difficulties of Knowing What Being Strategic Means!

The natural evolution of HR to embrace a more strategic role within organizations can be understood as part of the inevitable metamorphosis of a management function, amongst many others, that changes and becomes more sophisticated over time. Think about what was said in the previous chapter about the metamorphosis of Personnel Management 'into' HRM. Consider for example the way the marketing function has evolved to reflect and take advantage of the revolution in Web based communications, and the production function's adoption of just-in-time supply chain management principles—both of which reflect strategically important developments. The emergence of Strategic Human Resource Management, (SHRM) expresses the continuing evolution and refinement of HR, although as was pointed out in Chapter 2 this process is on-going, with new conceptualizations of what HR 'is' and what its focus should be.

The emphasis on HR's strategic role and contribution has been at the heart of much of the contemporary literature on HRM for the past 20 years, with important contributions coming from academics and experienced practitioners, many of whom are representing the view that people are a key, if not always the most important, organizational resource, but one that is critical to their performance. (Legge, 2005; Mabey et al., 1998; Salaman et al., 2005; Sullivan, 2005). But we have also highlighted the dangers of HR trying to 'look and claim to be strategic' for less reputable reasons, often to do with attempts to deflect criticisms that HR is not delivering and is still locked into a largely administrative and operational mind set and delivery model from which it cannot or does not want to escape. We have also made the point that 'becoming strategic is not as simple or straightforward as it might appear, partly because there is no consensus on what this means, particularly in a practical and applied context, where being strategic is more usefully understood as a relative rather than an absolute concept. The problems associated with equating 'being strategic' with what seems to be contemporarily 'fashionable' have also been referred to, a view shared by Haffendon who claims that:

> **There is a . . . large category of HR Directors who are faddists bent on chasing best practice and the latest quick fix, regardless of the needs of the business.**
> (Haffenden, 2002)

And, according to Michael Porter (1996), there is a real danger of failing to distinguish between operational effectiveness and strategy. He argues that if all organizations adopt similar operational practices, in other words how they use resources, no strategic competitive advantage will be gained by any unless such practices result in higher levels of profitability or other improvements *in strategic performance*. He states that:

> **Operational effectiveness means performing similar activities better than rivals perform them. Operational effectiveness includes but is not limited to efficiency. It refers to any number of practices that allow a company to better utilise its inputs by, for example, reducing defects in products or developing better products faster. In contrast, strategic positioning means performing different activities from rivals' or performing similar activities in different ways.**
> (Porter, 1996)

Porter's contribution to the debate on what makes something strategic is important for HR because his emphasis on difference is at odds with the 'best practice' approach to SHRM which suggests, in a somewhat simplistic way, that there exists a set of universally effective HR practices that are associated with organizational performance. However, according to Purcell (1999):

> **What is most notable about the best practice model is there is no discussion on company strategy at all. The underlying premise of this view is that organizations adopting a set of best practices attract super human resources, talent and competencies. 'These superior human resources will, in turn, influence the strategy the organization adopts and is the source of its competitive advantage.' (Milkovich & Newman, 2002, p. 30) Therefore, for this approach, policy *precedes* strategy.**

Supporters of this 'best practice' approach to HR strategy believe that there is sufficient evidence from research into the link between HR practices and organizational performance to suggest the existence of mutually compatible 'bundles' of HR policies that promote high levels of employee motivation and commitment (MacDuffie, 1995; Pfeffer, 1994). These are thought to include selective hiring, extensive training, employment security, a structure that encourages employee participation, and certain kinds of pay policies and practices. This list might also include other well known HR activities such as developing competency frameworks, 360 degree feedback, performance appraisal systems, and development centres. Questions that emerge from this way of providing HR with its route map to strategic contribution, but don't seem to be adequately answered, include:

- Where does the list stop and how many HR activities/elements constitute the bundle?
- Are all the individual elements of the bundle equally important?
- Does context play any part in influencing their strategic impact?
- Does it matter how the different elements are bundled together?

The point Porter makes about the difference between operational effectiveness and strategy is significant. HR functions that are successful in improving the way they do things do so because they deliver measurable improvements in cost reductions, productivity, cycle times, customer satisfaction levels, and so on, but to be strategically effective, HR needs to demonstrate the impact of what it does that goes beyond the operational level in ways that result in competitive advantage. But if all organizations are copying each other in their HR activities, then none will achieve a competitive advantage: they will only improve their operational effectiveness relative to how they were before but not in relation to organizations they are in competition with; if everyone makes the same operational changes then competitive advantage relationships remain largely unaltered. His view is that improvements in operational effectiveness only translate into strategic changes if similar activities are done in different ways or if there are differences between what one HR function does compared to another and that these differences are significant in generating and preserving a competitive advantage. Although Porter does not make this point, we would argue that his analysis also extends to HR Departments actually stopping doing certain things that have little or no operational value, but simply consume valuable resources. Strategic value and competitive advantage comes from either significantly reducing the costs of delivering HR services and/or reallocating professional resources to other and more value adding activities such as developing the function's ability to mobilise its resources to support corporate objectives.

Taking performance appraisal as an example, traditional performance review processes are still associated with the majority of UK organizations, but the questions that need to be asked are whether these processes contribute to operational effectiveness, and does this result in competitive advantage? If the answer to both questions is negative then a third question arises which is, what is the rationale for continuing to maintain such practices in their current form? There is a legitimate argument that is based on the premise that stopping wasteful HR activities that detract from operational effectiveness is itself a strategically valuable contribution.





**RESEARCH INSIGHT 3.1 HR in the Health Service Seeking a More Strategic Role**

This insight is based on the conference paper submitted by Morris and Mahoney.

**Morris, D. and Mahoney, M. (2005) 'Strategic reward systems: understanding the difference between "Best Fit" and "Best Practice"', Third Performance and Reward Conference, 7 April 2005, www.business.mmu.ac.uk/newsandevents/parc/morrismaloney.pdf. MMU**

This article applies the concepts of 'best practice' and 'best fit' to reward systems, arguably a crucial area of HR where the potential of creating strategically valuable contributions and competitive advantage is high. Read the article and answer the following questions:

1. In relation to reward systems and practices, what do the two approaches suggest HR practitioners should do in the way such systems are designed and implemented?
2. Does the evidence presented support one or the other approach?
3. In relation to reward systems and practices does the evidence suggest that there are in fact universally 'good' practices that are not contingent on organizational contexts and unique requirements?

The engrained belief that many of the activities HR engages in add value at the operational level and therefore have strategic significance may well express little more that 'taken for granted assumptions' that are rarely questioned or tested empirically.

References made in the previous chapter to the increasing interest in evidence based management suggest that the retention of existing HR practices and an unquestioning belief in their efficacy needs to be subject to a more rigorous process of questioning and evidence based evaluation to justify their continuation This point, that HR can act strategically by questioning rather than accepting the case for certain practices and policies is critical to the 'new HR' and is being increasingly reflected by those committed to looking carefully at the available evidence. For example, Beverly Alimo-Metcalfe during her presentation on engaged leadership at the 2008 CIPD National Conference, made it clear that she was not convinced by the argument that competences and being competent were strongly linked to organizational performance, yet she stated that many organizations are still developing competency frameworks and investing significant resources in their implementation and improvement. Is this justified, or is their growth more to do with 'fashion' and HR professionals simply copying what others are doing, based on the belief that if other organizations employ these then it must be right?

**STUDENT ACTIVITY 3.2 The Evidence For and Against Competency Frameworks and their Link to Organizational Performance**

This activity is research based and should be carried out in groups, possibly in the context of a seminar activity or an assignment. The tasks are:

1. Establish the extent of competency frameworks in UK organizations and whether there has been a growth in these.
2. Present the arguments in favour of competency and competency frameworks.
3. Evaluate the evidence on the effectiveness in improving employee and organizational performance.
4. Reach conclusions on their strategic value.

As is indicated in the following diagram, not all HR activities and contributions are at or should be at the strategic level; adding value and making contributions to the way an organization's human resources are managed can take place at different levels, and it is unrealistic to link each and every HR initiative and practice to a strategic intention and outcome. On the other hand, the consequences of not engaging at all at the strategic level are real and damaging to HR's standing in the organization. The hype about HR's strategic role may well have raised expectations which are difficult to meet without radical changes in how the HR function operates. This is particularly the case when line managers' perceptions still reflect a non-strategic HR function, a view confirmed by Lawler's research (2007) that found that the amount of time reported by HR professionals devoted to being a strategic business partner, in 2004, was no more than in 1995–23 per cent.

He also found that line managers believed that HR was 'far less involved in strategy than it thinks it is' (quoted in Hammonds). And despite the influence of their writings, the comment by Ulrich and Brocklebank (2005) that 'HR's role is to root out discrimination whenever it appears' hardly suggests that such a prioritization of activities will shift this perception.

If HR's strategic role and contribution is defined in terms of rooting out discrimination, the question is not whether this role is important or not but how it will be perceived by other stakeholders whose agendas and priorities may well be defined in terms of surviving the economic recession, coping with funding reductions and remaining competitive in an increasingly difficult world. Nor does it provide a convincing rebuttal to Hammonds' rather biting critique and challenge to HR expressed in his statement that:

> **After close to 20 years of hopeful rhetoric about becoming 'strategic partners' with a 'seat at the table' where the business decisions that matter are made, most human-resources professionals aren't nearly there. They have no seat, and the table is locked inside a conference room to which they have no key. HR people are, for most practical purposes, neither strategic nor leaders.**
> (Hammonds, 2005)

Such critical views are not necessarily representative of all line managers and senior executives, and many HR professionals are likely to take issue with them, but the point being made is that being aspirational is not enough and that in a stakeholder model of the organization it is those who depend on HR and are the recipients of its 'services' that will define what is adding value, what is strategic, and whether HR is acting effectively as a strategic business partner.

**PRACTITIONER INSIGHT Trevor Lincoln, People Director at eaga**

Eaga is a FTSE 250 company with headquarters in Newcastle, UK. Its main business is in home insulation but it also operates as an outsourcing arm offering a range of business services through call centre operations. These are the views on HR strategy for one of its senior executives.

For as long as I can remember during my career in HR there has been a debate about the contribution of HR to business strategy. My experience tells me that businesses will not be successful without HR not just supporting the delivery of business strategy but, more importantly, helping shape it. HR has the opportunity to either drive the business or become a passenger—a back seat driver constantly nagging at managers telling them what they should and should not do. The degree to which HR becomes the driver or takes a free ride is in my view determined by the qualities and competence of HR professionals:

1. Commercial acumen so that they understand the commercial world, and can influence the strategic plans the business has to conquer it.
2. Flexibility to interpret and apply the raft of employment legislation in a way which protects and supports the commercial intent of the business.
3. Most importantly of all, their ability to define a rock solid set of behavioural values which permeate the business influencing the development of the organization's culture and commercial orientation.

This does not mean plastering values posters on the office wall, or reproducing them in glossy brochures and doing nothing else. Quite the contrary, it means HR's role is to define these values in such a way that everyone in the organization understands them and how they fit within their role. When the organization reaches the point at which its values are strongly embedded, the strategic influence of HR flourishes.

In eaga we will not compromise our values for anyone or anything. We recruit, we promote, we performance manage, and we recognize talent through measuring performance against both performance objectives (what the individual achieves) and eaga values (the way in which they achieve this). Our values are underpinned by a set of job competencies so that employees know exactly what they need to do to demonstrate that they are living the eaga values. This applies to leaders at all levels of the organization. What has this to do with business strategy you might ask? The answer is that it has everything to do with business strategy and it has not come about by accident.

Three years ago eaga took the unusual step of taking all of its commercial Managing Directors plus their senior HR and Corporate Services colleagues out of the business for one week to visit some of the world's top companies. Over the course of the week the group studied these organizations and compared them to eaga. The majority of the discussions during that week were not at all about commercial imperatives—instead they were about the values which underpin our business. The discussions were led by HR and resulted in a strategy defined jointly by HR, Corporate Services and the Commercial MDs which has influenced our business ever since. These values are embodied in the following statement:

> **Eaga cares for its partners, customers and communities with integrity, respect and enthusiasm.**

It was agreed that the business could only be successful if we put our employees (partners in eaga's case) first. In doing so they would treat our customers and the communities we live and work in well, which would then lead to the long-term commercial success of the business. To reinforce this, HR now has peer representation on eaga's Executive, Operating, and Divisional Board's ensuring strategic influence at each.

What does the above statement mean in relation to our analysis of HR's role in strategy? Two points stand out. Firstly, that strategic impact does not come from the range of HR activities which tend to dominate the contents of HR textbooks but rather from HR focusing on shaping the behaviour of all the company's employees through the development and internalization of a set of corporate values that influence the way employees think about their work and what being a part of the eaga business involves. Secondly, there is a clear link between strategic impact and organization culture; it seems that it is *through* HR's ability to shape culture, through influencing how people think, perceive, and act, that the contribution that they make to the organization's business, commercial, or service provision objectives are maximized.

But at this point, the analysis of HR and strategy turns to a more academic direction and considers the contribution that certain well known writers on strategy have made to our understanding of the HR/strategy relationship.

See the Online Resource Centre extension material 3.1 for a more detailed summary of what being strategic means for HR

# What Can HR Learn from the Strategy Gurus?

Understanding the strategic issues facing HR and working to develop HR strategies that have a high impact—it does not necessarily follow that all strategies are strategically important because some might fail—is helped by drawing upon the thinking and contributions of influential writers on strategy and strategic management. To fully understand the complexities and challenges facing HR in its search for a more strategic role, we have to go outside of the strategic HRM literature and learn from the wider world of corporate strategy and strategic management. In doing so the intention is to identify key concepts and theories that can be applied to HR and from which HR practitioners can learn about strategy in the corporate world.

Perhaps the most influential book on strategy written in the UK in the last 15 years is by Johnson and Scholes, and more recently with Whittington (*Exploring Corporate Strategy* (2008) Pearson Education). In this latest edition, they define strategy as:

> **the direction and scope of an organisation over the long term: which achieves advantage for the organisation through its configuration of resources within a challenging environment, to meet the needs of markets and to fulfil stakeholder expectations.**

This definition addresses the question of what strategy involves rather than offering a conceptualization of strategy that is arguably more useful for the HR practitioner. This is what Minzberg offers in his influential 1987 article. In this article, he begins by stating that:

> **The field of strategic management cannot afford to rely on a single definition of strategy, indeed the word has long been used implicitly in different ways even if it has been defined formally in only one.**

He argues that explicit recognition of multiple definitions can help practitioners and researchers alike manoeuvre through this difficult field. Interestingly, although Minzberg accepts the existence of multiple definitions of the word strategy, he doesn't see this as a problem but an advantage, recognizing that there is not one way of making sense of this complex concept but several and each have their own uses and merits.

His five different interpretations of strategy are:

**1. Strategy as a Plan:** Seen as some form of consciously intended action, strategy represents a way forward, a set of actions and a use of resources that directs the organization (or the HR function) to do certain things in intended ways which are rational and consistent over time. Strategy as a plan represents a statement of the direction of travel, how we are going to get there and what resources we need to ensure we successfully achieve our intended objectives.

In an HR context, strategy as a plan has been strongly associated with Human Resource Planning, which involves the careful analysis of human resource requirements in the context of labour market conditions and the external product or service environment. The objective of such plans is to achieve the optimum balance between the demand and supply of labour over a given period of time. But strategy as a plan is not restricted to HRP, it could also be applied to the way an organization manages conflict with unions—think about the 2010 dispute between BA and the Unite trade union over changes to cabin crews' conditions of employment—what is the company's plan for dealing with this situation and has it been successfully implemented?

Unfortunately, plans do not always work out in the way intended; plans are often only as good as the information and analysis that informs them, and crucially plans can quickly become outdated and dysfunctional as external conditions change. Plans can also be 'good' and 'bad' in the sense that the assumptions, expectations and intelligence they are based on can be accurate and realistic or outdated and erroneous. Simply having a strategy—in the form of a plan—guarantees nothing other than you have a plan of action.

Strategies as plans can be intended and deliberate, following a rational line of thinking and pointing in a particular direction, or they can be emergent and flexible and much more closely related to the environment the organization operates in. Paradoxically, not having a formal plan but simply responding as quickly and as effectively as possible to environmental change can be equally strategic in the sense that this way of thinking and acting can have a more positive effect on the organization's performance than an HR plan that doesn't work! As an example, the speed of the onset of the 2008 economic recession invalidated many recruitment, development, and reward strategies (as plans) with these being rapidly abandoned and replaced by responses more in tune with harsh economic and financial realities. Not all HR plans are necessarily strategic in the sense that they may fail to generate operational change and enhance operational effectiveness and have little or no impact on the organization's competitive position. Paradoxically, HR plans might be counter-strategic!

**2. Strategy as Pattern:** According to Minzberg, strategy can also be understood as a pattern of behaviour, whether intended or not. In other words there is consistency as opposed to randomness in what organizations do. A helpful way of relating strategy as a pattern to the HR context involves contrasting what is described as HR's reactionary and fire-fighting role with one based on foresight and proactivity. Being forward looking and 'ahead of the curve'—and shaping rather than responding to events—is often represented as a more preferable strategic pattern, but given that we have emphasized that the strategic value of any action is to be found in its impact, either pattern could be more or less strategic than the other.

Another example of strategy as pattern can be found in an organization's approach to recruitment. One of the common threads linking companies rated highly by their employees as places to work, and which are often successful in a commercial sense, is the emphasis they give to developing and promoting staff from within. This pattern of action arguably produces a more reliable labour supply chain and greater employee engagement, both highly desirable and strategically valuable (see the *Sunday Times* Best Companies to Work for Survey referred to in Chapter 1).

**3. Strategy about What:** Whether plan or pattern, strategies need to be about something. The question that concerns the specific content, focus, and purpose of HR strategies is one that will be heavily influenced by the organization's unique history, position in its environment and internal competences. Specific HR policies and practices are always about 'something' and the relative emphasis given to each reflects a belief in their relevance and value to the organization, although put to the test many HR departments might be less than convincing in the way they defend every practice and policy they are involved in! But strategy as content and focus is also about implementation—it's not simply what HR does but how well it can implement its chosen policies. Returning to Porter's point, being strategic can mean performing similar activities in different ways and this can involve developing more effective ways of implementing chosen policies.

**RESEARCH INSIGHT 3.2 Implementing Strategy**

**Saunders, M., Mann, R. and Smith, R. (2008) 'Implementing strategic initiatives: A framework of leading practices', *International Journal of Operations & Production Management*, 28:11, pp. 1095–1123.**

Successful implementation is often key to any strategy and even though the strategy itself can be potentially effective, failure to implement it means its potential is never realized. The article to be read involves looking at strategic management implementation from an operations management perspective and aimed to highlight key practices associated with effective strategic implementation. Read the article and carry out the following tasks:

1. Identify the factors that seem to be associated with implementation failure.
2. Identify the main implementation frameworks the authors refer to and consider their relative merits and weaknesses.
3. Identify the main findings of the study, in particular what practices are associated with implementation success, and relate these to the role and contribution of HR.

Of the many strategies that HR is engaged with, in terms of content and focus, the following are some of the most frequently found in practice:

- Strategies for managing talent—should this focus on buying in talent and emphasize the criticality of the recruitment and selection process or should the emphasis be given to growing and nurturing existing employees? What are our plans or chosen pattern for this?
- Strategies for managing performance—this involves deciding on the use of different instruments and practices that are thought to stimulate employee performance. Do we rely on formal mechanisms such as appraisal processes, reward systems, and targets or rather emphasize the creation of a high performance work environment?
- Strategies for managing costs—does this involve reducing headcount, time worked, or wages/salaries and are reductions across the board or targeted?
- Strategies for managing rewards—are these based on a collective or individual approach to employees; are rewards linked to or independent of performance; what is the balance between financial and non-financial rewards?
- Strategies for managing trade unions—are TUs recognized and given negotiating rights? Is collective bargaining legitimized as the main form of decision-making in relation to the determination of and changes in terms and conditions of employment, and are employee communications directed through trade union representatives or based on direct contact with individuals?

Finally, strategies about 'what' fundamentally involves choice. Firstly, in the sense of which aspects of employment and HR are going to be emphasized, and secondly, choosing the specific way(s) in which the preferred action plans are going to be implemented to deliver the required outcomes and impact.

**4. Strategy as Position:** this can be understood in terms of strategy differentiation—how does an organization differentiate itself in relation to competitors. Perhaps the best example of this in HR is the way certain organizations position themselves within the labour market and relative to competitor organizations—the aim often is to be the employer of preferred choice. This positioning is more commonly known as employer branding and can be understood as:

> **How an organisation markets what it has to offer to potential and existing employees. Marketers have developed techniques to help attract customers, communicate with them effectively and maintain their loyalty to a consumer brand. Employer branding involves applying a similar approach to people management.**
> CIPD (2010a)

The deliberate positioning of an organization through distinguishing itself from its competitors involves making commitments and promises to provide a particular kind of working and employment experience to prospective employees and in so doing engage with people who are attracted to the particular kind of cultural environment being offered ((CIPD, 2010b) Martin and Hetrick, 2006).

**5. Strategy as Perspective:** The fifth conceptualization of strategy is arguably the most difficult to grasp but is potentially the most powerful because it is the most enduring. Strategy in this respect is, according to Minzberg, similar to what personality is to the individual. It might be better understood through such concepts as philosophy, ideology, and culture, or the character of the organization. The power of this way of understanding strategy is that it is associated with a collective and shared set of understandings and ways of being that transcend changes in the external environment and generate a sense of deeply-rooted commitment to patterns of behaviour.

In relation to strategy as plan, position, purpose, or pattern, then strategy as perspective stands out as the one where HR could make the most important strategically valuable contribution but realistically the one that it is least likely to understand and deliver on its own. The ability to shape the collective mindset and change organizational culture is one that HR could potentially contribute to but is unlikely to lead. This is the role of the organization's leader(s) whose vision and values help to shape the defining features of how the organization functions. (Examples of strategy as perspective can be found in Jim Collins' book, *From Good to Great* and in the quotation from Thomas J. Watson in Chapter 1 of this book, as well as the Practitioner Insight from Trevor Lincoln earlier in the chapter.)



# The Contribution of Hamel and Prahalad

The work of Gary Hamel and C.K. Prahalad has long been recognized within the world of business and business strategy as having a seminal influence on corporate and business leaders (Hamel and Prahalad 1990, 1993, 1994).

In their 1993 article, they present a summary of conventional thinking on strategy that emphasizes:

- Fit or the relationship between the organization and its environment; in the case of HR this idea translates into the fit between HR strategy and corporate strategy and the fit or integration between different HR strategies. (This relationship is more usually referred to as vertical and horizontal integration, and is illustrated by Figure 3.2 In the final section of the chapter.)
- The allocation of resources in ways that generate the best returns from investments made.
- A long-term rather than a short-term perspective.

Without rejecting the importance of these three elements, they offer an alternative view of strategy in which 'the concept of **stretch** supplements the idea of fit' and that '**leveraging** resources is as important as allocating them' (p. 77).

The concept of leveraging resources is one that is explored in more detail later in the chapter, but its importance for HR is self evident. Strategic contribution comes as much, if not more, from how human resources are used as having the right quantity and quality of resources in place at the right time. This position reflects O'Reilly and Pfeffer's belief that the problem with an HR strategy based on hiring the most talented people, whilst important for many organizations, detracts attention from the far more strategically significant requirement of increasing the talent and productive value of *all* of an organization's employees (O'Reilly and Pfeffer, 2000). And the notion of leveraging the human resource to increase its productivity is consistent with the point made in the first chapter of this book that one of management's fundamental objectives in the way human resources are managed is to constantly increase the level of resource utilization—getting more from the same or even better, more from less. The search for continuous improvements in employee productivity is not only important for operational effectiveness but also has strategic potential.



Examples of this relationship can be found in competitive advantage resulting from lower employment costs, increased employee flexibility and higher rates of creativity and innovation.

According to Hamel and Prahalad, there are two basic approaches to achieving greater resource productivity. These are:

1. Downsizing and head count reductions, or, as they say, 'becoming lean and mean'.
2. Resource leveraging that seeks to get the most out of the available resources, in other words to get more from what you have.

They argue that a resource leveraging strategy is more energizing than the downsizing route which is likely to have a demoralizing effect on employees and has the potential of reducing productivity which can result in further cutbacks; in other words what starts off as a planned reduction in resource costs can lead to a downward spiral of productivity as reduced costs trigger reduced human resource outputs which can often be proportionately greater that the savings from reduced input costs.

They claim that management can leverage its resources (including human resources) in five basic ways, four of which can be related to HR. These are:

1. **Concentrating Resources: convergence and focus.** They describe this in terms of organizations having a strategic focal point or strategic intent—it's what defines what the organization is about and

known for. In Marketing, this is known as the 'strap line'—a statement which summarizes its focus and represents a reference point for employees to use to help them stay aligned and in tune. In HR, the equivalent is what Purcell called 'The Big Idea'—that unifying concept that defines the organization's purpose or raison d'être. (Purcell, 2003).

They claim that convergence prevents the diversion of resources and that focus prevents their dilution at any given time, arguing that:

> **Without focused attention on a few key operating goals at any one time, improvement efforts are likely to be so diluted that the company ends up as a perpetual laggard in every critical performance area.**
> (Hamel and Prahalad,1993)

2. **Accumulating Resources: extracting and borrowing.** In an HR context this involves an organization maximizing its resource base through the way it learns from experience. Strategic advantage comes from harnessing the power of learning in ways that support operational effectiveness. This way of leveraging an organization's human resources touches on subjects such as the learning organization, organizational learning, and knowledge management and requires, according to Hamel and Prahalad, a corporate climate which allows people to challenge long-standing practices—not something many employees would feel comfortable about, or explicitly encouraged by many management teams. Learning from experience is a key source of leverage but which is paradoxically a source of threat because learning from and using experience invariably involves at least the potential for challenging the status quo. They make this point very clearly when they say that:

   > **Unless top management declares open season on precedent and orthodoxy, learning and the un-learning that must precede it cannot begin to take place.**
   > (Hamel and Prahalad, 1993)

   The implications of gaining strategic leverage through the use of experience for the HR function are obvious and not necessarily surprising. But this is not really the issue: what is, is the *ability* to deliver high impact outcomes based on learning strategies that go beyond the mere delivery of training that reflects a traditional training mind set, but are based on a clear understanding of how learning can be used to increase operational effectiveness and generate competitive advantage.

3. **Complementing Resources: blending and balancing.** This source of leverage is concerned with how organizations are structured and how this affects the way they function. It is about how organizations, based on hierarchy, levels, divisions, and departments create internal divisions and barriers to people working together. This is often expressed by reference to 'silos' which represent inflexible working arrangements and internal restrictions on what people can do and who they can work with. Blending, for Hamel and Prahalad, is essentially about the integration of organizational units and resources; it is about working together in ways that reflect a systems view of organizations. From an HR perspective, this has implications for the level of flexibility that exists within the human resource, whether managing is separated from the world of working and how well the human and technical systems are integrated (Rummler and Brache, 1995).

4. **Conserving Resources: recycling, co-opting and shielding.** This is about the productivity of resources—the extent to which any given skill, knowledge, or competence is actually used and how frequently it is used to drive the business forward. It is also about the ability of an organization to move its resources to wherever they can make a more valuable contribution. According to the authors, there are extensive opportunities for knowledge and resources to be recycled, but whether this happens depends on the state of the organization's internal culture and processes. Perhaps the best example of recycling and co-opting can be found in the idea of Communities of Practice (Wenger (2007); Hasan and Crawford (2007)). These involve people who have a shared or similar interest in a particular profession or area of work and involve the creation, processing, and sharing of knowledge. Membership can be flexible and involve co-optation. Essentially, such communities represent a key

resource that can be used to turn tacit knowledge into explicit knowledge and offer tried and tested solutions to different parts of an organization.

The interesting point about Hamel and Prahalad's concept of leveraging value and strategic contribution from stretching organizational resources is that it can so easily be related to developments in HR, whether in terms of new approaches to generating learning rich experiences, to unblocking existing sources of knowledge, to creating flexible and organic communities of people who have similar interests, and finally to working across boundaries in flexible and integrated ways. The crucial question is, however, whether HR professionals are aware of the potential such developments represent and whether they are able to realize this potential.

## Are HR Strategies Uniquely Different?

Whatever form HR strategies might take—and at this point it is important to emphasize the distinction between specific strategies that emerge from within HR departments in response to key human resource challenges and those that have their origins at the corporate level and relate to top management's strategic decisions—an important question to ask is whether these are specific and unique to each organization. How different are HR strategies and are they, in themselves, the source of competitive advantage? Boudreau and Ramstad (2007) argue that most HR strategies are similar in focus and content and it would be difficult to identify which strategy belonged to which organization. They claim that:

> **Talent and organisation decisions are often based on very broad and generic strategic goals such as 'increase innovation' or 'provide world class customer service'. Or they reflect workforce goals that are important but common to most organisations such as 'retain more baby boomer technical talent,' 'increase diversity,' 'or build next-generation leadership'.**

At one level, most HR departments would claim to have strategies, probably in the form of plans or patterns, but strategies that confer competitive advantage and generate high impact outcomes not only need to be effectively implemented but need to focus on aspects of behaviour, structure, and culture that if changed in the required way would make a significant difference to key dimensions of organizational performance. Boudreau and Ramstad describe these strategically important areas as 'pivot points'. Their argument is that HR strategy needs to reflect and focus on those key pivot points in the employment and management of people that have the potential to permanently change behaviour in ways that confer significant and sustainable improvements in performance.

What does this mean in practical terms? One way to make strategy 'real' is to look at what this meant for organizations in the 2008 recession. Many organizations linked strategy to survival, and for many this was the only strategically important objective they were dealing with, but others defined their strategy in terms of emerging from the recession stronger and better placed to take advantage of new opportunities. The key point here is that strategy, both corporate and within HR, reflects how people *frame* the problem(s) they are faced with and their ability to visualize a future desired state that they want the organization to be in.

Gary Hamel provides a continuing source of insight into business strategy and in a podcast for the CIPD applied his thinking and prescriptions to HR. In trying to make sense of what organizations needed to do he said:

> **we're going to have to find ways to get our employees to bring their creativity and their passion to work every day. I think the companies that do well over the next few months, the next few years are going to have a very important set of skills but those may not be the same skills that will see them through beyond this crisis. For that we need organisations that are fundamentally more adaptable, more innovative and more engaging places to work than they are right now. Some companies I think are already moving in that direction, most have a long ways to go.**
> **(Hamel, 2009)**

From his comments, we can see that the examples of strategically important pivot points are:

- The degree to which organizations are flexible and adaptable to environmental changes.
- The degree to which their employees are creative and innovative.
- The extent to which organizations engage with their employees and provide psychologically and emotionally rewarding places to work.
- Having the right leaders and leadership capabilities to confront new challenges and take advantage of opportunities to grow the business.

And why are these important? Because there is extensive evidence that positive measures of flexibility, creativity, and engagement are consistently associated with high performance at the individual and organizational levels (Khilji and Wang, 2006; Buckingham and Coffman, 1999). The task for HR then becomes one of establishing the strategic links between the specific aspects of employee and management behaviour and organizational performance and developing effective strategies that bring about the desired changes in the designated areas.

What makes HR strategies different between organizations is less to do with the strategic intentions expressed through mission statements and departmental strategy documents than their ability to identify the key things that need to be *changed*, rather than simply improved. This inevitably involves leading and leadership, and confronting conflict; HR to be effective as a strategic partner needs to be involved in these processes rather than on the periphery. The end of chapter case study offers a good example of how HR can be a strategic 'player' and what this involves. This case study helps to cast light on one of the most important questions facing managers in trying to bring about behavioural change. The question is:

> **does behaviour change as a result of changes in the structure and culture of an organization or does a change in behaviour precede and facilitate structural and cultural change?**
> (Pfeffer, 2005)

**STUDENT ACTIVITY 3.4**

Read the following article by Jeffrey Pfeffer and complete the tasks.

**Pfeffer, J. (2005) 'Changing mental models: HR's most important task', *Human Resource Management*, Summer, 44:2, pp. 123–128.**

1. What do mental models mean and why are they important?
2. What have mental models got to do with HR strategy?

How can HR change its own mental models and if successful what will this mean for its strategic role?

The importance of the link between strategy formulation, strategy implementation, and change is one that cannot be over-stated; successful strategy almost always requires change in one form or another.

For a model of the strategic change process and the relationship between strategic change and organizational performance see the Online Resource Centre extension material 3.2

# The Concept of Fit and Integration

The first of these strategically important contributions from the world of HR strategy lies in the concepts of fit and integration, considered briefly earlier in the chapter, and for our purposes we intend to treat them as synonymous. Farnham writing in the second edition of *People Resourcing* (Pilbeam and Corbridge, 2002) uses the familiar terminology of 'best-fit', as opposed to the concept of 'best practice' to describe a critical relationship which is that between what HR does and what the organization either needs or is capable of accommodating. He argues that:

> **Organizations need to identify the HR strategies which 'fit' their enterprises in terms of product markets, labour markets, size, structures, strategies, and other factors.**
> (Farnham in Pilbeam and Corbridge, 2002)

He offers three kinds of 'best-fit' models:

1. One that links HR to an organization's life or business cycle. The importance of this point lies in the realization that, whilst the fundamental objectives of managing people remain constant, their relative importance changes to reflect life cycle or business cycle requirements. HR then needs to adapt its contributions in ways that generate maximum value which is determined by the organization's position in each of these two life cycles. This point was again considered earlier in the chapter.
2. One that links HR's contribution to the different strategies and structural configurations of organizations. Here, the emphasis is on HR understanding how cultural and structural forms and preferences generate the context within which HR needs to operate in and make its contributions. For example, many public sector organizations are organized on hierarchical lines and operate in predominantly formal ways. The concept of best-fit in this situation suggests that the design and operation of appraisal systems, for example, will also reflect both hierarchy and formality. A second example of this particular model can be found in the design of performance and reward systems. In a cultural environment where individuals rather than teams are seen as the primary social unit, the design of jobs, the degree of functional flexibility and the use of individual rather than collective rewards will need to 'fit' this culture. On the other hand, in organizations that claim to be value driven, HR will be expected to reflect the importance of these values in every aspect of employee behaviour and in the way HR selects, develops, and promotes employees; hierarchy becomes less important than behaviour and HR needs to orientate its activities and contributions to reflect these different priorities. Think again about the Practitioner Insight from Trevor Lincoln and how some organizations define themselves in relation to basic beliefs and values.
3. The third best-fit model matches HR strategies to business strategies. This involves HR actively engaging with current and potentially different business strategies and working to support them. Strategies which stress creativity and innovation will require HR to tailor their selection criteria to ensure that creative and innovative people are employed and that these virtues are rewarded in the pay and reward systems more than conformity or length of service. The tight control of costs, reflecting a competitive strategy based on price, will require HR to be particularly sensitive to increases in wage/salary and employment costs, and seek to minimize labour costs without undermining productivity levels. In the 2008 recession, the survival of many private sector businesses depended on HR looking at ways of reducing costs, but in this recession, unlike previous ones, retaining skilled employees was considered to be strategically important in the context of expected future growth. This meant that simply reducing head count, whilst often a temporary 'survival' strategy ran in parallel with wage reductions, temporary lay-offs, and reduced working time rather than permanent and forced redundancies (Risling, 2010).

**STUDENT ACTIVITY 3.5 Managing in a Recession**

1. Choose an organization your are familiar with or research one on the internet.
2. If it has developed HR strategies for coping with recessionary pressures identify these and try to establish their effect and strategic impact.
3. An alternative involves deciding on what strategies should be adopted in a recessionary period, establishing what the approach to implementation should be and then linking these strategies to strategically important outcomes.

Be prepared to present your findings in the form of a PowerPoint presentation.

**KEY CONCEPT Integration**

The concept of strategic integration or fit can take three different forms:

1. **Horizontal integration.** In this form, the different activities and contributions associated with HR work need to be mutually supportive and designed in a holistic way rather than exist as unconnected and isolated interventions. The concept of connectivity is also useful in explaining what horizontal integration involves. Strategic impact comes from the synergistic effects of the different but closely interwoven activities.
2. **Vertical integration.** Here, HR is outward looking and connected to the wider organization, sensitive to its values and beliefs, its corporate strategy, and contextual challenges.
3. A third type, that we call **functional integration**, is less frequently referred to in the HR literature, but refers particularly to the way the HR and production functions work in conjunction rather than in isolation. Examples of this in action include work and job design, performance related pay systems, high performance team working, and production system design which can be seen as closely related to the concept of socio-technical systems.

Figure 3.2 shows more clearly how these first two forms of integration work, or should work, in symmetry. And the HRM Insight below illustrates the importance of the two forms of integration in a practical context.

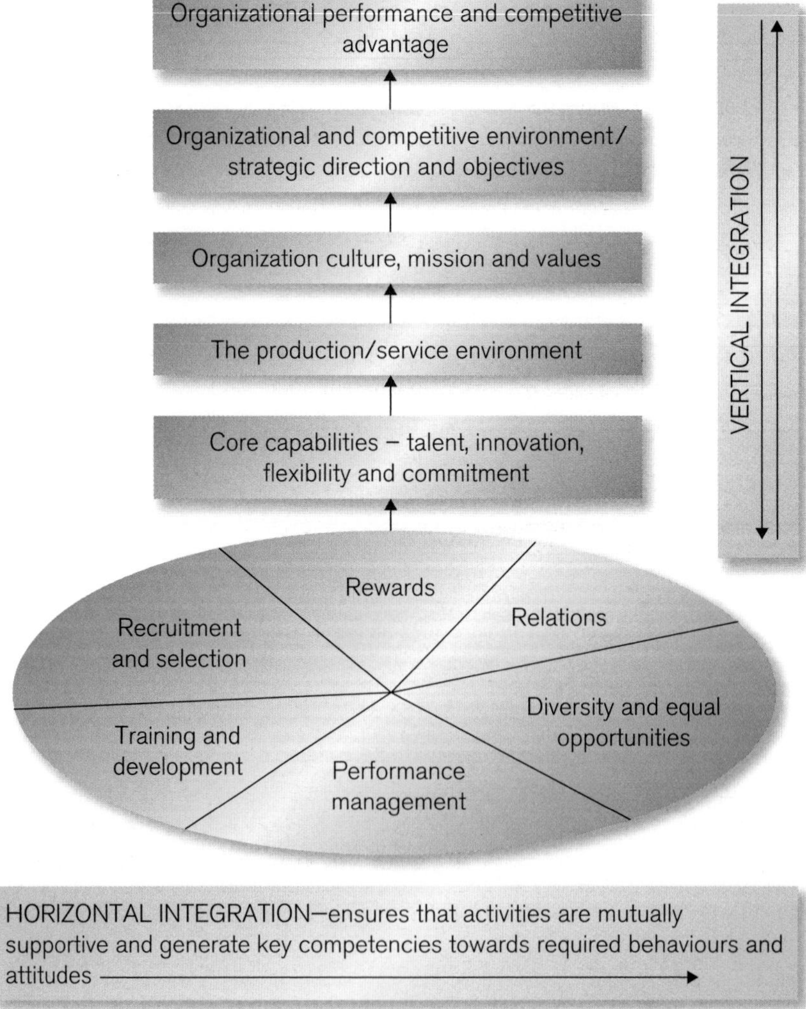


**Figure 3.2** A diagrammatical representation of vertical and horizontal integration as applied to HR

HRM INSIGHT 3.1 **Introducing a Leadership Training Programme at Midshire University**

Midshire, one of the UK's 'new' universities, had been structured around ten departments, each with its own management team and administrative support. Central functions, based on finance, marketing, the registry, facilities, and HR, coordinated a series of common services and procedures for all of the academic departments, with the 'centre' operating very much as a bureaucracy, exercising hierarchical control over its constituent parts.

Over time, the HR department had grown from rather modest proportions to what had now become a large and influential part of the university, employing approximately 60 staff, split evenly between professional and administrative employees. Its main operational role was in maintaining good relations with trade unions, providing advice to the senior management teams within the departments, managing grievance and disciplinary cases, and providing a centralized, course-based training service. Its reputation within the university ranged from being seen as an expensive overhead, through being seen as a well-managed but largely administrative service, to, for the majority of university staff, a somewhat remote and detached set of people who didn't have much interest in, and experience of, what most staff actually did and the environment in which they worked.

As a result of a major reorganization in 2002, which resulted in the merger of the ten academic departments into three new super colleges, it became apparent that many of the newly appointed senior managers lacked the strategic management skills that they needed to take on these important leadership roles. In addition, the results of the annual staff survey indicated that many employees, in both academic and non-academic roles, had considerable concerns about the quality of leadership in general and felt that this was an important matter that had to be addressed if the aspirations of the university's vice chancellor were to be met.

Responding to a request from the vice chancellor, the head of HR contacted an external provider of leadership training and held discussions about what would represent the most appropriate way of dealing with this problem. What emerged was a sophisticated course in leadership, delivered off-site and consisting of three separate two-day sessions using a mixture of both experiential and classroom-based learning.

The reaction of those who participated in the training was that, while the experience of being on the course had been interesting and developmental, the big problem was that little, if anything, had changed in the university and that the course on its own was not able to address the problem of a lack of leadership among management. The results of the staff survey the following year confirmed that staff continued to feel that the university had a serious leadership problem.

Questions

1. What action should have been taken and by whom prior to, during, and after the course to ensure that there was a high level of integration within the whole learning experience?
2. What other HR and management changes might the HR department have made to ensure that the new leadership course was horizontally integrated?
3. What should have been the respective contributions of the HR specialists and line managers in making sure that the investment in both time and money delivered the necessary outcomes?

# The Resource-Based View of the Firm

Arguably the most influential contribution to the development of a strategic dimension to HR is the idea that the organization represents a mix of different kinds of resources, one of course being the human resources. Central to this way of thinking is the belief that an organization's stock of human resource is not fixed but subject to renewal and expansion through carefully considered recruitment and selection policies, and increases in competence and capability through effective learning interventions, both of which can contribute to improvements in performance and productivity. In thinking about people as a flexible rather than fixed resource, the often unstated assumption is that the resource can only increase its contribution. This is not the case; people, depending on a number of influences can become less efficient and productive, and it becomes critical for HR to understand the reasons why this might occur and take appropriate action to prevent this happening. People can do more and less depending on a wide range of factors and influences.

This way of understanding the opportunities and challenges of managing people at the strategic level is consistent with Hamel and Prahalad's concept of resource stretching and owes much to the influential work of Barney (1991). In this article, Barney argues that the key relationship is that between the way human resources are used and the organization's chosen strategy to deliver competitive advantage and resultant changes in its performance.

The emphasis from the resource based view of organizations tends to be on the development of human capital capabilities so that 'the same becomes more' and through this improvements in operational effectiveness translate into increases in strategically important measures of organizational performance. According to Kamoche (1996), this means that people need to be seen as the 'source of resourcefulness' and that a central focus of HR is to grow as well as use the resource in ways that result in or contribute to competitive advantage. But if all organizations understand this and make similar commitments to and investments in training and development how does any single organization improve the value of its human capital at a greater rate or to a higher level than its competitors? According to Analoui (2007), to make a distinctive contribution to competency development an organization's resources must be unique and distinctive and Porter, who we referred to earlier in the chapter, argues that strategic advantage comes from organizations doing things differently from their competitors or doing different things better. So the dilemma for HR professionals, whilst sharing a common HR agenda with most comparable organizations, is that they have to find ways to improve efficiency and productivity that drive competitive advantage and which are unique to their own organization.

What does this mean in practical terms? Well, one way of making sense of this challenge is to take a concrete example: performance management. Doing something different might involve abandoning traditional forms of performance appraisals altogether, a strategy justified by a significant body of evidence that indicates many PA systems do not work, contribute little if anything of value to performance, and paradoxically can result in performance and productivity falls (Coens and Jenkins, 2000). Simply disengaging from what most other organizations do in this respect has the potential of saving significant resources and may prevent a reduction in what people actually produce and contribute to.

An example of doing things differently, again using performance appraisal as an example, would be to replace formal and highly structured systems driven by HR with informal systems owned and controlled by line managers and their teams of employees. What is lost is consistency and conformity replaced by diversity but relevant practice that reflects differences in how things should be done but where diversity of practice reflects common aims and outcomes.

Taking recruitment and selection as a second example, what different things could be done or the same things done differently? Instead of employing people directly organizations could outsource work and build flexible supply chain networks to deliver all but the core work of the organization. In other words, you stop most of the normal recruitment and selection activities and let other organizations take on this responsibility at a price which is considerably below the costs of undertaking this in-house. Doing the same things differently would involve retaining recruitment and selection responsibilities in-house but rely much more heavily on online recruitment and assessment—in other words leveraging technological resources whilst retaining human expertise and competency for the final stages of the selection process. Managed well, this approach could not only significantly reduce costs and cycle times but also result in better selection decisions. Related to the field of recruitment and selection, most organizations use job descriptions to help them draw up person specifications that in turn support the assessment and selection of applicants. Why? Some, but fewer, organizations don't use them for reasons which they fully understand. As an example, the highly successful engineering company Gripple, based in Sheffield, have rejected job descriptions completely. An article in the *Daily Telegraph* (Hurley, 2010) claims that the founder of Gripple has deliberately avoided the growth of formal structures and procedures as his company has grown into a £30 million pound business, and one of the things he has decided not to adopt are job descriptions. Hugh Stacey is reported as saying:

> **Job descriptions stop people doing things. If someone sees a ball dropping do they catch it or do they say it's not my ball?**

This might be a trivial example, although the management of Gripple certainly believe that job descriptions actually inhibit positive behaviour and flexibility, but the principle is what is important. Doing something differently from his competitors—and not having job descriptions is only one example of his approach to managing people—distinguishes him because, in his mind, the approach Gripple has adopted works and helps to contribute to competitive advantage. Why? Because his employees are so much more productive and value adding because, in part, they are free from traditional structures of formal control.

## Summary

Of all the different elements within HR, as it is taught in colleges and universities, the one that frequently causes students most difficulty is HR strategy. It's not obvious why this is the case. Is it the way it is taught, the abstract and academic nature of much of the material presented to students, or possibly because the 'theory' of strategy doesn't lend itself to easy application within HR? Whatever the explanation, this chapter set out to overcome some of these difficulties and to present an analysis of strategy and strategic contribution firmly within an HR context, but also using useful and important concepts and contributions from the field of corporate strategy. The following are some of the key points that we believe students, many of whom are likely to work in HR, need to reflect on:

- Despite having the potential to make strategically important contributions that support corporate objectives, HR is still subject to the criticism that it doesn't understand what this means and often fails to deliver.
- The reasons for this unfulfilled potential lie primarily in the behaviours, competences, agendas, and mind sets of HR professionals and in the unique ambiguities associated with the HR function.
- Being 'strategic' and making strategically important contributions is not something that happens because HR practitioners engage in a strategic discourse or associate themselves with the strategic dimension of HR. Being strategic comes from having a strategic as opposed to an administrative and operational mind set and from delivering contributions that other stakeholders define as being of strategic value.

  The concepts of 'fit' and integration suggest that HR needs to understand organizations as consisting of complex and dynamic sub-systems, and only by fully understanding these complex and dynamic relationships can HR move towards achieving what at best can only be a temporary fit and integration. Fitting and being integrated are temporary and provisional rather than absolute and permanent states. The challenge never ends!
- The idea of leveraging human resources to generate competitive advantage is central to what being strategic represents. This means that HR strategies which maximize the utilization of people and continue to grow their potential without undermining their commitment and level of engagement are those that are likely to make the greatest strategic contribution. One of the ironies of contemporary organizational life is that many people actually feel under-valued and under-used whilst others feel that work is too stressful and pressurized; both conditions suggest that management is failing to make the most of its people. What are the strategies that resulted in these two undesirable states and what strategies can change them?
- Finally, being strategic fundamentally means understanding the implications for behaviour and performance of the decisions managers make and the choices they are confronted with. We have argued that the available evidence suggests that the most successful organizations are those that relate decisions and choices to values, beliefs, and shared mind sets which endure and remain consistent through transformation and change. The key strategic choices involve:
  - whether to commit to an individualist approach to employee relations or to recognize and negotiate with trade unions;

- whether to reward employees on merit, performance, and potential, or on the basis of the jobs they do and their length of service;
- whether to employ only talented people or grow the talent of all employees those that are available;
- whether to base the development of employees on informal processes of learning and development or formal training programmes;
- whether to adopt a 'one size fits all' approach to the development of HR practices or to develop more tailored and individualized policies and practices.

always recognizing that these choices are not mutually exclusive but rather reflect question of preference, emphasis, and contextual relevance.

**Visit the Online Resource Centre that accompanies this book for self-test questions, weblinks, and more information on the topics covered in this chapter.**
**www.oxfordtextbooks.co.uk/orc/banfield_kay2e/**

## REVIEW QUESTIONS

1. What is the difference between strategy and being strategic?
2. When representatives of HR claim to be acting strategically, what might this mean?
3. What limits HR from increasing its strategic contribution to the organization?
4. In what way does HR's strategic contribution affect competitive advantage?
5. Thinking of an organization you are familiar with, what could HR do that would have a strategically important impact on employee behaviour and performance?

***See Online Resource Centre for answers.***

## CASE STUDY

### The Role of Human Resources in Strategic Change

In the following end of chapter case study, the experiences of one HR manager are recounted as part of a 'story' of strategic change and HR's role and contribution to this.

**Background to Organization:** Irish-based company ABC Ltd is the market leader in their sector and has been operating on the island for over 70 years. It is heavily unionized with 90 per cent of employees active members of four different unions and negotiates separately with production, distribution, sales, and clerical and management unions.

Prior to a takeover in the 1990s by an international company, the company was managed locally by a board of directors based in the Dublin head office. Traditionally the culture of the company has been very paternalistic—'We are one family and we all look after each other.' There was a very strong emphasis on the mentality that no one ever got kicked out of the family no matter how troublesome they were. Change never happened without complete consensus with the unions and without exchange of a monetary benefit to the affected group of employees. Traditionally the style of leadership within the company was very transactional and task orientated; employees' views and opinions were never sought for any strategic change projects.

The majority of the employees in the Irish Republic have been doing the same job for the past 30 to 40 years with little differentiation in their day to day tasks and therefore anything new or different that is asked of them is treated with suspension and mistrust. This group of 'Theory X' employees tends to be closed and secretive in their manner, risk adverse with low team spirit, and status. They adopt a predominantly 'what's in it for me?' attitude and are not open to change.

**Change in Ownership:** The international company that took over the Irish organization was very innovative and was successful in exploiting niche markets.

The company developed into an international organization by creatively adapting to the changing business environment. They established themselves as a leading participant in their markets. The organization believes that change creates opportunities—management analyse change and capitalize on it as effectively as they can. They look for the unusual and see how it can help their business—this helps differentiate them in the market place. The organization fosters a culture of learning from each other and ensures knowledge is shared internally. This is a culture they like to see mirrored throughout their individual companies and it represented a huge change for the Irish organization.

ABC Ltd not only wanted to change to 'better' practices as a company, it also wanted to introduce formal policies and procedures that would govern every aspect of the management of its people. Such formality had never existed in the business previously and the new management were convinced that this was critical to its future success. But they were also aware that there would be resistance to this change.

It was identified that to achieve the desired outcome they would involve and engage with everybody in a meaningful way. The desired outcome of ensuring that all our people are aligned and intrinsically motivated will be taken into account in both 'what we do' and in 'how we do it'.

The management initially communicated the need for this change in practice through an employee briefing session chaired by the CEO where all affected employees were invited to attend. This session was then followed up by a written business briefing which was not only issued to all staff but also copied to the union officials (an act that was never done before).

The management team made a commitment to all employees and union officials at the very offset of the engagement process stating the following:

People will not be surprised by what we do.

All the people within the area have the opportunity of contributing to suggestions and ideas before any decisions are made.

We engage with staff and give them the opportunity of contributing to planning the best way of implementing and achieving our plans.

We will work on the principle that the support of the people is critical to the success of any decision.

We will respect the union agreements that are in place in the business and will not change custom or practice without proper consultation and communication will all.

Taking into account all suggestions and ideas, ultimately it is the responsibility of the leader to make the decision. We must always make the best decisions in a timely fashion for the company in the long term.

**Role of Human Resources in this change program:**

Once the initial briefings took place with all affected employees and their union representatives the Human Resources Manager arranged a series of training days[4] for the senior and middle management teams where they could view the initial draft of the proposed policies and make their suggestions and recommendations on the content, the language and the tone of the policy and also to ensure that they understood the rationale of each one. The drawback of this method of engagement is that the pace of learning can be slow. It was identified though that due to the complexity of this change, that is, fundamentally changing the culture of the company, that the pace of change needed to be slow in order to allow all managers to fully understand and gain a sense of ownership of the processes so that they could in turn become agents of change.

Table 3.1 illustrates the time allocated to these offsite training sessions.

The middle management team of ABC was now in effect the change agent in this process and the CEO and the HR Manager now become the facilitators or sponsors of this project. Over the following 18 month period (change of this magnitude for a heavily unionized company is very slow) the middle management team started to move away from their traditional roles of instructing, directing, and controlling staff. They started to move away from focusing solely at the macro and micro levels within the organization

[4] Training days were held offsite and overnight so managers could focus on really examining what the rationale was behind each policy. Learning exercises used on training days were group exercises, role play, case study analysis, group discussion, and debate.

**Table 3.1** Overview of Facilitated Policy Training Days for Management

| Policy to be discussed | No. of Delegates | No. of Days allocated to Training |
|---|---|---|
| Disciplinary | 10 | 2 |
| Grievance | 10 | 2 |
| Dignity and Respect | 10 | 2 |
| Absenteeism Management | 10 | 2 |
| Leave Policy | 10 | 2 |
| Recruitment and Selection | 10 | 2 |
| Performance Management | 10 | 3 |

(transactional/autocratic leadership trait) and started to encourage commitment and engagement from their followers. We could start to see these managers moving towards the Resonant Leadership style in that they are in tune with those that surround them and they are intuitively aware and understood the needs and wants of others. Middle managers discussed and debated with their followers about the rationale of the policies. They then reported back to senior management and HR with their thoughts and suggestions so that a robust set of agreed and negotiated policies and procedures could be designed, agreed, and implemented in the business.

Figure 3.3 illustrates the methodology that the organization adopted during this change programme.

**Effectiveness of employee engagement and involvement in the change process:** Throughout the process of engagement and again once the policies had been agreed and implemented the HR Manager conducted an exercise with a sample group of individuals that were involved with the change programme. The purpose of this exercise was to ascertain on a continuum of employee involvement (Blyton and Turnbull, 1998) where they rated the level of employee involvement throughout the change programme. The group of employees sampled came from the following functions:

- Senior Managers (A)
- Union Shop Stewards (B)
- Union Officials (external stakeholder) (C)
- Middle Manager (D)
- HR Manager (E)
- Employee (F)

For comparative purposes these groups were ask to identify where they felt they fit best on the continuum at the initial stages of the programme and at the final stage. As illustrated in Figures 3.4 and 3.5, all groups moved along the continuum by the end of the process which illustrated to all that the methodology used in the management of this change process had indeed been effective.

The exercise clearly illustrated when an individual felt that they were involved in the change programme rather than the feeling that change was happening to them they became more aligned with the goals of the organization, thus allowing the change to be more effective.

In the strategic change programme the HR Manager was intrinsically involved in the offset of this strategic programme. She worked side by side with the CEO and Senior Management team advising on the communication rollout of the change and language to be used in order to relate to those affected the most by the change, that is, employees. She became a coach for the middle manager and an advisor for the employees. In this role the HR function moved away from a task-orientated administrative role to a more strategic business partner position. It was important that during this time the HR manager was able to converse to senior management in their language—business language—and relate everything back to how this change programme would ultimately add value to their business.

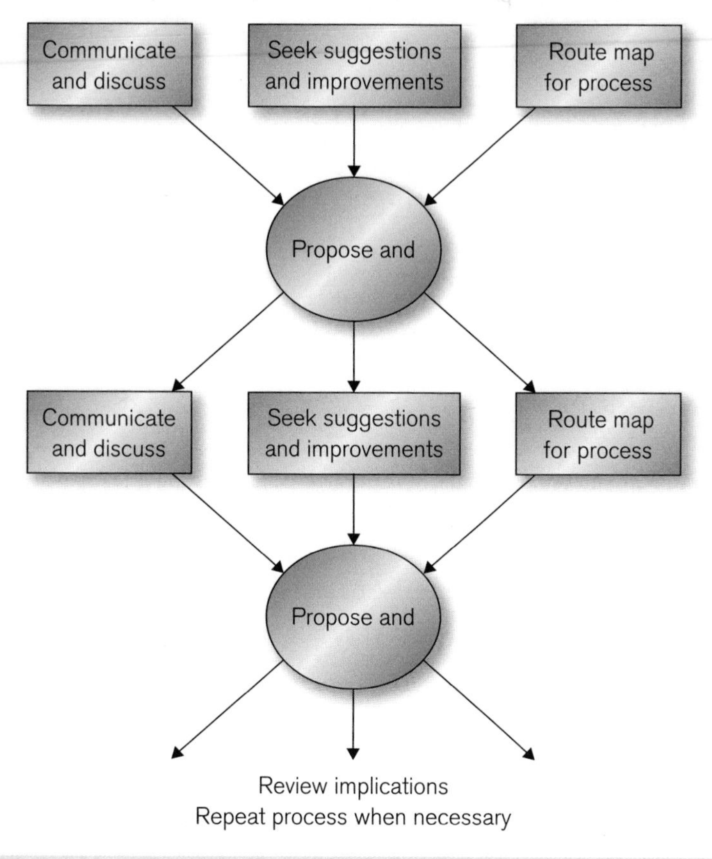


Figure 3.3 The methodology of introduction of change (we will constantly repeat the following sequence until we are satisfied that all issues are addressed)

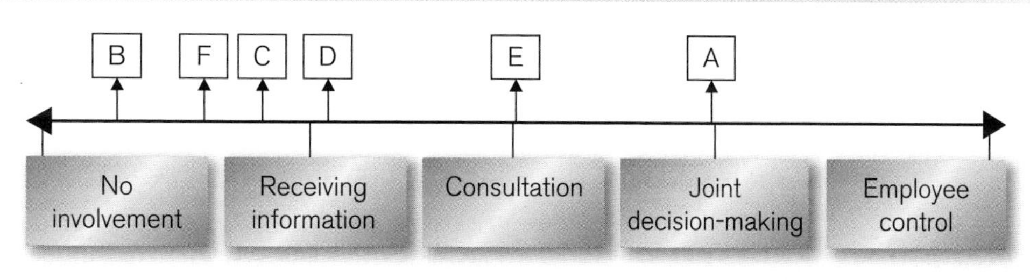


Figure 3.4 Continuum of Employee Involvement (Initial Stage of Change Program)

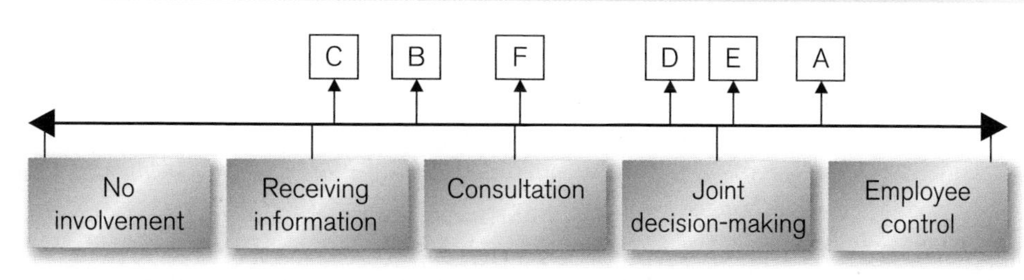


Figure 3.5 Continuum of Employee Involvement (Post Implementation of Change Program)

**Questions**

- Which of the five definitions of strategy can be seen to be in operation within the company?
- What were considered to be the key pivot points?
- What were the drivers for strategic change?
- Given that relying on training as a way of implementing strategic change so often fails, what was it about the way training was used in the company that achieved the desired changes?
- How could the company have dealt with managers and employees who resisted the changes being made?

## FURTHER READING

Eigenhuis, A. and Van Djik, R. (2007) *HR Strategy for the High Performing Business: Inspiring Success Through Effective Human Resource Management*, Kogan Page.

Kearns, P. (2010) *HR Strategy: Creating Business Strategy with Human Capital*, 2nd Ed., Butterworth-Heinemann.

Tovstiga, G. (2010) *Strategy in Practice: A Practitioner's Guide to Strategic Thinking*, John Wiley & Sons.

Wootton, S. and Horn, T. (2010) *Strategic Thinking: A Nine Step Approach to Strategy and Leadership for Managers and Marketers*, Kogan Page.

## REFERENCES


Analoui, F. (2007) *Strategic Human Resource Management*, Thomson Learning.

Barney, J.B. (1991) 'Firm resources and sustainable competitive advantage,' *Journal of Management*, **17**:1, pp. 153–182.

Bassi, L. and McMurrer, D. (2004) 'What to do when people are your most important asset', www.mcbassi.com/resources/documents/WhenPeopleAreYourMostImportantAsset.pdf.

Birdi, K. et al. (2008) 'The impact of human resource and operational management practices on company productivity: A longitudinal study'. *Personnel Psychology*, Autumn, **61**:3.

Boudreau, J.W. and Ramstad, P.M. (2007) *Beyond HR. The new Science of Human Capital*, Harvard Business School Press.

Buckingham, M. and Coffman, C. (1999) *First, Break All the Rules*, Simon and Schuster.

CIPD (2010a) 'Employer brand', www.cipd.co.uk/hr-resources/factsheets/employer-brand.aspx.

CIPD (2010b) 'Employer branding and total reward', www.cipd.co.uk/hr-resources/research/employer-branding-total-reward.aspx.

Coens, T. and Jenkins, M. (2000) *Abolishing Performance Appraisals*, Berrett-Koelher.

Gratton, L. (1999) *Strategic Human Resource Management*, Oxford University Press.

Hammonds, K.H. (2005) 'Why we hate HR', *Fast Company*, August, Issue 98, p. 40.

Haffenden, M. 'Strategic visions', *Personnel Today*, October 2002.

Hamel, G. (2009) 'Building leadership capability for change: An interview with Gary Hamel', podcast 32, July, www.cipd.co.uk/podcasts/_articles/garyhamel.htm

Hamel, G. and Prahalad, C.K. (1990) 'The Core Competence of the Corporation', *Harvard Business Review*, **68**:3, May–June, pp. 79–91.

Hamel, G. and Prahalad, C.K. (1993) 'Strategy as Stretch and Leverage', *Harvard Business Review*, **71**:2, March–April, pp. 75–84.

Hamel, G. and Prahalad, C.K. (1994) 'Competing for the Future', *Harvard Business Review*, **72**:4, July–August, pp. 122–129.

Harvey, J.B. (1996) *The Abilene Paradox and Other Meditations on Management*, Josey-Bass.

Hasan, Helen M. and Crawford, K. (2007) 'Knowledge Mobilisation in Communities through Socio-Technical System', http://ro.uow.edu.au/commpapers/558

HubCap (2010) *The Human Capital Handbook 2010*, http://alpha.hubcapdigital.com.

Hurley, J. (2010) 'Offshoring a false economy, says Gripple', *Daily Telegraph*, 15 October, www.telegraph.co.uk/finance/businessclub/8066470/Offshoring-a-false-economy-says-Gripple.html

Huselid (1994) 'Documenting HR's effect on company performance', *HR Magazine*, **39**:1, January.

Johnson, G., Scholes, K. and Whittington, P. (2008) *Exploring Corporate Strategy*, Pearson Education.

Kamoche, K. (1996) 'Strategic human resource management within a resource capability', *Journal of Management Studies*, **33**:2, pp. 213–33.

Kearns, P. (2004) 'How strategic are you? The six killer questions', *Strategic HR Review*, Vol. 3, March/April.

Keegan, A. and Francis, H. (2010) 'Practitioner talk: The changing textscape of HRM and emergence of HR business partnership,' *The International Journal of Human Resource Management*, **21**:6, pp. 873-898.

Khilji, S.E. and Wang, X. (2006) 'Intended and implemented HRM: The missing linchpin in strategic international human resource management research', *International Journal of Human Resource Management*, **17**:7, pp. 1171–1189.

Lawler (2007) 'Why HR practices are not evidence-based', *Academy of Management Journal*, **50**:5, pp. 1033–1036.

Legge, K. (1978) *Power, Innovation and Problem-Solving in Personnel Management*, Macmillan Business.

Legge, K. (2004) *Human Resource Management: Rhetorics and Realities*, Palgrave Macmillan.

Lester, D.L., Parnell, J.A. and Carragher, S. (2003) 'Organisational life cycle: A five stage empirical scale', *International Journal of Organizational Analysis*, **11**.

Mabey, C. et al. (1998) *Human Resource Management*. Sage Publications.

Macduffie, J. (1995) 'Human resource bundles and manufacturing performance: Organizational logic and flexible production systems in the world auto industry', *Industrial and Labour Relations Review*, **48**:2, pp. 197–221.

Martin, G. and Hetrick, S. (2006) *Corporate Reputations, Branding and People Management: A Strategic Approach to HR*, Butterworth Heinemann.

Milkovich, G.T. and Newman, J.M. (2002) *Compensation*, 8th ed., McGraw-Hill/Irwin.

Minzberg, H. (1987) 'The Strategy concept: Five Ps for strategy.' *Californian Management Review*, Fall.

Mooney, P. (2001) *Turbo-Charging the HR Function*, CIPD.

Morris, D. and Mahoney, M. (2005) 'Strategic reward systems: understanding the difference between "Best Fit" and "Best Practice"', Third Performance and Reward Conference, 7 April 2005, www.business.mmu.ac.uk/newsandevents/parc/morrismaloney.pdf. MMU.

Pfeffer, J. (1994) *Competitive Advantage Through People*, Harvard Business School Press.

Pfeffer, J. (2005) 'Changing mental models: HR's most important task', *Human Resource Management*, Summer, **44**:2, pp. 123–128.

O'Reilly, C.A. and Pfeffer, J. (2000) *Hidden Value*, Harvard Business School Press.

Pilbeam, S. and Corbridge, M. (2002) *People Resourcing*, 2nd Ed., *Financial Times* / Prentice Hall.

Porter, M.E. (1996) 'What is strategy?', *Harvard Business Review, November.*

Purcell, J. (2003) *Understanding the People and Performance Link: Unlocking the Black Box*, CIPD.

Purcell, J. (1999) 'Best practice and best fit: chimera or cul-de-sac?', *Human Resource Management Journal*, **9**:3, pp. 26–41.

Risling, C. (2010) '7 human resource strategies to use in a recession', http://ezinearticles.com/?7-Human-Resource-Strategies-to-Use-in-a-Recession&id=2216451.

Rummler, G.A. and Brache, A.P (1995) *Improving Performance*, Jossey-Bass.

Salaman, J.G., Storey, J. and Billsberry, J. (2005) *Strategic Human Resource Management: Theory and Practice*, Sage Publications.

Saunders, M., Mann, R. and Smith, R. (2008) 'Implementing strategic initiatives: A framework of leading practices', *International Journal of Operations & Production Management*, **28**:11, pp. 1095–1123.

Skinner, W. (1981) 'Big hat no cattle', *Harvard Business Review*, **59**:5, October/September, pp. 106–114.

Sullivan, J. (2005) *Rethinking Strategic HR*, Walters Kluwer.

Teo, S.T.T. and Rodwell, J.J. (2007) 'To be strategic in the new public sector, HR must remember its operational activities', *Human Resource Management*, Summer, **46**:2, pp. 265–284.

Ulrich, D. and Brocklebank, W. (2005) 'Role call', *People Management*, 16 June.

Wenger, E. (2007) 'Communities of practice. A brief introduction', *Communities of Practice*, www.ewenger.com/theory.

# Operational Challenges

# Recruitment and Selection

4

## Key Terms

**Hiring or employing** The overall process of taking on new staff from outside the organization.

**External recruitment** The process of identifying and attracting potential employees to an organization to fill current or future vacancies.

**Internal recruitment** The process of identifying current employees who may be suitable for newly created vacancies or for replacing staff who leave.

**Assessment** The tools and techniques used by an organization to identify and measure, either qualitatively or quantitatively, the skills, knowledge, and potential of applicants.

**Selection** The process, culminating in the decision to fill a vacancy from internal or external applicants, used by the organization to choose the most suitable candidate from a pool of applicants.

**Competency profiles/frameworks** These are statements of what people need to be able to do in order to perform their job to the required standard.

**Best practice** This term implies that in carrying out HR activities there is 'one best way' of doing things, irrespective of the context or circumstances.

**Best fit** This approach decides what should be done and how it should be done based on the unique circumstances that characterize every organization. It links action to specific requirements rather than following an established approach.

**Opportunity cost** This is the cost associated with not choosing to pursue one course of action in favour of another. This is a difficult calculation but is nevertheless an important consideration when deciding which course of action to take.

**Productive capacity/potential** Productive capacity expresses what employees can currently do and thus conveys their current value to the organization. Productive potential on the other hand represents employees' future value and contribution based on future learning and development.

## Learning Objectives

As a result of reading this chapter and using the Online Resource Centre, you should be able to:

- understand the importance of attracting high-performing employees to an organization;
- define and manage the processes involved in recruitment and selection;
- identify and develop different recruitment strategies for an organization;
- understand the professional and ethical standards that are appropriate in recruitment and selection;
- understand the relationship between recruitment and selection and other HR activities.

# Introduction

Figure 4.1 illustrates the relationship between the two connected fields of 'recruitment' and 'selection'. A more detailed 'map', which connects these two central activities to a more strategic understanding of what is involved in the acquisition of human resources, is provided later in the chapter. For the moment, Figure 4.1 shows how the two activities are related and what the key issues are. The bubbles on the left show the types of consideration to be made at each stage and the boxes on the right list some of the typical

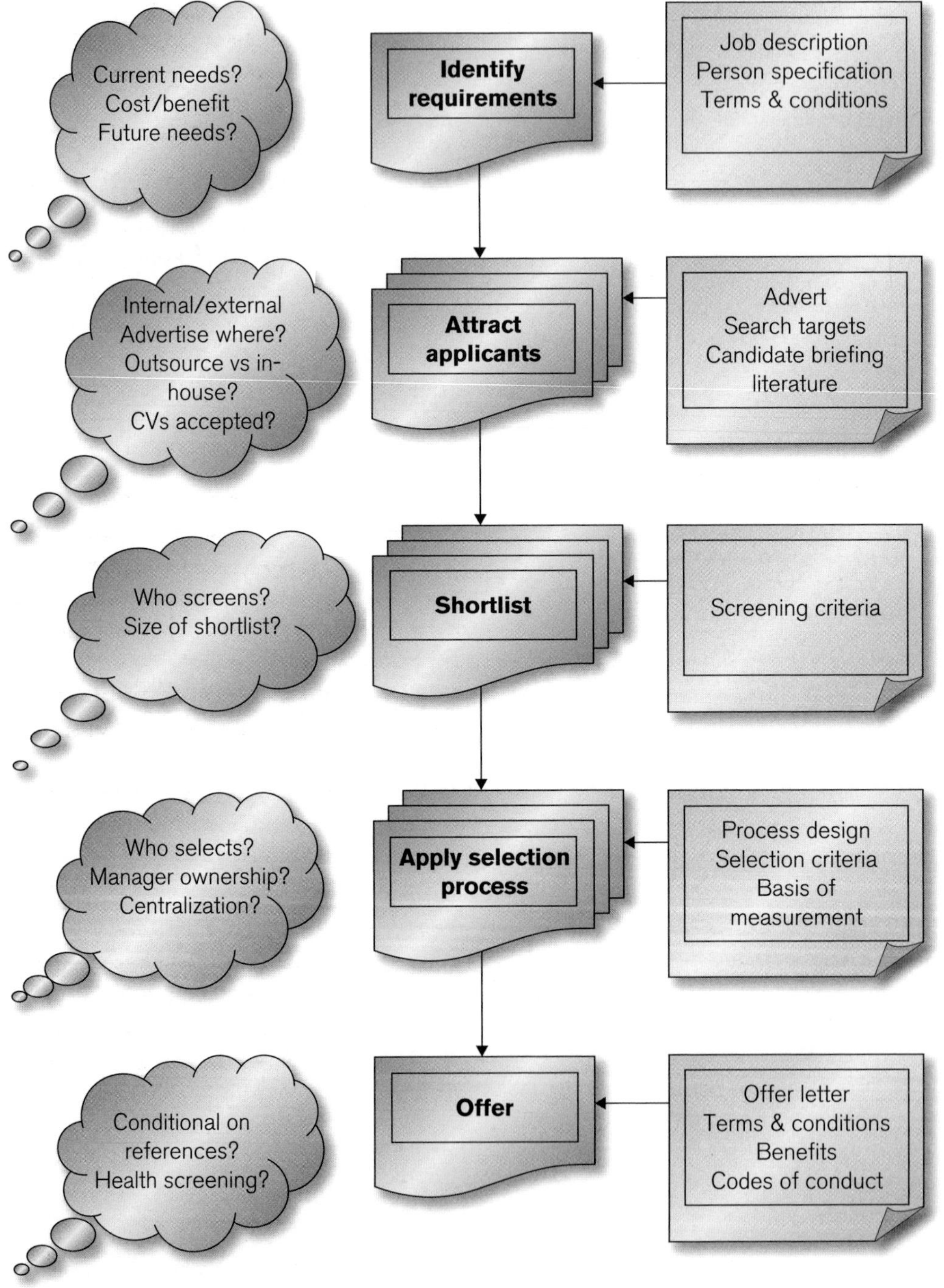


**Figure 4.1** The recruitment and selection process

documentation required at each stage of the process. As the chapter develops, a more detailed analysis of each of the three intermediate stages will be provided.



## Why is Recruitment and Selection So Important?

No matter how sophisticated the systems, processes, and technology of an organization, it is the capabilities and commitment of its employees that ensure its success. Without the optimum combination of people at different levels, with appropriate capabilities, knowledge, and motivation, individual and organizational performance will suffer. It is therefore essential to the success of the organization to ensure that recruitment and selection is effective, and delivers the highest calibre of employees at optimum cost. As many writers have maintained (e.g. Gratton, 2000; Michaels et al., 2001), by the beginning of the twenty-first century, an increasing number of managers had become aware that the only unique and sustainable source of competitive advantage came from the inspiration, knowledge, and effort of employees; that is, of the organization's 'human capital'. Human capital is a valuable asset for organizations, which resides within the people that comprise the workforce and can easily be lost through people voluntarily leaving the organization or as a result of organizational restructuring. Maintaining and strengthening the human capital base is one of the main strategic challenges facing the human resource professional, and recruitment and selection is key to achieving this goal.

It would be a mistake, however, to see these activities in isolation. Carrying out the various activities that result in the hiring of new employees is a necessary, but not sufficient, requirement. An organization's human capital base is enriched not only by the employment of new recruits from outside, but by the retention and development of the majority of its employees. Nevertheless, there is a strong case to be made for recognizing that recruiting and selecting the 'right' employees is absolutely critical to an organization's ability to grow and prosper. This view is reflected in the work of such writers as Jack Welch, a previous head of General Electric (GE), who argues that:



> **Nothing matters more in winning than getting the right people on the field.**
> (Welch and Welch, 2005)

But attracting and selecting the 'best' candidates is neither an easy task, nor is it risk free. Burrows (2004) justifiably argues that the challenges of introducing and integrating new recruits from outside a company cannot be underestimated or treated lightly. He also believes, however, that as long as the proper tools are used in the assessment process, applicants' ambitions and personal motivations are understood, and coaching is used to ensure the rapid integration of new recruits, the chances of meeting these challenges will be much greater than if these requirements were ignored or misunderstood. Notwithstanding this, mistakes can be made and the 'wrong' people hired, with unfortunate implications for the organization and for the employee.

Signpost to Chapters 11 and 12: Learning and Development and Managing Performance, for implications of underperforming staff

Collins (2001) offers an opinion on the importance of being as sure as one can about a person's suitability before making the job offer:

> **When in doubt, don't hire, keep looking . . . A company should limit its growth based on its ability to attract enough of the right people.**
> (Collins, 2001)

Pressures to fill positions quickly can often result in the wrong decisions being made—decisions that are not always easily rectified. HRM Insight 4.1 illustrates very clearly why it is preferable not to hire until a thorough assessment of each candidate's suitability has been completed.

If recruitment and selection is not risk free and may result in mistakes being made, can the assessment and selection of applicants be carried out in such a way that the 'best', or the 'right', person will always be identified, and the 'wrong' people kept out of the organization? The answer to this is, unfortunately, that 'no', it cannot be guaranteed. Recruitment and selection is not an exact science and, no matter how thorough and objective the processes undertaken are, there is always a possibility that the chosen candidate will not perform to the expected standard. Extraneous pressures can interfere with the decision-making process, and subjectivity and bias can undermine procedural rigour. It is important to recognize, however, that much better decisions and fewer mistakes can be made if a thorough process is followed, involving the gathering of as much relevant and objective information as possible, and using the expertise and judgement of different stakeholders. Consider the following HRM Insight, in which an important and costly mistake was avoided only by the timely intervention of an HR professional.

**HRM INSIGHT 4.1 The legal practice that nearly got it wrong**

Celia Johnson had been employed by Richard Curtis, senior partner in the law firm Curtis, Bowers and Smith, to bring some structure and order to the firm's HR provision. Up to her appointment, the HR function had effectively been limited to a part-time administrator and Curtis, who looked after all recruitment and reward matters. In an increasingly competitive recruitment environment, the firm had been struggling to attract and retain experienced lawyers, some of whom, in addition to their fee-earning roles, also had to manage different departments within the firm. Richard, aware of the need to strengthen his managerial team, was always on the lookout for new staff.

The firm had no recruitment strategy as such: recruitment was very ad hoc and relied on word of mouth, external networks, and on following-up enquiries and the CVs submitted by lawyers seeking to develop their careers. The firm didn't advertise positions and had no formal selection procedures, relying instead on informal mechanisms to hire new recruits.

This was of concern to Celia, who felt that even one bad appointment might have serious implications for the harmonious working relationships that characterized the firm. She wanted to replace the existing approach to hiring new staff with one that offered more rigour, checks, and a shared responsibility for the assessment and selection of candidates.

One Monday morning, not long after she arrived in the office, Richard called her to say that he had received a CV from someone who looked really promising and who would be worth having. As well as having a good track record as a fee-earner in a similar-sized law firm, Richard thought he might be useful in acting as temporary head of section for one of the partners who was about to go on maternity leave. Richard told Celia that he would give this person a call and ask him to come in to talk about the possibility of a job. Unfortunately, Celia could not be present at this meeting and was concerned when, after the two had met, Richard began to enthuse about the person's background and experience, concluding:

> He looks perfect. I'm sure he'll fit in and do a good job for us.

Unknown to Celia, it appeared that the first informal discussion had turned into a formal interview and that Richard was about to make an offer of employment. To pre-empt this, she suggested to Richard that this first meeting should be seen very much as the informal and preliminary stage of a more thorough selection process, and that the next stage should be a formal interview, preceded by a presentation on the applicant's strategy for enhancing the firm's fee-earning capability. Richard reluctantly accepted her advice and the necessary arrangements were made to invite the applicant back the next week. This gave Celia time to talk to the other partners and senior managers about the applicant's CV and whether they had an opinion on his suitability. She also arranged for one of the other partners to join her and Richard to hear the presentation and to interview the candidate.

The candidate's presentation turned out to be superficial and limited. Moreover, he failed to impress in the interview, coming over as one-dimensional and inflexible. This was despite the impressive list of achievements that he had claimed in his CV. In the discussion that followed the candidate's departure, Celia told the two partners that one of the firm's senior managers had spoken to her about the candidate and had said that 'he shouldn't be touched with a barge pole': it was alleged that, in one of his previous jobs, his behaviour had resulted in other staff leaving. Moreover, his claimed experience was, to say the least, clearly exaggerated.

A very different picture had now emerged from that which had originally been acquired by Richard Curtis and all three agreed that a letter would be sent informing the candidate that, in the light of all of the available evidence, it was not considered appropriate to offer him a position.

### Questions

1. What are the particular difficulties associated with recruiting knowledge workers?
2. What might the firm do to develop a more effective and reliable recruitment strategy?
3. What costs might the firm have incurred if the candidate had been offered a position?

## Why is it Important to Make the Right Recruitment and Selection Decisions?

Apart from the obvious importance of attracting talented people into the organization, why is the recruitment and selection process so important? It is important because:

- each employment decision can add to, or subtract from, the overall quality of the workforce;
- the ability of managers to continuously generate greater levels of added value from each employee is heavily influenced by what each new recruit brings into the organization and what each is capable of becoming;
- as a result of the increase in employment protection rights, it has become more difficult to correct mistakes in employment decisions once a person has been offered, and has accepted, a contract;
- employees who fail to meet the performance and behavioural expectations of managers can have a detrimental impact on the performance of others;
- the process of correcting a hiring mistake can be difficult, prolonged, and costly to all those involved;
- employing new and better qualified members of staff to replace those that are unwilling or unable to adapt to new requirements is often the only effective long-term strategy for improving the operational performance of functions and departments.

The aphorism 'if you can't change people, change the people' helps to explain the extent to which the introduction of new people with different attitudes, competency profiles, and, above all, a stronger work ethic can bring about transformation in performance capability throughout the organization. The Practitioner Insight looks at the importance of staff recruitment at Nottingham Trent University.

**PRACTITIONER INSIGHT Francesca Fowler, HR Director at Nottingham Trent University**

At Nottingham Trent University, recruitment is important to us for two reasons. It is not only an opportunity to bring new talent into the organization but we also challenge each vacancy that arises to be sure that we are recruiting for the right role. By following a thorough process we ensure we are legally compliant and give careful consideration on whether to replace like for like or redesign the role. We then make sure that we use a thorough selection process to bring the best people into the organization. The risks of getting it wrong are high and it would be difficult and costly to address problems should we make the wrong decision.

We tend to advertise most of our vacancies online as well as using either local or national media to ensure we have good accessibility for equal opportunities purposes. We sometimes use a recruitment agency, usually only for more senior posts that are more difficult to fill, as this is a very expensive option.

Line managers are trained to be able to chair our structured interview panels to ensure they ask the right questions and probe sufficiently to be able to identify the best candidates. We also use psychometric tests to support selection decisions for more critical posts.

We carry out surveys among our recent recruits to help us to evaluate our recruitment process as it is important to us that candidates feel they were given an open and honest understanding of the role and the organization and their feedback helps us to make improvements in our future recruitment.

Our own website is an important recruitment tool for us. All our vacancies are advertised on our website along with supporting documentation such as job descriptions and person specifications. We like to take applications through the website as it helps us to effectively track and monitor our recruitment process as well as easily gathering all the data we need about candidates.

In summary, the solution to many so-called 'people problems' is often associated with improving the effectiveness of the recruitment process, discriminating between potential stars and potential problem employees, and providing a workforce that delivers against current and future requirements (Ryan and Tippins, 2004). It is against this background that the role and contribution of the HR professional will be judged and evaluated. And if this is the challenge to be faced, there must be a debate about the way in which these objectives can be met, and about the specific practices and techniques that meet the criteria of 'best practice' or 'best fit', about which more will be said later in the chapter.

**RESEARCH INSIGHT 4.1**

To take your learning further you might want to read this article:

**Rioux, S.M. and Bernthal P. (1999), 'Recruitment and Selection Practices', *Development Dimensions International***

This article looks at the recruitment and selection strategies used by a number of organizations and shows that better strategies result in more positive organizational outcomes. The more effective these strategies are the more likely it is that the organization will recruit and retain satisfied employees. The article also highlights the importance of the internet for advertising vacancies and discusses what constitutes the most effective recruitment practices.

# Alternative Challenges and Perspectives

While an approach to recruitment and selection reflecting an overtly economic rationality, based on differences in individual productive capacity, is a persuasive one, it is not the only approach that the HR practitioner can adopt. For many organizations, the search for skilled and productive recruits takes on a more strategic and demographic perspective. For example, a report by the Women and Work Commission (2006) raised the issue of female under-representation in the science and engineering sectors, and the importance of developing strategic recruitment initiatives to overcome expected shortages in skilled engineers. The report also linked this under-representation to poor-quality career advice in schools, to continued male domination of the engineering profession, and to persistent pay differences between men and women. The objectives and challenges faced by those managing the recruitment process in this context are fundamentally different from those experienced when an employer is seeking to replace an employee who has left the organization or is advertising for a new position.

**For further insight into alternative challenges and the problem of skills shortage particularly in the public sector see the Online Resource Centre extension material 4.1.**

# The Impact of Economic Downturn

The impact upon recruitment of the recent economic downturn cannot be underestimated. From February 2008 to June 2008 the number of vacancies reported to the UK Office of National Statistics fell by almost 40 per cent and recovery was not seen until around October 2009. By February 2010 vacancies were still at only 70 per cent of March 2008 levels and at the same time UK unemployment rose from 1.6 million in February 2008 to 2.5 million in February 2010 with the biggest increase, excluding those over normal retirement age, among the 25 to 34 category (data available at www.statistics.gov.uk). There can be no doubt that the impact was very significant and the knock on effect upon the recruitment industry was devastating. Commenting about the Recruitment and Employment Confederations September 2009 report on jobs, Kevin Green, the REC's Chief Executive said:

> **The rapidly worsening economic outlook is now really starting to bite in the jobs market with temporary and permanent appointments dropping rapidly.**

During difficult times when organizations are facing tough decisions about whether to fill vacancies or not, recruiting the right person, where a genuine need exists, can be argued to be even more important. When jobs are at risk, whilst many more people may be available due to unemployment, it might be argued that the highest-calibre employees are those likely to still be in employment in many cases and they will be even more reluctant to risk moving to an unknown organization where they can perhaps be less confident about their future job security. So whilst it might seem that recruitment ought to be somehow easier in a downturn the challenges faced can be just as problematic.

# A Summary of Different Recruitment Situations

It should be clear by now that the recruitment and selection challenges facing management not only vary in their scale and complexity between organizations, but change over time and differ in terms of their rationale. Without necessarily being complete, the following list represents the situations most likely to be encountered by the HR professional.

- **Replacement recruitment**

  This might involve recruiting to replace any kind of employee, from the managing director of a plc to a manual worker in a factory.

- **Recruiting for a new position/job**

  The scale of this challenge may also be limited to one person, but because someone is needed to fill a new or revised position, the processes and implications are not identical to those of recruiting a replacement.

- **Recruiting for a new build**

  In this situation, the whole organizational unit is new—a new hotel or factory for example—and this creates differences in scale, complexity, and timescales.

- **Recruitment needs that reflect long-term distortions in the supply and demand for labour**

  These needs are often sector-specific or geographical in nature. Responses may involve developing new, and often overseas, labour markets and may feature an ethical, demographical, and political dimension.

- **Recruitment that is used as an instrument of social engineering**

  The challenge in this situation is less linked to labour shortages, than to desired or enforced change in the composition of the labour force and its political and social acceptability.

# An Economic Perspective on Recruitment and Selection

The ability to differentiate between applicants, in terms of their suitability and 'fit' with a person specification and the organization's culture, is at the core of what recruiting and selecting involves. But this still leaves unanswered the question: 'What difference does it make and can these differences be quantified?'

Cook (1988), in considering what the value of good employees actually means, offers an insight into the economic and financial dimension of employment decisions. His statement that 'The best is twice as good as the worst' and, by implication, the idea that the best adds at least double the economic value to the organization of a poor recruit has two important implications:



- Decisions about employing new staff can have either long-term financial costs or benefits for the organization. This means that the difference between the value of the contribution of the person employed, compared with that of one who was rejected, can be either positive or negative, depending on whether the 'right' employment decision was made. Of course, it is impossible to know precisely what the value of the contribution someone rejected might have been. It was explained earlier, however, that many organizations experience the negative outcomes of employing the wrong person, and have to bear the costs and losses of having to rectify decisions that, when taken, seemed rational and defensible. In economic terms, this is what is known as an 'opportunity cost' and, in extreme cases, such costs can be very high.
- It becomes even more important to understand both the 'real' costs of recruitment and selection, as opposed to those associated with direct expenditure, and the longer-term financial consequences that follow from the selection decisions.

According to Cook, failing to discriminate between the 'productive potential' of different potential employees can be detrimental, should the 'productive capacity' of employees differ greatly. He poses two questions to illustrate this:

- How much do workers vary in their productive capacity and value to the organization?
- How much are these differences actually worth?

As far as the first question is concerned, Cook believes that good workers do twice as much work as poor workers. In terms of the value of these differences, his opinion is that it roughly equates to the wage or salary that they are paid. In this context, the direct costs of recruitment and selection, the time of those involved and the value of production lost while positions remain unfilled must all be included in an overall cost-benefit calculation.

According to Edward P. Lazear (1998), however, the best and most productive employees are also likely to be the most expensive in terms of their recruitment and employment costs. This presents an interesting dilemma: is it better to employ the best people, irrespective of the costs involved, because their long-term value to the organization will be greater than the costs of recruiting and paying them, or is it better to employ the cheapest people and minimize recruitment and selection costs, irrespective of the quality of those employed? Decisions on whether a cost-reduction or productivity-maximization strategy is to be adopted can only be made within a specific context and if the implications of adopting one or the other have been fully explored. The reality for most organizations is that a position between the two extreme points on this continuum will be adopted, based on pragmatic considerations. Much will depend on contextual factors.

Fitz-Enz (2002) holds the view that:

> **The hiring decision is often made too lightly; few organizations have stopped to figure out how costly the decision to hire a new employee is . . . every time the recruitment system cycles, the company incurs a cost and runs the risk of making a poor hiring decision. Even if the new hire is good, there is a productivity loss as the person moves up the learning curve. Any way you look at it, hiring is expensive, and one cannot ignore the importance of the selection process.**

The implication arising from the contributions of Cook, Lazear, and Fitz-Enz are obvious. An economic approach to recruitment and selection must reflect the fact that decisions to appoint and reject an applicant will:

- affect the financial value of the contribution directly related to the newly employed worker over the duration of his or her employment;
- involve expenditure and costs.

Over the full period for which an employee remains with an organization, the costs associated with recruitment and selection become proportionately less as the net value of the employee's contribution increases, assuming that the most suitable person was employed. The reality is that few organizations have developed the kind of HR metrics that Lazear, in particular, has developed in the USA, which allow the value of contributions and costs to be calculated reliably.

## Calculating recruitment costs

Fitz-Enz (2002) offers the following formula for the calculation of what he calls 'cost per hire' (CPH):

$$CPH = \frac{AC + AF + RB + TC + RE + RC + NC + 10\%}{H}$$

Where:

AC = advertising costs;
AF = agency fees;
RB = referral bonus;
TC = travel costs;
RE = relocation costs;
RC = recruiter costs;
NC = the costs of processing unsolicited CVs;
H = the number of hires.

An alternative costing model, more appropriate to the UK, might be expressed as follows:

$$CPH = \frac{DA + GO + RE + C \text{ of } S + RC + EAF + TC + CLP + 10\%}{\text{Numbers involved}}$$

Where:

DA = direct administration costs—time plus rate of pay;
GO = a proportion of general overheads;
RE = recruitment expenses;

C of S = costs of selection—time of staff involved, selection materials;
RC = relocation costs;
EAF = external agency fees;
TC = training costs;
CLP = costs of lost production.

This is a potentially useful way of understanding and calculating hiring costs. But the other side of the equation involves estimating the net value of each hiring decision, recognizing that this can be negative as well as positive.

For guidance on how to avoid excessive recruitment administration see the Online Resource Centre extension material 4.2.

Signpost to Chapter 10: HR Planning and Measurement for a perspective on planning staffing requirements

**RESEARCH INSIGHT 4.2**

To take your learning further you might want to read this article:

**Barrick, M.R. and Zimmerman, R.D. (2009) 'Hiring for retention and performance', *Human Resource Management*, 48:2, March, pp. 183–206.**

This study looks at a number of variables with a view to predicting both the likelihood that recruited employees would perform well and be unlikely to resign from their jobs within the first one to two years of joining. A number of factors were identified that would predict performance and retention. Recruits who spent longer in previous roles, knew others in the organization, were conscientious and emotionally stable, were motivated to get the job, and who were confident in themselves and their decision-making were more likely to remain in their jobs and perform well in their roles.

**STUDENT ACTIVITY 4.1**

1. Test the validity and acceptability of the formula for calculating recruitment costs by asking organizations for information on how, if at all, they calculate overall hiring costs. Be prepared to amend the formula, in the light of what is found, to improve its usefulness.
2. Generate estimated or actual information on financial values for the above variables and calculate the CPH value for specific recruitment exercises.

As an example, one of the author's postgraduate students, completing a similar calculation but not necessarily using the same formula, came up with a figure of £6,000 as the cost of replacing a single administrative worker in a local authority. It doesn't take much imagination to realize that organizations which are growing organically, creating new productive units, or which have high turnover rates are likely to experience very substantial, and possibly recurring, hiring costs. Whereas recruiting in the context of the first two situations (replacement and new positions) can be considered to be necessary and an opportunity to invest in new and talented staff, recruitment that is linked to excessive rates of labour turnover is an unnecessary and unjustifiable cost.

The CIPD Recruitment, Retention and Turnover Survey 2009 provides more authoritative data on the economic costs of hiring. The survey found that the average cost of recruitment (i.e. of hiring someone) is estimated to be £4,000, rising to £6,125 when the full impact of turnover, training, and induction are taken into account. It also found that 47 per cent of organizations do not even measure the direct costs of recruitment. Whatever the methodology used, being able to put reasonably robust and consistently applied financial values on this important area of HR is becoming less an option, and more a requirement, if the 'true' economic costs of finding new and replacement labour are to be recognized fully.

## Labour markets

Labour markets can be virtual or physical, and they are important because they represent the source of an organization's supply of labour. External labour markets can be thought of as geographical areas within which potential employees are economically active. This means that these people are either in employment or unemployed and seeking work. The markets can be local, regional, national, or international in size, depending on the degree of scarcity and specialization of the skills and experience required, but many, particularly for professional, technical, and managerial work, are more virtual than real, with both applicants and employers using web-based recruitment practices. Historically, the physical limits of external labour markets were determined by travel-to-work times but, because work can now, for many, be from home and because many professionals are prepared to commute long distances, such physical limitations are less important than they used to be. Depending on the type of work and the degree of flexibility that an organization allows, potential employees can be found almost anywhere. Having said this, for many manufacturing businesses and 'lower level' service industries, the local or regional labour market represents the only realistic source of new and replacement labour.

However attractive, in terms of cost and time, an organization's internal labour market might be, there are dangers in over-relying on this source of recruitment. The main one can be expressed in terms of stagnation.

**KEY CONCEPT Stagnation**

**This term relates to the detrimental effect on creativity, change, and originality that is associated with relying largely, or entirely, on the existing workforce to fill job vacancies. The lack of 'new blood' from outside, which can bring new ideas, challenge, and vitality into an organization, can contribute to the long-term decline of an organization that is too inward-looking in its search for new talent.**

This importance of integrating recruitment and selection into a wider HR and business agenda has been supported by research conducted by Reed Executive, one of the country's leading recruitment firms (Carrington, 2004). The survey found that more than one in three of the organizations that responded admitted that their recruitment strategy was not aligned to business goals and nearly one in three said that recruitment had failed because it was not aligned to the internal motivation and retention of staff. Only 17 per cent said that recruitment strategies failed because of external skills shortages.

For a more detailed comparison of the pros and cons of using internal and external labour markets visit the Online Resource Centre extension material 4.3.

# The Role of Fairness in Recruitment

It is important that the recruitment and selection processes adopted by an organization are fair. This means that processes need to be as objective as possible and that only information relevant to the situation should be required. Decisions at all stages should be based solely on the merits of applicants and their suitability for the position in question. Employers have a legal responsibility to ensure that processes do not allow either direct or indirect discrimination to occur on the grounds of race, religion or belief, sex, sexual orientation, disability, and age.

The law allows for some exceptions to the above, known as 'genuine occupational qualifications', such as recruiting a male attendant for the male changing facilities at a swimming pool. Discrimination on the grounds of disability can, in some circumstances, be shown to be justifiable, but organizations are obliged to consider making reasonable adjustments in the work that needs to be done before excluding any such applicant for a job. A wheelchair user, for example, may have difficulties operating checkout facilities. It may be justifiable not to employ this person, but only if it can be shown that consideration was given to ways of altering the environment to allow the work to be done by a wheelchair user. A larger organization would be under a greater obligation to make this type of adjustment than would a small local shop, due to the relative affordability of such changes.

In practice ensuring a fair and lawful process is open to a wide degree of interpretation. This responsibility is perhaps set out in policy and more rigorously controlled in the public sector than elsewhere. For example a selection interview in the public sector is more likely to involve candidates being asked a series of identical questions to avoid the risk that any difference in treatment might be construed as discriminatory and all candidates who pass a benchmark in the initial screening of applications will be interviewed, whereas the private sector will more often simply interview those candidates who appear strongest on paper without scoring each applicant during screening and are more likely to follow a more flexible discussion and probing style at interview. Neither process is necessarily discriminatory and it might be argued that the private sector approach allows more flexibility to probe any areas of concern; however, there is a greater risk that a potential claim of discrimination will be more difficult to defend with the more flexible approach. The size of the HR function in the public sector is likely to be larger to administrate the increased bureaucracy that the greater control generates and the private sector might argue that the risk of a claim, potential consequences, and lack of flexibility this delivers do not make commercial sense in a competitive market. The role of diversity and equal opportunities are also considered in Chapter 7.

Signpost to Chapter 7: Equality in Employment, for more information on discrimination

# Identifying Recruitment Requirements

In most organizations, the costs associated with employing the required number of people represent a significant proportion of the organizational budget. Having too many people in a particular section will quickly impact upon either the profitability of the organization or its ability to deliver requirements within the specified budget. When a vacancy arises, it is therefore important to consider whether the need for the tasks carried out has changed, whether or not a different skill set may be required, whether or not tasks might be redistributed among others in the organization and whether forthcoming changes may impact upon requirements.

Signpost to Chapter 10: HR Planning and Measurement, for information on staffing requirements

As well as HR and the line manager, the person leaving the job and their colleagues may have a valuable contribution to make in reaching the decision about recruitment requirements. Contributions from these groups may be a useful consideration when deciding to update or amend the job description and person specification for the role.

**STUDENT ACTIVITY 4.2**

1. **In what way does the role of the line manager and HR specialist differ in recruitment decisions. What are the pros and cons of placing full responsibility for the recruitment of a direct report to the line manager?**
2. **Consider the role of the second level manager in a recruitment decision. What role does the line manager's manager play compared to the HR specialist and direct line manager in making a decision about whether to replace a role when someone leaves and what should his or her role be in the recruitment and selection process?**

## Defining recruitment requirements

There are often two important documents that are used to define recruitment requirements. The *job description*, sometimes referred to as the 'job specification', gives details of the purpose or the job, and of the tasks and responsibilities or areas of accountability that are assigned to the jobholder. The *person specification* details the skills, knowledge, and attitudes that should ideally be possessed by the jobholder to ensure he or she can meet objectives, while feeling that the job holds sufficient challenge and opportunity for growth.

## Job description

A job description, or job specification, is the document used to record what it is that an employee should be doing. At more junior levels, it is likely to be primarily concerned with the tasks that the post-holder is required to carry out on a day-to-day basis. At more senior levels, however, it becomes harder to define the exact details of actions required and job descriptions at this level are more likely to be primarily concerned with the overall responsibilities or areas for which the employee is accountable. Job descriptions are considered to be useful when jobs are relatively routine, if the work people do and the contributions they make are clearly defined and uncomplicated, and if organizational change is not a major factor. If these criteria are not met, however, then the value of the job description is more uncertain.

One of the questionable practices found in certain public sector organizations, in which there are many similar kinds of job, is the use of *generic* job descriptions. This has the advantage of simplifying the process of producing and amending job descriptions, but its disadvantage is that the distinctiveness and unique characteristics of each job are ignored. Does this practice also mean that generic job descriptions result in generic person specifications? If so, this has significant and worrying implications for the selection process, because effective teams need a balance of people with differing, but complementary, skills.

This is about achieving results, meeting targets, and overcoming problems.

## The person–organization fit

The idea that the assessment and selection process allows managers to identify someone from among those remaining 'in the pool' who is the 'best qualified for the job' informs the thinking of many HR professionals. 'Best' is, however, a relative term, and while the objective might be to eliminate weaker candidates and be left with the 'best', being the 'best' may not, in fact, mean that this person has the necessary personal and technical competences to perform the job to the required standards. An alternative approach to selection, often described as 'criterion-referenced selection', is based on the principle that the 'best' of applicants may not possess the required competences for the job. If this approach is taken, it is much more likely that a decision to appoint will not be made because none of the applicants meets the required standards. Such an approach is often associated with the re-advertisement of positions, after none of the original applicants have been considered suitable.

Both approaches fundamentally involve 'fitting' the person to the job and, in each, either the 'best fit' or the 'right fit' is chosen at the end of the process. This notion of fit can be seen as both attractive and yet, at the same time, worrying. It is attractive because it implies that, with sufficient preparation and care, it is possible to match the person to the job with the minimum of disruption and friction to the social fabric of the organization. It is worrying, however, because it implies that, as with physical objects such as machines, human beings can be treated as the equivalent of machine parts and somehow 'fitted' into the organization (i.e. the 'machine'). The belief that organizations can be understood as machines and managed as such is associated with the widespread use of the organization-as-machine metaphor, within which order, predictability, and control mechanisms are believed to result in efficient and non-problematical employee performance (Morgan, 1997). But the complex, and often unpredictable, nature of human behaviour and the high level of subjectivity that still surrounds the recruitment and selection process, despite its procedural regulation, means that seeing candidates as the equivalent of pieces in a jigsaw puzzle is both simplistic and unhelpful.

Part of the problem is not simply associated with the dangers of seeing organizations as machines, but with limiting the notion of 'fit' exclusively to the job. Fitting people into the organization, in terms of its culture and values, as well as into a job makes this task even more challenging. The identification of personal characteristics associated with being an effective part of a dynamic and challenging working environment is, arguably, of equal importance to the assessment of applicants against a more specific set of job competences. The emphasis on certain personal traits and strengths, described above by Welch and Welch (2005), suggests that, in some organizations, more importance is given to the ability of applicants to fit into the organizational culture and value system than is given to their fitting the requirements of a specific job. It has also been found that selecting someone who 'fits' both job and organization is even more problematical when the approach to hiring is opportunistic rather than planned (Levesque, 2005). An alternative approach is to look at fitting the 'job' to the person to maximize the potential performance.

For a more detailed discussion on this concept see the Online Resource Centre extension material 4.4.

## Person specification

In many cases of recruitment and selection, the person specification takes the form of a document that records the qualities of the ideal candidate for the job. The qualities are often prioritized in terms of importance, as shown in Table 4.1. Typically the person specification will describe the skills, knowledge, and attitudes required to carry out the job, the level and amount of experience necessary, the level of education and training required, and the personal qualities and competence of the ideal candidate. These are often prioritized in terms of essential and desirable characteristics. Care should be taken to ensure that criteria actually reflect requirements. For example if ten years experience is not necessary and three or four will suffice, requiring ten years could result in a claim of unfair age discrimination as this would automatically rule out younger candidates. More importantly, the best candidate may be excluded from the process for no good reason.

Once a person specification has been agreed upon, this then becomes the basis of the assessment process, where evidence about applicants from different sources is assessed against the requirements and standards contained with the person specification.

Table 4.1 Person specification for a payroll administrator

| PERSON SPECIFICATION<br>Payroll administrator<br>Grade 4 | |
|---|---|
| **Essential** | **Desirable** |
| **Skills, knowledge, attitude** | |
| Numerate | Motivated by repeated routine tasks |
| Accurate | |
| Team worker | |
| Trustworthy | |
| Works well to a deadline | |
| **Experience** | |
| Must have a minimum of one year's experience in an office environment, working with computers, and entering/processing data | Experience in a payroll, accounts, or HR environment |
| **Education and training** | |
| A good standard of education, including GCSE or equivalent in Maths and English | Training or qualification on tax and pay systems |
| **Personal qualities** | |
| Polite | |
| Helpful | |
| Able to relate to people at all levels | |
| Articulate | |
| Patient | |

**STUDENT ACTIVITY 4.3 Producing a job description**

1. Consider a role with which you are familiar in an organization of your choice, and produce a job description and person specification for that role.
2. What additional information would you want to know about the job and the ideal person to help you in the process of sifting applications and the assessment of shortlisted applicants?

# Job competencies

Some organizations are moving away from the more traditional job description and person specification due to the limitations of this approach and job competencies are becoming more widely used. Job competencies or competency frameworks refer to the range of behaviours that an employee must be able to demonstrate or develop in order to achieve the levels of performance required to be successful in a role. They are perhaps therefore more useful in a selection setting as they can give a more observable and tangible basis for selection decisions than knowledge or experience alone. Just because a potential recruit has experience of the types of situation they are likely to encounter in a job does not mean that they performed well in these situations, whereas an analysis of whether they behaved in a manner consistent with that required in the vacant role can give a better basis for the selection decisions. Job competency should not be confused with competence which refers to the minimum standard of performance required within a role although the terms are often confused and used interchangeably in practice. For a detailed exploration of managerial competence see Boyatzis (1982).

## Attracting the Right Applicants

A recruitment and selection strategy that focuses on hiring well-qualified high performers, or at least those with the potential to be this type of person, is likely to be more demanding and challenging than one under which lower standards are applied, or under which selecting the 'best' from a set of applicants is seen as the objective of the exercise. Even when unemployment levels in the external labour markets are relatively high, better workers are less likely to be unemployed or will only temporarily be so. The challenge of attracting them becomes, therefore, much harder than when recruiting less qualified people. This is because high-potential and top-performing candidates who can deliver the best results are often:

- well recognized, valued, and nurtured by their current employers;
- unlikely to be looking for another job, because they will have high current levels of job satisfaction;
- attractive to many employers when they do look and will often get more than one offer when they start looking;
- given a counteroffer to stay with their current employer;
- hard to convince that it is worth their while to move to a new job in an unknown organization.

The process of attracting the right candidates is that activity within which the HR function needs to give serious consideration to marketing the organization to potential candidates. There are many channels that can be used to make potential candidates aware of current and future vacancies, and these vary in degrees of formality and expense. Figure 4.2 shows the types of option available and the main features associated with each method. It should be noted that, while informal methods of recruitment, such as word of mouth and the use of 'now recruiting' banners, can be very cost-effective, they may limit the pool of applicants. The Commission for Racial Equality and the Equal Opportunities Commission warn specifically against the dangers of indirect discrimination inherent to word-of-mouth recruitment should the workforce consist predominantly of one gender or racial group.

**KEY CONCEPT Employer of preferred choice**

**This is a status that certain employers seek to attain in relation to prospective applicants. It means that, through its successful marketing of the organization, the development of challenging and supportive working environments, and the opportunity to enjoy good reward packages, applicants are attracted to the prospect of being employed by the organization. As a consequence, there is a natural flow of predominantly high-calibre people towards these organizations, which has the effect of reducing the time and costs of recruitment.**

Research into the effectiveness of different recruitment strategies offers interesting insights into what appears to work and what doesn't (CIPD, 2009). However, perhaps the biggest change in recruitment in recent years has been the move to online recruitment. The Internet Advertising Bureau (2008, available at www.iabuk.net) identified that online recruitment advertising accounted for 32.9 per cent of total online advertising spend of £1.7 billion in the UK, in fact without the growth of online recruitment advertising the overall online advertising market would have seen a 4.6 per cent decline. The shift to online recruitment advertising has happened so rapidly that it is as yet difficult to quantify the extent of the move as research thus far does not reflect the extent of this change. Research in this area still has to catch up, in fact the CIPD (2009) survey does not even ask participants in their annual survey a specific question about the extent

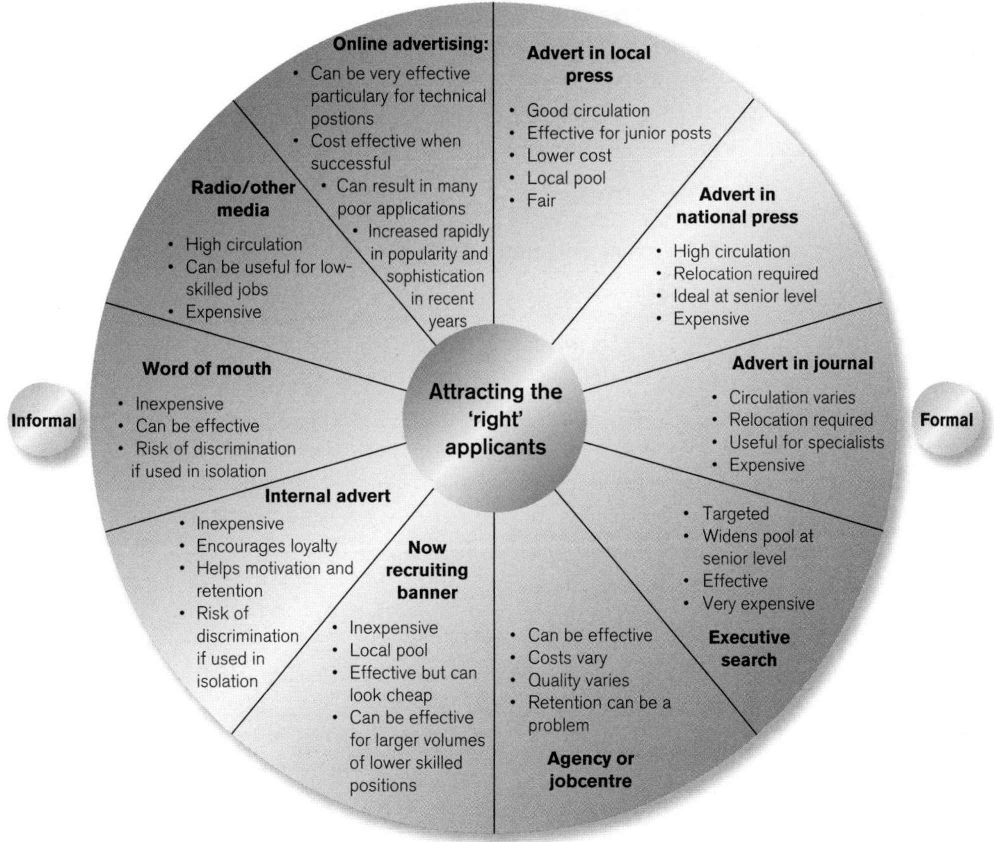


Figure 4.2 The recruitment 'wheel'—where and how to market vacancies



to which they use online advertising and only asks participants about the use of their own corporate websites for attracting applicants. However, it is the view of the authors that, once available, research will substantiate our view that the latter years of the last decade organizations have moved away from traditional methods of attracting applicants such as printed media advertising to online advertising and that whilst the use of recruitment agencies will still feature highly, the extent of use will have fallen as organizations become more selective. It is our belief that this change has been driven by both economic pressures on organizations and the increased capability and ease of use of recruitment websites along with an increase in the number of potential applicants who have access to the internet with the skills to be able to use this approach to look for work.

**STUDENT ACTIVITY 4.4 Approaches to attracting and selecting candidates**

1. Carry out your own research with local organizations and employers to establish how important online advertising has become in recent years.
2. What methods do the organizations you have contacted use to select the best candidates from their shortlist and to what extent do these methods influence the decision-making?

The important point to note about these different approaches and media for communicating with and attracting prospective employees is that, depending on the numbers of people being recruited, the level and type of worker, and the importance of time and costs, different organizations will develop and use a mix of techniques and methods that works for them. All have potential advantages and disadvantages, and it is unrealistic and misleading to think that there is any 'right' way in which to recruit. What *can* be said is that, through experience and the ability to relate outcomes to the methods used, HR professionals should be able constantly to reduce the costs involved and improve the quality of employees hired.

But recruiting new staff continues to pose problems and challenges, as the two following HRM Insights illustrate.

### HRM INSIGHT 4.2 Recruitment practices at Thompson

CW Thompson is a privately owned business with over 2,000 employees. The vast majority of its recruitment is via referrals from existing staff and customers. Many new recruits are, in fact, the friends and relatives of existing staff, and the manager believes that this is one of the reasons why there is a strong sense of loyalty and team working. Thompson is based in an area with a high ethnic minority population, but the manager has only employed three people in the last four years from an ethnic minority—and two of these have left.

A local resident submits a complaint to the Commission for Racial Equality, which investigates and on the basis of the evidence that is available decides to prosecute the company. The business' defence is that it cannot afford to advertise all vacancies in the newspaper and that changing recruitment practices would displease the existing staff.

#### Questions

1. What low-cost options might the manager have used to advertise more fairly?
2. How might the manager ensure that members of staff are not displeased by changes to recruitment practices?
3. Given that the business employs over 2,000 employees, to what extent do you feel that the cost of advertising should be taken into consideration?
4. What might explain the decision of the three people to leave?

### HRM INSIGHT 4.3 The case of LLT Solutions

LLT Solutions had a vacancy for a computer network administrator manager at one of its most prominent call centres, managing calls for global retail customers. The call centre was also a 'European hub', responsible for transferring queries to other European call centres. As this was a key role, the position was advertised nationally in the most widely recognized journal for network personnel and a thorough selection procedure was followed to select the preferred candidate.

The successful candidate accepted the offer and submitted one month's notice to his employer. That employer made the candidate a generous counteroffer, increasing his salary by 20 per cent, to beat the offer made, and promising to make a number of changes to the role to address previously unresolved concerns about issues such as effective communication and involvement in corporate decision-making and projects. The candidate consequently withdrew his acceptance of the newly offered post three days before he was due to join.

Because no other suitable internal candidate was available, the position was re-advertised the following month with a suitable closing date. The originally successful candidate applied again for the post, sending in an accompanying letter that explained that the promises made by his present employer had not been fulfilled and that he continued to be interested in joining the new business.

#### Questions

1. What are the pros and cons of making a 'counteroffer' if an employee resigns after an offer of employment is made by another organization?
2. In this example, what are the pros and cons to the recruiting organization of considering the same applicant a second time around?
3. What options does the recruiting company have in handling this application?
4. What would you do and why?

# Employer Branding

For many years organizations have invested in marketing their products and services to their customers, consumers, service users, and clients to help maintain loyalty to their brand, corporate image, or identity or to promote the services that they provide. Employer branding involves using a similar approach to human resources issues and is used to describe how an organization promotes what it has to offer to current and potential employees. This is an area of growing importance. Employer branding is therefore central to employee engagement and attracting a wide pool of talented applicants for any potential vacancy that arises.

The CIPD (2007) defines employer branding as:

> **a set of attributes and qualities—often intangible—that makes an organisation distinctive, promises a particular kind of employment experience, and appeals to those people who will thrive and perform to their best in its culture.**

**RESEARCH INSIGHT 4.3**

To take your learning further you might want to read this article:

**Davies G. (1999) 'Employer branding and its influence on managers', *European Journal of Marketing*, 42:5/6, pp. 667–681.**

This article looks at employer branding and what influences perceived differentiation, affinity, satisfaction, and loyalty, which are four outcomes relevant to employer brand. The study helps to clarify what employees regard as being important in these areas and shows that differentiation and loyalty are characterized by a combination of enterprise and stylishness, that affinity is characterized by agreeableness but also ruthlessness and satisfaction by agreeableness (being supportive and trustworthy).



## Recruitment advertising

The mostly widely used method for attracting applicants is recruitment advertising and the biggest change in recent years has been the move to online recruitment. The use of newspapers and trade journals for advertising has declined in popularity and it has become rare to not use an internet based-solution to advertise a vacancy and there are many websites including generic advertisers such as Monster (www.monster.com) and Totaljobs (www.totaljobs.co.uk) as well as regional websites and specialist websites for particular professions that are now widely used to advertise vacancies. Virtually all the newspapers and journals that have relied upon the revenue generated by recruitment advertising have developed their own websites and this sector is still changing rapidly. Many websites have become much more sophisticated in recent years offering services to candidates such as job alerts, and careers advice and services to employers allowing better branding, CV search facilities, screening tools, and online application options in order to remain competitive. Online advertising tends to be cheaper than the traditional methods and the switch away from printed media to online advertising was perhaps accelerated through the recent economic downturn due to the costs pressures faced by organizations.

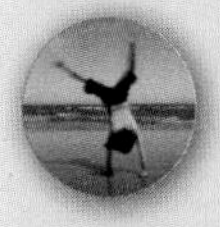

**STUDENT ACTIVITY 4.5 Looking at recruitment adverts**

Consider a selection of recruitment adverts from a variety of websites such as www.monster.co.uk, www.totaljobs.com, or www.fish4.co.uk for a job type of your choice such as an administrator, sales representative, or other role.

1. Identify the qualities that make some adverts stand out more than others.
2. Produce a checklist of items that must be covered in a recruitment advert, items that are often included but not essential, and the pros and cons of including these.
3. Add a set of guidelines to your checklist of areas to be checked to ensure that nothing which may discourage applications or that is potentially unlawful is included. You can draw from your own experience of applying for jobs and use the information in Chapter 7 on equality if you need guidance.
4. Rank the adverts according to the favourable impression they create and justify your decision.

## CV or application form?

A curriculum vitae (CV), or résumé is a document prepared by the candidate as part of his or her application, giving personal details, education and employment history, and other relevant information.

In any advert, details of how to apply should include whether to send a CV or to ask for a standard application form. It might be argued that an application form ensures that only objective and relevant information is gathered, and that it is fairer to consider similar information from all candidates. In practice, a tribunal claim for unfair selection is extremely unlikely to arise in relation to, let alone be found in favour of, a claimant on the strength of requesting only a CV. An application form does, however, make the life of those screening much easier because all data is in a similar format. For lower level jobs—for which applicants may be unlikely to have access to a computer or the necessary guidance to complete a CV—application forms can help to attract a wider candidate pool.



It cannot be denied that the first time writing a CV is time-consuming, but it is quick and easy to update, and few people relish the prospect of repeatedly filling in lengthy application forms. Particularly for senior roles, it is the recruiters that need to do the work to attract high performers, so applications via CV may be preferable.

## The role of social networking sites

Social networking sites have grown rapidly in popularity and there are an array of sites competing for members from more formal sites encouraging business networking such as LinkedIn to more informal sites such a Twitter and Facebook. LinkedIn (www.linkedin.com) now has over 60 million members, half of which are outside the USA. By its sixth anniversary since launch, Facebook boasted over 400 million global users, twice the number at its fifth anniversary. (www.facebook.com, 5 February 2010) and Twitter (www.twitter.com) had 75 million users by January 2010, although arguably many of these are inactive. There is no disputing the fact that social networking sites have direct access to so many people and that these sites therefore present an opportunity to employers to attract potential applicants. However the CIPD identified that only 7 per cent of employers use social networking sites such as LinkedIn to attract applicants. Employers are perhaps cautionary about using these sites due to their informal approach and reputation for the ease with which inappropriate comments and material can be circulated. Many employers bar or discourage their use whilst at work and we will see in Chapter 7 how such sites can present risk in terms of harassment linked to the work place. Inappropriate comments shared through such sites can have negative consequences at work should these come to the attention of employers.

A report commissioned by Microsoft (source www.euractiv.com, 1 February 2010) showed that 59 per cent of recruiters made use of data collected from the internet to evaluate candidates and that 41 per cent of UK recruiters, 16 per cent of German recruiters, and 14 per cent of French recruiters had rejected candidates on the basis of their online reputation. In the USA 70 per cent of HR professionals have refused job seekers based upon information found online. Whether or not this is morally or even legally defendable in light of discrimination legislation in the countries that such practices occur is arguable, nonetheless employees should take care about how their personal information can be accessed as it would appear that employers are increasingly gathering such covert information where it is available and are using this to support recruitment decisions.

## Handling applications

Before applications begin to arrive, the organization should consider how these are going to be handled. It is good practice to acknowledge all applications and often organizations will send a candidate pack, either upon first enquiry with the application form, or to those candidates who are shortlisted for interview.

It is important to consider and decide in advance on the process for shortlisting applications, and on the final assessment and selection stages. Larger organizations, particularly those from the public sector and those with large numbers of applications, are likely to use a scoring system based on agreed criteria, which are applied at the shortlisting and final assessment stages, or both. Often, this involves the allocation of points and the use of scoring matrices to express differences in applications/candidates in quantitative terms. If there are fewer applicants, it may be easier simply to rank the applications based on the closeness of the match with the person specification and chose an appropriate number for interview.

## Other checks

Organizations may have other obligations for checks, such as criminal record checks, checking eligibility to work in the UK, checking references, and health screening. Checks such as these can occur at different stages in the recruitment process, but they should always be applied consistently and fairly to avoid the risk of indirect discrimination. For example, checking eligibility to work in the UK should be handled consistently, to avoid a claim of racial discrimination, and health checks should be job-relevant, to avoid risking claims of disability discrimination.



# Assessing and Selecting

Assessing the suitability of applicants at each stage of selection, starting from reviewing application forms or CVs, to evaluating psychometric test results and rating performance in interviews, is central to the process not only of hiring, but of hiring the right kind of people. As a result of 'knowing' how well applicants match up to the requirements of a person specification or competency framework, the next stage in the assessment process can be planned. This involves the use of techniques and tools that are designed to discriminate between shortlisted applicants, using legal, relevant, and predictive criteria. The requirement to assess and distinguish is both challenging and difficult, and the people involved need to apply a range of skills to the task. It is also important to understand that the ability to make the 'right' selection decisions is as much of an art as it is a science, with, ultimately, professional judgement based on experience playing an important part.

Evidence from research carried out in the USA suggests a move away from restricting the assessment of specific applicant characteristics, such as educational attainments or cognitive ability, to a more holistic approach, as part of which assessors are interested in the 'whole person' and the full range of competencies that each person offers (O'Leary et al., 2002). Recognizing that effective job performance may be linked to other, perhaps less well-understood, skills and competencies is associated with the ideas of writers such as Daniel Goldman (1995, 1998), whose work on emotional intelligence has provided new insights into the relationship between what people are and how they behave, and job performance.

Signpost to Chapter 13: Case Study—Setting up an Assessment Centre

## The importance of predictive validity

According to O'Leary et al. (2002), the most important property of the assessment instruments used to measure or assess applicants against set criteria is their ability to predict future job performance, or job-related learning. In other words, does someone who scores well on the assessment instrument perform better on the job than someone whose score is poor? If the instruments and techniques are sufficiently reliable—meaning that they produce consistent results—the degree of predictive validity indicates which instruments and techniques are useful. Differences in test scores or ratings can then be used to identify which candidate is likely to be a better performing employee. This is the evidence upon which distinguishing between candidates is based. The challenge for managers is, therefore, one of identifying the degree of predictive validity for the assessment instruments in use, or of those that might be used.

One of the difficulties for those involved in using assessment instruments is, as Ryan and Tippins (2004) argue, that many of the research findings on recruiting staff have not been widely embraced by HR professionals. There are several reasons for this, including the failure of researchers to present their findings in an accessible and understandable way. The main reason, however, is perhaps that those using assessment instruments may have inaccurate beliefs about the predictive powers of the instruments they use. For example, in their USA study, Rynes et al. (2004) found that 72 per cent of the HR managers they surveyed thought that the degree of applicant conscientiousness was a better predictor of job performance than intelligence, whereas the reverse is true. They argue that evidence shows that structured selection processes are better than less structured ones and suggest that, often, those involved in making selection decisions rely too much on what they call 'gut instinct' and 'chemistry'. This is a complex and difficult issue, and however much evidence is presented that emphasizes the use of one or a combination of assessment instruments, it remains the case that the actual selection decision will involve some element of judgement and the application of personal experience of previous selection decisions.

As a result of reviewing a number of studies, Rynes et al. found the statistical relationships between commonly used assessment instruments and predictive validity shown in Table 4.2.

In the earlier study by O'Leary et al. (2002), those instruments found to have significantly lower levels of validity included those shown in Table 4.3.

These findings suggest that those instruments with a high predictive validity relative to others should be used, but this is an assumption that ignores the influence of contextual factors. For example, the skills and experience of interviewees will affect the actual level of predictive validity, with the use of inexperienced interviewers and deviations from 'best practice' resulting in considerably lower validity levels. What we need to emphasize here is not simply the use of particular instruments, but the way in which they are used, the qualities and experience of those involved, and the way in which different contributions to an assessment of

**Table 4.2** Statistical relationships between assessment instruments and predictive validity

| Assessment instrument | Predictive validity |
|---|---|
| Work sample tests | 0.54 |
| Cognitive ability tests | 0.51 |
| Structured interviews | 0.51 |
| Job knowledge tests | 0.48 |
| Unstructured interviews | 0.31 |
| Biographical data | 0.35 |
| Assessment centre results | 0.37 |
| Reference checks | 0.26 |

Table 4.3 Instruments with lower levels of validity

| Assessment instrument | Predictive validity |
|---|---|
| Job experience | 0.18 |
| Training and experience | 0.11 |
| Years of education | 0.10 |
| Graphology | 0.02 |
| Age | -0.01 |

the whole person are generated, evaluated, and combined with the judgement of the decision-makers to produce a final selection decision.

## Selection Interviews

The most widely used method of selecting candidates is interviewing. The CIPD (2009) identified that the competency-based interview is the most commonly used method, followed by interviews following a CV or application form, and structured panel interviews.

Interviews remain popular as they serve a number of purposes. From an employer's point of view they not only provide an opportunity to learn more about a candidate and assess the knowledge skills and experience described in an application in more detail but they also provide a chance to provide insight into the role and the organization and to sell the benefits of the organization to candidates. It is important therefore to see the interview as a two-way process of exchanging information. From a candidates point of view, in addition to persuading the potential employer of his or her attributes in relation to the role, applicants will use the interview as an opportunity discover more about the role and the organization and make a decision about whether to accept the role if an offer is made. An interview is therefore more than a series of questions to assess a candidate and needs to be properly structured. Typical structures will allow for introductions with the end aim to put the candidate at ease as well as explaining the format of the interview. Time will be set aside to ask a series of structured questions to assess the candidate's skills. There will also be time allocated to explaining more about the role and the organization and time for the candidate to ask questions of the interviewers. To ensure that selection interviews are both effective and that interviewers avoid any pitfalls in relation to legal considerations and avoiding any questions or behaviour that might be regarded as discriminatory it is good practice to ensure that interviewers receive appropriate training before taking part in an interview process.

More information on interviewing and the range of other selection methods that are available along with detailed guidance on how to put these together in an assessment centre can be found in Chapter 13.

Signpost to Chapters 13: Case Study—Setting up an Assessment Centre

Both legislation and culture in different countries will influence the selection process. For example in the USA the written details an applicant provides, often in the form of a one page resume are more brief and factual than that expected in a CV in the UK and it is more common for interviews to be on a one to one basis.

Qualifications are of particular importance in some cultures such as Japan and China whereas in other countries they are only of relevance to some job types. It is also more common in the Far East for applicants to attach a photograph to an application, whereas this is less common in European countries, perhaps due to the more rigorous discrimination legislation. For this reason also hobbies and pastimes are rarely included for example on a French resume and are becoming less widely used in the UK. There are also cultural changes over time, for example including date of birth on a curriculum vitae used to be standard practice in the UK and this is becoming less common since the introduction of age discrimination legislation.

These cultural differences are important to understand as HRM is increasingly operating in international arenas. It is important to understand and be sensitive to cultural differences and work within these in the country in which recruitment is taking place, whilst at the same time making allowances for these differences in order to avoid indirect discrimination when recruiting for roles with applicants from different backgrounds.

### RESEARCH INSIGHT 4.4

To take your learning further you might want to read this article:

**Branine, M. (2008) 'Graduate recruitment and selection in the UK: A study of the recent changes in methods and expectations',** ***Career Development International*****, 13, pp. 497–513**

This article looks at changes in graduate recruitment in the UK and shows that regardless of size or activity type, employers are using more sophisticated methods to attract and select candidates. Recruitment has become more person-orientated with employers interested in transferable skills such as personality and attitude; and whilst interviewing remains popular other methods of attracting and selecting candidates are being adopted.

### HRM INSIGHT 4.4 Using the right selection methods

FOC Inc is a large, highly successful global retailer with head quarters in the USA and a significant presence throughout the world in addition to the USA, particularly in Europe, the Middle East, and increasingly in the Far East. In the USA they have introduced strategic initiatives to increase the calibre of recruitment whilst reducing costs by moving to a third party online advertising solution for the majority of vacancies. This has significantly reduced advertising spend and the costs of using recruitment agencies to source candidates for vacancies and has been extremely successful in the USA.

Following significant pressure to adopt this approach globally, the UK management team have followed the US example and have backed on to the USA based online platform, which they have been using with mixed results. Recently the parent company insisted that a senior appointment for a UK based Sourcing Director could be recruited at much lower cost using the online route and decided to move away from the expensive retained recruitment consultant that they had used for senior posts in recent years. To assist with the process a highly rated, US based HR Vice President was seconded to the UK head office to oversee this process and other recruitment. To fall in line with US based practice, applicants were asked to submit a one page resume and then selection was based on a series of one-to-one interviews.

Despite a very large response for the Sourcing Director role, which created a high volume of work screening applicants, the calibre of responses to the online advert was generally of a low standard. The UK based senior managers insisted that the applicants who they interviewed were not of a high enough merit to appoint and criticized the US HR Vice President for the manner in which the recruitment was handled, the extent to which their time had been wasted and the delays in the recruitment that resulted. After significant delays a retained consultant was appointed to carry out an executive search to fill the post.

#### Questions

1. Why was the recruitment method that was so successful in the USA, unsuccessful in the UK?
2. What assumptions were made about recruitment and selection outside of the USA, by the American owners of the business?
3. What cultural differences might have impacted upon the situation?
4. How could the need to be cost effective and desire to increase US involvement have been better handled in this example?

# An Applicant Perspective

One of the distinctive features of this book is the emphasis given to making sense of HR from an employee perspective. In bringing this chapter to a close, it is necessary to ask the question: 'What does recruitment and selection mean to the person searching for a job?'

Inevitably, almost all of the research on this subject and, indeed, the approach taken by many writers of HR textbooks essentially reflect a managerial perspective. This managerial tendency is understandable and justifiable, but without considering the applicants and how their behaviour and attitudes are influenced by the experiences they are required to go through, it is a one-sided and limited perspective.

Chambers (2002) makes the important distinction between factors that influence behavioural reactions among applicants and the consequences that follow from these reactions. This distinction is important because it shows that the consequences of positive or negative experiences, particularly at the selection stage, continue after the selection decision has been taken. As an example, consider the situation in which an internal applicant has received negative feedback from the chair of an interview panel, who is also his or her line manager. The effect, while not inevitable, is likely to be a degree of demotivation and possibly a questioning of self-worth; the long-term consequences may involve rethinking the 'psychological contract', reduced levels of job performance, and a worsening of interpersonal relationships.

Signpost to Chapter 5: Managing Employee Relations, for more information on psychological contracts

Research quoted by Chambers (2002) points to the way in which applicant reactions to selection procedures are related to whether the procedures are perceived by the applicants as fair and just. The suggestion is that, if applicants perceive their experiences as unfair, unprofessional, or uncaring, they will take the decision not to continue with an application and to seek employment elsewhere. This reaction applies equally to internal and external job applications.

Chambers distinguishes between what he calls 'distributive justice', which is concerned with the perceived fairness of the outcome itself—for example, receiving or not receiving a job offer—and 'procedural justice', which is concerned with the perceived fairness of the procedures used to reach the outcome. This is to do with feeling that the procedures used in assessment and selection have been valid, fair, and managed in a professional manner. He also offers a further form of justice, which he describes as 'interactional justice'. This relates to the interpersonal treatment of applicants as procedures are enacted and the manner in which information is conveyed and managed.

The important point to emerge from this brief consideration of an applicant perspective on recruitment and selection is that managers and HR professionals need to recognize that applicants are human beings, who will become emotionally engaged in, and affected by, the way they are treated and what they are required to do. Decision-making is not something that only managers do; applicants are constantly evaluating their experiences and can decide at any point whether to continue with the process, up to, and including, declining the offer of a job. In tight labour markets and with an increasing proportion of knowledge workers in the labour force, traditional patterns of dependency, within which managers were 'in control', are being eroded, to the point at which talented employees with high performance potential are more selective about who they work for and the kind of work they do. The consequences for an organization that fails to understand this and bases its approach to recruitment and selection on twentieth- rather than twenty-first-century practices will almost certainly be costly and recurring.

# Summary

- Recruitment and selection are important to maintain the strength of the human capital of an organization. This area therefore represents one of the main strategic challenges faced by line managers and HR professionals.
- Recruitment decisions have costs associated with them in terms of the cost of recruitment and ongoing remuneration as well as there being a long term benefit to having the work required completed by a competent new recruit. It is therefore important to make the right decisions in terms of whether recruitment is necessary and to make sure that the candidate selected is likely to perform well in the role.
- When a vacancy arises organizations need to attract applicants from the available labour market. Employer branding is an important tool to ensure that the organization is attractive to potential applicants. The internet is growing in importance alongside traditional printed media and agencies for attracting applicants.
- Selection interviews remain one of the most popular mechanisms for selecting candidates in competency based, CV based, or structured interviews, however there are a broad variety of other methods to support selection decisions such as tests and assessment exercises which can be combined in an assessment centre to support effective decision-making.
- Despite developments in assessment instruments and high levels of procedural regulation, the final decision to hire or not remains, in many ways, a subjective one. It can be helpful to regard the process as matching jobs and people together rather than finding the best fit to a predetermined role and decisions are likely to be more effective if key stakeholders are involved in the process.
- Being able to visualize the experience from an applicant/employee perspective is a necessary part of being aware of, and sensitive to, the lasting effects that recruitment experiences can have on those who are selected and those who are not. These experiences can be positive and rewarding, but can also result in negative perceptions of the organization and of individual managers.

**Visit the Online Resource Centre that accompanies this book for self-test questions, web links, and more information on the topics covered in this chapter.**
**www.oxfordtextbooks.co.uk/orc/banfield_kay2e/**

## REVIEW QUESTIONS

1. Who should be involved in recruiting and selecting staff, and why? What roles will they play and why?
2. What are the arguments for fitting the organization to the person rather than fitting the person to the organization?
3. What do the concepts 'reliability' and 'validity' mean, and why are these important?
4. Making the right selection decision does not guarantee that the new recruit will stay—but what does?
5. From your own personal experiences of recruitment and selection, what role does the internet play and how do you feel organizations can get the maximum benefits from using internet based technologies in recruitment?

***See Online Resource Centre for answers.***

## CASE STUDY

### The Midlands Spring Company

The Midlands Spring Company manufactures a wide range of springs for the engineering and automobile industries. It was established by David Wheeler in 1986 and employs some 35 skilled and semi-skilled workers in its Peak District factory. David recently passed over management responsibility to his daughter, Jenny, and her husband, Alan Johnston. David comes in to work a couple of days a week but his main interests now lie outside the company. Jenny and Alan have been effectively running the business for the last 12 months and, while they have made considerable progress in sorting out some of the problems they faced, they are still struggling to deal with all of the issues that are preventing the business from developing. Alan has concentrated his energy on the sales and marketing side of the business, while Jenny has worked hard to develop the office and administrative systems. They are currently in the process of applying for the ISO 9000 standard, which is critical to getting orders from new customers who will only do business with suppliers who have been awarded the standard.

The main challenge is in the production area. Much of the plant and equipment is old, and maintenance costs are high. While the workforce is reliable and hard-working, there is little flexibility between the machine setters and production workers, all of whom are male and are full-time. The packers and dispatchers are female, and work under a variety of full- and part-time contracts. Quality has been a problem for some time, with scrap levels, waste, and faulty products worryingly high. Without significant and sustained improvements in production planning and control, and quality standards, the company faces a difficult future.

One of the first decisions Jenny and Alan made was to appoint a quality manager to work on the ISO 9000 application, and to introduce the necessary quality checks and procedures in the factory. Chris Openshaw had been recommended to them by a recruitment agency in Sheffield, and they appointed him after considering his CV and a short interview. Neither of them had any previous HR experience nor did they involve anyone else in the decision. In addition to having to pay the agency fee of £7,000, the appointment has proven costly. Despite his CV, which originally impressed them, it soon became apparent to Alan and Jenny that the appointment of Chris had been a mistake. He spent most of his time in his office working on statistical control procedures and showed little interest in the shop floor, where these measures would need to be implemented. He didn't understand the importance of developing good working relationships with either Jenny and Alan or the shop floor staff. Progress with the ISO 9000 application has been slow and the submission document is far from being complete.

Knowing what to do was key to making the right decisions. Jenny and Alan needed to address the issue of Chris' appointment and get help with finding someone else who could combine the quality role with that of production manager. They decided to terminate Chris' contract and gave him one month's notice. In fact, he hadn't been particularly happy in his job and the parting wasn't acrimonious. He decided to leave after two weeks. The second problem was addressed by talking to their local Training and Skills Council, who arranged for an experienced recruitment consultant to work with them on finding a replacement. After discussing their requirements, the consultant suggested that they create a new post of works manager, and develop a more effective recruitment and selection strategy than that used before. Jenny and Alan agreed, and went through a rigorous job analysis with the consultant. This resulted in a job description and person specification. They now had to decide on how to recruit and on the selection process. They knew another bad appointment could mean the end of the business, so they were determined to take advice from the consultant and work with him.



#### Questions

1. Where would the kind of applicants the company was looking for be found and how would you go about contacting them?

2. Using the information provided, plus further details on what similar jobs in the engineering and related sectors involve, prepare a person specification for use in the selection process.
3. Consider and decide upon a selection strategy, identifying the selection tools/instruments you would recommend that the company use if you were in the role of the consultant. Justify your recommendations.
4. What would be the key criteria you would use in producing a shortlist?
5. Who would take the final decision and what criteria would you use to establish whether the appointment was a success?
6. Produce an estimate of the costs of the whole process.

**Insights & Outcomes: visit the Online Resource Centre at www.oxfordtextbooks.co.uk/orc/banfield_kay2e/ to find out what the recruitment and selection strategy was and the outcome of the process.**

## FURTHER READING

Batata, A.S. (2005) 'International nurse recruitment and NHS vacancies: A cross-sectional analysis', *Globalization and Health*, **1**:7, www.globalizationandhealth.com.

Boyatzis, R.E. (1982) *The Competent Manager: A Model for Effective Performance*, John Wiley & Sons.

Cook, M. (2003) *Personnel Selection: Adding Value Through People*, 4th ed., John Wiley & Sons.

Dale, M. (2004) *A Manager's Guide to Recruitment and Selection*, 2nd ed., Kogan Page.

Horowitz, F.M., Heng, C.T. and Quazi, H.A. (2003) 'Finders, keepers? Attracting, motivating and retaining knowledge workers', *Human Resource Management*, **13**:4, pp. 23–44.

Incomes Data Services (2008) *Employer branding*, HR studies, IDS.

Office for National Statistics (2010) Labour Force Survey, www.statistics.gov.uk.

Sims, J. (2005) 'Weathering recruitment', *People Management*, 8 December.

*Sunday Times* (2010) 'Best 100 Companies to Work For', 7 March.

## REFERENCES


Advisory Conciliation and Arbitration Service (2007) *Recruitment and Induction*, www.acas.org.uk.

Barrick, M.R. and Zimmerman, R.D. (2009) 'Hiring for retention and performance', *Human Resource Management*, **48**:2, March, pp. 183–206.

Bozionelos, N. (2005) 'When the inferior candidate is offered the job: The selection interview as a political and power game', *Human Relations*, **58**:12, pp. 1605–31.

Branine, M. (2008) 'Graduate recruitment and selection in the UK: A study of the recent changes in methods and expectations', *Career Development International*, **13**, pp. 497–513.

Burrows, C. (2004) 'Enriching the talent pool: Injecting new blood from outside the industry', *International Journal of Medical Marketing*, **4**:4, pp. 390–2.

Carrington, L. (2004) 'Laws of attraction', *People Management*, 17 June, p. 26.

Chambers, B.A. (2002) 'Applicant reactions and their consequences: Review, advice, and recommendations for future research', *International Journal of Management Review*, **4**, December, pp. 317–33.

Chartered Institute of Personnel and Development (2007) *Employer Branding: A No-Nonsense Approach*, www.cipd.co.uk.

Chartered Institute of Personnel and Development (2009) *Recruitment, Retention and Turnover Survey*, www.cipd.co.uk.

Chartered Institute of Personnel and Development (2010) *Recruitment, Retention and Turnover Survey*, www.cipd.co.uk.

Collins, J. (2001) *From Good to Great*, Random House.

Cook, M. (1988) *Personnel Selection and Productivity*, John Wiley & Sons.

Davies G. (1999) 'Employer branding and its influence on managers', *European Journal of Marketing*, **42**:5/6, pp. 667–681.

Fitz-Enz, J. (2002) *How to Measure Human Resource Management*, McGraw-Hill.

Goldman, D. (1995) *Emotional Intelligence*, Bantam.

Goldman, D. (1998) *Working with Emotional Intelligence*, Bantam.

Gratton, L. (2000) 'A real step change', *People Management*, 16 March, pp. 26–30.

Internet Advertising Bureau (2008) www.iabuk.net.

Lazear, E.P. (1998) *Personnel Economics for Managers*, John Wiley & Sons.

Levesque, L.L. (2005) 'Opportunistic hiring and employee fit', *Human Resource Management*, **44**:3, Fall, pp. 301–30.

Michaels, E., Handfield-Jones, H. and Axelrod, B. (2001) *The War for Talent*, Harvard Business School Press.

Morgan, G. (1997) *Images of Organization*, 2nd ed., Sage.

O'Leary, B.S., Lindholm, M.L., Whitford, R.A. and Freeman, S.E. (2002) 'Selecting the best and brightest: Leveraging human capital', *Human Resource Management*, **41**:3, Fall, pp. 325–40.

Rioux, S.M. and Bernthal P. (1999), 'Recruitment and Selection Practices', *Development Dimensions International*.

Ryan, A.M. and Tippins, N.T. (2004) 'Attracting and selecting: What psychological research tells us', *Human Resource Management*, **43**:4, pp. 305–18.

Rynes, S.L., Colbert, A. and Brown, K.G. (2004) 'HR professionals' beliefs about effective human resource practices: Correspondence between research and practice', *Human Resource Management*, **41**, Summer, pp. 149–74.

Welch, J. and Welch, S. (2005) *Winning*, HarperCollins.

Women and Work Commission (2006) *Shaping a Fairer Future*, Department of Trade and Industry, http://news.bbc.co.uk/1/shared/bsp/hi/pdfs/27_02_06_wwc_paygap.pdf.

# 5 Managing Employee Relations

## Key Terms

**Trade union** An organization that is independent of an employer and funded by member contributions, the function of which is to represent worker interests in relations between workers and employers.

**Collective bargaining** The process of negotiation between trade union representatives and employers, or employer representatives, to establish by agreement the terms and conditions of employment of a group of employees.

**Collective agreement** A written statement defining the arrangements agreed between a union and employer, and the terms that will apply. Such agreements are only legally enforceable if this is expressly stated or if the collective agreement is referred to in individual written terms and conditions of employment.

**Psychological contract** The obligations that an employer and an employee, or group of employees, perceive to exist between each other as part of the employment relationship, comprising both expectations of each other and promises made to each other.

## Learning Objectives

As a result of reading this chapter and using the Online Resource Centre, you should be able to:

- understand the importance of maintaining good relations with employees, through involvement, and through effective communication and consultation;
- recognize the importance of the psychological contract at work and how to manage this to support organizational objectives;
- be able to evaluate the contemporary role of trade unions and how to manage effective union relationships through partnership;
- understand the difference between consultation and collective bargaining, and how to avoid disruption due to collective disputes;
- understand and apply key theoretical and conceptual contributions to the analysis of individual and collective behaviour.

# Introduction

The relationship between an employer and its employees lies at the heart of what makes an organization effective. The employees of an organization have the power to allow an organization to meet and exceed its objectives, or to fail. Highly motivated employees work more productively and, if they feel engaged with their employer, will make a greater contribution towards its overall direction and success. Demotivated employees, on the other hand, can also have an impact on the organization, but in different and more negative ways. This can include individual and less visible expressions of dissatisfaction, such as high absenteeism, poor timekeeping, and low productivity, as well as collective action, such as strikes and working to rule, all of which undermine the organization's ability to ensure its financial health and long-term competitiveness.

While the long-term decline in British manufacturing can, in part, be explained by the emergence of low-cost economies in the Far East, it is also worth remembering that those industries which experienced a rapid and close-to-terminal decline in the 1970s and 1980s—the most well known of which were motor manufacturing, shipbuilding, and steel production—were industries that were renowned for 'bad' industrial relations, low morale, and high levels of industrial conflict. As a general statement, organizations that are able to establish and maintain good relations with employees and their representatives are those that will not only avoid the weakening effects of an under-producing and uncooperative workforce, but gain the advantages that result from a workforce that is motivated and committed. The expectation is that this workforce will understand that its long-term interests are better served by working with management, rather than by challenging them in the pursuit of its own short-term interests. This theme of working with or against management, which is central to the whole of this text, will be explored in more detail later.

It is important to recognize that getting an organization's employment relations 'right' does not have the same significance as having an effective recruitment or training strategy. It is actually of *more* importance, because the state of an organization's individual and collective employment relations has a pervasive influence on how the other aspects of managing people are carried out. It is inconceivable that strategies to drive performance forward, initiatives to increase the level of employee utilization and attempts to access the world of discretionary effort will be successful if the general state of employment relations is poor and unsatisfactory, and if there is little trust between managers and employees. Effective employee relations provide a framework conducive to, and a positive psychological environment within which, performance discussions and other employment matters can take place. As a result, employees should be confident about expressing their views, in the expectation that these will be taken into account when final decisions are made. But to be able to manage performance or gain employee support for change, an employer must first have a constructive relationship with its employees.

Signpost to Chapter 11: Managing Performance, for perspectives on maximizing performance

# The Origins and Scope of Industrial (or Employment) Relations

What is now called 'employment relations' or 'employee relations' was originally known as 'industrial relations' and has its origins in the 1960s as a separate discipline or field of study. As was explained in Chapter 2, the importance of industrial relations in the second half of the last century shaped and influenced the development of personnel or human resource management as a specialist management function, and the agendas of those who had responsibilities in this area. But this does not mean that interest in the relationship between employee and employer is a relatively recent phenomenon. The contractual relationship that is at the heart of employment has been of interest to economists, sociologists, and lawyers since at least the middle of the nineteenth century and, arguably, since even earlier.

This contract provides a set of rights, responsibilities, and obligations that structure the behaviour of both parties, and represents the basis of what constitutes the normative system of regulation and control within the workplace. For many writers on political economy, the perceived and actual inequalities between the individual worker and his or her employer, based on the ownership of the means of production (*capital*), is closely associated with the rise of the trade union movement in the latter part of the nineteenth century. Even today, it is seen as being at the heart of what many believe to be the source of conflict between employers and workers (Clarke and Clements, 1977).

After the end of World War II, and in the immediate aftermath of reconstruction and readjustment to post-war conditions, trade unions and employers re-established relationships and proceeded to build new frameworks for the collective regulation of industrial relations, although many of those that came into being owed much to pre-war antecedents. The system of Whitely Councils, for example, established after the end of World War I to provide a comprehensive collective bargaining framework for a range of industries, survived well into the second half of the twentieth century, although almost all of those that remained were in the public sector. This fact reflects the way in which trade union presence and activity has become concentrated in public sector institutions, with only relatively few pockets remaining in the private sector (mainly in transport and communications).

What became a feature of post-World War II industrial relations was the increase in industrial conflict, particularly strikes, experienced by companies in heavy engineering, manufacturing, and, increasingly, in parts of the public sector. The so-called 'Winter of Discontent' of 1978–79 was the culmination of trade union activity in pursuit of pay claims that were higher than government pay policy allowed and began in private industry, before spreading to local authorities and other public sector employees.

The incidence and frequency of strike action were not on the same scale as that which was experienced in the 1920s, but, nevertheless, the disruption caused to production, competitiveness, and public service were considered to be serious problems that needed urgent attention. The so-called 'British Disease', represented by a strike-prone and inefficient workforce, became an uncomfortable, but not entirely unjustified, description of what was wrong with industrial relations at that time (Ingram and Metcalfe, 1991).

**RESEARCH INSIGHT 5.1**

To take your learning further you might want to read this article:

**Phillips J. (2009), 'Workplace conflict and the origins of the 1984–1985 miners' strike in Scotland', *Twentieth Century British History*, 20:2, pp. 152–173**

This article looks back at the causes of the miners' strike in Scotland in 1984–5 and discusses the role of the workforce's opposition to authoritarian management style in the strike in addition to more traditional views of an illegitimate strike, without a national ballot in response to the conservative government's proposal to close uneconomic pits. The article highlights the complexity of industrial relations and the importance of deteriorating relationships in creating a climate in which strike action becomes a more predictable outcome.

## The influence of academics

The 1960s saw the emergence of a group of academics who had a particular interest in trade unions and industrial relations. Among the most influential were John Dunlop (1958), Richard Hyman (1975), Alan Flanders (1970), and Alan Fox (1966). These, and others who shared their concerns about the state of industrial relations, were interested in trying to identify the underlying dynamics and structural forces that were 'determining' worker behaviour. They were particularly concerned with developing theoretical contributions that offered insights into:

- the political and institutional role of trade unions, and the impact that trade union activity had on employment and wages;
- the relationship between trade union leaders and members;
- the causes of strikes;
- the role and influence of management and employers in shaping the way in which industrial relations developed.

Dunlop (1958) developed a theory of industrial relations that saw industrial relations as a subsystem of society, on a par with the economic and political subsystems, which overlapped and influenced each other. Although the suggestion that industrial relations was equivalent in importance and impact to the two other societal subsystems is much more contentious now that it was in the 1960s, the central components of his theory are still relevant. They provide important conceptual and explanatory tools that can be used by those who are trying to interpret the way in which the 'system' functions, and can be summarized as:

- what he describes as 'actors' in the system. These are the representatives of management, employees and their representatives, and specialist government agencies that have an industrial relations function;
- the context or environment within which the actors operate and which determines the material conditions of work and employment;
- the ideology or belief systems that each 'actor' possesses and is influenced by, and which help to determine the way in which particular groups relate to other 'actors' within the system;
- the system outputs, which are expressed in terms of rules, that give the system a degree of stability and maintain order, although these should be seen as provisional and conditional rather than as permanent.

The importance of rules and rule-making processes are central to understanding the primary 'function' of the industrial relations system. One way of understanding why rules are important is to consider the limitations inherent in the formal contract of employment. By this, we mean that, while the employer agrees to the rate of pay, fringe benefits, holidays, and other conditions of employment, the commitment of the employee is quite different. He or she agrees to accept a role that is subordinate to that of management, in the sense of accepting managerial authority, and to carry out the duties associated with the job for which he or she been employed. But there is an important area of indeterminacy in the formal contract of employment, in terms of levels of job performance that will be delivered and sustained, and in acceptance of specific management orders. As Hyman and Brough (1975) argued, an employee makes a commitment to obey:

> **Yet such a promise is neither unambiguous nor conditional; and its interpretation is thus a source of potential conflict.**

They quote Gouldner (1954), who asks:

> **Which commands has the worker promised to obey? Are these commands limited to the production of goods and services only? Under the terms of the contract, may an employer legitimately issue a command unnecessary for production? Who decides this anyhow, worker or employer?**

This recognition that there is a degree of indeterminacy in all employment contracts means that one, or both, of the workplace actors, or an external third party, must establish rules to ensure that there is the necessary level of normative order, and therefore stability, within the national or local system. If this does not happen, the tendency will be for the lack of normative regulation to lead to higher levels of uncertainty, instability, and conflict than would otherwise have been the case.

## Rules in employment relations

Rules in employment relations fall into two main categories, as follows.

### *Procedural rules*

Procedural rules are those that establish how the actors in the system will respond and behave in given situations. For example, if managers and union representatives fail to reach agreement about annual pay increases, they may have already agreed on ways in which to resolve the impasse and avoid industrial conflict. This may involve third-party intervention, a cooling-off period, or some other mechanism for facilitating agreement. These rules fulfil the important role of maintaining system stability and avoid either party taking arbitrary action.

There is, however, a second category of procedural rules that has a quite different function. In this case, rules are agreed that determine how other kinds of rules will be determined. Again, a simple example will illustrate how these rules work: consider the important issue of what employees will be paid for the work that they do. Payment can be based on hours worked, production achieved, or performance attained—but who makes this decision? Is this something that management alone is to determine, or should it be decided by the employees themselves or through the intervention of a third party? These are important questions, the answers to which will have an important impact on the economic health of the organization and on the quality of the relationships between managers and employees. These rule-making processes are at the heart of any employment relations system and can be expressed in terms of:

- *unilateral regulation*, under which managers, unions, or employees create rules that regulate a particular part of the employment relationship. For example, on the question of overtime and what will be paid for such time, managers might feel that this is something that they alone need to regulate.
- On the other hand, trade unionism is based on the belief in, and commitment to, what is called *joint regulation*, more usually known as 'collective bargaining', under which both parties meet and, through the process of negotiation, reach a joint decision on rules, such as those that regulate the allocation and payment of overtime working, as well as other matters of importance. Unions have consistently strived to extend the application of joint regulation to as many aspects of the organization as possible, in an attempt to increase the protection they can provide to their members and to enhance their own influence.
- Procedural rules that originate outside of the employing organization or national institutions of the employment relations system can be created through *legal and judicial processes*. The British Parliament, the European Union, and associated judicial bodies make and interpret laws that regulate work and employment. In fact, it might be argued that the relative importance of each of these rule-making processes has changed significantly over the past 50 years, with the influence of judicial processes increasing, while that of trade union unilateral regulation and joint regulation has been decreasing in both frequency and influence. This view is consistent with the evidence of the relative decline in trade unionism and the increasing difficulty that unions experience in maintaining the idea and practice of joint determination, particularly those that represent workers in the private sector. Think about the Working Time Regulations (WTR) and the National Minimum Wage (NMW) as examples of how complex sets of rules over working time and payment are made by external parties rather than by unilateral or joint regulation.

### *Substantive rules*

These are the rules that are generated by rule-making processes, such as joint determination and unilateral decision-making. Once again considering pay as an example, these types of rules determine how pay rates and levels are determined, but represent the actual rules that say what a person's basic pay will be and what any additional payments for extra work done might be. As was explained above, the 'working week'—an

Table 5.1 Joint regulation of terms and conditions of employment

| Issue | Management decides | Informs | Consults | Negotiates |
|---|---|---|---|---|
| *Pay* | 70 (16) | 6 (10) | 5 (13) | 18 (61) |
| *Hours* | 71 (18) | 5 (10) | 8 (20) | 16 (53) |
| *Holidays* | 71 (19) | 9 (17) | 5 (13) | 15 (52) |
| *Pensions* | 73 (22) | 11 (25) | 6 (16) | 10 (36) |
| *Staff selection* | 78 (42) | 10 (26) | 9 (23) | 3 (9) |
| *Training* | 75 (36) | 10 (24) | 13 (31) | 3 (9) |
| *Grievance procedure* | 69 (15) | 9 (20) | 14 (36) | 9 (28) |
| *Disciplinary procedure* | 69 (15) | 9 (21) | 13 (35) | 8 (29) |
| *Staffing plans* | 75 (33) | 11 (26) | 12 (34) | 3 (7) |
| *Equal Opportunities* | 72 (22) | 10 (23) | 14 (40) | 5 (15) |
| *Health and safety* | 69 (17) | 9 (19) | 17 (49) | 5 (15) |
| *Performance appraisal* | 75 (33) | 9 (20) | 12 (33) | 4 (14) |

Source: *WERS 2004 First Findings*. © Crown Copyright/ESRC/ACAS/Policy Studies Institute.
(Note that the figures in brackets represent the managerial responses in workplaces that recognized trade unions.)





area of particular importance for both employees and employers—is now, for many workers, regulated by the EU and the substantive rules that have been established take precedence over any that were agreed by collective bargaining or imposed by employers. Substantive rules regulate how much people get paid, their hours of work, holiday entitlement, and so on. Many of these are contained in the formal contract of employment but, as explained earlier, this only regulates certain aspects of an employee's behaviour and performance at work. In a constantly changing environment, new conditions and situations arise that need to be regulated and, through the processes for creating new rules or amending old ones, the body of substantive rules is constantly being amended.

Table 5.1 summarizes the findings of the 2004 Workplace Employment Relations Survey (DTI, 2004) about the way in which rules are established and the degree to which management involves employees in the rule-making process.

**KEY CONCEPT Managerial authority**

The concept of managerial authority is central to understanding the sources of tension within employment relations and the ongoing struggle between managers and trade unions, in particular over the 'rights' and authority of each party. 'Prerogative' means the right to make decisions and to establish rules that are essential in allowing the production system to operate efficiently and effectively, and, historically, managers have tended to guard their prerogative and have tried to prevent trade unions from eroding it. If trade union power has increased as a result of economic or political change, and has strengthened their representative and negotiating role, managerial rights have been eroded and pushed back; if trade union power has been weakened by the movement of capital and restrictive legislation, managers have been able to reassert their rights 'to manage' and to restrict trade union involvement in the decision-making process. In extreme cases, this has involved the removal of recognition and the restriction or elimination of bargaining rights. This is an aspect of employment relations that is never completely resolved, but is rather in a state of dynamic tension.

**STUDENT ACTIVITY 5.1**

1. Summarize the information contained in Table 5.1 and compare it with the results of either previous workplace employment relations surveys on the same subject or the most up to date survey.
2. Explore the implications emerging from this comparison.
3. Consider the inferences that can be reached about changes in trade union influence and the significance of collective bargaining (negotiating) in contemporary employment relations.

## *Rules and legitimacy*

There is one further category of rules that needs to be explained, and this concerns the form that the rules take and their legitimacy. The idea that people at work operate within two organizational environments has long been recognized (Handy, 1993). At one level, the environment represented by the formal organization consists of the formally approved, usually by management, procedural and substantive rules. These rules are legitimized, through being known and approved by management, and regulate how people are supposed to behave at work.

The concept of the 'informal organization', however, suggests that this informal world, represented by the place of work and the day-to-day interaction between managers and employees, and within employee groups, can develop its own social and work-related norms (rules). These are often unknown to senior managers and may be in conflict with the formal rules that have emerged from 'more legitimate' processes. Such rules may lack the legitimacy of formally derived rules, but can nevertheless exert a powerful influence on the behaviour of the managers and employees affected by them. The reason why it is important to understand the importance of informal rules is that, while much of our behaviour is regulated and controlled in ways known to management, other aspects are not, for example:



- levels of discretionary effort;
- output and performance levels;
- the level of cooperation offered to management;
- the degree of employee flexibility.

In situations in which there is a lack of trust between employees and managers, and in which employees exercise control over the production/work process, it is likely that employees, either as individuals or groups, will limit their performance, creating a body of informal and, as far as management is concerned, often unknown rules that regulate what employees are prepared and not prepared to do. The challenge that contemporary managers face is not simply to discover and change these rules, but to understand the reasons why they exist.

**RESEARCH INSIGHT 5.2**

To take your learning further you might want to read this article:

**Macey W. and Scheider B. (2008), 'The meaning of employee engagement', *Society for Industrial and Organizational Psychology*, 1:1, pp. 3–30**

This article looks at what is meant by the concept of 'employee engagement' and the supposition that if this can be quantified then links may be established between employee engagement and competitive advantage. The article proposes a framework for understanding engagement and describes three elements of engagement, trait engagement (having a positive view of life and work), state engagement (feelings of energy and absorption), and behavioural engagement (extra-role behaviour).

**STUDENT ACTIVITY 5.2 The Wildcat Strike**

Alvin Gouldner's (1954) classic study of an unofficial strike and its causes remains one of the outstanding contributions to our understanding of the interaction between the formal and informal systems of work. The task is to read the first chapter of his text, *Wildcat Strike*, in order to answer the following questions:

1. What is meant by the term 'indulgency patterns'?
2. Why did the original managers appear to allow the workers to break the formal rules?
3. Why was legitimacy an important issue in the conflict that led to the strike?
4. What role did management play in events leading up to the strike?

Figure 5.1 represents a way of understanding the essential elements of an industrial relations system and how, as these change over time, the system produces new institutions, different patterns of rule making, and new ways of preventing and resolving conflict. The important point to note is that the system must be understood as dynamic, rather than static, and as influenced by forces that are often outside the control of the main participants and interest groups. A particularly good example of this inability to control the system can be seen in the way in which the effects of internationalization and globalization have changed the forces of competition in manufacturing and service industries. This has resulted in growth in the knowledge economy and the numbers of knowledge workers, a decline in manufacturing jobs and a corresponding fall in private sector union density. Because the public sector environment has so far remained relatively



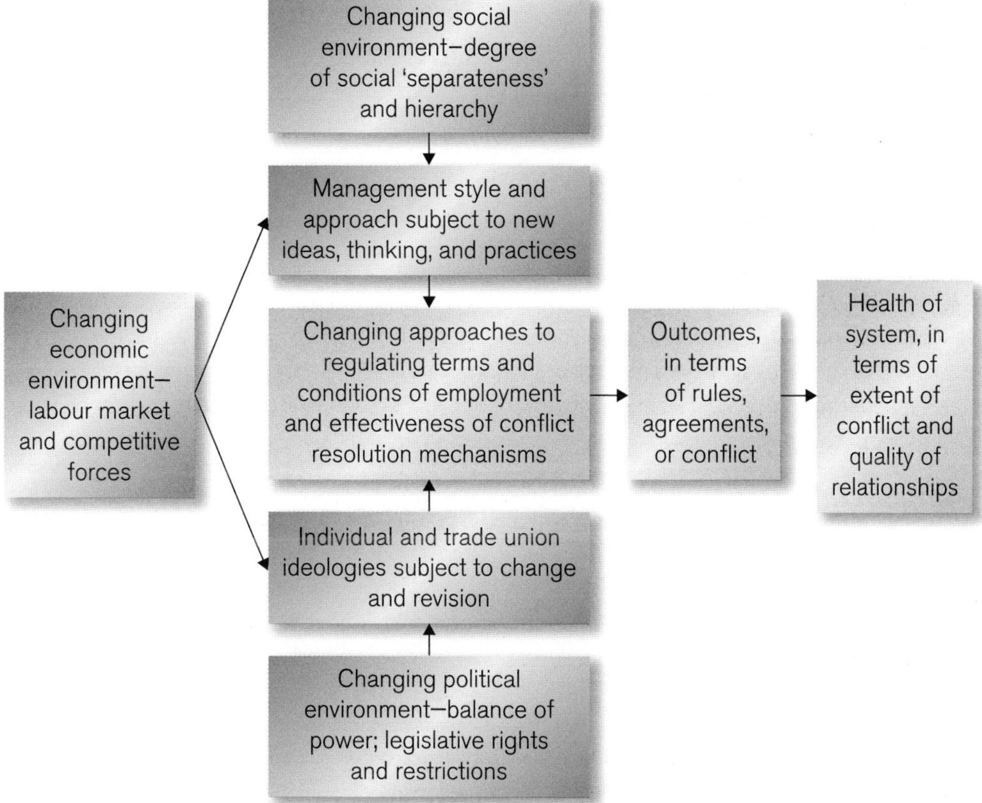


**Figure 5.1** A diagrammatical representation of an employment relations system

immune from the employment effects of the globalization of trade and competition, trade union membership and influence in this sector have been preserved. As the private sector increases its involvement in the provision of public sector services, however, and as old labour supply monopolies come under increasing pressure, it is inevitable that the form of regulation, union membership patterns, and the influence of trade unions will change.

Figure 5.1 is also useful in that it represents a model that can be applied both to national 'systems' and to those that exist within each organization. It can be used to explain why:

- the frequency and pattern of industrial conflict changes and differs between sectors and industries;
- new methods of reaching agreement on work and employment have been created;
- trade unions have a history of mergers and reorganization, and of developing new services for their members;
- more emphasis is now placed on individual, rather than collective, employment relations, as employers and managers—many of whom are from overseas—use different and more effective strategies to gain acceptance and commitment from their employees;
- governments periodically intervene in the system in an attempt to 'correct' any imbalances of power and to limit the ability of the main parties to damage the social or economic fabric of society.

## Perspectives on employment relations

One of the most important theoretical contributions made by the early industrial relations theorists, summarized by Salamon (2000), is the development of what are commonly known as perspectives on, or approaches to, the study and interpretation of industrial/employment relations. These perspectives are important because they express the different assumptions that academics and others make about the nature of organizations, the fundamental nature of the relationship between workers and employers, and the characteristics of the society within which work organizations exist and function.

The three perspectives that are most frequently referred to are:

- the unitary perspective, in which it is viewed that organizations and societies work together towards a common objective, with accepted hierarchical control and with all members having common values;
- pluralism, in which there are regarded to be many different groups with different roles and ideologies, which lead to differences in priorities and therefore conflict between groups which must be managed;
- the radical, or Marxist, perspective which suggests that class wealth and power creates a hierarchy in which workers at the bottom of the hierarchy are dependent upon those at the top for employment, but exploitation results in wealth being disproportionate to efforts. The trade unions therefore represent both political and employment interest and conflicts occurs in the pursuit of both economic and political change.

For a more detailed discussion about these perspectives see the Online Resource Centre extension material 5.1.

**HRM INSIGHT 5.1 ABC Pharmaceuticals**

ABC Pharmaceuticals is a global business with a manufacturing plant in the Republic of Ireland that is responsible for the production of the active ingredients used in a wide range of pharmaceutical products. The site employs over 400 skilled employees and has not had any union representation since the facility was built in the late 1970s. While the company does have union representation at some of its other manufacturing sites in Europe, its vision of the Irish site was that it would stay non-unionized. The decision by senior management not to recognize any union for either negotiation or representational purposes was based on the company's philosophy that its employees' best interests would be served through the creation of a single-status working environment. This would provide an excellent reward-and-recognition package and facilitate communication with employees at all levels.

From an operational perspective, it was also important to create a high level of flexibility in working practices, so that the plant could adapt and respond quickly to the continuing changes in product development, manufacturing processes, and market demand, all of which are features of the pharmaceutical industry.

To allow for employee representation, the company created the specific role of 'employee representative'. This role provides both individuals and groups of employees who have grievances or other difficulties with a route, involving defined procedure, by which they can raise issues and express their concerns to management. Management will then consult with the representative in solving the problem and in delivering a solution in the way that best meets the employees' and the business' needs.

There is a strong emphasis on communications at the site and it is a multi-level activity, involving crew/team meetings, individual discussions, general employee meetings, a newsletter (both internal and external), and the use of both email and intranet.

Because of the nature of continuous change, any changes that are mooted are discussed within teams that are both directly and indirectly affected, and within specialized forums, such as safety committees. For the majority of employees, this system works very well and representatives play an important part in dealing with a wide range of concerns and issues, very few of which, to date, have required outside intervention of any sort.

There is a small minority of employees, however, who feel that they would like the right to join a trade union and have its presence formally recognized. The effectiveness of the employee representative role and management's engagement with employees has not, however, resulted in any sense of dissatisfaction among the majority of employees about the way in which grievances and concerns have been dealt with.

### Questions

1. Is there a case to be made that the interests of employees would be better served by union recognition and negotiating rights?
2. Would recognizing trade unions result in an increase in differences and disagreements between managers and employees? If so, why, and what would they be likely to involve?
3. To what extent are the success of the plant and the stability of employment and wages a function of its non-unionized status?
4. If you were a national trade union official trying to achieve union recognition in the plant, what arguments would you present to management and employees to try to persuade them to accept this objective?



# What is a Trade Union?

A 'trade union' is a body that both collectively and individually represents the interests of its members, predominantly in the context of employment. The union is therefore concerned with the relations between workers and their employer. Many organizations formally recognize one, or more, trade unions for representation or negotiation purposes, but equally many, predominantly in the private sector, do not. The form of recognition adopted might be restricted to recognition of a particular union to represent individual employees, or groups of employees, in procedures such as dismissal and grievance procedures, but will often extend to the recognition of unions for collective negotiation over issues such as terms and conditions, including pay. It should be noted that formal recognition comes about when an employer is willing to negotiate, rather than simply to recognize or consult with, a trade union.

Trade unions are a worldwide phenomenon and are associated with industrialization, the fracturing of old social relations and dependencies, and the experience of greater economic uncertainty and insecurity.

Their form, practices, and ideologies differ between countries. For example, Japanese unions are based largely on individual companies, rather than on national associations, and are known for their commitment to a close working relationship with management. Their fundamental purpose is the same as that of British trade unions, that is, to offer their members protection and defence from the arbitrary action of management and from the economic system within which they are employed. What is different is the way in which each nation's trade unions try to deliver these outcomes and how successful they are.

Trade unions, in the absence of legal prohibition, thrive in situations in which:

- employees have limited, or no, protection from state or other judicial authorities;
- management show little concern for the interests or well being of their employees;
- individual workers are relatively powerless to challenge management and are unable to restrict their power;
- workers' experience of employment leaves them with a strong sense of grievance towards management, based on a feeling that they are being exploited and treated unfairly.

Of course, the corollary of this is that workers may experience none of the above and, as a consequence, may feel disinclined to join a trade union or to participate in any trade union activity.

Member commitment to the union can therefore be strong or weak, depending on the perceived need for unions and the degree to which members share the ideology of the union leadership. Those who subscribe to a radical and Marxist-informed ideology are likely to have a much more adversarial relationship with employers and managers than will the representatives of a union that adopts a pluralist perspective. It might be argued, therefore, that the contemporary existence of trade unions, and the relationship they have with employers and managers, is as much a function of the attitude and behaviour of employers and managers as it is of any independent motivation that affects the predisposition of workers to join, or to remain outside of, trade union representation. Employees may also have the option, as an alternative to joining a national trade union, of becoming a member of a company-based staff association.

**STUDENT ACTIVITY 5.3 A comparison between a trade union and a staff association**

This activity involves considerable research, which might include surveying people who are members of both types of representative body as well as looking at the literature on employee representation. Groups can concentrate on either trade unions or staff associations, or both, but the idea is to produce presentations that address the following issues:

- the motivation behind joining trade unions rather than staff associations;
- the functions of the two types of body;
- management attitudes to the bodies;
- the advantages and disadvantages they offer to employees and managers.

The most well-known definition of a trade union was provided by the Webbs, in 1920, when they said it was:

> **a continuous association of wage earners for the purpose of maintaining or improving the conditions of their working lives.**
> (Webb and Webb, 1920)

A more contemporary definition can be found in the Trade Union and Labour Relations (Consolidation) Act 1992, which defined a trade union as:

> **an organization . . . consisting wholly or mainly of workers of one or more descriptions whose principal purpose includes the regulation of relations between workers of that description and employers or employers' associations.**

Both definitions are similar and emphasize the union's regulatory and rule-making function, although the purpose of this activity, beyond reference to maintaining or improving the conditions of the working lives of members, is not made particularly clear.

Dunlop (2002), on the other hand, offers a much more helpful definition of what trade unions 'are for' and what this involves them in doing. He argues that, while people join unions for many different reasons, unions are fundamentally concerned with the following.

- Industrial jurisprudence

  This means that unions are involved in grievance and arbitration procedures, rules governing promotion, transfers, discipline and dismissals, and so on. Being able to participate in the regulation of such critically important policies and decisions provides a degree of protection and security from arbitrary action on the part of managers, but also helps to establish a more legitimate normative order. Dunlop calls this the 'human rights aspect of the workplace'.

- The economic regulation of employment

  This is concerned with what and how people are paid, the benefits they enjoy, their hours of work, and the terms of the wage-work bargain. This aspect of trade union activity is much more a reflection of the resource status of employees, the economic value they generate through using their physical and intellectual capital, and what they can expect in return from managers as rewards for their wealth-creating contributions.

## Union recognition

There is no obligation for employers to negotiate with a union. If no voluntary recognition agreement is in place, however, a union can apply for recognition to the Central Arbitration Committee (CAC) if it can show that it has at least 10 per cent membership among the group it wishes to represent and if it can secure a vote in favour of recognition from at least 40 per cent of the workers in that group. While recognition is usually expressed in some form of written agreement, it may be implied by the common practices undertaken by the organization.

It should be noted that the subject of unions, and the extent of their rights and immunities, has swung in different directions throughout recent history, depending on the government in power at the time. As a generalization, however, it might be argued that, since the curbing of trade union power during the years of the Thatcher government in the 1980s, subsequent legislative changes have concentrated on protecting the rights of individual workers and union members rather than on restoring the collective rights and power of trade unions.

**STUDENT ACTIVITY 5.4 Analysing changes in trade union membership**

There are a number of questions and issues that might be the basis of researching into changes in membership, but finding answers to the following questions will generate important insights into unionization.

1. Nationally, what are the current patterns of trade unionism and how have density levels changed from those of 25 years ago?
2. What explanations can be offered for changes in unionization and density levels?
3. What is the union situation in the private sector compared to the public sector?
4. Why do unions have such a limited presence and influence in the private sector?
5. Identify one union that you consider to be particularly successful and explain what the reasons for its success are.

(See Grainger (2006) for help in completing this exercise.)

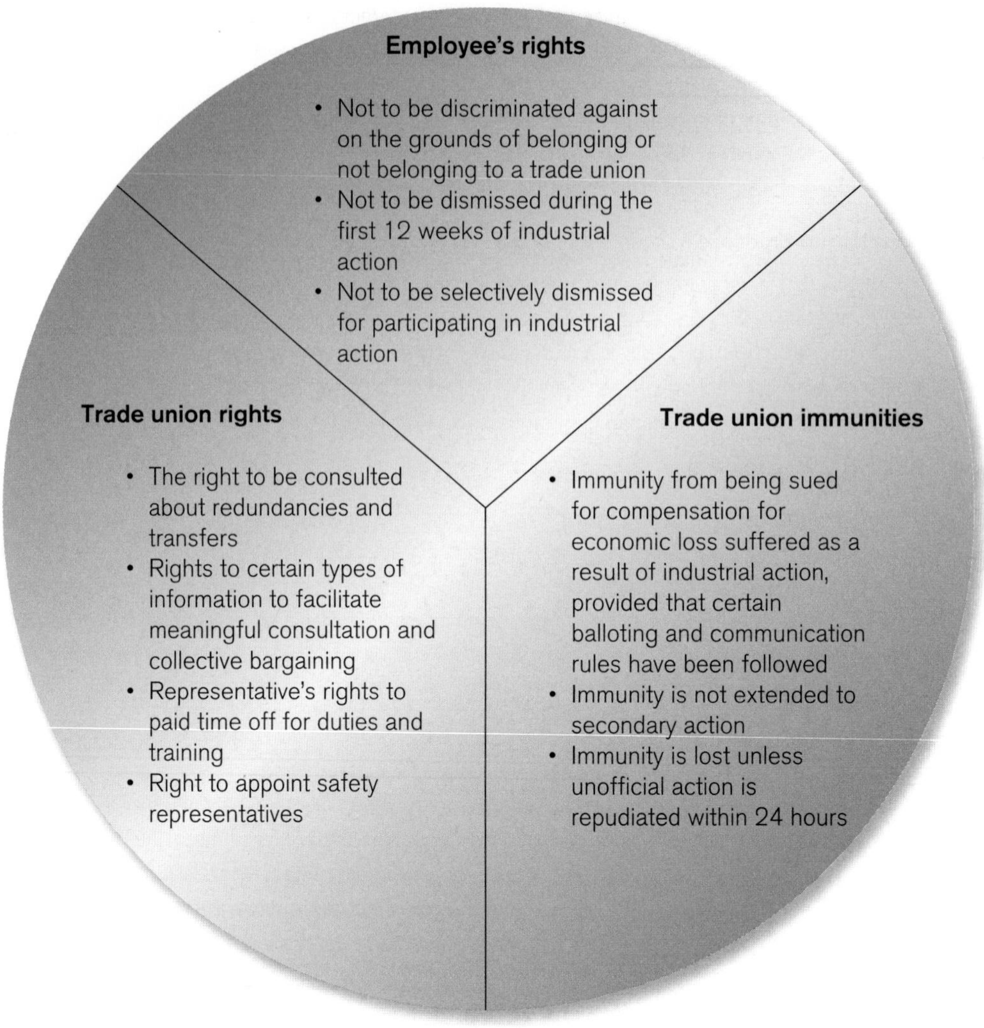

**Employee's rights**

- Not to be discriminated against on the grounds of belonging or not belonging to a trade union
- Not to be dismissed during the first 12 weeks of industrial action
- Not to be selectively dismissed for participating in industrial action

**Trade union rights**

- The right to be consulted about redundancies and transfers
- Rights to certain types of information to facilitate meaningful consultation and collective bargaining
- Representative's rights to paid time off for duties and training
- Right to appoint safety representatives

**Trade union immunities**

- Immunity from being sued for compensation for economic loss suffered as a result of industrial action, provided that certain balloting and communication rules have been followed
- Immunity is not extended to secondary action
- Immunity is lost unless unofficial action is repudiated within 24 hours

**Figure 5.2** Individual rights and trade union immunities

## Rights, obligations, and immunities of trade unions, members, and representatives

Within the law, employees have individual rights, such as the right against discrimination on the grounds of being a union member, and the trade union also has certain rights, obligations, and immunities from certain kinds of legal action, such as not being sued by employers in certain circumstances under which the union is representing its employees. These rights, obligations, and immunities are summarized in Figure 5.2.

## The contemporary role of trade unions

Like many organizations, trade unions have had to adjust to a rapid change in the arena of employee relations over the last 30 years. As earlier noted, unions were originally formed to provide a collective voice to assert and defend employee rights; today's trade unions have been forced to find an alternative role because successive governments have introduced legislation to regulate employees' treatment, terms and conditions of employment, benefits, and individual rights. In many instances, trade unions have struggled to come to terms with their changing environment and loss of influence, particularly with governments. The traditional and more confrontational approach, associated with the radical perspective, is unattractive to current and potential members who, in today's buoyant and more transitory employment market, can find alternative employment. Many have become less dependent on the unions and/or have been alienated by their ideologies.

If a collective agreement on pay and conditions is in place, union members and non-union members alike benefit from the pay deals negotiated. With the rise in 'no win, no fee' offers of legal assistance from certain firms of solicitors, the legal service offered by unions is less of a concern and many employees may choose not to pay a union subscription even if collective agreements are in place. Unions have, therefore, had to find alternative ways to attract members and have also been faced with the need to control costs, lose jobs, and reduce the burden of administrative expenses in much the same way as have many other organizations. In many ways, they have had to become more sensitive and aware of what their members or prospective members actually want, and become more 'business-like' in the way in which they operate.

Unions do, however, continue to play an important and influential role in many organizations and it is important that, if such a relationship exists, employers are careful to manage it in a constructive manner. Managed well, the relationship can promote useful dialogue, and can contribute towards effective decision-making and a positive working climate. If the relationship is managed poorly, then the results can be, at best, disruptive; at worst, if there is feeling of mistrust, there can be constant friction and outbreaks of conflict, and the consequences to both interest groups can be damaging.

More recent research by Blanden et al. (2006) suggests that the extent of the decline in union recognition has slowed since changes to recognition legislation introduced by the Labour government in 1999, with a significant increase in new union recognition being noted compared to a slight fall in the frequency of union de-recognition since 1997. This research does not suggest a reversal in the trends on union recognition but does find some evidence that the speed of the decline is perhaps slowing.





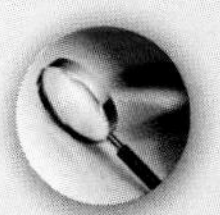

**RESEARCH INSIGHT 5.3**

To take your learning further you might want to read this article:

**Machin, S. (2000) 'Union decline in Britain', *British Journal of Industrial Relations*, 38:4, December, pp. 631–45.**

This paper examines the decline in trade union membership since the 1970s to examine the reasons why it has occurred. The article identifies that the main factor is not withdrawal of union recognition by the failure of trade unions to establish recognition in newly formed businesses set up in the 1980s and 1990s. It also identifies that negative association with unionization is linked to the age of the workplace rather than the age of the workers and that the negative association with unionization is found in workers of all ages in organizations set up after 1980.

**HRM INSIGHT 5.2 BA Cabin Crew**

In December 2009 the High Court blocked 12 day strike action by British Airways cabin crew, ruling that the planned action was illegal, due to balloting errors despite the fact that 92 per cent of those balloted were in favour of the proposed action. The dispute was triggered by BA introducing changes to working practices resulting in potential reductions in the number of cabin crew required during flights. The ruling was the result of members being balloted who had applied for voluntary redundancy and resulted in flight schedules being maintained over the busy Christmas period. However further ballots were held later in the year and staff subsequently took part in repeated periods of strike action throughout spring and summer in 2010 costing the airline estimated figures running in the hundreds of millions. The financial damage to BA could not have come at a worse time and coincided with further losses resulting from flights being cancelled due to the Icelandic volcano ash over European air space.

### Questions

1. What legal considerations would have come into play for BA and the UNITE trade union representing the strikers in this example?
2. What practical use was the protection offered by this legislation to BA staff?
3. What options might BA have considered to avoid the strike action?
4. What damage might this action have caused to the future security of BA and its employees compared with what staff might have gained as a result of the action taken?

More information on this dispute is available online at www.unitetheunion.co.uk, at www.guardian.co.uk (17 December 2009, 12 March 2010, 10 May 2010, and 9 June 2010) and at www.bbc.co.uk (17 December 2009, 12 March, and10 May 2010).

Links to these articles are provided on the Online Resource Centre accompanying this textbook.

## Why do employees join a trade union?



We have already considered the general reasons why employees join trade unions, but from the perspective of managers who are developing their strategy towards trade unions, a more detailed consideration of their motives is necessary. Historically, the reasons have often been negative, resulting from poor industrial relations and less favourable terms and conditions, leading to employees needing to feel supported by the strength of being part of a trade union. Changes in legislation and the employment market, together with increased awareness among employers of the need to engage their employees and to reward individual contribution, may have contributed to a decline in union membership over recent years.

Unions have, therefore, had to offer a wide range of benefits, and also appeal to a wide audience, in order to find members and hence maintain their funding through membership fees. In many cases, unions have merged to save costs and to offer better services.

Table 5.2 outlines some of the reasons why employees may choose to join a trade union. It is important for employers who maintain a non-union environment, or move to derecognize unions, to understand these reasons and, in so doing, avoid challenges to their non-union status quo.

**Table 5.2** Reasons why employees join trade unions

| Positive reasons for joining a trade union | Negative reasons for joining a trade union |
|---|---|
| Legal support | Peer pressure |
| Representation in formal meetings | Political persuasion |
| Credit union availability | Perceived lack of security |
| Cheap deals on insurance and other similar benefits | Lack of trust in employer |
| To benefit from union communications | To be able to participate in industrial action |
| Negotiating pay deals | To have support in expressing dissatisfaction |
| A shared identity and expression of common interest | High membership density |

**STUDENT ACTIVITY 5.5**

This activity comprises two parts (the first comprising questions 1 and 2; the second, question 3) and either one part, or both, can be undertaken. Given the potential research and scope involved, this is better as a collaborative activity, but can be undertaken on an individual basis.

1. Interviewing a number of different people in employment among your contacts, friends, and family, establish whether or not they are members of a trade union and the reasons for which they have chosen to join or not to join. Match these to the lists in Table 5.2 to establish the most common reasons for joining trade unions, adding any additional reasons that emerge. Put the reasons in an order that expresses their importance.
2. If people are trade union members, ask them what benefits they enjoy from union membership. Match these to information available on the union websites to establish how popular and widely known the benefits offered are.
3. Interview employers, or use a questionnaire, to establish why employers do, or do not, recognize and negotiate with trade unions. Establish what benefits those employers that do work with unions gain from such a relationship.

## Collective bargaining

An employer can recognize unions at a number of levels. We will see in Chapter 6 that all employees have the right to be accompanied by a union representative of their choice in formal disciplinary meetings; this may be expressed in the form of a recognition agreement with a particular union.

Signpost to Chapter 6: Managing Discipline and Grievance, for further information on disciplinary and grievance meetings

Employers can also recognize a union as the party with which they will consult about information affecting the organization and about issues such as redundancies, transfer of legal ownership, and changes to pension provisions, for example.

Some employers also recognize one, or more, unions for the purposes of representing the interests of members in collective bargaining arrangements. The distinction between consultation and bargaining is important and, from a managerial viewpoint, should not be confused. Trade unions will always tend to prefer to bargain, rather than be consulted, because 'bargaining' implies that any important decision has yet to be made, and is subject to trade union influence and, where appropriate, pressure and sanctions. 'Consultation', on the other hand, implies that management retains the final right to make the decision, but wishes to keep representatives informed of its intentions and is prepared to listen to what they have to say.

Signpost to Chapter 15: Case Study: The Role of HR in Closing a Factory, for an example of consultation over a factory closure

When a union is recognized for bargaining purposes, it has certain rights, which were summarized in Figure 5.2. The information that should be disclosed is covered by the Trade Union Relations (Consolidation) Act 1992 and includes information about the company's business, information relating to the categories of workers covered by the recognition agreement, and broader categories of information, such as information which, were it not disclosed, would impede the union ability to negotiate, and which it is good industrial relations practice to disclose. There are also exclusions if it might, for example, be damaging to the company to disclose the information. A union can make complaints for failure to disclose information to the Central Arbitration Committee (see www.cac.gov.uk).

Negotiating committees may consist of a number of union representatives, including company shop stewards and full-time regional officials employed by the union. For negotiation purposes, two or more unions may also form a joint negotiating committee. Negotiation may take place at different levels, from local negotiations covering a group of workers at one or more sites, to national-level negotiations, if there is a national agreement in place. Employers may be members of employers' associations and, should the need arise, may draw upon the advice and expertise of experienced management negotiators. There may also be scope to establish a second tier of negotiation, usually involving either more senior levels within the unions or management, or involving external bodies, in an attempt to resolve negotiations should the original negotiating committee fail to reach agreement.

Collective bargaining has four dimensions over which each party has an interest in influencing.

- Scope: This relates to the range of issues that are subject to joint regulation.
- Form: This explains whether the bargaining is formal or informal.
- Level: This relates to whether the bargaining is at company or national level.
- Unit: This relates to the bargaining unit, which identifies the group of employees covered by the resulting collective agreement. The unit can change, depending on what is being negotiated.

**HRM INSIGHT 5.3 Goldsmith's Pies**

Goldsmith's Pies employs around 800 people, manufacturing pies and ready meals for the retail sector. The 650 hourly-paid employees fall into two distinct groups for collective bargaining purposes. The food manufacturing team are represented by the FBCU. The maintenance team of 25 mechanical and electrical craft employees, who are responsible for maintaining and repairing all of the food processing equipment, are represented by Fidelity, predominantly an engineering union.

Earlier in the year, the FBCU negotiated a pay increase of 3.5 per cent for the manufacturing employees and this was accepted by ballot. The maintenance team negotiations are more problematic. This group feels that it is underpaid. The workers are particularly unhappy with the management team's suggestion that they should become multi-skilled (electricians learning mechanical skills and vice versa) to bring about productivity savings that will fund pay increases. They have also taken exception to new working practices, which include all employees being required to wear wellingtons in production areas and a move away from hairnets and cloth caps to disposable 'mop cap'-style headwear to reduce the risk of hair contamination in the products.

The local representatives of Fidelity have refused to recommend the offer of 3.5 per cent and, as a result, members have rejected this in a show of hands. The management team does not wish to offend the majority of its employees in manufacturing by offering bigger increases to one group compared to another.

**Questions**

1. What options might Goldsmith's Pies have to resolve this dispute?
2. What might be the potential consequences of industrial action?
3. What recommendations would you make to try and move discussions forward?
4. What recommendations would you make to avoid this type of dispute arising in future?

## Industrial action

Industrial action can have a damaging effect on an employer and its customers. It is the ultimate expression of force that a group of workers can inflict upon managers in an attempt to coerce management to agree to workers' demands. Equally, industrial action can have a negative effect on employees through loss of earnings, conflict between employers reflecting differences in the level of support for industrial action, and the possibility that prolonged action will result in job losses.

In organizing industrial action, a union is encouraging its members to break their contractual obligation to attend work and hence, in turn, cause the organization to break its contractual obligation to customers, clients, and suppliers. On the face of it, such actions are unlawful and, were it not for the immunities granted to unions in such circumstances, they would be sued for compensation for the economic loss that results from these actions. Interestingly, individual employees have no such protection and are reliant in the avoidance of claims on the fact that it would be difficult to prove the economic loss attributable to each individual.

### *Procedures required to secure immunity*

In order to secure immunity from being sued for damages (known as 'tort'), there are a number of conditions that the union must meet, which include:

- the action must be taken 'in contemplation or furtherance of a trade dispute';
- the union must conduct a secret postal ballot under strict conditions, involving every member who may be involved in the action;
- there are specific requirements about notifying the employer of the ballot, providing the employer with copies of the ballot paper, and with the numbers and categories of employee to be balloted;
- the ballot paper should state if the union is calling for either strike action or action short of a strike;
- specific conditions must be met with regard to calling action and notifying the employer of action to be taken.

(Further details of requirements can be found online at www.acas.org.uk. A link to this information is provided on the Online Resource Centre accompanying this textbook.)

### *Types of industrial action*

- Strike action

  A 'strike' is a temporary withdrawal of labour. This might involve a complete stoppage of work over a number of days or a series of shorter strikes of perhaps a day, or even a number of hours, at a time. Some strikes have lasted months and even years!

  Strikes are often accompanied by a number of employees 'picketing', that is, standing at the entrance to 'encourage' other employees, customers, and suppliers not to enter the premises or to cross the picket line.

- Action short of a strike

  Most types of action short of a strike still consist of a breach of contract. Examples include a 'go-slow', under which employees refuse to carry out a specific task, and 'blacking', under which trade union members refuse to work with another employee. Types of action that do not necessarily consist of a breach of contract include a 'work to rule', under which employees do the bare minimum to meet their contractual obligations or an 'overtime ban', under which employees withdraw from voluntary overtime.

- Unofficial industrial action

  If action is taken by members, or is called by a union representative, and does not follow the strict conditions for balloting for industrial action referred to above, then the union must repudiate or disown it within 24 hours to maintain its immunity. This involves the principal executive committee, president, or general secretary of the union writing to withdraw support from the union representatives who called the action and all those involved in the action. Writing to all of these participants deems the action to be unofficial and warns them that there is no protection from unfair dismissal, providing that *all* of those participating in the action are dismissed.

## Strategies for Improving Poor Industrial Relations

- Be clear on the rules and the distinction between normal working duties and union duties.
- Train, coach, and support the union representatives and line managers.
- Communicate directly with employees, as well as with union representatives, to prevent messages being distorted.
- Listen to employee concerns and rectify these wherever possible before the union representatives get involved.
- Apply the same consistent rules to union representatives as to all employees.
- Invite union representatives and managers to participate in joint training.
- Enlist help and support, and encourage senior dialogue with full-time union staff.
- Offer additional observer and participant places at consultation and negotiation meetings to other managers and representatives of non-union members to remove the mystery of such meetings.
- Take responsibility for the negotiations: managerial representatives should be given the authority to act, not be only a messenger.
- Brief managers and staff promptly, and publish minutes and notes following all collective meetings.
- Be consistent and clear.
- Ensure that all first-line managers are well trained to make appropriate decisions to avoid the need for an overruling decision to be made.
- Establish clear scope and objectives, along with joint commitment to outcomes of meetings, before commencing consultation or negotiation.



The Practitioner Insight gives a view from a professional about what constitutes effective employee relations. Table 5.3 shows characteristics of good and of poor industrial relations.

**PRACTITIONER INSIGHT Dan Goulding, former employee of an international motor manufacturer in the UK; currently occupies a senior HR role in the hospitality and leisure sector**

The role that Employee Relations (ER) plays within an organization has evolved during the past decade. As an HR professional working within Employee Relations you are there to deliver the requirements of the Company whilst ensuring employees are treated with fairness. This often means that a consistent approach needs to be applied to what people are paid and how they are treated.

When I first moved into HR I found it was essential to listen to my customers, understand what their requirements were and to try to accommodate these requirements within the wider HR framework. I have continued to develop and build relationships with my customers during my career and it is vital as an HR professional to devote time and effort to building trust and relationships with those who depend on you and need your advice and support.

To enhance the customer relationship it is vital as a HR professional that you ensure your customers are trained in ER if you want them to deliver the HR agenda, as by improving their competence and confidence in this area they will be better equipped to work with you. This relates particularly to line managers who need to be informed and aware of what the organization's key ER policies are and are able to buy into these.

ER can take two forms within an organization; it can be seen as the internal police within the organization that ensures compliance with policies and procedures or it can work in partnership with the internal customers of the organization to deliver its HR agenda. Working in partnership ensures that relationships are built which will allow the HR professional to influence other stakeholders and through this increase the chances of successfully delivering the HR agenda.

The ER framework within which an organization operates will be shaped by the legislation and the policies and procedures which are applied. It is essential as an HR professional that you are aware of these and also of any future legislation which will impact upon this area.

During my time in manufacturing I had good relations with the unions and found that it is possible to work in partnership together for the benefit of the company and union members. When this relationship has been strained, particularly around pay reviews, it has sometimes resulted in industrial action by union members which was detrimental not only to the company but to those involved in the industrial action. This is because even if the company accedes to union wage demands in order to avoid prolonging the action, the need to restrict increases in the overall wage bill is often associated with a reduced headcount and loss of employment.

When dealing with individual cases involving disciplinary action, it is essential to undertake proper preparation and collect and retain supporting documentation. My experiences have shown when this is not followed then management are exposed to claims of unfair or unreasonable conduct and any subsequent Employment Tribunals cases become more difficult to defend.

ER in the future will continue to be governed by legislation and by a company's own policies and procedures. Those working in this field of HR have an important opportunity and responsibility to work in partnership with other organizational stakeholders in such a way as to deliver the organization's HR strategy, which ultimately contributes to the bottom line.



**Table 5.3** Characteristics of good and poor industrial relations

| Good industrial relations | Poor industrial relations |
|---|---|
| Regular opportunities for dialogue between parties | Each party critical of the other |
| Accessibility to appropriate levels between both parties | Adversarial relationship between parties |
| Helpful, impartial, and realistic union support for employee in disputes and disciplinary matters | Unquestioning support of union for all employees in all disputes |
| Understanding of each party's role | Lack of union understanding of organizational objectives |
| Practical and realistic approaches | |
| Short, effective, and realistic bargaining | Little appreciation among union representatives of potential consequences of poor organizational performance |
| Open-minded parties | |
| Readiness of each party to back down and change direction | Lack of trust between parties |
| Well-defined and clear mechanisms for allowing and managing distinct time off for union duties | Unions encourage negativity towards organization to build their own power base |
| | Drawn-out, unrealistic bargaining |
| | Union representatives see union job as main role and union duties interfere with main job purpose |
| Organization takes responsibility for joint training and coaching of managers and representatives involved in the relationship | Over-reliance of organization on union to train representatives and lack of involvement of managers in training |
| Rapid resolution of issues at lowest possible level prior to union and senior management involvement | Over-reliance of organization on union and senior managers or HR to resolve disputes |

**HRM INSIGHT 5.4 The Case of Southlands Hospital**

Southlands Hospital Trust employs a wide variety of different employees. The ancillary hospital staff has a 39-hour working week, compared to a 37-hour working week for nursing and professional staff. Over the last three years, the union, as part of the collective negotiating process, requested a reduction in the working week of ancillary staff from 39 hours to 37 hours, to match those in professional positions, with no loss in overall weekly pay.

Negotiations for this group have previously involved local branch union leaders meeting with senior managers. The series of meetings has lasted several months and, if this has gone beyond the normal settlement due date, increases have been backdated. The hospital trust has resisted this claim in previous years by stating that, in years of low inflation, it is hard to find a way to accommodate this change without the organization incurring significant additional employment costs.

This year, the union supporting the ancillary workers has made it clear that this unfair term must finally be addressed and that, while it does not wish to pursue industrial action, it may have no alternative given the strength of feeling about this disparity among its members.

Questions

1. What mistakes have potentially been made in previous years' negotiations?
2. What options might be available to the Hospital Trust to help to resolve this disagreement?
3. What strategies might be employed over the course of the negotiations to resolve this issue?
4. What recommendations might you make to improve future negotiations?



# Employee Relations in Non-Unionized Environments

Maintaining effective employee relations in a non unionized environment is just as important as in a unionized environment. Many successful organizations both long-established ones such as Marks and Spencer and more newly informed companies such as Microsoft and Google have effective strategies in place to enable them to foster and maintain good relationships with their employees without the intervention and representation offered by trade union recognition. The models they have adopted, such as the use of staff associations at Marks and Spencer to provide effective mechanisms for consulting with their staff, have helped them to communicate effectively with their workforce whilst ensuring that the views of employees are sought regarding issues affecting the organization. The importance of employees having a shared consultation forum is regarded as very high in Europe and has resulted in legislation to ensure that this is a right shared by all employees in any organization employing even relatively small numbers of people.

## Information and consultation

Directive 2002/14/EC of the European Parliament and of the Council of 11 March 2002 establishing a general framework for informing and consulting employees in the European Community was implemented in the UK in the form of the Information and Consultation of Employees Regulations 2004 (ICE). The Regulations, which came into force in 2005, introduced a requirement for businesses to inform and consult with their employees. Introduction was phased to allow smaller businesses time to prepare for the requirements and the Regulations apply to all businesses employing more than 50 people.

The Regulations give employees the right to be:

- informed about the business' economic situation;
- informed and consulted about employment prospects;

- informed and consulted about decisions likely to lead to substantial changes in work organization or contractual relations, including redundancies and transfers.

Perhaps the easiest way to meet these obligations is through an existing communications forum, established under either a union recognition agreement or an agreement with, for example, representatives of an existing staff committee. These arrangements must meet the requirements set out in the Regulations, but there can be provisions to ensure that confidential information is protected and that any disclosure does not harm the business.

If no such agreement exists, the concern for managers might be that consultation, defined as 'the exchange of views and establishment of dialogue' between the employer and employees or employee representatives, may include pay and conditions if these have previously been determined without reference to the workforce. Unless companies in this position take the initiative to set up a voluntary agreement, there is a risk that employees will apply to the Central Arbitration Committee (CAC) to force the company to engage in an extended dialogue.

## Consultation in pan-European countries

If businesses operate in more than one European country, there are similar provisions covering the requirement to establish a 'European works council'. These provisions are aimed at larger employers, with over 1,000 employees and 150 employees in each of at least two different European countries. The regulations are complex and the implications are potentially extremely costly, given certain requirements to provide translation facilities at meetings. For more details on works councils, see ACAS' 2004 document, *Employee Communications and Consultation*.



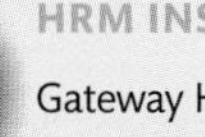

### HRM INSIGHT 5.5 Gateway Haulage

Gateway Haulage is a well-established and successful haulage firm, employing over 250 employees in the UK and with a number of distribution and transport contracts throughout the UK. Following its success, it is about to acquire another UK-based haulage business, which also employs 80 people, 20 of which are based at a depot in Holland.

Neither business has any formal union recognition agreement, nor do they have any arrangements in place covering consultation with employees. To date, each has relied on informal meetings held by managers with staff, on an ad hoc basis, to communicate with employees.

#### Questions

1. What is the risk to Gateway of not having a consultation agreement in place?
2. How does this risk change with the acquisition of the new business?
3. What recommendations would you make for consultation arrangements for Gateway Haulage?

### STUDENT ACTIVITY 5.6 What activities can employers use to foster and maintain good employee relations?

Consider the personal experiences of people within your group and their family and friends in terms of what has contributed towards both positive and negative views of the employee relations in the workplace. What approaches to employment practices and employee communication have been adopted to try and foster good employee relations? Combine this research with information given about the most recent *Sunday Times* Best 100 Companies to Work For (available online at www.timesonline.co.uk) and use your research to develop a set of guidelines for organizations to help them maintain good employee relations.

## The psychological contract

We began this chapter by explaining the importance of trust between employees and managers, and how the quality of relations between them impacted on other aspects of human resource management. Reference was also made to the importance of the informal dimension of employment—an idea that captures the day-to-day interaction between people who have to work together to produce goods and services. Both of these aspects of what can be described as the 'human', as opposed to the 'institutional', aspect of employment relations are expressed in the concept of the 'psychological contract' (Hiltrop, 1996).

The psychological contract refers to the obligations that an employer and an employee, or group of employees, perceive to exist between each other as part of the employment relationship, and consists of both expectations of each other and promises made to each other. Rousseau (1995) captured the relationship between the psychological contract, trust and performance when she wrote:

> **When two people working interdependently, such as a worker and a supervisor, agree on the terms of the contract, performance should be satisfactory from both parties' perspectives. As individuals work through their understandings of each other's commitments over time, a degree of mutual predictability becomes possible: 'I know what you want from me and I know what I want from you.' Commitments understood on both sides may be based on communication, customs and past practices. Regardless of how it is achieved, mutual predictability is a powerful factor in coordinating effort and planning.**

Arguably, the psychological contract is more important as a determinant of behaviour than is the formal contract because of the way it connects to employees' everyday experiences of work and of being managed. Indeed, as the frequency and intensity of strikes and other forms of formal, collective industrial action have diminished, perceived managerial violations of the psychological contract may explain the continued persistence of dissatisfaction and conflict, which is increasingly expressed at the individual and informal level.

The references made in Chapter 2 to the rise in the frequency of stress-related illness and absenteeism, high turnover rates, and the withholding of discretionary effort may suggest that conflict has not necessarily been removed from the system but has become expressed in different forms. Moreover, it seems now to be expressed in ways that do not fit easily with the formal and collective mechanisms of conflict resolution that are associated with the 'old' industrial relations.

The extent to which an employee feels 'engaged' with their employer and therefore feels duty bound, morally obliged, or genuinely motivated to do all that is within their capability to contribute towards an organization's success is heavily influenced by the psychological contract. Put simply, the psychological contract affects what an employee is willing to do, based upon the belief that over the long term the individual and group will be treated fairly by their manager(s) and be rewarded for their performance and contribution, but not necessarily on a day-to-day basis.

Signpost to Chapters 11 and 12: Managing Performance and Managing Rewards, for further insight into enhancing employee performance and linking this to reward

Good managers, perhaps instinctively, develop psychological contracts that result in high performance from those that report to them, from the first interaction during recruitment, through to all aspects of employment. Ensuring that high expectations are clearly understood and accepted by all employees, and are rewarded with promises about involvement, development, and recognition, is the key to utilizing the psychological contract effectively to the organization's advantage. This is perhaps easier to achieve in smaller, more flexible, organizations because managers and employees are more closely engaged in 'production', but the principle applies generally. Organizations that experience low morale, frequent complaints from employees, and a general lethargy may well be those within which the psychological contract may be perceived to have been broken by either party, with neither even aware that it has happened!

**Table 5.4** Employer/employee characteristics under positive and 'broken' psychological contracts

| Party to contract | Positive psychological contract | Broken psychological contract |
|---|---|---|
| *Employer* | Is supportive | Offers only subjective evaluation |
| | Encourages two-way communication | Pays lip service to employees' views |
| | | Engages only in pseudo-consultation |
| | Is consistent | Is single-minded |
| | Is fair | Reneges on commitments |
| | Sets clear standards | Is lacking in trust |
| | Keeps to commitments | Decision-making is controlled at senior level |
| | Offers objective evaluation of performance | Actions are motivated by need for personal approval and acceptance rather than team success |
| | Engages in meaningful dialogue | |
| | Offers a high level of empowerment and engagement | Feels threatened |
| *Employee* | Has strong sense of obligation | Questions job security |
| | Is trustworthy and honest | Lacks loyalty |
| | Makes maximum use of working time | Has low expectations |
| | Is reliable | Considers that appearances are more important than delivery of performance |
| | Is loyal | |
| | Is open-minded | |
| | Feels secure | |
| | Is confident | |
| | Has high expectations | |

Research from the CIPD (2005) shows that, while the majority of workers report major organizational change taking place where they work, they are not necessarily hostile to change, unless it is a major change resulting in redundancy. What does cause problems is management's failure to engage in meaningful communication and consultation, and to listen to what employees are saying. Worryingly for the general state of employment relations, the CIPD also found that employee trust in organizations is declining and that most people feel their organization is badly managed, which can be interpreted as a way of expressing dissatisfaction with the way employees are treated. Table 5.4 shows characteristics of employer and employees under positive and 'broken' psychological contracts.

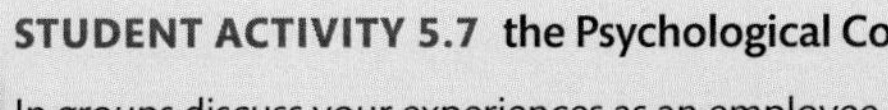

**STUDENT ACTIVITY 5.7 the Psychological Contract**

In groups discuss your experiences as an employee in both positive and negative scenarios.

1. What did group members consider to be their obligations under the psychological contracts where employment experiences were positive?
2. What expectations and behaviours were driven by negative experiences and why?
3. What is the impact upon the organization where perceived expectations and promises are not met?
4. What is the impact of a strong psychological contract in a positive constructive employment relationship and how can employers foster this within their organization?

# Summary

- What originally was known as 'industrial relations' reflected an era in which 'old industries', the collective institutions of employers and workers, and the management of industrial conflict were the dominant features. This 'area' of human resource management has, for some but not all, changed in important ways. Firstly, the tendency to talk about 'employment' rather than 'industrial relations' represents a broadening of the subject to include all employment contexts, irrespective of whether these involve the collective representation of workers or not.
- The change in emphasis represented by the renaming of the field meant that unionization and collective relations were no longer assumed to be the norm or the starting point, particularly for HR professionals and line managers. Nor was conflict seen as inevitable and, as new management practices were introduced by Japanese and other overseas companies, a different mindset and approach to relations between managers and employees began to emerge, based much more on a unitary perspective and cooperative attitudes.
- The notion of 'employee relations' takes this evolutionary trend even further, because of the emphasis this term gives to the primacy of individual over collective relations. This is consistent with the idea that the employment contract and the psychological contract are both important in understanding the dynamic behaviour of relations and relationships at work.
- In organizations where trade unions are recognized the terms and conditions of employment and the employment relationship are largely governed by agreements between the trade union and the employer. However, the extent of union recognition and union membership is declining. Many employment rights that were originally established through collective negotiation have been incorporated in to legislation and the extent of the role of trade unions is perhaps therefore seen as less important than it has been viewed in the past.
- European legislation has been a key factor in establishing obligations upon employers to consult with their workforce, whether or not there is a recognized union in place.
- In more recent years the emphasis on an employer in honouring the psychological contract that exists between an employer and its employees has grown in importance and is now recognized as a key element in maintaining positive employee relations.

**Visit the Online Resource Centre that accompanies this book for self-test questions, weblinks, and more information on the topics covered in this chapter.**
**www.oxfordtextbooks.co.uk/orc/banfield_kay2e/**

## REVIEW QUESTIONS

1. Are the causes of industrial conflict post-2000 similar or different to those of conflict in the 1970s and 1980s?
2. What are likely to be the most important consequences for the management of people of an increasing emphasis on the individualization of employment relations?
3. In the absence of trade unions and collective bargaining, what can employers do to ensure that their workers have the ability to communicate with and influence management?
4. What are the essential differences between a 'formal' and an 'informal' approach to employment relations?
5. How are organizations that are non unionized best advised to approach employee relations and consultation?

***See Online Resource Centre for answers.***

## CASE STUDY

### The claim for union representation

William Beckett Plastics is a small plastics manufacturing business based in Sheffield. It employs 50 people, the majority of whom are shop-floor operatives. The managing director, William Beckett, bought the company 20 years ago and has built it into a £3 million business that sells plastic components in over 30 countries. It has never been unionized, and relations between management and employees have always been fairly informal and amicable.

The MD's main contribution to the business was in the development of its business and marketing strategy, and he was heavily involved in expanding its national and international markets. While he maintained strategic control of the business, operational responsibility was in the hands of the production director and production manager, who were in day-to-day control of production and the two shifts of operatives that constituted 35 out of a total of 55 employees.

Unexpectedly, in 2000, William Beckett received a letter from the Transport and General Workers' Union (TGWU), seeking recognition and representational rights on behalf of the company's production operatives. He was initially surprised at the request—he had no idea that there had been discussions among his employees about union representation. Overcoming this, he remained unconvinced that there was sufficient overall support within the employee group for a change from the existing informal and direct model of employee relations, based upon management taking decisions on pay, benefits, and other employment matters in the best interests of the company. He decided, therefore, to write to each employee, reminding them of the benefits they had enjoyed in working for a company that, in his opinion, had treated them fairly and with consideration. At the same time, he wrote to the TGWU expressing the view that he did not believe their claim enjoyed sufficient support to be accepted.



In response, the union sought advice from ACAS and made an application to the Central Arbitration Committee (CAC) for union recognition. After passing the initial CAC test of acceptability, the union was given 20 days to agree on the representational and collective bargaining unit it wished to base its claim on. Believing that, at best, the union had the support of a handful of shop-floor operatives, the MD decided, with the assistance of the Electoral Reform Society, to ballot all 55 employees—a figure that included 34 operatives. He felt that any decision he might take needed to be based on a clear understanding of what all of his staff wanted, not only a small minority of them.

Almost all of the administrative staff voted for the status quo. Of the 34 shop-floor operatives, 24 returned valid ballot papers, of which ten represented a vote for union representation, two for a system of non-union employee representatives, and 12 for the status quo. As a result of the ballot, the union was disinclined to pursue the matter further, feeling that it had insufficient support from a bargaining unit based on all employees.

On reflection, the MD realized that there must have been something wrong for a significant number of shop-floor workers to feel that they needed independent union representation. After discussing the matter with his senior management colleagues, they all agreed that management had become complacent about the shop floor and had effectively become psychologically disengaged from the workers, even though it was in day-to-day contact with them. To avoid a similar situation occurring in the future, management had to make changes to the way in which employment relations were handled.

#### Questions

1. What procedures and criteria does the CAC apply in deciding on whether a union claim for recognition and representation rights succeeds?
2. What had management failed to do that resulted in the claim for representation being made and why had this happened?
3. What options were available to the MD in changing the way in which relations with his employees were managed?
4. As the MD, what would you have done and why?

**Insights & Outcomes: visit the Online Resource Centre at www.oxfordtextbooks.co.uk/orc/banfield_kay2e/ for an account of the developments that followed the final ballot.**

## FURTHER READING

Brown, W. et al. (1998) *The Individualisation of the Employment Contract in Britain*, Department of Trade and Industry/HMSO.

Fabr, H. and Western, B. (2001) 'Accounting for the decline in unions in the private sector 1973–98', *Journal of Labour Research*, **22**:3, Summer, pp. 459–86.

Hyman, R. (1984) *Strikes*, Fontana Press.

Millward, N., Forth, J. and Bryson, A. (2000) *All Change at Work? British Employment Relations 1980–98, as Portrayed by the Workplace Industrial Relations Survey Series*, Routledge.

## REFERENCES



Advisory Conciliation and Arbitration Service (2004) *Employee Communications and Consultation*, www.acas.org.uk.

Blanden, J., Machin, S. and Van Reenen, J.M. (2006) 'Have unions turned the corner? New evidence on recent trends in union recognition in UK firms', *British Journal of Industrial Relations*, **44:** 2, pp. 169–90.

Chartered Institute of Personnel and Development (2005) *Managing Change: The Role of the Psychological Contract*, www.cipd.co.uk.

Clarke T. and Clements, L. (1977) *Trade Unions Under Capitalism*, Fontana.

Department of Trade and Industry (2004) 'Workplace employee relations survey (WERS 2004)', www.bis.gov.uk/policies/employment-matters/research/wers/wers2004.

Dunlop, J. (1958) *Industrial Relations Systems*, Holt and Co.

Flanders, A. (1970) *Management and Unions*, Faber and Faber.

Fox, A. (1966) *Industrial Sociology and Industrial Relations*, Royal Commission Research Paper No. 3, HMSO.

Gouldner, A. (1954) *Wildcat Strike*, Antioch Press.

Grainger, H. (2006) *Trade Union Membership 2005*, Department of Trade and Industry.

Handy, C. (1993) *Understanding Organizations*, 4th ed., Penguin.

Hiltrop, J.M. (1996) 'Managing the changing psychological contract', *Employee Relations*, **18**:1, pp. 36–49.

Hyman, R. (1975) *Industrial Relations: A Marxist Introduction*, Macmillan.

Hyman, R. and Brough, I. (1975) *Social Values and Industrial Relations*, Blackwell.

Ingram, P. and Metcalfe, D. (1991) 'Strike incidence and duration in British manufacturing industry in the 1980s', CEP Discussion Paper.

Kaufman, B.E. (2002) 'Reflections on six decades in industrial relations: An interview with John Dunlop', *Industrial and Labor Relations Review*, **55**:2, pp 324–48.

Macey W. and Scheider B. (2008) 'The meaning of employee engagement', *Society for Industrial and Organizational Psychology*, **1:**1, pp. 3–30.

Machin, S. (2000) 'Union decline in Britain', *British Journal of Industrial Relations*, **38:**4, December, pp. 631–45.

Phillips, J. (2009) 'Workplace conflict and the origins of the 1984–1985 miners' strike in Scotland', *Twentieth Century British History*, **20**:2, pp. 152–173.

Rousseau, D.M. (1995) *Psychological Contracts in Organisations*, Sage Publications.

Salamon, M. (2000) *Industrial Relations: Theory and Practice*, 4th ed., Prentice Hall.

Webb, S. and Webb, B. (1920) *The History of Trade Unionism 1866–1920*, Longman.

# Managing Discipline and Grievance

6

## Key Terms

**Misconduct** Behaviour that transgresses contractual arrangements, work rules, established norms of performance or other standards that can be seen as reasonable and necessary for the effective employment and management of people at work; behaviour that is deemed to be unacceptable by reference to formally established norms.

**Discipline** The formal measures taken, sanctions applied, and outcomes achieved by management in response to perceived acts of misconduct.

**Grievance** The formalization of a claim that one or more persons, either co-workers or management, have acted wrongly towards another person(s) and, as a consequence, inflicted physical or psychological harm on that person, or others. This may involve an act, or acts, of misconduct.

**Mediation** A voluntary process where an independent facilitator assists 2 or more parties to explore options for resolving a dispute, disagreement, or problem situation by attempting to reach a mutually acceptable agreement.

## Learning Objectives

As a result of reading this chapter and using the Online Resource Centre, you should be able to:

- deliver an organization's approach to unacceptable behaviour and misconduct to reflect its wider managerial philosophy and values;
- understand what is meant by, and the role of, discipline and grievance at work;
- apply the law covering employee rights and procedural regulation thoughtfully and with regard to its consequences;
- understand the importance of acting ethically in discipline and grievance management;
- recognize the consequences of failing to manage effectively disciplinary and grievance issues in the workplace;
- develop effective processes for handling grievances at work.

# Introduction

## Context and culture

The management of discipline and grievance features highly on the HR agenda of most UK organizations. While it is difficult to quantify the frequency of cases involving grievance and discipline at work, the growth trend in the number of employment tribunal cases dealing with claims of unfair dismissal suggests that either employers are initiating more disciplinary cases, or that employees are questioning the legitimacy of such action, or both (Employment Tribunals Service, 2009). Further evidence for the growing importance of this aspect of HR can be found in the limited, but high-profile, number of cases of constructive dismissal, in which alleged failure by employers to respond adequately to employee grievances over issues such as harassment, bullying, and sexual discrimination have resulted in damaging and costly claims for compensation. Such cases highlight the danger of ignoring, or failing to investigate, behaviour at work that undermines the contractual, statutory, and human rights of employees.

The fact that employees are becoming increasingly aware of their 'rights' is neither contentious nor surprising. The preparedness of many managerial and professional staff to raise grievances over the way in which they have been treated suggests that organizations, and particularly their HR functions, will need to pay particular attention to this growing tendency and to the reasons for it. In a recent case, a female employee who left the army following disciplinary action after she failed to attend an evening parade due to child care problems and took her claim to an employment tribunal. Despite an attempt to claim over £1 million in damages, she was awarded just £17,010 for 'hurt feelings' as she was told she was not 'pulling her weight'. However the legal costs for the tax payer incurred by the MOD are estimated to have been in the region of £100,000. This demonstrates the need for organizations to manage discipline and grievance cases effectively and that the potential costs of getting it wrong are very significant.

Yet it would be unwise to assume that grievances are restricted to professional-level employees and it would be even more simplistic to assume that acts of misconduct resulting in formal disciplinary action are to be found only within the ranks of shop-floor workers and their equivalent. Of particular significance to our understanding of the challenges that management face in responding to both types of misconduct is the recognition that such problems occur at all levels within the organization and involve professional, white-collar, and manual employees.

Although small in number, some cases of serious misconduct involving financial irregularities and the breaching of important protocols involve top management. In a recent case in the USA, two hedge fund managers for Bear Stearns, who managed a pair of sub-prime laden hedge funds until their $1.4 billion collapse in June 2007 were accused of misleading investors about the health of the funds (*Daily Telegraph*, 11 November 2009). This was a very high-profile case given that this type of activity is widely regarded to have been what led to the credit crunch and subsequent recession recently. Whilst acquitted of criminal charges following a four-week trial, these types of case highlight that the ability of HR to deal effectively with different situations associated with inappropriate behaviour and misconduct are highly relevant at all levels and continue to be tested whatever the economic climate.

Despite the belief that the management of misconduct may become more significant in the years ahead, it would be misleading to suggest that the typical organization experiences more than a handful of cases each year. Factors such as size, sector, and employee characteristics have an influence on the actual number of cases that require resolution. Moreover, the preference by most progressive HR professionals for trying to manage grievances, as far as possible, at the informal level further complicates any meaningful attempt to establish the number of incidents of misconduct that actually occur. Even if such cases are limited in number, responding to them can consume significant amounts of management time and resources, and the more difficult and complex cases often generate intense emotional pressures for those directly involved. This may result in psychological damage to individuals who believe that they have been treated unfairly and without proper regard to the circumstances and explanations that led to the action resulting in disciplinary proceedings.

Organizations that consistently fail to act within defined legal and procedural frameworks, and which show scant regard for any wider ethical considerations, can also acquire damaging reputations as a result of the way in which they treat their staff. This, in turn, can affect their ability to recruit and retain top-quality people. The implications and consequences of 'getting things wrong' or, for reasons only known to those managers directly involved, of acting precipitously and without regard to the consequences can go beyond reputational damage. Collective responses, in the form of strikes and other expressions of industrial conflict, can be triggered by a sense of injustice and disproportionality or changes in what Alvin Gouldner (1954) called 'patterns of indulgency'.

**KEY CONCEPT Indulgency**

This relates to the situation in which managers, either deliberately or by default, allow and condone breaches of works' rules. This is essentially an informal understanding and is often associated with employees 'giving something in return'. Any new managers becoming involved are unlikely to have been party to this understanding and, viewing the behaviour of employees as being in breach of rules procedures, act accordingly. The point is that what is defined as misconduct may not be quite as simple and straightforward as it seems.

**STUDENT ACTIVITY 6.1 Indulgency**

Use Alvin Gouldner's book, *The Wildcat Strike* (1954). This is a classic text and well worth the effort of trying to get hold of a copy. The concept of indulgency is highlighted in Chapter 1 and is linked to the subsequent unofficial strike action.

1. Find out what the term 'indulgency' means in the context of this book and apply it more generally.
2. Consider its significance for alleged employee misconduct and employee behaviour.
3. Establish the relationship between changes in the indulgency pattern and the unofficial strike action.
4. Think of examples from your own experiences of uncertainty over what management has considered to be examples of employee misconduct.

## Failure to respond effectively

The important point is that the consequences of failing to act appropriately in the management of discipline and grievance do matter. Few senior managers will be so cavalier as to disregard these consequences in the lead they offer to those given specific responsibility for this key part of the HR agenda. One of the difficulties faced by HR professionals, however, is that they can never be sure that they are in full control of the situation that they are required to manage. Often, they become involved after an incident, or series of incidents, have already taken place, with initial action having already been taken by line managers. The type of question that a manager may ask, along the lines of 'I've sacked someone: is that ok?', illustrates that HR professionals are often faced with having to recover a situation that may already, by the time they are involved, have become more serious than it needed to be. As will be made clear later, the key challenge facing HR, beyond the procedural management of discipline and grievance, is the ability to influence the actions of other participants, particularly line managers, whose own agendas and interests may take precedence over any wider organizational interests.

While the arbitrary and inconsistent treatment of staff will never be entirely eliminated, there is an increasing awareness among line managers and HR professionals that their organizations need to develop more effective approaches and mechanisms for the management of discipline and grievance. This is not simply because of changing ethical, contractual and legal considerations, but stems from the simple recognition that getting it wrong can result in serious and damaging consequences for all parties. In terms of a discipline and grievance 'mind set' more emphasis should be placed on developing preventative strategies based on a better understanding of the conditions in which certain kinds of behaviours take place, in addition to appropriate and informed responses to such behaviours.

## Choices in the Handling of Discipline

Organizations that might claim to have efficient and well-used disciplinary and grievance procedures may have less reason to feel self-satisfied than organizations that only infrequently need such procedures to be invoked. In the latter type of organization, it is clear that employee behaviour is such that disciplinary and grievance procedures need rarely to be used. It is important, therefore, to distinguish between two very different situations:

- the causes of misconduct and its severity;
- how cases of misconduct are managed.

The position taken here is that the role of HR is not simply about managing the resolution of discipline and grievance cases, but includes investigating and addressing the reasons that contribute to their existence, however difficult and challenging this may be.

As far as acts of employee misconduct are concerned, the following may be relevant factors:



- deficiencies and failings on the part of the individual;
- external pressures and circumstances that have a temporary effect on individual performance and behaviour;
- management style and practices;
- the working environment;
- personal relationships;
- changes in people's employment status and security;
- misunderstandings and genuine mistakes;
- changes in standards, expectations, and social norms, resulting in behaviour that was previously considered acceptable becoming unacceptable.

From an HR perspective, it is important to establish which of the above explanations is relevant to each individual case of misconduct and whether, over time, any discernible patterns emerge that might justify a more strategic intervention to address particularly important causal factors. If a general criticism can be made of HR in the way that misconduct is managed, it is that often each case is treated individually, narrowly, and in isolation. Making sense of the situation by trying to locate incidents of unacceptable behaviour in a wider context can be seen as an important contribution to the effective resolution of that behaviour. 'Making sense' goes beyond a simple investigation of the circumstances surrounding an incident, and involves the application of a more holistic and integrated approach, including diagnosis, interpretation, and intention. Such an approach should both inform the way in which each case is handled and contribute to an outcome that is, as far as possible, fair to all parties and appropriate in the circumstances.

But the importance of choice in the management of misconduct goes beyond the question of exploratory processes and procedural regulation, and extends into the more complex world of management philosophy, values, and beliefs. Consider, for example, the purpose and function of discipline in contemporary organizations. Interestingly, the use of, and need for, discipline seems at odds with developments in contemporary management thinking, with its emphasis on commitment, employee-centred HR practices, and the search for higher levels of performance and discretionary effort. This emphasis on the importance of employees as the key, if not the only, source of competitive advantage has led many writers to question some of the more traditional approaches to managing people, which include the use of sanctions and punishment to 'manage misconduct'.

Pfeffer and Varga (1999; quoted in Frost et al., 2002), for example, argue that numerous studies have demonstrated that very significant economic benefits can be gained through the implementation of high-performance or high-commitment management practices, but that there is little evidence to suggest that disciplining staff contributes to these outcomes. On the contrary, there is extensive anecdotal evidence to suggest that disciplining—particularly, but not exclusively, if this is done in a way that is perceived to be arbitrary and unfair—creates exactly the opposite effect to that which is desired.

Moreover, the growth in the knowledge economy, in which highly skilled knowledge workers are increasingly replacing manual employees as an organization's key resource, might mean that traditional approaches to discipline, as well as hierarchical control, are unlikely to be appropriate and effective managerial practices when applied to such employees. In an economic environment of sustained low unemployment, growing flexible working arrangements, and an increasing body of legislative rights and duties that protect the individual from arbitrary and unfair disciplinary action, the ability of employers to maintain traditional approaches to disciplining staff has become increasingly compromised.

While the need for an appropriate response to instances of misconduct is a necessity for many organizations, what is increasingly important is that such responses are seen as proportionate, transparent, and fair, not only by those who are directly affected by them, but by their peers. A failure to deliver against these criteria not only undermines the integrity of HR, but affects the reputation of the organization, and is likely to have a detrimental effect on the attitudes and behaviour of other employees. In a somewhat perverse sense, the management of misconduct must involve a degree of consent and legitimization from those who are directly and indirectly affected by it. In the same way that applicants applying for jobs need to feel that they have been treated fairly and with 'procedural justice', so too do those subjected to disciplinary action (Konovsky, 2000).



# Alternatives to Disciplining People

This need to consider alternative ways of managing misconduct also emerges from the meanings associated with the act of discipline. Many dictionary definitions equate 'discipline' with 'punishment', seeing it as a way of exercising control, and enforcing compliance and order, along with obedience (Huberman, 1975). It is also seen in terms of a system of rules, the purpose of which is to improve and correct behaviour. Discipline is traditionally associated with 'what management does to employees' and usually involves the application, or implied use of, sanctions, ultimately ending in an individual being dismissed in cases of gross or persistent misconduct. But in less serious cases, the act of misconduct may require a less serious response: one that involves verbal or written warnings, demotion or job change. Whichever action is considered appropriate, the underlying assumption associated with the use of sanctions is that they will have the effect of dissuading the individual involved from continuing to act in unacceptable ways and will set an example to others. The analogy to the criminal justice system, under which laws, procedures, and punishments are applied to reduce or eliminate unacceptable behaviour in the wider society, is difficult to avoid. So, too, is the ongoing debate between those who favour harsher and more coercive punishments, and those who believe that an interest in understanding why people engage in criminal activities is the only way to develop more effective ways of dealing with such behaviour, based on prevention and education rather than punishment.

In fact, the word 'discipline' has its roots in the word 'disciple' and implies teaching or training. From this perspective, managers and employees might view disciplinary procedures as a mechanism for solving serious behavioural problems rather than as some sort of stick with which managers can beat or punish their employees. Of course, the reality for the majority of organizations is that a dual strategy, combining elements of both approaches, is likely to be seen as the most effective approach. This approach should neither be too 'hard' nor too 'soft', although the relative weight given to each is likely to vary in ways that reflect organizational values, management philosophy, and experience.

The conventional view that management needs to act firmly and fairly in dealing with acts of misconduct is one that few would argue against. Hence, the failure to respond to breaches of organizational rules and the failure to apply sanctions commensurate with the offence should be seen as a serious and unacceptable sign of managerial weakness. In other words, disciplining staff is necessary and inevitable in cases in which individuals clearly 'step out of line'. Reality is, however, often more complicated and challenging than this deceptively simple proposition suggests. Consider the following HRM Insight, which demonstrates the importance of proportionality in handling discipline.

**HRM INSIGHT 6.1 The case of the Queen's Medical Centre**

In March 2004, the Queen's Medical Centre suspended a consultant and senior lecturer in neurosurgery, who had 18 years' experience. The suspension resulted from an allegation that the individual had taken a second helping of soup in the restaurant without paying for it. In his defence, he stated that he had simply added more croutons to his soup. Three patients awaiting surgery on the day of suspension had their operations postponed. One week after his suspension, the brain surgeon was reinstated. The incident was featured in the national media throughout the week of his suspension, despite the surgeon's lack of willingness to comment.

Questions

1. Why was it considered necessary to invoke the hospital's disciplinary procedure?
2. What alternative forms of action might the HR function have taken in this example?
3. What was the overall impact of this incident likely to be in terms of the conduct and standards at the Medical Centre?
4. What recommendations might the HR function make following this incident?
5. To what degree do the likely consequences following from disciplinary action need to be considered in deciding on appropriate action?

(www.bbc.co.uk, 24 March 2004 and The *Times*, 24 March 2004)



# Consequences of Poor Decisions in Handling Disciplinary Matters

HRM Insight 6.1 may not have resulted in disciplinary action being taken against the consultant, but the damage done to his professional standing (he was, to all intents and purposes, accused of stealing), the stress and inconvenience caused to his patients, and the damage done to the hospital's reputation were all real. There is also a question of perceived fairness to employees of different status. The hospital, in this case, had established a precedent prior to this incident in dealing with similar situations, but with much more junior, and therefore less high-profile, employees. Without knowing the details and background to the case, it is difficult to comment on the motives and intentions of those who took the decision to suspend the consultant, but it can be seen as an example of a response that is almost pre-programmed. The stimulus, in this case, was the accusation of wrongdoing and this immediately triggered the formal response to 'invoke procedure'. This arguably excessive, and potentially dangerous, reliance on a predetermined course of action may be attractive in terms of its consistency and formal rationality, but it does raise serious questions about the exercise of managerial judgement and the role of HR in the decision-making process. Above all, it raises questions about the kind of organizational environment that elevates simple mistakes or relatively minor breaches of organizational rules to the status of major incidents.

The importance of an organization's environment to the frequency and management of both disciplinary and grievance cases cannot be overstated (Rollinson et al., 1996). Consider these two very different statements, which relate to the making of mistakes: 'If you make a mistake in this place, you get fired'; 'People should be able to work in a blame-free environment, where mistakes are both tolerated and encouraged.' Of course, these two statements, based on different student experiences of work placements, reflect two extreme points on a continuum of managerial tolerance and discretionary behaviour. The mid-point would be an organizational environment that has a balanced, and arguably more sensible, approach to the making of mistakes, but choices exist as to how individual organizations decide on the general principles they use to determine the way in which they approach cases of misconduct. The concept of mistakes is, however, more problematical than it may often seem. Mistakes differ in relation to their severity and consequences; many are the result of employees trying to do things differently and better, and errors or mistakes that result from this type of situation are often necessary parts of the learning experience. Clearly, disciplining a person who is acting in the best interests of the organization, however misguided, is probably not the most appropriate managerial response. But where behaviour is wilful, goes against clear operating procedures and standards, and has serious negative consequences, describing this also as 'a mistake' fails to do justice to the differences in the two situations.



## Unconventional Approaches to Discipline at Work



In Chapter 1, we referred to the case of the The Men's Warehouse, an American clothing company run by George Zimmer, which stood out from many other clothing retailers because of its distinctive philosophy of management, values, and employment practices. It also represents a company that takes a rather unconventional approach to misconduct and discipline: the distinctive philosophy of its founder shapes the way in which individual acts of misconduct are interpreted and managed. O'Reilly and Pfeffer's book (2000) is concerned with how great companies achieve extraordinary results with ordinary people. They use The Men's Warehouse to illustrate the point that its success is not because of tight hierarchical and financial controls or performance management systems, but rather because of its values and philosophy.

This commitment to creating an environment through which successful business and customer satisfaction emerges from satisfied and 'turned-on' employees means that the company puts its people first. But O'Reilly and Pfeffer found that the company drew on a pool of labour that was not always the 'best', recruited staff who had personal problems and difficulties, and those who may have had limited educational and achievement experiences. The implication is that some of the company's employees would 'break the rules', which, in most other organizations, would result in disciplinary action being taken. In The Men's Warehouse, however, an action such as stealing would not necessarily result in dismissal. The company's executive vice president for human development explains this rather surprising position:

> **what George has seen . . . are people who have never been treated particularly well, and that when you treat them well and give them a second and sometimes a third chance, even when they've ripped off a pair of socks, even when they've taken a deposit and put it into their pocket and not returned it for several days . . . you try to re-educate the person . . . We've looked at how to help ourselves and other people get better than most of the world thought we could ever be.**
> **(O'Reilly and Pfeffer, 2006)**

The obvious question that emerges from this brief account of the attitude towards employee behaviour and discipline at the Men's Warehouse is 'why?' Why does its management accept behaviour that would lead other companies immediately towards disciplinary action? O'Reilly and Pfeffer believe that the answer lies in the way such an approach generates a strong and sustained sense of reciprocation. They argue that:

> **By exceeding peoples' expectations concerning the chances they will be given, the dignity and respect with which they will be treated, and the opportunities they will have, the company builds an incredible sense of loyalty and commitment.**

In other words, there is a 'pay-off'. By not taking action that would be considered by others to be both legitimate and appropriate, the company's management is able to generate a powerful and sustainable response in terms of positive attitudes and performance-enhancing behaviours that would be difficult to achieve by other means. Paradoxically, choosing not to discipline someone in circumstances under which management would be entitled to do so can result in outcomes that are highly valued and, indeed, necessary for the long-term success of the organization.

## Admitting mistakes—encouraging openness

Part of The Men's Warehouse mission statement refers to 'admitting our mistakes' and it is this that provides a link to our second example of unconventional approaches to misconduct and discipline. It is taken from chapter 5 of Jerry Harvey's seminal work *The Abeline Paradox* (1988). In this chapter, Harvey tells the story of 'Captain Asoh and the Concept of Grace'; this account of motives, intent, honesty, genuine mistakes, and the power of forgiveness is summarized as follows.

Captain Asoh was the pilot of a Japanese airliner that landed in line with the runway at San Francisco airport but, unfortunately, two-and-a-half miles short, out in the Bay. No one was injured and very little damage was done, but a serious mistake had been made and those culpable needed to be identified. At a resulting inquiry, at which all of those who were involved in the incident attended, Asoh took the stand first and was asked by the chief investigator how he had managed to land his plane in the sea, rather than at the airport. To this, he replied: 'As you Americans say, Asoh, he f*** up!'



His admission of personal responsibility, refusal to attach blame to others, and honesty were both surprising and unexpected, to the point that the investigation had little more to do than tidy up the technical details. Perhaps people are not encouraged or supposed to display such characteristics in contemporary organizations, but the question that remained to be answered was: 'What do we do with Captain Asoh?'

Harvey's reference to this story is rooted in his earlier observation that, while it is now generally recognized that organizations need people who are prepared to take risks and, in the process, possibly make mistakes (on the grounds that, if you don't make mistakes, you are unlikely to have tried anything of significance), the managers of these organizations and those who support the managers (HR) aren't actually very good at forgiving those who make genuine mistakes! As a consequence of the fear of being found out and being punished, people at all levels become very adept at concealing the truth from others, and often from themselves, to the point at which it is difficult to distinguish truth from lies. Asoh was different, because he told the truth as he saw it, he didn't try to blame someone else and he didn't lie. We know why this behaviour is not as common as it arguably should be—but why is it important at all? Harvey's argument is that the truth is important because it provides the basis for human connection. It relieves our alienation from one another and prevents us from being psychologically separated from those upon whom we lean for basic emotional support, which, he believes, is a fundamental human need and is characteristic of a healthy psychological state.

One of the interesting things about Asoh's admission that he made a mistake and his being prepared to accept personal responsibility for this is, according to Harvey, that it is an increasingly rare phenomenon. The heart of the Captain Asoh story is not only about the acceptance of personal responsibility and honesty, but also about the reactions of those who were sitting in judgement over his wrongdoing. According to Harvey, what Asoh provided was an opportunity for these people to apply something that seems to be singularly absent from many organizations today: forgiveness. This can be thought of as 'the willingness to give up resentment, and in its highest form, the extension of grace', which is defined as 'forgiveness raised to the highest level in the form of unmerited favour' (Harvey, 1988).

So why should Asoh have been forgiven? There are two key reasons. Firstly, because he was honest enough to admit his mistake—he was an excellent employee with an unblemished record and he never intended to cause harm or danger to anyone, so what purpose would have been served by punishing him? Secondly, the act of forgiveness is also an act of giving, and giving is a particularly human need and characteristic. The act of forgiving is, therefore, an act of altruism from which both parties gain.

The story of Captain Asoh (and it is unclear even to Harvey whether it is apocryphal or not) often produces quite diverse reaction among those who are familiar with it. For some, the references to forgiveness, the extension of grace and altruistic behaviour have little relevance to HR as it tries to shed its humanist/welfare traditions along the road towards 'a seat at the top table' and strives to increase its contribution to the 'bottom line'. Harvey, on the other hand, would consider this to be a mistake for two reasons. Altruism is an experience that is fundamentally human and good, as well as deeply satisfying to the giver, but it is also an essential requirement for survival. As Harvey puts it, 'cultures that lack the capacity for altruistic forgiveness and grace die', or at least become dysfunctional and ineffective. But there is a more pragmatic reason: that forgiving and giving creates a reciprocal reaction from those in receipt. The sense of gratitude generated when someone in authority does not exercise the right to discipline and punish, or when management decides to give someone a second chance, can be a very powerful experience for those directly involved. It can also be the basis of an enhanced sense of obligation—the desire to show that the decision was the right one—and it can result in new, and stronger, personal relationships. These are the very outcomes that are associated with a high-commitment, high-performance environment.

**STUDENT ACTIVITY 6.2 Testing the hypothesis**

In classroom debates over the attitude of The Men's Warehouse to mistakes and acts of misconduct, several students presented with the justification that such leniency generates a greater sense of employee responsibility and commitment rejected the argument. They claimed that such leniency would be taken as a sign of weakness and that they would subsequently be taken advantage of. Your task is to share stories about situations in which an employee has either been disciplined or given a 'second chance' and to analyse what the effects of each management action were. You should also discuss whether more or less discretion and leniency in the disciplining of employees would be likely generally to strengthen or to weaken management-employee relationships.

# A More Conventional Approach to Misconduct

Despite raising legitimate questions about the purpose, form, and effectiveness of more traditional disciplinary practices, it would be unrealistic to argue against the necessity of some form of institutional framework and procedural regulation to help to manage cases of misconduct, even for the most forward-looking and employee-centred organization. The reasons for this are linked to:

- the existence of more prescriptive legislative provision in the field of employee rights, employer responsibilities, and procedural requirements. This means that all organizations need to develop a reliable and defensible capability for dealing with cases of discipline and grievance;
- the constant pressure to increase performance at the individual and organizational level has led many organizations to view 'poor or unacceptable performance', linked to absence, failure to meet

performance targets, and general 'bloody-mindedness', as potential cases of misconduct, with the implication that more, rather than fewer, cases will need to be dealt with;

- societal changes in what is considered to be acceptable behaviour, with respect to language, attitudes, and how people at work generally behave towards others, and the imposition of new standards and norms governing social interaction.

As a consequence of these influences, people's behaviour and conduct at work has become increasingly subject to more prescriptive normative frameworks and procedures that are designed to deal with breaches in these norms. For the majority of employees, and in most circumstances, such standards will be known and complied with. In other cases, in which conduct falls short of established standards, or in which action such as educational and training provision has been used in preference to formal disciplinary proceedings and has failed to produce the desired effect, the need for effective ways of dealing with misconduct becomes necessary, and it to this that we now turn (Younson, 2002).

Figure 6.1 represents a conceptual model of a generic disciplinary process.

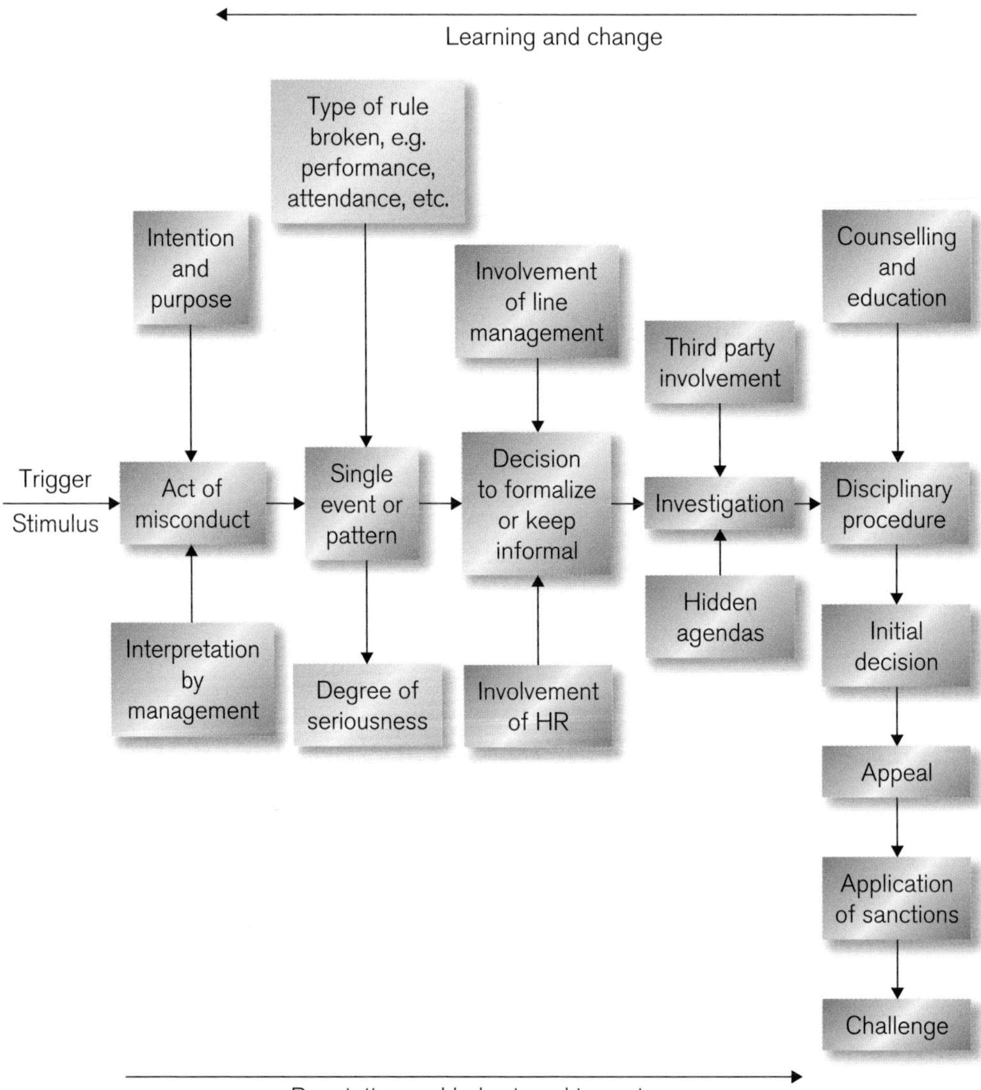


**Figure 6.1** A model of the disciplinary process

**RESEARCH INSIGHT 6.1**

To take your learning further you might want to read this article:

**Beyer (1984), 'A field study of the use and effects of discipline in controlling work performance', *Academy of Management Journal*, 27:4, pp. 743–64**

This study shows that supervisors tended to respond with disciplinary action to certain behaviours, when the work context was supportive of its use and showed a small but significant effect in terms of work behaviour for targeted employees.

**STUDENT ACTIVITY 6.3**

The model in Figure 6.1 helps to provide a clearer understanding of the different phases, parts, relationships, and challenges associated with the management of misconduct. After reviewing the model, try to improve it, by testing it against current practice, and discuss the challenges and responsibilities that each part of the model represents.

## The Relationship Between Minor and Major Breaches in Standards

The model in Figure 6.2 shows the relationship between minor and major breaches of standards at work and the relationship between the seriousness of the incident and formality of the response. For every major breach in standards, resulting in either dismissal or action short of dismissal, there will be more minor

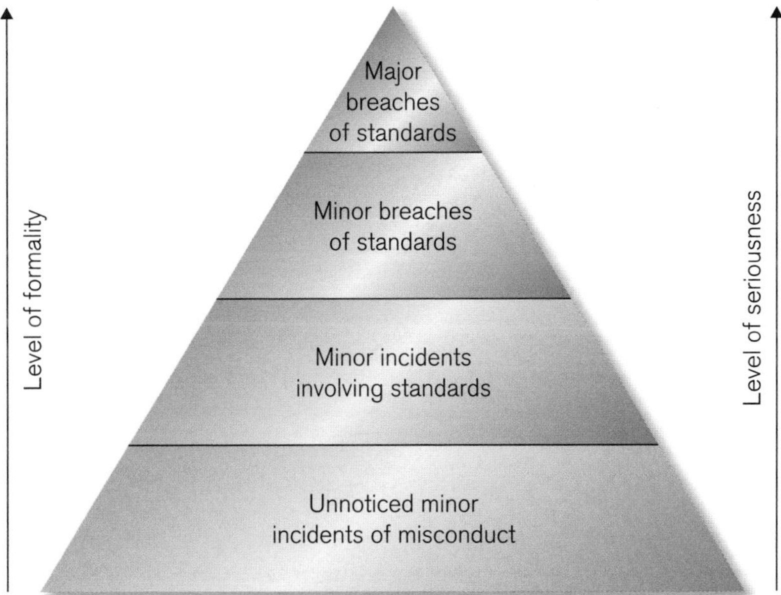


Figure 6.2 The conduct pyramid

breaches of behavioural standards and rules, which are formally addressed. There will in turn be more minor incidents involving standards addressed informally and even more incidents of non-conformity that go either unnoticed or unaddressed. The longer these are allowed to continue, the more management, by its own act of omission (i.e. by doing nothing) legitimizes them. Early intervention, almost inevitably by the appropriate line manager, is important to provide guidance and interpretation of the status of the action or behaviour, and helps to resolve any uncertainties over its acceptability and seriousness.

The key to managing behaviour successfully is to address standards of compliance/non-compliance at the informal and minor level in order to prevent any escalation in the frequency or seriousness of the problem. If an organization is over-reliant on the use of formal procedures to address conduct, this suggests that the standards and objectives of the organization are not being made clear and that the existing culture encourages non-compliance across the board. Again, we can see the importance of the organizational environment to the patterns of misconduct and to management responses to these.

As indicated earlier, the need to invoke formal disciplinary procedures can be indicative of other issues within an organization and might reflect, for example poor recruitment and selection practices, lack of training and development, ineffective pay and reward structures, or poor communications and employee relations. It may also reflect key characteristics of the labour force, such as position in the hierarchy, the type of work carried out, and the degree to which people work in what might be described as a 'factory culture'. This term is meant to cover any working environment in which employees have a more instrumental attitude to work, often involving less skilled or manually based work, and in which employees and management perceive themselves to be in an adversarial relationship. The greater the extent to which employees identify with the position of management and the wider interests of the organization, the less the likelihood of employees deliberately engaging in misconduct. As far as developing effective strategies for dealing with misconduct are concerned, this hypothesis offers a way forward that is not limited to using procedures to manage the misconduct, but includes its prevention.

The model in Figure 6.3 demonstrates how the extent to which management relies upon its formal disciplinary procedures will depend upon the make-up of an organization. Organizations employing younger employees to carry out roles requiring lower skills are likely to experience more disciplinary issues than those employing more mature and longer serving employees in jobs that require higher levels of skill and responsibility. This means that the frequency and seriousness of disciplinary cases is likely to be strongly correlated to the demographic characteristics of the workforce, knowledge of which can help management to pre-empt patterns of misconduct and to take appropriate preventative action.

There is a risk, however, that organizations which experience infrequent cases of misconduct will be less well equipped to deal with those that do occur, particularly if they are serious, because the HR staff and line managers who need to be involved may not have the necessary experience and competencies to manage these cases effectively.

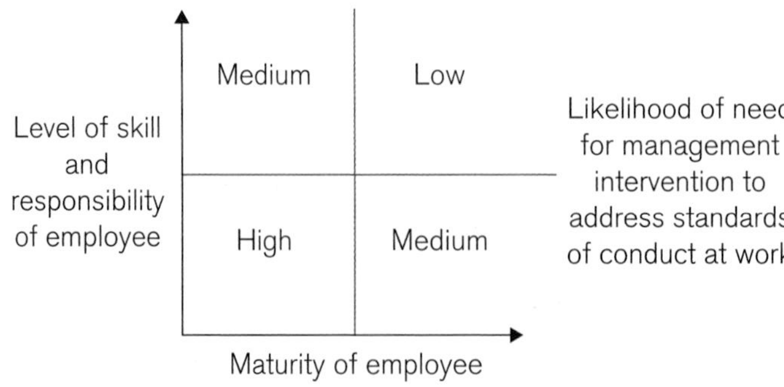


**Figure 6.3** The correlation of disciplinary cases with employee skill/responsibility and maturity

**STUDENT ACTIVITY 6.4 Developing the skills and competences needed to manage disciplinary cases**

This exercise requires students to think about what line managers need to know and be able to do in order to contribute to the effective management of misconduct, involving cases of discipline. In groups, your task is to design a two-day training programme entitled 'The role of the line manager in managing misconduct'. This activity will involve establishing the knowledge and behaviours they need, and how these can be learnt. It may well involve an element of research, and should result in a PowerPoint presentation and evaluation of what is proposed.

**HRM INSIGHT 6.2 The Belgian Chocolate Company**

The Belgian Chocolate Company was a small confectioners employing around a hundred people to produce speciality Belgian chocolates for a major retailer. A larger manufacturer acquired it and the company was placed under the management of Townends Chocolates, a large, well-established manufacturer. Townends recruited a new plant manager for the operation, to replace the previous owner who had managed the business for twenty years before selling the company and retiring. The new plant manager was given the objective of introducing more rigorous hygiene and performance standards as already established in the main Townends factory.

Eating on the shop floor was a serious hygiene concern, which had been highlighted as one of the unhygienic practices in a recent customer audit. Following advice from the HR department at Townends, a decision was made to stamp this out completely by making it a dismissible offence under the disciplinary procedure, in the belief that, if the consequences were so severe, then the behaviour would stop immediately. The Townends management team briefed the whole workforce by attaching a notice to their wage slips—and was shocked when the first offender was caught eating in the factory only days later. In the subsequent disciplinary hearing, the reason given was that sampling product on the shop floor had been standard practice for years to ensure the quality of the product. The staff representative in attendance stated that this was no more serious than office staff failing to wash their hands on each re-entry into the factory from the office area, which was a regular occurrence.

The plant manager issued a final written warning due to the mitigating reasons given and sent a further brief, via wage slips, that eating on the shop floor for any reason and failure to wash hands on entering factory areas would constitute dismissible offences. Several days later, the plant manager witnessed the staff representative entering the factory from the office without washing her hands. She was taken into the office for an investigation and was suspended pending a disciplinary hearing. When she informed a colleague later that evening of what had taken place, a petition was signed by the majority of employees, and submitted to the plant manager, that threatened that they would 'down tools' unless their staff representative was reinstated.

### Questions

1. What were the differences in culture between Townends and the Belgian Chocolate Company?
2. How might the HR function have sought to understand the issues at the newly acquired confectionery plant?
3. In the example above, what fundamental assumptions did the HR department and the new management team make?
4. What alternative measures might the HR team have recommended to identify and address the main issues facing them, given their new responsibilities?
5. How can the HR function contribute towards ensuring that the internal needs of the business are balanced with the requirements of the customer in this example?

**Insights & Outcomes: visit the Online Resource Centre at www.oxfordtextbooks.co.uk/orc/banfield_kay2e/ to find out details about what actually happened and how this situation was handled.**

# Disciplinary Procedures and the Role of the Law

The need to have disciplinary procedures is determined by ACAS codes of practice, which were first introduced in the 1970s and have been updated at regular intervals (ACAS, 2009a).

Most larger organizations have established disciplinary procedures that are in line with the ACAS guidelines, which recommend, among other things, that a disciplinary procedure is made up of several stages or warnings. Under the recommendations, if an employee is involved in a minor breach of work rules, in the first instance, the employer is advised to address what is essentially a minor problem through informal conversations, but if this fails to improve standards, the formal warnings demonstrated in Table 6.1 can be used progressively. The minimum standards in the 2009 ACAS code of practice (ACAS, 2009a), which was put in place when the Statutory Discipline and Grievance Procedures (set out by the Employment Act 2002) were repealed, must be complied with by all organizations and tribunals are legally obliged to take this into account when considering cases. For example, employers must offer employees the right to be accompanied to a disciplinary hearing by a work colleague or duly accredited union representative. In these circumstances, employees can insist that disciplinary proceedings are delayed by up to five days to allow arrangements for their chosen representative to be present at the hearing.

The additional recommendations from ACAS (ACAS, 2009b) no longer include the recommendation for a formal verbal warning stage that was in place prior to 2002 and instead place a stronger emphasis on the use of informal action wherever possible to resolve issues and encourage employers to consider the use of mediation to resolve disputes in the workplace.



## Disciplinary stages

If the actions of an employee are serious enough, then the procedure may be entered into at the appropriate stage. For example, a major breach of the rules might lead directly to a final written warning or, in the case of serious or gross misconduct, summary dismissal (i.e. immediate dismissal without notice being either served or worked by the employee).

**Table 6.1** Recommended stages in a disciplinary procedure

| Level | Recommended duration | Level of manager likely to implement |
|---|---|---|
| Written warning | 6 months | Line manager |
| Final written warning | 12 months | Senior manager |
| Dismissal | Permanent | Senior manager |

Procedures can vary between organizations in all aspects, including time limits for appeals, those permitted to be present, and the levels and duration of warnings. The important thing to note in an organization is that procedures should comply with at least the minimum requirements set by ACAS in their code of practice. Care should be taken to ensure that procedures, once in place, are properly communicated, including an appropriate reference in every employee's written statement of terms and conditions. It is also important in defending any potential claims for unfair dismissal to ensure that the procedures are always adhered to.

Applying disciplinary procedures fairly is a complex matter and many organizations have specific training in place for managers required to apply the procedures. These organizations will often have back-up provisions for advice from legal advisors, such as a solicitor or other appropriate professional. Many trade unions also have training for representatives and employ the services of their own legal advisors.

**For further discussion about record keeping and the use of witness statements see the Online Resource Centre extension material 6.1 and 6.2.**

## Gross misconduct

'Gross misconduct' is the term used to describe breaches of standards and rules that are serious and unacceptable in any circumstances. If a case of gross misconduct is identified, the likelihood is that, if the investigation provides evidence that supports the charge, the individual will face dismissal even though it may be his or her first offence. Examples of offences given by ACAS that can be regarded as gross misconduct are:

- theft or fraud;
- physical violence or bullying;
- deliberate and serious damage to property;
- serious misuse of and organisation's property or name;
- deliberately accessing internet sites containing pornographic, offensive or obscene material;
- serious insubordination;
- unlawful discrimination or harassment;
- bringing the organization into serious disrepute;
- serious incapability at work brought on by alcohol or illegal drugs;
- causing loss, damage, or injury through serious negligence;
- a serious breach of health and safety rules;
- a serious breach of confidence.

What constitutes acts of gross misconduct can be determined by individual organizations in the light of their particular circumstances and requirements. Examples should be incorporated into employee handbooks or made known to employees in other appropriate ways. As in all cases of discipline, procedural regularity and the reasonableness of management's action will be the criteria used by an employment tribunal in the event of a subsequent claim for unfair dismissal brought by the individual concerned.

## The roles of HR and line managers

The exact role of HR and line managers in carrying out disciplinary procedures varies between organizations (Rollinson et al., 1996). HR can be present in an active role, either as the party responsible for leading the investigation or the party taking the disciplinary action. In other organizations, one, or both, of these roles may be performed by two managers or by a line manager and a more senior manager, with HR taking more of an advisory role, either within the meeting or independent from the meeting. There is no correct way of doing things. It is, however, advisable to have at least two representatives present, in order to divide the roles of leading the investigation and making the disciplinary decision, so that there is a degree of impartiality in the decision-making process. Many organizations specify in their disciplinary procedures who will be in attendance, at what level, and in what capacity. For example, a larger organization may wish to involve a more senior level of manager in more serious offences, for which the consequences of making an incorrect decision are wider reaching. But, ideally, the investigations should be distinct from the hearing and should involve different parties. The Practitioner Insight discusses disciplinary processes and line manager involvement in small to medium sized business to give context to how procedures operate in practice.

**PRACTITIONER INSIGHT Katy Edmonds, HR Manager, IFA Ltd**

At Independent Forgings and Alloys Ltd, where I am currently employed as HR Manager, we have around 120 employees and it is very rare that we need to use formal disciplinary procedures. I have worked in larger organizations where line managers are not as confident and were therefore over-reliant on using disciplinary procedures to enforce rules and standards and needed much more support and intervention from HR to do so. More of my work in this area now involves coaching and supporting line managers to identify problems early on and to nip problems in the bud. I find that managers' behaviour is more important in maintaining standards than having an effective disciplinary procedure. If you've got good managers, you rarely need to use formal disciplinary procedures as they will set clear standards and identify potential problems early on and deal with them informally before problems escalate.

When it comes to grievances again having approachable managers helps avoid disputes escalating. If someone has a concern that could potentially be a problem this is best dealt with quickly at the lowest possible level. Where there is a problem and it is not possible to meet the employee's expectations it can be helpful for the employee to speak to their manager's manager and this may need a more formal process. When grievances arise this tends to be where employees are not happy about a proposed change and it is often possible to be flexible to try and accommodate employees. It is helpful to have an open mind and to make sure the employee feels they have been listened to. It also helps if managers have the maturity to be ready to change their mind in the face of good evidence rather than being belligerent.

**RESEARCH INSIGHT 6.2**

To take your learning further you might want to read this article:

**Klass, B.S. and Wheeler, H.N. (1990), 'Managerial decision-making about employee discipline: A policy capturing approach', *Personnel Psychology*, 43:1, pp. 117-34.**

This study examined how HR practitioners and line managers approached making disciplinary decisions and showed that different factors had varying impacts upon the two groups, with HR practitioners more influenced by institutional and legal factors and line managers more influenced by hierarchical factors. The study also showed a wide variation between managers in terms of the types of decision made.

**STUDENT ACTIVITY 6.5**

1. Consider the different roles and responsibilities with which the HR professional and line manager would be associated in the management of disciplinary proceedings. Where should final responsibility lie?
2. What are the most important difficulties that both the line manager and HR specialist face in managing disciplinary cases?
3. What would you include in a check list for line managers and HR specialists in carrying out disciplinary investigations and hearings?

## Appeals

Under the ACAS code of practice, employees must be given the right of appeal when dismissed or if action is taken short of dismissal. In fact, failure to offer the right of appeal may result in a tribunal finding a dismissal to be automatically unfair, that is, making such a decision regardless of the merits of the case. The

ACAS code of practice states that the right of appeal should be offered with all formal warnings. Procedures will often have a time limit and will state that the appeal must be in writing. Usually organizations, for clarity, will have a clear appeal process rather than rely on their grievance procedure as the mechanism for submitting appeals. Appeals should be dealt with speedily and, wherever possible, should be heard at a meeting by a person with greater authority than whoever took the original decision. If this is not possible, the appeal should nonetheless be as impartial a meeting as possible. The purpose is to hear grounds for appeal, paying particular attention to new evidence, and if the original decision is felt to be unfair or unreasonable, it should be overturned—although it would be idealistic to suggest that the decision on appeal is not, occasionally, influenced by other considerations.

**HRM INSIGHT 6.3 Sandy's Hairdressers**

Sandy's is a small, privately owned hairdressing business. There are three employees—two hairdressers and an apprentice/receptionist—and one hairdresser who works from the premises on a self-employed basis.

While the owner is on holiday, she asks the last person who leaves the premises to lock up and responsibility for the till is given to the more senior of the two employed hairdressers.

On returning from her holiday, she is informed by the senior hairdresser that the other employed hairdresser in the salon has been seen taking money from the till and that the till did not add up at the end of the day. When challenged, the person said that they had borrowed the money to get lunch and had intended to pay it back after lunch, but had forgotten. The incident happened three days ago. The owner's partner is a friend of yours and does not get involved in the business, but is registered as one of the directors. He has asked you for advice because the owner no longer trusts the person involved and does not want to continue her employment. There are no formal procedures in place due to the size of the business.

**Questions**

1. Consider what advice you would give.
2. What factors should the owner take into consideration and investigate?
3. What are the arguments for and against:
   i. taking a lenient line and allowing the person to continue to work, after discussing with her your concerns?
   ii. dismissing her on the grounds of stealing money from the till?
4. How should the owner handle the issue of any appeal that might follow from a decision to dismiss?

**STUDENT ACTIVITY 6.6**

Think about any disciplinary procedure with which you are familiar and consider the following questions. You can either use an organization with which you are familiar or look up disciplinary procedures online as many organization's procedures are publicly available.

1. How easy is it to read? Would employees easily understand it?
2. What impression would the procedure give if included as part of the induction material; or terms and conditions for an organization?
3. Given the ACAS codes of practice and guidelines on disciplinary procedures, rewrite the procedure to make appropriate improvements.

(See the ACAS website, www.acas.org.uk, for the most publicly up-to-date code of conduct and guidance.)

# Managing Specific Types of Behaviour

There are certain specific types of behaviour that may result in disciplinary action but often require organizations to consider wider implications and to have separate policies in place. The subject of harassment and bullying for example is complex and procedures for dealing with these issues are covered in more detail in the chapter on equality in employment. Where a formal complaint of harassment of bullying is made or comes to the attention of the organization, disciplinary action up to and including dismissal may be necessary. In these circumstances whilst it is the perception of the victim that constitutes harassment, an investigation will need to be conducted to establish what has taken place and where formal action is needed to address inappropriate behaviour then disciplinary procedures should be followed. It is advisable to have separate harassment policies in place alongside disciplinary procedures to deal with harassment and bullying.

Signpost to Chapter 7: Equality and Diversity Employment, section on Harassment and Bullying

Another area where separate policies may be required is that of 'public interest disclosure' or 'whistle blowing'. There are certain situations that arise where an employee has protection from disciplinary action from their employer if they make disclosures about inappropriate practices within their organization to a third party. For example, an organization may wish to take action if concerns about financial mismanagement are reported to an external body rather than to a more senior person internally, unless it is made clear with a separate policy how such concerns should be raised then the employee may have protection from dismissal or action short of dismissal. (More information on this subject is available at www.acas.ork.uk.)

Another area where it is advisable to have separate policies in place is misconduct relating to the use of alcohol or illegal drugs. Organizations will wish to have rules in place making it clear that it is unacceptable for employees to report to work under the influence of alcohol or illegal drugs; however, employees have a right to privacy under the Human Rights Act (1998) which extends to being tested for the presence of either alcohol or drugs. A clear policy can help make it clear when testing might be requested and what action might be taken should any employee refuse to comply with such a request. There may also be occasions where it is appropriate and reasonable to suspend disciplinary processes to allow an employee time to take professional advice and undergo rehabilitation in order to encourage those with difficulties to be open about seeking help and sorting out their problems.

HRM INSIGHT 6.4 **Alcohol abuse in the workplace**

Whitley Marketing Ltd is a small privately owned marketing solutions company. The main revenue stream for the business is supporting companies with marketing promotional material, web sites, and marketing campaigns.

Bob has been employed for nearly ten years and recently his manager has become concerned about his behaviour. His colleagues have noticed that his work rate has deteriorated since breakdown in a personal relationship and have reported that they have been able to smell alcohol in the office when Bob returned from his lunch breaks.

This afternoon when Bob returned from his lunch break he was over an hour late. His speech was noticeably slurred and he smelled of alcohol. He also had mud on his work clothes where it appeared that he had fallen over. Bob's employment record until recently has always been exemplary.

### Questions

1. Consider what action you would advise the manager to take.
2. How should the manager conduct an investigation, given that Bob does not appear to be in a fit state to even be at work?
3. What are the arguments for and against dismissing Bob?
4. What alternative action could be taken to address the problem?

# Absence Management

According to the Confederation for British Industry (CBI) (2008) absence from work cost the UK economy £13.2 billion in 2007 alone. The average employee took just under seven days (6.7 days) sickness absence during the year and rates of absenteeism were 55 per cent higher in the public sector at nine days per person than in the private sector (5.8 days). The control and management of employee absence is therefore an important role for both the line manager and HR practitioner as organizations cannot afford to fail to take steps to ensure that it is kept to the minimum level possible. Employees' absence can be controlled using either disciplinary procedures or distinct absence management procedures.

In either case the ACAS code of practice must be followed. The basic premise is that whilst it may be unavoidable for employees to take time off due to illness from time to time, organizations can monitor and review absence and where levels are high action can be taken as the employee is not capable of fulfilling their contractual obligation to attend work on a regular basis. Under UK legislation as long as the employer follows a fair procedure and takes all reasonable steps to support an employee to attend regularly then ultimately an employee may be fairly dismissed for sustained poor attendance.

From 1999 to 2002 Rolls Royce plc reduced employee absence from 2.9 percent to 2.4 per cent saving around £11 million. A level of 2.4 per cent is equivalent to 4.2 days per annum and is significantly below the average number of days even for the private sector (www.hse.gov.uk, case study, 'Rolls Royce: Improving Absence Management'). This was achieved through implementing a company-wide absence policy with clearly defined responsibilities for HR, line managers, and Occupational Health professionals, implementing early rehabilitation at four weeks absence including physiotherapy and introducing new IT software to monitor and record absenteeism and its cost. This is a typical example of the steps that an organization may take to minimize the impact of absenteeism.



In the UK, to qualify for 'statutory sick pay', employees are required to complete a self certification form for absences up to one week and obtain a medical certificate for absences greater than one week. Following wide spread criticism about the system in the UK over the ease with which employees can obtain the required medical certification for absences exceeding one week, a new 'fit notes' system was introduced in April 2010 allowing medical practitioners more scope to advise employers about the types of work an employee with health problems may still be fit to carry out. It remains to be seen whether this change will be effective in helping organizations in the UK to reduce the cost of absenteeism.

**STUDENT ACTIVITY 6.7**

In groups, consider how absence is managed in a selection of different organizations based on either research or your personal experiences. Produce a procedure for an organization of your choice to use to address absence levels using a compassionate but consistent approach, ensuring that the primary aim of your procedure is to assist employees to attend on a regular basis.

# Grievance Procedures

Grievances can be thought of as complaints made by one employee against another and, as such, they will not normally be raised by management against an employee. While having the potential to involve breaches of company rules, they do not relate to the most common causes of disciplinary action, which often involve unacceptable performance and poor attendance.

The ACAS code of practice defines grievances as:

**concerns, problems or complaints that employees raise with their employers.**

This may be considered to be too restrictive a definition in terms of the realities of employment, under which it is well known for a grievance to be raised by one employee against another, or by an employee against a manager, or by a manager against a manager. Such complaints are, in effect, claims that the behaviour of one party in relation to the other is unacceptable, in that it involves unfair and discriminatory treatment, failure to act within designated procedures, or the belief that the employer has failed to meet its common law duty of care. This means that the employer must take reasonable action to protect its employees from any harmful or damaging experiences that are not an inevitable part of the occupation or environment in question. For example, a soldier accepts that the risk of injury and even death are part of what being an infantry soldier involves, but being bullied during training, being denied proper equipment in the field, or failure to ensure psychiatric care to help him or her to come to terms with the after-effects of battle would be considered unacceptable and grounds for raising a grievance, or its equivalent, with the appropriate authorities.

As with cases of discipline, it is easy to make the mistake of seeing grievances in isolation from the social and work contexts in which they arise. Many grievances reflect what might be described as 'damaged relationships' rather than individual and isolated acts. It is well known, for example, that many employees who leave an organization often do so because of difficulties with working relationships: they don't 'leave their job', they 'leave their manager', or they leave because of the stresses of working with certain colleagues. This means that many grievances are never formally raised with management but are instead resolved by the 'aggrieved' party leaving the organization. Exit interviews can indicate whether an individual is being 'pushed out' by the inability or reluctance of management to resolve a stressful, damaging, or in some other way unacceptable situation. If HR is unaware of such situations directly or fails to use the information made available in exit interview records, the original cause of the grievance will continue to affect other relationships, with the likelihood of similar consequences.



## Grievance procedures and the law

The need to have grievance procedures in place is governed by the ACAS codes of practice, which were first introduced in the 1970s and have been updated by ACAS at regular intervals.

The ACAS code of practice lays out a process whereby, if an employee submits a grievance, this must be heard by an appropriate level of management and a response given within a reasonable time frame. The employee then has the opportunity to appeal against any decision given. Further details of codes of practice and guidelines can be obtained from the ACAS website (www.acas.org). Failure to comply with codes of practice can result in increased awards being made if a future complaint is found to be successful in an employment tribunal. These codes of practice do not govern collective disputes raised by more than one employee.

In reality, most companies have established procedures for handling employee grievances and recognize the value of handling complaints quickly and sensitively at the earliest opportunity, and of their being handled by the closest level of management to the employee who has made the complaint.

## Frequent causes of grievances

Most grievances can be linked to the following:

- unacceptable language and images, initiation rituals, and other forms of informal shop/office-floor behaviour;
- harassment and bullying;
- victimization and unfair discriminatory treatment;
- unreasonable and 'unlawful' requests to take certain action that might, for example, involve breaking health and safety regulations;

- failure to honour promises or obligations, for example, over the payment of bonuses or other forms of reward.

While the basis and legitimacy of certain cases of grievance can be more readily established by looking at the 'hard' evidence, the majority are more difficult to verify simply because they involve perceptions, expectations, and different views as to what is 'acceptable'.

Consider the two following scenarios.

- The captain of a Royal Navy warship is recalled from his ship because two members of his crew have lodged complaints about his 'authoritative style of management'. The remaining crew members may have shared this grievance but not formally recorded their concerns, or may have been perfectly happy with the captain's behaviour and have considered it to be within the bounds of what could be considered 'acceptable'.
- A male manager relieves a female subordinate of responsibility for one key account on the grounds that the employee has failed to meet basic performance criteria, and is subsequently accused of bullying and harassment.

Neither situation represents a 'clear-cut' case of harassment or bullying, but it is also obvious that the possibility exists for a grievance to be brought. In the second scenario, it might be argued that the female employee lodging a grievance might have done so to protect herself from possible disciplinary action and reflects the efforts of the individual to rationalize the damaging effect that the manager's decision has had on both her self-esteem and her standing within the company. The ACAS code of practice recommends that, if a grievance is raised during a disciplinary case, the latter should be suspended while the grievance is dealt with. Suffice to say that some grievances have their own 'history' and complicating factors, and cannot be taken at face value. On the other hand, many grievances are made by people who genuinely feel that they have been treated wrongly by some other member of the organization and who feel that the only way to resolve the situation, apart from leaving, is to lodge a formal grievance with the HR department.

While registering a grievance invariably implies some degree of formalization, the response from the HR department, at that early stage, may not itself be formal. Much depends on the approaches and philosophy of those involved, as well as the organization's grievance procedure, which, since the Employment Rights Act 1996, is a legal requirement for all organizations that employee at least 20 employees. Consider the situation of a female employee of an engineering company, who works in the dispatch department with several male colleagues. She complains to her supervisor about the language used by one of her male colleagues, which she finds offensive and unacceptable. On being informed of the 'grievance', which is not yet formally registered as such, the HR officer arranges an informal meeting with the two employees to establish the 'facts' of the case. During the meeting, it transpires that the offensive language complained about was also used by the female employee to her male colleague, and that the real problem is that their personal relationship has deteriorated over time. The response of the HR officer is, metaphorically, to 'bang their heads together' with a strong suggestion that they sort themselves out. Keeping the response informal not only avoids the consequences of early formalization, through which positions become entrenched, but also encourages the two parties to take responsibility for managing the problem themselves and probably results in a more satisfactory, and less damaging, outcome.

## Complaints about a manager

The experience of many specialist mediators suggests that interpersonal conflict cannot always be resolved by applying formal grievance procedures, and this has led to a greater emphasis on more informal and less threatening resolution mechanisms (see the Centre for Effective Dispute Resolution, www.cedr.co.uk). But the use of an informal approach to grievance resolution depends on both parties agreeing to this and this may not always be possible to achieve, particularly if it has proved impossible to agree on a mutually acceptable agreement and if the grievance procedure reflects an adversarial, rather than a resolution, approach to the management of grievances.

Interestingly, the growth in the number of grievances registered may not simply reflect an increase in incidents of interpersonal conflict, but also that organizations have failed to develop mechanisms and competences for dealing with such incidents. It may be that employers experience difficulties in managing the underlying causes of grievances because managers lack the awareness and skills to deal with conflict.

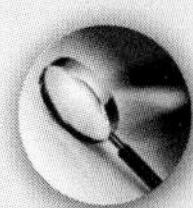

**RESEARCH INSIGHT 6.3**

To take your learning further you might want to read the following article by Suff which provides an up-to-date view on the management of discipline in the UK.

**Suff, R. (2010) 'Dispute resolution survey: Managing discipline'. *IRS Employment Review*, 26 April, http://www.xperthr.co.uk/article/101779/irs-2010-dispute-resolution-survey--managing-discipline.aspx.**

Signpost to Chapter 7: Equality and Diversity in Employment, for information about harassment and bullying at work

**KEY CONCEPT Interpersonal conflict**

Wherever people 'work together', the potential exists for differences to emerge and, if these are left to develop, conflict to occur. Often the conflict between people is contained and does not create problems, but, under certain circumstances, it can become manifest and be expressed behaviourally, through actions and language. Interpersonal conflict exists primarily in the informal domain of day-to-day interactions, but can become formalized as it becomes manifest and difficult to ignore. The importance of interpersonal conflict lies in how it is handled. Three choices exist: 'flight', 'fight', or 'unite'. All three strategies can be adopted, but the one that offers most opportunity for long-term resolution is 'unite' (CIPD, 2007).

# Summary

- The vast majority of employees will not need to be disciplined by their employer because their performance and behaviour will be well within the bounds of what is considered appropriate and acceptable. The need to discipline someone should be, therefore, an unusual, and possibly exceptional, act.
- There will always be circumstances, however, that require an organization to take formal disciplinary measures in order to deal with a situation that is, or has become, unacceptable. The reasons why such action is considered necessary are mainly to do with poor performance, absenteeism, and a failure to comply with works rules, such as those relating to safe working practices, along with dishonesty and behaviour that infringes the rights of others.
- Formal disciplinary procedures are typically used to address situations, but the adoption of a more informal and flexible approach, including the use of mediation as part of a more sophisticated and less prescriptive strategy is becoming more widespread and is actively encourage under ACAS guidelines. This is certainly the case when dealing with employee grievances.

- The role of HR in this field is to ensure that legal requirements are met, that consistency of treatment is maintained and that employee rights are protected, but it must be recognized that this role has to go beyond the implementation of procedure. The need to explore underlying causes and influences, and, wherever possible, to address these is also an HR requirement.
- Grievances can potentially present more challenges to management and require careful investigation of all aspects of each case. Often cultural and gender issues are involved, and behaviours that were acceptable in the context of a certain group of employees become less so when the demographic of the workforce changes. If grievances are individual in nature, the resolution of the complaint may be achieved more acceptably through informal processes of discussion and mediation, rather than through creating an adversarial situation by invoking formal procedure. If, however, there is a discernible pattern of grievances, for example, from female employees who are concerned about sexist behaviour, then HR is faced with a different challenge—one of influencing attitudes and changing perceptions.

**Visit the Online Resource Centre that accompanies this book for self-test questions, weblinks, and more information on the topics covered in this chapter.**
**www.oxfordtextbooks.co.uk/orc/banfield_kay2e/**

## REVIEW QUESTIONS

1. What are the respective responsibilities of HR and line managers in the management of discipline and grievances?
2. What contribution might an organization's CEO make to ensure that these issues are effectively managed?
3. How does the philosophy of management affect the way in which misconduct is managed?
4. What are the features of a working organization environment that might be associated with low levels of misconduct and interpersonal conflict?
5. What are the advantages and limitations of relying on formal procedures to manage misconduct?

***See Online Resource Centre for answers.***

## CASE STUDY

### Unauthorized breaks at Brown Packaging

David Brown Packaging is a small, but highly efficient, supplier of packaging materials to the engineering industry. David, who is both the owner and managing director of the company, set it up 18 years ago. Over the years, his business has expanded and now involves selling to national and regional customers, in addition to a growing number of overseas organizations. The company manufactures and supplies good quality products, produced to high technical specification and delivered through a just-in-time production system. This means that the company has to be highly responsive and flexible to changing customer requirements.

The culture of the company has been shaped by David and his two senior managers, Alan Davis, director of production, and Chris Wilson, who is in charge of quality and research and development (R & D). Through their emphasis on quality standards, individual responsibility, and efficient organization, the company has forged a well-deserved reputation for reliability and innovation. On the employee side, considerable resources have been invested in operator training, with all shop-floor staff qualified to at least NVQ Level 2. The company's employment policies are progressive, pay is locally competitive and there is little evidence that the workforce is either dissatisfied with their conditions of employment or with how management treats them. The company has been able to create an environment in which standards of performance and commitment are high, but not at the expense of employees feeling good about their jobs. It's essentially an 'OK' place to work.

On Friday, 29 May, David had been invited to play in a corporate golf day at one of the local courses and had invited one of his friends, Bob White, to join him. Bob, as well as being his golfing partner, was also an HR consultant who had helped David to develop his HR strategy some years ago and he was familiar with the set-up there. Bob arrived at the factory around 1 p.m., left his car in the car park and travelled on to the competition in David's car.

The factory was operating a two-shift system at that time and the afternoon shift ran from 2 p.m. to 10 p.m., with a 30-minute break at 6 p.m. There were, during this time, 12 people on the shop floor working on machines and dispatching products to customer orders. Each team of six operatives was led by a supervisor, who was responsible for meeting the production targets and for ensuring that the operatives knew what was expected of them. The works manager, Richard Allenby, who had overall responsibility for the shift, was not on duty that day and the two supervisors were left in charge.

At around 7 p.m., David and Bob arrived back at the factory to transfer Bob's golfing equipment into his car. On arrival, most of the shift was playing football in the car park outside of the normal break time and, despite recognizing David, continued to play. Clearly, this was both surprising and disturbing although, given the circumstances, it was difficult to know what might explain the situation. David Brown decided not to confront the situation there and then, but to raise the issue first thing on Monday morning. To say that he was angry and annoyed was something of an understatement and, as he drove away, he also expressed his disappointment with what he had experienced. Because of his professional interest, Bob asked David to let him know how the situation was handled.



### Questions

1. Consider the action that David Brown should take in response to the situation.
2. Is there any form of managerial response that might be considered more effective than initiating formal disciplinary proceedings?
3. What objectives would management be seeking to achieve in the way in which the situation was handled?
4. If some form of disciplinary response were to be considered appropriate, who should be disciplined and what form should this take?
5. What are the dangers inherent to management being perceived to be acting disproportionately and unfairly?

## FURTHER READING

Chartered Institute of Personnel and Development (2007) *Discipline and Grievances at Work*, www.cipd.co.uk.

Fowler, A. (1998) *The Disciplinary Interview*, CIPD.

IRS Employment Review (2001) 'Managing discipline at work', *IRS Employment Review*, **727**, May, pp. 5-11.

## REFERENCES

Advisory Conciliation and Arbitration Service (2009a) *Code of Practice 1: Disciplinary and Grievance Procedure*, ACAS April 2009, www.acas.org.uk.

Advisory Conciliation and Arbitration Service (2009b) *Discipline and Grievances at Work*, ACAS November 2009, www.acas.org.uk.

Beyer (1984) 'A field study of the use and effects of discipline in controlling work performance', *Academy of Management Journal*, **27**:4, pp. 743–64.

Chartered Institute of Personnel and Development (2007) 'Managing conflict at work survey', www.cipd.co.uk.

Confederation for British Industry (2008) 'Annual absence survey', www.cbi.org.uk.

Employment Tribunals Service (2009) *Employment Tribunal and EAT Statistics 1 April 2008 to 1 April 2009*, www.employmenttribunals.gov.uk.

Frost, P.J., Nord, W.R. and Krefting, L.A. (2002) *HRM Reality*, 2nd ed., Prentice Hall.

Gouldner, A. (1954) *The Wildcat Strike*, Antioch Press.

Harvey, J. (1988) *The Abeline Paradox and Other Meditations on Management*, Jossey-Bass.

Health and Safety Executive, 'Rolls Royce: Improving Absence Management', www.hse.gov.uk/betterbusiness/large/casestudies_rolls.htm

Huberman, J. (1975) 'Discipline without punishment lives', *Harvard Business Review*, **53**:4, July/August, pp. 6–8.

Klass, B.S. and Wheeler, H.N. (1990) 'Managerial decision-making about employee discipline: A policy capturing approach', *Personnel Psychology*, **43**:1, pp. 117–34.

Konovsky, M.A. (2000) 'Understanding procedural justice and its impact on business organizations', *Journal of Management*, **26**:3, pp. 489–511.

O'Reilly, C.A. and Pfeffer, J. (2000) *Hidden Value*, Harvard Business School Press.

Rollinson, D., Hook, C., Foot, M. and Handley, J. (1996) 'Supervisor and manager styles in handling discipline and grievance', *Personnel Review*, **25**:4, pp. 38–55.

Suff, R. (2010) 'Dispute resolution survey: Managing discipline'. *IRS Employment Review*, 26 April, http://www.xperthr.co.uk/article/101779/irs-2010-dispute-resolution-survey--managing-discipline.aspx.

Younson, F. (2002) 'A lack of discipline', *People Management*, **8**:12, 13 June, p. 17.

# Equality and Diversity in Employment

## Key Terms

**Equal opportunity** The process of ensuring that employment practices in an organization are fair and unbiased, and do not breach any of the legislative provisions that are in place to protect workers from unlawful discrimination.

**Diversity** A multifaceted approach to the management of employees, reflecting the changing social and demographic characteristics of the workforce. The approach reflects the belief that maximizing the potential and contribution of all organizational stakeholders is inextricably linked to recognizing and valuing difference, and to treating people with respect.

**Discrimination** Treating a person or group of people less favourably compared to another person or group of people.

**Harassment** Any unwelcome attention or behaviour from another that a person finds offensive or unacceptable and which results in the person feeling offended, uncomfortable, or threatened, and leads to a loss of dignity or self-worth.

**Bullying** The abuse of power, or of physical or mental strength, by someone in a position of authority towards a person (or group of people), resulting in harmful stress and undermined self-confidence.

## Learning Objectives

As a result of reading this chapter and using the Online Resource Centre, you should be able to:

- understand the legislative framework that governs equal opportunities in the UK;
- understand the nature and consequences of discrimination;
- define the range of managerial approaches to managing diversity at work;
- explain the limitations of HR strategies in managing equality issues in the workplace;
- recognize the types of behaviour that constitute harassment and bullying, and recommend managerial approaches to deal with these issues.

# Introduction

Fair employment is perhaps one of the most controversial and emotive of all HR issues. It is also a theme that permeates every other aspect of HR, in the sense that the requirement for managers to act in a fair manner and to avoid unlawful discriminatory practices is not restricted to any one part of HR, but extends to them all. While we have devoted a chapter exclusively to the subject of fairness in employment, in recognition of its growing importance, the topic features in many other chapters, particularly those dealing with recruitment and selection, rewards, grievance and discipline, and employee relations.

One reason why the focus on fairness in employment and the need to avoid certain types of discriminatory practice is growing is because employers are now required to cope with an increasingly complex and demanding raft of legislation. This legislation has been designed to protect the rights of groups of people who, historically, have been at a disadvantage in the workplace. An employer who 'gets it wrong' and fails to embrace the concepts of equal opportunities and non-discriminatory practices at work not only risks costly claims of discrimination through employment tribunals, but also loses status and respect.

**KEY CONCEPT Fair and fairness**

These can be understood as characteristics or outcomes of the way in which people are treated, for example, people being paid fairly, but the terms can also be used to describe characteristics of a person's behaviour or of a procedure. Phrases such as 'the managers in this company treat people fairly—there are no favourites' and 'the performance appraisal system doesn't contain bias' capture the practical importance of this concept. For the purposes of this chapter, 'fairness' encompasses a decision-making process that, when applied to employees, is based solely on merit. It is also important because of the effects of *not* treating employees fairly. As an example, research quoted in Chapter 3 shows that applicants who feel that the procedures used in recruitment assessment and selection are unfair may well decide not to continue with an application and may seek employment elsewhere (Chambers, 2002). Fair procedures in recruitment ensure that the best candidate is attracted and selected, based only on his or her individual merits, and focus on predicting the ability of prospective employees to carry out the job.

Any definition of 'fairness' normally involves some reference to equality of treatment, but another way of understanding its significance is to see fairness in the context of the distribution of benefits or obligations between two parties: in such an exchange relationship, there is—or should be—a reasonable balance between what the two parties give and receive. Fairness does not, however, necessarily mean equal treatment: unequal treatment can still be considered to be fair if it is possible to justify the different treatment experienced by an individual or group. Discriminatory treatment in the workplace is not only allowed, but actually necessary if HR is to make the contributions expected of it, but only in situations in which the criteria for treating people differently can be justified (Hyman and Brough, 1975).

# Unlawful Discrimination

While it is recognized that discrimination is an everyday feature of employment, it is clear that certain types of discrimination, not based on justifiable, merit-based needs of an organization, are unacceptable, offensive, and potentially damaging towards those who are disadvantaged by such treatment. Furthermore, such discrimination is likely to be offensive to the majority of those employed and the community in which the organization operates, and can impair the ability of the organization to provide goods and services.

**Table 7.1** Types of unlawful discrimination

| Basis of discrimination | Special provisions |
|---|---|
| Age | Retirement is no longer a fair reason for dismissal and there must be an objective justification |
| Disability | Special definition of disability and requirement to make 'reasonable adjustments' |
| Marriage or civil partnership | Employers should protect the confidentiality of the existence of a marriage or civil partnership |
| Gender reassignment | An employee does not need to be under medical supervision to be covered by protection. Time off for reassignment can be treated like other ill-health absence |
| Pregnancy or maternity | |
| Race | |
| Religion or belief | |
| Sex | |
| Sexual orientation | |

Since the 1970s, a number of Acts of Parliament have defined the types of discrimination that are unlawful in the workplace and in terms of the provision of goods and services. These were combined under the Equality Act 2010 (Commission for Equality and Human Rights 2010). The Act provides protection against discrimination on the grounds of 'protected characteristics' listed in Table 7.1.

**STUDENT ACTIVITY 7.1**

**This exercise is designed to explore the experiences of students in relation to discriminatory and/or unfair treatment, and should be undertaken as a storytelling activity.**

**In groups, share personal experiences of employment or social situations in which people felt they had been discriminated against. Explore the basis of the discriminatory treatment and identify who was the discriminating party. Finally, consider which situations presented to the group might be considered to be examples of unacceptable—or legitimate—discrimination.**

# The Origins of Equal Opportunities

The arguments used by those in favour of fair and equal treatment at work are based on the belief that many, historical and contemporary, employment practices have been based on personal and institutionalized ignorance and prejudice. Such characteristics have been increasingly at odds with a society in which those socially or economically disadvantaged by such practices were no longer prepared to accept them.

Signpost to Chapter 5: Managing Employee Relations, for perspectives on developments in relations between employers and employees

This led to the growth in what became known as 'equal opportunities' and also incorporated the notion of non-discriminatory treatment generally. At the heart of this movement was the strongly held conviction that people should not be treated differently on the basis of their gender, race, ethnicity, sexual orientation, age, or physical or mental impairment. This justification for not treating people differently is rooted in many of the world's great religions, but also in the humanistic philosophy that affirms the dignity and worth of all people. Such a commitment can also be found in the Treaty of Rome, signed in 1957, provisions of which have led to a Europe-wide movement to eliminate certain kinds of discriminatory employment practice (Hill, 2003).

In a somewhat simplistic, although helpful, way, the evolution from 'equal opportunities' to 'diversity', which many believe incorporates a commitment to equal opportunities, can be seen to be linked, in part, to a quite different justification. This is based on the so-called 'business', or 'pragmatic', case for treating people fairly, with respect and, where justified, equally. Again, at the core of this argument is the belief that employee morale and performance can be undermined by managers who fail to take the questions of equal opportunities and diversity seriously. This second justification relies on the belief that treating employees in a particular way is not only about legislative compliance and the avoidance of potentially expensive and embarrassing tribunal cases, but is based on the claim that advocating diversity in employment is 'good for business' as well as being ethically sound.

## The Business Case for Diversity

We can see, then, there are both legal and morale arguments in favour of diversity as an approach, but why should organizations adopt this approach unless it is to their advantage. The CIPD (2010) states that there are three broad factors which form the business case for diversity. Firstly there are people issues. The argument here is that by adopting a best practice approach to diversity, employees will be more highly motivated and committed and it will be easier to retain staff, thus reducing the need for recruitment. Employees will be less likely to suffer from stress, will have better attendance levels, and there will be less disruption in the workplace. It will also be easier to attract a broader talent pool and having a wider group of applicants will result in better calibre members of staff who are able to contribute in a more creative and innovative way to the organization. Secondly, there are market competitiveness benefits in that a more diverse workforce can help an organization to be more accessible to a wider potential pool of customers and can help improve service levels to a wider range of users through increased awareness. There may be benefits from being able to increase customer choice and service through a product offering that is better tailored to reflect the balance within communities and the global market place. There may also be enhanced opportunities to win contracts or business from other organizations that seek commitments to diversity from their suppliers as part of their sourcing policies. Thirdly, there are corporate reputation benefits. Corporate branding may be enhanced by being more representative of the communities and customers that the organization serves. Increasingly employers are adopting Corporate Social Responsibility policies that reflect their overall commitments, diversity being one part of many social commitments that reflect the image the company wishes to portray (Grosser and Moon, 2005).

Diversity is increasingly important to organizations that operate in a global market place both employing people and sourcing goods and services from countries that do not have the same levels of employment protection that we benefit from throughout Europe. The impact of adverse publicity relating to business activities, which are seen by global customers as unacceptable, particularly for large global consumer brands can be extremely detrimental. The role that multinational corporations can have in contributing towards ending or controlling exploitation in countries that do not benefit from protective legislation is both controversial and a source of concern and debate (Briscoe and Schuler, 2004; Oxfam, 2004), however there is also a positive and much more direct role that can be played by organizations in the way they market their products and regulate supplier employment practices. (See www.fairtrade.org.uk for more information.)

**STUDENT ACTIVITY 7.2 The influence of the global market on human rights**

In groups research the positive and negative influences that multinational organizations have had upon human rights. Answer the following questions:

1. How can multinational enterprises ensure that they adopt diversity practices that benefit both the countries in which they operate and source products and services and the organization as a whole?
2. What steps are necessary to ensure that a best practice intention is actually carried out?

**RESEARCH INSIGHT 7.1**

To take your learning further you might want to read this article:

**Arnold, D. and Hartman, L. (2005) 'Beyond sweatshops: Positive deviancy and global labour practices', *Business Ethics: A European review*. July, 14:3, pp. 206–22.**

This article discusses why so called 'sweatshops' exist and the arguments for mandated improvement of such conditions. There is more in depth consideration of what minimum standards should apply. Finally there are examples of multinational corporations who operate successfully in these environments and exercise a positive influence on economic activity and social conditions.

This is the view of the CBI (2008). In a joint report with the TUC and Commission for Equality and Human Rights it expressed the view that:

> **A firm's success and competitiveness depends on its ability to embrace diversity and draw on the skills, understanding and experience of all its people. The potential rewards of diversity are significant: an organisation that recruits its staff from the widest possible pool will unleash talent and develop better understanding of its customers. It will also enable it to spot market opportunities.**

The reality is that, when asked to identify the key drivers for diversity within their organizations, most of the organizations surveyed identified legal pressures as the most important influence. But other drivers, such as the improvement of business performance and its moral rightness, also figured prominently in employer responses. Table 7.2 summarizes the most frequently cited reasons for adopting a diversity approach to HR.



The impact of developments in equal opportunities legislation and diversity management is not only limited to the workforce and the workplace. Customers, suppliers, and the market or community in which an organization operates have increased protection and expectations as a result of a series of legislative provisions. This is particularly evident in the way in which employers operate in the labour market and in the hiring of external suppliers. For organizations such as the police, however, for which the workplace is also the community, the impact of legislative and social change governing behaviour has been profound (Macpherson, 1999).

Many employers have actively embraced the concepts of equality and diversity, and associated employment and managerial practices, recognizing that such a commitment is an expression of genuine support for these developments and of an understanding that they have been in business' best interests. For example,

**Table 7.2** Key drivers supporting a diversity approach in employment

| **Drivers for diversity** | **Percentage of respondents** |
|---|---|
| Legal pressures | 68 |
| To recruit and retain best talent | 64 |
| Corporate responsibility | 63 |
| To be an employer of choice | 61 |
| Because it makes business sense | 60 |
| Because it's morally right | 60 |
| To improve business performance | 48 |
| To address recruitment problems | 46 |
| Belief in social justice | 46 |

**Source**: This material is taken from 'Diversity in Business: A Focus for Progress Survey Report' (CIPD, 2007), with the permission of the publisher, the Chartered Institute of Personnel and Development, London.

in the 1980s, being an 'equal opportunities employer' was seen as a desirable badge that helped to attract talented applicants from a more diverse social and ethnic labour market. More recently, organizations competing in tight labour markets, particularly for knowledge workers, have recognized the importance of being perceived as an 'employer of choice' or an 'employer of first choice'. Employers who seek this status frequently emphasize the importance they attach to fair employment practices and to opportunities for all of their employees, and the value they place on diversity within their workforce. In a recent Singapore survey of entry-level graduates, looking at which employers were considered to be employers of choice and what they needed to offer to attract new graduates, the most important factor cited was good career growth and opportunities. Other factors given a high rating in the survey included corporate culture and whether the company was socially and environmentally responsible. All three factors, either directly or indirectly, relate to an organization's position on equality and diversity matters (JobsFactory, 2006; Backhaus and Tikoo, 2004).

As an example of diversity in practice, it is worth looking at the Irish economy and the influence of multinational corporations on diversity practices and management. At one level, it is simply the degree of diversity in the workforce that helps to explain the growing interest in diversity management. Microsoft, for example, attracts talented people from all over the world and about 20 per cent of its 2,000 employees employed in Ireland are not Irish, with almost 40 different nationalities represented on-site. Google represents a similar story. Since opening in Ireland in 2003, it has developed to such an extent that it also employs staff from 40 different countries, speaking 30 different languages. But the commitment that such companies make to diversity policies and practices also reflects the philosophy and values of the company as well as the legal requirements for equality of opportunity. In the Irish national 'Best Companies to Work for in Ireland' recognition scheme, Intel Ireland won the overall national diversity award for 'presenting new and effective ways to promote diversity in the workplace'. Speaking at a conference on women in science and technology, the head of HR development at Intel Ireland claimed that its diversity initiative was not something new, but reflected a long-established commitment to developing leadership and diversity policies, of which gender is a part. She went on to claim that such commitment is the driving factor behind her company's economic performance:

> **By promoting a better and more equitable environment for all its employees, Intel retains the best people and gives them the support to grow and productively use their individual insights and talents to increase our leadership across the industry worldwide.**

Although organizations ignore equal opportunities at their peril, changing attitudes and behaviours to difference and diversity cannot easily be ignored, particularly because unacceptable behaviours are often culturally or institutionally embedded. Cases such as the resignation of a number of police officers from the Greater Manchester Police force, following the screening of an undercover documentary by the BBC in 2003 featuring shocking coverage of the officers' racist attitudes, reveal how, despite careful selection methods and compulsory diversity training, discriminatory practices can survive and inflict serious damage on an organization's reputation.

In summary, the trend in the UK seems to be a movement away from what can be considered the more limiting concept of 'equal opportunities' towards the more sophisticated and less prescriptive notion of 'diversity'. Given the lack of precisions in language and meaning, however, it would be unwise to see this as anything other than a generalized and, to a degree, controversial movement. In terms of what these two related ideologies represent, we have argued that:

- an equal opportunities approach is essentially about compliance and making sure that minimum standards and good practice are in place;
- a diversity approach places a greater emphasis on the economic benefits of an all-encompassing approach that looks not only to minimize the risks to the organization of claims of unlawful discrimination, but seeks to maximize the economic benefits of having a diverse workforce from many different backgrounds in order to provide a better service either to the customers or to the community that the organization serves.

If this is a useful distinction, we can also argue that diversity is the more strategic of the two concepts, with implications for an organization's competitive advantage generated through a creative and productive labour force, and the leveraging of potential to support key organizational objectives. For some, these objectives may be financial; for others, the reputational benefits may be more important.

**RESEARCH INSIGHT 7.2**

To take your learning further you might want to read this article:

**Kochan, T. et al. (2003), 'The effects of diversity on business performance', report of the Diversity Research Network, *Human Resource Management*, 42, pp. 3–21.**

This article shows evidence that it is extremely complex to quantify the benefits of diversity in terms of performance and that it is difficult to identify many direct links between adopting a diversity approach and performance. However, there was some indication that gender-balanced teams performed either at similar levels or slightly better and there was also evidence that negative effects of diversity may manifest where there is a highly competitive context between teams, with positive outcomes being more likely where the organization promotes learning from diversity.



**STUDENT ACTIVITY 7.3 Testing meanings and perceptions**

This activity can be carried out within organizations, if students have access, or within the college/university. Working in groups design a questionnaire to investigate and generate evidence on what people think about equal opportunities and diversity in relation to their meanings and values/contributions. The questionnaire does not need to be particularly long or complicated, but must address the following questions:

1. What do employees/managers think 'equal opportunities' is concerned with?
2. What do employees/managers think 'diversity' is concerned with?
3. Rather than assuming that they are a 'good thing', identify what the advantages are to different organizational stakeholders of developing HR policies and practices around both concepts.
4. What do employees/managers feel are the disadvantages and problems of organizations committing to one, or both, positions?
5. On the basis of analysis of the data collected, produce a presentation entitled 'Equal opportunities and diversity: a balanced assessment' and discuss the issues raised.

# Stereotype, Prejudice, and Discrimination

In trying to understand what unacceptable and unjustifiable discriminatory practices are based upon, it is important to appreciate the influence on behaviour of the concepts of the 'stereotype' and 'prejudice'.

**KEY CONCEPT Stereotype**

A stereotype is a fixed idea or popular misconception about an individual or group of people. It can similarly be thought of as a conventional, formulaic, and oversimplified opinion or image that one person has of another, which has the effect of conditioning that person's perceptions of, and attitudes towards, the other. One effect of stereotypes is that we tend to see everyone from a given group, race or category in very similar and pre-determined ways, with the result that we don't recognize differences.

**KEY CONCEPT Prejudice**

A prejudice can be thought of as a preconceived view of someone, despite knowing little or nothing about that person. Prejudices are triggered by someone reacting to superficial characteristics, such as gender, race, or colour. They are formed through conscious and unconscious socialization processes, as well as through general experiences that predispose the person towards a positive or negative view of another.

As far as HR is concerned, both the influence of stereotypes and prejudices are not simply an issue for managers: they potentially affect everyone. In areas such as recruitment and selection, and promotion and career development, they can be particularly important and can help to explain how discriminatory decisions are influenced by subjective and distorted perceptions, rather than by those based on objective and rational considerations.

The process of appraising employees is also an area of HR in which the potential for error, bias, and prejudice is high. Coens and Jenkins (2002) talk about the tendency to categorize, that is, the process of psychologically locating a person into a particular group that is associated with either positive or negative value judgements. This is then associated with the instinctive allocation of behavioural patterns that reflect these value judgements to individuals and groups.

It is, of course, human nature to evaluate a person when we meet him or her for the first time and, often, we will begin to make judgements very quickly, based on other people we have met or stereotypes that we have acquired. 'Liking' and 'disliking' may also be the product of what we might call 'chemistry', although this is not something that can be rationally explained. People will automatically make value judgements about others, often on the most limited of information, and will feel more comfortable and able to build rapport with those who they perceive to be like themselves. When meeting someone for the first time, we will often try to establish what we have in common to help to 'break the ice' and to ease the conversation. It is important then to recognize that these processes go on all the time and often at the subconscious, rather than conscious, level. The point to note is not that basic human traits and tendencies can, or should, be suspended when we enter the workplace, but rather that we all need to be aware of them and to make a conscious effort not to allow prejudice and bias to affect rational and objective decision-making (Rick et al., 2000).

# Approaches to Fair Employment

Figure 7.1 demonstrates the three different approaches that organizations can take to fair employment.

## Partial or non-compliance

The first approach is described as 'partial compliance' or 'non-compliance'. This approach is perhaps more apparent in smaller, more stable firms which perhaps do not feel that they have sufficient time and resources to be able to adopt all of the measures that would be regarded as 'best practice'. At the risk of being controversial, many small firms operate very successfully in environments in which there are few explicit fair employment policies and often inconsistent implementation, but do not experience the level of claims that might otherwise be associated with such practices. It may also be that organizations falling into this category come from the small to medium-sized enterprise (SME) sector, in which the pressures for survival and financial stability are such that matters of equal opportunities and diversity have less impact and importance than they might in larger, and in many public sector, organizations. Context, resources, and awareness are important differentiators indicating which model organizations are likely to identify with or be capable of adopting.

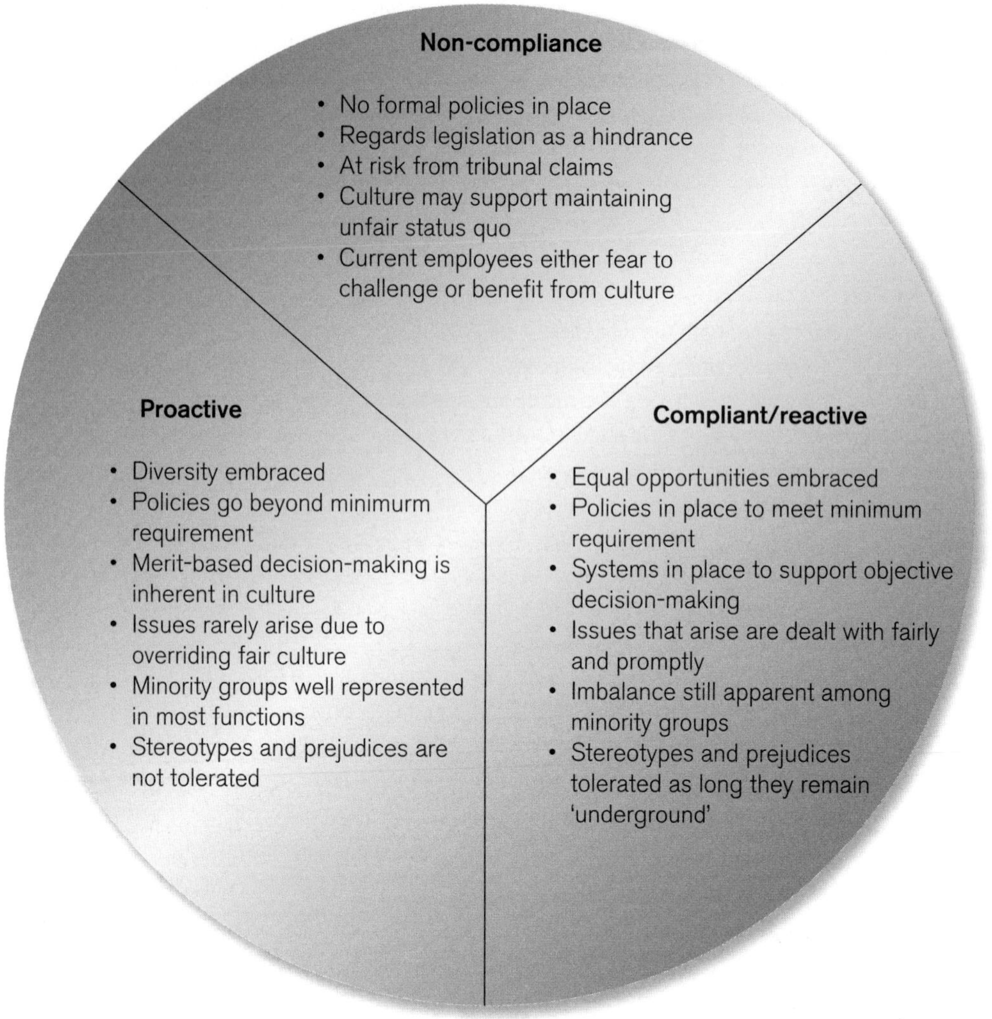

**Figure 7.1** Characteristics of different organizational approaches to fair employment

Merit may not be the only basis for discriminating between employees in terms of jobs, rewards, and developmental opportunities. Familial connections may have an important influence in companies that seem to adopt a more idiosyncratic approach to issues of equality and diversity. Employees who fear the consequences of challenging unfair, and possibly discriminatory, practices may be less inclined to put pressure on employers to develop more consistent, and objective, HR and employment practices. It is also possible that an unfair and subjective decision may sometimes be masked by what appears to be an objective justification, making it difficult to challenge. In other words, unfair and unlawful discriminatory treatment might be difficult to prove if the reason for a candidate failing to get a job or to be promoted is presented as a more acceptable justification, such as lack of experience and potential, rather than grounds of race or gender, or another unlawful reason.

Applicants are unlikely to challenge decisions not to appoint them if they have been treated respectfully and if the reasons for non-selection seem to be merit-based. Decisions on recruitment and promotion that are not linked to job performance criteria and evidence-based assessments may still be, in the minds of those who take them, rational and defendable. In other words, the person who is appointed for reasons to do with family connections and considerations of loyalty may, in the mind of the owner making the decision, be the 'best person' even though others might consider themselves better qualified using more conventional selection criteria and approaches. This kind of organizational culture survives in many owner-managed companies, particularly in countries within which family, and the importance of trust and loyalty, are held in high esteem. Rather than condemn such thinking and practices, it is important to try to understand why this type of approach still exists and is valued, even though it challenges many of the presumptions and tenets of equal opportunities and diversity.

Signpost to Chapter 8: International HRM

## Compliant/reactive

The second commonly experienced approach can be described as 'reactive' or 'compliant'. This approach can be found in many successful organizations. A full set of equal opportunities and diversity policies are likely to have been developed, with a particular emphasis on assessment, recruitment, and training. In organizations within which this approach has either evolved or been explicitly adopted, issues are generally dealt with promptly and effectively using established procedures, but there is likely still to be some cultural resistance to embracing fully the idea of a balanced and diverse workforce. This may be because the business case has either not been properly developed or communicated, or, if the business case has been made, has not been backed up by the predicted outcomes. In other situations, the reactive approach reflects a degree of uncertainty about how far a commitment to equal opportunities and diversity should extend. There are genuine questions raised about whether equal opportunities and diversity are ends in themselves or simply means to ends, in which case, they would need to compete with other HR and managerial strategies that might be considered more effective in meeting organizational objectives.

While managers and staff can be 'fully trained' and briefed about their obligations under both legislation and organizational policy, it is perhaps not seen as being in the interests of the organization to go beyond this minimum requirement. Prejudices and stereotypes may still be held by some managers and some staff but, due to the 'rules', everyone knows that these must not be expressed. Those in under-represented minority groups may be singled out as examples of equal opportunities good practice, but whether this can be considered fully representative is open to question. For example, 'politically correct' recruitment literature featuring female engineers, male nurses, or ethnic minorities in managerial positions are impressive at one level, but the reality may be that these groups are consistently under-represented in the organization. The HR department may have all the correct policies in place but, behind the scenes, there may continue to be unchallenged biases in recruitment, training, and promotional decision-making.

## Proactive

A 'proactive' approach is often adopted by larger organizations in ways that can be considered to be systemic or culturally embedded. A proactive approach often reflects a broad array of policies and procedures that go beyond the minimum required to be compliant with legislation and recommended good practice. For example, holiday policies that include special provisions for observance of the religious holidays of different faiths, or extended maternity, paternity, and flexible working provisions, may be adopted. While the HR function can ensure the development of comprehensive, broad-reaching policy, communications, and training programmes, it is the extent to which diversity is embraced at all levels of the organization and particularly by those in senior positions that distinguishes a proactive organization from one that is reactive. Diversity goes beyond simply treating everyone in the same way, recognizing instead that different groups of people have different needs and expectations of work and employment. This might be expressed in the nature and length of the working day, flexible working arrangements, the types of food offered in the cafeteria and opportunities for worship. To be a fully proactive organization, diversity issues need to inform every aspect of organizational decision-making and may well extend into the field of positive action (see later in the chapter). The overriding feature of this proactive approach is a culture of tolerance that embraces the value of difference.

**HRM INSIGHT 7.1 Intel**

Intel, which is the world's leading producer of computer chips and operates globally, is a good example of a company that has embraced equal opportunities and diversity in a proactive and systemic way. In Intel, all employees are required to behave in ways that reflect its position on these matters.

As far as equality of employment opportunities are concerned, this is what the company has to say:

> We respect, value, and welcome diversity in our workforce, as well as in our customers, our suppliers, and the global marketplace. Our policy is to provide equal employment opportunities for all applicants and employees.
>
> We do not discriminate on the basis of race, color, religion, sex, national origin, ancestry, age, disability, veteran status, marital status, gender identity or sexual orientation. This policy applies to all aspects and stages of employment from recruitment through retirement. It prohibits harassment of any individual or group.

This commitment is supported by a genuine desire to encourage openness and a feeling among individual employees that their views and opinions are valued. The company goes on to say that:

> Our long-standing Open Door guidelines encourage employees at every level, regardless of their title or role, to raise issues and to expect a timely response and resolution. We regularly conduct worldwide internal organizational surveys that include diversity aspects, and we share these survey results and their related action plans with our employees. This open exchange of ideas and concerns promotes a fair and respectful workplace for all of our employees worldwide.
>
> (www.intel.com)

Questions

1. What advantages does this policy offer to Intel?
2. Is this an approach that might be recommended to an SME? If not, why not?
3. Is there an inconsistency between the concept of 'equality' and that of 'diversity'?

**STUDENT ACTIVITY 7.4**

Consider all of the types of provision made in your organization to promote diversity.

1. List as many types of provision that have not been considered as you can think of, which may support the agenda for improving diversity.
2. Compare your thoughts with those of a colleague with a different gender, age, or ethnic background.
3. Consider the significance of any differences that may emerge.

# Legal Framework

The first elements in the legal framework for equal opportunities legislation were introduced in the 1970s, when it became unlawful to pay an employee a lower wage for doing the same job as a colleague of the opposite sex. It also became unlawful to discriminate against employees on the grounds of their gender or marital status and their race, nationality, and ethnic or racial origin. In more recent years, protection has been extended to many other groups.

## Direct discrimination

*Direct* discrimination occurs if an individual treats a person, or group of people, less favourably than he or she treats another person or group. Yet, in employment, we discriminate between people all the time: for example, managers are usually on more favourable terms and conditions than are those at more junior levels. The difference is that direct and unlawful discrimination occurs if the less favourable treatment is specifically due to one of the items in the listed in Table 7.1, which includes sex, race, or age. In addition the Equality Act 2010 also makes it unlawful to discriminate by 'association', that is to discriminate because of a person's association with another person with a protected characteristic or by 'perception', where a person is perceived to have a protected characteristic even where this is not the case.

For further discussion on positive action and positive discrimination see the Online Resource Centre extension material 7.3

## Indirect discrimination

*Indirect* discrimination occurs if a requirement or condition, while applied equally, cannot be justified and results in less favourable treatment of a person from one group compared to others not of that group. Examples of indirect discrimination might be:

- an organization introducing a dress code that is not suitable for persons of a particular religious belief. Although that dress code would apply equally to all, it would indirectly discriminate against people of that particular religious belief;
- an organization requiring candidates to undertake a fitness test for a job, which includes lifting a 20kg weight, when the job regularly involves lifting weights of no more than 10kg. This requirement would indirectly discriminate against women, because fewer women than men would be able to meet the criteria, and it would not be justifiable given the capabilities required for carrying out the job;
- an organization deciding to advertise a senior job internally when the current ethnic or gender mix is unbalanced. This may restrict access of minority groups to more senior posts.

## Genuine occupational qualification

Discrimination can be justified if there is what is known as a 'genuine occupational qualification'. For example, if an actor is required to play the part of a black person in a film, applications might justifiably be restricted to those from black people. Another example might be insisting on a particular language being spoken by a support worker or social worker employed to work specifically with people from a particular ethnic group among which spoken English tends to be limited.

# Disability Discrimination

## What is a 'disability'?

Under the Equality Act 2010, 'disability' is defined as a physical or mental impairment that has a substantial and long-term adverse affect on a person's ability to carry out normal day-to-day activities. Normal day-to-day activities can now include any number of elements and the restricted list included when disability legislation was first introduced (The Disability Discrimination Act (1995)) which included elements such as mobility, manual dexterity, and speech has been removed in favour of the general definition in itself. Discrimination is now defined as a 'detriment arising from disability' (Eversheds, 2010). Case law has helped to

**Table 7.3** The questions asked by a tribunal in deciding if a claimant has a disability

| Question asked | Considerations |
|---|---|
| Does the claimant have an impairment? | Both the cause of the impairment and its effects |
| Does the impairment have an adverse effect on the claimant's ability to carry out day-to-day activities? | Prior to the introduction of the Equality Act 2010 the 'considerations' were restricted to a defined list, but this list has been replaced by a general requirement and so any impairment that results in a substantial impairment may be considered |
| Is the effect of the impairment substantial? | Whether the effect is minor or trivial |
| | That effects can be cumulative |
| | Also required to deduce what the effects of the impairment would be 'but for' treatment, i.e. without treatment |
| Is the effect of the impairment long term? | Whether the impairment has lasted, or is likely to last, for at least 12 months |

define further the types of impairment that are likely to distinguish someone as disabled and include not being able to apply make-up for a woman (*Ekpe v Commissioner of Police for the Metropolis* (2001) IRLR 605) and playing football, snooker, and cycling for a 29-year-old man (*Coca-Cola Enterprises v Shergill* (2003) EAT 5–21). There are exceptions to conditions that are not classed as disabilities: people whose eyesight can be corrected by wearing spectacles, for example, and those suffering from addiction are not classed as disabled.

Table 7.3 shows the questions that are now addressed by a tribunal in making a decision about whether or not a claimant is disabled.

## Reasonable adjustments

If a person is disabled, an employer is expected to consider making reasonable adjustments to accommodate the person's particular needs. This might include alterations to a person's working conditions, to their workplace, or to access to goods, facilities, and services. Adjustments might include, for example, altering someone's hours, modifying instructions or procedures, and modifying or acquiring equipment. In deciding what is reasonable, it is not only the cost that should be taken into consideration, but the effectiveness of the adjustment and the resources available to the employer, as well as the disruption to the employer.

This is a very complex area and many organizations employ specialist medical and advisory services to help to assess the extent of a person's disability and what adjustments are reasonable. In cases of disagreement, employment tribunals may be called upon to make the definitive decision. It is therefore important that medical opinions are supported by additional information, which might include details of exactly what a person can and cannot do, because medical opinion alone will be insufficient to defend a claim to a tribunal.

The types of adjustment that an employer should consider in accommodating a disabled person include:

- improving access to the premises or changing its physical features;
- reallocating duties;
- altering hours of work;
- assigning a different place of work;
- acquiring or modifying equipment;
- providing auxiliary aids;
- modifying instructions manuals or procedures;
- providing a reader or interpreter.

# Facts and figures behind disability

In 2001, around one in five people of working age in private households had a long-term disability (Smith and Twomey, 2002). This is a surprisingly high number of people and encompasses a very wide number of conditions, from those more traditionally associated with disability, such as visual impairment or use of a wheelchair, to more recently defined conditions, such as dyslexia and depression. A more recent analysis of the statistical data produced the following results:

- 1.3 million disabled people in the UK are available for and want to work.
- 50 per cent of disabled people in the UK of working age are in work compared with 80 per cent of non disabled people.
- Employment rates vary according to the type of impairment a person has; only 20 per cent of people with mental health problems are in employment.
- 23 per cent of disabled people have no qualifications compared to 9 per cent of non disabled people.
- 7 million people of working age have a disability.
- The average gross hourly pay for disabled employees is £11.08 compared to £12.30 for non disabled employees.

**Source**: Office for National Statistics (2009)

Meager et al. (1999) concluded that the most common impairments among applicants to tribunals are problems with hands or arms, problems with the back or neck, and mental impairments such as depression and anxiety. Moreover, they showed that less than one in ten cases involved recruitment decisions. Hurstfield et al. (2004) found that less than half of the applicants to a tribunal had even considered themselves to be disabled prior to their case being submitted.

It would therefore seem that, from an employment perspective, the disability legislation is of more benefit to those in employment who lose their jobs through becoming disabled while in employment than it is to those with what might be regarded as more severe disabilities. These people may find it hard even to enter employment because the adjustments that would be required to accommodate them may be beyond that which would be considered reasonable.

**HRM INSIGHT 7.2 The extent of the requirement to make reasonable adjustments**

**John has worked for a large retail outlet for four years. Two years ago, he suffered a breakdown in personal relationships outside work and he has experienced three separate spells of absence due to depression since this time. Over the two years since the breakdown, John's conduct at work has been a problem. He has received a succession of warnings for failing to follow instructions given to him by his supervisor, for taking unauthorized breaks, for smoking in an unauthorized area and has now been dismissed, following an incident in which he made an abusive hand gesture at a manager. At each stage, his employer followed disciplinary procedures that were fully compliant with ACAS guidelines on managing conduct issues.**

**Following his dismissal, John submitted a claim for unfair dismissal and disability discrimination. He argues that his depression is a disability and affects day-to-day activities, such as his abilities to concentrate, to be able to get out of bed in the morning and his ability to sustain normal relationships with people. He states that his depression led to his inappropriate behaviour at work, and that the company should have made reasonable adjustments and not pursued disciplinary action for minor breaches of conduct rules at work.**

**Questions**

1. **Considering Table 7.3, what arguments might the claimant and respondent in this case make in favour of and against John having a disability?**
2. **Consider the list of reasonable adjustments: would it be reasonable for any of these to be made for John?**
3. **What arguments might the respondent use to defend this case?**

# Age Discrimination

Like disability discrimination, age discrimination legislation varies slightly from other discrimination legislation. Firstly, age is a continuum and the boundaries that distinguish one group from another can only be arbitrarily set. ACAS, in its guide for employers (2006a), recommends a series of age bands, each comprising broadly ten years, with which employers will be able to monitor numbers of employees in different age groups.

In addition to the usual aspects of the legislation, which make direct and indirect discrimination unlawful, there are specific references to elements of treatment that, until the introduction of the legislation, were common practice in many organizations. What is interesting is that it is not necessarily the old that discriminate in favour of the old and the young in favour of the young: Oswick and Rosenthal (2001) demonstrated that older workers are often subject to discrimination at the hands of managers of a similar age.

## Service-related benefits

To prevent service benefits from automatically being classed as age discriminatory, there are special provisions. Any benefit earned by having service of up to five years is exempt, that is, a pay increment automatically earned after five years of service is more likely to be gained by an older employee, but the legislation cannot be used to challenge this. There may also be examples of non-pay benefits earned over five years, such as extra holidays, which have been put in place to reward loyalty or to increase motivation. If an employer can provide evidence that this is the case—such as an attitude survey, for example—there may be an objective justification for the practice.



## Retirement provisions

The legislation originally introduced 'retirement' as a fair reason for dismissal. Employers typically set their normal retirement age (NRA) at 65 years old, because it was hard to justify using a lower age. This provision was subject to fierce opposition and the provision was removed in April 2011 requiring employers to demonstrate an objective justification should enforced retirement be in place for any group of employees at any age.

# Equal Pay

Legislation about equal pay is an extension of sex discrimination legislation relating to the pay and benefits awarded to men and women in employment. The principle is that a man or woman engaged in 'like work', 'work of equal value', or 'work rated as equivalent' should receive the same contractual pay and benefits. For example, if a man and a woman are employed in similar jobs, but the man receives a higher salary than the woman, she can apply to an employment tribunal on the grounds that she has been unfairly discriminated against. If she is successful, the organization will be required to pay her the higher rate of pay. Awards can be backdated and comparators need not be current employees, so it would be possible for a woman who is paid less than her male predecessor to bring a claim.

In order to defend an equal pay claim, an employer will need to have in place an objective job evaluation scheme that helps to justify any differences in terms of the relative value of the work. The subject of job evaluation is covered in more detail in a later chapter.

Signpost to Chapter 12: Managing Rewards, for more detail on job evaluation

## The burden of proof

If an employee elects to take a complaint of discrimination to a tribunal, he or she simply has to show that there is reason to believe that he or she may have been discriminated against. It is then up to the employer to provide a 'written objective defence' against the claim, which, in effect, means that the burden of proof is upon the employer: it must demonstrate that discrimination did not take place, using whatever documentation it has available.

It is therefore important to make sure that decision-making, in all aspects of employment, is fully recorded. Even if an employer has not discriminated against an employee, it will be impossible to defend a claim without such a written record. Ironically, a claim for unlawful discrimination may succeed, not because the discrimination did take place, but because the employer could not disprove it!

# Recommended Best Practice in Equal Opportunities

The concept of 'best practice' has increasingly become part of the language of HR and its value, as well as its limitations, was explored earlier in the book. In the context of equal opportunities and diversity, there is a strong prescriptive element to many of the reports and guides available to the HR practitioner (see ACAS, 2009), and a wealth of advice is available for those seeking help in implementing equal opportunities in the workplace and wishing to embrace the concept of diversity. In contrast, the 'best-fit' approach to HR—where each organization decides on the basis of its unique circumstances and requirements on equal opportunities and diversity practices—is rarely considered, in part because of the universality of legislative requirements.

However, the concept of 'best practice' is unfortunately associated with the idea that there is only one way towards reaching a stated objective and that this is, in some way, 'better' than any other. While this is an attractive prospect, it is also simplistic and misleading. Best practice does not guarantee the outcomes that are being pursued and, indeed, what might appear to conform to best practice may result in unintended and unhelpful consequences. The Key Concepts of formal and material rationality found in Chapter 2 are helpful in understanding this point.

What is being argued here is that there is no single correct solution to ensuring equality of opportunity within an organization. Adopting a contingency perspective, the approach taken will need to be tailored to suit the needs of the particular organization, having regard for its size, resources, and ability to implement whatever policy positions are agreed. It is also worth recalling that HR always needs to be aware of the importance of showing how it adds value and contributes to organizational objectives. It cannot be assumed by HR practitioners that a commitment to equal opportunities and diversity will result in universal acceptance and approval, particularly if this is perceived to be based on coercion rather than consent and if there is little concern to show how such a general commitment or specific practice is in the organization's interests.

For example, it might be argued that insisting that all applicants for jobs complete a standard application form for any vacancy is an approach to recruitment that is consistent with good practice and avoids claims that people who submit CVs are at an unfair advantage. But this policy might mean that many good applicants who do not have the time needed to fill out numerous application forms will decide only to apply to organizations that will accept their CV. Is the loss of potentially talented applicants worth more or less than recruitment policies that strenuously attempt to provide 'a level playing field'?

While the use of application forms might be recommended, this does not mean that an organization that accepts CVs has unfair recruitment practices, nor is it the case that using application forms inevitably results in a fair screening process. Having policies, training, and systems in place can help promote equal opportunities, but it is the actions and decisions of managers and employees that are key to ensuring the development of a fair, diverse, and merit-based culture within which all employees can thrive and contribute to their potential. The challenge is not in developing the appropriate written policies and procedures, but rather in influencing the behaviour and generating commitment of those who have to implement these (CIPD, 2006).

What does come through from various sources (CIPD, 2005b) is the important role that senior managers, and particularly those at the head of the organization, can take in leading the organization towards a more diverse culture and fairer employment practices. But what also needs to be understood is that this involves a continuous process of change and improvement, rather than a one-off initiative. As such, its success will depend as much on the ability to implement and manage change as on the desirability and relevance of the proposed changes themselves.

But even endorsement of equal opportunities and diversity policies by the CEO and Board is likely to be ineffective if this is an action only of paying lip service to political correctness or if it is perceived to be such. Those at the top of an organization will have a greater impact by and through the standards and expectations they set in employing and managing people, and through the extent to which their own formal and informal behaviours reinforce this endorsement. It is also essential that senior management take responsibility for challenging any undesirable behaviour and for making clear, to all employees, the consequences that may follow from breaches of the organization's code of behaviour.

There are many activities that organizations can engage in to promote equality of opportunity. Figure 7.2 shows a number that can help to promote such practices and, in so doing, minimize the risk of claims for unfair and unlawful discrimination.

**STUDENT ACTIVITY 7.5**

This activity involves looking at the equal opportunity practices currently in operation and reaching a judgement about their effectiveness. This exercise can be done in groups, but it is recommended that it is undertaken on an individual basis.

1. Identify the criteria you would use in evaluating an organization's equal opportunities policy.
2. Evaluate the equal opportunities policy of an organization with which you are familiar. (Note: you will need to collect information from within the organization to help you to complete this task.)
3. Which of the elements recommended in this chapter are included in the policy and what other commitments are also included in the policy?

For more information about what should be contained in an equal opportunities policy see the Online Resource Centre extension material 7.1

# Work–Life Balance and Family-Friendly Legislation

Work–life balance is about recognizing the importance to employees of non-work, as well as work, commitments. A concern with getting the balance between work and non-work commitments 'right' is not only a reflection of the diverse nature and needs of the workforce, but also of the belief that a lack of recognition and concern on the part of management can affect productivity and motivation. Work–life balance can be

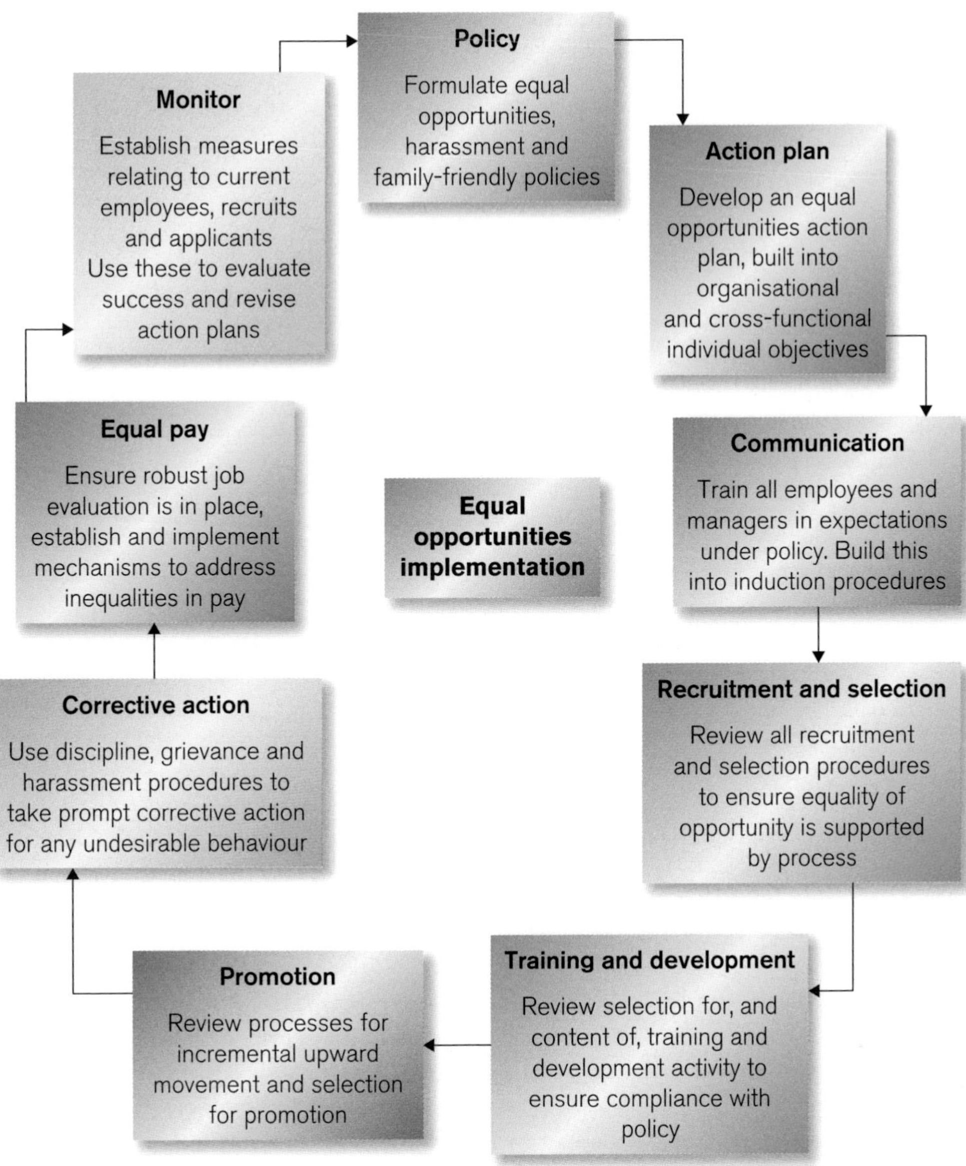


**Figure 7.2** Nine recommended activities to promote equal opportunities

understood, therefore, as being concerned with providing employees with a degree of choice in terms of how they allocate their time and energy between work and non-work commitments (www.Flexibility.co.uk, 2010).

## The impact of poor work–life balance

The impact of having a poor work–life balance can be far reaching upon the employees in an organization. Long hours and the stress of balancing work and home life can impact upon both work performance and relationships at home.

A study by the CIPD (2005a) found that:

- 45 per cent of respondents indicated that working long hours had put strain on personal relationships;
- 11 per cent of respondents believed that this strain had contributed towards a divorce;

- over 60 per cent of respondents stated that working long hours had a negative impact on their work performance, including making mistakes and taking longer to complete tasks.

Such findings are also consistent with the increasing prevalence of stress in the workplace and problems of stress-related absenteeism. They reinforce one of the central themes of this book that ignoring the human dimension of employment can undermine employee productivity and contribution.

**RESEARCH INSIGHT 7.3**

To take your learning further you might want to read this study:

**Chartered Institute of Personnel and Development (2009) 'Flexible Working: Working for families, working for business', available online www.cipd.co.uk**

This study highlights a lack of availability of flexible full-time work, that this affects the choices that people make in terms of their work, and that as a result many women are working below their potential. The findings are consistent with the view that employers are still unwilling or unable to meet employees' aspirations with regard to flexible working in order to improve work life balance. After reading the report:

- Identify the different factors and considerations that affect an organization's decision to either offer or limit opportunities for flexible working.
- Decide, on balance, whether the costs of providing flexible working are greater or less than anticipated benefits.
- Consider how an organization can reduce costs and increase the value of the benefits.



## Addressing work-life balance

There is a great deal of legislation that has been introduced in support of work-life balance. Working hours, breaks and holidays are regulated by the Working Time Regulations 1998, and there are now extensive provisions for maternity and paternity leave, provisions for time off to look after a dependent in an emergency and the right for parents of small children to request flexible working. Details of these rights can be found on the ACAS website (www.acas.org.uk). Many employers will have policies that clarify how these are implemented in their organization. Others extend these policies to groups that are not covered by the legislation, offering, for example, the right to request flexible working to all staff. Some organizations also develop more extensive policies to support work-life balance, such as extended leave, that is, allowing employees to take longer periods of unpaid holiday above normal allowances. Other polices might include career breaks, allowing longer periods away from work, and compressed hours policies, allowing employees to work the same hours over fewer days (see business case studies for work-life balance at www.tuc.org.uk).

**STUDENT ACTIVITY 7.6**

This activity is designed to deepen your understanding of the ways in which organizations implement work-life balance policies. If undertaken in groups, the exercise allows for comparisons of organizational practices and their effects.

1. Investigate the range of 'family friendly' and 'work-life balance' policies currently used by an organization of your choice.
2. Establish the extent to which these policies go beyond what is legislatively required and the objectives that they serve.
3. Collect information on one or more of these policies that will help you to form an opinion about whether or not they are working and reflect on whether the policies are meeting objectives.

Despite the attractiveness of such policies, it is important to recognize that there is a cost associated with them. While the benefits to employees of enjoying legislative rights at work are well understood, the problems that these may generate for employers, particularly those in the SME sector, also need to be recognized. The Practitioner Insight gives a view from a SME business about the effects of family friendly legislation in practice.

**PRACTITIONER INSIGHT Leigh Thomasson, Managing Director, Robinson Healthcare**

Robinson Healthcare employs in the region of 160 people manufacturing a range of products for the professional, home, and animal health care markets both in the UK and overseas. As a relatively small business we are able to have a human touch that can be difficult in larger businesses. We have a loyal and hardworking team and when employees are in genuine difficulty we do our best to support them. For example, we will regularly pay additional discretionary company sick pay especially where we have loyal, long-serving employees.

We recognize that employees need time off for family reasons and we understand that employees need time off, for example taking paternity leave and maternity leave when an employee or their partner has a baby. It is of course disruptive to the business when people are away and the majority of the recent improvements in provisions for employees place a burden on the employer. When businesses compete in a global market where labour costs are much lower, this can make things very difficult. There are market segments where we simply cannot compete for this reason. We will usually employ resource to cover maternity leave but other time away for family reasons is hard to cover and places more pressure on colleagues. For these reasons it is very hard for us to accommodate requests to work reduced hours, flexi-time, or home working. We can be a little more flexible in the factory as job share is less disruptive as it is easier to maintain consistency with different people, but we have core hours that we operate and need everyone to be available as far as possible during those hours. In the office areas, part-time hours and job share are very difficult, particularly at more senior level where each person has a unique role, as we lose continuity and the ability to react and respond to everyday situations when people are not available. When any member of staff is away for any reason, be it holidays, training, sickness, or for family reasons, it puts pressure on everyone else and having part-time working just compounds these difficulties. It is possible to plan around this but then we end up either delaying actions until the person returns or spending a lot of time working around it and this is not ideal in such a fast moving competitive business environment.

Research carried out by Tenon, one of the UK's top ten accountancy firms, into the views of the owners of small firms found that over 70 per cent felt that, as a result of the growth in employment rights, their businesses were now run for the benefit of their staff instead of their staff working for them. According to Michaela Johns, director of Tenon, there is a growing frustration with employment legislation that penalizes the majority of firms who develop progressive working practices:

> **My clients find it tougher to be a good employer, with the whole work-life balance drive, and also to make money, which is why they are in business in the first place.**
> (Tyler, 2007)

# Harassment and Bullying

## What is 'harassment'?

The range of behaviour that may constitute harassment ranges from extreme forms, such as physically assaulting someone, to more subtle actions, such as excluding someone from a conversation or social group. Table 7.4 comprises a list of behaviours that might constitute harassment. While some forms of harassment are a deliberate abuse of power on the part of the perpetrator, it can be the case that a person

**Table 7.4** Examples of types of harassment

| | |
|---|---|
| **Physical** | Pushing; causing physical harm; patting; being touched by another person; repeatedly or intentionally bumping into someone |
| **Verbal** | Shouting; lewd remarks; personal questions; derogatory comments; gossip; mimicking someone's accent; insults; abusive language or innuendo; offensive text messages or placing inappropriate remarks on publically accessible social networking websites |
| **Non-verbal** | Rude gestures; graffiti; display of suggestive pictures; mimicking mannerisms; offensive flags or emblems; ignoring someone or 'freezing' someone out; publishing inappropriate pictures or footage on publically accessible websites |

accused of harassment may be unaware of the impact of their behaviour upon another person. It is, however, the perception of the person that is subject to the harassment that should be taken into consideration when considering accusations of harassment. It should also be noted that behaviour that is considered to be acceptable by one person might be considered unwelcome by another.

There is an increasing risk from harassment via electronic media and organizations should be mindful of their responsibilities for any harassment that occurs 'in the course of employment'. The case of Jones v Tower Boot Co Ltd (1995) established that the test of 'in the course of employment' should be interpreted broadly. Certainly organizations should consider banning or restricting the use of social networking sites whilst in the workplace and may also wish to have policies in place that go beyond this. Some organizations are introducing polices such as preventing manager and employees having links outside work through such sites due to the risks and are making it clear that if any derogatory remarks impact upon working relationships this will be included within the harassment policy at work. The extent of responsibility for employers in this arena has yet to be fully tested within case law so caution should be exercised.

The effects of harassment can be far-reaching. Left unaddressed, harassment can affect the attendance and motivation of employees, and, in extreme cases, can result in mental health problems, such as depression and anxiety. The costs to an organization can be very high if allegations of harassment are not managed swiftly and effectively. For example, in 2006, Helen Green was awarded £80,000 in compensation for the bullying she was subjected to while employed by German-owned Deutsche Bank. The harassment, which included insults such as blowing raspberries, resulted in Miss Green suffering a nervous breakdown (Fresco, 2006).

In more serious cases of harassment, there may also be a risk of criminal charges being brought under the Protection from Harassment Act 1997.

**STUDENT ACTIVITY 7.7**

1. Consider which types of people, or groups of people, in an organization are most likely to be at risk from harassment and why.
2. Within your group, ask whether anyone has suffered from harassment and share your stories. Find out how the victim felt, what happened as a result of their experience and whether any action was taken to deal with the situation.

HRM INSIGHT 7.3 **Discrimination in the workplace**

A young male recruit of a non-white ethnic origin is recruited to work in a team led by a female team leader. Throughout the three-week probationary period, the team leader has difficulties with the new recruit, who specifically refuses to carry out what he states are menial tasks, is late back from breaks on a number of occasions, and, on one occasion, uses offensive language towards the team leader. When challenged by the team leader, the new recruit accuses her of being racist and alleges that she is picking on him because of his ethnic origin.

The team leader consults her male colleague, who covered her role for two days while she was on holiday, and he tells her that he found the new recruit to be cooperative and hard working. She approaches her male line manager about the problems she is experiencing to ask for advice.

### Questions

1. What information should the team leader's line manager establish as part of the discussions with the team leader and the new recruit?
2. What are the possible scenarios that might have given rise to the current situation?
3. What advice and support might the line manager give to the team leader in each of these different scenarios?
4. Should the employee be involved in the discussions and, if so, what might be communicated to him?

**Insights & Outcomes: visit the Online Resource Centre at www.oxfordtextbooks.co.uk/orc/banfield_kay2e/ for information about what actually happened to address this situation.**

### STUDENT ACTIVITY 7.8

1. In working groups, write a set of operational guidelines for line managers on how to handle a complaint of harassment or bullying in the workplace.
2. Consider the relative merits of an approach to the management of harassment and bullying claims based on procedure regulation and conciliation.

For more information on what should be contained in a harassment and bullying policy or 'dignity at work' policy for students with less familiarity with this topic to use to support this activity see the Online Resource Centre extension material 7.2.

### HRM INSIGHT 7.4 Józef's case

Józef is a Polish worker who has been employed for five years within his current organization, which manufactures components for electrical equipment. Up to six years ago the workforce were predominantly white British, but now the company employs 10 per cent ethnic minorities, mostly from other European countries, eligible to work in the UK. As economic conditions have become less favourable many European workers have left, often returning to their country of origin.

Józef alleges that he has been subject to harassment from co-workers since the organization announced that many employees were at risk of redundancy against a background of declining sales, as follows:

- Last month, a colleague said, 'I don't know why you don't go home. There's loads of jobs compared to here, it's not fair us losing our jobs while you're still here';
- Two weeks ago, the same colleague shouted across the office in front of colleagues 'Have you put your voluntary redundancy request in yet, Polish boy?';
- Yesterday, one of Józef's friends at work told Józef that the colleague had been contacting other colleagues via Facebook and had been extremely rude stating things like 'Józef should go home and not take our jobs' and 'it would serve him right if someone were to follow him home and put a brick though his window to give him the message'.

Józef reports this to his line manager in confidence. Józef says he has had enough of this individual. He does not want to make a big issue of things, but simply wants it to stop.

Questions

1. What are the options for dealing with Józef's complaint?
2. What actions should Józef's line manager consider taking?
3. What other actions might be necessary to prevent further escalation of problems?



## Summary

- Under UK legislation and the legal frameworks of many countries globally, employees enjoy protection from being unlawfully discriminated against.
- What was originally described as 'equal opportunities' has now become known as 'diversity' or 'diversity management', and is essentially concerned with how people behave at work in relation to each other and what are considered to be acceptable and unacceptable practices.
- Legislation has created a much stronger foundation of 'human rights' in the workplace, which means that discriminatory practices in the workplace relating to gender, race, disability, and age have now become unlawful as well as unacceptable.
- In addition, UK legislation has been introducing support of families and promotion of work-life balance, including enhancing support to employees who need to spend more time with families and giving greater consideration to flexible and part-time working.
- There is a developing interest in the business benefits or 'business case' for diversity and there are mixed views as to the strength of the economic rationale in favour of organizations adopting a diversity approach.
- Organizations need to take steps to prevent harassment and bullying in the workplace as this can have far reaching and serious consequences both morale and economic.
- The choices available to line managers and HR practitioners go beyond complying with legislation and creating an environment where people are treated based on merit and with respect and can include encouraging individuals and teams to maximize their contribution by embracing the opportunities that a diversity approach can offer.

online resource centre

**Visit the Online Resource Centre that accompanies this book for self-test questions, weblinks, and more information on the topics covered in this chapter.**
**www.oxfordtextbooks.co.uk/orc/banfield_kay2e/**

## REVIEW QUESTIONS

1. How does equal opportunity differ from diversity management? What is then the relationship between the two?

2. Does the recent emphasis on diversity imply that organizations have become more diverse in relation to their geographical coverage and recruitment patterns, and therefore that they need to develop employment policies that reflect this diversity—or do those advocating 'diversity' want organizations to become more diverse and, if so, why?

3. What bases can organizations rightfully, and necessarily, discriminate on and what kinds of discriminatory practices are now unlawful?
4. Do cultural differences justify certain types of discriminatory practice?
5. What is the role of the line manager and HR specialist in establishing fair and acceptable standards of behaviour in relation to preventing bullying and harassment?

***See Online Resource Centre for answers.***

## CASE STUDY

### Recruitment at Melbourne Finance

Jenny is a female manager at Melbourne Finance, a large financial organization with over 15,000 employees at more than a hundred locations throughout the UK. Part of the success of the organization is down to comprehensive training and performance management, supported by detailed assessment of key personnel and a high degree of internal promotion. The organization has clearly established equal opportunities policies and recognizes the importance of these in all aspects of its operation.

Jenny is an assistant branch manager at a larger branch. Her line manager approaches her to inform her that a promotional opportunity has arisen in another operating site. She is informed that senior executives in the company would like her to apply for the role because they think she would be an ideal candidate. Jenny is also informed that the position is to be advertised internally only at this stage.



Jenny then discloses to her line manager that she would be very interested in the position, but explains that she has just discovered that she is six weeks' pregnant. She asks that this information not be disclosed to any other party.

Shortly afterwards, her line manager informs Jenny that she is required to attend an interview. She then informs her line manager of her intention to disclose her pregnancy during the interview, to which her line manager responds by saying that she has already informed those on the interview panel, having felt obliged to do so.

Jenny attends the interview and, despite being the only internal candidate, she is turned down for the job and is told that the recruiting managers felt she did not have enough experience. The post is then advertised externally and an external candidate is appointed.

Towards the end of her maternity leave, another opportunity arises on a different site and Jenny is, again, approached to apply. This role is perceived to be more senior than the first. This time, her application is successful and she is offered the job on returning from maternity leave.

Jenny is convinced that the reason she did not get the first job was due to her pregnancy. Both of her interviews were conducted in a professional manner, with no reference to her pregnancy or maternity leave, so she has no direct evidence to support any claim. She contacts her line manager from her first job and shares her concerns, but the manager responds by advising her to 'let the issue go', suggesting that Jenny has secured a good promotion and it would not be wise to jeopardize her career by making an issue out of not being awarded the first post.

#### Questions

1. What mistakes were made by the organization in recruiting to fill the vacancy?
2. What action might Jenny have taken when turned down for the first vacancy?
3. What impact might this have in the longer term for Jenny?
4. What approach to fair employment is being taken by the organization that employs Jenny?
5. What improvements should the company make to the way in which it manages similar situations?

## FURTHER READING

Advisory Conciliation and Arbitration Service (2010) *Delivering Equality and Diversity*, ACAS, www.acas.org.uk.

Arnold, D. and Hartman, L. (2005) 'Beyond sweatshops: Positive deviancy and global labour practices', *Business Ethics: A European review*. July, **14:**3, pp. 206–22.

Briscoe, D. and Schuler, R. (2004) 'Global ethics and labour standards in international HRM', *International Human Resource Management*, 2nd ed. Routledge.

Clements, P. and Jones, J. (2005) *The Diversity Training Handbook: A Practical Guide to Understanding and Changing Attitudes*, Kogan Page.

Confederation for British Industry (2008) 'Talent not tokenism: The benefits of workplace diversity', www.cbi.org.uk and www.equlalityhumanrights.com.

Daniels, K. and Macdonald, L. (2005) *Equality, Diversity and Discrimination: A Student Text*, CIPD.

Illes, P. (1995) 'Learning to work with difference', *Personnel Review*, **24**:6, pp. 44–60.

Ozbil, M. (2009) 'Managing Diversity and the Business Case', CIPD.

Storey, J. (1999) 'Equal opportunity: Retrospect and prospect', *Human Resource Management*, **9**:1, pp. 5–8.

## REFERENCES



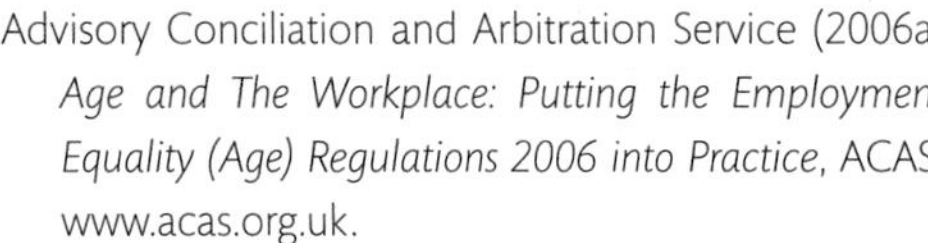


Advisory Conciliation and Arbitration Service (2006a) *Age and The Workplace: Putting the Employment Equality (Age) Regulations 2006 into Practice*, ACAS, www.acas.org.uk.

Advisory Conciliation and Arbitration Service (2009) *Flexible Working and Work Life Balance*, ACAS, www.acas.org.uk.

Advisory Conciliation and Arbitration Service (2009) 'Bullying and harassment at work: a guide for managers and employers', ACAS, www.acas.org.uk.

Backhaus, K. and Tikoo, S. (2004) 'Conceptualizing and researching employer branding', *Career Development International*, **9**:5, pp. 501–17.

Chambers, B.A. (2002) 'Applicant reactions and their consequences: review, advice, and recommendations for future research', *International Journal of Management Review*, **4**, December, pp. 317–33.

Chartered Institute of Personnel and Development (2005a) 'Flexible working: impact and implementation: an employer survey', www.cipd.co.uk.

Chartered Institute of Personnel and Development (2005b) 'Managing diversity: People make the difference at work—but everyone is different,' www.cipd.co.uk.

Chartered Institute of Personnel and Development (2006) 'Diversity: An overview', www.cipd.co.uk.

Chartered Institute of Personnel and Development (2007) 'Diversity in business: A focus for progress survey report', www.cipd.co.uk.

Chartered Institute of Personnel and Development (2009) 'Flexible Working: Working for families, working for business', www.cipd.co.uk.

Chartered Institute of Personnel and Development (2010) 'Diversity: An overview', www.cipd.co.uk.

Coca-Cola Enterprises v Shergill (2003) EAT 5-21.

Coens, T. and Jenkins, M. (2002) *Abolishing Performance Appraisals*, Berret-Koehler.

Ekpe v Commissioner of Police for the Metropolis (2001) IRLR 605.

Equality and Human Rights Commission (2010) Equality Act guidance for employers, www.equalityhumanrights.com.

Eversheds (2010) 'Equality Act 2010: What does it mean for employers?', www.eversheds.com.

Flexibility.co.uk (2010) 'Balancing work and the rest of life—the role of flexible working'.

Fresco, A. (2006) '£800,000 payout for bullied City secretary', *The Times*, 1 August, www.business.timesonline.co.uk.

Grosser, K. and Moon, J. (2005) 'Gender mainstreaming and corporate social responsibility: Reporting workplace issues', *Journal of Business Ethics*, **62**:4, pp. 327–40.

Hill, M. (2003) *Understanding Social Policy*, Blackwell.

Hurstfield, J., Meager, N., Aston, J., Davies, J., Mann, K., Mitchell, H., O'Regan, S. and Sinclair, A. (2004) *Monitoring the Disability Discrimination Act 1995*

*Phase 3*, Disability Rights Commission Report, Department for Work and Pensions.

Hyman, R. and Brough, I. (1975) *Social Values and Industrial Relations: A Study of Fairness and Inequality*, Blackwell.

JobsFactory (2006) 'JobsFactory employers of choice for entry-level graduates survey', www.careercentral.com.sg.

Jones vs Tower Boot Co Ltd (1997) IRLR 169, CA.

Kochan, T. et al. (2003) 'The effects of diversity on business performance', report of the Diversity Research Network, *Human Resource Management*, **42**, pp. 3–21.

Macpherson, W. (1999) *The Stephen Lawrence Inquiry*, HMSO.

Meager, N., et al. (1999) *Monitoring the Disability Discrimination Act (DDA) 1995*, Department for Education and Employment.

Office for National Statistics (2009) Labour Force Survey, January–March.

Oswick, C. and Rosenthal, P. (2001) 'Towards a relevant theory of age discrimination in employment', in Noon, E. and Ogbonna, E. (eds) *Equality, Diversity and Disadvantage in Employment*, Palgrave, pp. 156–217.

Oxfam (2004) 'Trading away our rights: Women working in global supply chains', www.maketradefair.com.

R (on the application of Age UK) v Secretary of State for Business, Innovation and Skills (2009) IRLR 1017, HC.

Rick, J. et al. (2000) 'Institutional racism: Where's the prejudice in organisations?', Presentation to the British Psychological Society Occupational Psychology Conference.

Smith, A. and Twomey, B. (2002) 'Labour market experiences of people with disabilities', *Labour Market Trends*, August, Office of National Statistics.

Tyler, R. (2007) 'Employees too powerful, say employers', *Daily Telegraph*, 12 April.

# 8 International Human Resource Management

## Key Terms

**Global organization** An organization that employs a workforce in different countries throughout the world, with a view to maximizing performance by sourcing or providing goods and/or services in a globally based market, and in which decisions are driven by markets rather than by geography.

**National cultures** A complex system of norms, social values and behaviours, expectations and legal frameworks that gives an identity to a particular country.

**Multinational companies (MNCs)** Multinational companies that have a national base, but which operate and trade multinationally.

**Expatriate worker** An employee deployed overseas, usually sourced from his or her country of origin.

## Learning Objectives

As a result of reading this chapter and using the Online Resource Centre, you should be able to:

- understand the implications of employing staff from overseas, deploying staff to other countries, and employing staff in other countries;
- recognize the social and cultural differences between countries, and their effect on employment and management practices;
- understand the concept of a global organization, and the implications for global employment and for global HR policy and practice;
- understand the role of the international HRM (IHRM) practitioner and the responsibilities that he or she has.

# Introduction

International HRM (IHRM) is a field of growing importance in the human resources arena, and there are a growing number of UK organizations that operate in more than one country. The emphasis on maximizing performance by treating resources as global, rather than country-specific, applies increasingly to human resources, and this perspective informs how they are employed and managed. With the onset of more cost-effective transport systems and swifter, more effective, methods of communication, organizations that previously operated in a number of countries, but with each country being responsible only for local sourcing and the supply of products and services to markets in its own country, are now seeing the benefits of global sourcing and supply. Equally, economic expansion, particularly in China and India, and the forecast for higher growth rates overseas has led many organizations to the conclusion that they need to have the organizational capability to operate in these countries and across national borders, in order to benefit from this predicted growth.

To be a truly global organization, it is not sufficient simply to operate in a number of countries. The global organization has the capability of operating and managing at a level at which service to its customers is not restricted by local geographies. Products and services can be sourced from the optimum location, and price and quality, rather than national identity, become critical business criteria. The search for raw materials to fuel world economic growth, and the search for markets for goods and services as this growth creates new wealth and greater demand, are having a profound effect on the way in which senior executives think about business. Success in this global arena is a function of a number of key factors, but the ability to generate and sustain the organizational capability to operate in these markets is absolutely critical. The human resource is an integral component of the competitive organizational capability that global companies need to maintain their international presence (Hira and Hira, 2005).

Few, if any, HR practitioners are now immune from the effects of globalization and the internationalization of business, and the aim of this chapter is to explain the implications of this inexorable trend for those with specific responsibilities for managing people. But, before we outline those areas of HR that have been influenced either directly or indirectly by the opening up of borders and the increasingly free movement of goods, services, and people, it is worth remembering that this is not a new, or indeed recent, phenomenon. The pace of change has undeniably increased over the past 20 years—but remember our reference in Chapter 1 to the building of the Pyramids: it is unlikely that many of the workers used in their construction came from outside the borders of Egypt, but for certain of the more skilled trades, workers may well have been brought from other parts of the Middle East. This is a view that accords with the research of David (1997), who, based on the evidence of ancient artefacts in the building area, argued that:

> **The workforce at the town may therefore have included elements from a number of countries, as well as native-born Egyptians.**

The construction of Britain's canal and rail networks in the eighteenth and nineteenth centuries certainly depended heavily on 'foreign' labour, in the form of Irish 'navvies'. Before this, the forced migration of the French Huguenots into England in the sixteenth and seventeenth centuries represented a major source of skilled labour, expertise, and know-how that transformed the country's cloth industry. More recently, in the nineteenth century, the expansion of the British Empire was dependent on engineers, traders, and others living and working overseas. In the twentieth century, immigrants from the West Indies and the Asian subcontinent provided a much-needed source of labour for the UK's textile and steel industries. The point is that flows of labour into the UK, doing business abroad, and the employment of UK technical experts and managers on overseas contracts, are not new ideas; what *is* new is the scale and complexity of these developments, and their implications for the HR practitioner.

In the context of an introductory text, it is not practical to try to cover all aspects of IHRM and, for the purposes of this chapter the following are the areas to which we will pay particular attention:

- the use of UK expatriate staff to work on overseas projects;
- the cultural issues related to establishing overseas businesses and outsourcing the production of goods and services;
- employing and managing a diverse workforce;
- new developments in HR in Asia;
- competencies of the IHRM manager and those needed for working successfully abroad.

# International HRM

International HRM, as an area of academic study, followed the emergence of HRM, and shares the same strategic focus and emphasis on vertical and horizontal integration. Its antecedents lay in the comparative study of industrial relations, which focused on national differences in employment and managerial practices, the collective organization of labour and conflict resolution mechanisms (Ferner and Hyman, 1998). It has, however, evolved into a distinctive, and increasingly recognized, subject in its own right, as the implications of globalization and international business have impacted on the use of human resources and the role of the HR professional (Scullion and Linehan, 2005; Edwards and Rees, 2006).

As far as IHRM is concerned, academics have tended to adopt one of two approaches.

- **It is seen as essentially HRM 'writ large', and associated with a domestic and national agenda transferred and relocated into an international arena.**

  A definition that fits this approach is given by Scullion (1995), who claimed that IHRM could be understood as:

  > **the HRM strategies, policies and practices which firms pursue in response to the internationalization of business.**

  This approach gives particular emphasis to the international context and transnational requirements associated with such activities as:
  - recruitment and selection;
  - performance and reward strategies;
  - the management and control of diverse workforces.

- **It is viewed in a more strategic sense, in ways that mirror the HRM/SHRM debate, and highlights the importance of leveraging maximum contributions from an organization's global human resources in the pursuit of competitive advantage. Seen in this way, IHRM encompasses the above three sets of activities, but additionally involves:**
  - facilitating organizational learning and knowledge management across borders and between internationally dispersed operating units (Glaister et al., 2003);
  - the internationalization of management throughout the organization, reflecting its global presence and operations;
  - the internationalization of organizational culture to reflect multiple dimensions of diversity.

From the perspective of the HR practitioner, the internationalization of business has had the effect of adding new responsibilities to those previously restricted to a regional and national perspective, such as the employment and management of expatriate workers and 'foreign' nationals. It has also created new levels of complexity and challenge, resulting from organizations extending their operations internationally and, as a consequence, having to come to terms with the implications of different cultures, business environments, and legal systems.

Harris et al. (2001), in their study of the implications of globalization on HR, capture the essence of these challenges when they argue that:

**Whilst managers in organisations working in a single-country environment are still subject to the twists and turns of external events, the manager working in an international environment must try to assess the impact of multi-country, regional and global trends. Hardly surprising, choices in this context become complex and ambiguous.**

They suggest that a domestically-based company developing an international dimension will need to think carefully about:

- the kind of HR strategy that will facilitate the transition and operation as an international organization;
- the implications of such a transition for the kind of managers the organization requires and the competences they will need to be effective in a different context;
- whether it will be appropriate to develop a standardized set of employment policies and practices, or to allow flexibility and variability to reflect local and regional differences;
- strategies for resourcing, rewarding, and managing the performance of employees;
- employee recognition and representational issues.

**PRACTITIONER INSIGHT Edin Veljovic, HR Consultant, Serbia**

How is HR different in Serbia, for example, how do laws, customs, and attitudes to work differ?

Being an HR consultant in various sectors in Serbia (both in profit and non-for profit organizations) provided me with insights about typical challenges that stand in front of HR managers in these sectors. One has to be careful and to distinguish three main sectors of HR features. The first sector consists of multinational companies that operate in Serbia. Employees who work in these companies pose more (pro)Western attitudes to work, that is, they are task-oriented, well-educated, familiar with the life-long learning (training) concept of work, and they spend long hours on their jobs. The main challenges of the HR managers in this sector are related to layoffs and job uncertainty.

The second sector consists of Small and Medium Enterprises (SMEs). The SMEs' owners are predominately entrepreneurs and they do not have clearly developed structures and functions within organizations. Given that, in local SMEs, the role of HR is attached to one of the existing functions (marketing, quality, or administration) or the owner/CEO is the main HR figure, these functions are very fragile. Such unstructured and vulnerable partnership between business and HR function creates enormous potential for development of HR capacity within the company. Only recently, CEOs of SMEs realized that they have to bring both more structure and (international) experience into SMEs' HR functions. There is a huge need for training of HR people especially in the domains of recruitment, selection, creating of job descriptions, employee development, and reward system. Employees in this sector, usually, have attended a state university that has obsolete learning methodologies, and which favours knowledge rather than the skills to engage that knowledge. Commonly, employees from SMEs lack critical skills and their attitude to work is more reactive than proactive in spite of owners' entrepreneurial influence that cascades right through the businesses. Their view of business is that it belongs to the owner(s) and it is not their role to nurture it. Nevertheless, once exposed to interactive training or consultancy their reaction/response is highly positive.

The third group consists of employees from public sector or state (pre)owned companies. There is usually an HR function which is connected with the legal department. It is predominantly administrative and bureaucratic, solving employees' different legal issues such as salaries, sick and maternity leaves, team building activities, and similar. The employees in these organizations have less flexible attitudes to work. They are time-driven, that is, they rarely work long hours and are more interested in their rights than duties, tasks, and deadlines. The layoffs, usually, happen if a company is privatized and new shareholders want to make it more efficient and effective. However, these companies have strong union history as heritage from socialistic times that protect employees' rights.

The above Practitioner Insight focuses on the challenges organizations in transition face from changing internal and external environments and the implication such changes have for HR.

**HRM INSIGHT 8.1 TNN International**

TNN International is a UK-based global manufacturer and supplier of air-conditioning systems. Due to predicted expansion in overseas markets, TNN would like to appoint a sales manager to manage South American operations and to coordinate the activities of a potentially growing team of sales representatives based in Mexico. This position has been advertised internally. Applicants include an expatriate British sales representative, who is employed on a considerably more generous package than are the other candidates due to his expatriate status and who was involved in the start-up of the South American operation because of personal contacts with local agents. There are two Mexican applicants, both of whom joined the operation from a competitor, and both have had a significant influence in growing sales. Finally, there is a female sales representative, currently based in South Africa, who has been extremely successful in developing this market and, for family reasons, is looking to move to Mexico.

The successful candidate will be responsible for managing the remaining team members who have, to date, reported to the international business manager in the UK. You have heard unofficially from other international sales agents that the expatriate British worker is adamant that he will not work for a Mexican because this will affect his credibility with his customers. You have also independently heard that the two Mexican male candidates have expressed a determination to not work for a woman for 'cultural' reasons, stating that the Mexican customers will not accept working with a female manager. The UK business has a clear fair employment policy that it extends to all of its international businesses.

**Questions**

1. How should the informal complaints of the expatriate British worker and the two Mexican workers be addressed prior to the selection process?
2. What selection methods might be used to establish a fair basis for making the recruitment decision?
3. What action might need to be taken after the conclusion of the selection process?

However, international companies, particularly those that are relatively new and are in the fast-moving IT sector, face a much wider range of HR challenges that go well beyond those associated with overseas recruitment. Many have relatively undeveloped HR functions and little in the way of strategies that address the kind of questions that Harris et al. (2001) suggest are associated with the 'road to internationalization', which is often driven by the attractiveness of favourable tax environments, and of educated and skilled labour forces.

Such companies often experience rapid growth, linked to technological advantages and market demand, but sometimes in the absence of anything other than the most basic HR activities, such as recruitment and selection, and payroll. The need to develop a more effective HR function, linking its operation explicitly to an HR strategy for the business, is likely to be recognized, at some point, as a necessary development in building the organization's capability to sustain its growth and expansion.

Interestingly, many of the HR challenges and problems that these companies face when they become 'international' and seek to build for future expansion are similar to those faced by organizations operating only in a domestic context. There are, however, important differences to do with managing change, creating consistency and uniformity of practice, and challenging entrenched perceptions about gender, culture, and contribution. HRM Insight 8.2 tells the story of the difficulties that one HR professional encountered in introducing an HR department into an environment that had previously operated without one.

**HRM INSIGHT 8.2 Developing the HR function in an international company**

The following illustrates the challenges, and some of the key issues, facing the HR manager in a French-owned electronics company operating in Ireland. The case concentrates on the experiences of establishing HR in an environment that had not previously had a centralized HR function and the difficulties of implementing agreed HR policy in the face of managerial inertia and resistance.

Jean LeFebre, an innovative entrepreneur who understood the fast-changing electronics industry and recognized the potential that leading-edge technologies offered in the rapidly growing telecommunications sector, established International Electronics in France in 1986. Despite some initial problems, the company grew from a €20 million company in 1995 to a company with a turnover of €350 million ten years later.

As the company increased its production and turnover, the strategic decision was taken to establish a manufacturing plant in Ireland; its Cork factory was established in 1995. Because of its success and the favourable economic environment in Ireland, Cork became the predominant manufacturing site for the company's complete product range. The company does, however, have distribution and research and development (R&D) facilities, along with software engineering sites, in Germany, Sweden, Hong Kong, and Japan. It recently opened a manufacturing site in China, but this only supplies the local Asian market. In terms of its general HR approach, the company has slightly different policies to reflect differences in local legislation but, overall, has a set of corporate policies and practices to which it expects all of its subunits to adhere.

From its inception, the company coped with its rapid growth, an ever-changing environment, and the difficulties associated with managing the company on a global basis without an HR function, but in 1995, the decision was taken that things had to change and an HR director was appointed. The HR director was based in France, where the head office was located, with a brief to introduce formalized systems and procedures into the company. As a result of her appointment, Catherine Dupre oversaw the recruitment of several key managerial personnel, one being the head of human resources in Cork. The appointee, Ciara O'Sullivan, who qualified as an accountant before moving into HR, began work in January 2006 when the headcount stood at 180.

As the only female in the eight-strong management team, Ciara was faced with a number of important questions: where to start; what to do first; how to begin the contribution of the HR function to the company's operational and strategic objectives. It soon became apparent that her first priorities were to find out what policies were in place, who was responsible for what, and whether any procedures had been established to support these practices.

One of her first tasks was to conduct an audit of the organization from a HR perspective. This involved one-to-one meetings with colleagues on the senior management team to establish their levels of need in areas such as recruitment and selection, induction, the socialization of new employees, contracts of employment, and general administration, training and development methods and records, and, finally, performance management and appraisal.

As it transpired, this was only the tip of the iceberg. As well as dealing with all of the above, Ciara experienced a significant degree of negativity towards the HR function that was, in certain respects, more difficult to deal with than some of the more straightforward matters. As she remarked:

> While most would see this function as necessary and indeed useful, some find it the complete opposite: literally a thorn in the side of progress.

In trying to introduce change, she was constantly confronted with the phrase 'but this is the way it's always been done', and began to wonder what it was about change and the introduction of new processes that upset a small minority of individuals. One explanation was that they felt threatened by the introduction of some form of control or that they would have to conform to the same standards as the rest of the employees. Whatever the case, their initial reaction was a defence of the status quo.

One event that captured the difficulties facing Ciara was the need to shed a small number of temporary workers, due to a short-term downturn in business predicted to last four weeks. The management team had agreed the need for this and the situation was not unusual for those workers who were employed on a contingent basis. The key decision, however, was which employees should be let go? Although not in itself a difficult question to answer, it led to a great deal of discussion and disagreement.

One suggestion was that the LIFO ('last in, first out') method should be used because it was a practice that had been used in the past, although not very successfully. The problem was complicated because Ciara had, in the preceding period, implemented an intensive recruitment drive to find suitable, flexible, and adaptable employees for one particular area of the factory. Having heavily invested in this process, and having spent valuable resources on medical examinations and training, she felt that the application of the LIFO criteria was not in the best interest of the company. She preferred to use the criterion of functionality, which meant that employees would be chosen on the basis of their role and value to the company.

One part of the plant was chronically overstaffed and had a surplus of staff working on contingent contracts. It seemed obvious to Ciara that the small number who needed to be let go could be selected from this group, but this suggestion was immediately rejected by the relevant manager, who told Ciara (politely) to mind her own business and 'stop interfering in things [she knew] nothing about'.

The manager in question, in defence of the LIFO approach, argued:

> This is the way it's always been done. Why fix it, if it isn't broken?

Tensions arose between Ciara and several of the management team over the way in which to handle the situation and, the longer the impasse continued, the more the company was haemorrhaging valuable resources in the form of higher wage costs and unproductive workers. She decided to pick up the phone and talk to the managing director about the problem and, if necessary, involve the HR director. Politically, however, this was not without its problems because, while the group HR director had overall responsibility for employment matters, she left the Cork site very much in the hands of Ciara.

### Questions

1. Why is Ireland such a popular location for international manufacturing companies? What are the distinctive features of the Irish labour market that attract overseas investments?
2. Why did the company feel it was necessary to establish a centralized HR function in 1995 and what challenges did the HR director face in establishing the function?
3. What support might Ciara have expected from the HR director and managing director in her efforts to get HR embedded in the Cork plant?
4. What action might Ciara have taken to overcome the resistance to change generally and the employment problem specifically?
5. Should she have involved senior managers from headquarters? If yes, in what capacity and what might the consequences have been?

**Insights & Outcomes: visit the Online Resource Centre at www.oxfordtextbooks.co.uk/orc/banfield_kay2e/ for an explanation of how the issues confronting the HR manager were resolved.**

## Globalization

The internationalization of management has, for some, become an expression of what has become known as 'globalization' (Edwards and Rees, 2006). Accepting that there is an ongoing debate about what this actually means, Edwards and Rees believe that, as far as IHRM is concerned, the most important aspects of globalization are:

- *global production*, meaning that transnational corporations produce, distribute, and sell goods and services around the world;
- *global organizations*, for which the ability to resource and manage global production systems impacts directly on HR and management, both of which have to come to terms with social and cultural differences.

Each of these is facilitated by the growth in global financial systems and the expansion of global communications networks.

Globalization is also associated with the rapid, and relatively recent, development of a 'global economy'. What this means is that national economic and social identities and differences are becoming less distinctive, and arguably more irrelevant, as market forces and free trade move national economies and economic organizations towards a more convergent and universalistic state (Edwards and Rees, 2006). While the effects of globalization are clearly accelerating, including the ideas of systems of finance, production, and trade that are 'without boundary', care must be taken not to overstate the effects that this has on national employment systems, and on the social and cultural differences that not only exist between national economies, but within them.

Thinking about the debate on globalization and the impact that this is having on HR, what does it actually mean for the HR practitioner in terms of his or her work? Without representing an exhaustive list, the following represent situations that are related to the growth of transnational corporations and a converging global economic system.

- More people are working for transnationals in an HR capacity. Increasing numbers of newly qualified and experienced HR practitioners are employed by 'global' enterprises, such as Gazprom (the Russian gas supplier), or work for overseas companies that set up UK or Irish subsidiaries. These new employment contexts raise interesting questions about the way in which social and cultural differences are managed within the workplace and the status that HR enjoys within these organizations. A particularly important issue here relates to gender and the extent to which females working for overseas companies face problems of acceptance and discrimination (Wirth, 2002).

**Signpost to Chapter 7: Equality in Employment, for examples of discriminatory employment practices**

- UK-based organizations are, because of inward migration and a more diverse indigenous workforce, employing more people from diverse social, cultural, and religious backgrounds. Managing diversity has become less of an aspiration for those organizations seeking to adjust to demographic change and more of a reality. The CIPD reports that one in three UK employers is actively recruiting migrant workers to work in such diverse industries as the NHS, agriculture, food processing, and hospitality, and the implications for recruitment and selection, and induction practices, as well as for communications, welfare and training, are obvious.
- Increasingly, HR practitioners, particularly more senior ones, have to undertake overseas assignments or secondments, or are responsible for organizing the expatriation and repatriation of other managers.
- HR professionals are developing new approaches to individual and organizational learning, and generating knowledge-sharing networks that connect to the different parts of the transnational/global organization.
- HR professionals in global organizations are also developing ways of communicating with people in different parts of the world, and building the capability to track and monitor employment numbers, costs, and the outcome of management development programmes across national boundaries.

Figure 8.1 presents the different challenges and responsibilities facing the international HR manager at the strategic level.

**RESEARCH INSIGHT 8.1 Outsourcing Practices in South East Asia**

The article by Chiang et al. (2010) focuses on the strategic significance of outsourcing in the Asian context. The article draws on several important HRM perspectives in explaining outsourcing practices and concludes that the practice is still in its development phase and subject to number of key constraints and considerations.

After reading the article and relating its findings to Western outsourcing models and developments, you are required to:

1. Summarize the main features of outsourcing practices identified in the article.
2. Consider whether these practices reflect operational rather than strategic considerations.
3. Identify the circumstances which have influenced companies to consider outsourcing aspects of the HR function.
4. Establish whether what is being outsourced in South East Asia is similar to or different from that found in Western companies, and explain any significantly different practices.

**International transactions and administration**
- Pay and conditions
- Legal issues
- Recruitment and selection
- Induction
- Database maintenance
- Managing expatriation and repatriation

**Building capability and resource development**
- Fast-tracking and developing managers
- Career and succession planning
- Developing knowledge management systems
- IT-driven learning

**Business-driven activities**
- Reorganization
- Efficiency drives
- Supporting overseas start-ups, e.g. new factories
- Outsourcing, e.g. overseas call centres

**Developing and implementing strategy**
- Strategic HR planning
- Performance and reward management
- Managing closures, acquisitions and mergers
- Culture building

Figure 8.1 The four dimensions of the international HR manager's role and contribution



One of the growing trends in HR that is extending beyond its Western origins is outsourcing—the contracting for HR services from external contractors. The question which arises from this development is whether the way in which HR outsourcing works in regions such as South East Asia reflects Western models and practices or has its own distinctive characteristics. The following Research Insight offers an opportunity to answer this question. As a source of information on HR outsourcing in Western economies, refer to Lawler III et al. (2004).

# The International HR Manager and Culture

**KEY CONCEPT Culture**

Culture, as a force and a phenomenon, exists within professions, religions, organizations, and geographical regions. Our interest is primarily in national cultures. 'Culture' can be understood as the shared beliefs, values, and understandings that define and distinguish one group from another. It is what Hofstede and Hofstede (2004) call 'the collective programming of the mind'. The culture with which people identify influences and shapes their behaviour in relation to their environment. Cultural clashes exist if people are exposed to different belief and value systems, but fail to learn to adapt to such differences. From an IHRM perspective, the inability to understand and manage culture and cultural differences is often the reason why expatriate assignments fail, and why some immigrants and migrant workers in the UK find difficulty in assimilating into the British way of life.

Despite the feeling that globalization and the convergence of economic systems is reducing national differences, it would be wrong to ignore the continued existence of cultural differences between nations—differences that impact both directly and indirectly on the employment and management of people. At one level, such differences manifest themselves in restrictions: for example, on the employment of women and the types of work they are allowed to do. While the emancipation of women in Western societies has resulted in very high labour market participation rates and increasing female representation across occupational boundaries, in other societies, there remain significant cultural and legal restrictions on what women are allowed to do and be.

Less obvious cultural differences restrict, or make it socially unacceptable to engage in, certain behaviours that might be taken for granted in other cultures. For example, in certain countries or organizations, the status and position of people in the organizational hierarchy carries far more formal importance than it would in other national contexts, creating a strong sense of deference from those of lower status and in subordinate positions. In itself, the reluctance on the part of those lower down the hierarchy to question those in more senior positions may not be a problem, but it will affect the ability of the organization to introduce more egalitarian and democratic practices, such as 360-degree appraisal systems and open discussion forums. Cultural sensitivity and the ability to manage in situations of cultural difference, and indeed of cultural conflict, consequently becomes an important requirement for the manager with international HR responsibilities.

### HRM INSIGHT 8.3 A different approach to selection

Ahmed Hassan is head of The International Computer Group operating throughout the Middle East. The business involves designing and contracting for the installation of computer networks and the supply and maintenance of component parts. His, and the company's, reputation is based on a strong underpinning philosophy about doing business, wherever that might be, with reliability and international quality standards. The business has grown in size and profitability and continues to develop new markets in the region and beyond. Ahmed's approach to recruitment and selection is heavily influenced by the concept of the family, and family relationships transferred into the world of business. He relies heavily on members of his extended family to run the business and several occupy key management positions.

Ahmed's approach to management, is based on strong values and beliefs and trust in his staff. He offers attractive remuneration packages and expects his employees to reflect his personal and business values. The quality of his staff is the key to the success of his business and new recruits need to buy into the ethos of the company. Because of the expansion of the business a new senior technical post was created, but because of limited availability in the local labour market Ahmed advertised in India and received several responses with CVs. One in particular caught his attention and he arranged to fly over to Delhi to interview him. He invited the applicant for dinner and began to ask him about his background and experience. The conversation continued until towards the end of the meal Ahmed put his hand in his pocket and pulled out an employment contract and said 'I would like to offer you the job'. This surprised the applicant who, after recovering his composure said that he needed time to think. Later the following day the applicant called and said he would accept the job and they met to agree the details around salary, conditions, and start date.

This event took place quite recently and the following questions need to be thought through very carefully if you are to understand that the UK approach to recruitment and selection reflects our legal system and social values, but is not intrinsically better than anyone else's.

#### Questions

1. What was Ahmed basing his decision to offer the job on?
2. How does this way of deciding if someone is suitable or not differ from the general approach taken in the UK?
3. Is the UK approach likely to produce a decision that means the integrity of procedure will always identify the applicant who will add value to the organization and perform the job to the required standards?
4. What do you think happened in the following years?

online resource centre

**For comments on this story see the Online Resource Centre www.oxfordtextbooks.co.uk/orc/banfield_kay2e/**

National cultures are important because they help people to understand:

- what they are and how they fit into society;
- how they relate to each other;
- what social conventions are important and why;
- how they perceive work and what it means in the broader context of their lives;
- the importance of time and the significance of space in relation to personal and professional relationships.

Successfully working across cultural boundaries is often associated with the person moving into, and feeling comfortable within, a different cultural environment. This inevitably involves being prepared to learn new social and business conventions, and to adjust psychologically to different values and cultural norms. The corollary of this is equally valid: the inability to cope with cultural difference is associated with ineffective performance and failed overseas assignments, secondments and postings. As Hofstede (2004) points out:

> **Culture is more often a source of conflict than of synergy. Cultural differences are a nuisance at best and often a disaster.**
> (www.geert-hofstede.com.)

Hofstede's work has been particularly influential in identifying national cultural identities and the differences in the ways in which people behave and organizations function. As a result of his research, he found that nationality affected many cultural assumptions and business practices, with the key cultural differences being explained by the following five variables.



- Power distance

  This refers to the degree to which members of a society or organization accept and expect that power is distributed unequally. This dimension also represents the degree of inequality that exists within social institutions and, while all societies reflect differences in the distribution of power and the resulting pattern of inequality, some are more unequal than others.

- Individualism

  This represents the degree to which people identify themselves as individuals or as members of a social group (or 'collectivity'). In certain Western societies, social ties are loose and the interests of the individual are given primacy; in other societies, such as that of Japan, there is a strong collectivist ethic and group identity. This might mean, as a generalization, that effective team and group working is more difficult to achieve in the USA than it is in Japan, or at least in Japanese companies that reflect Japanese cultural work practices. Equally, Japanese culture might inhibit individuality and creativity.

- Masculinity/femininity

  This concept refers to the distribution of roles and relationships between genders. In different cultures, men are characterized, to varying degrees, by a tendency to be assertive and competitive, while women are regarded as caring and modest. Women working in cultures that are closer to the masculinity pole have a tendency to 'behave like men', that is, they become competitive and assertive, believing that becoming 'more like men' is necessary to achieve personal and professional recognition and success.

- Uncertainty avoidance

  Uncertainty avoidance represents the extent to which a society exhibits a tolerance for uncertainty and ambiguity. On an individual level, it helps to predict how well a person from a culture that has a low tolerance of uncertainty and ambiguity would cope if, for example, he or she were to work in an organization within which uncertainty and ambiguity were frequently experienced. Uncertainty-avoiding cultures try to minimize the possibility of the 'unknown' by developing strict laws and rules, and by adhering to philosophical and religious teachings that produce a greater number of social 'absolutes'. People who live and work in uncertainty-accepting cultures are more tolerant of different opinions, rely on fewer rules, and adopt a more questioning and relativist approach.

- Long-term versus short-term orientation

  This describes the 'time horizon' of a society or organization, or the importance that it attaches to the future as compared to the past and present. From the point of view of working and doing business in different cultures, knowing where they score in this dimension can be very important because it can help managers to appreciate the time needed to build relationships, to become accepted, and to be trusted. Eastern nations tend to score especially high on this dimension, while Western nations score low and developing nations very low (high, in this sense, meaning a long time horizon).

**STUDENT ACTIVITY 8.1 Reflecting on cultural experiences**

This is an exercise that can be done in seminar groups and can result in a presentation, or more informally and based on individual reflection. Each approach will depend on an ability to reflect on experiences of cultural difference and to make sense of these.

1. Share stories of overseas travel or working that has involved experiencing different cultural situations.
2. Think of the most powerful or difficult problem that you have experienced or had to deal with while overseas and share this with the group.
3. Explain what effect this had on you and how you dealt with it.
4. As a group, discuss the implications of these cultural experiences in relation to working abroad and the support that HR professionals might need to provide for those working in different cultural environments.

## Key cultural concepts

**Ethnocentric**—this can refer to the practice, often unconscious, of judging other cultures from the perspective of one's own. The starting point therefore in anyone taking an ethnocentric position is with that person's own national culture.

Closely related to this meaning is a second one that is potentially more significant—the tendency to see one's own culture as inherently superior to that of other countries.

**Polycentric**, on the other hand, describes a position and perspective that recognizes the existence of many different national cultures which are, in principle equally valid and justifiable be reference to national identities and difference. No one culture is seen as inherently better than another.

## Culture shock

'Culture shock' is a term used to describe the anxiety and feelings of surprise, disorientation, and confusion felt when people have to operate within a different culture or social environment. It is often the outcome of the negative experience of moving from a familiar culture to one that is unfamiliar. But it is not simply the effect of the new that is potentially destabilizing: it is also linked to the shock and discomfort of being separated from family, friends, and the other things that matter in a person's life, such as church, social club, pub, and local shops.

For many people, the experience of moving to a different cultural environment, without the benefit of any acculturation experiences, can be expressed in terms of four stages. Not everyone passes through all of the phases, of course; much depends on the individual, their duration in the new location, and whether the move involves an individual or group.

1. **The 'honeymoon' phase**

   This is not always experienced and depends on the nature of the new location, but when everything new seems to be 'different and better', those affected may experience a temporary sense of pleasure.

2. **The 'distress' phase**

   At this point, which may occur after a few days, weeks, or even months, new things are seen in a different light and begin to be compared unfavourably with those 'at home'. Small irritations become exaggerated, and feelings of loss and loneliness can develop.

3. **The 'autonomy and independence' phase**

   After a period of time, people become more confident in and familiar with their 'new' environment. They have, either consciously or subconsciously, engaged in a social learning process, which changes their perceptions of their new environment from being different to being normal. Entering this phase also implies a degree of social integration, as opposed to social and psychological isolation.

4. **The 'reverse culture shock' phase**

   Perhaps the most well-known example of this phase is that of soldiers coming home after time spent in a war zone: coming to terms with the very different conditions and relationships in a peacetime environment can produce very serious and lasting psychological effects. Although not as intense as those of soldiers the experiences of expatriates and their families returning to the UK after a two- or three-year secondment or assignment abroad can involve similar psychological stresses and difficulties of adjustment (Gunn, 2003).



For a detailed analysis of the issues and of the challenges involved in the repatriation of managers returning to their country of origin after an overseas assignment, see Scullion and Linehan (2005).

HRM Insight 8.4 illustrates the problems associated with overseas secondment, for which family considerations need to be taken into account, and is a good example of the challenges facing those in HR.

**HRM INSIGHT 8.4 Virginia Power Tools**

Virginia Power Tools is a large multinational company quoted on the New York Stock Exchange. It manufactures and sells high-precision power tools to the automotive industry worldwide. The resignation of the managing director of the UK arm of the business, who has been headhunted by a competitor company, has prompted Virginia to place the executive immediately on garden leave for the duration of his notice, pending negotiations over his departure, because Virginia is concerned about conflicting interests. Virginia estimates that it may take up to 12 months to select and recruit a replacement, and the company has therefore decided to second an existing US employee, Bob Homer, vice president of a similar-sized operation in the USA, to the UK. He will both run operations and lead the recruitment of a replacement.

While it is anticipated that this secondment will initially last for 12 months, there is a possibility that the company's commitment to acquire businesses overseas as part of its global expansion programme may result in further UK-based assignments for Bob. Bob is married with two children, aged three and six years.

**Questions**

1. What alternatives, in terms of benefits and support, might form part of the package to encourage Bob to move to the UK?
2. What arrangements might need to be considered to support Bob's family?
3. What arrangements will the UK HR team need to put in place to enable Bob to be employed in the UK?
4. Is there a case to use external specialist companies to provide support for Bob and his family? If so, what might this involve?

From a UK ethnocentric perspective, the study of international HRM often involves looking at the HR practices found in other developed countries, but more usually in the emerging economies of South East Asia, and considering how they might be different from those found in the UK. In others words, the point of departure is HR in the UK and the UK context becomes the reference point against which comparisons are made. The recruitment and selection case study will almost certainly be read by UK students and practitioners in terms of their practices and experiences and many will interpret the actions of the company head as not only different from what would have happened in the UK but wrong too! However, the important point to make is that it was only 'wrong' in the context of UK practices and legislative requirements. From a different social and cultural perspective Ahmed Hassan's approach was perfectly understandable and from a business perspective eminently sensible. He knew the company and what the job involved in detail; he also knew the technical and personal competencies he needed to find in applicants. It may not have been written and formalized and he may not have followed 'procedure' but if his decision was validated by how well the successful applicant subsequently performed then we can say that, to use a concept developed in Chapter 1, his behaviour was materially rational; that is he achieved a successful outcome. Limitations in the UK approach to recruitment and selection, based on the balance between how processes and procedures are designed and implemented and the quality of applicants recruited are probably more familiar to managers and business leaders rather than academics, but an article by James Hurley, entitled 'Employers a risk to recruitment,' (*Daily Telegraph* Business Section, 8 February 2011, p. B7) indicated what some of these might be. He writes:

> **Companies that complain about skills shortages preventing them from hiring are just as likely to be undermined by their own recruitment processes as weak applicants.**

He continued by quoting a senior UK manager who said:

> **Too often, internal 'specialists' take insufficient time to understand requirements, define the job description and then turn those into an operating brief.**

Although this is an example of how similar things are done in different ways in other countries, it provides another indication of where the UK can learn from others rather than assuming that our model of HR is the given starting point in any consideration of international practice. It is also worth remembering the point made by Michael Porter in Chapter 3, that acting strategically often involves acting differently from competitors in the way the same activities are carried out. And research undertaken by the CIPD and Bridge Consulting (CIPD, 2010) provides more extensive evidence that companies in South East Asia in particular are not merely following UK and Western practice but are developing their own distinctive approach to HR. In his report Jerry Connor asks how relevant HR can be if the so-called best practice approach to HR failed to alert UK businesses to the recession that hit in 2007/8. He goes on by stating that:

> **In Europe this has been extrapolated by the tendency, especially where the Ulrich model had been implemented without a truly compelling overriding purpose, for the function to become ever more specialised and fragmented.**

He continues by asking the rhetorical question:

> **Is it enough to build a function built on a collection of expertise around core people priorities? Or do we need to be bolder and build the capability to generate rule-breaking insight and to act as guardians of the long-term commercial success of our organisations?**
> (Connor, 2010)

His research, based on interviews with leaders of Asian businesses, suggests that the new form of HR being developed there appears to by-pass and avoid the issues that are being raised in Europe. The different HR agenda reflects very different situations and requirements where growth and expansion and technological change define the context in which business is done and the role and contribution HR is expected to play. Clearly the legislative framework in that part of the world is different but the report also suggests that there is a different HR mindset, particularly amongst companies operating in an international context and global market place. According to Connor:

> **Asia represents one of the most fast-moving and creative business environments in the world today. And it has some of the world's most dynamic and creative HR leaders.**

This relationship between rapid economic growth and an innovative approach to HR is not a coincidence but an inevitable outcome of the interplay between economic forces and the international war for talent. As Yeung et al. (2008) claim:

> **the growth and globalisation of firms in Asia and the evolution of HRM in the region are two faces of the same phenomenon.**

The four elements of Asia's 'new' model of HR indicate the degree to which practice in emerging and growth orientated countries not only reflects economic conditions and imperatives but also national and regional cultures. These elements are:



- **Insightful thinking** The report by Connor indicates an important paradox: on the one hand Asian culture and business practice is based on the idea of telling people what to do and expecting them to do it unquestioningly. But the economic challenge requires much more insightful thinking that has to go beyond top business leaders, affecting the organization as a whole. Again we see parallels with Porter's idea that to be strategic HR needs to explore opportunities to be different and being different requires the ability to question, challenge, and have insight. One of the examples given of what being insightful involves relates to a rejection of the distinction between corporate strategy and HR strategy. According to Connor:

  > **There is no need to talk about the HR strategy supporting the business strategy. They are one and the same thing.**

- **Community** Building a particular type of social organization or organizational culture is seen as one of the key priorities for the new Asian model of HR, and one of the key influences on this is the importance of the family and family type relationships within business organizations. Many of those interviewed as part of the research project questioned the perceived Western emphasis and value of individualism and internal competition, which can be seen to conflict with core values such as community and family type relationships that generate high levels of mutual loyalty. However, such distinctions are now ones of degree rather than kind and, as is seen later, the value of competition and competiveness is recognized much more in Asia today than in earlier phases of its economic development.

- **Purpose** The report highlights the importance and power of what it describes as 'purpose'—the sense of identification and pride that many aspiring professionals seem to have and to want. National pride and a self-belief in the 'rightness' of what organizations do and the contributions they make are key drivers that help to explain the zeal and commitment of employees to their organizations and what they stand for. Self-interest co-exists with a belief in a higher interest, whether this be organizational, national, or cultural, and HR is seen to have an important role in facilitating this fusion of different levels of engagement and involvement. The report notes that HR leaders:

  > **are looking to build deep and enduring engagement, tapping into the passion, dreams and aspirations of their people to power long-term growth.**

- **Performance** Again, the emphasis given to individual performance is potentially in conflict with cultural values and loyalty to employees, but the report offers insights into the way HR leaders are increasingly trying to create a stronger commitment to achieving high performance and managing this effectively without undermining the strength and importance of traditional values. For some organizations this involves encouraging a degree of competition that is not inconsistent with Asian educational systems where the pursuit of excellence is a defining feature. In others, the coaching by expatriates of indigenous staff creates a pool of people who able to replace those on short-term contracts. A third example of creating high-performing organizations links back to the recruitment of talented new people whose personal drives and capabilities are seen as far more important that their ability to undertaken specific jobs.

# International Management Competences

Understanding the cultural and business environments in which international managers have to operate and the potential difficulties associated with the repatriation process helps HR staff in the decisions they have to make in the recruitment, selection, and development of these managers. Integral to the successful management of these processes is the ability to identify the key skills and competences that those working overseas need to possess. The case study at the end of the chapter provides insights into what these might be, but this is only one person's account of what major overseas assignments involve and it is important to look carefully at what research tells us about these competences. Moreover, how are these skills and competences actually acquired? Are the 'real' challenges of HR in the areas of assessment and selection, or in designing learning experiences that build on what these managers already know and can do?

**RESEARCH INSIGHT 8.2 Support for expatriate workers**

The article by Stroppa et al. (2010) provides insights into the support provided for expatriate workers. The role of support networks is analysed as is the mediating effects of company size. Read the article and:

1. Explain the different kinds of support available to expatriate workers on overseas assignments.
2. Identify the different sources of support and comment on their relative importance and contribution.
3. Establish how company size affects the provision of support.
4. Reach general conclusions about strategies for supporting expatriates before, during, and after their assignment.

One of the most interesting findings from recent research into the recruitment and selection of international managers, and one that confirms a view expressed elsewhere in this book, is provided by Paul Sparrow (2006). As a result of his work, commissioned by the CIPD, he found that:

> **The majority of expatriate skills are learnt through experience–they learn how to manage across cultures in most instances without education in cross-cultural skills.**

This suggests that the key HR decision is taken at the assessment and selection stage, at which point evidence of the ability to learn from experience and to be able to cope with potentially stressful environments becomes an important differentiator.

The report identified the following characteristics as being associated with the successful expatriate manager.

- Professional and technical competence, and experience on the job

  This area also included general maturity, knowledge of the company, and experience of performing the job in the 'home' organization.

- Personality traits and relational abilities

  Included under this head are also important communication skills, but not only those involving language ability. The category also relates to personal maturity, tolerance, respect for the host country, and adaptability.

- **Perceptual dimensions and life strategies**

  This area relates to, among other things, the ability to learn from experiences, and the avoidance of being judgemental and evaluative in relation to different social values and social conventions. In other words, it relates to avoiding an ethnocentric stance.

- **Self-maintenance factors**

  These characteristics relate to the ability to function independently, to cope with stress and pressure, and to exhibit confidence in carrying out specific tasks.

- **Leadership and motivational factors**

  This final area of competency relates to the development of relationships, the use of initiative and the ability to take appropriate action, and a general interest in working overseas.

The outcome of Sparrow's research into relevant managerial competences is certainly consistent with the personal account of Chris Atkin, and with other individuals' 'stories' of what working overseas involves and the demands such work makes of managers who have to carry out important duties in an often unusual and demanding environment. Based on his work, Sparrow offers an interesting and useful competency framework, which rests on the three fundamental attributes that those working overseas need to have: emotional stability; confidence and relationship building; openness to different experiences. This framework is presented in Figure 8.2.

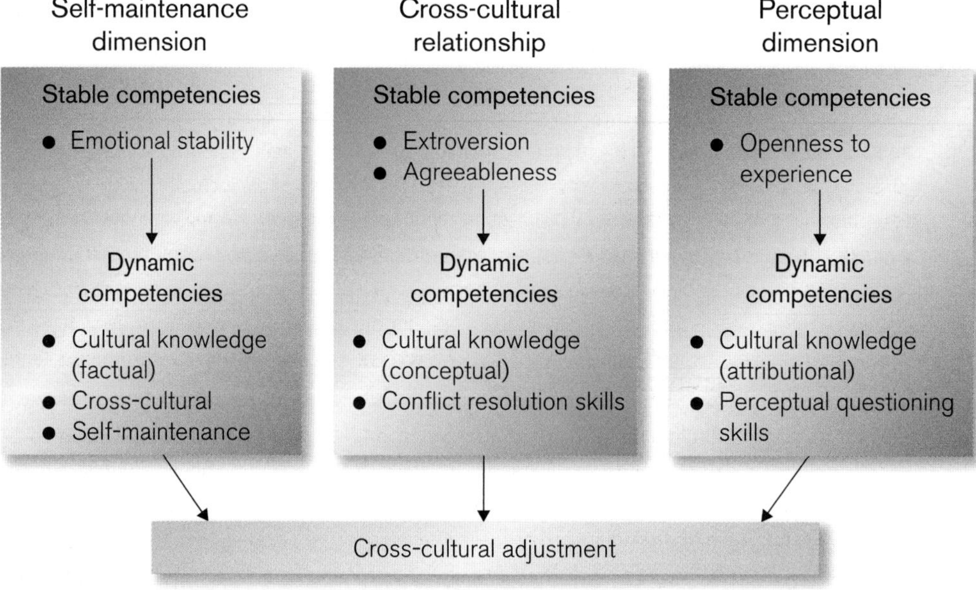


**Figure 8.2** A competency model for overseas working

**Source**: This material is taken from *International Recruitment, Selection and Assessment* (Sparrow, 2006), with the permission of the publisher, the Chartered Institute of Personnel and Development, London.

**STUDENT ACTIVITY 8.2 Designing an assessment centre for managers working on international assignments**

This is a demanding activity that requires careful planning and preparation. It is also one that needs to be done collaboratively. Groups can set their own parameters on the scale and level of sophistication of the exercise, and can add detail to the context. To give the exercise extra realism, your tutor might play the role of the managing director and give you feedback on your proposals.

You are a team of HR practitioners working for a global engineering company, with manufacturing and distribution centres in India, China, and Japan. Currently, these centres are managed by local staff, who report directly to the UK-based head of overseas production. Because of continuing expansion of the centres and the building of an additional unit in Malaysia, the managing director has decided that the current reporting lines are no longer appropriate. He has decided to create the new position of managing director for Asia, with executive responsibilities for all of the company's business in that region. The appointee would report directly to the UK-based MD. Your job is to provide the MD with a shortlist of three candidates from which he will make the final choice.

He wants to be kept informed of developments on this new appointment and wants you to report back to him with answers to the following questions:

1. What is your recruitment strategy?
2. What is your person specification?
3. What activities will you use in the assessment centre? He also wants to know how this will operate.
4. What will be the main criteria for deciding on who is to be included in the final shortlist?

# Summary

- Diversity in employment is not only being driven by the ethnic, age, and gender differences within UK society, but by globalization, the internationalization of the labour force, and economic migration. All of these are trends that are likely to continue. In Chapter 2, we explored the different historical influences that shaped the development of the specialized management function that became known as Personnel Management and then Human Resource Management, and identified the key influences of social and religious values, management theory, trade unionism, and industrial conflict. Today, we can add further seminal influences on what HR is becoming and its agenda: internationalization and globalization. Workforce diversity is only one manifestation of this; others include managing expatriate workers and supporting their families, developing new management strategies for recruiting and developing in a global labour market, coping with cultural differences, and complying with different employment regulations and traditions. At the same time, HR continues to be tasked with delivering administrative efficiency and providing operational support to managers, while not forgetting the importance of maintaining effective communications with staff, gaining employee commitment, and providing a positive working environment.
- The implications for HR of these challenges are profound, and are unlikely to be met unless organizations develop the 'right' level of HR capacity and capability to equip them to operate in this new, and more demanding, context. This may not involve employing more HR staff: interestingly, some of the organizations that have been in the forefront of developing new models of HR have employed outsourcing, IT-enabled HR services, and service flexibility to generate their status as truly international and global (examples being the Royal Bank of Scotland and Diageo).
- It is not only the shape of the HR 'architecture' that changes: perhaps as significant are the implications for the HR professional. New, business-related skills are becoming increasingly critical, both for personal and professional credibility, and for the function's standing with other stakeholders. New competences linked to operating and managing in an international context will be crucial in the development of new HR tools and interventions, such as those needed to facilitate learning and knowledge sharing within the international organization. And, as always, the ability to develop and relate HR strategies to operational performance will continue to be valued and expected from those in HR. Not only is HR being shaped by the forces of internationalization and globalization, so too is the profile of those who work in the function.

**Visit the Online Resource Centre that accompanies this book for self-test questions, weblinks, and more information on the topics covered in this chapter.**
**www.oxfordtextbooks.co.uk/orc/banfield_kay2e/**

## REVIEW QUESTIONS

1. How do cultural differences affect HR and the management of people?
2. Why do individuals and organizations have to become less ethnocentric and more polycentric when operating in an international context?
3. What key attributes and competences does the HR professional working for an international company need?
4. What is the link between diversity and internationalization?

***See Online Resource Centre for answers.***

## CASE STUDY

### Chris Atkin's story



The following is based on an interview with the subject.

Chris Atkin can be reliably described as an 'international manager', with over 39 years experience of travelling and 'doing business', in Europe initially, then in the Middle and Far East, in South Africa and in Australasia. He might best be described as an 'international commuter', because his job as sales director for Dormer Tools meant that he was frequently away for up to four weeks at a time. Dormer Tools was a world-class producer of engineering cutting tools, used in almost all metal manufacturing processes. It sold a range of high-quality products through a network of international distributors and agents. Starting out as a management trainee, he spent the first five years with Dormer in manufacturing, and then moved into sales and marketing, after the managing director suggested that his outgoing personality might make him well suited to that function.

Early experiences of working in the Middle and Far East created an element of culture shock, when he was exposed to very different traditions, values, and ways of working. It became clear to him that becoming culturally aware and sensitive was a precondition of building trust and mutual understanding with potential business partners and clients. Using Saudi Arabia as an example, it was clear that it was very much a 'man's world', certainly during the time he worked there, and there would be no contact or socialization with female family members. Of course, times change and, at the recent wedding of the daughter of one of his business associates in Dubai, around a hundred people attended, and although males and females dined separately, they all came together afterwards.

Reflecting on 'doing business abroad', Chris thought that the following were important points to remember.

- Don't make promises that can't be kept—people have long memories and, if you let them down, they will remember and refuse to do business with you again.
- Be aware of how business is conducted in different parts of the world—Saudis, for example, like to barter before agreeing a deal and the need for them to feel that they have achieved a good deal means that negotiating skills, and the ability to keep something in reserve as a concession, are important.
- Preserving a strong ethical stance in business dealings is important—realistically, in certain countries, potential customers will seek additional commissions or will link a sale directly to an 'illegal payment'. It is important, when negotiating contracts, to remember the long-term benefits to one's personal reputation and the safety of avoiding questionable business dealings.

One of the points that came over clearly in the interview was the need for UK managers working abroad to have certain competences, the most important for Chris being as follows.

- **The ability to work alone, along with personal endurance and resilience**

  In the early period of his international role, there was little backup from the home company and telecommunications were far less developed than they are now. The ability to make business decisions in relative isolation was an important requirement.

- **Understanding the implications of 'getting business'**

  This means thinking about whether the manufacturing plant's capacity to produce and deliver products in the quantities agreed and on time was an important requirement.

- **Problem solving and problem preventing**

  This involves seeing beyond 'the deal' and taking a longer term, more holistic, perspective, as well as being able to resolve difficulties that might be preventing a deal from being concluded.

- **The ability to help customers to solve technical problems**

  This means not only selling the cutting tools, but offering advice on the machines that will use them, helping with maintenance issues and advising on operative training.

- **Language and cultural understanding**

  Learning the basics of Arabic, for example, was very helpful for the business side of his work, but also facilitated social interaction and personal acceptance.

Talking about the support he received from what was called 'personnel' in those days, Chris accepted that, in the 1970s and 1980s, the function in his company was not as developed and influential as it is now. Even so, he admitted that he never really understood what it was about! The people who worked in it always seemed busy, but were not business-orientated and lacked a real identity, although this changed under the influence of developments in HRM, with the HR manager now sitting in on commercial discussions with other senior managers. Chris' main recollection of his 'own HR people', however, was that they were 'a race apart', physically isolated from other management functions in the same building and only visible during a strike or the threat of industrial action.

The main 'HR' interventions with Chris were conducted by the managing director, rather than by HR staff, and involved annual appraisals, the setting of performance targets and the development of strategies for developing new markets. His advice to HR is to spend more time with the people who are working abroad, discover what they need to know and the support they require, and find out where they are going, so that intelligence can be gathered about these countries to help the managers to prepare for their assignments, particularly if families are also involved.

Finally, one particular experience that Chris had is worth recounting. Invited by a Saudi sheik to a traditional Bedouin feast, he was presented with a dish of rice that contained sheep's eyes—a delicacy in certain parts of Saudi Arabia. Knowing that, when offered one, he could not refuse to accept it because to do so would be construed as an insult to his hosts, he accepted it and a second when this, too, was offered. The experience wasn't particularly pleasant, but on the basis of understanding the importance of social etiquette, he built up a lifelong friendship with his host, who later presented him with a complete set of traditional Arabian clothing as a token of his respect, something that Chris experienced as a very humbling occasion.

### Questions

1. With international secondments and overseas business travel now much more frequent than they used to be, what is the role of HR in supporting this?
2. What competences do members of HR staff need to have to be effective in preparing and supporting expatriates?
3. What can be done to avoid or limit the effect of culture shock?
4. Consider HR's role in developing an ethical code of practice for managers working and doing business abroad.

## FURTHER READING


Briscoe, D.R., Schuler, R.S., and Claus, L. (2009) *International Human Resource Management: Policy and Practice for Multinational Enterprises (Global HRM)*, 3rd ed., Routledge.

Chartered Institute of Personnel and Development (2005) *International Organisations: Assessing the Effectiveness of Their HR Function*, CIPD practical tool, available online to CIPD members at www.cipd.co.uk.

Hofstede, G. (2001) *Culture's Consequences: Comparing Values, Behaviors, Institutions, and Organizations Across Nations*, Sage.

Ozbilgin, M. (2005) *International Human Resource Management*, Palgrave Macmillan.

Perkins, S.J. (2006) *International Reward and Recognition*, www.cipd.co.uk.

Scullion, H. and Collings, D. (2010) *Global Talent Management*, Routledge.

Seers, L. (2010) 'Next Generation HR', *Time for change—Towards a Next Generation for HR*, February.

Trompenaars, F. and Hampden-Turner, C. (1997) *Riding the Waves of Culture: Understanding Cultural Diversity in Business*, 2nd ed., Nicholas Brealey Publishing Ltd.

Wil-Harzin, A. and Pinnington, A. (2011) *International Human Resource Management*, Sage.

## REFERENCES




Chiang, F., Hau-Siu Chow, I. and Birch, T.A. (2010) 'Examining human resource management outsourcing in Hong Kong', *International Journal of Human Resource Management*, **21**:15, December.

Connor, J. (2010) *The Growth Option: Turbo-Charging HR's Impact in Asia*, CIPD.

David, R. (1997) *The Pyramid Builders of Ancient Egypt: A Modern Investigation of Pharaoh's Workforce*, Routledge.

Davison, L. (2005) 'How to recruit migrant workers', *People Management*, 1 September, p. 50.

Edwards, T. and Rees, C. (2006) *International Human Resource Management*, FT/Prentice Hall.

Ferner, A. and Hyman, R. (1998) *Changing Industrial Relations in Europe*, Blackwell.

Glaister, K.W., Husan, R. and Buckley, P.J. (2003) 'Learning to manage international joint ventures', *International Business Review*, **12**:1, pp. 83–108.

Gunn, N. (2003) 'Repatriation the right way', *Expatica HR*, www.expatica.com.

Harris, H., Brewster, C. and Sparrow, P. (2001) *Globalisation and HR*, CIPD.

Hira, R. and Hira, J. (2005) *Outsourcing America: What's Behind Our National Crisis and How We Can Reclaim American Jobs*, AMACOM.

Hosftede, G. and Hofstede, G.J. (2004) *Cultures and Organizations: Software of the Mind*, McGraw Hill.

Hurley, J. (2011) 'Employers a risk to recruitment,' *Daily Telegraph* Business Section, 8 February, p. B7

Lawler III, E.E. et al. (2004) *Human resources business process outsourcing: transforming how HR gets its work done*, John Wiley & Sons.

*People Management* (2006) 'Migrants plug city skills gaps', 28 December, p. 9.

Scullion, H. (1995) 'International human resource management', in Storey, J. (ed.) *Human Resource Management: A Critical Text*, Routledge.

Scullion, H. and Linehan, M. (2005) *International Human Resource Management*, Palgrave.

Sparrow, P. (2006) *International Recruitment, Selection and Assessment*, www.cipd.co.uk.

Stroppa, C. and Spieß, E. (2010) 'Expatriates social networks: The role of company size.' *International Journal of Human Resource Management*, **21**, 13 October.

Wirth, R. (2002) 'Breaking through the glass ceiling: women in management', Presentation at the First ILO International Conference on Pay Equity Between Women and Men: Myth or Reality.

Yeung, A., Warner, M. and Rowley, C. (2008) 'Growth and globalization: Evolution of human resource management practices in Asia', *Human Resource Management*, **47**:1, February, pp. 1–13.

# HRM Processes

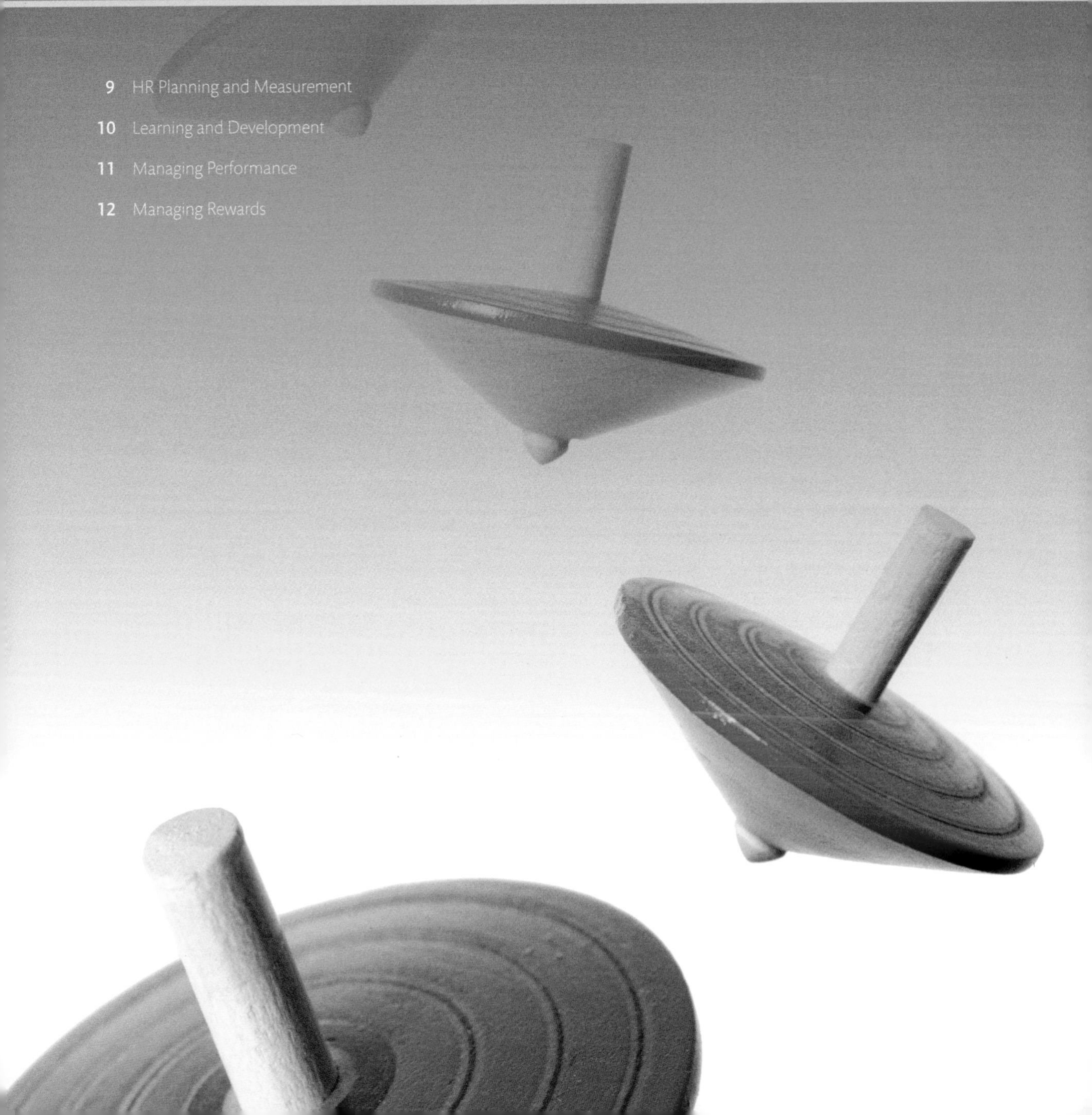

# HR Planning and Measurement

9

## Key Terms

**Planning** Can be understood as a set of techniques, an approach and a mindset, all of which relate to achieving specified objectives. It should be understood as a process, rather than a time-constrained event.

**Human resource planning (HRP)** Originally known as 'manpower planning', this is concerned with planning and controlling the quantity and quality of labour available to an organization.

**Metrics** Relates to what and how something is measured. HR metrics focus on key aspects of the labour force, its behaviours, and its costs and contributions. The use of measures is increasingly associated with important features of the HR function, as part of the process of evaluating its efficiency and effectiveness.

**Bradford absence index** This technique calculates the impact on business of an individual's absence pattern based on the frequency and number of days lost.

## Learning Objectives

As a result of reading this chapter and using the Online Resource Centre, you should be able to:

- understand the importance of human resource planning (HRP) and measurement;
- recognize the different approaches to HR planning that can be adopted;
- identify the range of metrics that can be used to measure HR management;
- understand the limitations and problems associated with the use of metrics in HR.

# Introduction

Think again about the building of the Egyptian Pyramids and other great monuments to human civilization: where did all of those workers come from? How many were required and what skills did they need at each stage of construction? Who decided when their employment was over and how did they know how many might need replacing, as a result of death, illness, and absence, during the period over which the particular project lasted?

If there had been any HR professionals around at that time, these would have been the kinds of challenges and issues that they would have been faced with:

- how many people do we need?
- when do we need them?
- what skills and competences do they need to have?
- where can we find them?
- what is it going to cost us to employ them?
- how can we ensure that we have neither too many nor too few in relation to construction or production requirements?
- how can we reduce our labour force in ways that reflect social and legal norms, and maintain our reputation as an employer, ensure that labour costs stay within budget, but also maintain the organization's commitment to the welfare of its employees?



These are deceptively straightforward questions that are as relevant today as they were in the past. Successful organizations are successful, in part, precisely because they have been able to provide consistently effective answers to these questions, even though their internal and external environments are constantly changing and evolving in response to economic and social forces. The HR professional, working with line managers, has a key role to play in ensuring that an optimum balance is struck between the number and quality of people employed, the associated employment costs, the organization's requirements for productive capacity and associated budgetary constraints.

Although the economic and financial imperatives vary between the public and private sectors—and most commentators would argue that, historically, these are much more influential in the private sector—people are rarely employed for any reason other than that they are an economic resource necessary for the creation of goods and services. This means that human resource planning (HRP) is not simply about meeting the demand for labour, but also involves understanding and managing the costs associated with employing any given number of people. As has been seen recently, the NHS has found that successfully recruiting the required numbers of doctors and nurses to meet establishment numbers is not the whole story. Budgetary constraints have led to situations in which many hospital posts have been axed and staff redeployed, temporary contracts not renewed, the use of agency staff reduced or curtailed, and, in extreme circumstances, staff made redundant. HRP is about getting the right number of people with the required skills and competences in post at the right time, but this has to be achieved within changing budgetary constraints and has to reflect the organization's ability to pay the costs of employment (Royal College of Nursing, 2007).

From an economic perspective, employees represent a cost as well as a source of added value and while the costs of employing someone are relatively easy to calculate, the value they bring is not. This is key to understanding that HRP is not simply about the production of 'manpower plans' and futuristic scenario planning, but needs to be seen as an important dimension of almost all aspects of HR. In particular, it connects to the implementation and effectiveness of an organization's recruitment strategies, its labour reduction strategies, the continual search for improvements in productivity, and the consequences that follow from this in relation to changes in the demand for labour. Going back to the example of the Egyptian Pyramids, if they were being built today, what would be the essential differences in the employment and use of labour? There would be fewer people employed, all would have a greater range and depth of skills, they would be more flexible and productive, and the strategies for employing and managing them would be more sophisticated. All of these changes relate to improvements in the planning and control of the labour resource: a requirement that, in the context of tight labour markets and high labour costs, is increasingly important for the vast majority of organizations.

From a managerial and economic perspective the continued search for efficiency savings and productivity improvements that may well involve reduced headcounts and lower overall employment costs is a rational response to a tighter fiscal framework, but its impact on the interests of individual employees and trade unions is often perceived quite differently. These situations demonstrate once again that the interests of employers and employees, together with their trade unions, come into conflict. Generally speaking those affected by job insecurity and pay/benefit cuts will resist them in whatever ways they can; employers will seek to find ways of pushing through changes in the numbers of people they employ and/or wage cuts. Unless trade unions can mobilize sufficient political power to resist or delay these changes the question that sooner or later has to be answered is how do we deliver the required cutbacks in employment that are needed or required? The following HRM Insight, with associated student activity, is based on events that happened in 2008.

### HRM INSIGHT 9.1 Reducing employment costs

Multiplex Manufacturing is a family run business based in a Northern industrial city. It employs 120 people in total who are all employed on one site. The breakdown of the 120 staff is as follows:

30 are skilled workers on full-time contracts which equate to 38 hours per week. All 30 have been with the company for five years or more and are key to the business. Seven of the 30 are female. Turnover levels are low as the company has a good reputation for paying above market rates and is known as a 'good employer' in the area. Overtime has been running at approximately 10 per cent per week.

65 are operatives who assemble the products, package them, and prepare them for dispatch. Some are responsible for stock control and materials handling. Approximately half of this group are female and the length of service varies from several weeks to 20 years. Annual turnover is above that of the skilled group and averages 10 per cent. Overtime has been approximately 15 per cent.

20 are administrative and technical workers who work in the office and are engaged in production planning, secretarial work, sales and marketing, and finance. Unlike the 'factory floor' staff, those in this group are paid monthly salaries.

The final group consists of five managers. The MD is the daughter of the original owner, her brother is production director, and the other three head up Sales and Marketing, Production Planning and Quality Control, and Product Development and Technical Support.

Over time, more and more of the company's products have been exported and now exports represent 80 per cent of output. It has an annual turnover of £5 million, with plans to grow this to £10 million, and is in the process of negotiating a bank loan to fund its expansion plans. Employment costs represent 50 per cent of turnover.

After having its best year ever, with profits reaching three quarters of a million pounds in 2007, the world recession hit and within weeks orders fell by 30 per cent and it quickly became apparent to the MD that things would remain very difficult for some time. At that reduced level of output, the finance director calculated that the business would cease to exist as a viable concern within three months. At that point it was impossible for management to know how long the recession would last, but there was a belief that, with the depreciation of the pound against most other currencies and economic growth in the Far East, if the company could survive, and make the necessary changes in its workforce and employment costs, it would be well placed to take advantage of these opportunities. But it needed a survival strategy!

Because the company has very little internal HR expertise, you have been hired to advise them on what actions need to be taken to cut employment costs by 20 per cent over a 12 month period. Whilst you have a relatively free hand, you must identify actions that have the potential to achieve the required costs savings, but it is equally important that the changes do not undermine employee motivation and commitment to the company. It is equally important to retain 'core' employees whose skills are critical to the company's future success yet at the same time trying to ensure that what is being proposed is as fair to everyone as possible.

Working in groups and with the intention of producing a presentation that summarizes your thinking and ideas, you are required to:

- Outline your general strategy for achieving the required employment costs reduction.
- Making realistic assumptions about wages and salaries, show in detail where the savings would come from.
- What actions would you take to ensure the cuts were perceived as fair?
- What would you do to ensure motivation and productivity levels remained high?

**Insights & Outcomes: visit the Online Resource Centre at www.oxfordtextbooks.co.uk/orc/banfield_kay2e/ for a summary of what actually happened and the results that followed.**

The long-term trend in Western economies is for organizations to operate effectively with fewer employees—a fact that reflects increasing labour productivity and the increased use of technology. This does not mean, however, that fewer people are economically active or that there are fewer jobs available. Part of the difficulty is that new job creation, whilst increasing the number of economically active people, often involves part-time or casual work. The *Daily Telegraph*, quoting recent NIESR statistics, reported that just 6,000 of the 200,000 jobs that have been created since Britain emerged out of recession pay a full-time wage. So whilst certain organizations may be adding to their labour force the actual numbers employed may well be associated with a relative fall in the hours the organization needs. Conversely, where the public sector is shedding jobs and/or reducing employment costs, many job losses will be full time and permanent, which is where the greatest long-term costs savings can be made (Philpott, 2010).



But managing a gradual and planned reduction in the labour force is not always easy. Organizations can face unpredictable changes in competitive and financial conditions, such as cheap imports, unfavourable movements in exchange rates, increased costs of employing people and tightening budgetary constraints. As a result, they can quickly find that they are employing too much labour at too high a cost and quickly need to reduce either employment numbers or overall employment costs. Given the relative inflexibility of wage rates and salaries, which means that it is difficult to force through pay reductions, by reducing supply levels, either in terms of hours or people employed, HRP strategies need to be developed that allow organizations to respond quickly to changing demand conditions.

The following situation represents the kinds of environmental change that impact directly on employer's costs.

In response to proposed increases in the number of statutory holidays from 20 to 28 days, Bob Cotton, the Chief Executive of the British Hospitality Association, commented that the change represented an additional 3.5 per cent on payroll costs. Whatever the social case for such changes, the impact on employment costs cannot be avoided:

> **If you start pushing up the wage bill too high you start shedding labour to pay for those left in work.** (Wallop, 2006)

His comment captures the pressures and dilemmas with which employers have to work in deciding on their employment strategies. But one of the most significant consequences of the recent recession has been the emergence of pay freezes and absolute pay reductions in organizations that have had to respond in a much more radical way to budgetary and market changes. For the first time in many years, organizations have been confronted with the challenges of not having to accept pay increases but rather pay decreases; it has become increasingly possible to achieve financial flexibility not only by reducing headcount and hours worked but also by wage and salary reductions.

On the other hand, a numerical shortage of labour or qualitative imbalances can have a serious effect on the organization's ability to meet demand for its goods and services. This can result in reduced revenues, lost orders, and dissatisfied customers: having too few employees of the right quality can have equally serious financial consequences as having too many employees! Depending on the degree of volatility and change in the product market, organizations can be faced by quite rapid turnarounds in their financial situation, where labour force reductions are quickly followed by the need to expand employment in critical areas. The challenge of HRP is to reconcile changes in the supply and demand for labour, and to produce, as far as possible, a labour force that can be flexed in terms of numbers and quality in response to changes in demand. To achieve this while avoiding the creation of damaging conflict with the employees and their representative institutions is, it might be argued, the 'holy grail' of HRP. The fact that few organizations seem to have been able to achieve this goal is testimony to the difficulties and challenges facing the HR professional in this aspect of their work.

**PRACTITIONER INSIGHT Dean Royles, Director NHS Employers**

In the NHS, Workforce Planning (WFP) is driven by the rapid pace of technological and organizational change and the rising expectations of patients and service users. Another key factor is the long-term planning timelines involved in training medical staff today for situations that can only be predicted 10 or 15 years ahead.

Making better WFP decisions means that management has to be 'more savvy' about the situation we are faced with. In particular, we need to be able to have much more confidence in the indicators we use to tell us what the situation is in relation to number, capabilities, and costs and avoid the mistake of simply relying on the data themselves. We need to avoid the situation of being 'data rich and insight light'.

Contemporary WFP is no longer a purely internal function about headcount and resources—this is only one of its dimensions. It also needs to have an external focus, looking at the changing environment in which we have to operate and ensuring that we can meet the ambitions of the health service and support it on its ongoing transformational journey.



WFP today is not just about headcount numbers: it also involves contributing to the challenge of improving employee and service productivity. This can be achieved in two ways, firstly by looking at wage costs and efficiency levels, and secondly looking towards increasing the level of employee engagement which we know plays a major part in levels of discretionary effort—'going the extra mile', which in turns affects productivity.

But a major challenge over the next five years is to address the financial costs of employment which can involve pay freezes, reductions in sick pay costs and agency spend, as well as productivity increases, which means the cost of inputs falls in relation to outputs. As an example, by not making premium payments for working on the royal wedding bank holiday this year, we would save £30 million. Although significant, this has to be placed in the context of a £40 billion pay bill.

The tools of HRP are becoming more sophisticated and reliable and allow managers to demonstrate a more direct link between cause and effect and returns on investments. But we still have to avoid the errors of previous years, particularly the mistake of seeing planning as a simple linear process—it's not quite as simple as that! We also need to be better at building contingencies into our plans and recognizing the virtue of flexibility so that we can mitigate the effects of things that we can't predict now. The new reality is of a WFP system that needs constant refinement in order to get it as good as we can; perfection is a dangerous illusion.

Several references have already been made in this chapter to the choices available to organizations faced with shortages, or surpluses, of labour. Table 9.1 offers an indication of the most frequently used strategies, some of which can be thought of in operational terms, while others have a more strategic dimension. In considering these options, think carefully about the costs and benefits each involves and the consequences to employee relations, on both an individual and a collective basis, of adopting each one.

For an explanation of the different interests between employers and employees in relation to the challenges of balancing supply requirements with demand see the Online Resource Centre extension material 9.1.

# The Planning Process

Planning, generally, is integral to any organized activity. It often is not only an option but also a necessity, and most organizations, particularly larger ones, engage in some form of planning as part of the process of strategic and operational management. Given that people are a critical organizational resource and source of significant cost, it is logical that managers need to plan for meeting the organization's human resource requirements. This is particularly the case if labour markets are tight and if the time taken to train people in the required skills, for example, as doctors, can take a number of years.

Planning, however, is a process that has been associated with spectacular failures and white elephants. In the 1960s, the Labour Government under Harold Wilson produced a 'National Plan', which claimed to be a blueprint for managing the whole economy—but its use and value, and indeed relevance, were soon questioned, as the economic environment on which it based its assumptions and forecasts changed. The eventual failure of Communism can be linked to the inefficiencies and defects of its centralized economic planning system, under which resources, production targets, and markets were determined centrally, with little regard for what people wanted and needed.

The assumptions that both of these centralized planning models were based upon quickly lost their validity as social, political, and economic forces changed the environments to which the economic plans related. A plan, as with a strategy, is only as good and as useful as the assumptions about the future internal and external environment on which it is based are accurate. Understanding the limitations and fragility of planning and plans is as important to the HR planner as is the potential value that the planning process and the resultant HR plans offer. Given the rapidly changing environments in which most organizations operate, human resource plans must be flexible, that is, they must be adapted constantly to reflect changes in the environment if they are to retain their potential utility. Planning that is seen more as discrete events and mechanistic activity than as an ongoing and adaptive process is unlikely to contribute much of value to organizational effectiveness.

HRP, if based on poor data, limited forecasting models, and an inability to see the wider HR and business picture, can result in inaccurate and misleading estimates of supply and demand numbers, resulting in either a costly surplus or shortage of employees. As John Bramham, one of the most influential writers on HRP, states:

> **In preparing 'plans' the need for flexibility is stressed. No plan in any fixed sense will be relevant for long. The success of planning in an organization will be judged by how well the organization can anticipate or adapt to the unforeseen.**
> **(Bramham, 1994)**

This is a view supported by Bratton and Gold (1999) who state that:

> **The domination of equations, which mechanistically provide for solutions for problems based on the behaviour of people, may actually become divorced from the real world and have a good chance of missing the real problems. Hence the poor reputation of manpower planning.**

We are in an era in which almost all organizations are struggling to cope with an unprecedented level of change and it would be too simplistic to see planning as being able to 'see' or predict at any point in time. The prevalent approach to planning an organization's human resources in the 1970s and 1980s is seen, in retrospect, as having been overly prescriptive and inflexible (bin Idris and Eldridge, 1998).

This view was echoed in an earlier Institute for Employment Studies (IES) report that concluded:

> **When it concerns human resources, there are the more specific criticisms that it is overquantitative and neglects the qualitative aspects of contribution. The issue has become not how many people should be employed, but ensuring that all members of staff are making an effective contribution.**
> **(Reilly, 1996)**

The importance of this statement lies in the recognition that numbers, in themselves, are less important than what people contribute, the behaviours they exhibit, and the potential they possess. The HR planner, and the whole approach to planning, now need to reflect the importance of distinguishing between:

> **the numbers of people in employment from what they actually do and are capable of doing at work.**

Many of the problems associated with what was known, in the 1980s and early 1990s, as 'manpower planning' were linked to the following:

- the planning process was more a series of activities than an ongoing process, meaning that information from the internal and external environments was often outdated and irrelevant;
- the idea that a plan, in the form of a single document, once written, was complete was attractive but misguided. The danger is that people come to believe that the contents of the plan and what it forecasts are fixed in time rather than contingent and provisional;
- it focused too heavily on the quantitative aspect of employment and neglected issues of variability in contribution and performance;
- the lack of flexibility and ability to frequently change planning scenarios and forecasts meant that many plans quickly became out of date;
- forecasting and predicting future economic conditions, and attempts to reconcile these with the organization's workforce requirements, were often carried out in an isolated and detached way.

More recent attempts to explain and justify the role of HRP emphasize the need not to try to predict the future, but to use planning to challenge assumptions about the future and to engage in more sophisticated 'scenario planning' activities. HRP is now much more about finding ways to achieve a better internal integration of HR activities in order to be clearer about what the workforce requirements will be in the future, in terms of skill and competency requirements, and how these needs can be met. Quality, potential, and 'fit', rather than simply numbers, of employees required is seen as a particularly important dimension of the planning process and its outcomes.

Table 9.1 provides a summary of the essential features of the HR planning process, and the actions needed to ensure that each key feature can be effectively managed and add value to the organization.

Signpost to Chapter 14: HR and the New Opening

# Manpower Planning or HRP?

As was made clear in Chapter 2, human resource management (HRM) is associated with a degree of terminological complexity and confusion that is rarely found in other management functions, with the result that both students and practitioners are often confused about the meaning(s) of commonly used terms and expressions. In the context of this chapter, the central question is whether the term 'manpower planning' carries essentially the same meaning as 'human resource planning' (HRP).

At the conceptual and philosophical level, these two terms and their meanings can be seen to be analogous to those of 'Personnel Management' and 'Human Resource Management', and result in a similar debate about the relationship between the two. To add to the terminological confusion, the equivalent term used in the USA is 'workforce planning', but as far as this chapter is concerned, that term will be seen as equivalent to HRP (Watson, 2002).

According to Bramham:

> **There is a big difference between human resource planning and manpower planning . . . in terms of process and purpose.**
> **(Bramham, 1994)**

**Table 9.1** Features of effective HR planning

| Essential feature | Essential actions |
|---|---|
| *Based on organization's objectives* | The HR plan should grow out of the organization's objectives and strategic aims. For example, expansion plans may require a greater focus on recruitment, while upgrading skills may be necessary if technological advancement is required. |
| *Flexible* | The HR plan may need to change in order to ensure that organizational objectives are met in the event of unseen demands or change. These might be market changes, such as a recession resulting in job losses to save costs, or internal unexpected change, such as the resignation of unexpected numbers of key personnel, leading to refocused efforts in recruitment and retention. |
| *Built-in contingencies* | There may be aspects of the plan that allow for resource to be diverted elsewhere in the event of unplanned events. For example, temporary or interim staff may be required to cover unexpected absence. |
| *Defined value-added outcomes* | All activity should be carefully scrutinized to examine whether or not it truly adds value. For example, an increased number of staff committee meetings with the intention of improving communications may actually escalate the number of complaints and encourage more time away from productive work. |
| *Regularly reviewed* | Objectives set early in the year may no longer be relevant as the year progresses. For example, there may have been plans for a programme of management training, which might be cancelled in the event of a decision to make a layer of management redundant. |
| *Overall strategic direction* | All aspects of the plan should directly or indirectly contribute towards the overall strategic direction of the business. For example, improved induction procedures may enhance productivity, despite more time away from direct work in the initial weeks, because of enhanced long-term retention of staff. |
| *Timelines identified* | Plans should include a timeframe over which activity will be completed. For example, succession planning may be an annual activity, reviewed at a set time each year. |
| *Priorities identified* | There may be some aspects of the HR plan that are more important than others and activity may be prioritized, particularly if there are seasonal demands. A retail chain may be more focused on recruiting, rather than training, new staff during the lead-up to Christmas and may focus on training for development during the quieter times of the year. |
| *Resource identified* | Different levels of HR support may be required for different aspects of the plan and the plan should take account of the availability of staff to support activity. |
| *Acknowledges reactive requirements* | Remember that allowing time for the day-to-day reactive issues is just as important and often more valued. A prompt reaction to an unexpected challenge can stop problems from quickly escalating further; effective plans acknowledge this valuable role. |

He argues that HRP is concerned with motivating people and involves processes in which costs, numbers, control, and systems interact, whereas manpower planning is concerned with the numerical requirements of forecasting. Despite this, he accepts that there are important areas of overlap and interconnection (see Bennison and Casson, 1984).

It might be argued that Bramham's position on this issue has, to a degree, been superseded by a simple change in definition, driven by the need to avoid the use of discriminatory language, and by the incorporation of the more restrictive forecasting function into the wider and more encompassing HRP activity. If there is a meaningful and useful distinction to be made, it is probably based on the differences between strategic and operational requirements and focus; if this is a defensible point of view, it justifies Bramham's position and allows HRP to be defined as:

> **involving the strategic alignment of an organization's human capital with its business direction, and employing the use of methodical processes in analysing the current workforce, determining**

**future workforce needs, identifying the gap between the present and future, and implementing solutions so the organization can accomplish its mission, goals, and objectives.**

Manpower planning, meanwhile, is:

**part of the wider HRP function, but having a more operational focus and purpose that involves identifying the numbers of people required at appropriate skill levels across a given shift or production pattern in order to meet production or work requirements.**

**RESEARCH INSIGHT 9.1 Researching the case for family friendly policies and more flexible working arrangements**

The report into Flexible Working: working for families, working for business published by the CIPD was based on work undertaken by the family friendly working hours task force, sponsored by the UK government.

**Chartered Institute of Personnel and Development (2009) 'Flexible Working: Working for families, working for business', www.cipd.co.uk.**

Read the report, and other sources, and answer the following questions either as an individual or as part of a seminar group. If the latter, then produce PowerPoint summaries of your key findings and be prepared to defend the positions you have taken.

1. Is it the case that family friendly working arrangements are equally beneficial to employers and employees?
2. Is the business case in support of such working arrangements conditional on the state of the labour market or not?
3. What specific HR actions and practices would be helpful in facilitating family friendly working arrangements?
4. Are such practices likely to result in increases or decreases in the productivity of the employees concerned and of the organization as a whole?
5. As an employer, what reservations might you have on this subject?

In summary, HRP has evolved from what was originally a process involving forecasting changes in the demand and supply for labour into a more sophisticated and integral part of HR (see Table 9.2 for management strategies related to changes in the demand and supply for labour).

**Table 9.2** Management strategies related to changes in the demand and supply for labour

| | |
|---|---|
| A **short-term fall** in the demand for labour can involve:<br>• reducing or eliminating overtime working<br>• postponing the recruitment of workers to replace those who have left<br>• freezing establishment numbers<br>• ceasing the use of agency staff | A **long-term fall** in the demand for labour can involve:<br>• moving some employees from full-time to part-time contracts<br>• introducing short-time working<br>• introducing voluntary or compulsory redundancy |
| A **short-term rise** in the demand for labour can involve:<br>• increasing advertising spend and improving its effectiveness<br>• increasing the use of temporary staff and short-term contract workers<br>• using 'golden hellos' to attract new recruits<br>• increasing overtime | A **long-term shortage** of labour can involve:<br>• developing alternative labour markets, e.g. overseas recruitment<br>• substituting technology for labour<br>• increasing the degree of functional flexibility through changes in training strategies<br>• introducing flexible working strategies<br>• improving the perceived value of the reward package |

While an ability to predict changes in the external environment is still valued as a contribution to effective decision-making in the employment of people, the limitations and uncertainties of 'knowing' what the external environment will look like at any point in time are better understood today than they perhaps used to be (Bennison, 1980). What have also changed and become increasingly important influences on what HRP represents can be expressed in terms of:

- the importance of the organization's internal environment, particularly the impact on its labour requirements of such activities as succession planning, competency development, retention levels, productivity, and efficiency initiatives;
- a movement away from the notion that organizations can always be proactive when it comes to planning human resources, based on the unsustainable belief that future environmental conditions can be accurately predicted;
- a greater recognition that HRP is increasingly associated with both strategic and operational dimensions;
- the importance of flexibility in HR plans;
- the critical need for management thinking and organizations to be able to adapt quickly to environmental changes;
- the need for HR practitioners to develop appropriate planning tools and provide managers with a range of options in terms of known and 'predicted' environmental conditions.

**KEY CONCEPT Whole-time equivalents (WTEs)**

This is a quantitative measurement of the number of staff available to or in the establishment that allows for staff on different employment contracts to be reflected in the 'head count'. A simple system of weighting operates, under which a full-time employee working a nominal 35 hours—or whatever is the company or industry standard working week—is allocated a weighting of 1. A part-time worker who works half the standard hours is weighted 0.5; one who works two days each week is weighted at 0.4. As organizations, particularly the NHS, move to more employee-friendly and flexible contracts, the actual numbers of nurses and doctors, for example, can increase while the WTE figure falls. Expanding the output of medical schools can, paradoxically, be associated with a fall in general practitioner WTEs because more GPs work on a part-time basis.

From a senior management perspective, the perceived effectiveness and value of HR's contribution to the planning and management of human resources is less to do with whether those involved are reactive or proactive, or whether they have a 'manpower plan' or not, and more to do with whether they are effective in meeting the organization's labour requirements, within existing budgetary constraints. They must also provide 'solutions' that fit the strategic and operational requirements of the organization. The general criticisms levelled against the HR department outlined in Chapter 2, in terms of the relevance of its priorities and activities, can be revisited in the context of HRP. The HR department is likely to be criticized because of its inability to distinguish between the HR plan and an HR plan for the organization, and because it is slow to respond to changing resource requirements. Such criticism is likely to be compounded by a perception that its contribution to HRP is marginal and ineffective, at least as far as delivering against the organization's capacity and capability requirements is concerned. This may well mean that it is as legitimate and appropriate for HR to concentrate energy on actions that help to overcome unexpected problems in meeting quantity and quality targets as it is for HR to engage in pre-planned and proactive activities, such as forecasting future demand and supply conditions. HRP has a short-term relevance and value as well as a long-term dimension and, as was pointed out recently to one of the authors, the long term is getting shorter!

Despite the recognition that making effective contributions in the field of HRP sometimes involves the HR practitioner reacting to unforeseen events, constructing some sort of HR plan, the key features of which

Table 9.3 Constructing the HR plan—key questions and sources of information

| Key question | Useful sources of information |
|---|---|
| What are the purpose, strategy, and objectives of the HRP function? | • Organizational objectives<br>• Department objectives<br>• Job descriptions |
| What are the strengths and weaknesses of the current labour force? | • SWOT analysis<br>• Customer service survey |
| How do we classify positions and grades? | • Manpower plan<br>• Grading structure<br>• Job evaluation scheme<br>• Job descriptions |
| What are the external labour market changes? | • Market data<br>• Jobcentre Plus statistics |
| What are the age, skill, gender, and ethnicity profiles? | • Personal records<br>• Training files |
| What forthcoming legislation may affect us? | • Consultation Papers<br>• Recently reported case law<br>• New Regulations |
| What is our current demographic and ethnic spread compared to the community? | • Equal opportunities monitoring data demographics analysis<br>• Data from Commission for Racial Equality and Equal Opportunities Commission |
| How do we retain specialist skills? | • Turnover data<br>• Skills audit<br>• Appraisal data |
| Do we have the right organizational structure for future demands? | • Organizational structures<br>• Organization's strategic aims and objectives |
| What skills will we need in future? | • New product development strategy<br>• Organization's strategic aims and objectives |

reflect a detailed understanding of the organization's internal and external environments, is still considered to be an important tool for the management of employment numbers, employment costs and the quality of an organization's human resources. Its construction and format are likely to differ depending on the requirements of different organizations, but, as a guide to the key issues against which the plan needs to deliver, Table 9.3 provides a useful summary.

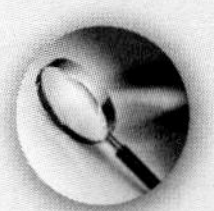

**RESEARCH INSIGHT 9.2 Contemporary Developments in Workforce Planning**

The CIPD report on workforce planning provides insights into three key issues based on contributions from experienced practitioners.

**Chartered Institute of Personnel and Development (2010) *Reflections on Workforce Planning.***

After reading each of the three main sections of the report, you should be able to explain:

1. The evolution of workforce planning and the contemporary forces and factors that have re-awakened interest in the process and its contribution to organizational needs and success.
2. The relationship between financial and workforce planning and the role of the line manager in implementing and monitoring workforce plans.
3. The strategic dimension of workforce planning and how this can help to achieve competitive advantage for the organization.

## HRP Measurement and Metrics

Historically, measurement in HR was very much associated with HRP and involved the production of estimates or 'precise' measures covering:

- Changes in the existing supply of labour as a result of:
  - people leaving the organization, often described as 'labour wastage', or 'labour turnover' if losses are replaced by the recruitment of new employees;
  - people being absent from work because of illness or other reasons;
  - the loss of productive time resulting from wasteful working practices and lower-than-acceptable performance levels.
- Changes in the demand for labour, which can only meaningfully result from an assessment of changes in:
  - production levels and work requirements;
  - establishment numbers;
  - changes in employment budgets;
  - the expansion or contraction of productive capacity;
  - changes in labour productivity and working methods;
  - the application of new technology.



Developing reliable demand forecasting models has always been more difficult to achieve than measuring changes in the supply of labour, for the simple reason that variations in the demand for an organization's products or services can never be predicted with a sufficient degree of certainty. Consider, for example, the loss of jobs resulting from mergers, which can be both significant and sudden, as the (at the time of writing) proposed link between Barclays and ABN Amro illustrates (Dey and Power, *Daily Telegraph*, 2007). Difficulties of accurate demand forecasting are particularly acute in the private sector, but even in the public sector, in which product markets are less volatile, changes in funding and budgetary pressures can also affect the ability to make long-term predictions about demand requirements.

Changes in demand can often be linked to known changes in labour supply, for example, a known level of wastage, and can be used to establish demand requirements, in terms of replacing people who leave. Knowledge of wastage levels is also an important factor in making decisions about demand requirements over the longer term. On the one hand, if an organization is expanding, simply replacing labour that is lost will not deliver the numbers and quality of employees required, leading to the need for additional recruitment. On the other hand, an organization that needs to make reductions in its labour force as a result, for example, of a decision to outsource may be able to avoid or limit the need for compulsory redundancies by not replacing the numbers of people who are predicted to leave over a given period.

Before we move on to consider some of the most commonly used measurement techniques, it is important to make the point that the results of these calculations do not, in themselves, represent anything other than a contribution to subsequent decisions about how organizations manage situations of labour surplus or shortage. Depending on expectations of future requirements, managers may choose to accept a short-term surplus in the knowledge that demand will increase in the medium term and that the cost of a short-term reduction strategy, followed by the costs of hiring new staff, would be more than the costs associated with running a short- to medium-term surplus. Much depends on the organization's ability to live with short-term surpluses, and on its philosophy towards its employees and their welfare.

Equally, shortages of labour do not necessarily result in new recruitment. There are other ways to meet demand requirements, through, for example, the use of overtime working, reorganizing working methods, and introducing new contractual arrangements for existing staff. There is no single 'correct' strategy for managing surpluses or shortages for all organizations; rather, it is a matter of choosing the one that best fits, or a combination of several that fit, the particular circumstances of each individual organization in ways that minimize costs, maximize productivity, and, as far as possible, reflect the interests of employees. As shown in HRM Insight 9.2, the situations faced by managers in responding to changes in their workforce, even though the numbers involved might be relatively few, can be complicated and challenging.

**HRM INSIGHT 9.2 The case of Sunside Leisure**

Sunside Leisure is a privately owned business, which operates a number of leisure facilities: including hotels, leisure centres, sports facilities, gyms, and swimming pools. The organization employs around 500 staff in total. The HR team consists of an HR director, an HR manager, and two administrators. In three months' time, the HR manager is due to start maternity leave and will therefore be out of the business for between six and 12 months. She has indicated that she will probably take only six months off and, after this time, intends to return on a full-time basis. Additionally, one of the HR administrators is due to go on maternity leave in six weeks' time. She has indicated that she will probably be on leave for 12 months and may wish to return part time, for two or three days each week.

The team is committed to the following activities in addition to the normal day-to-day recruitment, administration, induction, performance management, and communications activity:

- delivery of equal opportunities training to 50 managers and team leaders (consisting of five one-day workshops, which were originally going to be delivered by the HR manager in four months' time);
- wage negotiations covering 50 staff who transferred under TUPE from facilities that were originally managed by the local council, which are likely to be sensitive due to a disparity in rates between the different facilities;
- restructuring of the catering teams, including outsourcing to third-party caterers of ten employees and potentially reducing the requirement for a team leader;
- a recruitment campaign to increase headcount at two leisure centres for the increased summer demand and to provide 'out-of-school' summer sports clubs for 5–12 year olds in the area.

Questions

1. What options might the HR director consider for covering the periods of maternity leave in the department?
2. What additional resources might be required and where might they be found?
3. How might the HR plans be affected by the current situation and how can these effects be minimized?



# Absence

Absence through sickness or other reasons represents a significant cost to most organizations, with sickness absence alone estimated to cost UK businesses over £13.4 billion each year (CBI, 2007). While it is inevitable that the majority of employees will be unable to attend work from time to time due to ill health, it is a fact that some employees will take more time off than others. Employers tend to expect that employees will only take time off when they are genuinely unable to work, but there will always be occasions on which employees take time off, claiming ill health, when they might have come to work, known euphemistically as 'taking a sickie'.

Absence rates vary between different organizations and between different types of job. It might be argued that it is easy to manage with minor illness if the working environment is warm and comfortable, compared to more physically demanding environments, and that more motivated employees with a greater degree of responsibility will be less inclined to take time off when they are ill. The propensity to take time off may also be linked to the extent to which the psychological environment is positive and supportive.

Whatever the reason for absence, there is no doubt that it impacts on the organization's ability to meet its objectives and puts pressure on those who have to cover the extra workload. According to ACAS (2006), the effects of high absence levels are wide-ranging and affect everyone in the organization; managers and employees, together with their representatives, need to work to keep absence under control and to minimize its costs.

The costs of unacceptably high levels of absence are normally expressed financially, and are based on calculating the value of lost production and sick payments. These financial measures also include:

- the costs of additional staffing levels and overtime working to cover anticipated absences;
- the cost of replacement labour;

- costs associated with delayed production and disruptions to planning schedules;
- costs associated with loss of quality or service levels;
- costs resulting from low morale and dissatisfaction.

Monitoring absence rates forms a key element of absence management and most organizations track absenteeism on a weekly, or monthly, basis to monitor the effectiveness of absence management strategies. This often involves calculating absence using a formula and comparing the resultant figure with an internal or external benchmark standard.

The *absence rate* is usually calculated as follows:

$$\frac{\text{Number of days absence within team}}{\text{Number of working days available}} \times 100$$

For example, a team of five people who each work five days a week, less bank holidays, can work a total of (365–104–8) 253 days each, making a team total of 1,265 potential working days. If 50 days were to be lost through absence, the team's absence rate would be:

$$\frac{50 \times 100}{1{,}265} = 3.95$$

A calculation for the whole organization is similarly based on the time lost as a result of absence. The formula usually used for calculating the *lost time rate* is:

$$\frac{\text{Total absence in days/hours over a given period}}{\text{Total time in days/hours available over the period}} \times 100$$



In the case of a hotel, for example, we can work out total hours available per month by multiplying each employee's monthly contracted time (remembering that this figure will reflect different employment contracts) and adding the individual totals together. This assumes, of course, that the hotel actually monitors and records absences, aggregates the time lost through absence, expressed preferably in hours, and calculates the lost time rate. By using the same calculation on a departmental basis, it is possible to develop a more detailed pattern of absences that will be useful in deciding on what corrective action to take.

One of the limitations of the lost time rate calculation is that it cannot distinguish the pattern of absence in terms of whether few employees are taking long periods of absence or whether many employees have infrequent bouts of absence. Consequently, the calculation of what is known as the *frequency rate* is often preferred to, or used in conjunction with, the lost time rate. The formula for this is:

$$\frac{\text{Number of spells of absence over a given period}}{\text{Number of workers employed over the period}} \times 100$$

A similar calculation can also be used to establish the individual frequency rate, expressed in terms of:

$$\frac{\text{Number of employees with one or more spells of absence over a given period}}{\text{Number of workers employed over the period}} \times 100$$

The Bradford absence index is useful because it gives weighting to the frequency of absences, reflecting the belief that many frequent spells of absence are more disruptive and costly than fewer, longer absences, which can be more easily managed because it is easier to make contingency plans. The index is calculated by using the formula:

$$\text{Index} = S \times S \times H$$

Where:

S = the number of recorded absences;
H = the total number of hours absent.

The formula can be applied to each individual and to the organization as a whole.

As an example, consider two hotel employees, one a porter and the other a chef. If the porter were to be absent on five separate days during a month, totalling 40 hours, his or her absence index would be:

$$\text{Index} = 5 \times 5 \times 40 = 1{,}000$$

The index for the chef, who was absent only once during the month for one week, would be:

$$\text{Index} = 1 \times 1 \times 40 = 40$$

The problem with this method of calculating absence, as with the others, is that it cannot show the actual costs of any given level or individual pattern of absence. It might be argued that, although the index for the chef is much lower, his or her absence in the month might be more of a problem than that of the porter simply because of the chef's more valuable contribution and the revenue lost in the restaurant because of his or her absence. Not all employees have the same value in terms of their contribution to the organization and the costs of absence will vary in relation to the value of work that is lost. This point is developed in more detail later in the chapter.

**HRM INSIGHT 9.3 Sickness absence in the public sector**

A belief that recorded sickness absence in the public sector is higher than in the private sector and represents a huge cost to the taxpayer is supported by research carried out by the government, using results from two other contemporary surveys into sickness absence (CBI in association with AXA, 2004; CIPD, 2004—see Table 9.4).

Of particular interest here is the cost of sickness absence. Figures presented in the report suggest that, at an annual average of ten days per person, sickness absence among the 523,000 civil servants costs over £375 million and, in local authorities, up to £900 million per year. With a target reduction of 30 per cent in civil service sickness absence rates alone, it is estimated that approximately 1.7 million working days would be saved, equivalent to more than 7,000 additional employees. Expressed in a different way, reducing the absence rate by this amount means that the current level of work undertaken by civil servants could be achieved, broadly speaking, with 7,000 fewer employees.

**Questions**

1. How might the differences in sickness absence between the two sectors be explained?
2. What short-term actions could the managers with responsibility for reducing sickness absence rates by 30 per cent take that might contribute to achieving this target?
3. What actions could the HR practitioners take over the longer term to complement the short-term measures?
4. Research developments in absence trends and construct an up to date table based on Table 9.4. Discuss the changes observed and comment on reasons behind them.

**Table 9.4** Summary of 2004 absence surveys—average recorded days absence per employee per year in public and private sectors

| | 2003–04 | 2002–03 | 2001–02 | 2000–01 |
|---|---|---|---|---|
| *CBI (all)* | | 7.2 | 6.8 | 7.0 (estimate) |
| *CBI (public sector)* | | 8.9 | 8.9 | 10.1 |
| *CBI (private sector)* | | 6.9 | 6.5 | 6.7 |
| *CIPD (all)* | 9.1 | 9.0 | | |
| *CIPD (public sector)* | 10.7 | 10.6 | | |
| *CIPD (private sector)* | 7.8 | 7.0 | | |

## Turnover

'Turnover' differs from 'wastage' only in the sense that the use of the former term relates to those who leave an organization and are replaced, while the latter relates only to the number of those who leave. For practical purposes, both relate to the loss of people and the terms can be used interchangeably.

According to the latest CIPD survey (CIPD, 2007), the overall employee annual turnover rate for the UK is 18.1 per cent. The report found that annual turnover levels vary considerably from industry to industry, with the highest average rates (22.6 per cent) found in private sector organizations and, within this sector, the hotels, catering, and leisure industry reports rates of turnover at 10 per cent higher than the average for the sector (32.6 per cent). The public sector has an average turnover rate of 13.7 per cent. While there are situations in which high wastage rates may actually help an organization to resolve a situation of labour surplus, persistently high rates outside of the organization or industry benchmark range are usually a cause for concern: when skilled and experienced employees decide to leave, it usually represents a significant loss and a cost to the organization. Finding suitable candidates to replace leavers takes time and resources in terms of recruitment and training (remember the estimates of recruitment costs explored in Chapter 4).

It is inevitable, however, that, from time to time, employees will choose to leave and either pursue careers elsewhere, retire, take a career break, or return to education. These are examples of what is known as 'voluntary quits'. In addition to employees who choose to leave, there are a number who are dismissed or who are performance managed out of the organization. High turnover rates create particular pressures for the HR department, which is primarily responsible for replacing those who leave, but also for line managers who face disruption to production and service standards. This is the necessary result of having to induct and train new employees, who are usually less experienced and productive compared to those they replace: it takes time before new recruits perform at their optimum levels. The result is a reduced ability to meet objectives, reduced levels of productivity, and higher unit costs. It is therefore important for managers to measure labour turnover, monitor its impact, and take appropriate action to minimize its effects. As far as the latter is concerned, this should at least involve operating efficient and effective replacement procedures, but the effective management of turnover also involves understanding and dealing with its underlying causes.

### *Measuring turnover*

Turnover is typically measured over a 12-month period to smooth out seasonal differences, but can be tracked weekly or monthly to provide a more detailed and contemporary understanding of what is happening.

Turnover is calculated as follows:

$$\frac{\text{Number of leavers over a given period}}{\text{Number employed at the period end}} \times 100$$

For example, if 25 people left over the last 12 months and the current number of employees is 275, turnover would be calculated as:

$$\frac{25}{275} \times 100 = 9.09\%$$

Variations on this method involve taking the average number employed during the period. For example, in an organization employing 235 people at the start of the period and 275 at the end, with 25 leavers, the calculation would be:

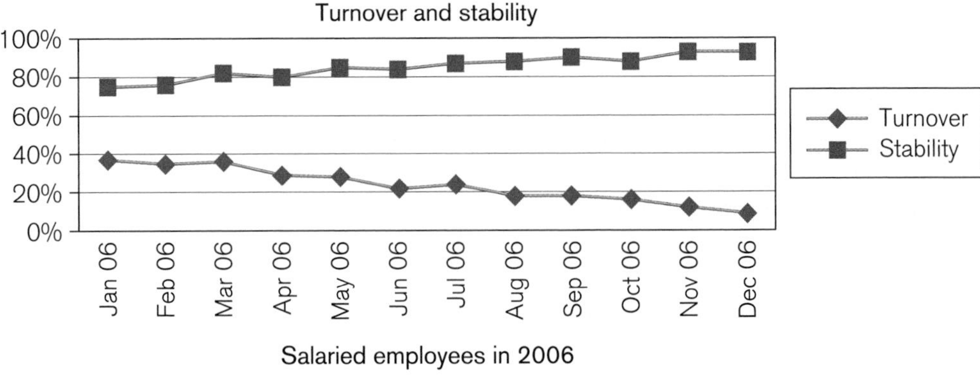


**Figure 9.1** Annual labour turnover and stability tracked monthly as a percentage through 2006

$$\frac{25 \times 100}{(235 + 275)/2} = 9.8\%$$

Figure 9.1 shows how annual turnover can be tracked on a monthly basis to show trends. In the graph, annual labour turnover within this organization is showing a downward trend throughout 2006.

## Stability



'Stability' is a useful measure to accompany turnover and can give a better reflection of the retention of employees than can turnover. If turnover is high, it is difficult to establish which employees are those that are leaving without carrying out more in-depth analysis. It may be that new employees are poorly inducted and often leave within the first few weeks, and that longer-serving staff tend to stay. Or it might be the case that a large portion of longer-serving employees is nearing retirement and that the increase in turnover is due to a demographic 'surge'.

Stability is a measure of the percentage of employees with more than a stipulated amount of service. For example, it may be useful to know what percentage of staff has over one year's service and can therefore be assumed to have become experienced and qualified. Stability can be calculated as follows:

$$\frac{\text{Number of staff with over one year's service over a given period}}{\text{Number of staff employed at the period end}} \times 100$$

For example, if the organization of 275 employees in the turnover example were to have 259 employees with over one year's service, stability would be calculated as follows:

$$\frac{259}{275} \times 100 = 94.18\%$$

This information is particularly useful to establish the kind of problem from which the organization is suffering. For example, if annual turnover is 45 per cent and stability is 90 per cent, then it can be seen that it is mostly shorter serving employees who are leaving and that retention seems to be better among longer-serving employees. It is also important to assess both turnover and stability against the overall change in numbers employed. For example, stability figures will fall during expansion, due to the number of new positions created, and turnover may be very high, along with very high stability, if an organization reduces in size resulting in little recruitment and large numbers of redundancies. Figure 9.1 also shows an organization with increasing stability among its workforce throughout 2006.

## Vitality

Some organizations, particularly larger ones with a variety of more senior positions, may have policies that encourage and promote the development of staff, and which try to balance external recruitment to more senior positions with internal promotions. 'Vitality' is a method of measuring the balance of internal promotion versus external recruitment or loss of employees. Although much less commonly measured than turnover, it can be a useful measure of career development and employee satisfaction.

*Recruitment vitality* is measured as follows:

$$\frac{\text{Number of roles filled by internal promotion} - \text{number of roles filled externally}}{\text{Number of positions filled}} \times 100$$

High negative scores indicate a preference for external recruitment, suggesting that if there is little opportunity for internal promotion and that it is likely that internal potential is not being tapped. High positive scores indicate that most posts are being filled internally and that external markets are not being fully exploited to bring in new ideas, skills, and methods of working.

A similar calculation can made for *turnover vitality*:

$$\frac{\begin{array}{c}\text{Number of roles vacated due to internal}\\ \text{promotion} - \text{number of roles vacuated due to departure}\end{array}}{\text{Number of roles being vacant}} \times 100\%$$



High negative scores indicate that employees are leaving to advance their careers, while high positive scores indicate that employees rarely leave to pursue careers externally and benefit from internal promotion as a preference.

Signpost to Chapter 4: Recruitment and Selection

**HRM INSIGHT 9.4 The case of Lincester Passenger Transport Executive**

Lincester Passenger Transport Executive is responsible for providing the majority of local passenger transport for the town of Lincester. One hundred and fifty drivers are employed across a variety of shifts, providing a bus service seven days a week to the general public. The organization also employs ten maintenance and 20 administration and managerial staff. Turnover has risen among drivers over the last five years, from 10 to 25 per cent. Driving staff are expensive to recruit and train. In addition, 25 per cent of the drivers will be eligible for retirement in the next five years.

### Questions

1. List as many reasons as you can think of that might contribute to the high levels of labour turnover among driving staff. How might you establish the 'real' reasons for the turnover of drivers?
2. What range of HR activities might the Lincester Passenger Transport Executive consider over the next 12 months to help to improve retention?
3. What HR metrics should the organization track and how might information be gathered to monitor any improvement in employee retention that might be achieved?
4. What strategies might managers consider to deal with the retirement problem?

**HRM INSIGHT 9.5 Developing New Technologies to support Workforce Planning**

Early attempts to develop statistical models to support HRP were generally limited to demand and supply forecasting; planners felt that the main requirement was for managers to be given accurate information on future scenarios which provided the basis for decisions on either shortfalls or surpluses in human resource capabilities. Unfortunately, the ability to accurately predict the future by extrapolating from past trends was constantly being compromised by changes in the external environments and human resources plans quickly proved to be outdated and of little value.

More contemporary developments in developing 'tools' to support HRP activities are much more sophisticated, realistic, and focused on things that really matter—the relationship between inputs and outcomes that reflect numerical and financial metrics. An example of this is the eWIN computer portal introduced by the North West Region of the NHS. It offers a platform to facilitate improved engagement, collaboration, and the sharing of workforce intelligence. It was designed specifically to support the Region's strategic agenda which focused on Quality, Productivity, Innovation, and Prevention and allows changes in key input and existing variables to be tracked into these four outcome areas as decisions are taken to change human resource numbers, capabilities, and locations. According to its supporters:

> eWIN is the tool that can help organisations to plan and model future workforce configurations which will deliver sustainable patient services.

It does this by:

- Providing online access to a set of workforce benchmarking metrics.
- Sharing examples of productivity and quality improvements within NHS NW organizations which can be used as a basis to improve productivity.
- Sharing knowledge and generate innovation and ideas about new/different ways of working, including through data analysis.
- Highlighting potential problem areas for improvement.
- Allowing managers to model future outcomes and generate estimates of cost savings. For example, reductions in sickness absence can be expressed in cost savings.

Given the size of the NHS overall, the large numbers and variety of staff it involves, and the complexity of its employment contracts and practices, this kind of interactive tool that employs key benchmarking and cost data offers a much more effective and useful tool in the management of people, particularly in relation to their costs, service provision, and productivity levels. However, as will be seen later in the chapter, the attractiveness of this kind of rigorous and analytical approach is not without its challenges, particular with regard to the use of benchmarking.

# Measurement in HR—the Wider Debate

One of the central objectives of this book is not only to provide insights into what skills and knowledge HR practitioners and line managers need to manage employees effectively, and how these activities might be carried out, but also to explain why these activities are important and the consequences that might follow from doing them, not doing them well or not doing them at all, as the case may be. This approach is particularly important as far as measurement and the use of metrics in HR are concerned, and the issues surrounding the development of wider and more sophisticated approaches to measurement now need to be considered.

To put this issue into a wider context, it is necessary to recognize that the increasing use of metrics to monitor organizational performance is not restricted to HR. The public sector, in particular, has been subject to the development and application of many different performance measures and targets, and there is an extensive literature on the experiences and effects of performance measurement strategies (Propper and Wilson, 2003).

In the USA, the work of writers such as Jac Fitz-Enz (2000) and Wayne Cascio (1991), in measuring the economic value of employee performance and producing measures that allow the financial costs of employee behaviour to be calculated, has been instrumental in bringing the debate about measurement in HR to centre stage. In the UK, the contributions of Kearns (2000), Mooney (2001), and Mayo (2001) are increasingly influencing the approach to the priorities and agenda of HR professionals.

Mooney, in particular, provides a powerful argument in support of the use of measurement in HR. He starts off his chapter on 'HR Metrics', in *Turbo-Charging the HR Function*, by quoting W Edwards Deming, who said:

> **You don't have to do this—survival isn't compulsory.**
> (Mooney, 2001)

This is Mooney's way of stressing the importance he attaches to the extensive use of measurement in HR. He is particularly critical of the HR community because of its reluctance to understand why measurement is important and the value it can provide. He claims that, while almost every other facet of business has committed to measuring its contribution and effectiveness, HR has been reluctant to go down this route, and argues that this is directly linked to the lack of status and respect from which many in HR suffer.

> **The absence of quantification forces HR departments to remain on the periphery of strategic decision-making, rather than occupying the central role which the importance of the function requires.**
> (Mooney, 2001)

With this comment, Mooney reinforces the importance of the distinction that Ulrich (1996) makes between HR activities and HR outcomes, under which what HR 'does' is less important to its organizational standing and reputation among other stakeholders than is what it achieves, or its outcomes. Measurement of these 'deliverables' and the added value they represent is now seen as a critical part of what managing the HR function involves.



Part of the problem with measurement in HR is the belief that the economic value or effectiveness of people and HR activities cannot be calculated, and Fitz-Enz (2000) accepts that there are difficulties associated with measuring the economic effectiveness of people, particularly in service and professional work, although less so in manufacturing. He, like Mooney, is a strong believer in the importance of incorporating rigorous measurement systems into the HR function, arguing that:

> **The bottom line is that although it is not easy to evaluate staff work in quantitative terms, it can be and is being done.**
> (Fitz-Enz, 2000)

This strategic approach to measurement has significantly different implications for HR practitioners than the measurements associated with HRP and its association with absence and turnover rates. Mooney argues that it is the management and effective reduction of absence and turnover that has the potential for reducing the financial costs of employment, not the measurement of the rates alone.

Training is another key HR activity, representing, according to Mooney (2001), up to 6 per cent of many organizations' payroll costs. In a worst-case scenario, training can be wasteful, disconnected from an organization's HR and business strategy, and a net consumer of resources, rather than a net contributor. In such circumstances, the logical course of action would be to overhaul the training function radically, to outsource it, or simply to stop those training courses for which there is little, or no, evidence of the actual delivery of added value, in terms of new or enhanced competences and improved performance levels.

Expressing the contribution of training in terms of total spend, training days delivered or numbers of employees 'trained' is no longer considered by those critical of HR's approach to measurement to be particularly useful. Such measures say little about outcomes or the value of training. The costs of training, both direct and indirect, need to be known so that the allocation of physical and financial resources can be accurately correlated with the value of the benefits associated with each training activity. Training needs to be seen as an investment, rather than as a consumer of resources, and to this end, being able to calculate or estimate the value of the returns is as important as knowing what the costs of training are.

**STUDENT ACTIVITY 9.1 Calculating the costs and benefits of training**

1. In groups, discuss the different types of costs associated with training employees. You can choose any type of training with which you are familiar, including:
   - induction training;
   - skills training;
   - management development.

   The objective is to produce a formula that incorporates all of the costs associated with the type of training you have chosen.
2. Estimate the financial values of each type of cost, and use your formula to produce an overall cost and a cost per trainee, making your own assumptions about the structure of the chosen course and numbers involved.
3. Devise a formula for estimating the value of the benefits or outcomes associated with the type of training chosen. These do not necessarily have to be expressed in financial terms. This is likely to be more difficult, but is nevertheless a worthwhile exercise.

Research by Anderson, commissioned by the CIPD, into organizational evaluation practices has led to important developments in how the returns from training can be conceptualized and calculated (Anderson, 2007). Her work highlights different approaches to calculating returns on training with the concept of 'return on expectations' replacing or co-existing with more conventional ideas about return on investment. Anderson argues that different organizations have different evaluation requirements and that a 'one size fits all' approach is misleading. Importantly, she considers the strategic significance of engaging in meaningful evaluation activities and how this can help to generate stronger integration with training and other HR activities.

Mayo is another influential writer who believes in the importance of quantification in HR. He is committed to the principle that everything can be quantified, and in ways that facilitate management and change. He claims that:

> **Whether we are talking about the capability or potential of people, the culture in which they work . . . measures for these can be found and tracked.**
> (Mayo, 2001)

Mayo's main contribution is in his work on measuring the asset value of employees, rather than on measuring absence or turnover levels. His more sophisticated approach involves measuring:

- people's human capital, which varies between employees, can rise as a result of personal and competency growth, and collectively represents the totality of human capital available to the organization;
- aspects of the working environment, such as leadership, the level of practical support, the extent of team and cooperative working, the extent of learning and development, and the effective use of rewards and recognition;
- the financial and non-financial value to the organization generated by each/all employees.

He argues that, while employees do represent a cost in terms of their wages/salaries and other benefits, they are also an asset, in the sense that they create and add value. He is also clear that some employees represent a net cost, in the sense that the value of their contribution is less than the costs of employing them. Some employees are, or become, 'liabilities' and it is important that managers are able, through appropriate measurement activities, to identify these employees, as well as those who represent a high positive asset value.

The ability to calculate each person's *human asset worth* (HAW), and give it a numerical value that can be tracked over time and which can be compared with that of other employees, is based on the following formula:

$$HAW = \frac{EC \times IAM}{1000}$$

Where:

HAW = human asset worth;
EC = employment costs;
IAM = individual asset multiplier.

Essentially, Mayo's model is based on knowing what it costs to employ a person, and this is not only their wage or salary, but a more complete understanding of the costs associated with employment and the value of those factors, such as capability, potential, contribution, and what he terms 'alignment to organizational values', that collectively express the person's gross asset worth or value (see further Mayo, 2001, pp. 82 and 83).

There are, of course, questions that can be asked about the methodology and assumptions that underlie Mayo's model, but his concern with finding ways of measuring, and thereby distinguishing, individual asset values is understandable when so little is known about this area.

A more recent contribution to the search for effective and reliable ways of calculating key human resource costs, benefits, and outcomes comes from one of the UK's leading HR consultancy's—Mercer Human Resource Consulting (Bucknall and Wei, 2006). In their introduction, the authors set out the rationale for using measures in HR. The reasons are to:

- To determine how well HR is operating and contribution.
- To determine how efficient and effective the HR function is overall.
- To help establish the organizational climate and how well it is performing.
- To improve the productivity of all staff.
- To maximize the return on human capital.



They also set out certain important principles which reflect Mercer's extensive experience in the field of workforce management. The following are important because they reflect a clear focus and approach to planning and resource management; they provide a set of guidelines that indicate how best to create maximum value for an organization's human resources. They suggest that managers:

- Recognize that workforce planning and management should be seen as a form of asset management based on business needs and performance drivers. This emphasis implicitly rejects the notion that jobs can be created and people employed, or continue to be employed, for reasons that cannot be justified by key business considerations.
- Segment employees and focus of groups that have the greatest potential impact for adding value or reducing costs.
- Consider and focus on three critical dimensions of the workforce:
  - capabilities;
  - behaviours;
  - attitudes.
- Determine which workforce characteristics contribute most to the creation of value and at what cost.
- Establish priorities and drive through changes in how things are done.

**STUDENT ACTIVITY 9.2 Calculating and interpreting key HR ratios**

Obtain a copy of *Magic Numbers for Human Resource Management* (Bucknall, H., and Wei, Z. (2006) John Wiley & Sons) and look at chapter 8 which shows you how to calculate HR staff as a percentage of total staff.

1. Use the ratio provided to calculate the HR ratios in organizations from which it is possible to collect the required data.
2. Compare the different ratios and explore the reasons for the differences.
3. Establish whether organization's that have a high HR staff to total staff ratio are more or less productive than those with low ratios and how this can be measured 4. Think of strategies that reduce the HR ration, and as a consequence the costs of running the HR function, whilst increasing current levels of HR contribution and productivity.

# Measurement in HR—Some Important Reservations

Despite the enthusiasm for measurement, the debate about its relevance, value, and consequences is by no means one-sided. The purpose of this part of the chapter is to address some of the concerns associated with the increasing use of measurement and its extension to different areas of the HR function.

The first point to make relates to the collection of data that allows measurements to be made of the chosen parameter or variable. Without appropriate monitoring and recording systems, and without the accumulation of reliable data, managers can often find that they are presented with 'snapshots' rather than meaningful trends. Actions based on partial, flawed, unreliable, or misleading data will undermine, rather than advance, the ability of measurement to improve HR's contribution to organizational performance: they might result in the wrong decisions being taken. Mooney (2001) suggests that managers need to consider the following criteria in deciding on their strategy on measurement.

- The relevance of the chosen measure to the overall business performance

  If the data relates to an aspect of employment or HR that is of no, or limited, value (defined by the appropriate stakeholders), little is gained from expending energy and resources in measuring it. Becker et al. (2001), in their work on measurement in HR, make a similar point when they question how well existing HR measures capture the 'strategic HR drivers'. They go on to claim that there is often:

  > **a disconnect between what is measured and what is important.**

- The amount of control that the HR function has over a particular measure

  The phenomenon or behaviour that is of interest to managers—for example, employee satisfaction with organizational leadership—is a result of a wide range of experiences outside the control of HR. The question arises: 'Is this something that the HR department should measure if it can't do much to influence these experiences?'

- The ease and reliability of data collection

  This raises questions about whether decisions on what to measure are unduly influenced by the ease with which data can be collected and analysed, rather than driven by the value and importance of the phenomena to which the data relates.

- Data quality

  This point relates to the reliability and integrity of the data, and the way in which it is analysed and interpreted. The key question is: 'What does the data actually show and can it be relied upon?'

Pfeffer and Sutton (2000) are two writers who, while accepting the potential value that appropriate and reliable measures can bring, are concerned to highlight the pitfalls and problems that managers face when the measurement process 'goes wrong'. They begin their chapter, 'When Measurement Obstructs Good Judgement', by claiming that:

> **Measures and the measurement process, especially badly designed or unnecessarily complex measures, are amongst the biggest barriers to turning knowledge into action.**
> **(Pfeffer and Sutton, 2000)**

They are particularly concerned about the many examples of measurement processes that fuel destructive behaviour, rather than helping managers deal with it. They also claim that, even when such destructive measurement practices are identified, little is done to correct things.

Perhaps the most well-known, but nevertheless important, observation that they make is that measures focus particular attention on what is measured, often at the expense of other equally—or perhaps more—important behaviours. They point out that measures affect what people do, as well as what they notice and ignore, arguing that, as a consequence:

> **everyone knows that what gets measured gets done, and that what is not measured gets ignored.**

In addressing the potential and actual problems that managers experience with measurement, Pfeffer and Sutton offer the following suggestions:

- effective measurement systems that drive behaviour need to be simple enough to focus attention on key elements and fair enough that employees believe in, and support, them;
- measurements need to guide and direct behaviour, but not be so powerful and coercive that they become substitutes for judgement and wisdom. Managers need to interpret and ascribe meanings to what the measures are producing. The meaning may not be immediately apparent and managers may be unwilling to accept the 'correct' interpretation if this seems to reflect badly upon their actions;
- managers should avoid the overuse of 'end-of-process' measures, which can provide insights into how well or badly something has gone—but, because these are 'end' measures, it is often too late to correct a problem. Consider the use of evaluation questionnaires that ask students what they feel about a module after they have completed it. 'In-process' measures instead allow for the correction of mistakes and for more effective control in time to make a difference.

In their later book, Pfeffer and Sutton address the wider issue of the evidential basis upon which managers take decisions and decide on strategies that impact on their employees (Pfeffer and Sutton, 2006). As part of a powerful critique on management practices that lack a strong evidential support base they consider the widespread practice of benchmarking and whether this 'best practice' HR activity will deliver the outcomes expected of it. The point they make is that there is far too much 'casual benchmarking' taking place, with practices being copied without those who are basing what they do on what they consider to be 'better' failing to understand the underlying logic that drives these practices. In other words they really don't understand why someone else's strategies, policies, and HR practices are in fact better and end up trying to imitate what others do. They argue that much of what successful organizations do and achieve is less to do with superficial behaviours, rituals, and practices and much more to do with the organizations basic values and beliefs—in other words its philosophy. They quote one senior executive who realized the mistake he and other colleagues had made when he is quoted as saying:

> **We have been benchmarking the wrong things. Instead of copying what others do, we ought to copy how they think.**
> **(Pfeffer and Sutton, 2006)**

They also make the important point that comparisons with other organizations, particularly where external benchmarking is involved, fail to reflect the different strategies, competitive environments, and business models that define the uniqueness of the comparator organization. The implication is that external benchmarking runs the risk of establishing a disconnect between the underlying rationale and drivers of success from the more obvious measures of their success.

The following student activity provides a very powerful example of what can go wrong when performance measures and targets are imposed on one organization simply because they worked somewhere else.

**STUDENT ACTIVITY 9.3**

Read the case:

**Kerr, S. (2003) 'The best laid incentive plans', *Harvard Business Review*, 81:1, pp. 27–37.**

1. Explain what the case has to say about the relationship between data and actual behaviour.
2. In groups, discuss the examples of employees responding in unexpected and undesirable ways to the measures to which they were subject, and, in particular, try to explain their motivations and objectives.
3. Explore the underlying assumptions made by Hiram Phillips and his consultants about the use of the measures and the behaviour of employees.
4. Evaluate the choice of the performance measures imposed on the company and its employees, and consider alternative, and more effective, ones.
5. Given the original objectives, present your own ideas on the use of measures to improve performance.

# Summary

- HR professionals are increasingly required to take a more strategic role within their organizations, but the ability to operate strategically and the invitation to do so are heavily dependent on their ability to show clearly and consistently how their contribution can add value and contribute to organizational performance.
- Understanding how employees create value and measuring the value-creation processes is the challenge that the HR professional faces.
- Organizations, because they are unique, need to develop different approaches to the measurement of the things that are important to them and which help them create value, either through the reduction of costs (e.g. those of sickness absence) or through increasing the asset value of their employees.
- One of the most important things that HR needs to know about are the consequences of its actions and policies, and whether these are positive, neutral or negative.
- Workforce planning is an obvious aspect of HR that requires reliable and useful measurement tools and approaches, but there are many others that seem to be increasingly subject to measurement and evaluation.
- In considering what to measure and how, two things stand out. Firstly, measures are not ends in themselves, but means to ends. In other words, they contribute to the achievement of objectives and outcomes that matter to organizational stakeholders; if they don't, they fail the functionality test. Secondly, as the case study that ends the chapter shows, getting it wrong can have serious consequences.
- What many managers often fail to realize is that the introduction of HR measures does not simply represent a technical innovation or initiative. For those affected by measures and targets, their significance and impact is likely to be perceived and experienced in a rather different way: measures and targets can become instruments of coercion and punishment, and, because employees react to this perception, they can distort behaviour.
- The notion of unintended consequences considered in Chapter 2 is particularly relevant in such cases.

**Visit the Online Resource Centre that accompanies this book for self-test questions, weblinks, and more information on the topics covered in this chapter. www.oxfordtextbooks.co.uk/orc/banfield_kay2e/**

## REVIEW QUESTIONS

1. How is human resource (or workforce) planning (HRP/WP) different from what used to be known as 'manpower planning'?
2. What are the quantitative and qualitative aspects of HRP/WP?
3. What is the link between HRP and flexible employment patterns?
4. Why can the use of targets and measurements of performance distort behaviour and lead to the manipulation of figures, and how can this consequence be avoided?
5. What are the key contributions to effective HRP that HR professionals and line managers must make?

***See Online Resource Centre for answers.***

## CASE STUDY

### Absence management—the case of Northwood Council

Northwood Council employs over 13,000 employees and is the largest employer in its local area, which has a population of 200,000 people. A brief overview of its workforce characteristics is as follows:

- 51 per cent work on a part-time basis;
- 32 per cent are male;
- over 50 per cent are aged 40 plus;
- 90 per cent are classified as white British;
- less than 1 per cent consider themselves to have a disability;
- over 30 per cent have worked at Northwood for over ten years.

Compared to the overall national average of eight days' absence per employee per year, Northwood continues to have a high level of absence. Over the past few years, managing absence has become a strategic priority for the Council, and it has invested considerable amounts of time and resources to try to reduce absence levels.

The average number of days absent per employee for each of the last few years is as follows:

- 2001–02: 10.66 days;
- 2002–03: 11.31 days;
- 2003–04: 15.7 days;
- 2004–05: 13.21 days;
- 2005–06: 12.29 days.

It can be seen that there was a significant reduction in absence between 2003–04 and 2004–05, and this can be attributed to some of the absence management interventions that were put into place. This included providing absence data to managers, the introduction of new absence management policy and procedures, and the provision of training for managers.

The absence management policy is a comprehensive document, which details the responsibilities of all parties when managing absence and also shows all of the procedures that have been followed. This includes the requirement that managers carry out a return-to-work interview after every absence. Northwood has also identified a set of 'trigger points', which means that, after a specified number of days or occasions of absence, a counselling interview will take place between the manager and the employee. Associated absence management practices include an emphasis on accurate recording and monitoring of absence data, and the use of departmental targets. Northwood has also tried to demonstrate its commitment to improving the well-being of its staff by promoting a series of health-based events, such as routes for lunchtime walks and basic health checks during the working day.

The organization has been making steady progress in reducing its absence levels and has also set some ambitious future targets for the average number of days' absence per employee over each of the coming four years, as follows.

- 2007–08: 11.25 days;
- 2008–09: 10.75 days;
- 2009–10: 10.25 days;
- 2010–11: 9.9 days.

There is confidence that the absence levels can be reduced further because of the commitment of the organization to achieving this. Senior managers have this as one of their strategic priorities, and this has been communicated to managers and employees throughout all layers of the organization. Northwood has also looked to address some of the associated HR areas, such as work–life balance, general employee satisfaction, and the content of job roles.



**Questions**

1. How might you explain the huge rise in absence levels between 2001–02 and 2003–04?
2. Why do you think that the interventions used to reduce absence between 2003–04 and 2004–05 managed to reduce absence so significantly?
3. Does the demographic profile of the organization have an impact on absence?
4. Are there any absence management interventions that the organization has not covered?
5. How do you think the trade unions have viewed the organization's growing focus on absence management?

## FURTHER READING

Chartered Institute of Personnel and Development (2007) *New Directions in Managing Employee Absence*, CIPD.

Chartered Institute of Personnel and Development (2009) Absence management annual survey report, CIPD.

House of Commons Health Committee (2007) *Fourth Report on Workforce Planning*, www.publications.parliament.uk.

*IRS Employment Review* (2006) 'Recruitment and Retention', Issue 839, www.irser.co.uk.

Liff, S. (2000) 'Manpower or human resource planning: What's in a name?', in Bach, S. and Sisson, K. (eds) *Personnel Management: A Comprehensive Guide to Personnel Management*, 3rd ed., Blackwell.

Mintzberg, H. (1994) *The Rise and Fall of Strategic Planning*, Prentice Hall.

Turner, P. (2002) *HR Forecasting and Planning*, CIPD.

## REFERENCES


Advisory Conciliation and Arbitration Service (2006) *Managing Attendance and Employee Turnover*, www.acas.org.uk.

Anderson, V. (2007) *The Value of Learning From Return on Investment to Return on Expectation*, CIPD.

Becker, B.E., Huselid, M.A. and Ulrich, D. (2001) *The HR Scorecard*, Harvard Business School Press.

Bennison, M. (1980) *The IMS Approach to Manpower Planning*, IMS.

Bennison, M. and Casson, J. (1984) *Manpower Planning Handbook*, IMS.

Bin Idris, A.R. and Eldridge, D. (1998) 'Reconceptualising human resource planning in response to institutional change', *International Journal of Manpower*, **19**:5, pp. 343–57.

Bramham, J. (1994) *Human Resource Planning*, IPD.

Bratton, J. and Gold, J. (1999) *Human Resource Management*, 2nd ed., Macmillan Business.

Bucknall, H., and Wei, Z. (2006) *Magic Numbers for Human Resource Management*, John Wiley & Sons.

Cascio, W.F. (1991) *Costing Human Resources: The Financial Impact of Behaviour in Organizations*, PWS-Kent.

Chartered Institute of Personnel and Development (2004) *Employee Absence: A Survey of Management Policy and Practice*, www.cipd.co.uk.

Chartered Institute of Personnel and Development (2007) *Recruitment, Retention and Turnover*, www.cipd.co.uk.

Chartered Institute of Personnel and Development (2010) *Reflections on Workforce Planning*.

Chartered Institute of Personnel and Development (2009) 'Flexible Working: Working for families, working for business', www.cipd.co.uk.

Confederation of British Industry (2004) 'Workplace absence rises amid concerns over long-term sickness: CBI/AXA survey', press release, www.cbi.org.uk.

Dey, I. and Power, H. (2007) 'Bloodbath at ABN in London', *Daily Telegraph*, 1 April, p. 7.

Fitz-Enz, J. (2000) *The ROI of Human Capital*, AMACOM.

Health and Safety Executive (2004) *Managing Sickness Absence in the Public Sector—A Joint Review by the Ministerial Task Force for Health, Safety and Productivity and the Cabinet Office*, www.hse.gov.uk.

Holbeche, L. (2002) *Aligning Human Resources and Business Strategy*, Butterworth-Heinemann.

Kearns, P. (2000) *Measuring and Managing Employee Performance*, FT/Prentice Hall.

Kerr, S. (2003) 'The best laid incentive plans', *Harvard Business Review*, **81**:1, pp. 27–37.

Mayo, A. (2001) *The Human Value of the Enterprise*, Nicholas Brealey Publishing.

Mooney, P. (2001) *Turbo-Charging the HR Function*, CIPD.

Pfeffer, J. and Sutton, R.I. (2000) *The Knowing-Doing Gap*, Harvard Business School Press.

Philpott, J. (2010) *The 2010 Jobs Recovery*, CIPD.

Propper, C. and Wilson, D. (2003) 'The use and usefulness of performance measures in the public sector', *Oxford Review of Economic Policy*, **19**:2, pp. 250–67.

Reilly, P. (1996) *Human Resource Planning: An Introduction*, IES Report No 312. www.employment-studies.co.uk.

Royal College of Nursing (2007) *Our NHS—Today and Tomorrow*, www.rcn.org.uk.

Ulrich, D. (1996) *Human Resource Champions*, Harvard Business School Press.

Wallop, H. (2006) 'Bank holidays time off law "will penalise firms"', *Daily Telegraph*, 28 August.

Watson, T.J. (2002) *Organising and Managing Work*, FT/Prentice Hall.

# Learning and Development 10

## Key Terms

**Learning** A fundamental and natural human process involving growth and change. Learning is about behavioural modification. It cannot be seen, but is inferred from differences in what we know, believe, and can do. Learning is the way in which we can improve and be different from that which we were. Learning needs to be understood as both a process and an outcome.

**Training** Can best be understood as planned, structured, and often formalized learning experiences that seek to develop specific skills and knowledge needed for effective job performance. Historically, employees have learnt many of the competencies they need to perform effectively by being trained.

**Development** A term often used to describe changes in the whole person and what they can do. It reflects the belief that all people have the potential to be more and do more, and that this potential needs to be developed as well as utilized. People can develop to a limited degree through training, but development implies the employment of a much wider range of learning experiences and methods, such as coaching and mentoring, not all of which are necessarily connected to the working environment.

**Competence** The combination of skills, knowledge, and experience that results in a person's ability to carry out specific tasks and procedures to a required standard. Can be equated to 'know-how' (Gladstone, 2000). A specific competency can also be understood as an underlying characteristic of a person, that is, a trait, a belief, an ability, or an attitude, that distinguishes one person from another and explains differences in job performance (Rothwell, 2004).

**Human resource development** This term came into usage in the late 1980s and early 1990s, and is used by many writers, but fewer practitioners, in preference to training. Its relationship to training is similar to that between Human Resource Management (HRM) and Personnel Management, in that it represents a more holistic and strategic approach to learning than does training (Walton, 1999).

**Coaching** A process in which a 'coach' supports an individual to develop his or her skills through a series of structured conversations by exploring the nature of challenges faced at work and helping the individual to identify the best approaches to those challenges to achieve the desired outcomes.

**Mentoring** The development of a relationship between a much more senior person in an organization and more junior person, often as part of a development programme, involving the experienced person using his or her greater knowledge and expertise to accelerate the junior colleague's development.

## Learning Objectives

As a result of reading this chapter and using the Online Resource Centre, you should be able to:

- understand how people learn and recognize that training represents only one way in which people can learn at work;
- understand and explain why training and development are important to an organization and to its employees;
- identify different approaches to delivering learning;
- understand the importance of evaluating training and other approaches to work-based learning.

# Introduction

Humans are designed to learn: people who don't learn rarely survive or prosper. While we are born with different levels of inherited capabilities and potential, we are all programmed to learn and, through learning, grow as individuals. But some people seem to learn more than others, learn more quickly and attain higher levels of performance. Learning is a common characteristic, but also one that distinguishes one person from another in that some people seem to be 'better learners'.

From the day we are born, we embark on a lifelong journey of learning. We are the most versatile of all animals and are able to adapt to the widest variety of environments, because of our capacity to learn the skills, knowledge, and best approach to be successful in the environment in which we find ourselves. The make-up of the human brain is much the same whether we choose to live and work in a fast-paced city environment or to adopt a subsistence lifestyle in a remote area with very low population density. However, the capabilities we must acquire to survive and succeed in these different environments are themselves vastly different and we require very different learning experiences to enable us to develop the necessary skills to survive and do well in each.

Most people will thrive when exposed to positive learning experiences and will continue to enjoy learning throughout their lives, but it is important to recognize that people can also be damaged by negative experiences of learning, particularly as children. This can have a lasting effect on their motivation to learn later in life, as adults. Nevertheless, learning new skills and acquiring knowledge, and therefore becoming better equipped to survive and succeed, are important to everyone because these connect to a person's sense of achievement and self-esteem.



**STUDENT ACTIVITY 10.1**

The following appeared in a CIPD examination paper in 2006:

**Reading about what looked like an interesting website that invited people to write in with 'their most dangerous idea', you checked it out and found that the head of learning at an American university claimed that schools were bad for children and should be closed. His argument was based on the belief that learning in schools involves children being spoon-fed information and repeatedly tested to see if they can regurgitate it. This creates stressed-out children and adults who avoid all learning because it reminds them of their school experiences. He concluded his entry by saying that 'we need to produce adults who love learning and can think for themselves'.**

1. In the context of your own experience of learning, what were the things that you enjoyed about learning and what didn't you like?
2. Think about the learning achievements that have been particularly important to you. Why were they important and how did you develop as a result of these experiences?
3. How can we make learning enjoyable and meaningful for adults, particularly those who have experienced learning failures?

We can learn in many different ways, not all of which produce the kinds of outcomes to which either the individual or the training professional is committed. Learning at work, and for work, involves particular difficulties and challenges. Training, as a way of learning, is, from a managerial perspective, usually seen in instrumental terms. This means that learning is linked to the acquisition of new or increased competencies and capabilities which are used in the production of goods or services. These competencies and capabilities are only needed because they help to create value and wealth for the company. Quite simply, people and their capabilities are used by those who employ and manage them to generate goods and services that have a social or financial value.

People are employed not only for what they already know and can do, but also for what they may subsequently learn to do. Because of the dynamic nature of the working environment, employees are constantly expected to update their knowledge, learn new skills and acquire new capabilities. There is a presumption, therefore, that all employees will not only work, but will also continue to learn. To be effective and to continue to make a positive contribution to the employing organization, employees need to be active learners. But it is also important to recognize that, if an employee believes that the only beneficiary from his or her improved competence is the employer, learning through training will inevitably be seen as something he or she is required, rather than wants, to do. The positive motivation to learn cannot be taken for granted and must be nurtured, so that employees see learning as important for themselves as well as for the organization.

**KEY CONCEPT Motivation**

This is about the drives and needs within each person that direct and influence their behaviours. People are constantly interpreting their environment by reference to their own and others' interests, and act accordingly. Unless employees *want* to learn, they will try to avoid it. Coercing people to learn rarely works and is often counterproductive. If they are forced to participate in training, the most that will happen is that they will 'be there'. The reality is that the desired learning will not take place because those attending the activity lack the motivation to learn from it.

**HRM INSIGHT 10.1 Team briefing training at Delta Ltd**

Delta Ltd employs over 200 people providing an outsourced call centre response for a large financial company. Each team has a team leader who is responsible for the day-to-day performance and management of the teams, ensuring that customers receive a prompt and friendly response to telephone queries. As part of Delta's strategic intention to improve communications across the business the management team decided to revise their team brief as feedback from a recent opinion survey suggested that employee interest in the briefings was low, that the briefings were rushed and largely consisted of a manger reading a script of information from a piece of paper. The senior management team therefore redesigned the briefing format to include sections about local performance and local news that were to be completed by the line manager along with an interactive section which would consider a particular problem area chosen by the team leader and their team to discuss and resolve issues.

Prior to the introduction of the new briefing the senior managers met with the HR and Training Advisor to design and deliver an interactive training workshop to support the Line Managers to develop skills and confidence in delivering team briefing. The senior managers assisted with the training and agreed to attend a sample of briefings before and after training to support the desired improvements. The line managers all attended training and the feedback was very positive with everyone agreeing that the training was informative, enjoyable, and helpful. Two months after the training another opinion survey was conducted and the results from this survey showed no improvement in the responses from staff about their team briefings. The senior managers gathered further information from team members to suggest that briefings continued to be rushed and read off a script with low interest for those involved.

Questions

1. What might be the reasons for the failure to change behaviour?
2. What alternatives might have been considered to embed a positive and sustained behavioural change in this situation?

# 'Learning' was 'Training'

Think again about our reference, in Chapter 1, to the people building the Egyptian Pyramids and the British railway and canal networks: how did the workers acquire the knowledge and skills that they needed to carry out all of the tasks and operations they were required to perform? They learnt primarily by 'doing', which means that they learnt from the experience of working, but also, as operations became more complex and challenging, they would have learned by being trained. Obviously experience played its part, as it still does today, but increasingly more focused and directed learning, which involved people being taught and instructed by others who already possessed the required knowledge and skills, would have been the way in which more and more employees acquired the behavioural capabilities they needed to do their jobs.

Over time, learning became increasingly structured, planned, and formalized. Training was seen as the means by which people could learn what they needed to know and do. Training itself became a profession. As Davis and Davis (1998) conclude:

> **Training, with great impetus from the exigencies of two world wars became a function within organizations, and its processes became formalised. Like other work, training itself became work and was assigned to the people who performed it. This became the basis assumption about the place of training in organizations for almost half a century and is still the basic concept that governs how learning takes place in most organizations.**

## Why train employees?



Consider for a moment how training and development fits into HR and the strategic organizational agenda. In Chapter 1, the development of the human resource was explained as a key objective of organizations that, in order to remain competitive and efficient, need constantly to refresh the skills and competencies of their employees. Developing the resource is one of the fundamental objectives of people management, because it is through employees' growth and development that they increase their asset value and acquire new, or higher, capabilities that organizations need and managers can utilize.

But training can also be seen to be in the interests of employees who, through planned and structured learning, can acquire new competencies and capabilities, which they own. It adds to the value of their human capital. This not only increases their value to the employer, but increases their attractiveness to other employers: it enhances their employability and value in the labour market. In practical terms, this can result in increases in pay (skill and qualification-based pay are part of many organizations' reward strategy) or lead to offers of more rewarding jobs elsewhere.

**KEY CONCEPT Human capital**

The knowledge, skills, abilities, and capacity to develop and innovate that is possessed by people in an organization (CIPD, 2006).

As well as supporting both employee and managerial interests, training is important because of the way in which it has the potential for facilitating:

- organizational change;
- functional flexibility;
- attitudinal change;
- statutory compliance.

**Table 10.1** The six 'Es' of training—why organizations train employees

| | |
|---|---|
| **Engage** | Effective training provides the opportunity for employees to connect with the organization, and with its policies and methods of working. It helps to ensure that employees 'buy into', or engage with, the organization's culture. It helps to make employees feel valued and develop working relationships with their colleagues. |
| **Educate** | Training can help to educate or increase the knowledge and awareness of individuals and teams. |
| **Enhance** | Training can help to enhance or improve the skills and competence of individuals and teams within an organization. |
| **Empower** | By properly training employees, an organization can increase the accountability of teams and individuals, and can ensure that faster, better quality decisions can be made, while avoiding the need to pass decision-making unnecessarily up the organizational chain. |
| **Energize** | Participation in training can help to energize, motivate, and inspire employees. It provides an opportunity to take a step back and allows people to consider how they can best contribute towards the effectiveness of the organization. |
| **Enlighten** | Training can also be an effective means of helping individuals to see things in a different way. It can help employees reach an often sudden conclusion that there is a better, more effective, way of doing something and can help to unlock previously untapped potential. |

Using a mechanical metaphor, training, as part of a strategy for learning and personal development, is arguably the most powerful 'lever' managers can use to achieve these important objectives.

It is rare for major new organizational initiatives not to be linked to training of some sort or another, but there is a danger that training can be overloaded with expectation and used inappropriately or unrealistically. Training can be ineffective as well as effective—much depends on whether training is the 'right' lever to pull and, of course, on who is pulling it (Boydell and Leary, 1996).

Training can also be an expensive activity and the resources needed to equip a specialized function do not come cheaply. Off-the-job training will incur the cost of either purchasing the professional training support or of providing a skilled person in the organization to design and deliver the training. Often both will be involved. On top of this, there is the cost of releasing employees and covering their work for the period during which they are undergoing training. Additionally, there will be cost involved with expenses that are incurred by trainers and trainees, including facilities and materials. So why do organizations bother with all of this expense? Why not simply recruit someone who is fully trained already?

More often than not, it is not possible to recruit the ideal person with the exact skills needed for the job. Even when good candidates are available, they will still need to learn the unique systems, processes, and procedures operating within the organization. In addition, change is a feature of most organizations and, as a consequence, so is the need to learn the new skills necessary for adapting to changing products, technologies, and markets. Technology, in particular, is constantly being improved and updated; new working arrangements are frequently introduced as a result of reorganization and attempts to re-engineer operating processes and procedures, and all of these require the employee to learn new things.

Training, for many, is therefore an essential part of surviving change and maintaining the currency of what they know and what they can do.

Table 10.1 summarizes the potential power that training possesses.

**HRM INSIGHT 10.2 Taylor's Laundry Services**

Taylor's is a medium-sized, privately owned business, employing around 200 people. It supplies industrial clothing to a variety of private and public sector customers, and provides a regular laundry service for those customers who require it. Most employees work in the laundry, ensuring that garments are properly washed, dried, and sorted for return to customers within a short timeframe. Most jobs have relatively low skill requirements and new recruits are regarded as being able to pick up the work very quickly on the job. They are therefore put straight on the job on their first day in the business, having been shown where the fire exits are and how to operate the washing and drying machinery.

Time off the job for training is seen as costly and so people pick up the job by asking more experienced staff what to do. Staff turnover is high, with even relatively new employees passing on skills to new recruits.

### Questions

1. What kind of training would this organization benefit from?
2. What cost is the company incurring as a result of the lack of effective training provision?
3. How is the lack of a training function impacting on other HR issues?
4. How would you design a realistic training intervention(s) that would address the above problems?

## Criticisms of training

While the theoretical case for training is undeniable, the reality is often disappointing. There is a sense that training—or, perhaps more accurately, those with training responsibilities—have too often failed to deliver what has been promised and expected, to the point at which the credibility of the training function has been compromised. Criticisms of the effectiveness of training are not new (Megginson et al., 1993), but, worryingly, persist. Davis and Davis (1998, ch 2) suggest that one explanation for training's credibility problem is because 'learning got left out'.



They, at least, would agree that, if not left out, learning must either have been neglected or that the central role of learning in training has not been fully understood or articulated. They offer two reasons for this worrying neglect.

- Training, frequently seen as a response to a performance problem, has become routinized and, under pressure to provide a response, trainers have failed to reflect on the reasons for its successes and failures.

  Particular factors that have a bearing on whether training 'works' are:
  - trainee motivation;
  - the importance of practice and application;
  - the critical role of the line manager in supporting trainees.
- Trainers themselves often lack sufficient understanding of learning theories and, while they may be knowledgeable about the technique, subject matter, or procedure, many are not professional trainers. This is an important point because it suggests that, whatever the inherent limitations of training are, the key to its success or failure are the personal and professional qualities of those who train, and the extent to which they can effectively manage the whole training process.

**RESEARCH INSIGHT 10.1**

To take your learning further you might want to read this article:

**Sloman, M. and Webster, L. (2005) 'Training to Learning', *Training and Development*, 59:9, pp. 58–63**

In this article Sloman and Webster offer an interesting insight into the problems of training. Partly, they argue, these are due to changes in the nature of work and the kind of employees on which organizations increasingly depend for their long-term success, that is, those they describe as 'knowledge workers'. They claim that traditional classroom-based training courses are likely to be of limited value to the learning and development of this category of employee and that a 'shift is taking place from training to learning'.

Increasingly there is a shift in emphasis, due to highlighted limitation of training and the need to focus on generating learning through more effective approaches. The CIPD (2008) learning and development survey noted that within the companies surveyed, the use of training courses remained static, whereas the use of both coaching and in-house development programmes is on the increase. The *IRS Management Review* emphasizes the trend away from training to learning. Describing training as a reactive activity designed to resolve short-term operational deficiencies rather than being connected to the long-term needs of the individual or the business, the point is made that:

> **organisations have recognised that the traditional ad hoc approach to training is incompatible with the need to adapt quickly to changing business circumstances.**
> (*IRS Management Review*, 1998)

This distinction between training and learning was explored in an earlier article by Sloman (2004), who reflected on the limitations of course-based training and its emphasis on content, instruction, and the passive involvement of trainees, leading to prescribed behavioural change. He concluded that learning was the way forward, generated by:

- motivated participants;
- self-direction;
- work-based processes and locations.

In addition to uncertainties over whether learning is, or can be, generated through training, there is the added problem of line managers failing to understand their responsibilities with regard to the use of training. According to Cosgrove and Speed (1995, cited by Rothwell, 1996), senior managers often fail to specify what they expect from the training function and training professionals, in an attempt to please everyone and gain support for their work, raise unrealistic expectations of what training can deliver. They fail to understand the importance of integrating it with corporate strategy.

Rothwell (1996) shares with Ulrich (1998) the view that, historically, training has been focused too much on activities, such as organizing and delivering courses, rather than on hard results and valued outcomes. Moreover, Rothwell believes that many customers of training mistakenly believe that high-profile training activity automatically means results and that offering more training inevitably improves performance. Both assumptions are questionable. In his critique of traditional approaches to training, he argues that the main problems that need to be overcome in any attempt to 'reframe' training are as follows.

- Its lack of focus

  There are too many terms in the field—education, development, etc.—and different job titles within the training community create confusion about what people actually do and what training actually means.

- Its lack of management support

  Senior executives and line management often express concerns over training's importance, costs, credibility, and effectiveness, and fail to understand their own responsibilities.

**HRM INSIGHT 10.3 Paul Kearns' story of an unhelpful director**

Many years ago, when I had only been in my new job as head of training for a couple of weeks, our technical director came into my office and asked me if I could organise some presentation skills training for his team of engineers. I have to admit that I did not particularly like the way he just expected me to deal with his requests immediately, without any prior discussion. So my first reaction was, 'can we sit down and talk about exactly what you want?' This was not the reaction he had been used to from my predecessor. He seemed impatient and more or less intimated, 'What is there to talk about?' As far as he was concerned it was a simple matter of sending his engineers on a course.

(This material is taken from Kearns, P. (2005) *Evaluating the ROI from Learning*, with the permission of the publisher, the Chartered Institute of Personnel and Development, London.)

Questions

1. What did Kearns want to talk to the director about and why?
2. If Kearns had simply done what he had been asked and organized presentation skills training for the engineers, what might the outcome have been?
3. What strategy might Kearns adopt to try to change the attitude of the director towards training and the role of training experts?

- **It is not conducted and managed systematically**

  Poorly carried out training needs-analysis fails to identify the nature of the performance problem; training methods and materials are not carefully matched with training requirements and little is done to ensure that transfer of learning takes place.

- **It is not linked to other organizational initiatives**

  Training is often undertaken in isolation from other HR practices and management initiatives, and, however effective it might have been, quickly loses its impact because of this 'lack of connectivity'. Training becomes something that is 'bolted on' rather than integrated and embedded.

- **It can be used unrealistically to try to achieve attitudinal change, which is rarely, if at all, achievable through conventional training interventions**

  In such areas as diversity, equal opportunities, and racial awareness, deeply rooted prejudices, beliefs, and behaviours are unlikely to be touched and changed through instruction or course-based training. Training can, if properly designed and managed, help employees to acquire knowledge and skills; it is much more difficult to believe that it can change the way in which they think and see the world.

**STUDENT ACTIVITY 10.2 'Fixing the problem'**

Look carefully at Figure 10.1, which represents a model of what might be described as a 'flawed approach to training', and answer the following questions.

1. Taking each stage in turn, identify what changes and improvements should be made.
2. How might the trainees contribute to each stage of the model?
3. What might line managers contribute?

As a result of answering the above questions, design your own improved model of the training process. You can carry this out as a group activity, and present your results for discussion and evaluation.

For more information about the Systematic Training models, which were popular during the 1970s and 1980s, see the Online Resource Centre extension material 10.1.

Figure 10.1 shows why these models have declined in popularity. If the employee's experience of training reflects even parts of the approach to training illustrated in Figure 10.1, the probability of any positive and lasting outcomes being created is likely to be low or non-existent. In fact, it might even be negative, because employees may be deterred from any further participation in training by the negative experiences of

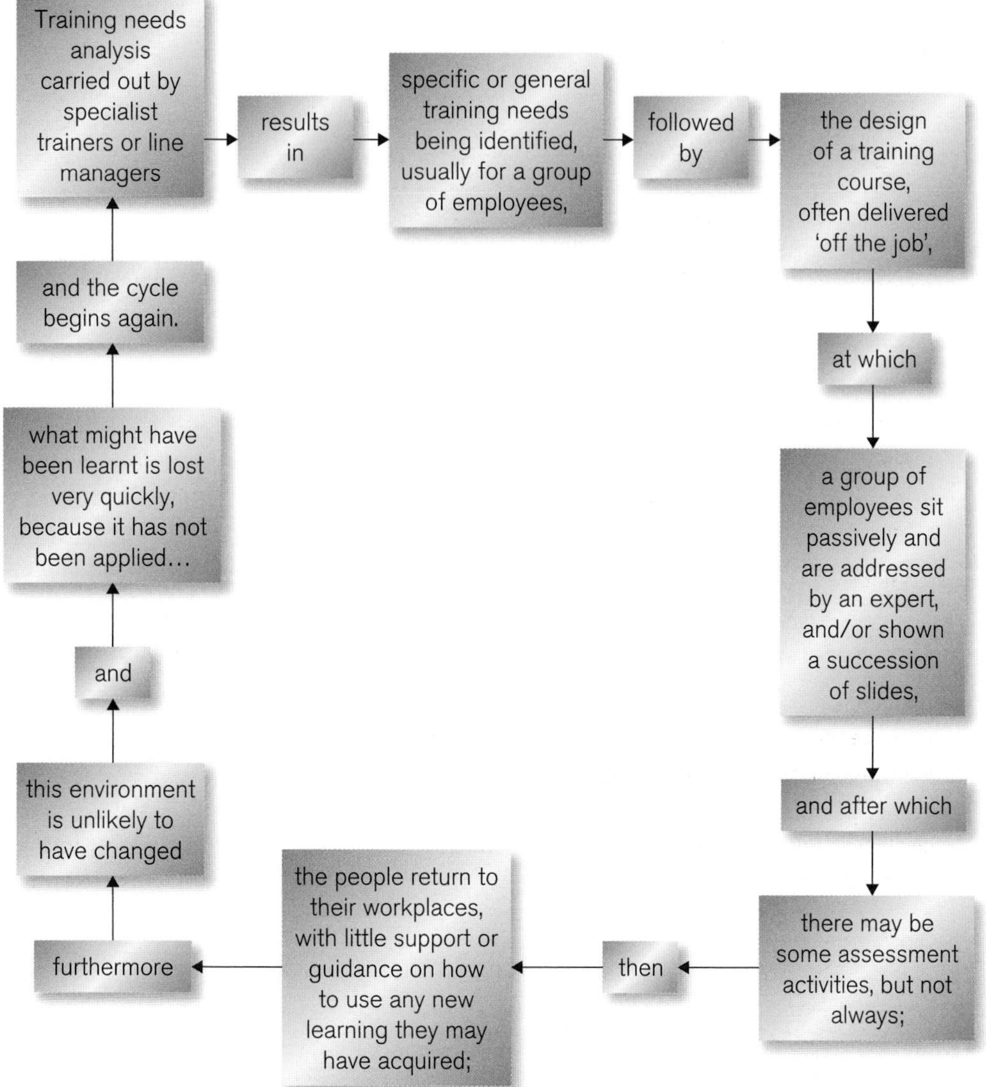


**Figure 10.1** A flawed model of the training cycle

a flawed process. The specific weaknesses and problems associated with this model are not difficult to identify and include:

- the lack of direct involvement and ownership of trainees;
- the assumption that other people—line managers and trainers—know what employees need to learn and that reliable processes exist to identify learning requirements;
- the practice of subjecting employees, who may have quite different interests, skills, knowledge, and motivation, to the same training programmes;
- the belief that taking employees 'off the job' and out of their working environment facilitates learning;
- the belief that the transfer and application of any new learning that might occur is not problematical;
- the failure to recognize that employees learn as much, if not more, from informal processes and interactions than they do from planned and formalized interventions;
- the idea that training can be wholly managed and controlled by others and still be effective.

## On a more optimistic note

A combination of budgetary pressures and the need for training to re-establish its credibility as a 'value-adding' activity has resulted in an improved understanding of what training can and cannot achieve, and a more effective use of training interventions. According to Peter Cresswell (in Hope, 2006), general manager for consultancy services at Siemens:

> **Over the years training has improved considerably. We are now looking at how effective the training has actually been. It is important that organizations know what they want out of training and are able to measure it, to prove that they have achieved their objectives.**

Evidence from recent research, into the way in which many organizations have redefined and aligned their training and development functions, shows that traditional models and thinking about training have been replaced with more effective and valued approaches, based in part on a closer integration between training and business strategy. Of particular interest is the way in which the 'business partner' model of HR is driving training in a more strategic and focused direction (see Hirsh and Tamkin, 2005a,b; Smethurst, 2006a).

Signpost to Chapter 2: HRM: An Academic and Professional Perspective, for insights into the value of the HR function



Many organizations are reporting major new training and development initiatives (see Warren, 2006; Smethurst, 2006a). Research carried out by the Adult Learning Inspectorate and published in its 2004–05 report (Scott, 2005) provides evidence of more widespread improvements in training. It found that 75 per cent of providers of learning at work had passed inspections in the previous 12 months, compared to only 40 per cent four years before.

What emerges from many of these examples of new thinking and practices in training is the importance of the following (Hope, 2006):

- employees who want to participate actively in their own learning;
- close working relationships between trainers and line managers that result in agreement on training plans, skill and competency needs, and line support for learners;
- accurate diagnosis of training and development needs;
- opportunities for the reinforcement of learning through practice;
- designing bespoke training solutions rather than offering 'courses for all';
- a connection between the delivery of training, its evaluation, and the planning and design of future training interventions, i.e. a cycle of learning and application;
- a strong relationship between the required learning outcomes and the learning methods employed.

# Different Perceptions of the Value of Training

In addition to the debate about whether, and under what circumstances, training delivers the required learning outcomes, significant differences have been expressed over the economic status of training (Kearns, 2005).

## Training as a cost

As argued earlier in the chapter, there are direct and indirect costs involved in training employees that have to be paid for, either from a central training budget or from budgets devolved to line managers. Training can also be perceived as an overhead, that is, a charge on all income-generating departments irrespective of whether they actually benefit from any centralized training provision. Seen as a cost, training is likely to be limited in scope and intensity: costs, generally, are something to be reduced. It might be thought that organizations that employ low-skilled workers are more likely to see the costs of training in a negative way, believing that adequate supplies of labour in the external labour market can meet all of their skill requirements. Surprisingly, however, the perception that training is a cost to be minimized is not restricted to such companies. Pfeffer (1998) provides evidence of national differences in the amount of training provided among motor manufacturing plants. He presents data that shows Japanese plants providing 364 hours of training in the first six months for new employees, while the respective figures for European and Australian plants are 178 hours and 40 hours respectively. One can speculate that, in the latter two examples, training is seen more as a cost to be controlled rather than as an investment.

In their study of human resource practices in UK companies, Truss et al. (1997) provide similar evidence of minimal levels of training being provided. In one large retailing and distribution company it was found that less than half of the employees received any training in the year prior to the research. In only two of the other seven organizations studied did more than half of the respondents indicate that they had received the training they needed to do their job.



## Training as an investment

Seen from this perspective, training represents a key instrument in developing capacity and capability to support organizational objectives. During periods of economic difficulty, such as that seen towards the end of the last decade, it is particularly important that organizations are able to see the economic benefit of investment in training. The training budget can be seen as an easy target to reduce costs and unless spend can be justified then it is likely to be one of the first things to be forfeited. As Kearns (2005) states:



> **We should think of it as an important lever through which we can gain competitive advantage.**

This means, however, that the contribution which training makes needs to be systematically evaluated and that some attempt must be made to calculate the returns on investment in training. Pfeffer (1998) again provides interesting examples of organizations that spend heavily on training and relate this spend to changes in key performance indicators. He cites the Men's Warehouse, whose sustained growth in revenues and net earnings is linked to its investment in training. According to Pfeffer:

> **The key to its success has been how it treats its people and particularly the emphasis it has placed on training, an approach that separates it from many of its competitors.**
> (Pfeffer, 1998)

Interestingly, while claiming that training is an investment, Pfeffer accepts that return on investment calculations are difficult, if not impossible, and that successful firms who invest heavily in training:

> **do so almost as a matter of faith and because of their belief in the connection between people and profits.**

HRM Insight 10.4 illustrates that, while the financial quantification of the worth of training is (for most practical purposes) not an option, a belief in its value and relevance shapes many organizations' support for it.

### HRM INSIGHT 10.4 The German engineering company

Some years ago, one of the authors was part of a group of staff and students on a visit to West Germany. The purpose of the visit was broadly educational, and involved visiting different organizations to learn about management and how businesses in Germany were run. One of the companies visited was a medium-sized engineering company that manufactured a range of products used in the construction industry. At that time, and as with other European economies, West Germany was in the grip of a recession and demand for the company's products was falling. Similar businesses in the UK were shedding labour and cutting back on their training programmes, particularly those for craft apprentices. Training resources tend to be plentiful when companies are doing well, but in periods of economic difficulty, they tend to be the first to be cut. It is a cost that can easily be identified and from which, consequently, savings can be made.

Talking to the training manager in the German company, I asked him whether his company was planning a similar cost-reduction strategy. His answer was, in many ways, surprising because it represented a more forward-thinking and strategic approach to training. He said that the company was definitely not planning to cut the number of apprentices it employed, nor the training they received. When asked why, he asserted that these apprentices were the future of the company and that, when business picked up, they would be fully-skilled and able to meet the expected increase in demand for the company's products. He also made the point that, within reason, employees not engaged full-time on production might use their time in developing new skills that would increase their functional flexibility and value to the company.

### Questions

1. What are the implications for training of an organization's shedding of labour and cutting back on training when demand falls?
2. How can underutilized resources be used to provide training?
3. The German company's approach to training reflected part of a wider management philosophy: how might this be characterized?



# The Measurement and Evaluation of Training

The need to evaluate and measure the effectiveness in training is intrinsically linked to the justification for carrying out training activity to enhance the contribution that employees and teams make to the organization. The evaluation of training has been the subject of debate over the last 50 years, nonetheless it is still difficult to directly quantify training outcomes and the link between any attending training and subsequent changes in behaviour and the effect these have upon the organization. One of the earliest studies on the evaluation of training was that of Kirkpatrick (1998), who first proposed four levels of training evaluation in 1959 and developed these to become perhaps one of the most widely known descriptions of what trainers should evaluate. Kirpatrick explains that the levels are increasingly more complex, and perhaps more costly to evaluate, but that for evaluation to be meaningful it should be across all four levels:

1. Reactions—what the trainees thought and felt about the training.
2. Learning—the increased knowledge and skills.
3. Behaviour—and the change in behaviour and improved performance on the job.
4. Results—the impact upon the organization of the training.

Where Kirkpatrick's model describes what should be evaluated Easterby-Smith (1994) highlights four reasons why training should be evaluated:

1. Proving—to prove something has happened as a result of training and development activity.
2. Controlling—to demonstrate that the standards of delivery have been monitored.
3. Improving—to demonstrate that the review of current programmes and activities will ensure that they become better in future.
4. Learning—to demonstrate that evaluation is an integral part of the whole learning and development process itself.

It can be helpful to consider both of these models when designing training evaluation so that consideration can be given to what to evaluate and why. There are, however, difficulties in measuring the above in an objective manner that is valid in relation to the required outcome. Traditional post-course questionnaires may measure the satisfaction of trainees following attending training, however this does not mean that learning has taken place or that this learning will be transferred to the workplace and within what time frame. Similarly an evaluative test at the end of a training event may be helpful to assess knowledge but this does not mean that it will be applied to the benefit of the organization who arranged the training event. It is therefore difficult to accurately measure return on investment (ROI) in training, nonetheless this area remains a key focus for HR and training specialists as well as line managers to justify this continued expense. The Practitioner Insight highlights the importance of the measurement of training at Northern Foods.

**PRACTITIONER INSIGHT Beverly Hodson, Group Learning and Development Manager, Northern Foods plc**

Learning and Development is widely recognized at Northern Foods as being an important part of our success. We are made up of a number of business units and these have different cultures. Some units are more proactive and more forward thinking than others and here training and development is further up the agenda and is more targeted. Those units demonstrating best practice have mapped out their strategic plan and have clear and measurable outcomes and an associated return on the investment for training and development that link to this plan.

Measuring the return on investment for training is an area with which many businesses struggle, however for us it is critical to show this return to justify the training budget and to ensure that it is not an easy target for cuts when considering our annual budgets. Training is only part of this picture and individual development supported by good line managers is recognized as being one the most effective way of learning with the strongest long-term benefit.

Our most effective learning is targeted development, where individuals are given the opportunity to learn new skills by engaging in real experience outside their normal responsibilities, like a project, with good line manager support. We have found it is better to focus on building an employee's strengths and mitigating their weaknesses rather than focusing on weaknesses. Effective line manager support is so important in ensuring that employees reach their maximum potential, that this is a key area of focus for us in terms of learning and development. We have a broad range of managers with different levels of skills and it is important for us to improve consistency in this area. This goes beyond learning and training and has involved us identifying what 'good management' looks like in our organization, identifying current capabilities and helping managers move towards best practice. This entails developing management tools such as our 'Capability Model', which maps out the skills, knowledge, and talent required, as well as developing managers to be able to manage as effectively as possible.

**STUDENT ACTIVITY 10.3**

In groups, consider training events or activities that group members have attended at the request of an employing organization or a skills development course that you have attended as part of your studies.

1. What was the objective of the training?
2. What changes in behaviour were anticipated by the organization that required group members to attend and how would these be of benefit to the organization?
3. What were the costs associated with the training?
4. How could the training be evaluated and how might the return on investment be calculated?
4. Was there a case for employees paying part of the costs of their own training and, if so, what is it?

**STUDENT ACTIVITY 10.4**

Choose a development need identified in an organization with which you are familiar and design an actual training event or activity that would deliver specified learning outcomes.

For some ideas about the types of training you might consider see the Online Resource Centre extension material 10.2.

Make any realistic assumptions you want to, and think creatively about what you need to do and how to achieve the objective of generating the required learning. Present your ideas for discussion and evaluation.



## Developments in Workplace Learning

The debate referred to earlier in this chapter about training and learning involved two key issues.

Firstly, questions were raised about the limitations of training, particularly with regards to over-reliance on training courses and the role of the trainer as 'expert', and whether such criticisms undermined the credibility of training as a planned and structured source of learning. We concluded that training continues to have a role to play, but only if the responsible parties respond to criticisms from participants and line managers, and begin to develop practices that are grounded in appropriate theories and principles of learning, which also reflect actual business requirements.

Secondly, the trend away from 'training' towards 'learning' suggests that non-course-based approaches and practices need to be developed to reflect developments in the nature of work and of workers. This means that structured learning, that is, learning that is planned and is associated with specific outcomes, should be more individualized and learner-centred rather than 'imposed from above', and must be embedded in the working environment.

This recognition that the workplace, rather than the training room, should be the primary context in which learning is located is a theme shared by many of the writers to whom we have already referred. 'Workplace learning', or 'work-based learning', is associated with the following contemporary beliefs:

- that the workplace, in terms of its physical and social environments, is a site for learning and offers a range of learning opportunities;
- that many of these opportunities are informal and opportunistic rather than formal and planned;
- that the workplace needs to be understood as a learning, as well as a working, environment;
- that working and learning are inextricably linked.

What emerges from this brief reference to the learning environment is the importance of context. Whether learning emerges from the ongoing social interaction at the place of work or as a result of more planned and structured training interventions, the influence on these experiences of a wider set of factors cannot be ignored. If HR professionals are genuinely interested in increasing the effectiveness of workplace learning, it will be necessary to address barriers to learning that may exist in the workplace itself, in addition to developing more effective learning interventions.

For further insight into the relationship between learning and work see the Online Resource Centre extension material 10.3.

**STUDENT ACTIVITY 10.5 Designing a learning environment**

This is a group exercise and requires access to a working environment, which can be the university or college if you are full-time students. The objective is to discover people's views about the extent to which their working environment facilitates learning.

1. Design a questionnaire that seeks to measure the extent to which the working environment affects learning. The questions should focus on key influences, practices, and behaviours that are linked to learning, as well as barriers to learning, and should be completed by a representative sample of employees/students.
2. Present the findings of the survey and discuss the results.
3. Establish what are the main barriers, or obstacles, to learning.
4. Discuss changes that might be made to the learning environment that would increase the amount of learning created or which would remove the blockages to learning.

# Coaching

Coaching is becoming a more commonly used tool to support employee development at work. The CIPD 2009 Learning and Development Survey reported that 70 per cent of organizations surveyed use coaching as a method of developing their workforce. However, there is a broad understanding of what is meant by coaching and it can easily be confused with mentoring and counselling.

Coaching in a work context is generally quite different from a sporting context. Where sports coaching is largely instructional in its nature, workplace coaching more typically refers to a process where a coach supports an individual to develop his or her skills through a structured conversation which explores the nature of challenges faced at work and helps the individual to identify the best approaches to those challenges to achieve the desired outcomes. This may, for example, involve discussing situations at work to analyse the root cause and identify desired outcomes, followed by a process to choose the best options for achieving the outcome and evaluating the impact of actions taken. This should not be confused with either mentoring or counselling, however sometimes there is overlap between these terms. Mentoring has some similarities but tends to involve a much more senior person using their greater knowledge and expertise to support the development of a more junior person within an organization. Coaching, in comparison, is perhaps more associated with developing a specific skill set that has been previously identified either formally or informally as an area for development. Whilst it may be a line manager who is coaching a team member it may also be a functional expert, more experienced colleague or third party appointed for the specific purpose of developing that skill set further. Counselling more typically refers to a process of support for an individual with personal problems often relating to either mental or physical health.

Coaching can be a very effective mechanism for developing employee skills, particularly in complex environments. Many organizations are investing in either coaching training for managers or are employing the expertise of externally sourced coaches to support the development of their employees.

**RESEARCH INSIGHT 10.2**

To take your learning further you might want to read this article:

**Baron, L. and Morin, L. (2010) 'The impact of executive coaching on self-efficacy related to management soft skills', *Leadership and Organization Development Journal*, 31:1, pp. 18–38**

This article study looks at executive coaching in its context as an increasingly common method of skill development. It examines the links between the number of coaching sessions and with post training self efficacy or confidence and self belief in their personal capabilities. The study shows a significant positive link between the number of coaching sessions and self efficacy and concludes that to improve return on investment with regard to coaching, organizations should implement systematic coaching programmes with multiple coaching sessions spread over several months.

# The Growth of e-Learning

Martyn Sloman's influential book on e-learning (2001) places this new approach to learning in a wider context. He argues that this development is not simply about the use of technology, claiming that:

> **Today's training professionals are operating at the beginning of a revolution. Importantly, it is about much more than the arrival of a new platform for the delivery of training. The context in which the trainer operates, internal and external relationships and the role itself can be expected to undergo profound changes.**

**KEY CONCEPT e-learning**

This can be understood as learning that is delivered, enabled, or mediated using electronic technology for the explicit purpose of training in organizations (CIPD, 2007a).

As with most new developments in HR, the emergence of e-learning has not been without controversy, central to which has been the role of technology. Elliott Masie (www.masie.com), for example, not only argues that e-learning is not about computers and computing, but that the 'e' should be an abbreviation for 'experience', not 'electronic'. The point being made is that there is real danger in concentrating on systems, portals, and technology-driven 'learning solutions', and in seeing them as ends rather than means. As Sloman says:

> **There is a danger of becoming seduced by the functionality of the technology rather than concentrating on its use.**
> (Sloman, 2001)



## Forms of e-learning

- Web-based training

  In corporate training, technology is used primarily to deliver content to the end user without significant interaction with (or support from) training professionals, peers or managers.

- Interactive online learning

  Particularly used in further and higher education, but also in organizations with their own intranet, the emphasis here is on the delivery of courses and support material online. Platforms such as 'Blackboard' also provide opportunities for exchanges of information, interaction with tutors, collaborative activities, and, depending on the nature of the course, assessment and online feedback. There has also been a very significant growth in the private sector, with specialist companies offering a range of generic and bespoke e-learning solutions (Alcock, 2005).

- Informal e-learning

  Beyond these 'course-based' approaches to e-learning are the growing opportunities for technology to support informal learning in the workplace. In many knowledge-intensive organizations, technology is linked with knowledge management strategies and developing intranet capabilities to facilitate knowledge exchange linked to 'communities of practice'.

- Standalone e-learning materials

  These take the form of CD ROM-based learning. In this case, there is no support provision or interaction outside of the CD ROM-based material.

For further information on the business case for e-learning see the Online Resource Centre extension material 10.4.

## Understanding and Managing the Learning Process

So far, this chapter has focused on *what* people at work need to learn and why, and the different *methods* that can be made available for them to learn. What has only been indirectly alluded to—the actual way in which learning takes place—must now be addressed.

Learning, as a process, has several important characteristics:

- you cannot see it happening—it is essentially a cognitive process;
- you can only see that learning has taken place through changes in the way people think, behave and work;
- people may well have learnt something new or already possess a valued competency, but may choose not to use and display it;
- 'real' learning relates to knowledge, skills, and attitudes that are embedded within the individual. Some learning can be described as temporary and superficial, which can be easily lost;
- no one can learn for you. HR professionals and line managers can help others to learn, provide 'learning-rich' learning environments, and support learning with a wide range of resources, but learning is only something that individuals can do, i.e. learning lies within the domain of the individual;
- we may choose not to engage in certain kinds of learning because of being apprehensive about what we might learn about ourselves or about others, or because we cannot see its relevance. This means that employees need to feel positive about the outcomes of the learning process before they make a commitment to learn.

**STUDENT ACTIVITY 10.6 How people learn**

Consider the following set of statements about the relative effectiveness of different learning experiences.

People remember (learn):

- 10 per cent of what they read;
- 20 per cent of what they hear;
- 30 per cent of what they see;
- 50 per cent of what they see and hear;
- 70 per cent of what they talk over with others;
- 80 per cent of what they use in real life;
- 95 per cent of what they teach someone.

(Glasser, 1986)

1. What explains the differences in the learning associated with these seven ways of learning?
2. Which of these ways of generating learning are associated with your own experiences at university or in the workplace?
3. Is there any relationship between the way in which you are required to learn and how effective learning experiences are?
4. What are the implications of your conclusions for the design of learning interventions?

One of the aims of this chapter has been to clarify the often-experienced confusion between training and learning. It is a mistake to think of these as separate and independent activities. Training is a way of generating learning, based on the use of certain techniques and methods. Magee and Thayer (1961) explained this relationship when they said:

> **The central process in training is learning.**

Training has, however, been subject to sustained criticism precisely because it is felt that it does not represent a powerful and reliable means of generating the learning managers and employees require. The problem that people such as Martyn Sloman (2001) have with training is twofold. Firstly, it is often badly designed and delivered, or based on a faulty diagnosis of training needs; secondly, it is considered an inappropriate way of meeting certain learning requirements for which other, more individualized, learning methods, such as coaching and mentoring, are likely to produce the required results. While the purpose of training is to generate learning, whether it does so and whether it meets the expectations of different stakeholders is problematical and uncertain.

Tom Boydell (2003) summarized the position of many who feel that HR professionals have placed too much emphasis and reliance on training when he asserted:

> **I think most learning does not arise as a result of training. If you ask yourself, or a group of people, to identify 4 or 5 or whatever really important things you or they have learned in the past year/2 years/life so far, I would be surprised if many came as the result of training–i.e. of someone else telling or showing you, deciding for you, what the right answer is, the best way to do things, the correct way to be.**

The critical question then becomes: 'Can training be reformulated and reframed, so that it can overcome many of its limitations and deliver valued contributions to the development of employees?' Perhaps one way in which this can be achieved is for those responsible for the management of training to incorporate principles and practices associated with the theory of accelerated learning. It seems to us that the shift within the training profession from an emphasis on training to one of learning is, in one sense, absolutely appropriate and justified. Learning is the key to change, improved performance and personal growth. The central question is: 'How can we achieve this in the most effective and efficient ways possible?'

It also must be recognized that, in the same way that 'learning got left out [of training]' (Davis and Davis, 1998), we might also conclude that 'people have been left out of learning'. Perhaps there is even a link between these two statements. Certainly, we would argue that understanding the human dimension of learning is critical to any efforts to make training more effective: if training is seen only in terms of models, procedures, budgets, activities, and roles, it will continue to disappoint and fail to deliver. The human dimension has to be at the heart of the training experience. As learning becomes less an option and more a necessity, the failure to create learning is increasingly unacceptable and costly to employees and organizations. The problem is not one of not knowing how to meet this challenge, but of learning how to use what we know about what works and what doesn't, and understanding why.

## The Kolb learning cycle

Perhaps the best-known representation of how learning is created was presented by David Kolb (1984). His 'learning cycle' (see Figure 10.2) offers important insights into the different ways in which people can learn, and into the choices and preferences that exist in our own learning.

The theory is based on the fact that our learning experiences are not discrete experiences, but form part of the constantly evolving view that we develop of the world around us. It is a model that reflects the importance of learning from the consequences of our own, and others', actions. This enables us to understand, interact with, and manipulate our environment to our advantage. For example, children initially learn to eat with their fingers and to associate eating with pleasure, not only because of the taste, but also because it removes the discomfort of being hungry. They then learn to use a spoon, so that they can eat food that

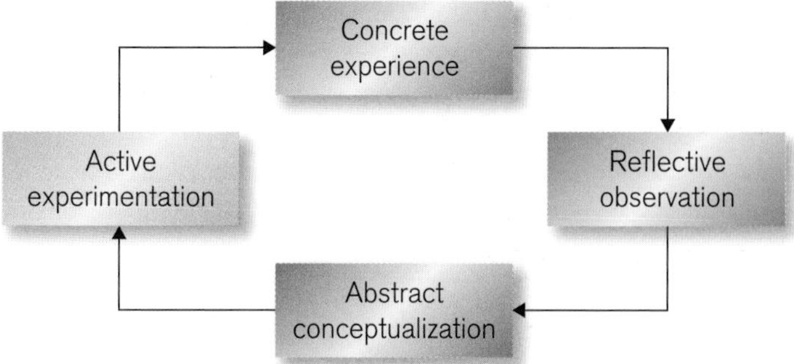


**Figure 10.2** Kolb's experiential learning cycle
**Source**: Kolb, David A, *Experiential Learning: Experience as a Source of Learning*, © 1984, p. 42, Fig 3.1. Adapted with the permission of Pearson Education Inc, Upper Saddle River, NJ.

cannot be eaten easily with their hands and, eventually, they learn to use cutlery to enable them to eat without making a mess. Each of these learning experiences builds on the last and becomes part of an increasingly complex pattern of behaviour, including social skills and rules used at mealtimes. This learning process is cyclical and each part of the learning builds upon the last.

Kolb defined how people learn from their experiences by going through the four following steps.

- Concrete experience

  This is the stage in learning during which the learner carries out an action that has observable consequences. Kolb used the example of a child touching a hot stove. In a work context, it might be easier to imagine selecting a computer icon that you have not previously used and the function of which you do not understand.

- Reflective observation

  This is the stage in learning during which the learner reflects upon their action and the outcome of that action. In Kolb's action, the child realizes that the stove burned his hand and that this hurts. In our work context example, you might reflect upon the fact that the icon in a word processing package created a large indented dot on the page.

- Abstract conceptualization

  This is the stage in learning during which the learner develops a theory that can be applied to similar scenarios. In Kolb's example, the child theorizes and draws the conclusion that touching a hot surface will hurt. In our example about learning to use a computer, the learner may draw the conclusion that the icon can be used to create a bullet point in a piece of text.

- Active experimentation

  This is the stage in learning during which the learner tests the theory out to see if the correct conclusion has been drawn. In Kolb's example, the child may put his hand near the stove to see if it feels hot. In our word processing example, the learner may type text and select the icon again to see if, in fact, this icon does enable the learner to create bullet points within a document.

In turn, this cycle can lead to further experience. For example, Kolb's child might begin to learn about other items that are hot; our computer learner may go on to explore other icons, such as numbered bullet points, and so on. Hence the learning process is ongoing and cyclical.

## Experiential learning at work

What relevance, then, does this have in a workplace? It is important to understand that to 'grow' individual and group capability, and therefore increase or change the supply of labour to the organization, employees need to be engaged in some kind of planned and structured learning. Failure to recognize this will inevitably result in a less qualified and less productive workforce than that which might be achieved using workplace learning. Unplanned and unstructured (informal) learning will almost inevitably take place, but, depending on the nature of the experience, it may not be what is required from a managerial perspective. For example, bad habits and negative attitudes may develop as part of an ongoing socialization process.

We can also help people to learn by helping them through the learning cycle. The job of a driving instructor is to take the learner driver through a series of learning experiences in a safe and structured manner, to ensure that the full set of driving skills and knowledge needed to pass a driving test are learnt; the workplace is no different. By helping to shape not only the actual experiences, but also the reflection, conceptualization, and experimentation stages of learning, managers can facilitate the required learning outcomes and permanent learning.

If the objective is to help an employee to learn about a new computer system, effective learning will require the individual to be given the opportunity to experience every aspect of the system. Reflection should be structured to help the learner to draw conclusions, such as 'this really isn't that difficult' rather than 'I don't like this new system'.

Conceptualization may include helping the learner to draw conclusions such as 'I can use the manual to work out quite a lot about how to write reports, without needing too much assistance', rather than 'this new system is useless'. Ideally, the learner will then feel comfortable experimenting with the new system. For example, the learner might be able to make enquiries and enter more complex data, in the knowledge that they can do so within parameters acceptable to the organization. Although associated with the way in which children learn, 'playing' with the new system—almost seeing it as a toy or puzzle—is a powerful form of experimentation that is equally appropriate to certain kinds of adult learning.



## Learning styles

There are a range of different theories on learning styles. For example Honey and Mumford (2006) proposed a model of 4 learning styles which they referred to as activists, reflectors, theorists and pragmatists, corresponding to the learner's preferred entry point on Kolb's learning cycle.

**For more information about the Honey and Mumford (2006) model of learning styles see the Online Resource Centre extension material 10.5.**

One of the more recent theories of learning is that put forward by Jackson (2005). In this 'Hybrid Model' of learning, 'Sensation Seeking' is described as the basis of learning. Jackson argues that sensation seeking is the core biological drive which leads us to be curious, explore, and learn. Those with a high drive to explore can have dysfunctional learning experiences unless these are regulated by factors such as goal orientation, conscientiousness, deep learning, and emotional intelligence. In the workplace it would therefore be important to recognize that some employees have a higher drive to explore and therefore learn than others, but that in all cases, learning experiences need to be structured to ensure a positive outcome.

**RESEARCH INSIGHT 10.3**

To take your learning further you might want to read this article:

**Jackson, C.J. (2009). 'Using the hybrid model of learning in personality to predict performance in the workplace', 8th IOP Conference, Conference Proceedings, pp. 75–79**

This article contrasts the hybrid model of learning, in which Jackson argues that 'Sensation Seeking'—a biological drive for curiosity and exploration that results in functional or dysfunctional learning outcomes—is more effective than other models of learning to predict workplace behaviour.

The training centre recommended that the groups follow the Kolb learning cycle by doing an activity, receiving feedback, and producing guidelines and action plans as a team for the next exercise. The training therefore consisted mainly of outdoor activities, followed by discussions about what had gone wrong in order to learn from mistakes made and to improve team performance in the next exercise. The exercises throughout the week were of increasing duration and complexity, and trainees were encouraged to develop weaknesses by having a go at roles they wouldn't normally play. Feedback included detailed comments about personal style from the trainers and from other group members. People who were not natural leaders were expected to lead the group; people naturally good at problem solving were expected to let others try out their ideas and be more considerate to team members, and so on.

To make the most of this expensive training, underpinning theory on subjects including management, team working, motivation, and communication was given to trainees as documents and books. These were to be read outside of the structured activity (managers were expected to be capable of studying this in their own time).

### Questions

1. Consider Kolb's experiential learning model: how was reflection interpreted? Was true reflection time given?
2. Which learning styles were not catered for by this training course?
3. Which learning styles would not respond well to this training programme?
4. With reference to the conscious competence model, which steps were missed out?
5. What recommendations would you make to improve the quality of the training provided?

**Insights & Outcomes:** visit the Online Resource Centre at www.oxfordtextbooks.co.uk/orc/banfield_kay2e/ for an insight into the outcomes of this training course

**STUDENT ACTIVITY 10.8**

Consider learning or training situations in which you have been involved recently. Identify an experience that you thought was effective and one that was ineffective. Using the models described above and/or other models of the learning process, explain why the two experiences produced different outcomes. Reflecting on this explanation, produce a set of guidelines that trainers can follow to ensure the effectiveness of any structured learning experience.

## Moving forward—the power of accelerated learning

A consistent theme in this chapter is that looking at, and correcting, deficiencies in how people learn and how they are trained can improve the value and effectiveness of training. We would argue that, through understanding how these two processes can be improved, both employees and managers will benefit. What 'accelerated learning' offers is a set of principles, values, and practices that represent an alternative to conventional approaches to learning, particularly the use of course-based training, which have the potential of generating enjoyable and productive learning experiences. Proponents of accelerated learning reject learning based on mechanization, standardization, external control, 'one size fits all', behaviouristic conditioning, and an emphasis on instruction and passive listening, suggesting instead a very different, but more effective, approach (Meier, 2000).

Meier compares what he calls 'traditional learning' with 'accelerated learning', using the dimensions shown in Table 10.2.

Meier argues that any approach to, or philosophy of, learning is underpinned by a set of assumptions about what people need in order to optimize their learning. As far as accelerated learning is concerned, these assumptions are as follows.

Table 10.2 A comparison of traditional and accelerated learning

| Traditional learning | Accelerated learning |
|---|---|
| Rigid | Flexible |
| Sombre and serious | Enjoyable |
| Single-pathed | Multi-pathed |
| Competitive | Collaborative |
| Behaviouristic | Humanistic |
| Verbal | Multi-sensory |
| Controlling | Nurturing |
| Cognitive | Cognitive, emotional and physical |
| Means-centred | Results-based |

- A positive learning environment

  People learn best when their social, physical, and emotional environments are positive, supportive, and stimulating.

Signpost to Chapter 1: The Management of Human Resources, for insights into the importance of a learning environment to employees



- Total learner involvement

  Active involvement and responsibility are key to effective and sustained learning. Meier points out that learning is not a spectator sport, but participatory.

- Collaboration among learners

  People generally learn best in an environment characterized by working together with others. Learning can, and often does, happen through what a person does on his or her own, but effective and deeper learning is often associated with groups and teams engaging in a shared learning experience.

- Variety that appeals to all learning preferences and styles

  Learning becomes 'accelerated' and more effective when the full range of people's senses and energies are engaged and used in learning (see Figure 10.4).

- Contextual learning

  Again, the importance of context is emphasized. Learning 'out of context' and in isolation from the working environment is harder to absorb, and can easily be lost. Meier believes that:

  > **the best learning comes from doing the work itself in a continual process of 'real world' immersion, feedback, reflection, evaluation and re-immersion.**

Based on the characteristics and assumptions of accelerated learning, Meier offers what he describes as a 'universalistic' model of learning (2000, p. 53). This features four phases, or components, all of which must be present in one form or another, or, according to Meier, no real learning occurs. The four phases or components are:

- *preparation*—the arousal of interest;
- *presentation*—the initial encounter and involvement with new areas of knowledge or skill;
- *practice*—the integration and embedding of the new knowledge or skill;
- *performance*—applying the knowledge or skill to the job.

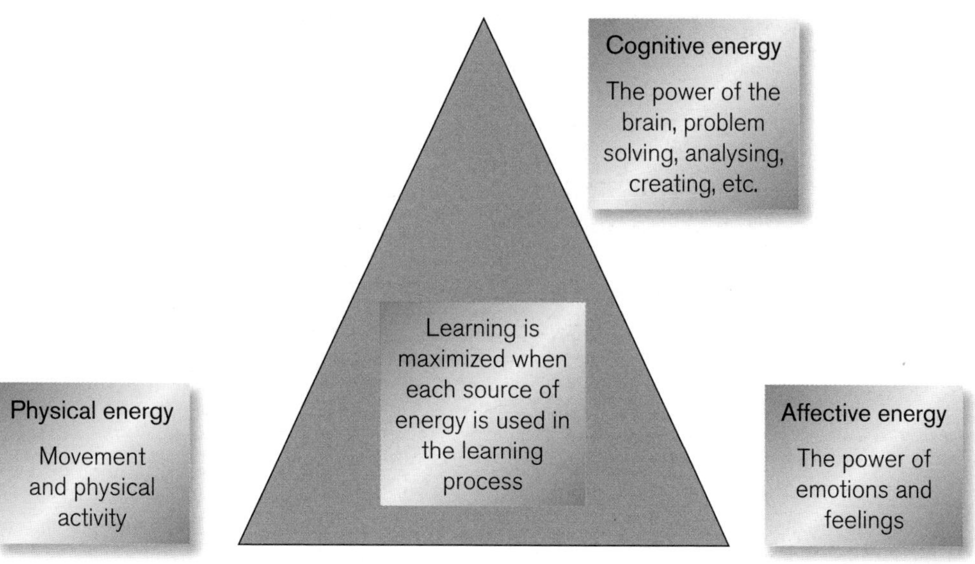


**Figure 10.4** The energy triangle



Finally, and to continue the thinking behind the ideas associated with accelerated learning, we want to offer an interesting and challenging hypothesis: that enjoyment and learning outcomes are positively correlated to the amount and variety of energy consumed in the learning experience. Consider, as an example, being involved in business simulation or skills development exercises, as opposed to sitting in a lecture theatre listening to a PowerPoint presentation. Which learning experience consumes most energy and which is likely to be the most productive type of learning? The concept of the 'energy triangle' presented in Figure 10.4 describes the three types of energy that need to be utilized in learning and what they involve.

**STUDENT ACTIVITY 10.9 Testing the hypothesis**

1. Think of two learning situations, one of which was enjoyable and productive, and one that wasn't. Rate both on a scale of 1–10, with 10 the most enjoyable and productive.
2. On a scale of 1–10, rate each of the two experiences in relation to the three types of energy generated. Add the three values together.
3. Compare the ratings from task 1 to the aggregate energy score in task 2 and establish whether the hypothesis has validity.

# Summary

- Human beings learn throughout their lives and in order to be effective, and to continue to make a positive contribution to an employing organization, employees need to be active learners. Equally to get the best from their employees organization's should provide an environment that ensures that the learning and development of their employees is structured to help them to achieve their maximum potential.
- Training is one method of bringing about learning among employees and whilst it forms an important part of learning and development, it is not always the case that learning from training is effectively transferred to a change in behaviour to enhance the performance of individuals and teams. Effective evaluation of training and development is essential to show a positive return on investment for an organization and to therefore demonstrate that the activity is valuable and worthwhile.

- Emphasis is moving away from seeing training in isolation as the solution for developing employees towards creating a learning environment at work. Development is more effective if it is well designed taking employee requirements, support, and the working environment into consideration, and organizations are placing increased emphasis on coaching and in-house development programmes to enhance the skills of their workforce.
- E-learning and online solutions are growing in importance and are becoming more sophisticated to ensure effective, supported learning with a greater flexibility to allow learners to work at their own pace at a time that suits their needs.
- There are many useful models such as Kolb's learning cycle (1984) and Honey and Mumford's learning styles (2006) that can help learning providers to better understand what makes learning effective, although these can be regarded as over simplified and therefore also subject to criticism.
- Accelerated learning is about enhancing the effectiveness and uptake of learning by ensuring all the factors are conducive to effective learning. Learning is the key to change, improved performance, and personal growth. The central question is: 'How can we achieve this in the most effective and efficient ways possible?'

**Visit the Online Resource Centre that accompanies this book for self-test questions, weblinks, and more information on the topics covered in this chapter.**
**www.oxfordtextbooks.co.uk/orc/banfield_kay2e/**

## REVIEW QUESTIONS

1. What does 'from training to learning' mean and why has this shift in emphasis come about?
2. What changes need to be made in the assumptions upon which current approaches to training are based?
3. What does an employee-centred approach to learning involve and what are its implications for trainers?
4. What are the respective roles of the HR professional and the line manager in generating learning at work?
5. Why is the motivational state of learners important to the outcome of learning interventions?
6. How can HR demonstrate the economic and business case for learning and development activities?

***See Online Resource Centre for answers.***

## CASE STUDY

### The provision of online training by Learndirect

Learndirect is a provider of online training and is operated by UFI Ltd in England, Wales, and Northern Ireland. As the UK's leading provider of online adult learning, since 2000 it has helped over 2.5 million people to gain skills that they, their employer, or the economy needs to support them into further training or employment. Many Learndirect courses are provided on a funded basis through 'Train to Gain', a government funding initiative to enhance skills. Learndirect's research shows that in 2010, 41 per cent of people were feeling insecure about their jobs. With £14.5 million of Train to Gain-funded programmes delivered in 2008/2009, and over 14000 e-courses sold during the year, Learndirect is set to play a key role in helping people gain the skills they need as the UK emerges from the economic downturn. (See www.ufi.com for more information about what goes on behind the scenes and www.learndirect.co.uk for more information about the training it provides.) Learndirect was originally created in response to the then-Chancellor Gordon Brown's vision for a 'University for Industry' to improve the skills of the British workforce. Its remit was to use technology to transform the delivery of learning and skills throughout England, Wales, and Northern Ireland. Its selling point is that students can study anytime, anywhere.

The majority of learners are below the UK's NVQ level 2 or have a 'skills for life need' such as basic literacy or IT skills, and hence the learning has to be accessible for learners with a previously low level of academic achievement. There are learning support centres throughout the UK to support people with their training. Learndirect's websites show a number of success stories such as people learning new skills to enhance their careers and go on to university, with people gaining jobs that they would otherwise have been unable to acquire. It is undoubtedly a very successful organization that has helped a broad number of people to gain new skills.

A similar service is provided in Scotland by Skills Development Scotland which, in contrast to UFI Ltd, is a public body (see www.skillsdevelopmentscotland.co.uk) and has a slightly different remit in terms of the scope over which learning support is provided. The Learndirect Scotland website (www.learndirectscotland.com) gives details of the types of learning experiences that are available in Scotland and, in common with the rest of the UK, there are many case studies describing how people have moved on to successful employment and further education as a result of the support provided by Learndirect Scotland.

Online training will continue to play a very important role in skills development in years to come. With more and more homes having computers and internet access, and initiatives such as home access designed to provide computers for low income households (see www.homeaccess.org.uk), the availability of accessible training via online providers will continue to be an important issue. However, it is also important to understand how this technology will be funded. If public funding is to continue then economic justification will be required, given the pressures on public finances following the downturn.

Sources: www.ufi.com, www.learndirect.co.uk, www.learndirect.scotland.com.
(see Royle, K. et al. (2008) 'Lessons and challenges for the system from the evaluation of Learndirect pedagogy and materials: A policy summary', *CeDAR*, University of Wolverhampton. www.wlv.ac.uk/PDF/sed-res-learndirect-fullreport.pdf)





**Questions**

1. To what extent has Learndirect been successful in contributing to developing skills that are valuable to the economy?
2. There can be no long-term guarantee about the level of public funding available for activities delivered by Learndirect and its Scottish counterpart. What evidence can you see from their websites of activity that might offset the risks of changes to funding in future?
3. What key differences do you notice between the Learndirect and Learndirect Scotland websites in terms of the accessibility of their websites and the services that are offered by the different organizations to their clients? To what extent do you feel that this is influenced by the different managing organizations for both organizations?
4. What arguments can Learndirect and Learndirect Scotland put to the government to encourage it to continue to invest in funded training of the type they provide?

## FURTHER READING

Baron, L. and Morin, L. (2010) 'The impact of executive coaching on self-efficacy related to management soft skills', *Leadership and Organization Development Journal*, **31**:1, pp. 18–38.

Beard, C. and Wilson, J.P. (2002) *The Power of Experiential Learning*, Kogan Page.

Bramley, P. (1996) *Evaluating Training*, CIPD.

Corely, A. and Eades, E. (2004) 'Becoming critically reflective practitioners: academics' and students' reflections on the issues involved', *HRD International*, **7**:1, pp. 137–44.

Cotton, J. (1995) *The Theory of Learning*, Kogan Page.

Le Deist, F.D. and Winterton, J. (2005) 'What is competence?', *HRD International*, **8**:1, pp. 27–46.

Macpherson, A., Elliot, M., Harris, I and Homan, G. (2004) 'E-learning: Reflections and evaluation of corporate programmes', *HRD International*, **7**:3, pp. 295–313.

Quinones, M.A. and Ehrenstein, A. (1997) *Training for a Rapidly Changing Workforce*, American Psychological Association.

Slotte, V., Tynjälä, P. and Hytönen, T. (2004) 'How do practitioners describe learning at work?', *HRD International*, **7**:4, pp. 481–99.

## REFERENCES

Alcock, M. (2005) 'Time for e-learning to be handed back to the trainers?', www.trainingreference.co.uk.

Boydell, T. (1970) *A Guide to Job Analysis*, BACIE

Boydell, T. (2003) 'Difference between training and learning', www.trainingzone.co.uk.

Boydell, T. and Leary, M. (1996) *Identifying Training Needs*, CIPD.

Chartered Institute of Personnel and Development (2005) *E-Learning Survey Results Report*, www.cipd.co.uk.

Chartered Institute of Personnel and Development (2006) 'Human capital', www.cipd.co.uk.

Chartered Institute of Personnel and Development (2007a) 'E-learning: Progress and prospects', www.cipd.co.uk.

Chartered Institute of Personnel and Development (2007b) 'Training and development survey report', www.cipd.co.uk.

Chartered Institute of Personnel and Development (2008) 'Reflections on the 2008 learning and development survey: Latest trends in learning training and development survey report', www.cipd.co.uk.

Clark, N. (2005) 'Workplace learning environment and its relationship with learning outcomes in healthcare organizations', *HRD International*, **8**:2, pp. 185–205.

Davis, J.R. and Davis, A.B. (1998) *Effective Training Strategies*, Berrett-Koehler.

Donelly (1987) 'The Training Model: Time for a Change?' *Industrial and Commercial Training*, **93**:3, pp. 3–6.

Easterby-Smith, M. (1994), *Evaluating Management Development, Training and Education*, Gower.

Gladstone, B. (2000) *From Know-How to Knowledge*, Spiro Press.

Glasser, W. (1986) *Choice Theory in the Classroom*, HarperCollins Publishers Inc.

Hirsh, W. and Tamkin, P. (2005a) 'Piece by piece', *People Management*, 8 December, pp. 32–4.

Hirsh, W. and Tamkin, P. (2005b) *Planning Training for Your Business*, IES Report 422.

Honey, P. and Mumford, A. (2006) *The Learning Styles Questionnaire*, 80-item version, Peter Honey Publications.

Hope, K. (2006) 'Class act', *People Management*, 15 September, p. 16.

IRS (1998) 'Using human resources to achieve strategic objectives: Learning strategies review', *IRS Management Review*, Issue 8.

Jackson, C.J. (2005). *An Applied Neuropsychological Model of Functional And Dysfunctional Learning: Applications for Business, Education, Training and Clinical Psychology*, Cymeon.

Jackson, C.J. (2009). 'Using the hybrid model of learning in personality to predict performance in the workplace', 8th IOP Conference, Conference Proceedings, pp. 75–79.

Kearns, P. (2005) *Evaluating the ROI from Learning*, CIPD.

Kenney, J. and Reid, M. (1986) *Training Interventions*, CIPD.

Kirkpatrick, D.L. (1998) *Evaluating Training Programs*, 2nd ed., Berrett-Koehler.

Kolb, D.A. (1984) *Experiential Learning: Experience as a Source of Learning*, Pearson Education.

Lave, J. and Wenger, E. (1991) *Situated Learning: Legitimate Peripheral Participation*, Cambridge University Press.

Little, S., Quintas, P., and Ray, T. (2002) *Managing Knowledge*, Sage.

McGhee, W. and Thayer, P. (1961) *Training in Business and Industry*, John Wiley & Sons.

Megginson, D., Banfield, P. and Joy-Matthews, J. (1993) *Human Resource Development*, Kogan Page.

Meier, D. (2000) *The Accelerated Learning Handbook*, McGraw-Hill.

Pfeffer, J. (1998) *Hidden Equation*, HBS Press.

Rothwell, W.J. (1996) *Beyond Training and Development: State-of-the-Art Strategies for Enhancing Human Performance*, AMACOM/American Management Association.

Rothwell, W.J. (2004) *Beyond Training and Development: The Groundbreaking Classic on Human Performance Enhancement*, AMACOM/American Management Association.

Royle, K. et al. (2008) 'Lessons and challenges for the system from the evaluation of Learndirect pedagogy and materials: A policy summary', *CeDAR*, University of Wolverhampton www.wlv.ac.uk/PDF/sed-res-learndirect-fullreport.pdf

Scott, A. (2005) 'Quality of work-based training improves', *PM online*, 7 December, available online to CIPD members at www.peoplemanagement.co.uk.

Sloman, M. (2001) *The e-Learning Revolution*, CIPD.

Sloman, M. (2004) 'Learner drivers', *People Management*, 2 September, p. 36.

Sloman, M. and Webster, L. (2005) 'Training to learning', *Training and Development*, **59**:9, pp. 58–63.

Smethurst, S. (2006a) 'Course of treatment', *People Management*, 9 March, pp. 34–6.

Smethurst, S. (2006b) 'Staying power', *People Management*, 6 April, p. 34.

Stern, E. and Sommerlad, E. (1999) *Workplace Learning, Culture and Performance: Issues in People Management*, CIPD.

Taylor, H. (1991) 'The systematic training model: Corn circles in search of a spaceship?', *Management Education and Development* **22**:4 pp. 258–78.

Truss, C., Gratton, L., Hope, V., McGovern, P. and Stiles, P. (1997) 'Soft and hard models of human resource management: A reappraisal', *Journal of Management Studies*, **34**:1, pp. 53–73.

Ulrich, D. (1998) 'A new mandate for human resources', *Harvard Business Review*, **76**:1, pp. 125–34.

Walton, J. (1999) *Strategic Human Resource Development*, Pearson Education.

Warren, C. (2006) 'University challenge', *People Management*, 9 March, pp. 30–3.

Zuboff, S. (1998) *In the Age of the Smart Machine*, Basic Books.

# 11 Managing Performance

## Key Terms

**Performance** Can be interpreted as expressing the relationship between a person's capabilities and what the person actually achieves, usually related to a person's job.

**Performance management** 'A broad term that has come to stand for the set of practices through which work is defined and reviewed, capabilities are developed, and rewards are distributed . . .' (Morhman and Morhman, 1995). 'A strategic and integrated approach to delivering sustained success to organizations by improving the performance of the people who work in them and by developing the capabilities of team and individual contributions . . .' (Armstrong and Baron, 1998).

**Performance appraisal** A process for reviewing the past performance of an employee, and agreeing future objectives and development activities. It can be seen as '*the process of evaluating and judging the way in which someone is functioning* . . .' (Coens and Jenkins, 2000).

## Learning Objectives

As a result of reading this chapter and using the Online Resource Centre, you should be able to:

- understand what managing performance involves and how performance can be conceptualized;
- understand and appreciate the different approaches to modelling performance;
- recognize the importance of measurement in performance management, and appreciate the arguments for and against the use of targets and objectives;
- debate constructively the arguments for and against the use of the appraisal process in managing performance;
- critically evaluate different performance enhancement strategies.

# Introduction

One of the difficulties in trying to make sense of what performance management 'is' and what it might mean for managers and employees, as Armstrong and Baron (1998) state, is that:

> **performance management is a fairly imprecise term, and performance management processes manifest themselves in many different forms. There is no one right way of managing performance.**
> (p. 7)

What can be said with some certainty is that performance management is not synonymous with the appraisal process, which is one technique (or instrument) used by many organizations to 'manage' performance. Unfortunately, appraisal techniques often constitute the only method of managing performance. A much more sophisticated and useful conceptualization is provided by Lockett (1992), who emphasizes the need to see performance management in an ecological way, within which the different elements of a living system interact and influence each other, rather than as a series of unrelated functions.

In Chapter 1, we identified employee utilization as one of the fundament objectives of management; in contemporary organizations, performance management is that aspect of management that is associated with delivering this objective. Simply having a performance management system in place does not, however, guarantee higher levels of performance than would otherwise have existed without the 'benefit' of the system features. As with many other aspects of HR, formal and material rationality are not necessarily synonymous.

The search for higher levels of individual and team performance is important to all organizations, and ways must be found to ensure that performance levels are sustained and enhanced. Despite improvements in equipment, materials, and processes, organizational performance is still linked to the quality of people that an organization employs and what they do at work. You can have the best equipment and systems in your sector, and the most up-to-date processes, but if you don't have the right number and quality of people doing what is needed, the organization will not function properly. 'Managing performance' fundamentally means that employees know what is expected of them and act in ways that contribute to the best interests of the organization, but what this means and how it is delivered for each individual organization will inevitably differ, because each faces a unique set of circumstances and challenges. There are no universal solutions to performance management problems and each organization must, through a process of diagnosis, action, evaluation, and learning, develop its own strategy and practices.

According to Mabey et al. (1998), performance management refers to a set of techniques and procedures that serve to:

- provide information on the contribution of human resources to the strategic objectives of the organization;
- form a framework of techniques to secure the maximum output for any given level of inputs;
- provide a means of inspecting how well individual performance-enhancing processes actually deliver performance in relation to targets and objectives.

They define performance management as:

> **A framework in which performance by individuals can be directed, monitored, motivated and refined.**
> (Mabey et al., 1998)

There are, then, a number of common principles that are useful in understanding what needs to be done.

# Basic Requirements of Managing Performance

- Everyone should know what to, and what not to do

  Performance management is not something that will be successful if it is 'done' once a year: it is more of a process than an event. These ongoing processes need to be connected not only to each other, but also to every aspect of the organization's activities. (This is a practical example of the concepts of vertical and horizontal integration discussed in Chapter 3.) Moreover, it is as important to establish what *not* to do as what *is* to be done: doing 'more' is not particularly helpful or sensible if this involves doing more of the wrong thing! Simply asking the individual to undertake more activities, without first establishing if there are any that are no longer required or which should be replaced with a more efficient activity, can be both detrimental to the organization and demotivating to employees, who may struggle with a seemingly ever-increasing workload.

- Everyone contributes

  It is important for employees, as well as managers, to contribute to the effective management of performance. Line managers do not know everything, nor should they be seen as the only stakeholder capable of contributing to improving performance. The position adopted here is that employees are fundamentally responsible for their own performance, in the same way that they are responsible for their own learning and development, and excluding them from any initiatives to improve performance makes no sense and will almost certainly result in failure. Even if such initiatives involve only annual objective setting, employee involvement in the process is likely to contribute to higher individual motivation, legitimation of the process, and increased commitment. Contemporary thinking about improving employee performance has moved away from simply communicating what needs to be done, towards achieving the employee's active support, and engagement in the process.

- Everyone develops the necessary skills

  For an organization to maximize its performance, every employee should be encouraged to grow by acquiring new skills and competences that will enhance their effectiveness. Development need not be restricted to HR-organized training courses, but can include a range of formal and informal learning experiences, including secondments, coaching, and project work.

Signpost to Chapter 10: Learning and Development, for further information on training and development

- Managers must have the necessary skills

  Ask a group of managers if they are effective in managing the performance of their teams and most, if not all, will probably say that they are. But if you were to ask those that they manage the same question, a different picture might emerge. The existence of this 'perception gap' suggests that there are important issues around what is known by managers, and how this is interpreted and valued. For example, employees might feel that they are working hard and trying to do their best, but, for differing reasons, some of which will be to do with the quality of interpersonal relationships, this endeavour is not recognized. What is critical to the effective management of performance is the contribution of line managers to the engagement of their staff in the delivery of performance. To be effective in this role, managers need a range of technical and process skills, without which their ability to influence employee performance will inevitably be compromised. It might be argued, therefore, that employee performance is as much a function of the quality of managers as it is of the skills and competences of employees.

- Managers measure and monitor

  We have already emphasized that effective performance management cannot be 'done' once a year. The process is ongoing and, to be effective, managers need to measure performance on an ongoing basis, to ensure that it remains on track and that employees continuously develop their skills. Distinguishing performance management as a process, rather than an event, helps to identify the nature of the management engagement process and avoids situations developing in which it is 'the time' to do something, such as 'the time' to carry out annual staff appraisals.

## The Performance Management Cycle

Figure 11.1 presents the key activities and areas of responsibility associated with an integrated and holistic performance management system. The fundamental importance given to evaluating the effectiveness of the individual and the cumulative effects of these activities is consistent with Ulrich's emphasis on the outcomes of HR interventions rather than on activities per se (Ulrich, 1998).

Performance management should not be seen as a once-a-year task, but as an ongoing process or cycle. The model in Figure 11.1 shows that the first step in this cycle is for the organization to define its long-term strategy and strategic intentions. The objectives of the organization define the goals and targets over a shorter period and will need to be regularly assessed to establish their alignment with the strategy. For example, these might express the levels of service to be provided, or the level of sales or profitability, or the activities planned in the near future.

In order to be able to measure success at regular intervals, the key measures, or metrics, need to be established. Unless an organization defines what is important and how this will be measured, it will be difficult to assign the necessary resource to ensure that the objectives are, as far as possible, achieved. Once this is agreed, it is easier to decide which team will be responsible for each element that goes towards the overall objectives. The organizational objectives can then be translated into departmental and team goals, and then into individual goals and objectives. The individual objectives are often agreed and finalized during an appraisal interview, which will be explored in greater detail later in the chapter.

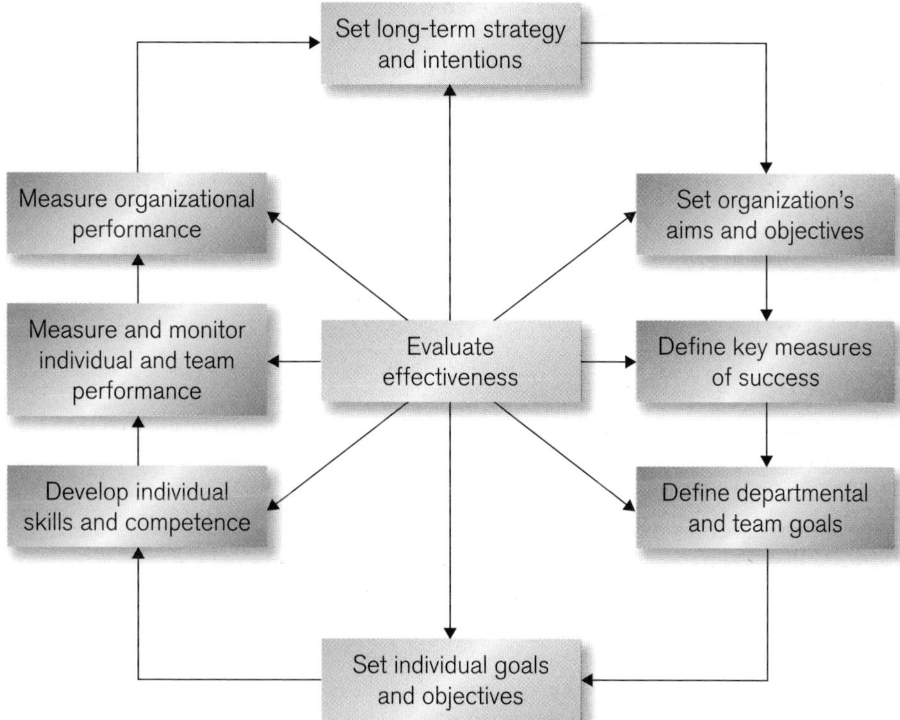


**Figure 11.1** Activities associated with performance management

Signpost to Chapter 9: HR Planning and Measurement, for further information on metrics and measurement

The next step in the process is to develop the skills and abilities of the individuals and teams, to ensure that they are able to maximize their efforts in achieving their objectives. The performance of individuals and teams is then measured, and the results can be pooled to establish a regular measure of the organization's performance. Increasingly, key performance outcomes are a function of teams rather than of individuals, although the relative importance of one or the other depends on the nature of the work being undertaken and the social organization of work.

# Making Sense of Performance

'Performance' is a term used frequently in HR, but it has no precise or agreed meaning: it can mean different things to different stakeholders and this can create problems in 'what' is managed. Just let your mind wander and think of what you associate the word 'performance' with. You may think of actors who 'perform' on the stage or cinema set, who entertain an audience. Those who have delivered an outstanding performance can then be nominated for awards, with those considered to have performed better than any of the other nominated persons receiving the highest award—perhaps an Oscar. You may also associate performance with sport and athletes, who constantly strive to reduce the time they take to run a set distance, increase the weights they can lift, or the height they can jump. Such initial associations confirm that 'performance' is not something that is restricted to the world of employment and work, and there may be much that we can learn from these other contexts in which improved performance is an important objective.



But performance is also of vital importance to the way in which organizations are managed and to what people do at work. How well businesses perform often determines their status, financial value and survivability, and the performance of each employee and how well they work together as teams is an enduring managerial concern.

Whatever the industry, the level at which people function or the jobs being performed, managers are faced with four fundamental questions:

- What are the key determinants of organizational performance?
- How well are my staff currently performing in their jobs?
- How can their performance be improved?
- What are the causes of underperformance?

## Employ only talented people?

Pfeffer and O'Reilly's book, *Hidden Value* (2000), provides a useful starting point to the analysis of organizational performance. They begin by asking the question:

**What's the most important factor for success in today's knowledge-based economy?**

In other words, what will make some organizations more successful, and therefore more likely to survive and prosper, than others? Pfeffer and O'Reilly quote from the McKinsey report, 'The War for Talent' (McKinsey Co, 2000), to present the 'conventional' answer to these questions—that superior organizational performance will come from the superior performance of talented people. The implication of this view is, therefore, that the performance 'problem' is solved by employing only the most talented people, who, it is assumed, will naturally perform to their capability and deliver the high levels of performance that organizations require. If it were only that simple!

One important drawback to adopting this performance management strategy is that there are a finite number of exceptionally talented people around and, if all organizations are trying to employ them, the following might happen:

- because demand will exceed supply, the cost of employing such talent will increase to the point at which their productivity will fall;
- because they can command high prices, these people are much more likely to change employers more frequently than other employees, which means that what they can give to an organization is transitory;
- undue emphasis on potentially high performers may well result in 'ordinary' performers becoming disillusioned, and less committed to their work and organization, which can result in reduced performance;
- there is no guarantee that even the most talented staff will always perform to their potential—capability has to be engaged and harnessed, and this cannot be taken for granted.

There is, of course, persuasive anecdotal evidence that those with exceptional talent are often crucial to organizations becoming, and remaining, successful and the importance of recruiting the best possible employees or of refusing to employ those that don't meet a minimum specification is undeniable. So, too, is the need to retain talented staff, so that their capability and potential has a chance of being realized.

But the real challenge facing organizations in understanding the 'secret' of high performance, according to Pfeffer and O'Reilly (2000), is that of creating cultures and systems in which talented staff can actually use their talents. They go beyond this, however, and emphasize that the key to long-term organizational success is to ensure that management practices are in place that ensure extraordinary results from almost everybody (Pfeffer and O'Reilly, 2000, p. 2). Their emphasis on the environment in which people work and perform, which can liberate the potential of all employees, is an important step forward in understanding the limitations of concentrating a performance management strategy on individuals without having any regard for the quality and characteristics of the social and psychological environment in which they work.



Having made the point that organizational success comes from driving the performance of all employees, rather than simply recruiting highly talented people, the McKinsey report offers insights into what companies should do to become successful, suggesting that recruiting high performers is only part of a set of requirements that drive performance of both people and the organization.

**STUDENT ACTIVITY 11.1**

**Working either individually or in groups, and using the links on the Online Resource Centre to access the McKinsey report (2000), undertake the following tasks.**

1. **Summarize the seven key points made in the report.**
2. **Taking each one in turn, consider the implications for HR of trying to implement each requirement.**
3. **Consider the risks and benefits associated with each requirement.**
4. **Consider what is left out or underemphasized in the report.**

Despite the arguably over-blown rhetoric about the importance of talented employees and its impact on performance above the level of the individual worker, talent management continues to enjoy considerable popularity amongst HR professionals and academics and is likely to remain at least part of an organization's overall strategy for managing performance (McCartney and Garrow, 2006; Capelli, 2008).

We will be returning to the ideas and contributions of O'Reilly and Pfeffer (2000) and others later, particularly in the search for evidence that links managerial strategies and practices to employee performance. Before we do that, however, we need to continue to search for clarity over the meaning of the term 'performance' and how this relates to similar terms.

## The search for conceptual clarity—what does 'performance' actually mean?

One of the difficulties that students and managers face is the confusion that can exist when we talk about performance and how it can be managed. The following concepts are sometimes used interchangeably and are related, but each has its own distinctive meaning and significance.

- Productivity

  This is a concept that links the inputs to a production process to its outputs, expressed in quantitative or financial terms. Applied to the individual, it can be thought of as being close to performance, but is much more precise and is subject to quantitative measurement. In engineering and manufacturing contexts, in which it is easier to measure labour inputs and outputs, productivity has traditionally been the preferred concept that managers use and measure.

For further discussions about this important aspect of performance see the Online Resource Centre extension material 11.1.

- Effectiveness

  This can be understood as the relationship between targets or objectives set and what is actually achieved. If the targets or objectives are not particularly stretching or are impossible to meet, however, whether an employee is considered effective or not is more a function of the target or objective-setting process than of anything that the employee might do.



- Effort

  This is a difficult concept that is often linked to the intensity of work, that is, how hard an employee works, but not necessarily linked to outcomes. People who have a strong work ethic are, however, likely to put a great deal more effort into their work compared to those who are less strongly motivated, and are also likely to be committed and high-performing employees.

- The effort bargain

  This is a powerful concept that captures the often imprecise relationship between what employees 'do' at work and the rewards that they receive.

- Discretionary effort

  This term captures the belief that employees only give a part of what they are capable of and that moving to higher levels of performance, effort, or contribution is at their discretion, rather than subject to management control.

- Contribution

  This is a broader concept than performance. Contribution is seen as what employees can do in addition to doing their jobs. This is particularly important if jobs actually limit what people are allowed to do, with job descriptions representing barriers to what people are allowed to do.

Fundamentally, performance is about achievement, but reflecting the definition offered at the beginning of the chapter, it combines achievement with capability—what people are capable of achieving. Two important consequences follow from this definition.

- Not all employees are capable of the same levels of performance. All organizations contain people who have different existing capabilities and differences in potential. Employees, in other words, are different in terms of their innate capabilities and in terms of what they want to, and can, achieve. Using a sporting analogy, however hard most footballers try, the majority will never perform at the level of David Beckham or Wayne Rooney, or others who are exceptionally talented and driven. While effort is important, it is not the same as inherent or acquired talent or capability. 'Trying hard', if this effort is focused and directed to desired outcomes, is clearly an important element in performance, but effort alone is rarely sufficient to explain high-performing employees. In observing changes in management thinking and philosophy, driven by the ideas of such writers as Charles Handy and Tom Peters, John Lockett (1992) argues that one key feature of this shift in thinking is the emphasis from effort towards performance:

> **There is an urgent need for people at work to achieve results—results which meet the company's performance requirements. Scoring 'A' for effort is no longer relevant, unless that effort is harnessed towards those requirements.**

- Simply achieving set objectives is not necessarily an indication of high performance if the targets or objectives set are too low and do not realistically stretch an individual or reflect his or her capability. This means that, while one individual might achieve more than another, they might actually be seen as a lower performer because, while one achieved all that they were capable of, the other did not. Using objectives to manage performance, while an attractive proposition, can therefore be difficult and fraught with dangers, particularly if objectives change and if they are expressed in qualitative, rather than quantitative, ways.

If performance can be conceptualized as the relationship between what people are capable of achieving and what is actually achieved, how does this differ from 'effectiveness'? Quite simply, someone who is 'effective' is someone who meets expectations or achieves the objectives set for them. Critical to understanding the significance of this distinction is the recognition that, while both performance and effectiveness are related to achieving standards and meeting expectations, an employee can be effective and not a high performer because the standards and expectations against which their performance is being measured were pitched at too low a level. The key point here is that maximum performance is achieved when employees use their capabilities to the fullest, drawing on all of their physical, intellectual, or emotional energies, and when they are set targets and objectives that stretch the individual (or team) to the highest sustainable level of performance.

**STUDENT ACTIVITY 11.2 Performance and productivity in the NHS**

A recent newspaper article with the title 'Billions spent on extra NHS wages but productivity falls', raised a number of challenging questions about the way in which increased inputs into the service, in the form of extra funding over several years, had led to improved performance in particular areas, for example, reduced waiting times, speedier treatment, and improvements in meeting many of the service's key performance indicators, but measures of productivity had fallen by an estimated 14 per cent since 2000. The article, based on a report, 'Management of NHS Hospital Productivity', commissioned by the National Audit Office (2010), found that despite significant real growth in the resources going into the NHS, the evidence shows that productivity in the same period had gone down, particularly in hospitals.

This exercise is best done as a group investigation and seminar presentation based on the above report. The tasks are to:

- Read the ORC extension material 11.1 about productivity.
- Read the National Audit Office report and summarize the key findings.
- Identify how the additional resource inputs had been used and whether they were being used to drive productivity improvements.
- Address the issue of how hospital outputs are measured and whether the methodology is sound or could be improved.
- Present your recommendations for reversing the decline in hospital productivity and consider the HR implications of your recommendations.

## Motivation and Performance

The subject of motivation properly belongs to the discipline of psychology and the study of human behaviour, but it has long been used in HR to try to generate insights into the behaviour of people at work and the factors and conditions that impact on their performance. It is not the intention here to provide a systematic account of motivational theories, nor of the extensive range of research outputs that have been produced on this subject (Latham, 2007; Herzberg, 2008; Porter, 2003).

However, it is worth noting the growing interest in what is called Positive Psychology (Peterson, 2006; Compton, 2005) which represents an interest in and emphasis on positive aspects of human behaviour and using the power of positive emotions to focus attention on what people can do well and what they find rewarding and self-fulfilling. Positive Psychology is associated with the Humanist tradition in psychology, linked with such writers as Maslow, McGregor, Herzberg, and Gerry Harvey the author of the *Abilene Paradox* which was referred to earlier in the book to explain why people behaved in ways that were inconsistent with their personal beliefs and preferences.

One of the common themes of this group of writers is the importance of understanding motivation as an inner force, often associated with sets of enduring needs or drives that shape and direct behaviour in the workplace, where either the failure or success in achieving desired needs has further consequences for employee behaviour. The implicit assumption that connects motivation to performance is that the more managers know about the dynamics of motivation the more they can acquire insights into what employees value from their work which in turn allows them to develop mechanisms and provide opportunities that allow employees to achieve their needs and at the same time increase their performance.

The simplicity of this association is also its main weakness. The search for a universalistic answer to the question 'how do you motivate workers' has produced numerous answers. And that is the point; there are many different answers to the question, all of which have the potential to address specific performance problems and situations, but none relate to all. What complicates this relationship even further, is that the question itself is both problematical and potentially misleading. Asking 'how do we motivate workers' implies that they are relative passive players in a relationship that is largely controlled by others. This is sometimes described as *extrinsic motivation*, where factors and decisions 'outside' the individual represent the main context for understanding and influencing employee behaviour. But if we ask the question in a different way, for example, 'how does the worker motivate himself/herself', then the focus of interest and understanding moves to within people and the challenge then is one of self motivation. An internal focus is often associated with the concept of *intrinsic motivation*, where forces and processes with the individual interact with the external environment and specific external influences such as reward systems, performance standards, and managerial expectations (Thomas, 2009).

One of the most stimulating and original contributions on employee motivation and performance produced in the past five years is that from Amabile and Kramer (2007). Whilst accepting the importance of talented people and the use of external influences their research findings lead them to attach primary importance to peoples' perceptions, motivational for work and emotional states which are not only in a state of dynamic equilibrium within the individual but are also influenced by the environment the person is working in. They argue:

> **If your organisation demands knowledge work from its people, then you undoubtedly appreciate the importance of sheer brainpower. You probably recruit high-intellect people and ensure they have access to good information. You probably also respect the power of incentives and use formal compensation systems to channel that intellectual energy down one path or another. But you might be overlooking another crucial driver of a knowledge worker's performance—that person's inner work life.**
> (Amabile and Kramer, 2007, p. 72)

For them, perception involves making sense of their environment and giving it meaning and significance; emotions represent their reactions to these external events and activities and determine 'how they feel', whilst the motivation for work determines how they will perform their duties, when, to what standard, and indeed whether to do it at all. Amabile and Kramer claim that:

> **Every worker's performance is affected by the constant interplay of perceptions, emotions, and motivations triggered by workday events, including managerial action—yet inner work life remains mostly invisible to management.**

It may be that in searching for ways to motivate people to improve their performance managers have been over-emphasizing, as well as over-stating, their ability to shape the external environment and failing to recognize that behaviour is fundamentally determined by what goes on within people.

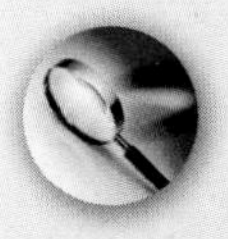

**RESEARCH INSIGHT 11.1 The inner self**

Read the article by Amabile and Kramer (and summarize the key points they make.

**Amabile, T.M. and Kramer, S.J. (2007) 'Inner work life', Harvard Business Review, 85:5, May, pp. 72-83**

- Identify the key emotions and emotional states that are likely to have a positive and negative effect on performance and link these different states to specific experiences workers can be exposed to in the workplace.
- Identify the actions managers can take to increase the worker's experience of positive emotions and decrease the frequency or intensity of negative emotions.

You can extend this activity to an individual or group project which aims to test certain claims and conclusions the authors make.

The work of Amabile and Kramer has implications for the way managers can use the insights generated by their research to develop a more strategic approach to 'managing motivation'. Adopting a strategic perspective involves:

- framing the problem and challenge in the 'right' way—that is basing the assumptions made about human behaviour and motivation on verifiable propositions and a tested body of knowledge;
- developing practices that impact on the majority if not all of an employee group;
- ensuring that subsequent affective and behavioural changes have a significant and positive impact on performance.

One of the strategically important conclusions that can be reached is that however much importance is attached to the 'inner working self' people work and function in a social and managerial context, the characteristics of which inevitably impact on individual motivation and behaviour. As such, strategies that reflect the internal drives and emotions of people (intrinsic) *and* the working environment (extrinsic) need to be developed. Given the generally recognized importance of the line manager in understanding employee behaviour, it is not surprising that Amabile and Kramer recognize this key influence when they claim that a manager can dramatically shape their employees' inner working lives, but not necessarily through more conventionally understood 'levers'.

The work of Nohria et al. (2008) offers further insights into the strategic value and implications that come from understanding what explains human motivation. They theorize that motivation is based on, and driven by, four basic things. These are:

- The drive to acquire. This may be largely seen as a materialistic need but extends beyond the obvious things such as money and better jobs to positive experiences that individuals value and gain satisfaction from.
- The drive to bond. This emphasizes people's need to form relationships, be part of something more than their own existence and where success results in powerful positive emotions. Equally, where the need is not met or frustrated, powerful negative emotions are often released.

- The drive to comprehend. This need reflects the fundamental requirement for people to make sense of their situation, what they are being asked to do and why. Knowing why is arguably more important than knowing what in terms of explaining behaviour! Humans are naturally curious and whilst differences between individuals do exist, most seek to become more aware of their environment.
- The drive to defend. This need to protect oneself and others from threats, uncertainty, unknown change, and the 'unfair' decisions of managers.

Nohria et al. link these basic four drives to related motivational and performance strategies in the following way:

| Basic drive | Strategic focus and response |
|---|---|
| Acquiring | Reward System |
| Bonding | Culture Building |
| Comprehending | Job design and work organization |
| Defending | Develop trust and fairness |

**STUDENT ACTIVITY 11.3 Researching the relationship between motivation and performance**

This activity should be based on group work with each group undertaking the same tasks, but then comparing results at the end through presentations.

- The first task is to design a piece of research that can be easily undertaken using fellow students, most of whom will have some work experience. Each group needs to agree on one or two key research questions which, if answered will illuminate the relationship between motivational state and performance. The hypothesis might be that positive motivation is linked to performance.
- Data has to be collected that helps to answer the research questions.
- Review the evidence and present your conclusions, together with any reservations in the form of a PowerPoint presentation.
- Finally, use the conclusions to re-consider the motivational theory presented by the Nohria team of researchers.

The emphasis on these four strategies or 'management levers', whilst in one sense attractive, does suggest the use of the 'lever' metaphor that may be less than helpful in trying to explain actual rather than assumed behaviour. The question is not whether these drives exist, or that the associated managerial strategies are inappropriate, but that the notion of levers is itself problematical and simplistic. None of the four strategies are subject to easy changes; in fact each takes considerable time to develop and implement and the idea that culture can be changed by 'pulling a lever' is difficult to reconcile with what we know about the challenges associated with managing and changing organizational culture, and of course with the idea that people rarely play active and passive roles in the way they respond to changes in their environment. However, notwithstanding these reservations, the work of Nohria et al., taken together with the conceptual model development by Amabile and Kramer, lends justification to the belief that there is a strong relationship between peoples' motivational state and their work performance. This means that unmotivated workers are likely to perform well below their capabilities and those who are highly motivated close to what they are capable of, and probably beyond because these limits will be expanding as a result of the positive motivational forces.

But the assumed associations between motivated people and high performance and weakly motivated staff and low performance rests on a questionable assumption—that highly motivated people will be high performers. This may not always be the case although it is an assumption that managers often believe in or want to believe. The point is that 'pulling levers' in whatever form they take does not always result in the changes in behaviour that managers are looking for and expect. Think about the concept of the paradox unintended consequences we explored in Chapter 1 and read the HRM Insight below.

**HRM INSIGHT 11.1 A performance improvement strategy that went badly wrong**

This case study is based on a Harvard Business School article by Kerr (2003).

The scenario is not unusual; a new senior manager comes into a company and introduces a new performance management system based on incentives, targets, standards penalties, and a new system of performance measurements.

The outcome is not what he expected, even though he thought he had been acting rationally using what he believed were tried and tested practices.

**Questions**

1. Consider the assumptions Hyram was making when he developed his performance management system and whether these are justified.
2. What was the impact on worker motivation of his new system? Were they acting rationally in the way they reacted to the new practices and standards?
3. Why didn't Hyram know things were not going according to plan before his final board meeting?
4. Which elements or parts of the two previously quoted Harvard Business Review articles are helpful in explaining worker behaviour?
5. Advise Hyram on what he should do to re-design the performance management system to produce the intended consequences.

# Understanding What Influences Performance

Earlier in this chapter, we suggested that one of the important questions to which managers need to know the answer is what explains low performance, and how can this problem be addressed? The use of a sporting analogy, to which some readers will be directly able to relate, helps to identify explanations for low and unsatisfactory performance problems.

An experienced golfer with a handicap of 15 regularly performs to this standard at the club of which he is a member. On a golfing holiday with some friends, he played three of the top links courses in Scotland and returned scores well in excess of his handicap; in other words, he performed badly. Consider the possible explanations for this.

- It might be that the three courses were more difficult than his own, and that his poor performance was simply a function of the newness and level of difficulty of the courses. He played as well as he normally did, but because the courses were harder than he was used to, his performance fell relative to the challenge he faced.
- The playing conditions might have played a part in his poor performance. The wind might have been blowing and it might have been raining. In other words, the physical environment might have been a factor.
- Although appropriate to his own course, his clubs might not have been right for the different challenge he faced. In other words, he might have lacked the right equipment to play well.

- He might also have lacked the level and range of skills to perform well in a more challenging environment. Limitations in his ability to perform might have been a factor.
- There might have been something about him on those days that affected his performance: he might not have been in the right frame of mind, or he might have been nervous or a little overawed by the occasion. He might have been physically below par and have not had the energy to deliver a sustained performance over all 54 holes or he might have lacked sufficient motivation to go out and play well. Collectively, these factors relate to the person's state of mind, and his psychological and physical well being.
- Finally, he might have been missing help from his club professional or coach, who would normally give him tips on what he was doing wrong and offer constructive advice on what to do differently to improve his performance. In other words, he lacked some of the necessary support to help his performance.

The use of this sporting analogy is useful because it suggests that we can draw upon our own experiences of performance, many of which may lie outside the world of work, to help us to understand human behaviour and the factors that influence our performance at work.

In addition to the possible explanations offered above for performance problems, W.E. Deming, cited in Rothwell (1996, p. 12), provides a further insight into where the most frequently experienced performance problems are to be found. As does the French consultant cited a little later in this chapter, Deming holds the view that what workers do or do not do is not the main reason why organizations experience these problems. He argues:

> **The workers are handicapped by the system, and the system belongs to management.**



Rothwell (1996), in supporting this emphasis on managerial responsibility, claims that:

> **As little as 20% of all human performance problems is attributable to individual employees; as much as 80% of all such problems is attributable to the work environments or systems in which employees work.**

Explanations are closely linked to 'solutions' and, as far as the effective management of performance is concerned, accurately diagnosing underlying causes is the basis for the 'right' solutions. Get the diagnosis wrong and any attempt to manage a performance problem is unlikely to have any significant impact; it might even worsen the situation. The following situations are often linked to performance problems, but the appropriate managerial responses are quite different.

## Understanding different performance situations

Managers are faced with a wide range of situations that create very different kinds of performance problems and it is necessary to consider these in more detail.

- People absent from work

  If people are not at work, they cannot perform and their absence will also result in falls in productivity levels. Sick pay and fixed employment costs mean that, even though people are absent from work, the costs of employing them largely remain the same, while their added-value contributions become zero. The higher the level of absence and the longer the time for which people are away from work, the bigger the performance loss becomes. The challenge for management then becomes one of finding effective ways of reducing absenteeism.

Signpost to Chapter 9: HR Planning and Measurement, for information on measuring and managing absenteeism

- **People at work who don't perform**

  Given the need to become as competitive and efficient as possible, pressures to increase performance are found in most organizations. Employees who are physically absent from work represent one kind of problem, but those who just turn up to 'do their jobs' and no more present a different challenge to management. If people don't want to perform at any level other than that with which they are comfortable, then there can be a serious underutilization of labour that, sooner or later, affects the performance of the organization itself. Examples of employees who do as little as possible are more likely to be found in parts of the public sector that are protected from financial and competitive pressures. In serious cases, a culture of underperforming can develop, which can be more difficult to change than cases of individual underperformance. How can these problems be managed? Consider the approach adopted by an internationally renowned CEO in HRM Insight 11.2.

**HRM INSIGHT 11.2 The case of the GE 'people factory'**

In his book about his experiences as the CEO of GE (General Electric), one of the most successful USA-based global businesses listed on the New York Stock Exchange, Jack Welch (Welch and Byrne, 2003) describes the mechanism used throughout GE to manage performance. In this approach, an employee's performance is described in terms of their performance against last year's objectives with 'A' performers being in the top 20 per cent, 'B' performers being in the middle 70 per cent in terms of performance, and 'C' performers defined as the bottom 10 per cent. Under this model, the company insisted that every manager identify the lowest performing 10 per cent. Failure to do so would result in the manager being categorized as a 'C' performer. In Welch's words, 'the underperformers generally had to go', presumably meaning that, in most cases, those identified as the lowest performing 10 per cent would generally lose their job or be encouraged to leave. Welch also expresses the view that anyone in this category should not have received any pay rise.

**Questions**

1. What advantages might be achieved by an organization in implementing this model?
2. What might the disadvantages be to the organization and what impact might this approach have on the employees of the organization?
3. Consider the above model from the point of view of a manager of a team of ten people. What dilemmas might a manager face if asked to rate his or her team against this model?
4. What are the legal, moral, and ethical implications of using this system to identify the poorest performing 10 per cent of the salaried workforce, given the intention to terminate the employment of employees in this group under the strategy described?
5. How might the top 20 per cent of performers be positively and negatively affected by this policy?

- **Legitimizing low standards**

  Although not obviously a problem, the existence of high performers who coexist with those who are satisfied with, or are allowed to deliver, lower levels of performance does create certain challenges and difficulties. If there are no negative consequences for being a low performer, why should a low performer want to improve? Moreover, what message does this send to high performers, if it doesn't matter? Not addressing the problem of low performance can, paradoxically, result in its legitimization, making subsequent attempts to address the problem more difficult than they would otherwise have been.

- **Raising performance expectations and standards**

  How can managers stimulate people to raise their 'average' level of performance to sustainably higher levels? This is not about raising performance on a temporary basis, although this can be important under crisis circumstances, but about leveraging up everyone's performance to a new and higher level that becomes the new performance base line. The Hay Group (Jirasinghe and Houldsworth, 2006) has found that many organizations adopt a performance enhancement strategy that combines elements from two broad approaches. Some give an emphasis to improving performance through the development of employees (a 'soft' approach), while others prefer one based on measurement (a 'hard' approach). The conclusion reached is that the most successful companies adopt a balanced and rounded approach, combining elements of both, including measures on teamwork, long-term thinking, building human capital, developing and managing talent, and maintaining of customer loyalty.

- Removing the barriers to higher performance

  The final situation that has to be managed is fundamentally different to the other four. If management feels that there are performance problems, the often-implicit assumption is that employees need to be encouraged, induced, or paid for additional effort or performance, and an effective mix of antecedents and consequences are designed to impact on employee behaviour. In many cases in which job performance and wider contribution linked to the exercise of discretionary effort give cause for concern, the problem is less to do with lack of ability or motivation and more to do with the existence of 'organizational blockages'. Quite simply, this means that there are influences that originate in the culture, working environment, or management behaviour that act to suppress employees' natural desire to 'give more'. The challenge is, therefore, to clear the blockages that are preventing people from improving their performance.

**STUDENT ACTIVITY 11.4**

**This activity relates to the situation in which management is attempting to build performance to permanently higher levels. According to the Hay Group's research (Jirasinghe and Houldsworth, 2006) into what companies actually do to achieve this there are two quite distinctive approaches: developing performance and measuring. Your task is to construct a matrix for each strategy, in which the theoretical advantages and disadvantages of each approach are listed. You should also record your views on the roles of HR professionals and line managers in supporting both strategies.**

Signpost to Chapter 9: HR Planning and Measurement, for information on linking performance and reward

# The Role of the Manager in Performance Management

Several years ago, one of the authors was attending an international conference on Human Resource Management in Beirut. One of the speakers was a Frenchman, who had worked for more than 20 years as a senior HR executive for American Express and who, after leaving, had built up his own performance management consultancy. During a conversation about his work as a consultant, he made an interesting comment about his thinking on where most performance problems lie:

> **Whenever I am asked by the CEO of a business to try to sort out their performance problems, I always say that I will only agree to work for them on the basis that I will not be recommending any of the employees are made redundant as a way of solving the problem. Almost all problems of organizational underperformance are not due to what employees do or don't do—they are generally because of deficiencies in management.**

The point of the story is that, while individual performance is an important factor in explaining organizational success, it rarely explains organizational failure. People can be working hard and achieving performance targets, but a business can still fail. As an example, consider the case of MG Rover and think about the reasons this company went into receivership (Holweg and Olive, 2005).

The need to ensure that each employee is performing close to his or her potential is, however, one of the most important objectives in any performance management system and, arguably, the most frequently used single instrument for managing individual performance is the appraisal process. The Practitioner Insight gives a view form an HR consultant of what performance management means and entails.

**PRACTITIONER INSIGHT David Lloyd, Performance Management Consultant: an HR consultant's view of performance management in practice**

One of the most challenging questions managers need to address is precisely what is meant by performance management? All too often people in the same organization hold different views about what it means and what it involves the organization doing. Very often it is seen in a very limited way—being equated to the pursuit of targets and individual objectives. Whilst there is nothing wrong with the pursuit of targets, on its own it can damage long-term performance, e.g. by producing unintended consequences. Emphasizing quantitative targets can negatively impact on the quality of goods and service and indeed lead to unethical behaviour with damaging consequences.

The performance management system in any organization must be capable of understanding and describing the value its goods and services create for its customers and the processes that create this value. All targets whether at an organizational, team, or individual level must be aligned to and support customer value and the processes that create this value in terms of goods and service. Without this understanding and alignment goods and service can be created that meet targets but which are not fit for purpose and do not create meaningful customer value.

Performance management, in my experience involves prioritizing three key elements. Firstly, the organization needs to have a sense of where it is going—knowing what its long-term vision for itself is and continually reinforcing this to all levels and all employees. The second element is the organizational philosophy and core values that will guide the organization along its journey particularly at times of uncertainty and change, and thirdly a coherent set of policies and practice that define the framework within which individual and team contributions can be assessed and validated. So, the three elements of any performance management system are a vision and certainty of purpose, a coherent business and management philosophy, and a set of policies and practice to define effectiveness and efficiency.

An organization is a work system and therefore performance management must be a system to support the overall purpose and goals of the organization as a work system. Remember 80 per cent of the purpose of a work system is dependent on the design and management of the work system and only 20 per cent is dependent on the performance of individuals. The performance management system must also be aligned to other support systems and initiatives, e.g. communications, quality, investment, technology, etc.

It is essential and critical that HR does not design performance management policies and practices that create 'silos' whether these be functional or process based, but rather to work to integrate and connect different aspects of the wider performance system. This means they need to take a holistic and systems approach to performance and avoid an unduly bureaucratic emphasis on procedural conformity. Above all, HR needs to understand the concept of added value and the importance of meeting internal and external customer requirements.

## The performance appraisal process

A performance appraisal is a process that is commonly used throughout many organizations to evaluate or appraise employees' performance in the past and to consider how to maximize the employee's future contribution. The timescale under consideration is often a year, but performance may be appraised over a shorter period, from as little as a few weeks for a newly hired employee.

Signpost to Chapter 14: Case Study: HR and the New Opening, for examples of the importance of measuring performance of newly hired employees

The process usually includes a preparation stage, completed by both the employee and the manager. This may involve filling in either a pre-appraisal form or a draft copy of the appraisal form, so that these can be brought together for discussion during an appraisal meeting. To avoid favouritism and to ensure that a consistent approach is adopted across the organization, there may be some input in the preparation stage from the manager's manager. Often appraisals will cascade through an organization and the appraisals are completed in order of seniority to ensure that objectives are passed down through each level of employee.

The appraisal then typically takes place at a meeting between the employee and his or her manager, and discussions take place covering each of the elements of the employee's job that the manager and employee wish to consider. Table 11.1 gives some examples of the elements that are often included in an appraisal process.

A final record is then made of what was discussed and agreed at the meeting, including performance in the past, objectives for the future, and development plans to support the employee to achieve these targets. This document is then copied for each of the parties and forms the basis of ongoing assessment against the objectives set. The whole process is shown in Figure 11.2.

**STUDENT ACTIVITY 11.5**

1. Working in groups, design and produce an appraisal form for use with members of your seminar group, or a group of employees with which you are familiar. This form must record all relevant information on an individual's performance over a given period and should have a section outlining future objectives to improve performance.
2. Write a set of guidance notes to help you and your lecturer, or other employees and their manager, to prepare for and complete the appraisal effectively.
3. Reflect on what you learnt by engaging in this activity.



## Rating performance

Many appraisals require the manager to rate the performance of each employee in order to compare performance among colleagues. Rating systems can also be used to link performance to pay. Rating systems can be a useful indication to an employee of the extent to which the company recognizes their contribution; a lower score can be an effective way of alerting an employee that there is need for them to improve their work performance (Coens and Jenkins, 2000).

Signpost to Chapter 12: Managing Rewards, for more details of using rating scales to link performance and reward

- Manager-allocated rating scales

  Rating scales vary in complexity. A simple method of rating performance might be to ask the manager to choose a rating using a scale, an example of which is shown in Table 11.2. In this example, the manager chooses the rating that is felt to be most appropriate for the employee, given the manager's knowledge of that employee's overall performance since the last appraisal. While this system is easy to implement and relatively simple, the rating is highly subjective and will be susceptible to a manager making a judgement based upon his or her overall perception of the employee, rather than on hard indicators of actual performance.

Table 11.1 Items that might be covered in an annual performance appraisal

| Item | Details | Why might this be included? |
|---|---|---|
| Personal information | Name; department; service details; date commenced in role; date of appraisal meeting | A record of personal information and dates to give context of the appraisal |
| Last year's objectives | Details of objectives set at last year's appraisal | To clarify what level of performance was required for the preceding year |
| Performance against last year's objectives | Details of the extent to which objectives were met | To assess the extent to which performance last year reached the expected standard |
| Performance rating | A grade or score relating to overall performance | To give a score relative others in the organization—often linked to performance-related pay |
| Additional achievements | Other achievements during the previous year | To establish additional contribution during year that was not anticipated as part of objectives initially set |
| Summary of last year's development activity | Details of training and development activities last year and the benefits of these | To assess the effectiveness of development activity over the previous year |
| Employee's strengths | Manager's view about what an employee is good at | To praise and recognize the employee's best qualities |
| Employee's weaknesses | Manager's view about areas in which performance could be improved | To identify areas of skill, knowledge or attitude that might be improved |
| Planned training | Training activity and courses scheduled for forthcoming year | To identify training courses to address training needs identified |
| Other planned development activity | Other development activity, such as projects, coaching or secondment | To identify other planned activities to help to address weaknesses or to build skills and knowledge that will be required in the near future |
| Next year's objectives | Details of objectives for the forthcoming year, including measures and constraints | To agree the standards expected of the employee over the coming 12 months |
| Manager's summary | A summary of the manager's overall view of performance during the year | To record the manager's overall view of the employee |
| Senior managers' comments | A summary of the next level of management's view of the employee's performance | To provide an opportunity for the next level of management to ratify the process and provide feedback |
| Employee's comments | An opportunity for the employee to make his or her own comments | To provide an opportunity for the employee to comment, including on areas of agreement or disagreement |
| Signatures | Signatures and dates of acceptance of the record of meeting | Ensures all interested parties acknowledge receipt of the formal record |

- Objective-based rating scales

  One way of trying to avoid the subjectivity of a rating scale is for the manager to assess an employee's performance against the objectives set and to allocate a rating based upon the extent to which these objectives are met. An example of this type of rating is given in Table 11.3. Providing that the objectives were set in such a way that the required target level of performance was clearly defined, then the rating allocated can reflect this.

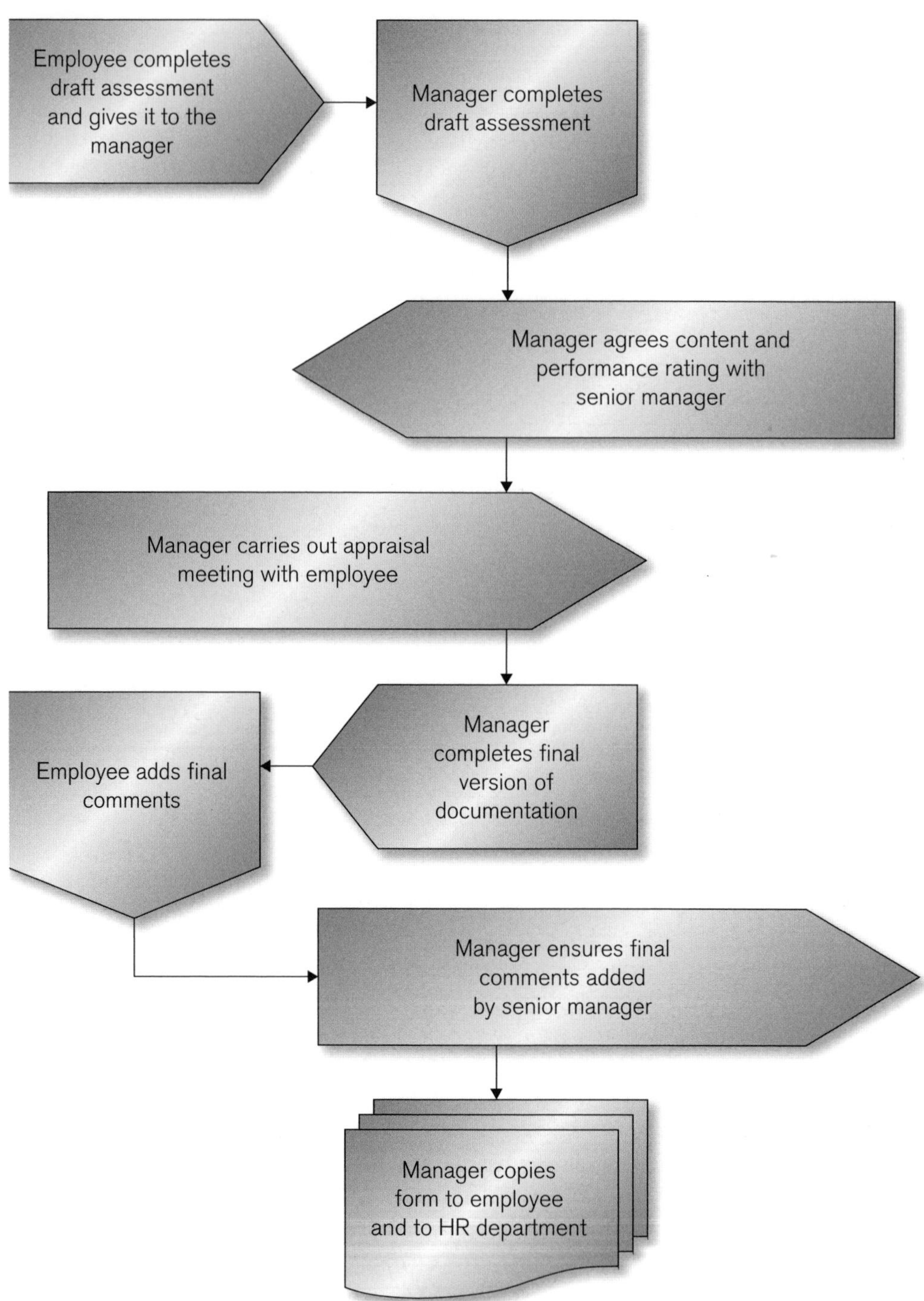


**Figure 11.2** The performance appraisal process

The advantage of linking the rating to objectives is that the rating will more closely reflect the employee's actual performance. You will notice, in the example in Table 11.3, we have referred to the level of support and supervision provided to an employee, which may exceed that normally expected for any given level of performance. It is possible that an employee has only reached certain objectives as a result of levels of support and supervision that should not be necessary, and the organization may wish to take this into account in rating performance. Ratings such as these are often then linked to the pay award given to an employee.

Table 11.2 Example of a performance rating scale

| Rating | Description |
|---|---|
| *Outstanding* | Employee demonstrates a level of performance that substantially exceeds that expected. Demonstrates an outstanding ability to meet all challenges within current role |
| *Above standard* | Employee has demonstrated a level of performance above that expected and has met challenges with a high degree of proficiency |
| *Satisfactory* | Employee's performance is at a standard that is satisfactory and acceptable |
| *Needs some improvement* | Some areas of performance need to be improved to reach a satisfactory level; more than a typical level of supervision required to meet objectives |
| *Poor* | Performance falls below the expected standard and unsatisfactory performance needs to be addressed, with considerable input required from supervision |

Table 11.3 Example of an objective-based rating scale

| Rating | Description |
|---|---|
| *Exceeds* | Employee measurably exceeds all objectives in every respect |
| *Fulfils* | Employee has met all agreed objectives to a standard that is fully satisfactory |
| *Developing* | Employee is relatively new to role and has met objectives to a satisfactory level, given level of experience and training |
| *Below standard* | Some areas of objectives not met, and employee requires more support and supervision than should be necessary to achieve objectives |



- Points-based rating scales

  There are also a variety of systems for rating job performance that allocate points to different aspects of the job that employees perform. To be effective, points-based appraisal rating systems require comprehensive, reliable, and consistent information on performance against each job element or objective. Unless it is possible to meet these criteria, these systems are unlikely to possess the necessary credibility to be accepted and legitimized.

## *The value of rating performance*

In general, the more objective a system is, the more value there is to rating performance because the rating given will actually relate to job performance. In reality, there are many jobs in which it is relatively easy to measure and rate performance, such as the sales levels achieved by a sales representative or the number of calls answered per hour by a telephone enquiry receptionist. Even in these examples, however, outside factors, such as the demand for these services, will influence performance levels.

The more complex a system is, the more effort and time needs to go into designing, maintaining, and implementing it. HR professionals, often seen as the guardians of the appraisal process, must have regard for the time spent by managers in carrying out appraisals and completing the associated paperwork or online forms. A degree of sensitivity, and awareness of the loopholes and 'short cuts' that can develop, is also required, otherwise the appraisal process can become increasingly detached and ineffective as a positive contribution to improved performance. The criticisms levelled at performance appraisal by Coens and Jenkins (2000), which were highlighted in Chapter 2 and particularly in relation to rating errors, illustrate many of the pitfalls and deficiencies that organizations have experienced in implementing and maintaining such approaches to performance management. Coens and Jenkins (2000) argue that their research suggests that the majority of such schemes not only do not improve individual performance levels, but actually undermine them (Grint, 1993). This is to do with the undermining effects of managers sitting in judgement on their subordinates and the biases that inevitably intrude into the assessment not only of an employee's performance, but of the person.

Signpost to Chapter 2: HRM: An Academic and Professional Perspective, for details of Coens and Jenkins' criticisms of performance appraisals

# Setting Objectives

A key factor in the success of any organization is its ability to ensure that everyone clearly understands what they are required to do to contribute to its success. Everyone has a part to play in achieving the organization objectives, and setting objectives for individuals and teams is an important part of any performance management process.

*SMART* is an acronym used to describe key characteristics of appraisal objectives. Each of the letters stands for the following:

**S** specific (one end result is clearly described);

**M** measurable outcome (the outcome can be measured);

**A** agreed (manager and report agree the outcome);

**R** realistic (i.e. 'what is the maximum we can realistically achieve including target and stretch?');

**T** timely (i.e. 'by when will it be achieved?').



It is also important to remember that objectives can become outdated as circumstances change, and management must respond quickly to new situations and demands.

Tracking progress and amending objectives to reflect new conditions and priorities is an essential part of 'managing objectives' if employees are to stay focused on what's important, rather than on what was originally agreed. Whatever objectives are agreed and possibly changed should limit employee performance, in that they prevent or inhibit employees from responding to other needs or engaging in other value-added activities that are not incorporated in an employee's formal objectives.

## Direct objectives

Most organizations will have a financial budget to which it must adhere. Some sections of the organization will be responsible for bringing money in through bidding for funding, achieving sales, or raising funds. Other teams will require resources that have a cost attached to them and the team may be responsible for securing the most effective resource possible within the predetermined cost. If an individual or team is responsible for a section of this budget, this might be expressed as a direct objective as follows:

**Achieve sales of £500,000 in lingerie by the end of December 2011.**

Many objectives that can be quantified, either by using financial values, percentage changes, or physical quantities and expressed in these ways, represent a stronger motivational influence on employee behaviour because progress towards the agreed objectives can be monitored and displayed. If this is not possible, an alternative approach to agreeing objectives is required, possibly expressing these in a qualitative way. The problem with this approach, however, is that it becomes more difficult to agree on measures that accurately express progress and achievement.

## Indirect objectives

- Key performance indicators (KPIs)

  It may also be possible to have a measure in place the achievement of which, although not referred to directly in the organization's central objectives, contributes to these objectives being met. Such objectives become supportive or secondary, rather than primary. It is therefore important to adopt these measures and set targets, which are often referred to as 'key performance indicators', or 'KPIs'. An example might be:

**Attract an average of 5,000 visitors per month to Mayfield Hall Museum throughout the summer season in 2012.**

In this example, the 'KPI' is visitor numbers and this directly correlates to revenue generated from ticket sales.

- Project measures

  If objectives cannot easily be expressed in terms of numbers that are directly or indirectly related to the organization's main aims and objectives, then targets might also be expressed in terms of delivery of a project that, if completed successfully, will contribute towards the organization achieving its strategic objectives. An example might be:

  **Re-tender the combined schools' catering contract for the Stokehampton district, incorporating government guidelines on healthy eating and maintaining current overall costs for the three years commencing on 1 April 2012.**

## The drawbacks of setting objectives

It should be noted that some jobs lend themselves more readily to objective setting than do others. For example, a sales representative with a clearly defined sales target is perhaps in a role better suited to objectives than an administrator, who may need to respond flexibly to manage a variable, and at times unpredictable, workload.

Setting objectives presumes that required actions or outputs can be predicted and sometimes this simply is not the case. Many jobs consist of complex patterns of decision-making and long-term strategic planning, and the flexibility and creativity needed to deliver success in these roles can be stifled by rigid objectives. Many employees will have the self-motivation and capability to add value to an organization, identifying what needs to be done and how best to contribute to this in the absence of, or regardless of, what objectives are set. Furthermore, this creative capability can be further stifled if the attainment of prescribed objectives is related to future pay awards.

# Giving Effective Feedback

Employees and managers generally benefit from honest, objective feedback about how things are going. A constant exchange of information, often generated through what might be described as 'performance conversation', helps everyone to stay on track and the organization to stay competitive. Problems come to the surface before they get out of hand, information that can improve performance gets to the right people before it's too late, and people build stronger working relationships because of feedback.

Effective feedback helps an employee to understand how others perceive their behaviour and performance. It may not always be welcome if it contains implied or explicit criticisms, but it is an essential part of any performance management system. The purpose of giving feedback is not to change employees and try to mould them into what their manager would like them to be, but is about furnishing them with information about their behaviour and performance. Helping employees to understand how they are perceived at work, and not only by their line manager, gives them the opportunity to learn about themselves and to decide whether they need to change in some way or another.

Effective feedback, then, offers people information about themselves in a way that leaves them with a choice about how to act. The objective of giving feedback is to clarify and not judge. To be effective, the receiver needs to feel empowered and motivated to change and this can be achieved if the feedback is delivered in ways that do not damage the employee's self-esteem. Any negative feedback needs to be balanced by feedback that is positive and encouraging, so that the overall effect of the experience works to improve the employee's sense of worth and value, and motivates them to do better.

**STUDENT ACTIVITY 11.6 Giving constructive feedback**

Consider the following statements:

**We all think you could answer the phone more politely. You are always upsetting people on the phone.**

**I usually find you to be very helpful, but I think you might be more effective when you are explaining technical problems if you were to use diagrams and check that people understand as you go.**

**You are too aggressive when you are trying to get patients to explain why they need an urgent appointment.**

**You are efficient with all the administration and I feel you could use this to build a better rapport with your colleagues, when under pressure, if you were more sympathetic when they aren't as quick as you. For example, when Mary was busy last week, she might have appreciated an offer of help with understanding the system.**

**Good effort. Well done with the Samuels contract.**

**I am delighted with how you handled the Johnson case. The customer particularly valued the level of detail and layout in your report and summary. I think we will see a real benefit if we take this approach with our other accounts when you get the opportunity.**

1. Decide whether or not you think the feedback statements given above are constructive or not constructive and consider what aspects of the statement make it more or less constructive.
2. Research the literature on giving constructive feedback and give a presentation to your group on what are considered to be essential features of the process.
3. After seminar presentations, practise giving constructive feedback and ask those receiving it what impact your comments had.



## 360° feedback

One of the more recent developments in the use of appraisals to manage performance is 360-degree (360°) feedback. This involves seeking contributions about what a person achieves and how he or she operates not only from the line manager, but from others who are in contact with the person and are in a position to offer such feedback. Using this process, an employee, but more often a manager, can receive structured feedback from a variety of sources to assist him or her in improving performance. Typically, a questionnaire is sent to a selection of colleagues, subordinates, and, possibly, external contacts. The completed questionnaires are returned anonymously to an independent third party. The same questionnaire is also completed by the employee and by his or her manager, and the responses are compared between each group.

To be effective, feedback to the employee of the results should ideally be undertaken by a trained facilitator, who can help the employee to understand his or her own strengths and weaknesses, and can use the information to produce a development plan. While this tool can be extremely effective in helping an employee to understand exactly how he or she is perceived, the process must be properly managed. The employee is unlikely to benefit unless he or she remains open-minded and willing to participate in the process. Without a reasonable degree of trust, the process of seeking feedback at different levels might be detrimental to working relationships. Other staff may be reluctant to comment, and may need encouragement to be open and honest, and reassured that responses are anonymous. The feedback will also be more meaningful if any scores and responses are supported by examples and written comments to aid clarification. The design of the questionnaire is also crucial. While generic, 'off-the-shelf' questionnaires are available, organizations may benefit from designing their own process relevant to the skill sets they deem to be important to their own managers and teams (Coomber, 2006).

## Development Plans

A development plan is an important tool to help an individual plan how he or she can best maximize his or her skills and knowledge. This can form part of an appraisal process, but a more detailed development plan can help to enhance the development of any individual. For example, an organization may wish to use development plans to fast-track employees who are identified as having high potential (Stringer and Cheloha, 2003). Typically, development plans will list all structured activity that is designed to address specific development needs. This might be to help build upon weaker areas, to develop existing skills and knowledge, or to develop new skills and expertise in readiness for future challenges. An effective development plan will encompass a broad range of developmental activity and will have only a small element of development reliant on attendance of training courses. Other activities may involve coaching or mentoring, participation in project work, secondment to another role or department, and opportunities to carry out new tasks or be exposed to new situations and challenges in the workplace.

## Managing Problem Performance

Earlier, we made reference to a situation with which managers are often confronted—that of performance that is consistently below what is reasonable and acceptable. In a worst-case scenario, managers will ignore the problem or rationalize it away, interpreting it as less of a problem than it really is. But problems of underperformance are rarely solved by pretending that they don't exist, and the effective management of performance not only involves developing systems and procedures, but also engaging with those employees whose behaviour is unacceptable.

In serious cases involving managerial staff, this may involve managing people out of the organization through the use of what are referred to as 'compromise agreements'. These are forms of contracts that end the employment relationship by mutual agreement and involve the employee giving up his or her employment protection rights in exchange for a financial payment, and often a favourable reference. In cases in which the problem is considered irretrievable, often involving a breakdown in the relationship between employee and management, rather than invoke disciplinary procedure leading to dismissal, management may wish to consider a solution to the problem that is less damaging for both parties.

In less serious situations, management can consider the mechanisms that normally lie outside an existing appraisal process.

- An informal performance review

  This involves a meeting between a manager and an employee to highlight areas of concern with the employee's current performance, to discuss and set targets for improvement, and, if appropriate, to arrange support and training to achieve these targets.

- A formal performance review

  This is a meeting between a manager, often with an HR practitioner or another manager present, and the employee, who should be informed of the right to be accompanied by a representative. At a formal meeting, concerns about performance can be discussed, targets set for improvement and consequences of failure to improve can be highlighted, which may ultimately include demotion, transfer or termination of employment. A timescale for improvement, training, and support can also be agreed.

Both types of review are, or should be, based on the principles that employees need to be given the opportunity to improve their performance before further action is taken and that raising concerns informally first is preferable to invoking formal procedure or action. Both types of meeting are, however, likely to cover the same content, including:

- discussing areas of concern;
- setting targets and timescales for improvement;
- agreeing appropriate training and support.

**STUDENT ACTIVITY 11.7**

1. As a group, develop a manager's guide to effective appraisal interviewing.
2. Design and, if possible, pilot a training session for first-line supervisors on 'effective performance appraisal interviewing'.
3. Survey a group of employees who have experienced performance appraisals, and present and discuss your findings with the group.

# Summary



- Managing employee performance is rarely an option in contemporary organizations, simply because of the pressure that managers are under to remain competitive and to deliver productivity improvements. One way in which these can be achieved is by getting employees to perform at sustainably higher levels. This can be achieved through increasing effort levels, by accessing effort that is discretionary and under the control of the employee, through working more efficiently, or through reducing the amount of unproductive time due to absence and wasteful activities.
- At a more strategic level, management can remove relatively low performers and replace them with new recruits, who either can perform at higher levels or have the potential to do so. This kind of strategy is associated with a high-performance culture in which high standards of effort and commitment are expected from all employees; in this type of culture, low performance is simply not acceptable from either employees or managers.
- The culture of an organization and the expectations held by its senior management are critical factors that influence what people do at work and what they want to do. Often employees want to do more, but are inhibited from doing so because, paradoxically, high performance from a few employees, compared to the majority, focuses attention on an endemic problem that some managers prefer to remain hidden. In such situations, the problem of low performance has little to do with the skills and capabilities of employees, and is rather a symptom of weak and ineffective management.
- Employee motivation is an important factor in performance and has been the subject of many theories and studies. This area is extremely complex and influenced by many factors, which may be linked and which can both motivate and demotivate a person at work.
- Appraisal schemes are widely used to both set objectives and rate performance against these and to encourage employee development, however the ability of such schemes to drive performance upwards remains a highly debatable question. Some authors argue that such schemes not only do not improve individual performance levels, but can actually undermine them.
- The belief that higher levels of performance can be achieved by offering incentives or other inducements is historically associated with certain industries, such as construction and engineering. In such

industries, there is an often explicitly accepted assumption, held by both managers and workers, that there are two levels of performance: one linked to the basic wage and a higher one, up to 33 per cent higher, that is associated with additional incentives.

- Organizations are increasingly looking to improve productivity by creating a working environment that encourages employees to use their potential to the full, rewards them for this (but not necessarily in a financial way), and generates higher levels of employee engagement with the organization and its objectives.

online resource centre

**Visit the Online Resource Centre that accompanies this book for self-test questions, weblinks, and more information on the topics covered in this chapter. www.oxfordtextbooks.co.uk/orc/banfield_kay2e/**

## REVIEW QUESTIONS

1. What are the key features of the working environment that have an impact on an employee's level of performance?
2. How does 'performance' differ from 'productivity' and what is the relationship between the two?
3. What kind of appraiser biases might be found in the performance appraisal process and how might these be managed?
4. What are the features of 'high-performance work practices'?
5. What does the concept 'discretionary effort' mean and why is this important in managing performance?
6. Strategically, what are the advantages of developing the performance capabilities of existing staff compared to recruiting high-performing people?
7. What are four motivational strategies proposed by Nohria et al.?

***See Online Resource Centre for answers.***



## CASE STUDY

### The case of the light machine shop

In situations in which managers are under pressure to increase pay in a way that does not increase wage costs, which might decrease labour productivity, agreements with groups of employees to link increases to changes in employee behaviour can result in improvements in productivity. In other words, agreements can generate added value or reduced cost, with either the savings or increased output values becoming the source of increased payments. Employees, through greater utilization of their intellectual and physical labour, effectively pay for their own pay increases. The management of United Steels, within which the light machine shop (LMS) was located, was faced with a similar situation. The shop stewards representing the 50 workers employed in the LMS had submitted a pay claim, but after discussions with Peter Wilson, employment relations manager for United Steels, had agreed to consider a proposal for a productivity agreement.

The LMS was one small department in a complex of steel-producing and heavy engineering facilities, and was physically on the perimeter of the complex, well away from where most of the senior managers were located. It was essentially a fabrication shop, in which products such as steel frames, tables, and panels were made.

Peter discussed the options with his team and it was decided that a scheme should be designed that would generate increased revenue, which could be shared between the company and the employees covered by the scheme. He asked George Black, one of the employee relations officers, to come up with an idea that might deliver the required objectives. George looked at the current system of working and payment, and found the following.

- All of the employees were paid an hourly rate based on their skill level. This was known as the 'consolidated time rate' and was paid irrespective of the amount of work each individual completed. There was an unspoken understanding within the shop of the level of output that was needed before management began to show a concern about performance levels.
- Each job allocated by the shop foreman to an individual worker had a time allowance attached to it. This allowed time figure was the result of a time study, under which the foreman would apply time study practices to arrive at a time that was neither too easy nor too difficult to meet. All new jobs had to be timed by the foreman and an allowed time determined. Existing jobs were often subject to retiming as design changes altered the 'amount of work' that was involved.
- Workers were able to increase their weekly wages by completing jobs that had an aggregate allowed time in excess of 40 hours (a 40-hour week was in place). If, for example, an individual completed jobs having an allowed time of 47 hours, he would receive 47 times his hourly rate.
- Individual performance could only effectively be increased by workers increasing their focused effort, i.e. by working harder and smarter, and by using their skills to full effect.
- Current management attitudes and practices meant that the decisions on performance levels were largely in the hands of the workers.
- The shop foreman was only in contact with his line manager infrequently and the HR representatives were rarely seen on the shop floor. He spent most of his time with the workers he was managing and was particularly influenced by the strong trade union presence, manifested by two experienced shop stewards who had worked in the shop for many years. He didn't want any trouble that might involve senior management and he was very much interested in a 'negotiated order'.

George was relatively inexperienced in designing 'productivity' schemes, but, after discussing the best approach to take with a colleague, he came up with the following proposal.

- The scheme would be based on the ability of workers to earn a non-consolidated bonus by increasing their weekly output of steel components.
- The principle underpinning the scheme would be the relationship between allowed times and actual times. The time the workers *actually* took to complete each job or part of a job would be recorded, along with the *allowed* time, on each job card issued by the shop foreman.
- All job cards for the previous six months would be collected and the aggregate allowed times calculated. The aggregate actual times would also be calculated and compared to the allowed times using the formula:

$$\frac{\text{Allowed times}}{\text{Actual times}} \times 100 = \text{productivity index}$$

The data collected produced the following base-line index:

$$\frac{57{,}850}{52{,}000} \times 100 = 111$$

- A 13-week moving average would be used to iron out weekly fluctuations in output, with the first bonus payment being paid in week 13.
- Bonus payments would be paid to each worker pro rata to his or her skill grade, with skilled workers receiving 100 per cent bonus, semi-skilled workers receiving 90 per cent and those designated as unskilled, 80 per cent.

- Actual payments, at 100 per cent, would be £3 per week for every percentage point by which the productivity index exceeded its base line.

**Questions**

1. What were management's objectives in designing this scheme?
2. Was the scheme about performance or productivity?
3. If the index were to increase from its base line, what might the explanations for this be?
4. Are there any potential flaws in the scheme?
5. How do you think the behaviour of the workers in the LMS would have changed as a result of the scheme being implemented? Would their behaviour have reflected what the HR staff expected?

**Insights & Outcomes: visit the Online Resource Centre at www.oxfordtextbooks.co.uk/orc/banfield_kay2e/ for an account of why the bonus scheme failed and the lessons that were learnt.**



## FURTHER READING

Boice, D.F. and Kleiner, B.H. (1997) 'Designing effective performance appraisal systems', *Work Study*, **46**:6, pp. 197–201.

CIPD (2010) 'Talent Management: An overview'. CIPD.

Fisher, C.M. (1994) 'The difference between appraisal schemes: Variations and acceptability Part II', *Personnel Review*, **24**:1, pp. 51–66.

Incomes Data Services (2003) *Performance Management*, IDS Study.

Incomes Data Services (2010) 'Talent management'. *HR studies*, No. 918, IDS.

IRS (2003) 'Performance management: Policy and practices', *IRS Employment Review*, Issue 781, pp. 12–19.

Maslow, A. (1998) *Maslow on Management*, John Wiley & Sons.

Soltani, A., Van der Meer, R., and Williams, T. (2005) 'A contrast of HRM and TQM approaches to performance management', *British Journal of Management*, **16**:6, pp. 403–17.



## REFERENCES

Amabile, T.M. and Kramer, S.J. (2007) 'Inner work life', Harvard Business Review, **85**:5, May, pp. 72–83.

Armstrong, M. and Baron, A. (1998) *Performance Management: The New Realities*, CIPD.

Cappelli, P. (2008) 'Talent management for the twenty-first century', *Harvard Business Review*, **86**:3, March, pp. 74, 76–81.

Coens, T. and Jenkins, M. (2000) *Abolishing Performance Appraisals*, Berrett Koehler.

Coomber, J. (2006) 'Feedback—360 degree', www.cipd.co.uk.

Grint, K. (1993) 'What's wrong with performance appraisals? A critique and a suggestion', *Human Resource Management*, **3**:3, pp. 61–77.

Holweg, M. and Olive, N. (2005) *Who Killed MG Rover?* Cambridge-MIT Institute Centre for Competitiveness and Innovation, www.innovation.jims.cam.ac.uk.

Jirasinghe, D. and Houldsworth, E. (2006) *Managing and Measuring Employee Performance*, Kogan Page.

Kerr, S. (2003) 'The best laid incentive plans' *Harvard Business Review*, **81**:1, January, pp. 27–37.

Lockett, J. (1992) *Effective Performance Management: A Strategic Guide to Getting the Best from People*, Kogan Page.

Mabey, C., Salaman, G. and Story, J. (1998) *Human Resource Management: A Strategic Introduction*, Blackwell.

McCartney, C. and Garrow, V. (2006) *The Talent Management Journey*, Research report, Roffey Park Institute.

McKinsey Co (2000) 'War for talent II—seven ways to win', *Fast Company*, **42**, p. 98, www.fastcompany.com.

Morhman, J.R. and Morhman, S. (1995) 'Performance management is running the business', *Compensation and Benefits Review*, **27**:4, pp. 69–76.

National Audit Office (2010) 'Management of NHS hospital productivity'.

Nohria, N., Groysberg, B. and Lee, L.E. (2008) 'Employee motivation: A powerful new model', *Harvard Business Review*, **86**:7/8, July–August, pp. 78–84.

Pfeffer, J. and O'Reilly, C.A. (2000) *Hidden Value*, Harvard Business School Press.

Rothwell, W. (1996) *Beyond Training and Developing*, AMACOM.

Stringer, R.A. and Cheloha, R.S. (2003) 'The power of a development plan', *Human Resource Planning*, **26**:4, pp. 10–17.

Taylor, F.W. (1998) *The Principles of Scientific Management*, Dover Publications Inc.

Thomas, Kenneth, W. (2009) *Intrinsic Motivation at Work: What Really Drives Employee Engagement*, Berrett-Koehler.

Ulrich, D. (1998) 'A new mandate for Human Resources', *Harvard Business Review*, **76**:1, January–February, pp. 124–34.

Welch, J. and Byrne, J.A. (2003) *Straight from the Gut*, Warner Books.

# Managing Rewards

12

## Key Terms

**Rewards** Can be both material and symbolic in form, and are outcomes of the employment and psychological contracts.

**Pay** Regular and contractually agreed monetary rewards, usually linked to position or job and paid as a wage or salary.

**Bonus** An additional, but variable, payment associated with individual, group, or organizational performance.

**Incentive** The prospect or promise of a reward that is conditional upon an agreed outcome being achieved.

**Benefit** Normally contractually agreed 'additions' to the wage or salary, provided by an employer as part of the overall employment package.

**Reward system** All of the practices, procedures, and methods of rewarding employees either in use by, or potentially available to, management.

## Learning Objectives

As a result of reading this chapter and using the Online Resource Centre, you should be able to:

- understand that rewards can take different forms and serve different purposes;
- understand the principles that underpin different types of payment system and how these systems work;
- understand how to link the use and management of rewards to employee behaviour, particularly that which relates to job performance;
- contribute to the processes involved in changing reward structures and making them more effective;
- identify the factors that influence an organization's use of reward practices.

# Introduction

## Putting rewards in context

According to the CIPD (Arkin, 2005), there has never been a better time to become a specialist in reward management. This view is based on evidence generated by the Institute's 2005 annual reward survey (CIPD, 2005), which found that demand for such expertise is growing, with more organizations taking on specialist reward practitioners. Interesting as this trend might be for those wishing to develop a career in this field, the real significance of the report lies in the way in which it casts light on the forces and pressures influencing reward practices, and the challenges facing managers in the way in which they respond to these pressures.

But why are rewards, and the way in which they are managed and experienced at work, such an important part of human resource management? A useful starting point is recognizing that rewards are a basic element of the employment relationship, and have a critical influence on the satisfaction and commitment of employees. Organizations that fail to understand this fundamental relationship are likely to be less competitive and successful than those that do, and which deliver consistently effective reward policies and practices. Quite simply, employees who are frustrated and dissatisfied with the rewards they receive will express this through how they behave and perform in their jobs; in ways that are unlikely to be in the interests of the organization. Organizations that make mistakes in the way in which they manage rewards are almost certainly going to experience damaging consequences, in the forms of low productivity, higher turnover, and a general lack of employee engagement. The bigger the mistakes, the higher the costs that the organization will experience.

It is similarly important to recognize that the way in which rewards are managed will also, either directly or indirectly, impact on other aspects of HR. For example, a sense of unfairness and dissatisfaction with pay will probably have an effect on the form and level of industrial conflict, and the preparedness of employees to participate with management in a more collaborative approach to employee relations. As Paul Bissell (in Arkin, 2005) observed:

> **Organizations are realizing what a powerful lever reward is and how it needs to complement their other business strategies, whereas historically people have tended to view it in glorious isolation.**

What this means is that reward management is not simply about the basic issues of paying people fairly in relation to market rates, the job they do, and how well they perform in the job, but extends to the impact of reward decisions on recruitment, retention, training, flexibility, and performance, in addition to their effect on morale and commitment. It is self-evident that, without satisfactory rewards, the organization will not be able either to attract or retain the calibre of employee it requires, with the right skills and competencies to deliver the contributions that the organization needs in order to be successful and competitive. In fact, it would not be an exaggeration to suggest that rewards have a significance that pervades almost every aspect of employment and work. It is not surprising, therefore, that interest in reward management is growing.

**KEY CONCEPT Fairness**

There are issues relating to pay and rewards generally that generate subjective feelings of what is, and what is not, 'fair'. This often involves employees looking to other employees, and comparing what they do and what they get paid in relation to these 'comparator' employees. If there is a perception of unfairness, there is great potential for disharmony and the impact upon motivation can be significant. Judgements about what is fair and what is not fair are also found in relation to the rewards experiences of male and female employees doing the same or similar work, and if differences in pay or benefits exist that cannot be justified by differences in the value of jobs, the feeling of unfairness that often follows can ultimately involve the aggrieved party challenging the employer through an equal pay claim.

But while the issue of pay and reward is fundamental to the behaviour and performance of employees, it is arguably one of the most contentious and difficult areas of HR to manage. It is perhaps for this reason that the remuneration packages of reward specialists tend to be significantly greater than those enjoyed by the majority of HR generalists (CIPD, 2005). This level of recognition of the important role and contribution played by reward specialists is partly due to the scale and range of reward matters. From managing the payroll, pensions, and other contractual benefits, those involved also have to make critical decisions on wage and salary levels, pay increases, and sort out the never-ending disputes and disagreements over bonus payments. The costs of the pay and of the total reward packages represent, for most organizations, a significant proportion of their total budget and these costs need to be managed effectively to ensure that they remain within acceptable limits. Reward specialists not only have to ensure that employees are fairly and adequately paid (both highly subjective), but must also avoid significant overpayment, in the context of what the organization can afford to pay to remain competitive and in business.

Managing rewards can also involve large-scale, sector-based pay modernization projects, which seek to replace ageing and ineffective pay policies with common pay structures, based on national job evaluation frameworks and harmonized conditions of employment. The NHS' Agenda for Change project is a good example of a major reward management initiative and, in this case, links the development of a new national competency framework to a simplified structure of jobs and payment levels (Department of Health, 2004).

The challenging nature of reward management is also the result of the increasingly complicated nature of the 'reward package'. Rewards are far from being solely about pay. According to Thompson (2002):

> **the era in which reward was just about cash and benefits is gone forever; increasingly the emphasis in leading organizations is on a total reward approach, including more intangible rewards like the work environment and quality of life considerations, the opportunity for advancement and recognition, and flexible working.**

Moreover, as reward systems are integrated with other areas of HR, and have to respond to external pressures and legislative change, it becomes increasingly difficult to envisage a situation in which managers have, in some finite sense, 'solved the problem'. It is much more sensible to conceptualize reward management as an ongoing engagement—an attempt to reconcile the interests and expectations of different organizational stakeholders—that is undertaken in the knowledge that these different interests and expectations can never be fully met or reconciled. As Daniels (2000) alleges:

> **Few organizations are satisfied with their reward and recognition systems. Furthermore, every change in these systems results in someone else becoming unhappy. Most often, management becomes cynical, because no matter what they try, nobody is satisfied.**

Differences over what constitutes 'fair' and 'effective' reward systems, and uncertainties about the behavioural impact of particular rewards and reward practices, makes the job of the HR practitioner working in this field particularly problematical and challenging. There are no simple or universalistic answers and prescriptions that are guaranteed to work. What emerges from the different academic contributions, research findings, and individual experiences is that there is no consensus on how organizations should be rewarding their employees, nor is there any certainty that the use of particular rewards will actually generate the behaviours and outcomes desired by managers. Furthermore, not all commentators hold the same views as to the effects on behaviour of particular types of reward.

A good example of the polarization of opinion over the use of rewards can be seen in the arguments relating to the use of rewards to encourage higher levels of individual performance, that is, those relating to performance-related pay. Many managers and employees genuinely believe that rewards used in this way do have a positive impact on employee motivation and, used appropriately, can increase individual performance levels. This is often described as the 'incentivized' level of performance. On the other hand, writers such as Herzberg (2003) and Kohn (1993a) have consistently taken the view that such rewards not only fail to deliver the intended outcomes, but actually distort behaviour and have a long-term detrimental effect on productivity. Kohn even equates these additional payments with bribes and argues that they should not be used, despite the fact that many managers and employees believe that people will do a better job if they have been promised some kind of reward or incentive.

The difficulties faced by managers in determining the most appropriate and effective reward strategy for their organizations are not only highlighted in the academic literature, but also in the realities of organizational life. The dilemma they face is that, while employees value rewards and generally would like more of them, rewards can be very costly for the organization and if pay is the predominant form of reward, overpaying employees can be an expensive mistake—remember that it is much easier to give rewards than it is to take them away! At the same time, it is natural to expect that employees will want to maximize their remuneration and reward levels, to reflect their views about their value and the contribution that they believe they make to the organization. This tension between what employees feel they are worth and what managers consider it is economically prudent to pay is often at the heart of disagreements and conflict between the two parties, particularly if financial rewards are involved.

It is quite easy to establish the existence of tensions and disagreements over pay. If an organization were to seek the opinions of its employees on this subject, it would be far more likely to find that employees consider themselves underpaid rather than overpaid. Whether they would consider themselves to be under- rather than over-rewarded is a separate question, but given that pay is the most visible and, arguably, the most important reward provided by employment, the tendency for employees to believe that they are paid less than they feel they deserve helps to explain why pay is often the cause of many outbreaks of industrial conflict.

Student Activity 12.1 is designed to provide insights into the complexities and apparent paradoxes associated with the use and perception of rewards.

**STUDENT ACTIVITY 12.1**

Language and perception are critical to understanding the meanings associated with certain reward situations. Consider the following statements and explain what they mean, giving examples if possible:

- a reward can be seen as a punishment;
- a reward can become a bribe;
- the award of an annual bonus can result in disappointment and a sense of rejection;
- the offer of a pay increase is rejected by union officials as 'insulting';
- a pay increase is also perceived as a pay decrease.

# Current Issues in Reward Management

## What do we mean by rewards?

We should not take it for granted that all of the main organizational stakeholders share the same views about what constitutes a reward and the value that any particular reward represents. For too long, rewards have only been equated with pay and this perception needs to be challenged. As Thompson (2002) argues:

> **we need to re-think what is and what is not a reward.**

Rewards can, in one sense, represent instruments for controlling behaviour. Consider their use, first of all, in a non-employment context. Anyone who has visited Disney SeaWorld theme parks will almost certainly have observed the use of rewards to reinforce desired behaviour in animals. When a seal, dolphin, or killer whale performs an act correctly, the trainers pat it, praise it, and feed it fish as a reward for doing the right thing. This is what is known as 'instrumental conditioning', under which desired behaviours are immediately followed by a reward. The animal quickly begins to associate certain behaviours with particular consequences, i.e. the reward, and because the reward is desired, it quickly learns to associate one with the other.

Children similarly learn through the use of various kinds of reward. Being well behaved can become associated with sweets and chocolate, extra TV time, and special rights. Interestingly, however, while the use of rewards to train animals seems to work most of the time, the same can't be said for children, who don't seem to play to the same set of rules as animals!

So what if rewards are withheld? Does this constitute a form of punishment? It is important to remember that, just as rewards have the potential to give pleasure and satisfy a fundamental need if they are given, withholding or withdrawing them has the potential to hurt. From a behavioural perspective, managers need to try to predict the reactions that follow from using rewards in different ways.

Kohn (1993a) argues that rewards and punishment are not really opposites, but different sides of the same coin. He suggests that the giving and the withholding of a reward each represent strategies that amount to manipulating the behaviour of an animal, child, and an employee. In this sense, a reward represents an extrinsic—that is, an externally located—source of motivation that, according to Kohn, does not alter a person's emotional or cognitive commitment, which are the keys to understanding and influencing behaviour.

But managers are not dealing with animals or children, and the questions they are particularly interested in are:

- can rewards be used to condition the behaviour of employees and, if so, in what circumstances?
- what types of reward have the greatest impact on employee behaviour?
- is the distinction between extrinsic and intrinsic rewards a useful one, and, if so, why?
- are there any problems and costs associated with the inappropriate use of rewards?



Failing to reward in circumstances in which the employee honestly believes that the reward is deserved and rightful can have a destabilizing effect on the employment relationship.

For a case study example of a breakdown in the employment relationship because of issues over rewards see the Online Resource Centre extension material 12.1.

It could be argued that employees are not simply interested in material rewards and that, if organizations are seeking to strengthen employees' commitment through the management of rewards, paying them more is unlikely to achieve this. Most people would not reject an increase in their pay, but only when the wage or salary becomes seriously out of line with expectations or long-established comparators does pay, in the sense that the level is perceived to be too low, begin to have a significant impact on employee behaviour, or when its real value falls. Managers need to recognize that the absence or withholding of opportunities, a lack of recognition for achievement or a feeling that the organization doesn't value its employees all have the potential to create dissatisfaction and disagreement with management's behaviour and decisions. Some will resign and move to other employment; others will, through different circumstances, stay, but do less; those who feel particularly strongly may openly challenge management from within.

## Characteristics of rewards

We would argue that, whatever form it takes, a reward must have the following characteristics:

- It must have a value in itself or because of what it represents. In other words, its value is linked to the fulfilment of a basic human need or one that is socially acquired.

- It must be relevant and important to the individual. A company car, for example, is not important to the employee who either cannot drive or has no need of a car, and free membership of a fitness club is unlikely to be attractive to someone who has no interest in physical activity.
- It must be associated with, or serve, a purpose. A reward is something that can be used to achieve an outcome that is desired by one party or the other.
- A reward needs to have a behavioural effect on the person receiving the reward, although the actual effect may not be that which was intended.
- There must be conscious recognition on the part of the receiver and giver that an act of rewarding has taken place.

Whatever the intention of the 'giver', it is the receiver who effectively gives meaning to an exchange or transaction, and managers must be at least aware of the possibility that their motivation and intentions may be misinterpreted or misconstrued by the receiver. Although the nature of a reward is often seen as unproblematical, this is far from reality and this is not only a question of conceptual clarity. Managers' reward strategies are, in part, based on their own views about what employees' value, the assumptions they make about the behavioural impact that might follow from the use of particular kinds of rewards, and the operation of the reward and payment systems that they use. If their assumptions are flawed, it is likely that the objectives associated with a particular reward scheme will not be achieved.

## Rewards categories



Rewards are usually placed in the following categories:

- Monetary rewards
  - Basic pay
  - Bonuses
  - Commission payments
  - Overtime
  - Condition payments
- Benefits associated with working for the organization
  - Pensions
  - Health care
  - Subsidized meals, loans, etc.
  - Membership of health and fitness clubs
  - Company cars or petrol allowances
  - Flexible working arrangements
- Psychological rewards

  The source of these is embedded in the work that people do and the environment in which they work.
  - Recognition
  - Praise
  - Being valued
  - Being part of a social community
  - Achievement
  - Recognizing that work is important and has an intrinsic value
  - Fun and enjoyment

- Personal rewards
  - Promotion
  - Advancement and development
  - Acquisition of new competencies
  - Increased employability

The recently developed concept of 'total rewards' is important because it provides managers today with the opportunity to identify, and use, a much wider range and variety of rewards than was perhaps available or understood by earlier generations. Many of these are non-materialistic, relate to the psychological well being of employees, and exist in the working environment. Recognizing the importance of these types of reward, Pfeffer (1998) argues that:

> **Creating a fun, challenging and empowered work environment in which individuals are able to use their abilities to do meaningful jobs for which they are shown appreciation is likely to be a more certain way to enhance motivation and performance—even though creating such an environment may be more difficult and take more time than merely turning the award lever.**

This view that pay may have far less of an impact on employees' day-to-day behaviour than other forms of reward is supported by research undertaken by Sanders and Sidney, the HR consultancy. Quoting from their findings that employees value work friendships as much as pay, Deeks (2000) reported that:

> **Of the 313 employees surveyed, 80 per cent claimed that they enjoyed going to work mainly because of the people they worked with. Two-thirds indicated that the workplace community influenced whether they stayed with an organization. A further 62 per cent said that the workplace community had alleviated other areas of dissatisfaction, such as pay.**

The idea that managers can manipulate employee behaviour by having control over different reward levers is as dangerous as it is attractive, but the belief that certain kinds of rewards, particularly monetary incentives, can deliver significant improvements in performance is shared by many managers and employers. This belief was brought to the fore by the experiences and writings of F.W. Taylor (1998). Taylor believed that workers who placed a high value on money and were not of high intelligence would respond positively to the prospect of earning more through increasing their performance. Such circumstances as Taylor describes are not fundamentally different to those we thought about earlier in relation to animals performing at SeaWorld centres, where careful training regimes linked to performance standards were reinforced by rewards that the animals valued.

Despite challenges from writers such as Kohn (1993a, 1993b) and Herzberg (2003), the influence of the Taylorist belief in the use and effectiveness of financial incentives is still pervasive, and not only among managers: many employees in sales, construction, and engineering would probably hold similar views. What unites both managers and employees is the notion that there are, in fact, two levels of employee performance. One can be described as the 'normal' level, which corresponds to employees providing effort and output levels reflecting what they consider to be fair and appropriate in relation to the contractually based reward package. This is often expressed in the phrase:

> **A fair day's work for a fair day's pay.**

But over and above this exists what is thought of as the 'incentivized' level of effort and performance, which can only be accessed through additional monetary payments, in the form of incentives. Those who adopt this view also tend to believe that the incentivized level of effort and performance can only be accessed through additional financial payments that are between 25 to 33 per cent of pay.

The case that individual performance levels can move significantly between different performance levels is not, in itself, the central question; crucial is whether increased performance can only be delivered through the use of financial incentives and whether the use of such payments, under certain circumstances, can actually be dysfunctional. These are the questions that those critical of the use of financial incentives are asking and, in so doing, these critics are beginning to point to other, more effective, forms of reward that can be used to improve employee performance.

## The Case For and Against Incentive-Based Rewards

**PRACTITIONER INSIGHT Judy Crook, HR Consultant**

I want to say a few things about the use of payments linked to performance or production, based on my experience of working in manufacturing and sales environments.

The most important difference between manufacturing and service based organizations, including the public sector, is the ability to carry out meaningful, objective, and consistent measures of performance. Many performance-related payment schemes outside of the manufacturing sector may look good on paper but they often fail because the reward/bonus is often based on questionable measures of performance; this not only undermines the integrity of the scheme but can be costly to the company. Manufacturing and sales environments allow for the physical measure of production/sales and the translation of this into financial values which support easily constructed measures of individual and team performance.

But even in environments where measurements are relatively easy to establish, things can still go wrong. Any bonus scheme needs to be designed carefully to ensure that the scheme is driving the behaviours the company wants from its workers. This is not always fully understood.

There are two key objectives that need to be met in designing bonus schemes. Firstly to ensure that the behaviours the bonus scheme is designed to encourage are linked to company, team, and individual targets. For example, if you design a bonus scheme for sales people that only rewards sales it will result in behaviour that maximizes sales numbers. But the problem with this is that important considerations, like the margin the salesperson generates, are not seen as important because they have not been recognized in the scheme. The result is likely to be more sales but at the expense of lower margins. A sales person should be targeted on sales and margin to make sure they don't sell at the lowest price.

Secondly, ensure the bonus scheme targets are stretching but achievable, otherwise they can de-motivate and employees will not be interested in them. This is not always easy to achieve, but HR professionals and line managers need to work together to try and get the right balance between targets that are too easy and those that are too hard. The introduction of such schemes also needs careful consideration. For example, making sure that all those employees involved know the purpose of the scheme and its operating rules well in advance of the scheme starting. Regular monitoring and updates should be undertaken throughout the year to increase the motivational effect of the schemes, to drive performance, to create healthy competition and to share best practice. Bonus schemes don't manage themselves!

It is also important to look at the 'small print' of these schemes. For example, what are the rules governing eligibility? Do workers need to have been employed for a certain time to participate; will bonuses be paid on a proportionate basis depending on how long they have worked and what happens if someone leaves but is still entitled to a bonus that is only realisable after the date of leaving? These are important questions that need answering before the scheme is introduced. Finally, from a management point of view it is vital that these schemes and bonus payments are not seen to be part of the terms and conditions of employment of the participating workers and may be changed at any time by management in accordance with the rules of the scheme.

In my experience, well designed and managed bonus schemes can benefit the business and the employees but these outcomes don't happen by accident; they happen by applying the right kinds of design principles and operating rules, and by adopting performance measures that can be relied on.



Although the annual bonus payment made by some organizations could be considered to represent an incentive to higher performance, the 'incentive' effect of the promise of an annual bonus is only one of many influences on employee behaviour. It is meant to act as a reward rather than operate as a direct incentive—a subtle but important distinction and not always one that is easily understood. But there are numerous historical and contemporary reward practices that are based on a much more powerful 'incentive effect' where there is a very clear and intended relationship between improvements in performance, or however outputs are measured, and additional financial payments, either on an individual or group basis. Increases in output above a pre-determined level or in excess of targets, result in variable and conditional bonus payments. This is the underlying principle of Payment by Results reward schemes. At a behavioural level, such schemes work, or are expected to work by reflecting the importance of pay and the prospect of earning more, in an individual's motivational profile. More pay is the carrot and people are assumed to want more carrots to eat! But, is this belief justified in relation to the motivational drives of all workers or only those with a strong drive for accumulation of material things, or in certain conditions and contexts but not others? Is this belief culturally or ideologically based or is it supported by a consistent pattern of evidence based on the experience of operating such schemes? These are questions this section seeks to answer.

One of the most consistent critics of the use of incentives and incentive-based payment systems is Alfie Kohn (1993a, 1993b, 1995). The starting point for Konh's critique is the acceptance that, as in the UK, many US managers, and those that advise them:

> **believe in the redemptive power of rewards.**

But his research—based on numerous articles, studies, and experiments, not all of which are industry based—indicates that rewards:

> **typically undermine the very processes they are intended to enhance.**

These problems appear to go beyond the design and implementation of incentive-based pay systems. Kohn argues that:

> **the failure of any given incentive programme is due less to a glitch in that program than to the inadequacy of the psychological assumptions that ground all such plans.**

Kohn suggests that incentives, in their many different forms, not only achieve (at best) temporary compliance or short-term behavioural changes that may be manifested in improved performance, but do not alter the attitudes that underlie behaviour. This is a very similar view to that expressed by Herzberg (2003) in his famous article on employee motivation, in which he distinguished 'movement' from 'motivation'. Herzberg saw incentives as having the capacity to 'move' people, with further movement only being achieved by more incentives. Motivation, on the other hand, was based on an inner force, under which behaviour comes primarily from a person wanting to do something rather than from external stimulation, which he describes as being equivalent to bribes.

What, then, are the reasons why rewards, in the form of incentives, fail? Kohn suggests the following factors.

- Pay is not a motivator

  This is not meant to imply that money is unimportant or that paying less than is considered fair is acceptable, but rather that paying people more will not encourage them to do better or more work over the long term.

- Rewards punish

  This is about feeling controlled and manipulated by managers, if the rewards that employees expect or hope to receive are withheld or withdrawn.

- Rewards rupture relationships

  The pursuit of personal rewards has the effect of reducing cooperation and fracturing relationships: rewards individualize work.

- Rewards ignore reasons

  The use of incentives is often an easier way of trying to address problems of behaviour and performance than exploring and understanding the underlying causes of the problems.

- **Rewards discourage risk taking**

  Because employee behaviour is increasingly focused on trying to achieve the incentive, behaviour that is not seen to be relevant to this is downgraded, even though it still might be important to the organization.

- **Rewards undermine interest**

  This is about the way in which the use of extrinsic controls and influences are thought to undermine employee commitment and interest in their work, because they reduce interest in anything else.

Kohn's article and criticisms of using rewards to generate commitment and improved performance produced a predictable response from many managers, consultants, and other academics, whose views were also published in the *Harvard Business Review* (Bennett Stewart et al., 1993). In the article, the contributors argued that:

- rewards should not be confused with incentives and people should be rewarded for a job well done. Companies should not stop paying for performance, but should avoid using incentives;
- while much of what Kohn says about the limits of behaviourist psychology and the instrumental use of incentives has a degree of validity, integrating the use of incentives and gain-sharing, as part of wider strategy of work reorganization and participative working, can achieve very significant results;
- incentive schemes have a limited time during which they can be effective and, within this timeframe, they can be important elements of a wider reward package;
- many rewards are not perceived as bribes, but as equitable outcomes that reflect the contributions that people have made;
- while the negative aspects of using of piece rates and merit pay to reinforce task-orientated behaviour are understood, appropriate rewards for improved performance make sense intuitively and practically, and they are neither wrong nor intrinsically demotivating.



It is possible to reconcile the differences between Kohn's position and those who, while accepting some of his arguments, believe that he has gone too far in appearing to reject any positive outcomes from using rewards to influence employee behaviour. Both are, to a certain extent, 'right' and, while incentive-based rewards may have a part to play in influencing employee performance, over-reliance on such rewards is dangerous. Metaphorically, in rejecting the possible beneficial effects of incentives, we might be 'throwing the baby out with the bathwater'!

Pfeffer and Sutton (2006) address the role and impact of financial incentives directly in chapter 5 of their book. Their starting point is to accept that many, if not all of management's decisions on pay policy and the use of incentives are based on several deeply held, widely shared, and inter-twined beliefs and assumptions about what motivates people at work. But they are also clear that these basic assumptions are part of the problem—they are only assumptions! And because organizations fail to adequately test their validity and contextual applicability, they often result in pay policies and practices that fail to produce the kind of employee behaviour that managers want. A view that supports much of what Kohn argues.

The assumed motivational effect of financial incentives is based on the twin beliefs that the desire for more 'pay' does or can affect the behaviour of most employees, and that performance can be increased primarily or only through increase in employee effort levels and that these will indeed respond to the prospect of gaining financial rewards. But Peffer and Sutton quite rightly point out that if performance problems result from factors other than restricted effort, then using financial incentives to raise effort and through this individual performance will inevitably fail. The diagnosis of performance problems then becomes a critical element in the decision whether or not to employ an incentive scheme.

But their review of the evidence on the use of financial incentives allows them to claim that 'There is no question that financial incentives motivate people and, under the right conditions, can drive big increases in performance and productivity' (p. 121), whilst recognizing that critical to this outcome are the conditions and contextual features of the environment in which such schemes are applied. It is clear from their research that whilst the basic assumption about the motivational impact of financial incentives may well have a degree of general validity, many of the failures associated with such schemes are caused by:

1. The failure to accurately diagnose the underlying causes of performance problems.
2. Weaknesses in the design of financial incentive schemes.
3. Organizational factors and conditions which are not consistent with or accommodative to what are relatively simplistic and one-dimensional interventions.

**RESEARCH INSIGHT 12. 1**

Read Chapter five of the Peffer and Sutton book.

**Pfeffer and Sutton (2006) *Hard Facts, Dangerous Half-Truths, and Total Nonsense: Profiting from Evidence-based Management*, Harvard Business School Press**

1. Identify the organization's conditions that need to be in place before financial incentives can be effective.
2. Explain what they mean when they say that the failure of many such schemes is not because incentives don't work but because they work too well.
3. In addition to the motivational effect, explain how else financial incentives drive performance.
4. Review the evidence they present on why financial incentives fail to deliver the expected performance outcomes and list the explanations in the order of their importance.



# The Status of Rewards

Our earlier reference to the use of rewards in training animals and conditioning the behaviour of children is useful in the sense that it draws attention both to the use of rewards as an expression of power and to their functionality. Rewards have also been categorized in relation to the form they take. We need now to consider the conceptual basis of rewards and how rewards that are seen in quite different ways affect behaviour.

## Rewards as rights

Rewards become rights largely through the process of managers offering employment, and through the prospective employee agreeing to accept the terms and conditions embodied in the contract of employment. Many of the expressed terms of the contract refer to what the employer is contracted to provide to the employee, in the form of a set wage or salary, holidays, pension, sick pay entitlements, and so on. These represent what the Americans call forms of 'compensation for having to work', and the benefits that employers provide over and above the financial package. These rewards, or forms of compensation, need to be understood as a set of rights associated with being employed by a particular organization, which continue to be provided for as long as the contract remains in place.

Consider the weekly or monthly pay cheque. When employees open their pay slips, do they see what they have been paid as a reward or as something to which they have a right because they have earned it? Here, again, we see evidence to support the argument that rewards need to be seen in the context of reciprocation, that is, an exchange relationship, rather than as isolated and detached acts of benevolence. It is also worth considering the behavioural effect on the employee of being paid as opposed to not being paid. Being paid (i.e. rewarded through pay) may not elicit any obvious behavioural consequences. It might generate a sense of reassurance; it might reinforce the degree to which the individual identifies with the organization; it might create a sense of obligation to those in control. But these effects can be difficult to discern and may not be obviously expressed in what the employee does or in how he or she performs at work. Ask yourself the question: 'What motivational effect follows from opening the monthly wage or salary pay slip?'

**KEY CONCEPT Reciprocation**

Reciprocation relates to the effect that certain kinds of rewards generate. This can take the form of an obligation or predisposition to give something back to the person or organization responsible for the original reward. Reciprocation also suggests that rewards are never simply one person giving to another, but represent a more complex, and often unspoken, exchange that has positive outcomes for both parties. The concept emphasizes the idea that the act of rewarding, particularly if rewards are discretionary, valued, and represent genuine motives, can, in turn, result in the recipient rewarding the giver, albeit in different, but no less important, ways.

What is more predictable, however, is the effect on the employee's behaviour of not being paid, not being paid on time, or not being paid the right amount, and of not being given the benefits to which he or she is entitled. Failing to deliver rewards that have the status of rights will almost certainly generate a much more obvious, and potentially damaging, response simply because these rewards are both expected and contractually determined.

## Rewards that are conditional or contingent



Within the employment relationship, many rewards made available to employees are additional to those prescribed in the employment contract. This means that they are linked to, and dependent on, certain conditions being met. These might involve acquiring new competencies, for which extra pay would be given, achieving agreed levels of output or production, meeting sales targets or meeting personal and business objectives. It would be too restrictive to suggest that this type of reward is only associated with performance criteria, but many of the reward schemes that are based on the 'conditionality principle' are associated with some measure of job performance and are frequently linked to what is generally understood as performance-related pay.

The point about this category of rewards is that they are not 'freestanding', in the sense that they are acquired simply as a result of being employed, but are related to some measure of how we actually behave or perform at work, and are experienced only if predetermined conditions and criteria are met. An incentive is a particular kind of reward that, according to Armstrong (2002), can be understood to be the promise of a specified reward that only becomes realizable after the achievement of previously set and known targets. He makes the following important distinction:

> **Financial incentives aim to motivate people to achieve their objectives by focussing on predetermined specific targets and priorities . . . Financial rewards provide financial recognition for achievement.**

Certain kinds of rewards can, therefore, take the form of promises of what will, or might, be experienced by employees at some future date. While many promises provide a clear understanding of what the employee has to do or achieve for the reward to be given, some are more ambiguous.

Consider, for example, an employer who is struggling to make money in difficult trading conditions and who pays his staff below market rates for the jobs they are doing, on the grounds that he 'can't afford to pay more', but with 'promises' to increase pay when conditions and profitability improve. In this case, it is the employer who decides when levels of profitability justify increased pay and, despite the reasonable expectations of his employees, the pay increases may never materialize, with fairly predictable consequences for the quality of relationships between those employees and management.

**KEY CONCEPT Expectation**

This is one of the most powerful and important concepts in the field of reward management. It focuses attention on the behavioural impact of different 'reward experiences' and on whether the amount or form of any given reward creates a positive or negative response. The more people expect, whether this is considered reasonable or not, is not the point; what is the point is that expectations, if not met, will result in disappointment and behaviours that reflect this emotional state. Conversely, the less an employee expects, the lower the likelihood of disappointment with what he or she receives.

Expectation is closely tied into the Psychological Contract and is arguably the most important factor that explains a weakening or breakdown in this unwritten, and often, unacknowledged, relationship. Expectation is also linked to beliefs about what is fair—fairness in rewards and fairness in the way employees are treated generally; the problem with determining whether anything is fair or not is that it is an inherently unfair concept and is open to wide interpretation.

The following HRM Insight offers an insight into contingent rewards—often based on a clear relationship between behaviour, performance outcomes, and reward. It also allows students to become familiar with their basic design principles and gives them an opportunity to construct one that will deliver the intended outcomes. The insight is based on a real life scheme and details of its operation can be found in the online resource centre.

For details of how the scheme worked in practice see Online Resource Centre extension material 12.2

**HRM INSIGHT 12.1 New England Tools Ltd**

New England Tools Ltd distributes a wide range of high quality tools to the motor trade, garages, repair centres, and mobile workshops. Its products enjoy a strong brand reputation within the trade and lie at the top end of the market in terms of quality and price. It does not operate in the retail sector but sells through a national network of distributors who order products from the regional manager, who in turn submits these orders to the company HQ. The distributor applies a mark up to cost and this becomes the price the end user pays. Each distributor operates as a franchise but has to buy and sell on only the products offered by New England Tools. Quite simply, the more they can sell to the trade, the more business they generate for themselves and for New England Tools.

The national network of distributors is managed by a team of nine regional managers who on average are responsible for ten distributors. The key role of the regional managers involves recruiting new distributors, developing their business acumen and awareness, and providing training in selling skills and customer relationships. They also have to provide direct support to their distributors in the development of their customer base.

Jenny Bingham, the HR manager for New England Tools has been working closely with the company MD, David Wilson, on a strategy for improving company performance through the use of incentives and rewards and has been looking at the way the District Managers are currently rewarded. This is what she has found.

- Each district manager is paid a fixed salary with benefits.
- Each district manager is set an annual target of purchases of products they make from the company which reflects the sales their distributors make to the end user. This is their annual budget—the value of purchases they are expected to achieve. The annual targets are not the same—such differences reflect the geographical size of their districts and the number of distributors they have.
- Recruiting new distributors, training them, and offering them advice and support in the way they operate their franchises is also an important part of their job.

Jenny is convinced that the managers will respond to a bonus scheme if it is carefully designed by encouraging them to work more effectively with their distributors to boost end user sales.

Your task is to prepare a proposal for Jenny that represents the design principles and operating rules for this bonus scheme.

Specifically, you are required to produce a PowerPoint presentation, which presents your ideas. These need to, minimally, cover the following requirements:

1. Decide whether the bonus scheme should be individual or collective, justifying your decision
2. What would the bonus be based on?
3. What would be your base line from which any bonus calculations would be based?
4. What would your bonus line look like? This is the relationship between increases in performance and the bonus paid at any level of performance within the limits of the scheme
5. What form would the bonus take?
6. What checks would you build into the bonus scheme?



## Rewards that are discretionary

These are rewards that are neither based on contractual rights nor on meeting specified conditions, but which result from managers and employees deciding to reward others in ways that only make sense in the context of their own particular circumstances and working environment. For example, without it being part of any formal agreement or incentive scheme, an owner of a business might, in the light of a good year's results, decide to give his or her staff a week's fully paid holiday in the Mediterranean. Alternatively, he or she might provide a one-off payment to reflect the contribution of the workforce to the organization's success, as was the case with the American Shoe Corporation (see HRM Insight 12.2). There is no promise of repeating the reward and, even if the company achieves similar results in the future, the owner may decide to invest the sum potentially available as a bonus, in new capital equipment, or even pay it as dividends to the shareholders. Discretionary rewards are often not planned and, therefore, employees have no expectation of receiving them. Discretionary rewards that become regular and predictable can, however, increase employee's expectation that they will receive them, with predictable consequences when they cease.

**HRM INISGHT 12.2 The American Shoe Corporation**

The American Shoe Corporation (ASC) is a long-established and family-owned business, with manufacturing plants in West Virginia and Pennsylvania. It has some 250 employees, many of whom are from the same families and have worked for the company for many years. In recent years, the industry generally had been damaged by overseas competition from low-cost producers and several other US shoe producers had outsourced their manufacturing operations, laid off part of their workforce, or, in some cases, gone out of business.

On the day before the company was due to announce its results for the preceding financial year, employees received letters asking them to attend a meeting on the following Monday morning with the works manager of the two respective factories. The reaction to this letter was predictable. Many anticipated bad news and expected that some would be told their jobs had to go, and, by the time of the meeting, there was an air of pessimistic apprehension among the two groups of workers.

Both works managers began the meeting by sharing the same message with their staff. The head of the company, in the light of a reasonable set of results and to reflect his gratitude and appreciation for the commitment and loyalty showed by his staff, was awarding each man and woman $1,000 for each complete year of service, with a pro rata payment for those with less than one year's service. For some, this meant payments of over $20,000 and for those whose husband or wife worked there, this meant a combined amount of even more.

The reaction of many employees was a mixture of surprise, disbelief, and a deep sense of appreciation, with some reduced to tears. They knew that this would be unlikely to be repeated, but they also knew that the payments genuinely reflected the beliefs and philosophy of the company's owner, who did try to treat his employees as part of a wider family.

### Questions

1. What might the motives of the company's owner have been in deciding to reward his staff in this way?
2. What effect do you think the decision had on the behaviour of his staff?
3. Would the same effects on employee behaviour have been achieved by giving the same overall amount paid as an increase in base pay over the next three years or as improvements in the benefit package, rather than in the form of a 'loyalty reward'?
4. Are there any negative consequences that might follow from this act?
5. Think of other examples of circumstances in which discretionary rewards might be used to positive effect.

The final activity in this section requires students to reflect on and share their own experiences with being paid and rewarded and should result in a deeper understanding of the impact on behaviour of different reward practices and lend support to certain of the theoretical positions presented in the chapter.

**STUDENT ACTIVITY 12.2**

1. In groups, list all of the rewards that members have experienced throughout their working experiences.
2. Consider the effects that the different rewards had on their behaviour and performance—which have been associated with generally positive behavioural and attitudinal changes or alternatively have had a negative impact?
3. Present your findings to the class and be prepared to discuss the implications of your results for the management of rewards. What general conclusions are you reaching?

## Determining pay

A great deal of effort goes into determining the level at which to pay employees. Pay too much and the organization may suffer due to not being competitive in its marketplace: being over budget may result in management being unable to employ sufficient numbers of people to carry out the required work. Pay too little, however, and this can lead to an inability to recruit and retain the necessary calibre of employees, and can result in disputes over pay. Determining pay properly in the first place might involve activities as simple as a short investigation into the appropriate rates, by scanning through the jobs pages in the local press, or might involve complex systems of evaluating a job, involving examining its content and the skills required to be able to carry out the tasks and responsibilities of the post. This is known as 'job evaluation'.

The rate of pay that the organization chooses to pay will also be determined by external factors, such as the levels of unemployment and typical rates of pay locally. If unemployment is very low, this will usually drive pay rates higher. In the UK, for example, rates of pay for similar positions will typically be higher in the south-east of the country. There may also be regional differences due to variations in the availability of labour.

For details on how Job Evaluation works see Online Resource Centre extension material 12.3

# Typical hourly payment systems

## *Flat rate*

Most payment systems are based on a flat rate or have a flat rate element to them. A flat rate is that under which an employee is given a fixed amount for a fixed period of time. This might be an hourly rate (e.g. £7 per hour), an annual amount (e.g. £20,000 per annum), or a set amount for any period between these two. There are also a variety of payment systems that are designed to improve the productivity of the workers to whom they are paid. The so-called 'market rate' helps organizations to fix hourly rates and many salary levels. Differences in skills and competencies also help to explain differences in basic pay levels.

Figure 12.1 shows the relationship between the level of skill and the band into which market rates fall. The more skilled a position, the higher the rate of pay and the broader the range of pay rates applied to the position in the marketplace.

The model in Figure 12.2 shows a typical distribution of rates of pay across different organizations for jobs of a similar value. By comparing rates of pay within an organization to those paid in others, it is possible to determine whether or not employees are overpaid or underpaid against market rates. There are no wrong or right answers for an organization about the level at which to pay compared to market rate. If the employer has a good reputation and a relatively stable workforce, along with other benefits for employees, then being at the lower end may not result in recruitment and retention problems. A highly profitable organization may, however, choose to pay at the top end to give wider choice in attracting and selecting the very best candidates.

## *Piece rates*

A piece rate is that under which an employee is paid for each item of work completed. Piece rates were more commonly found in manufacturing before the 1980s, but versions of piece rates still exist today. An

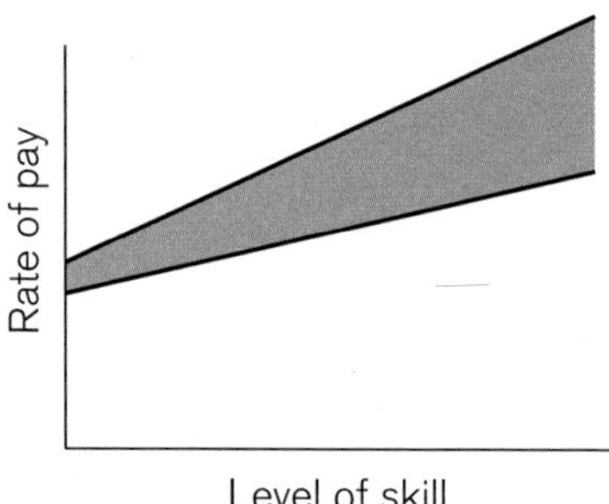


**Figure 12.1** Relationship between pay and skills

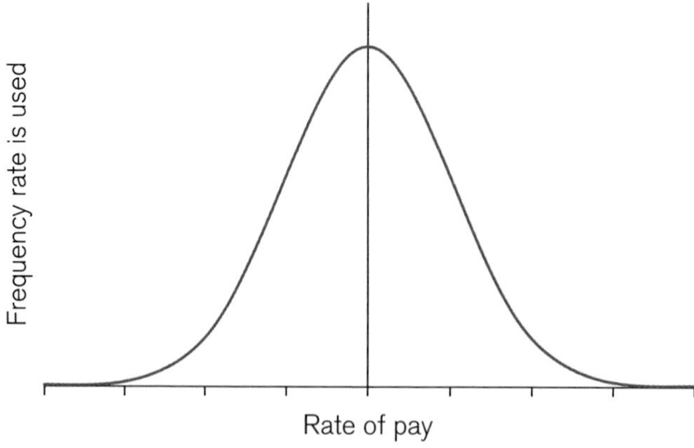


**Figure 12.2** Distribution of pay rates

example of an industry using a piece rate might be garment manufacture, in which each task is divided up into components and is timed, to establish how long it should take to carry out that particular task. The employee can then increase their rate of pay when carrying out these tasks by working at a faster rate than is average. Often this is capped at a maximum of, for example, 20 per cent extra.

While it can be argued that this system does enhance productivity, there are many factors that have led to its demise. Modern manufacturing techniques have increasingly favoured more flexible manufacturing. Piece rates become more complicated, the more component parts there are, and the administration of these schemes can be excessive. Many organizations have adopted cellular manufacturing systems, within which one item is taken through to completion before the next is started, to avoid having a large amount of expensive stock as work in progress and to avoid having leftover obsolete stock if orders change. There is also no doubt that a large part of the reduction in the use of the piece rate is due to the decline of manufacturing in the UK, with a large proportion of manufactured goods, including electrical goods, toys, and textiles now being imported from China and the Far East.

Piece rate systems encourage workers to try to stick to the jobs that they can do best and naturally tend to make employees reluctant to do work that does not attract the higher rates. Staff can therefore be reluctant to participate in off-the-job training or meetings to help improve productivity, because of the loss of wages that this involves. Production changes may not be welcomed because these can result in tasks being retimed at less favourable rates; staff may be tempted to compromise on both quality and health and safety, in order to maximize their output to achieve higher rates of pay. Repeating the same task over a long period of time can cause medical conditions known as upper limb disorders or repetitive strain injuries. Regularly rotating people around different tasks and allowing employees to take regular breaks can reduce the risk of this type of injury, but piece rate systems can make it harder to implement measures to minimize the risk of employees developing these types of problem at work.



### *Group/team bonus*

Another payment system, frequently used to encourage employees to complete more work in the time given, is a group bonus. Schemes vary depending on the organization, the nature of the work, and the number of people employed, but typically involve measuring the performance of a group of people and awarding a payment to the group for increased output. The group either receives an equal portion of the bonus or pro rata payments that reflect different contributions. For example, certain team members may receive 100 per cent of the bonus, while others are paid 80 per cent. Different factors can affect the success of these schemes. If the group to which it is applied is too large, then there may be little personal reward for extra effort from the individual so effectiveness may be reliant on the quality of supervision rather than on the efforts of any one individual. Other factors can be linked to payment in addition to output levels. These can include, for example, the team's health and safety record, quality achievements, or the team's attendance records. The more factors that are included in the calculation of the team or group bonus, however, the more complicated pay administration becomes.

### *Rates for skills, shift premium, and overtime premium*

We have already established that higher skilled positions attract higher rates of pay. In addition to determining the basic hourly rate, an employer should also consider the time by which the work needs to be carried out and the possibility that additional hours might be required to complete the job or work in progress, for which 'premium' payments may need to be paid.

If employees are required to work at unusual times of the day, then 'shift' pay may be included as a pay item. For example, employees may work only at night, which can attract an additional payment that is typically in the region of 25 to 35 per cent of their normal rate. This is often expressed as a separate pay item, but may be incorporated into an employee's basic wage. There may be payments for early starts or late finishes, or a combination of payments if hours vary on a rotating basis.

There may also be extra payments above the normal rate of pay for extra hours worked either at the end or beginning of a working day, or on days that are not normally worked, i.e. overtime. A typical payment for overtime on a normal working day might be 'time and a half' after eight hours (i.e. an extra 50 per cent on top of the normal hourly rate). Working at weekends, if this is not the normal working pattern, may typically attract time and a half on Saturday and double time (i.e. 100 per cent on top of the normal hourly rate) on a Sunday.

**STUDENT ACTIVITY 12.3**

Overtime working has a long tradition in UK industry, particularly in manufacturing. Yet many organizations, such as Rolls Royce, are abandoning systematic overtime payments, instead moving towards paying increased hourly rates and annualized hours. After researching the literature available and looking at changes in company practices, answer the following questions.

1. What does 'institutionalized' overtime mean and how does this come about?
2. What are the disadvantages of excessive overtime?
3. What adverse behavioural and performance effects does it have?
4. What might be the effects of reducing or withdrawing overtime completely?
5. What strategies are available to management to maintain production in the absence of overtime?

# Performance-Related Pay (PRP)



Earlier in the chapter, we explored the arguments for and against the use of financial incentives to reward employees. Here, we will consider rewards to drive performance from a more practical perspective.

Performance-related pay uses financial incentives to link an individual's pay to his or her performance. Rather than simply awarding a bonus payment, performance-related pay usually refers to the system used to calculate the pay rise awarded to an individual, which is linked to a measure of his or her performance over a given time period. Pay rises tend to be awarded annually for salaried and professional staff, but might be awarded at other intervals depending on the schemes in place. The performance element might be the whole of the award or an additional amount over and above the standard cost-of-living award.

Often, performance-related pay is linked to performance objectives set for the individual as part of an annual appraisal process. The goals for the entire organization are broken down by department and by seniority, and each employee on the performance-related pay scheme is set a number of objectives to achieve in a given period. Measures are put in place and these are then reviewed at the end of the period to determine the extent to which they have been achieved. The pay award reflects the extent to which the measures are met. A key requirement in the employment of PRP is, therefore, the ability to measure accurately and consistently what performance is defined as.

Signpost to Chapter 9: HR Planning and Measurement, for insight into measuring the HR function

Incentive schemes and commission payments, as examples of the PRP principle, potentially apply to all categories of employee. Consider, for example, commission payments, which are frequently used for sales staff. The sales representative or manager will be given a target, usually an amount that he or she must sell or a profit level that he or she must achieve over a given period. The amount of commission earned during the period will depend on the extra sales or profit achieved above a minimum target. For example, a sales representative may be able to earn up to an extra 25 per cent of his or her salary at the end of the year as a bonus payment, if he or she can sell more than 10 per cent above the minimum target set.

Bonus schemes can also apply to senior executives in an organization. In a private company, this might be linked to the profit levels, sales, and cash generated by the business or might relate to achievement of objectives or budgets (Blanchflower, 1991).

**HRM INSIGHT 12.3 The case of Bradley Distribution**

Bradley Distribution is a provider of third-party distribution services, with locations across the globe. Pay for more senior and salaried employees is performance-related, using the following model.

Employees' performance is described in terms of their performance against last year's objectives, with 'A performers' exceeding their objectives, 'B performers' meeting their objectives, and 'C performers' not meeting their objectives. The behavioural style ratings from '1' to '3' represent the way in which the individual goes about meeting his or her objectives, with '1' representing 'always follows the required behaviour', to '3' representing 'rarely displays the required behaviour'. Under this model, the organization asserts that 20 per cent of all employees should fall into the 'A' category, 70 per cent into the 'B' category and 10 per cent into the 'C' category.

The overall budget set for pay reviews is 4.5 per cent and the actual amount paid is at the discretion of the departmental manager within the bands set, dependent on the employee's rating in the matrix.

**Questions**

1. What advantages might be achieved by an organization in implementing this model?
2. What might the disadvantages be in terms of cost, and in terms of the impact on the employees and managers of the organization?
3. Consider a typical salary within an organization with which you are familiar. Work out the difference in annual salary for an A2 and a B3 performer in this model. Consider the positive motivational impact of receiving this extra payment and the potential de-motivational impact of receiving the lower payment.
4. Consider the above model from the point of view of a manager of a team of twenty versus a manager of only two people. What dilemmas might each manager face if asked to rate his or her team against this model?
5. What are the legal, moral, and ethical implications of using this system to identify the poorest performing 10 per cent of the senior salaried workforce, given the intention not to award any pay increase at all to up to 10 per cent of the workforce each year?

Signpost to Chapter 11: Managing Performance, for more detail on performance rating scales

# Incremental pay schemes

The defining feature of this type of pay scheme is the way in which length of service drives pay increases, in addition to annual increases linked to cost-of-living adjustments. Incremental awards are generally limited to salaried employees, particularly those who work in the public sector. Such increases, according to Brown and Armstrong (1999):

> **inevitably seem to generate into automatic progression.**

Such increases are less popular among private sector employers for the simple reason that increases in pay have nothing to do with performance, contribution, or any appropriate criteria other than length of service. Upward movement from one point in a salary grade to the next is relatively unproblematical, although so-called 'bars' are sometimes applied to progression to the top of the grade. 'Going through the bar' can, however, be relatively easy, if meeting the criteria for progression is not difficult to achieve. Teachers, lecturers, civil servants and local government officials are most closely associated with payment structures that provide for annual incremental increases. Since the introduction of legislation on age discrimination in 2006, however, rewards relating to service levels exceeding five years are potentially unlawful, particularly if these relate to remuneration.

Signpost to Chapter 7: Equality and Diversity in Employment, for more information on age discrimination

# Contemporary Reward Practices

The penultimate section in this chapter provides an overview of the reward practices and priorities associated with the results of the CIPD's annual reward survey (CIPD, 2010). National surveys are useful indicators of what organizations are actually doing and, assuming that they are broadly representative, they also provide insights into the reward agendas with which organizations are engaged. They also point to trends in reward management practices—indicating how organizations are changing their ideas in relation to the challenges they face and expect to face in the future.

Some of the key findings of the 2010 CIPD survey are:

- An increasing number of organizations have developed a reward strategy, and many others indicate their intention to develop one. Associated with this trend is the increase in the number or organizations developing a 'total reward approach'. It is difficult to know what these trends actually mean; it could well be that these answers reflect not what is actually happening but what the respondents aspire to or feel they want to be associated with. Being associated with strategy, as we discussed in Chapter 3, through talking about it does not necessarily mean that the reward management practices have a strategic impact.
- Cash-based bonus and incentive schemes, (they essentially mean the same) are widespread in the private sector. There are several reasons for this. In certain industries, such as banking and finance, they are considered to be necessary to attract, retain, and motivate staff. But in the private sector it is also easier to design incentive schemes in ways that connect behavioural change with desired business results and outcomes. This is because of the greater opportunities for establishing meaningful measures of performance through such variables as sales, customer service levels, production targets, etc.

  Decisions about basic rates are heavily influenced by external market comparisons, internal pay structures, often based on job evaluation systems, and the ability to pay. Certainly, the ability to pay criterion has become much more prominent during the recent recession, with downward movements, mostly temporary, linked to organizations reducing their employment costs without necessarily shedding valuable labour resources. Maintaining rather than increasing the real value of wages and salaries will probably be a feature of the post-recession period although unless the economy experiences a 'double-dip' effect, pressure from organized labour and individual employees for increases that at least maintain the real value of wages and salaries will almost certainly develop.
- Reflecting the continuing debate about final salary pension schemes just under one-fifth of employers indicated that they intended to change their pension arrangements, either by increasing employee contributions, amending final salary schemes or through other means. Again, the evidence suggests that the costs and efficacy of employee rewards are coming under increasing scrutiny.

  The four main priority areas in 2010 were:

  - ensuring reward strategies and practices were aligned with the business;
  - ensuring that market rates are competitive;
  - ensure high levels of fairness in relation to internal reward levels and relationships;
  - achieving and maintaining cost minimization.

**STUDENT ACTIVITY 12.4 Bankers' bonuses**

This activity should be undertaken by two groups of students, each group taking on one of the two tasks and then combining for the third.

Bankers' bonuses have, in the past few years, been the source of continuing debate and controversy. Whilst ideological differences can explain the attitudes of different people towards bankers receiving 'high' annual bonuses, the debate needs to go beyond such positions and engage in more serious and meaningful questioning about their justification, and this is the purpose of this activity.

1. Each group should research the issue of bankers' bonuses and become familiar with the debate and issues.
2. Members of both groups should decide individually whether they are broadly supportive or against the practice—hopefully there will be a reasonable split!
3. The group that is in favour of bonuses then has to prepare a presentation—three or four slides only—which presents the case against them! And the group that was against them has to prepare a presentation in favour of them.
4. Collectively discuss what the basis for support and opposition was and establish how the concept of fairness was applied.
5. Also discuss the consequences that might follow if bankers' bonuses were eliminated or significantly reduced through taxation or rewards caps.





## Evaluating the effectiveness of reward management practices

These four priorities may not be shared by all organizations—differences between the public and private sectors and those operating in a largely domestic rather than international context will obviously make a difference in relation to their relative importance. Other research into reward management suggests that the effectiveness of reward strategies and practices is also becoming an increasingly important consideration. (Bevan, 2006; Armstrong et al., 2011; Brown, 2008). Much of the interest in the intended impact and actual effects of reward practices is linked to the 'evidence-based management' approach referred to earlier in this book; it also reflects Ulrick's emphasis on the importance of outcomes in HR rather than activities. But despite the development of more sophisticated approaches and techniques associate with measuring the costs and benefits of HR costs and benefits much remains to be done in the field of reward management to reflect this imperative. According to Brown (2008):

> **despite the very obvious costs of pay budgets, incentives and benefits plans, the spread of sophisticated HR information systems and shared service centers, the widespread adoption of balanced scorecards and near-universal pay benchmarking, very few organizations seem to have any concrete evidence to evaluate or justify their reward practices.**

Reference to 'fads', 'me-tooism', and 'history' (Bevan, 2006), and casual benchmarking of certain reward practices suggests that many decisions about what to introduce, what to change, and what to stop doing are often made without fully appreciating the evidential base for such decisions; essentially reward managers at best only have an imprecise understanding of the relationship between the workings of reward practices, the effects on employee behaviour and the impact on key organizational outcomes. And despite indications from the CIPD's reward survey that an increasing number of organizations are trying to develop useful evaluative tools and techniques, there is very little hard evidence that the situation generally has significantly improved. The inability to establish causal relationships between practices and outcomes may not be of particular concern where the costs involved are insignificant, but this is not the case with regard to rewards. With the costs of compensation averaging between 65 and 70 per cent of total costs in the USA, and not far below this in the UK and other Western economies, not only are there substantial opportunities for cost savings but also for generating higher value outcomes for the organization. Whilst basic pay and benefits might be less easy to change—linked as they often are to market conditions and collective agreements, other types of rewards may offer more realistic scope for revision, based on the answer to the question—are they working? Many practices become institutionalized over time and their legitimacy is not based on their efficacy but on tradition and custom and practice. Unfortunately, although understandably, many managers, when faced with the challenge of establishing whether a practice is working in intended ways or has lost its effectiveness would probably prefer not even to have to confront this question, let alone try to answer it. Why? Because a problem only becomes a problem, and therefore requires a solution, when it is officially recognized as such. Often it is easier to simply leave things as they are rather than 'manage' them in an active way, but unfortunately the problems don't go away, they often become acute and damaging. Yet, as Brown (2008) argues:

> **the whole point of being strategic about reward management is to set out how reward can best support the organization's success, establish the criteria to assess success, and to make changes and improvements to close the gaps.**

**STUDENT ACTIVITY 12.5 Making rewards strategic!**

Having reward strategies is not the same thing as achieving strategic impact as a result of your chosen reward strategies and practices. This exercise is designed to sharpen awareness of the strategic value of different reward practices and of the link between strategic value and cost.

1. Re-read Chapter 3 on strategic HR and look carefully at how being strategic was defined.
2. After reading the CIPD latest annual reward survey, identify those reward practices that could be seen to have a potential strategic impact, explaining why they possess this potential.
3. Prepare a presentation on the subject of strategically powerful reward practices and compare these with those that do not possess this potential.
4. In the presentation, establish whether those reward practices that possess high strategic value are also those that have a financial cost.
5. Finally, construct a graph which has two dimensions—high cost and high strategic value—and locate the full range of reward practices on the graph.



The final Research Insight in this chapter involves a much more detailed assessment of the recent work on evaluating the effectiveness of reward management practices. It also connects to the idea of what being strategic means and supports the need for 'hard' evidence that either justifies continuing with existing reward practices or legitimizes changes.

**RESEARCH INSIGHT 12.2 Evaluating the effectiveness of reward practices**

Read the article by Duncan Brown and individually or in groups:

**Brown, D. (2008) 'Measuring the effectiveness of pay and rewards: the achilles'heel of contemporary reward professionals', *Compensation & Benefits Review 2008*, 40:23, pp. 23–41.**

1. Summarize the reasons why he argues that knowing whether reward practices are effective or not is an important requirement.
2. List the principles and objects associated with making reward practices more effective.
3. Summarize the different ways, with examples of measures, that reward practices can be directly linked to key business requirements and outcomes.
4. Apply the model contained in exhibit four to any specific reward practice and for each of the ten criteria, show what each of these would mean in practice.
5. Identify the challenges associated with changing reward practices and briefly indicate how these might be addressed.

# Summary

- Rewards and how they are managed constitute an important part of what HR professionals are responsible for, and this importance is likely to grow as the new class of knowledge workers applies different requirements and priorities to what they want their employers to provide for them.
- Managing rewards has never been particularly easy; it is certainly becoming more challenging as employers have to meet the reward expectations of an increasingly diverse labour force. Inevitably, this means that reward packages and 'solutions' will become more individualized, rather than be the product of collective negotiations, and will reflect changes in personal circumstances.
- The evidence suggests that rewards that meet an individual's intrinsic needs, that is, those that connect to his or her 'humanness', have a stronger and longer lasting effect on his or her perception and behaviour than do those that are essentially materialistic in nature, which are used by managers in an instrumental way. Many of these rewards are generated in the working environment, and are given and received in an often informal and hidden (from HR) way. Examples of these might include praise from a manager, colleague, or customer; recognition for achievement; and opportunities to learn new skills.
- The psychological environment is, once again, identified as the context in which major influences on how an employee feels and behaves are located.
- As far as the formal reward arena is concerned, pay and benefits continue to remain contentious issues for management and this is, in an era of increasing competition and outsourcing of production and jobs, much to do with costs as well as the effectiveness of different pay practices.
- The concept of flexibility, which is so critical to management, theoretically means that pay can go down, for all or certain employees, as well as up. But this does not mean that the value of rewards has to fall as well as rise.
- One of the challenges facing HR and line management is to increase the overall value of the reward package without increasing its cost and this is being achieved by those who understand the value of non-financial rewards.
- Critically, organizations need to 'know' whether their reward practices and strategies are working in the intended way and if they are not, take the necessary actions to address the problems encountered.

**Visit the Online Resource Centre that accompanies this book for self-test questions, weblinks, and more information on the topics covered in this chapter. www.oxfordtextbooks.co.uk/orc/banfield_kay2e/**

## REVIEW QUESTIONS

1. Why do organizations use job evaluation as the basis for their pay structures? What are the advantages and disadvantages of paying people according to the job they do?
2. What is performance-related pay, and what are the pros and cons of implementing a performance-related pay system?
3. How do intrinsic and extrinsic rewards differ, and why is this distinction important?
4. Why have organizations moved away from the piece rate pay systems that were so popular in the 1970s?
5. What reward strategies are contemporary organizations using and what are the objectives to which these strategies relate?

***See Online Resource Centre for answers.***

## CASE STUDY

### The Star Hotel

The Star Group of hotels has twenty-six hotels throughout the UK, operating in the business, conference, and banqueting markets. While there is a London-based corporate headquarters, hotel general managers have considerable discretion for deciding on wage and salary levels, and over any incentive or bonus schemes they may wish to introduce.

Strict financial controls are established through the budgeting process, and managers have to produce monthly revenue and expenditure forecasts for head office. The expectation is that agreed budgets will be met, because this allows HQ to be confident about revenue and cash flows. Strict control over staff and employment costs are expected to be in place and maintained, which should not exceed an agreed percentage of each hotel's monthly turnover figure.

Beating the performance standards represented by the monthly and annual budgets is seen by managers as the way in which to demonstrate to senior management that the hotel is being well managed and is financially successful. Equally important is the need to ensure that customers are satisfied with the services they receive when they use the hotel. This helps to ensure a strong customer base and long-term prosperity. A key role played by the conference and banqueting department, and by reception/reservations, is increasing the proportion of 'repeat business', as well as finding new business.

The Sheffield Star Hotel is located on the edge of the city, which is itself seeing a growth in the number of hotels operating within the city limits. The growth in competition without a corresponding increase in overall demand for hotel facilities might be a potential threat to the Sheffield Star and its general manager is keen to find ways of responding to this. He is also under pressure to increase bottom-line performance and is considering different cost reduction strategies to achieve this. He is, however, convinced that increasing revenue and cash flow has to be the main way forward, because most obvious areas for cost savings have already been explored.



The following information summarizes the hotel's key financial, employment and operational situation.

| | |
|---|---|
| Annual sales turnover | £6m |
| Gross profit | £1.2m |
| Employee WTEs | 48 |
| Annual payroll | £1.4m |
| Average monthly wage/salary bill | £278,000 |
| Average room occupancy rate | 69 per cent |
| Average monthly sales ledger, i.e. outstanding debt | £187,000 |
| Average monthly restaurant sales | £89,000 |
| Average monthly conference and banqueting sales | £215,000 |

The hotel has the following departments and related numbers of employees:

| Department | Numbers | FT | PT |
|---|---|---|---|
| Housekeeping | 15 | 3 | 12 |
| Reception, including telesales | 7 | 7 | 0 |
| Restaurant, including waiting staff | 28 | 7 | 21 |
| Sales and banqueting | 5 | 5 | 0 |
| Bar staff | 11 | 3 | 8 |
| Finance | 3 | 3 | 0 |
| Secretarial and admin | 5 | 3 | 2 |
| General manager | 1 | 1 | 0 |
| Operations manager | 1 | 1 | 0 |
| Maintenance | 1 | 1 | 0 |
| Total | 77 | | |

**Note**: A significant proportion of the bar and restaurant staff is casual workers. The remaining members of staff are either on part-time or full-time contracts.

### The task

The general manager believes that the way forward is to incentivize his staff to perform at higher levels of effectiveness and holds the view that, if the right kind of incentive schemes can be designed, most of his employees will respond positively. He has invited your company of reward management consultants to work with him on this task.

These are the guidelines you have been given:

- as many employees as is practical to be included;
- individual, functional/departmental and organizational schemes can be considered;
- a close relationship between changes in employee performance and contribution to the bottom line should be established;
- schemes should be based on the ability to measure changes in performance;
- the expectation is that benefits, in all cases, should exceed costs;
- different incentive schemes for different groups of employees can be considered.

The task is to prepare a presentation to the general manager, in which you outline your ideas for incentivizing the hotel's employees. The presentation should include details on the following:

- who should be and who should not be considered for incentivizing, with reasons;
- your ideas/plans for incentivizing any two groups of employees, showing clearly how you would measure the performance of each group (note that a group can be one person or all of the employees);
- the problems that the hotel might encounter, in general, from its attempts to incentivize staff and the specific problems that might be experienced in the two schemes considered as part of the above point.

**Insights & Outcomes: visit the Online Resource Centre at www.oxfordtextbooks.co.uk/orc/banfield_kay2e/ for examples of incentive schemes that were developed by the hotel's management.**

## FURTHER READING

Chartered Institute of Personnel and Development (2010) 'Employee attitudes to pay annual survey', www.cipd.co.uk.

IRS (2001) 'The new reward agenda', *IRS Management Review*, Issue 22.

Marsden, D. (2004) 'The "network economy" and models of the employment contract', *British Journal of Industrial Relations*, **42**:4, pp. 659–84.

Marsden, D., French, S. and Kubo, K. (2001) *Does Pay De-Motivate, And Does It Matter?* Centre for Economic Performance.

Pfeffer and Sutton (2006) *Hard Facts, Dangerous Half-Truths, and Total Nonsense: Profiting from Evidence-based Management*, Harvard Business School Press.

Rousseau, D. (1995) *Psychological Contracts in Organizations: Understanding Written and Unwritten Agreements*, Sage.

Thorpe, R. and Homan, G. (2000) *Strategic Reward Systems*, FT/Prentice Hall.

Wilson, T.B. (2003) *Innovative Reward Systems for the Changing Workplace*, McGraw-Hill.

Zingheim, P.K. and Schuster, J.R. (2000) *Pay People Right*, Jossey-Bass.

Armstrong, M., Brown, D. and Reilly, P. (2010) *Evidence-Based Reward Management: Creating Measurable Business Impact from Your Pay and Reward Practices*, Kogan Page.

## REFERENCES


Arkin, A. (2005) 'Eyes on the prize', *People Management*, 10 February, p. 28.

Armstrong, M. (2002) *Employee Rewards*, CIPD.

Armstrong, M., Brown, D. and Reilly, P. (2011) 'Increasing the effectiveness of reward management: An evidence-based approach,' *Employee Relations*, **33**:2.

Bennett Stewart, G., Appelbaum, E., Beer, M. and Lebby, A.M. (1993) 'Rethinking rewards', *Harvard Business Review*, **71**:6, pp. 37–49.

Bevan, S. (2006) New Realism in Reward Strategy, e-reward, Stockport.

Blanchflower, D.G. (1991) 'The economic effects of profit sharing in Britain', *International Journal of Manpower*, **12**:1, pp. 3–9.

Blyton, P. (1995) *The Development of Annual Working Hours in the United Kingdom*, International Labour Office.

Brandt, R. (1995) 'Punished by rewards? A conversation with Alfie Kohn', *Educational Leadership*, **53**:1, pp. 13–16.

Brown, D. (2008) 'Measuring the effectiveness of pay and rewards: the achilles'heel of contemporary reward professionals', *Compensation & Benefits Review 2008*, **40**:23, pp. 23–41.

Brown, D. and Armstrong, M. (1999) *Paying for Contribution*, Kogan Page.

Chartered Institute of Personnel and Development (2005) *Reward Management*, www.cipd.co.uk.

Daniels, A.C. (2000) *Bringing Out the Best in People*, McGraw Hill.

Deeks, E. (2000) 'Mates lighten workload', *People Management*, 12 October, p. 9.

Department of Health (2004) 'Agenda for change: What will it mean for you? A Guide for staff,' www.dh.gov.uk.

Gouldner, A. (1954) *Wildcat Strike*, Antioch Press.

Herzberg, F. (2003) 'One more time: How do you motivate people?', *Harvard Business Review*, **81**:1, pp. 87–96.

IPA (1997) *Towards Industrial Partnership: New Ways of Working in British Companies*, IPA report, executive summary available online at www.ipa-involve.com.

Kohn, A. (1993a) *Punished by Rewards*, Houghton Mifflin Co.

Kohn, A. (1993b) 'Why incentive plans cannot work', *Harvard Business Review*, **71**:5, pp. 54–63.

Pfeffer, J. (1998) *The Human Equation: Building Profits by Putting People First*, Harvard Business School Press.

Taylor, F.W. (1998) *The Principles of Scientific Management*, Dover Publications.

Thompson, P. (2002) *Total Reward*, CIPD.

Waring, A. (1992) 'Working arrangements and patterns of working hours in Britain', *Employment Gazette*, March, pp. 88–100.

# Case Studies

# Case Study: Setting up an Assessment Centre

13

## Key Terms

**Selection criteria** The overall skills knowledge and abilities that are either essential or desirable from candidates in order for them to be successful in their role against which selection decisions are made. These may include qualifications or specific experience as well as broader skills and abilities. Usually a minimum standard is required against specific selection criteria to be successful. This term is a much broader term than assessment criteria and could include criteria that are used to screen applicants to go forward for further assessment such as minimum qualifications and experience. The application of the selection criteria at the point of the whole process where a final decision is made on which candidate, if any, is offered the job/position can be based on an aggregate numerical score which reflects how well candidates have met specific selection criteria or through a discussion amongst the panel of selectors, or both. At this point, additional selection criteria may come into play, consciously or subconsciously, where the decision-makers attempt to ensure the 'right' applicant is selected. See Chapter 4 on Recruitment and Selection.

**Assessment criteria** Predetermined qualities involving both skill and knowledge against which candidates are scored in a particular assessment activity to assess their suitability and potential for success in a job. The basis of assessment criteria is that the higher the score the stronger the likelihood that a candidate will perform well in the job role. Scoring against assessment criteria can be done subjectively by the assessing team or against pre-determined performance standards. The choice of standards, whether subjective or objective will clearly affect the ease or difficulty applicants will experience in meeting the standards in use.

**Assessment centre** A collection of activities designed to assess the suitability of a number of candidates for a job. The assessment typically involves several assessors evaluating the performance of a number of candidates in a series of exercises and tests. Candidates are normally presented with individual or group based exercises and tests which can extend to two or three days, the results of which determine whether the candidate progresses to the next stage in the selection process or is considered not to be suitable for the specific job in question or for employment by the organization (CIPD, 2010).

**Validity** It is important that any test or assessment used in selection has a high degree of validity. If the scores obtained by a sample group of job holders in a test correlate highly with job performance the test has a high degree of validity and can be regarded as effective in predicting job performance.

**Reliability** A test with a high level of reliability means that candidates who repeat the test consistently gain similar scores. It is important that assessment tests and exercises have a high level of reliability.

## Learning Objectives

**As a result of reading this chapter and using the Online Resource Centre, you should be able to:**

- understand the benefits to be gained by using assessments centres in recruitment;
- be able to set up a competence matrix against which to plan and design an assessment centre;
- be able to write assessment centre exercises to enable assessors to assess different skills;
- be able to design and implement an assessment centre.

# Introduction

The first of the three case study chapters deals in much greater depth with the use of assessment centres to select the 'best' candidate for a job. The IDS report (2008) indicates that assessment centres are widely used by employers to gain insights into key behavioural tendencies and patterns which correlate strongly to the organization's culture and to specific job requirements. The two critical questions assessments centres are designed to answer are:

1. Will this person fit into the organization and work well with others, where the job involves social interaction with others, and are the applicant's personal values and 'ways of behaving' consistent with those of the organization. This is an increasingly important question in situations where organizations recruit largely on the basis of values and behavioural traits rather than, or in addition to, specific job related skills and knowledge.
2. Does the applicant currently possess, or could through planned learning experiences easily acquire, job specific skills and knowledge.

The CIPD identified in their annual report on recruitment, turnover and selection (2009a) that 35 per cent of companies used assessment centres for recruitment purposes. This figure has risen over recent years and seems to be unaffected by times of economic downturn, suggesting that the value of assessment centres is increasingly recognized despite the relatively high costs associated with their use. The report claims that:

> **Assessment centres can improve the predictability of selection processes when well designed with a clear job description and person specification in mind**



It is, however, dangerous to assume that any assessment centre will offer a high degree of predictive ability, simply because there are so many variables involved and choices to be made in how they operate and who is involved. According to the CIPD Guide to Assessment (2007), the following points affect the level of predictive validity and therefore the value of assessment centres in identifying talented and qualified people.

- Clarity over objectives and focus—this involves ensuring that information is presented to participants about the job and the organization as well as information generated about participants. It fundamentally also involves being clear over what competencies any particular centre is prioritizing and which are critical for effective job performance.
- Accurate representation of the organization environment in which the person(s) selected will be working—this is significant for the design of the exercises/activities and the extent that theses reflect as closely as possible the actual working environment. As an example, if a global organization relies heavily on telephone, email, and web-based communications, it makes little sense emphasizing assessment activities that focus on presentational skills, and if the work that has to be done exists in a pressurized environment, this is a key variable that has to be designed into an activity.
- The number and complexity of the competencies being measured—many organizations, particularly those in the public sector, tend to create over-complex competency frameworks with excessive numbers of individual competencies existing at several levels. Having more competencies than it is realistically possible to assess and measure is not only an unnecessary complication but it could also result in loss of focus and the ability to distinguish core competencies from those that have less of an impact on job performance.
- The range of exercises and activities involved—few participants will excel in everything and consequently there is a need to have a sufficient range of exercises and activities that cover the core competencies being assessed. This may involve having more than one activity that measures the same competency and/or not assuming that the only competencies that are important are the ones that have been identified by the assessment centre designers; be prepared to recognize 'talent' that doesn't

conform to conventional definitions, and to recognize it means it has to be given an opportunity to be expressed. The concept of opportunity cost helps here to understand that too much conventional thinking on the part of HR can result in competent people being employed, (but also unfortunately incompetent people too) and talented people not being hired! These two paradoxical situations may be difficult to understand, but using the concepts of formal and material rationality explored in Chapter 2 will certainly help in resolving them!

- **The range and quality of assessors**—the obvious point here relates to those who judge participant behaviour and assess their competencies. Are they sufficiently trained and experienced and have their prior judgements and decisions been validated by the performance and career development of those they selected or scored highly? It's not just a question of the competency of the assessors to make sensible and informed judgements, but of who they are and their functional background and level within the organization. Careful consideration needs to be given to ensuring the right mix of assessors is available and in place to participate in the assessment centre. This will help to ensure that a line manager and senior manager perspective and experience is in place and undue emphasis is not given to trainers, HR specialists, and even psychologists as judges of talent, suitability, and performance.
- **Feedback**—consistent with the insights developed by Chambers (2002), and referred to in Chapter 4, is the belief that feedback should be given to both successful and unsuccessful candidates. The notion of procedural justice and its importance to applicants suggests that those who are unsuccessful will be more pre-disposed to the organization and the outcome if they are treated with respect and consideration. And this can be achieved with sensitive, realistic, honest, and (whenever possible) positive feedback for all applicants, ensuring that their self-esteem and the image of the organization they take away is itself positive and enduring.

Assessment centres usually consist of a series of activities and exercises that are undertaken by a number of candidates at the same time in a scheduled, structured, and managed way. This process typically takes place over a day or more either at the employer's premises or a suitable location such as a conference centre or hotel. Usually a number of trained assessors either observe the candidates during the exercises and make an assessment of the candidates' contribution or assess the final product of the exercise such as a written report or test or the content of a presentation. The final decision normally reflects a consensus amongst the assessors based on discussions and evaluation of the evidence from all the activities rather than a simple aggregation of scores and a numerical ranking of the participants. There are advantages and disadvantages to using assessment centres, shown in Table 13.1

**Table 13.1** The advantages and disadvantages of using assessment centres in recruitment

| Advantages | Disadvantages |
|---|---|
| Higher predictive validity than some other selection methods but depends on factors identified above | Inflexibility of arrangements—little opportunity to accommodate individual circumstances and availability |
| Realistic preview of future performance | Number of suitable candidates can be low in relation to those invited to participate, but this depends on initial filtering of applicants |
| Get to meet people—the social aspect of work and working is emphasized | Cost of development and maintaining relevance and currency of activities and exercises |
| Mix of assessors and consensus decision | Costs of assessor time, venue, and in certain situations high resource costs |
| Broader range of information upon which to made decisions | Pressure and intensity of experience may deter some candidates |
| High face validity, equal treatment for all participants | Possibility of social and cultural bias in design of activities which may disadvantages certain ethnic groups? |

In the current economic climate the costs of running assessment centres can become prohibitively high and to reflect one of the key themes of this book, that the decision to engage in certain HR activities needs to be seen in the context of costs and the expected value of the associated outcomes, the decision to use them may be linked to such considerations as the criticality of the appointment, where the cost of making the wrong decision is high, the expected return on investment, and the efficiency of the whole process where numerous applicants can be assessed in the context of the centre.

Assessment centres are widely used in graduate recruitment as they can be very effective in assessing generic skills that generate important insights into prospective future job performance.

In the graduate market candidates are more willing to commit the time required to participate in the process when compared to those in other positions who are more likely to have to use holidays in order to attend. Assessment centres can also be effective in recruiting at a senior level where it is likely that candidates will be more able to take time to participate in the process. Public sector school head teacher recruitment might be such an example in that it is extremely important to recruit the best candidate in an objective and transparent process and it is perhaps likely that candidates will already be employed by schools in the same or neighbouring authorities, so will be more readily available to participate over the required time frame. In larger organizations, such as councils and big businesses, internal applicants may be encouraged to apply for promotion and are permitted paid time to attend recruitment selection events for internal moves. The point being made is that careful consideration has to be given to the assumptions made about who can attend and whether attendance issues are potentially important considerations when organizing these events.

Signpost to Chapter 4: Recruitment and Selection



As seen in Chapter 4, Rynes et al. (2004) showed that assessment centres were more able to predict job performance than an unstructured interview. Rynes also showed that work sample tests and structured interviews were effective in predicting job performance. It would therefore seem to make sense to improve the predictive validity of assessment centres by using a combination of the most effective selection methods and include these in the process. The level of predictive validity achieved with any given assessment centre will vary and reflect differences in their design, the skills of the assessors, the types of activities used, and how accurately behaviour and performance are measured. Roberts (1997) argues that whilst assessment centres generally have high predictive validity they can take many forms and it is therefore difficult to apply a common standard and expect to deliver against the general expectation that they offer more useful ways of assessing applicants than other methods. Comparing assessment centres with other assessment and selection methods is itself somewhat misleading as many individual 'assessment instruments/methods' are often found to be employed in many assessment centre designs. It is clear, however, that in order to be effective care needs to be taken to ensure that the assessment criteria are relevant to the job in question, that the exercises included in the assessment centre are effective in providing evidence of performance against these criteria, and that those assessing candidates are competent. It is the authors' experience that where care is taken in designing appropriate assessment centres and where line managers are supportive of the process and the design, are trained to assess and are actively involved as assessors, then they are an extremely effective mechanism for selecting high-performing candidates.

In this chapter we will explore these in more detail and provide guidance and advice whilst providing an opportunity to put this into practice by guiding readers through the process of designing an assessment centre for selection purposes. This, like the other two chapters in the final section of the book, is designed to allow readers to generate 'real' understanding and competency in major HR projects—in this case setting up and running an assessment centre. The student activities have been designed to replicate as accurately as possible those that experienced HR professionals see as central to this particular task.

# Background to Fulney plc

Fulney plc is a distributor of construction products and materials to the professional and trade sectors of the market. Their products, including heating, plumbing, and electrical products are sold primarily to building contractors either 'off the shelf' or as an order specified by a consultant or architect in a larger scale construction project. Whilst primarily UK based they also have a significant presence in a number of European countries including France, Germany, Denmark, and Portugal. They have a nationwide network of trade counter branches which are supplied through regional distribution centres via an in-house distribution fleet. In total there are around 8,000 employees in the UK and a further 7,000 employees internationally, based at over 1,000 locations in the UK and a further 500 locations overseas. They have an ethos of developing strong employee relations, and employee incentive and recognition schemes promote high levels of employee satisfaction.

Like all construction-related sectors they were adversely impacted by the most recent economic downturn and this resulted in both their national and international graduate training programmes being suspended for new recruits. They now intend to relaunch these programmes and wish to design a new assessment centre as part of their drive to recruit highly talented graduates, particularly from management- and engineering-related disciplines, to support the development of a cadre of internal leaders who will be expected to be promoted to senior positions in the future. They are looking to fill twenty UK based and ten international graduate roles to functions such as branch management, sales and marketing, finance, HR, supply chain and logistics, and purchasing and sourcing. Candidates do not need specific experience in these fields but must be able to demonstrate a broad range of management skills in the assessment centre to succeed. Candidates for the international programme must be able to speak both English and a language of one of the main European businesses. The two equally weighted objectives that the assessment centre experience is designed to meet are:

- Identify candidates who have the potential to become successful managers within the company.
- Identify candidates who have the potential to be successful managers and eventually to become corporate leaders of the business.

# Elements of Construction of Assessment Centres

Once an organization has made the decision that an assessment centre is the most appropriate means of selecting candidates the next step is to plan and design the assessment centre. There are many consultants and professional organizations that can assist with assessment centre development and design and there are also 'off the shelf' assessment exercises that can be bought in. These can be expensive and charges can be incurred for design, development, validity testing, and assessor training and often it will be a requirement that a package is bought including all these features. Elements of these packages are often only available to practitioners who have undertaken minimum training requirements to ensure that tools provided are not used improperly and purchased materials have strict copyright rules to protect the integrity of the materials and the intellectual property of the organization involved in its development. An alternative approach is to develop the assessment centre in-house.

Figure 13.1 shows a number of elements in constructing and assessment centres, and we will explore these in more detail to understand why they are important.

## Assessment Criteria

The first step is to establish the assessment criteria against which candidates will be assessed. A starting point for this will often be either the person specification for the role or there may be competence frameworks

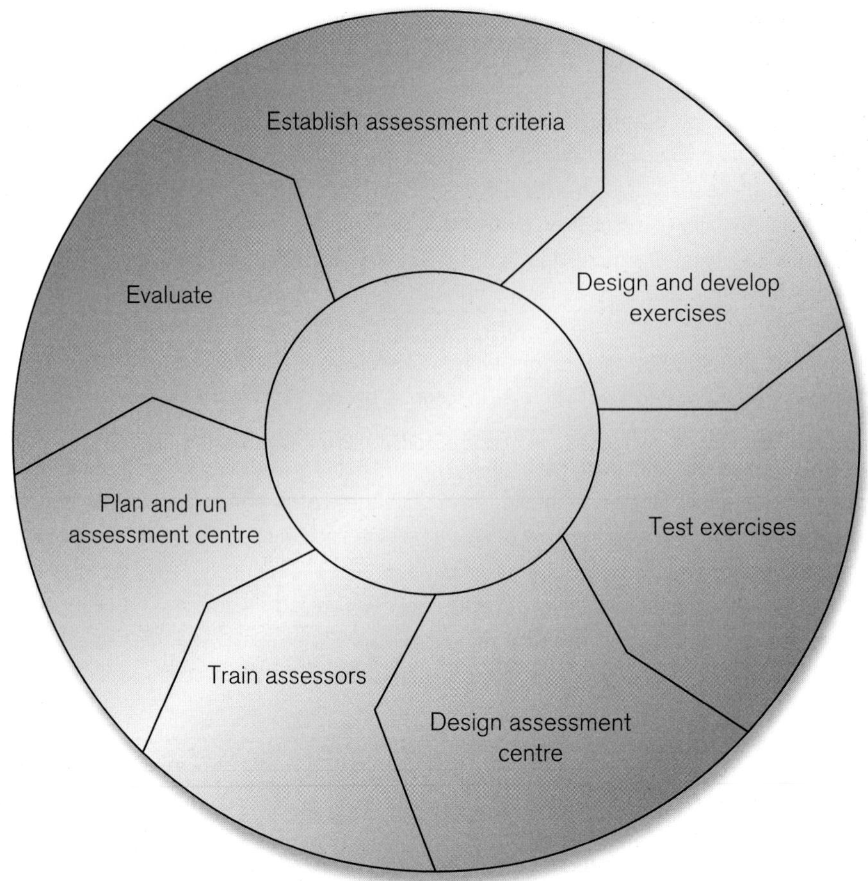


**Figure 13.1** The steps in developing assessment centres

that have already been written for the role. There may be minimum criteria on the person specification against which candidates will have already been screened, such as their level of qualification or the amount of experience they have. These are the types of criteria that are usually excluded from assessment centres as they do not relate to measurable behaviour. For example, there may be a level of qualification that is required and only those who have this qualification will be put forward.

Assessment criteria are typically behavioural in form and can be used in combination to predict performance in a job or type of job. Generic criteria might include skills such as communication skills, leadership skills, and problem solving abilities. These are skills that are relevant to many people in a variety of jobs but can be defined in terms of observable behaviour and the demonstration of positive examples of these behaviours can readily be assessed and measured. There may also be skills which are more specific to a particular job which are also observable and measurable, for example, it might be possible to measure the ability of a sales representative to sell the features and benefits of a particular product line with which they are expected to be familiar or a chef may be required be able to create an appetizing dish from a selection of basic ingredients. These types of skills often form part of the assessment criteria and can be expressed in terms of a competence matrix. This is typically a structured way of representing skills or competencies, breaking these down into examples of behaviours or indicators that might demonstrate the level of skills a person has. An example of this is shown in Table 13.2.

There is no correct number of criteria against which to assess candidates. Too few criteria and you will not get a balanced view of the candidate, too many criteria and they may overlap and it may be difficult for assessors to objectively judge on all criteria. An organization may also feel that some criteria are more important than others and therefore add more weight to these. The typical number of criteria is around eight to ten. Scoring systems also need to be considered. Too many options and the scoring system may

**Table 13.2** An example of one element of a competence matrix

| Communication Skills | |
|---|---|
| Demonstrates the ability to vary communication style, conveying information clearly and persuasively whilst actively listening to and taking on board the view of others | |
| Positive Indicators | Negative Indicators |
| Listens effectively to others | Interrupts others |
| Expresses views clearly and concisely | Gives too much or too little explanation to points made |
| Uses examples to demonstrate a point | Makes little contribution in groups |
| Speaks persuasively | Points do not follow on appropriately from others in discussions |
| Builds upon what others have contributed | Is abrupt or dismissive of others views |
| Seeks appropriate clarification from others to help understanding | Lacks confidence in making contribution or stating views |

be unreliable. Assessors cannot be expected to consistently and objectively chose a score out of 100 for a single criteria as it will be hard to justify the difference between each percentage point. Having an even number eliminates the tendency to choose the middle value on any range with an uneven number of values. A scoring system might be 1-6, with 6 being a strong score and 1 weak score.

**STUDENT ACTIVITY 13.1 Developing a competence matrix for graduate recruitment.**

The key point to remember is that the matrix has to identify behaviours, the presence or absence of which is believed to have an important bearing on their ability to perform successfully as managers and future leaders. The tasks are:

- Identify an appropriate number of key generic skills that would help Fulney plc to assess new graduates for their graduate training programme.
- For each generic skill develop a set of positive and negative indicators that would assist the assessors in making informed judgements about the extent to which each candidate possess the required generic skill.

**Note**: You may format these in a similar way to Table 13.2 or create an alternative format that better suits your organization of choice.

You should also develop your own scoring/rating scale, with weightings if appropriate.

Competence frameworks may reflect generic skills such as those required by all managers in an organization or may reflect skills and knowledge that are more relevant to a specific job or group of jobs. Due to the amount of time and resource used to develop competence frameworks, these are typically either more generic frameworks that apply to a wide number of different roles with core skills or would more often be used in larger organization where there are a number of people who hold similar jobs. It is also more likely that competence frameworks will be used where it is of greater importance to select and develop job holders to match the framework to improve individual and, therefore, organizational performance. For example, it might result in a greater direct impact on profitability to invest in developing a framework and working to maximize peoples' ability against this in a direct sales role with a high level of accountability and may be seen as less critical in a back office function with lower accountability, such as more administrative roles. Competence frameworks may also be more commonly used where the risk of error has a potentially greater impact, such as air traffic control or similar critical roles, where it is essential to ensure that job holders have the maximum level of competence.

Signpost to Chapter 4: Recruitment and Selection

## Presenting the Organization

Assessment centres also present an ideal opportunity to give the candidate additional information about an organization to help them understand the role they have applied for and how this fits into the organization. It's important to understand that whilst, from an organizational perspective, assessment centres function to generate information and insights into applicant skills, behaviours, and values, from an applicant perspective they provide indications and clues that help them answer the question—'what would it be like working for this organization?' Equally, if time and effort is put in to designing and developing tailor-made exercises which accurately reflect the types of scenarios and challenges that will be faced by the successful candidate then the exercises in themselves can give candidates an insight in to the actual role/job that the organization is seeking to fill. There are consultants who can be appointed, often at considerable cost, to work with an organization to develop an appropriate assessment centre and all the exercises and processes that are required. Where there is sufficient expertise, the assessment centre materials can be developed in-house. Care should be taken when developing in-house material that the competencies and criteria against which you assess are relevant to the role and that a representative selection of different types of exercises is used to accurately assess the candidates' capability against the required criteria.

An organization will also need to give consideration to where the assessment centre should be held. There are advantages to holding the assessment centre on the premises where the job is required in that the candidates can gain a view of the working environment and have a better understanding of the role as a result. Assessment centres do require a high degree of coordination and there may not be sufficient numbers of suitable, private rooms available on-site so hotels and conference centres provide a professional alternative, but with cost involved.



## Exercises

There are a wide variety of exercises that might be used to assess capability in an assessment centre. Organizations will typically select a variety of individual and group exercises. Assessment is either based on observed behaviour during an exercise in which candidates interact with others in a group or one to one setting, or the assessment may be carried out after the exercise by analysing written answers. Presentations are particularly important ways of assessing communication and group work skills and allow assessors to begin to gain insights into personality traits and key behaviours.

Table 13.3 describes some of the types of exercise that are typically used and what these entail along with information about the sort of information that can be gained by using this type of exercise. It is important to note that there isn't a 'best' approach to putting together or selecting exercises although a balance of individual and group exercises and written and assessed behaviour exercises is typical. The relevance will depend on the skills required in the job and how best this can be assessed. The list of exercises, along with the criteria that each is designed to demonstrate is often represented in a matrix to make it easy for assessors to understand the requirements in each exercise. Assessment scoring sheets which are exclusive to each exercise can also help ensure that only those criteria that are targeted in each exercise are assessed.

### Testing exercises

Where exercises are newly designed there may be ways in which an organization can test these to establish if they are effective. Ideally the exercises would be trialled using a number of recent recruits to the type of position for which the assessment centre is designed to be used. The scores of recent recruits would then be compared statistically to the actual job performance of this group, determined, for example, by supervisor

Table 13.3 Examples of the types of exercises used

| Type of exercise | Description | Details |
|---|---|---|
| Group discussion—non assigned role | Candidates discuss the contents of the same brief and alternatives to reach a consensus | These exercises are designed to bring out information about candidates ability to interact in a cooperative environment |
| Group discussion—assigned role | Candidates are given slightly different information and are required to represent different interests | These type of exercises are designed to be more competitive and to bring out more information about ability to influence others |
| Group presentation | Candidates discuss information and are required to present their conclusions to assessors | This type of exercise can bring out similar skills to group discussions but also assess presentation ability |
| Group activity | Candidates are given a task to complete as a group | This type of exercise analyses group behaviour in a more practical context and can reveal more delegation and leadership qualities |
| Written exercise (e.g. letter of response, case study) | Candidates are required to analyse a set of information and produce written recommendations or answers | This type of exercise can be used to assess problem solving and analytical ability along with written communication skills |
| In tray | An in tray exercise usually consists of a variety of items such as emails or an 'in basket' and candidates must respond appropriately | In tray exercises can be used to assess problem solving and communication skills in a multi-task environment where ability to prioritize is important |
| Individual presentation | Candidates study a brief, and present their findings to an assessor | These exercises asses similar analytical ability to a written exercise along with presentation skills and provide an opportunity to analyse ability to respond to questions or pressure |
| Role play—how would you handle this scenario | In a role play exercise the candidate is given a brief and is required to interview another person with an undisclosed brief to achieve a positive outcome | Role play exercises can be useful to assess interpersonal skills and coaching, questioning and listening skills in a one-to-one setting |
| Criteria-based interview | Candidates are required to give examples of evidence, in an interview, which demonstrate their ability against specific assessment criteria | Interviews can be a useful part of an assessment to analyse any area of skill so are useful to balance an assessment centre by targeting criteria that are less measurable elsewhere |
| Mini interviews | Candidates rotate round a number of assessors for a series of short interviews each of which assesses only one criteria | Mini interviews can be used to give a number of assessors a view of candidates and can assess ability to respond in a more dynamic and pressured setting |

ratings or the results of appraisals, to establish which criteria and exercises are most effective in predicting job performance. This is only possible where there are a number of roles. Where the organization is recruiting to fill a single or small number of roles then it is still useful to find someone in a similar role to trial the exercises to try and establish if the exercises are achievable in the time given and give the type of information that they are designed to provide.

**STUDENT ACTIVITY 13.2 Write a group discussion exercise**

Write a group discussion exercise which would be suitable for assessing at least three different areas of generic competence among a group of four recent graduates who have applied for the graduate leadership development programme at Fulney plc. Specifically:

1. Prepare a set of instructions which can be read aloud by the exercise administrator to inform candidates exactly what is required of them.
2. Identify one or more scenarios that may be faced by the successful candidate in which he or she may be expected to reach a consensus with colleagues about the required outcome. You will need to decide whether to give the same brief to all candidates and develop a 'non-assigned role' discussion, or whether to vary the brief to each candidate and create an 'assigned role' discussion exercise.
3. Design an observation sheet so that assessors can make a record of the exercise and develop and assessment summary sheet which enables assessors to score each of the criteria being assessed, giving evidence to support their decision.

**STUDENT ACTIVITY 13.3 Develop a written exercise**

Produce a written 'case study' exercise which would be suitable for assessing at least three different areas of generic competence among recent graduates who have applied for the graduate leadership development programme at Fulney plc. Specifically:

1. Identify a typical scenario that might be faced by a successful candidate and provide a description of what the exercise entails and how answers should be structured.
2. Provide a detailed description of the challenge faced and background information to allow the candidates to be able to weigh up the pros and cons of different potential outcomes and then chose a preferred outcome, justifying the reasons why they would make this choice.
3. Design an assessment summary sheet which enables assessors to score each of the criteria being assessed, giving evidence to support their decision.



# Other Activities

There is also a variety of other activities which can be used to assess candidate behaviours which may be included as part of an assessment centre. Those identified below represent the most common instruments and techniques currently in use.

## Aptitude tests

Candidates may be asked to complete an aptitude test such as a verbal or numerical reasoning test. Their scores in these tests can then be compared to a sample group to determine how they score compared to the sample group. Aptitude tests are usually bought 'off the shelf' from a professional organization that has developed the test and used robust methodology to ensure the test is fair. Where an in-house test is to be developed, care should be taken to ensure the extent to which the test can accurately reflect performance in the role (validity) and that the scores can consistently be reproduced by the same candidate in different situations (reliability). The danger with such tests is that whilst there may be a significant degree of correlation between job performance of the sample group and the scores in the test in terms of both the reliability and validity of the test, it is possible that someone who scores very highly may not perform well and vice versa.

It can also be difficult to weight their importance versus performance in the exercises designed to relate to the assessment criteria. Aptitude tests are perhaps therefore more useful for pre-screening large numbers of candidates and often will not form part of an assessment centre.

Signpost to Chapter 4: Recruitment and Selection

## Personality tests

Personality tests are also on offer from a number of different professional providers, usually an organization with significant occupational psychology capability. They are more complex in design than aptitude tests and are rarely developed in-house for this reason. They vary from aptitude tests in that rather than assessing skill in answering questions correctly of a similar nature, they are designed to give a view of a candidate's preferences in different situations compared to a sample group. Answers are therefore not correct or incorrect but are typical or untypical compared to a majority or normative standard. Personality preferences assessed vary in number depending on the test and whilst there may be a correlation in some roles between some of the scales they describe and job performance they are less likely to be used because of the difficulty of establishing their predictive validity. The information they provide can, however, be very useful in helping assessors to gain a more in depth understanding of how a person might prefer to behave at work and if the results are fed back with probing questions by a trained assessor the information gained can be helpful in selecting the most appropriate candidate for a role.

## Presentation about the organization

Often part of the introduction to the assessment centre, and often presented by a senior manager, a presentation about the organization can be a very useful way of giving a view of the organization as well as answering many questions candidates have and helping to set the scene for the event. A presentation may be prepared or might take the form of a more informal question and answer session. This, again, is part of the event that organizations may wish to keep assessors from to prevent subjective judgements being made abut the extent of interaction and the types of questions asked if this is not relevant to the selection criteria.

## Social event

An organization may decide to give an opportunity for assessors and candidates to socialize at some point during the event. Whilst this can help candidates to understand more about the organization and provide an informal setting to answer questions it does increase the risk of subjective opinion developing based on views that are not relevant to assessment criteria and that these subjective views might influence the final decision. It is important that assessors remain impartial throughout the assessment process. Organizations may, therefore, wish to consider providing additional rooms for assessors and candidates to retire for breaks and between exercises so that the contact with candidates is restricted to assessed, structured activities and there is less chance of information being discovered in an informal setting, over lunch for example. It might also be better for a social event to involve people in the organization other than those who are responsible for making assessment decisions. Alternatively, if there is to be a social event involving candidates and assessors it might be more appropriate to hold this after exercises are marked, but before a discussion to pool information to make the final decision. An unsuccessful candidate might feel subject to discrimination if a discussion over dinner revealed that he or she had different religious or political beliefs to assessors and other candidates. It might also make a candidate uncomfortable if social chatter about families and commitments outside work disclosed information about a candidate having different carer responsibilities or sexual orientation to the majority. If organizations decide to adopt this approach it may be advisable to make sure that all assessors are equal opportunities trained and are well briefed in advance about both expectations from this activity and the need to remain impartial and objective when assessing after such an opportunity to get to know candidates and to ask assessors to limit discussions to answering candidate questions and chatting about the organization and job responsibilities rather than more personal topics.

## Tour of the workplace

There may also be an opportunity to have a guided tour of the workplace as part of the event to help sell the organization and to allow candidates to see the environment in which they will be working. Where the assessment centre is to be held away from site there might be an opportunity to have a look round the site at the beginning or end of the day or as a separate element of the recruitment process. Again it may be sensible to not ask assessors to lead such a tour if possible to maintain their impartiality.

# Design Elements

Designing a timetable and arranging a day that flows for both assessors and candidates can be challenging. Assessment usually takes place over one or two days depending on the number of exercises being used and the timetable will need to include sufficient breaks for assessors and candidates as well as time for assessors to mark exercises as they go, whilst the information is still fresh in their mind. There may also be time set aside for candidates to give feedback about exercises and some time when candidates are asked to provide their views of other candidates. Typical numbers of candidates range between perhaps six and twelve candidates and assessor number will vary depending on how exercises are marked but may be either one or two assessors for every two candidates.



Typically assessors will either rotate around both candidates and assessors, seeing a selection of candidates in a series of exercises or the same assessor will see everyone in the same exercise. Some assessors may have a tendency to mark more leniently than others. This can be mitigated by asking assessors to assess in pairs to reach a consensus. It is also important to properly train assessors and use the training to ensure that consistent marking standards are applied.

To ensure that candidates have an independent person to support them through the process, that everyone is in the right place at the right time, and that someone is always on hand to answer questions, assessment centres may have an additional member of staff who is independent of the assessing team to run and/or administrate the process. This is more likely to be the case where there are larger numbers of both candidates and assessors. An administrator's role is to ensure that all materials are available and that exercises are fairly administered. To ensure that the integrity of an assessment centre in which exercises are to be used more than once is maintained, an administrator may also be responsible for making sure that all materials are gathered in from candidates at the end of the process. The person who runs the assessment centre is also responsible for the smooth running of everything and can provide advice to assessors to ensure consistency and fairness. They will also chair discussions to assist assessors in reaching an objective consensus about who to select at the end of the process.

Assessors need to understand their role in behaving consistently with each candidate and that they objectively score against each of the targeted criteria. It is advisable that assessors do not discuss candidates until the final discussion to avoid any influence between assessors before all marking is complete. Time should be set aside at the end of the exercises, once they have all been marked for assessors to discuss evidence gained in each exercise against each of the selection criteria to reach a consensus score. This may not necessarily be the average of all scores as lack of evidence in one exercise may be more than offset by strong evidence in other exercises and so a score higher than the average score may be justified. Only once a consensus is reached against all criteria for all candidates should scores be added up to analyse which candidate has performed the best.

**STUDENT ACTIVITY 13.4 Produce an assessment centre timetable**

Consider the types of exercises that you would use to assess graduates for the leadership development programme at Fulney plc.

1. Produce a matrix showing which selection criteria can be assessed as a result of which exercises.
2. Produce a timetable that would be effective for both assessors and candidates in a one or two day assessment centre. You should decide how many candidates and assessors will be involved at what stages and should include appropriate breaks for both. You should also ensure that there is sufficient time for assessors to properly carry out the required assessments and take care that neither candidates or assessors have long periods of time where they are unoccupied.

# Assessor Training

Assessor training is an important element of running an assessment centre as it is important to ensure that assessors understand how the process works, the content of the exercises, and how they are expected to score candidates behaviour and responses against the selection criteria. All assessors should, therefore, attend structured training to ensure that they are familiar with every exercise and how to observe and then assess each element of the exercises. There may be instances in some exercises where assessors are expected to ask candidates questions to challenge their understanding or their proposals and it is important that assessors are trained to handle this consistently and fairly. It is also important that assessors understand their wider obligations under legislation governing unfair discrimination to ensure that their behaviour throughout is in line with these requirements.

Signpost to Chapter 7: Equality and Diversity in Employment

**STUDENT ACTIVITY 13.5 Develop a training workshop for an exercise or exercises that you have designed**

Consider an assessment exercise or exercises that you have designed. Specifically:

1. Produce a training workshop for assessors to ensure that they are fully informed about the exercise and how to observe, record, and assess this exercise. You should consider how best to make the training practical.
2. Develop examples of training materials you might use to help trainee assessors acquire the required knowledge and skills.
3. Develop a tool for evaluating the effectiveness of your training and a mechanism for determining the standard required for an assessor to pass and be regarded as competent.

# Measurement and Evaluation

It is important to evaluate assessment centre validity, wherever possible. If the assessment centre is a one-off event to recruit a single or small number of posts, then it is difficult to do this objectively. However, feedback from assessors and candidates can provide useful information for understanding what worked well, what proved problematical, and what could be improved if similar events were to be used for recruitment purposes in future. Where there are a larger number of roles to be filled over a period of time, the scores obtained by successful candidates can be statistically compared to scores across different exercises and assessment criteria within the assessment centre to gain an understanding of which criteria and exercises are most effective in predicting future job performance. This data can be very helpful in making improvements to the assessment centre for future use.

# Summary

- Assessment centres can be an extremely effective mechanism for selecting high performing candidates and although they are costly to run this can still be the most appropriate way of selecting, particularly where there are a number of similar posts to fill and where there is a compelling justification in terms of the importance of the role.
- The first step in designing an assessment centre is to determine the assessment criteria that are to be used. The expectation is that candidates who score highly across these criteria are likely to deliver a strong performance in their role, but this critical relationship needs to be validated. The selection criteria need to be comprehensive enough to ensure that all essential criteria for the role are met either in the assessment centre or as part of the preselection.
- There are a variety of different types of exercises that can be undertaken during an assessment centre to give candidates an opportunity to demonstrate their level of competence; and assessors observe, assess, and record their assessment through all exercises. At the end of the process this information is used to reach a consensus about who is the best candidate.
- Care should be taken to design assessment centres well so that they run smoothly and are both reliable, in that the results are repeatable, and valid in that they are an effective means of predicting future job performance.
- It is important to assess fairly and consistently and to ensure that any recruitment process is fair and objective in line with current legislation. The design of the assessment centre is an important element in ensuring objectivity and fairness and it is also important to ensure that assessors are properly trained.
- Evaluation of an assessment centre is important to make sure that it is as effective as possible, particularly given the expense, time, and resources that go into running an assessment centre. The most effective evaluation, involving comparisons of scores against job performance is only possible with larger numbers but anecdotal feedback can also be very helpful.

## CASE STUDIES

The final part of this chapter involves dealing with some of the issues that arose during assessment centres run by Fulney plc. There are no correct answers as such but you should use your best judgement and experience to suggest potential solutions to these issues.

### The difficult candidate

You are the co-ordinator for the assessment centre and during the first group exercise that you are administrating you very quickly become aware that the behaviour of one candidate is causing difficulties for the group. Her style is very domineering and aggressive and not only has she commandeered the group to the extent that at least half of the discussion time has been taken over by this person but she has also forced the group down decision routes that others do not appear to be comfortable with. You are concerned that this person's extreme behaviour may inadvertently lead the assessors to mark other group members lower than they might have scored if placed in a balanced group. This may potentially result in scores being deflated for otherwise high scoring candidates with strong potential to succeed.

1. What are the options with regard to sharing your concerns with your assessors, what are the pros and cons of sharing your concerns and if you do raise this, when do you feel it is appropriate to do so?
2. What are the potential implications of either sharing these concerns or choosing not to raise this with assessors and how might you mitigate these?
3. What is your preferred course of action and why?

### The candidate with dyslexia

During the break following an exercise that you are about to mark, one of the candidates approaches you and explains that he has found the written exercise that he has just been asked to complete particularly challenging as he is dyslexic. He explains that during his written examinations at university he is always allowed additional time to complete written papers to compensate for his condition. He has not raised this issue until now as he did not realize that it would be a problem in the assessment centre.

1. How would you handle the conversation with this candidate and what information do you think it would be prudent to ask for?
2. What are the potential legal implications for the company regarding this candidate or other candidates given the competitive nature of the assessment centre and the condition that the candidate has?
3. What course of action would you recommend?

### The problem assessor

During your assessment centre, your over hear one of your assessors make inappropriate comments to other assessors, which are derogatory and could be construed as discriminatory, about a number of the candidates. These comments were made in a private break-out room, away from the candidates, during a period when assessors are marking exercises that they have just been observing. The assessor is a senior manager within the business and is an experienced interviewer and assessor who has attended the assessment centre training that you ran.

1. What are the potential consequences of the comments that have been made by this assessor?
2. What course of action, if any would you take in this situation?



## REFERENCES

Bourne, A. (2009) 'Screening: Best practice', *HR Director*, **55**, February, pp. 28–30.

Chambers, B.A. (2002) 'Applicant reactions and their consequences: Review, advice, and recommendations for future research', International Journal of Management Review, **4**, December.

Chartered Institute of Personnel and Development (2007) 'Assessment centres for recruitment and selection', www.cipd.co.uk.

Chartered Institute of Personnel and Development (2009a) 'Recruitment, retention, turnover: CIPD Annual Survey Report', www.cipd.co.uk.

Chartered Institute of Personnel and Development (2009b) 'Selection interviewing', www.cipd.co.uk.

Chartered Institute of Personnel and Development (2010) 'Selection methods', www.cipd.co.uk

Clifford, B. (2008) 'How to evaluate your selection process,' *People Management*, **14**:1, January, pp. 42–3.

Furnham, A. (2008) 'HR professionals' beliefs about, and knowledge of, assessment techniques and psychometric tests', *International Journal of Selection and Assessment*, **16**:3, September, pp. 300–5.

Incomes Data Services (2004) 'Psychometric tests [and] guide to suppliers'. *HR Studies Plus*, IDS.

Incomes Data Services (2008) 'Assessment centres', *HR Study* 876, IDS.

Landon, T.E. and Arvey, R.D. (2007) 'Ratings of test fairness by human resource professionals', *International Journal of Selection and Assessment*, **15**:2, June, pp. 185–96.

Murphy, N. (2008) 'Trends in recruitment methods in 2006 and 2007 (3): Selection'. *IRS Employment Review*, **893**, 20 March, 8ff.

Pearn Kandola Occupational Psychologists (1996) 'Tools for assessment and development centres', CIPD.

Roberts, G. (1997), *Recruitment and Selection: A Competency Based Approach*, CIPD.

Rynes, S.L., Colbert, A., and Brown, K.G. (2004) 'HR professionals' beliefs about effective human resource practices: Correspondence between research and practice', *Human Resource Management*, **41**, Summer.

Spence, B. (2009) 'How to filter job applications', *People Management*, 12 March, p. 45.

Taylor, S. (2010) *Resourcing and Talent Management*, 5th ed., CIPD.

Woodruffe, C. (2007) *Development and Assessment Centres: Identifying and Developing Competence*, 4th ed., Human Assets.

# Case Study: HR and the New Opening

14

## Key Terms

**Organizational structure** This relates to aspects of the formal organization, particularly the roles and responsibilities that people have, the hierarchy and reporting lines, the different departments and sections within the organization and how they are connected, formal communication channels and the way in which power and authority are distributed. Organizational structure is analogous to the human skeleton or the framework of a new building: it is what gives the organization shape and influences how it operates.

**Induction** This needs to be understood as a multistaged process rather than as a single, course-based event. It represents the introduction of new employees into the organization, into the department in which they work and into the job they have to do, although it can also relate to the transfer and promotion of existing employees. It should introduce the employee to the social environment, the technical aspects of work, and the rules and procedures of employment.

**Blended learning** This technique uses several different but complementary learning methods, which, when used together, are considered to be more effective at generating the required learning outcomes than one single method.

## Learning Objectives

As a result of reading this chapter and using the Online Resource Centre, you should be able to:

- understand the HR issues and requirements associated with opening a new productive facility;
- appreciate the role that HR plays in supporting the business;
- be aware of the way in which operational pressures and demands drive HR in a competitive, customer-focused environment;
- contribute actively to the delivery of key HR outcomes linked to 'new openings', particularly in recruitment and selection, organizational and job design, induction, skills training, and performance review and appraisal.

# Introduction

The first of the three integrated HR case study chapters that comprise this part of the text focuses on the activities and challenges associated with the role of HR when organizations expand or open new facilities, engage in mergers and acquisitions or relocate overseas. In this particular case, it involves opening a new hotel, and ensuring that it is staffed and ready to open on time. The term 'greenfield site' is sometimes used to describe a new plant in a new location, for which nothing is inherited other than the company's existing philosophy and operating systems. With significant new developments such as a new opening, HR has the opportunity to be much more creative in the sense that they are working with a blank sheet of paper and can really influence key decisions and outcomes: many HR interventions tend to be based on much smaller scale actions and contributions that are made within existing cultures and structural forms. Where HR is required to play a more formative and strategic role the metaphor of builder or architect is often used to emphasize a different kind of contribution to organizational success. (Tyson and Fell, 1986; Ulrich et al., 2008; Monks, 1992).

The specific example used to illustrate HR's role in supporting such a new opening is based on the recently built Robinson Hotel, located in the centre of Birmingham. The following section provides details about the company, the hotel, and labour market conditions: but before we move on to this, it is important to understand that, while the case study chapters in Part 4 share some features with those found in the preceding chapters, they are different from them in important ways.

Because they are based on real events and much of the content is based on interviews with the HR practitioners who were closely involved, they represent unique insights into the pressures and challenges that these practitioners faced—and how they dealt with them. All three chapters provide examples of HR making important contributions to the 'business', and of HR professionals who have a very clear conception of what is expected of HR and of what they have to do to meet these expectations. The chapters are about 'delivering', to use Ulrich's (1996) word, but they also demonstrate what and how things were done to achieve the required outcomes. In addition, the three chapters show how important it is to link different activities together and to approach the practice of HR with a very clear understanding of the importance of maintaining an integrated and holistic perspective on what needs to done. They also give a sense of the operational and strategic value of these activities.

In this chapter, particular emphasis is given to the task of finding and employing staff, inducting and training them, and using performance reviews and appraisals. The ultimate test of whether these activities are done effectively is in the behaviour of employees—whether they fit into their jobs and the social environment which they need to be part of; whether they stay and develop or leave because they are either unsuitable or are dissatisfied with their job and working conditions; and whether they are comfortable working in a service orientated business. The chapter emphasizes the essential connectivity of what can often become separate and detached activities. The case study shows that a competent, efficient, and motivated workforce, possessing the right attitude and performing to the required standards, is one of the key determinants of organizational success, and this is where HR can add value—through its ability consistently to deliver these outcomes.

The approach taken:

- provides information on the location, organizational context, and specific requirements associated with meeting all staffing requirements leading up to, and shortly after, the opening of the hotel;
- offers academic insights into key HR activities and responsibilities, using appropriate research and literature contributions to provide an academic perspective on these activities;
- provides realistic exercises that reflect the tasks and challenges faced by the HR practitioner involved;
- offers insights into the actual experiences of the people involved in the project and, through this, allows the student to understand more realistically the pressures, dilemmas, successes, and failures of those involved, and what they learnt from their experiences;

- puts the student in the key role of HR manager and other stakeholders;
- provides extensive opportunities to research and practise important aspects of the HR function.

## The Background

Robinson Hotels & Resorts is the UK's largest independently owned hotel group, with over sixty properties spread throughout the UK. It operates within the four-star deluxe sector of the market, and is committed to providing a full range of services and facilities to its customers. As a result of its strategy of growing organically rather than through mergers and acquisitions, it acquired a site in the heart of Birmingham and developed plans for a brand new, 120-bedroom hotel, with an opening date of 1 November 2009. Failure to meet this deadline had obvious implications for the ability of the general manager (GM) to take advantage of the busy Christmas and New Year period, and would have adversely affected his planned revenue budget. This contextual factor shows how HR failing to deliver its key contributions by a specific date has real and material outcomes for the organization's business profile and performance; getting it wrong matters!

The GM, Daniel Martin, was appointed in January 2009, followed in June by Marjory Hughes and Claire Wilson, sales director and HR manager respectively. Claire's initial tasks during the critical six month pre-opening period were to:

- design the organizational structure, and prepare job descriptions and person specifications for each job;
- agree the headcount and workforce budget;
- recruit and select staff for all posts;
- plan for and deliver an effective induction and skills training programme;
- devise an effective performance review and appraisal system.

All of these tasks had to be successfully completed at the latest two weeks before the hotel opened its doors to paying customers, thus allowing for a short period of final testing and preparation.

## Designing the Organizational Structure

The ability to meet the November opening deadline was heavily dependent on having a fully staffed and trained workforce in place by that time, but before any recruitment could begin, agreement had to be reached over the hotel's establishment numbers and its internal structure. In thinking through the implications of creating a functional structure, it is worth noting Child's comment that:

> **The design of jobs and work structures should not only take into account the nature of the work and the characteristics of personnel; it also has to be consistent with the philosophy of management that is being followed. The structuring of jobs needs to be matched by an appropriate design of organisational systems and an appropriate managerial style.**
> (Child, 1984)

This way of conceptualizing structure suggests that it is more than simply a technical task, involving creating roles, jobs, relationships, and lines of accountability; decisions on these issues also reflect something about the beliefs and values of the organization's senior managers, and about the functional requirements associated with delivering a specified level of service to meet customer expectations and service standards. Structure is also, as Watson (2002) argues, about:

> **the regular or persisting patterns of action that give shape and predictability to an organisation.**

This means that the hotel's structure of work and jobs needed to deliver behavioural patterns and standards that were known and understood, regularly repeated, and fit for purpose. But structure is not to be

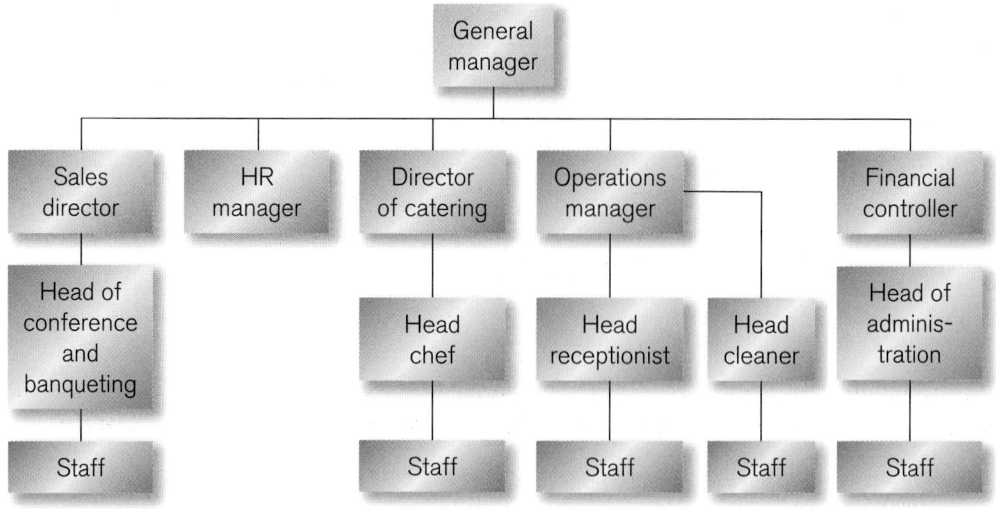


**Figure 14.1** The structure of the Birmingham Robinson Hotel



interpreted as a state of permanence. A central theme of this book is that of the importance of adaptation to environmental changes at the organizational, HR functional level and on the part of individual employees. Any structural configuration has to be seen as one that reflects requirements and circumstances at any given time and is subject to a process of ongoing modification. Increasingly organizations, in their search for productivity gains, need to change roles, create more demanding tasks, and remove layers of work or people from the organization. In such circumstances a rigid organization structure becomes an impediment to effective adaptation strategies.

At the time of opening, the hotel employed 160 people from seventeen different national groups, although not all of these were full-time employees. The management structure reflected the industry's traditional emphasis on heads of departments reporting to functional heads, who, in turn, reported to the general manager, as indicated in Figure 14.1.

The first three senior management appointments had responsibility for appointing the remaining functional heads and, with these in post, the heads of department. The people who filled these three positions were clearly critical to all subsequent employment decisions, and to the effective and profitable operation of the hotel.

**STUDENT ACTIVITY 14.1 Preparing job descriptions and person specifications**

Either individually or in groups, prepare job descriptions for the general manager and HR manager. The structure and content of these should be sufficiently detailed to allow for the following tasks to be completed.

1. Produce person specifications for each position, detailing the necessary and desirable features that applicants should possess, and specifying, where appropriate, the level of attainment or standard.
2. Design an advertisement for the post of HR manager and indicate what your recruitment strategy would be.
3. Design an assessment and selection strategy for the HR post, based on a shortlist of six applicants, indicating clearly the chosen assessment methods and key criteria, with weightings, if considered appropriate.

**Note**: You should explore all opportunities to collect data on both roles and validate the outcome of this exercise by contacting actual hotel General Managers and HR managers and generate primary data yourselves.

**Note**: In carrying out task 3 you can use the information and insights gained from reading Chapter 13 which involves using assessment centres as a selection strategy.

Once in post, the focus of the management team in the pre-opening phase was agreeing the establishment numbers, allocating jobs to departments, and recruiting staff. Staffing models used in other hotels influenced the numbers of posts agreed upon, but particular use was also made of the following.

- Ratios

  For example, the number of bedrooms that might be cleaned to standard in one shift divided by the number of bedrooms, subject to a projected occupancy rate. With 120 rooms, with one cleaner able to clean six bedrooms per shift at an average projected occupancy of 80 per cent, the number of WTE cleaners needed would be calculated as follows:

  $$\frac{120}{6} \times 0.80 = 19$$

  **Question** To ensure that as far as possible the number of cleaners required the amount of work needed to be done, what employment contract would you offer the cleaning staff and what would the main terms and conditions be?

- Size of facilities

  For example, the range of facilities offered in the leisure centre would indicate not only the numbers of staff needed, but their different jobs and skill sets.

- Projected usage rates

  The number of guests and visitors expected to use the restaurant, for example, would inform decisions on the number and variety of restaurant/bar posts needed.

  **Question** How would you ensure that the right staffing levels were available to reflect different restaurant usage levels?

**STUDENT ACTIVITY 14.2 Annual hours contracts**

**In order to achieve the required level of flexibility, many organizations are turning to annual hours and zero hours contracts.**

1. **Research the use of annual and zero hours contracts, and report on the available evidence of the experiences of both employers and employees.**
2. **Explain how annual hours contracts differ from zero hours contracts.**
3. **In the case of the Birmingham Robinson Hotel, consider the advantages and disadvantages of guaranteeing a minimum number of hours/shifts per month to its casual workers (CIPD, 2005; Stredwick and Ellis, 2005).**

# Staffing the Hotel

Unlike established workplaces, with a new opening, there are no opportunities to draw upon the internal labour force as a source of labour supply unless staff employed in different parts of the business are transferred in. All recruitment had to be based on the external labour market, which effectively meant the Birmingham region for the majority of employees. The bulk of the pre-opening budget of £300,000 was allocated for staffing purposes, compared to a starting employment budget of £2 million. The difference between the two is explained by the fact that recruitment to the full-establishment figure gradually took place over the full pre-opening period. The recruitment strategy was based on four elements:

- unsolicited CVs sent in on a speculative basis;
- the use of online applications and processing, using the hotel's electronic database and search facilities. The CIPD has found that the trend for online recruitment is growing, with almost two-thirds of organizations using technology to support this activity (CIPD, 2006b, p. 3);

- local advertising and the use of industry-specific publications;
- recruitment agencies, but limited to posts that required specialist skills and experience.

Selection for senior managers was based on interviews, with the HR manager undertaking the first and the GM, the second interviews. Interestingly, psychometric tests were not used for any position, the emphasis being placed instead on a person's CV, experience, and ability to 'fit' the hotel environment. This involved having the required skill set, being flexible and adaptive, being able to work under pressure, and understanding the need to meet customer expectations.

For all other positions, responsibility for selection was devolved to the appropriate head of department, with the HR manager conducting the initial assessment of applications and then agreeing with the appropriate head of function or department which candidates would be invited for interview. Effectively, the criteria used in deciding on this and the subsequent decision whether to offer a job or not were related to the following factors.

- **The employability of the applicant**

  This was based on a review of his or her work record, education and qualifications, and experience.

- **The legal status of the applicant**

  This involved reviewing any criminal records that an applicant might have and reaching a judgement on whether this disbarred him or her from working in the hotel. It also included establishing the candidate's right to work, defined in terms of his or her national status.

- **The technical skills of the applicant**

  This was particularly important in recruiting to areas such as bars, restaurant, leisure club, and conference/banqueting.



Three other features of the hotel's recruitment strategy deserve mention:

- building and maintaining links with institutions that represent a long-term source of labour supply. In this case, one of Birmingham's universities provided, via its course in hotel and leisure management, a regular supply of casual and part-time workers, many of who came from abroad and had previous experience of the hotel industry;
- the development of a 'talent bank' of applications and CVs that might be used to fill new vacancies as they came on-stream or to provide replacements for those who left;
- the decision to pay above the local labour market rate for hourly paid staff. This may have cost more in one sense, but attracted better quality applicants, which, in turn, allowed the hotel to deliver a 'deluxe' level of service (CIPD, 2010).

# Induction

According to the CIPD (2006a):

> **Every organization, large or small, should have a well-considered induction programme.**

Although the Institute claim that designing an appropriate and cost-effective induction package is a complex task, it need not be, and in the context of a hotel, the induction experience is driven by two requirements.

1. The need to meet legal requirements surrounding employment. This involves communicating information on issues such as pay and benefits, sick pay, holidays and conditions, company rules, and health and safety procedures. This might be termed the formal dimension of induction.

2. Job induction. This is a dimension of induction covering duties and responsibilities, working location, reporting lines, and job standards.

The CIPD claims that:

> **[an] induction programme has to provide all the information that new employees and others need, and are able to assimilate, without being overwhelming or diverting them from the essential process of integration into a team.**

Conceptually, induction needs to be seen as a process rather than a discrete event, and as multifaceted. This is consistent with Mullin's view that 'orientation' (as he describes it) is basically a natural extension of the recruitment and selection process (Mullins, 1995).

It might also be argued that, from the perspective of line managers working under considerable financial and service/production pressures, induction needs to be delivered without compromising operational requirements. Realistically, of course, there will always be tension between the need to provide a comprehensive and satisfactory induction experience that goes beyond the basics, and operational pressures. This tension may help to explain some of the frustrations and disappointments that new employees sometimes experience with the way in which they are inducted into an organization.

In explaining why the hotel suffered from a higher than expected level of turnover, Claire Wilson offered the opinion that some new employees came with unrealistic expectations of what hotel work was like, that is, tending to imagine it as glamorous, when in reality it was hard work and demanded a high level of commitment. In their book on the hospitality industry, Boella and Goss-Turner (2005, p. 94) similarly emphasize the potential importance of misplaced expectations that are built up during the recruitment and selection process. Not only are these expectations important in understanding subsequent behaviour, but so too are the first impressions that are created as a result of starting to work. According to Boella and Goss-Turner:

> **First impressions are often the most lasting impressions, and the first impressions formed by many employees upon starting employment with a new employer may not be good ones . . . The first hours and days are critical and if properly dealt with can create the right relationship that contributes to employees staying with an employer.**

Figure 14.2 offers a more realistic insight into the induction experience and the challenges that this presents to the HR professional.

The so-called 'induction crisis', a term used to explain the higher levels of wastage among newly recruited employees, helps to explain the relationship between unrealistic expectations, ineffective induction practices, and the propensity to leave. Such losses are not only costly, but often unnecessary: the individual might not have left if the induction experience had created a positive, rather than a negative, impact on the person's 'feelings' about the organization and job (Ramsay-Smith, 2004; Cheng and Brown, 1998).

This view is supported by the experience of Claire Wilson, who saw a clear correlation between the people who left full-time posts and the inadequacy of their induction, training, and development—limitations that created a feeling of not being valued on the part of the employee. One of the key points here and one which again reflects a key theme of the book, is that traditionally induction 'was perceived as something that was done to people' and frequently involved information overload.

Rather induction can be seen as something 'done for people' and done moreover in ways that reflect a stronger inductee orientation instead of something that reflects the interests of those managing the process. And rarely do organizations consider the economic costs of poorly designed induction programmes. Research quoted in *Personnel Today* (2006) claims:

> **UK businesses are losing up to £2bn a year in employee productivity due to inefficient staff induction processes**

Thus, in evaluating the effectiveness of any induction process the question is not only whether the objectives of both parties were met, but at what cost?

| Party with responsibility for provision | Legal aspects of employment | Company procedures and rules | Organizational culture–values and expectations | Working environment and job performance | Social and informal environment |
|---|---|---|---|---|---|
| HR professionals | ✓ | ✓ | ✓ | | |
| Senior manager(s) | | | ✓ | | |
| Line/ departmental manager | | | | ✓ | ✓ |
| Co-workers | | | | ✓ | ✓ |

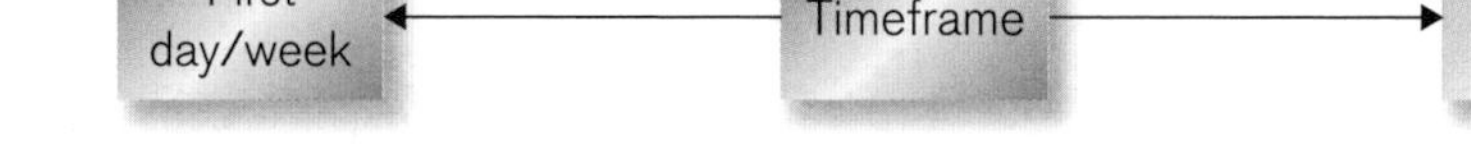




Figure 14.2 The induction process

**STUDENT ACTIVITY 14.3 Designing the induction experience**

What Figure 14.2 doesn't offer is an answer to the 'how' question: how is induction to be structured and experienced so that employees don't simply learn about the organization and their job, but do so in a way that connects with their affective domain (their attitudes and what they feel), and begins to build a relationship between the employee and the organization? This is the challenge that is found in this set of activities, which can be undertaken either individually or in groups.

1. Design a one-day induction experience for fifteen new, hourly paid, employees working as cleaners, bar staff, and receptionists, and who have been employed three weeks before opening.
2. Design an induction experience for the head chef, head receptionist, and head of operations, all of which began work eight weeks before opening.
3. Discuss the role of employee feedback in induction and give examples of how this can be built into the induction experience.

# Training

Responsibility for training is shared between different stakeholders and, for the majority of employees, follows on from induction. The Robinson Hotel Group, as a whole, provides a centralized training facility available to all of its hotels, offering course-based training in key areas of the business, such as food preparation, hygiene, and 'back office' procedures. Hotel staff can be nominated for these courses. Suppliers of equipment and products also have an important contribution to make, offering on-site training in the use and maintenance of equipment, as well as product knowledge training. Heads of department, as the key line managers, carry out operational training covering specific procedures, techniques, and performance standards. This is provided in the form of on-the-job training, and is designed to provide staff with the necessary skills and knowledge to perform their jobs to the required standards and to display appropriate customer service behaviours. Finally, the HR manager is responsible for meeting statutory training requirements that all staff must meet, particularly in the fields of discrimination in employment and health and safety. This is the only form of what might be described as 'awareness training'; much more emphasis and time is given to specific and job-orientated training that supports operational requirements. The distinction between 'knowing about' and 'being able to do' is important, particularly in understanding training priorities and the appropriateness and effectiveness of different training methods. Training in hotels does reflect statutory requirements, but is primarily driven by what employees need to know and be able to do, that is, it is business focused. If staff can't perform their jobs properly and with the right attitude then customer satisfaction levels will inevitably fall, resulting in lower revenue and profitability.

Given the difficulties of taking staff away from their work to experience classroom-based training, the prominence of on-the-job training methods is understandable, although not all of the things that staff must learn can be acquired in such a way. This is particularly the case with the knowledge that has to be acquired about the legislative framework within which both managers and employees are required to work. Training for this is based on the use of CDs and laptop computers. These are made available to new employees, who can progress through the specially designed structured training programme at their own pace and in their own chosen location. The package has a self-assessment element and staff can complete this when they feel that they are ready. An external verifier then checks the submitted assessments and the results are communicated to each individual. Certificates of attainment are sent to successful candidates, and the HR manager updates their personal records and the hotel's training records. The advantage of using this form of e-learning lies in its potential to provide a consistent level of training whenever, and wherever, needed (IDS, 2006).

The use of a mix of training approaches and methods that fit different and changing requirements is consistent with the idea of blended learning.

Signpost to Chapter 10: Learning and Development

In the hospitality industry, much of the work of staff is performed in direct contact with customers, and the behaviours and skills needed to be effective cannot easily be taught using conventional course-based learning, but must be learnt through direct experience or simulation. According to Boella and Goss-Turner (2005, p. 123), on-the-job training, if handled correctly, can be particularly effective for learning manual and social skills, but much depends on the technical skills of the instructor/manager and his or her ability to deal sympathetically with the difficulties experienced by staff in learning new skills in a pressurized environment.

One of the more challenging tasks faced by Claire Wilson was training the hotel's heads of department in appraisal skills. Because this is a common requirement for all of the hotels in the group, Claire has discussed with Ahmad Khan, the group HR manager, the idea of designing a programme open to managers from other hotels. He is keen to promote more centralized training, if this makes sense and can be justified, and has asked Claire to meet with him to explore how this can be achieved. He is bringing an open mind to this challenge and is looking for some practical, realistic ideas. This is the background to the next student activity.

**STUDENT ACTIVITY 14.4 Training managers in appraisal skills**

This exercise can be done in a number of different ways, but is more productive if students take the roles of Claire Wilson and Ahmad Khan, and work together to complete the following.

1. Design the outline of a one-day, course-based appraisal training programme for heads of departments, assuming around twenty attendees in the first group, showing very clearly how you would spend the time and the learning activities that you would include. You should agree learning outcomes and specific behavioural competences that you want each participant to achieve. You need to consider how these outcomes

and competences can be realistically assessed and where, and what pre- and post-course activities you want participants to commit to. The training will be carried out in hotel conference facilities.

2. One of the elements of the training programme you design must include a session on 'giving and receiving effective feedback'. Research this subject and explain how you would develop this capability in the managers.
3. Construct a visual model of the feedback process in the context of appraisals and develop a power-point slide based on your model. Present this to the class and, in the light of feedback, refine your model and slide.
4. Produce a training budget for the course and any associated activities.
5. Devise an evaluation strategy to establish the effectiveness of the training.

# Performance Review and Appraisal

The need 'to know' whether an employee is meeting reasonable expectations of his or her performance and establishing whether the employee 'fits' into the organization are not the same thing, but each is important for both employee and manager. A formal system of appraising employees is used by many public sector organizations and larger private sector businesses, but more flexible and informal systems for answering these two questions are increasingly being explored as the limitations and disadvantages of traditional performance appraisal methods are better understood.

As far as the Birmingham Robinson Hotel is concerned, the approach taken to appraisal was practical and realistic. All employee contracts contained a provision relating to a three-month probationary period, at which point the contract could be terminated if job performance or general behaviour failed to meet expectations. At weeks four and eight, employees participated in a performance review with their head of department. This was a relatively informal exchange between the two parties to establish how each one 'felt about how things were going', with the results of the exchange recorded and placed in the employee's personal file. The twelve-week exchange was, according to Claire Wilson, 'more of a performance appraisal', in the sense that it followed a clearer structure and confirmed continuation (or otherwise) of employment. Criteria used to establish whether the employee was performing at an acceptable level included:

- punctuality;
- customer service skills;
- attendance.

What is rarely, if ever, considered under the performance appraisal heading is the significance of an equivalent process involving the employee appraising management and the organization. By this, we mean that employees go through a similar, if more individual and unstructured, process of reaching decisions about how well the organization has performed in relation to the promises it made, that is, the expectations that employees had of how they would be treated and rewarded, in the light of the actual experience of working and being managed. The decision by some people to leave—and this is probably the main reason for the majority of voluntary quits—is that they feel disappointed, let down, or badly treated: the performance of the organization and its managers has, in the perception of those leaving, been consistently below reasonable standards and what was promised or at least intimated. Often the most important source of disappointment and frustration is the lack of opportunity for development and progression, but also how people are treated is equally important. Are staff treated as human beings—as people—or rather as economic resources; this is the same dilemma and choice outlined at the very beginning of this book, and the admittedly very general principle we have advocated is that treating staff as people, respecting their individuality and circumstances, and knowing them personally is often associated with a high performing employee. The frequently referred-to aphorism that 'people leave their managers not their jobs' strongly suggests that the process of reaching judgements about performance is not one-sided.

At the Birmingham Robinson, managers received a performance appraisal, based on a formal interview with their line manager, after three months in post and just before twelve months. The second is significant in the sense that, after twelve months, all employees acquire employment protection rights, and cannot have their contracts terminated without good reason and in the absence of a proper procedure. After this, appraisals were held annually, and involved a formal interview and completion of an appraisal form.

**STUDENT ACTIVITY 14.5 How to appraise the performance of managers in the hotel**

This activity requires students to design an appraisal instrument that reflects the context and requirements of a hotel environment.

1. Design an appraisal matrix that has two dimensions. Identify on the left-hand side the appraisal criteria and, along the top, you need to have a scale that reflects the extent to which each criteria has been met. You may wish to consider weighting the criteria and quantitatively assessing these to produce an overall rating or assessment score, with a minimum achievement level, below which performance would be considered deficient or unacceptable. Be prepared to defend and amend your matrix as a result of feedback from a presentation you may be asked to give your group.
2. Identify the kind of evidence you would use to allow proper decisions to be made in reaching conclusions about managers' performance and consider what form this might take and where it would be found.
3. Consider what action would be appropriate to deal with situations of:
   - excellent performance;
   - average performance;
   - unsatisfactory performance.

   Highlight the possible implications of each action.

In carrying out these tasks, remember the points made in Chapters 2 and 11 about the general problems that managers and employees experience with performance appraisals.

Signpost to Chapter 2 HRM: An Academic and Professional Perspective and Chapter 11 Managing Performance

According to Claire Wilson, the effectiveness and value of reviews and appraisals—they mean the same thing in different organizations—depends very much on who is involved as the appraiser and how appraisals are carried out, particularly how feedback is given and received. This means that the skills of the appraiser and appraisee may be important factors in determining the extent to which the experience of appraising and being appraised is positive and functional, rather than negative and unhelpful. As was pointed out in Chapters 2 and 11, simply having an appraisal scheme or system does not, in itself, mean that it will generate the desired outcomes. In considering the key features of an effective appraisal scheme, ACAS (2006) suggests that the following are desirable:

- written records of the appraisal to provide feedback and to allow more managers to monitor the effectiveness of appraisals;
- a job description that focuses attention on the employee's performance at work, thus ensuring that assessments are based on objectively verifiable requirements rather than on the person;
- the use of a rating system, under which categories of performance can be numerically scored;
- the use of assessments based on objectives, standards, or other reasonable and agreed criteria, thus reducing the degree of subjectivity (note that it would be unrealistic to expect to eliminate subjectivity completely);
- the provision of a genuine procedure that allows people to be able to appeal against their assessment.

## Summary

In reviewing the experiences of the six-month period prior to opening the Birmingham Robinson Hotel, the following are some of the key learning points that the HR manager made.

- Much more training might have been carried out during the pre-opening phase to prepare staff for the pressures and demands on their skills and knowledge that would arise once the hotel became fully functional. The general point here is that operational pressures *do* interfere with employee training and it is often difficult to undertake required training when such pressures take priority. It might be argued that the HR practitioner must find creative, effective solutions to this tension rather than force managers to release staff for training when this causes operational problems. It also suggests that some of the training provided failed to reflect the pressures that staff experienced doing their jobs; in other words the training to reflect the conditions in which skills and knowledge would be applied.
- The heads of department might have used the pre-opening time more effectively to build their teams, and to create a better understanding of operating procedures and standards. This may be about the important role that line managers play in building the social organization of the business, under which employees' feelings and attitudes towards their work, and towards their work group, is a key variable in determining how they actually perform their jobs. It's not only about having the technical skills, but about wanting to use them.
- There was a degree of over-recruitment in the pre-opening phase, partly because of the successful recruitment campaign, and as the headcount was reduced through non-renewal of casual and temporary contracts and through voluntary quits, the impact on wastage rates created the impression that there 'was a problem here'. The point to note is that any measure of HR—in this case, wastage and turnover—can be misunderstood in terms of its seriousness or cause. What was a natural adjustment to a temporary oversupply situation might have been interpreted by people taking the statistics in isolation as some kind of problem that needed a solution, as well as a failure on the part of management.
- The departure of two heads of department, who left the hotel during its first eight months of operation, was not a surprise and, according to Claire Wilson, she realistically knew at the time that the two appointments might be problematical. The decision to employ was heavily influenced by the urgent need to make appointments and to fill key posts. Her comment that 'you need to have the confidence to hold off' reinforces the point made in Chapter 4 that it is better to resist short-term pressures to recruit, if at all possible, particularly if key managerial jobs are involved, and to make sure that the 'right' manager is in place from day one. It is just as important *not* to recruit if there is real doubt about the suitability of the applicant.

Signpost to Chapter 4: Recruitment and Selection

- Finally, the experiences of managing the HR dimension of the new opening offer persuasive support for those arguing that a link does exist between what HR does and organizational performance. Claire Wilson made this clear when she remarked that the staff that had left had been those whose induction, training, and development had not been satisfactory and had it been better they may have stayed; in general, those that stayed had benefited from more positive and supportive experiences in these key areas of HR.

**Visit the Online Resource Centre that accompanies this book for self-test questions, weblinks, and more information on the topics covered in this chapter.**
**www.oxfordtextbooks.co.uk/orc/banfield_kay2e/**

## CASE STUDIES

The final part of this chapter gives students the opportunity to consider how to address the types of issue that arise when managing projects of this sort. Due to the different pressures facing organizations in this type of situation, the responses to staffing issues can and often do vary from that which appears appropriate in a more stable environment. In the debate between 'best practice' and 'best fit' HR, lack of awareness of and sensitivity to context and operational pressures can undermine HR's standing with other stakeholders and limit their ability to maximize their contributions. 'Best fit'!

In the following mini case studies, students can use their knowledge and judgement to offer practical solutions that will overcome the challenges described.

### Joe's case

Joe was interviewed for the position of head chef. As an Australian national, he noted during his interview that, if offered the post, he would require the support of the hotel in obtaining a permit to work in the UK. He explained that he already had a work permit to work at a different organization and that it should be relatively easy to get a permit for the new hotel. Joe had a very impressive CV and had extensive experience in similar positions at different hotels, both UK-based and elsewhere in the world. The director of catering felt that Joe was, by far, the best candidate for the post and, despite the delay expected in obtaining a work permit and the associated cost, was still keen to offer the position to Joe. He was therefore offered the post, conditional on eligibility to work in the UK. As part of the application process for a work permit, the hotel asked Joe to supply supporting documents, including his passport and current work permit. It transpired that he did not have a work permit and that his visa granting permission to work in the UK had expired some months before. The HR manager explained to the catering director that it would be much more difficult to get a work permit in these circumstances, due to the new restrictions on employing non-EU workers.



#### Questions

1. What options might the HR manager and catering director have considered?
2. Investigate the new rules, post-2010 on employing non-EU workers in the UK. What would be the potential penalty for employing Joe without eligibility to work in the UK?
3. How should the catering director and HR manager have handled the situation, given this problem?

### Cathy's case

Cathy was appointed as a waitress and bar attendant at the hotel when it first opened. Although, when at work, she proved to be a real asset, being both efficient and capable, and establishing good relationships with her customers, her attendance and timekeeping were a real problem. During her first few weeks, she was absent with a cold for two days, took one day off when her car broke down, and took two further separate days due to a migraine. She was also late for her allotted shifts on four different occasions. Ordinarily, she would have failed her initial three month probationary period, but due to her excellent performance when at work, and the fact that staff turnover had made it exceptionally difficult to recruit and train a replacement, Cathy's probationary period was extended. When challenged about her absence, she mentioned problems at home, including a recent breakdown in her marriage, and problems with childcare, including having to rely on family members to look after her children when she worked in the evenings.

#### Questions

1. What were the pros and cons of continuing Cathy's employment beyond her probationary period?
2. To what extent do you feel that attendance and timekeeping issues were relevant to her probationary period?
3. What options might the hotel have considered? What action would you have taken?

## Ben's case

Ben was employed as a hotel porter and, during his probationary period, demonstrated that he was extremely keen and conscientious. He also had an exemplary timekeeping and attendance record. He did, however, find it difficult to pick up new tasks and, despite being shown by his supervisor on numerous occasions exactly what he was required to do, he kept forgetting many instructions and making simple mistakes. Prior to taking the job, he was out of work for a long time and he got very nervous during any meetings with his supervisor to discuss the difficulties he had in learning new tasks. He failed to pass his probationary period and, although this was extended, he became very agitated and upset: he was very concerned that he might lose his job because he enjoyed the work at the hotel and really needed the money.

### Questions

1. What were the potential implications to the hotel in continuing Ben's employment?
2. What options might the hotel have employed to help Ben to learn more systematically the required tasks in the role?
3. What was the likelihood of Ben's difficulties proving to be a problem in the long term?

## Allegations of bullying

During recruitment, the hotel worked closely with a recruitment agency to provide large numbers of staff, particularly for the lower paid positions in the hotel. During the initial weeks after opening, the agency continued to supply staff to replace those who decided to leave. As part of its efforts to re-employ some of those who left the hotel, the agency discussed the reasons why these people left and raised a delicate issue with the hotel about why some of the staff left. In a discussion over staffing requirements, the agency informed the hotel that bullying might be a problem among some of the cleaning staff and that three of those who left had raised this as being a problem. For reasons of confidentiality, it could not disclose more information because those who had informed them of the issue had specifically asked not to be named, but the agency felt that it might help the hotel to raise the issue so that steps could be taken to ensure that this did not continue to be a problem in the future.



### Questions

1. How might the hotel have investigated these allegations?
2. How might the hotel have gone about establishing the opinions of the remaining staff about their employment?
3. What recommendations would you have made to reduce the risks of bullying and harassment among staff?
4. How might the hotel have gone about gathering information from those that had left to help to reduce staff turnover?

## REFERENCES

Advisory Conciliation and Arbitration Service (2006) *Employee Appraisal*, www.acas.org.uk.

Boella, M. and Goss-Turner, S. (2005) *Human Resource Management in the Hospitality Industry*, Elsevier Butterworth Heinemann.

Chartered Institute of Personnel and Development (2005) *Flexible Working: The Implementation Challenge*, www.cipd.co.uk.

Chartered Institute of Personnel and Development (2006a) 'Induction factsheet', www.cipd.co.uk.

Chartered Institute of Personnel and Development (2006b) *Recruitment, Retention and Turnover*, www.cipd.co.uk.

Chartered Institute of Personnel and Development (2010) 'Recruitment factsheet', www.cipd.co.uk

Cheng, A. and Brown, A. (1998) 'HRM strategies and labour turnover in the hotel industry: A comparative study of Australia and Singapore', *International Journal of Human Resource Management*, **9**:1, pp. 136–54.

Child, J. (1984) *Organisation: A Guide to Problems and Practice*, Harper Row.

Incomes Data Services (2006) *e-learning*, IDS HR Study 818, summary available online at www.incomesdata.co.uk.

Monks, K. (1992) 'Models of personnel management: A means of understanding the diversity of personnel practices?' *Human Resource Management Journal*, **3:**2, December, pp. 29–41.

Mullins, L.J. (1995) *Hospitality Management: A Human Resources Approach*, Pitman.

Ramsay-Smith, G. (2004) 'Employee turnover: The real cost', *Strategic HR Review*, **3**:4, p. 7.

Stredwick, J. and Ellis, S. (2005) *Flexible Working*, CIPD.

Ulrich, D. (1996) *Human Resource Champions*, Harvard Business School Press.

Ulrich, D. Brockbank, W. and Johnson, D. (2009) 'The role of strategy architect in the strategic HR organization', *People & Strategy*, March.

Tyson, S. and Fell, A. (1986) *Evaluating the Personnel Function*, Hutchinson.

Watson, T.J. (2002) *Organising and Managing Work*, FT/Prentice Hall.

# 15 Case Study: The Role of HR in Closing a Factory

## Key Terms

**Collective redundancy** This arises when an organization intends to dismiss, because of redundancy, twenty or more employees at one establishment within a ninety-day period. In such cases, dismissal is not related to individual performance or behaviour, but is for business reasons, such as plant closure, reorganization, or reallocation of work.

**Consultation** A process that can be individual and collective, and involves managers and employees, or their representatives, jointly examining and talking about issues of mutual concern. There is also an expectation that the discussions will seek to produce jointly acceptable solutions through a genuine exchange of views and ideas (Dix and Oxenbridge, 2003).

## Learning Objectives

As a result of reading this chapter and using the Online Resource Centre, you should be able to:

- plan a closure and understand how the role of HR fits in with the project plan;
- understand what is involved in the communication processes relating to a closure and the options for managing this process;
- identify and contribute to the management of the different HR activities needed to promote continuing performance during, and following, a closure;
- understand the legal and ethical issues facing managers in a closure situation.

# Introduction

This chapter has two general aims. The first is to provide insights into what is involved in closing a manufacturing unit, although the closure 'principles' and requirements are broadly similar whatever the sector or industry. The second is to facilitate, through a series of integrated tasks, the development of the knowledge and competences needed to participate in, and contribute to, this type of project. Participation in closing an operating unit, particularly one that has been in existence for many years, takes the HR professional out of his or her 'normal', and often routinized, world. It requires the HR professional to operate in a context full of new, and often unpredictable, challenges—a world in which measures of success and failure are much more obvious and known, and in which there are very clear expectations about what HR needs to deliver. In many ways it represents HR operating very clearly in the wider business context which involves working with others in a project team to implement strategic decisions. It means the HR personnel involved become 'business partners' whether or not they are aware of this or choose to describe their role in these terms.

From a practitioner perspective, the textbook world of neatly packaged and sequentially arranged HR activities, devoid of context, complications, and pressure, is at odds with the kind of organizational reality found in the demanding and stressful work of delivering planned change, particularly where this involves job losses and possible redundancies. During closure situations, in addition to maintaining core HR activities, the HR professional must work across functional boundaries, plan and deliver HR outcomes that are scheduled sequentially and in parallel, and cope with conflicting and changing priorities. Particularly at more senior levels, the boundary between HR management and what might be described as 'general management' can become less clear, and frequently HR is only one element of a team of 'managers' grappling with the demands of the challenges set by the organization. Professional and functional boundaries become blurred as people come together to plan, solve problems, and achieve objectives.

The exercises built into the chapter are closely related to those in which the HR professionals assigned to the closure were actually involved. All can be done individually, but the tasks are better undertaken as group activities. The learning experience is enriched even more if all of the activities and tasks are undertaken as part of a skills development study block, into which learning experience opportunities for research, presentation, reflection, and feedback can be built.

In trying to make the case study as experiential as possible, we have tried to strike a healthy balance between providing information on what is involved in closing an operational unit and leaving important areas of information to be researched by the student. While much background information is provided and explanations of processes are given, the emphasis is on students working together to make their own decisions and to provide answers to the tasks set.

Signpost to Chapter 10: Learning and Development

Additional exercises that concentrate on more specific situations that developed during the period of planned closure have been included at the end of the chapter, with questions that offer further opportunities for students to deepen their knowledge of what can happen in closure situations. These exercises provide opportunities to solve the kinds of specific problem that emerged as a result of implementing agreed policies on how redundancies and transfers were going to be managed.

# Background to Standard Tools

Standard Tools is an American-owned manufacturing company, with factories and distribution units located throughout the USA and Europe. It manufactures and sells a wide range of hand tools, hardware, and DIY products. It has annual European sales of $2.7 billion, of which $150 million is generated in the UK. Its UK sites are as follows.

- Northton Central

  This site employs the following staff:

  - 150 employees in tool manufacturing;
  - twenty engineering and design staff;
  - twenty IT support staff;
  - twenty finance and administrative staff.

- Northton (outskirts) *(seven miles from Northton Central)*

  This site employs the following staff:

  - fifty employees in garden furniture manufacturing;
  - fifty commercial and customer service employees;
  - fifty field sales representatives, selling doors, tools, and decorating products.

- Bramham *(15 miles from Northton Central)*

  This site employs 350 staff in tool manufacturing, along with managerial and administrative staff.

- Beechford *(40 miles from Northton)*

  This site employs 150 staff in gardening products and distribution.

- Midsleigh *(200 miles from Northton)*

  This site employs the following staff:

  - 100 distribution employees;
  - fifty customer service and commercial sales staff.

## Union involvement

Unite is recognized at the Northton Central and Bramham sites for the purposes of procedural representation of salaried staff and the negotiation of terms and conditions of employment for hourly paid employees (manual workers). Shop stewards are an accepted part of the recognition agreement and have regular meetings with management as part of their representational role. The full-time district officer may become involved in negotiations if disputes cannot be resolved internally. The other sites are non-unionized.

The company has a severance agreement with the union in the event of compulsory job losses. Any employee made redundant, or volunteering for redundancy, receives twice the statutory entitlement without a cap on weekly earnings level, inclusive of all statutory and notice entitlements. The agreement states that, in the event of redundancy, volunteers will be sought in the first instance. A performance-based selection method has been agreed for salaried staff in the event of redundancy, but no agreed selection method exists for hourly paid employees.

# Background to the Decision to Close

Standard Tools' parent company is registered on the New York Stock Exchange and its headquarters is in Columbus, Ohio. The CEO and his vice presidents take strategic business decisions for manufacturing and human resources. The problem for the HR team in the UK is that the approach taken by American-based companies in closing factories and the legal framework that regulates such actions are different to the UK. In the USA, the decision to close comes first and, once it is announced, there follows a period of 'impact bargaining' to lessen the impact of the closure on employees. There is therefore little understanding or appreciation within corporate headquarters of the UK requirements for consultation and of other legal requirements. The CEO simply wants the closure to be announced and completed within the shortest possible time, and is not too interested in the protestations of the UK managers charged with achieving this objective.

The reasons for closing Northton Central are entirely business driven and directly relate to the economics of production. Employment and production costs, as well as overheads, are much higher for two manufacturing units than for one, and it has been obvious for some time that significant cost savings might be made by closing the much older, and less efficient, Northton Central site, transferring production and employees to the newer factory in Bramham.

Production requirements for both Bramham and Northton Central sites (only fifteen miles from each other) have reduced in recent years, due to what is referred to as 'strategic sourcing from low-cost countries'. Not only might costs be saved by closing one of the sites and concentrating all activity on the other, but the land and buildings might be sold to release cash, which can either be invested back into the business or used to fund other projects, such as acquisitions. Unless these efficiencies are delivered, the ability to compete with low-cost producers in the Far East will be undermined, which might mean the end of manufacturing in the UK.

The possibility of closing the Northton Central site has been an agenda item at senior meetings for a number of years. In terms of priorities, it took this time for it to reach a point at which the decision was made to investigate the feasibility of closing the site. The information-gathering team involved manufacturing, sourcing, financial, and engineering representatives from around the world, along with key UK-based managers, including the HR manager. This team worked in the UK for three days at the end of January 2011 to gather all of the necessary details and to establish a cost-effective closure plan. This was presented, two days later, to the US executive board in order that it might make a decision.

The decision was made to close the site. The company wants the estimated savings of £1 million per year to be released quickly and all activity to be completed within five months from the end of January 2011. In addition to estimated closure costs, including redundancy, of £1 million, every week that the site remains occupied after the five-month period incurs costs of approximately £20,000 per week.

From a legal point of view, it has been accepted by the UK management team that the outcome of the executive board meeting was a proposal subject to consultation, rather than a final decision to close, although as far as the Americans are concerned, it is a final decision. The UK HR team has been given responsibility for producing the HR plan and for ensuring that this is in line with the operational plans for the closure.

## Implications

The detailed implications of the closure decision are as follows:

- ninety manufacturing jobs will be transferred to the Bramham factory;
- sixty manufacturing jobs will be lost because the manufacture of certain products will be outsourced;
- twenty design and engineering staff will transfer to Bramham;
- thirty manufacturing jobs at the Bramham factory will be lost because the manufacture of certain products will be transferred to the company's French plant;
- the forty non-manual employees at Northton Central will be transferred to a new administration building on the outskirts of Northton, two miles away from the garden furniture plant.

Responsibility for managing the HR part of the closure project is in the hands of the HR department that is based at the Bramham site. The team consists of the HR manager and two HR officers, all of whom are permanent, full-time staff. They have been required to commit 50 per cent of their time for the next six months to support the project.

Other managers at Bramham and Central Northton can be used to provide additional resources to support the project, as long as the demands made on them are not excessive. The sum of £25,000 has been allocated from the total project budget to help to resource HR activities, for which existing resources are not available. This money can be spent on anything to do with the HR project plan and is controlled by the HR manager.

**STUDENT ACTIVITY 15.1**

In working on this activity, you can draw upon other resources that might be available to help deliver or support certain activities, but you cannot spend more than £25,000. You can also make any reasonable assumptions about the company, its workforce and its environment, if these help you to undertake the different activities associated with the project.

Produce a project plan covering all of the HR issues relating to closing the factory, transferring staff to Bramham and dealing with planned job losses and possible redundancies. This plan must identify and schedule all of the key activities that need to be undertaken to achieve the objective of a successful closure within the five-month timeframe. The plan should not include activities that are to do with production transfers, plant movement, or other non-HR matters, although, in reality, the HR activities would be integrated within a comprehensive project plan.

The project plan can be constructed in one of two ways.

There are different software packages that can be used to produce the plan, with Microsoft Project being the best known and most available of these. The ability to use a software-based system is dependent on possessing certain basic skills, but these can be acquired with a minimum of three hours' training provided by someone experienced in using the software.

Alternatively, a paper-based approach can be used. The same principles and techniques incorporated into project-planning software are used in a manual approach and either will be suitable, provided proper preparation and training are given. It is recommended that, if possible, a software-based approach is adopted, because this will provide opportunities for significant skill development in project management.



**Note**: This activity should be undertaken by a group of people working creatively to produce the plan. On completion it should be subject to either peer review and amended in the light of the feedback given or checked by a tutor. Significant weaknesses in the project plan will compromise the whole project and need to be identified at this stage.

# Project Management

Projects, of different types and complexities, are becoming increasingly common in HR and represent a different kind of challenge to the more discrete approach to HR work. Projects, and the ability to manage them, require new and different skills that many HR professionals lack. Not only are these skills an essential part of an HR professional's 'toolkit', they also represent a prerequisite for being able to work across functional boundaries.

According to Bee and Bee (1997), projects can be differentiated from other activities because they:

- are goal-oriented, with specific and clear objectives;
- require members of project teams to work cross-functionally;
- involve careful coordination of interrelated activities, requiring accurate scheduling;
- are of a finite duration, with start and finish times;
- are usually unique in terms of context and experience.

Invariably projects, although differing widely in size and scale, involve a team of people working together, under the direction of a project leader or manager, and the ability to meet the project's objectives is closely related to the way in which the project team works together. These members not only have the responsibility of directly delivering individual parts of the project plan, but are also required to organize and coordinate the contributions of other internal stakeholders and external resource providers.

Projects tend to have a distinctive life cycle, with five recognized phases:

1. Project definition, with agreed aims and objectives.
2. Planning and resourcing, using either computer software or paper-based systems.
3. Implementation, with ongoing learning and adaptation. This is, arguably, the most intensive part of the project and involves:
   - devising a detailed list of tasks and activities that contribute to the achievement of the project's objectives;
   - agreeing on timescales for the carrying out and completion of activities, including milestones. 'Milestones' are important points in the life of the project and represent key achievements;
   - agreeing on the resources that the project needs to complete all activities on time. Resources can include time, money, skills/knowledge and facilities;
   - agreeing on the roles and responsibilities of team members.
4. Project completion.
5. A post-completion stage, at which features of the new situation need to be managed.

## Working as a Team

The ability to work effectively as a project team member is closely related to being sensitive to the internal dynamics within the team itself. A useful model that can help to explain what these dynamics are and how they develop was developed by Bruce Tuckman in 1965 and revised in the 1970s (Tuckman and Jensen, 1977). Tuckman's model is based on the premise that teams go through the following different phases and activities before they reach full effectiveness.

- Forming

  The team comes together with little clear understanding of its structure and leadership or team roles. Relatively high levels of uncertainty will be experienced over how the team will function and its priorities.

- Storming

  There is an increase in the degree of clarity about the purpose of the team, but some uncertainty remains. Competition for leadership roles may be experienced, and energy can be expended on relationship and emotional issues at the expense of project objectives. Decision-making is often difficult and compromises may be required to facilitate progress.

- Norming

  Agreement and consensus emerges, and the roles of leader(s) and member(s) are accepted. Emerging commitment to each other and to project objectives develops, with team members engaging in social activities. More open discussions about how the team functions take place.

- Performing

  There is growth in the level of confidence among team members and a strong commitment to deliver against project objectives. There will be more independent working within a framework of understanding and agreement. Decisions about how the team functions are taken collectively.

- Adjourning

  This is the stage at which the team breaks up after the end of the project. This is more to do with the well being of the team members and their relationships with each other and the organization, than it is about the project itself. Nevertheless, how people feel about their experiences will affect their future roles and status.

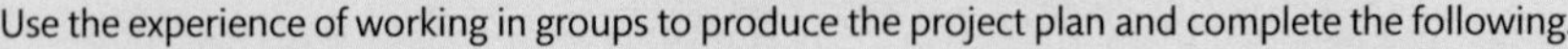

**STUDENT ACTIVITY 15.2**

Use the experience of working in groups to produce the project plan and complete the following.

1. Review the way in which the group is operating in relation to the four stages of Tuckman's model.
2. Discuss any interpersonal conflict that may have been experienced, explore its origins and how the group managed this, if at all.
3. Agree on changes in the way in which the group functions that will improve its effectiveness.
4. Explore any patterns of leadership behaviour that have emerged and discuss their effects on group performance and effectiveness.

# Communicating the Decision to Close

If a reorganization or closure involves the possibility of redundancies and the consequent legal requirements for consultation, it is important to express any initial announcement as a proposal rather than as a plan. This avoids the criticism that consultation is not meaningful and preserves the integrity of the consultation process. Representatives of employees affected by these changes are likely to attempt to challenge the decision to close and, again to meet legal requirements, it is necessary to avoid giving the impression that the decision has already been made. For example, moving towards seeking volunteers for redundancy at an early stage might be inferred as evidence that the company is refusing to engage in meaningful consultation.



Announcements that are sympathetic, offer strong justification for the closure, and express genuine concern for employees are likely to be received more positively than those that are ambiguous, uncaring, and complicated. For example, you can announce what the proposal is, why this has come about, and state that the process of consultation will be commencing at the earliest opportunity. You can also express support for those who may be affected by the proposals and give a commitment to consider all alternatives put forward. It is not helpful to any party, however, to make promises that might compromise the company, raise unrealistic expectations among the workforce about the size of any redundancy package or misrepresent the number of people who might be faced with compulsory redundancy. From a managerial perspective, the critical objective is to achieve as early as possible acceptance, however grudging, of the principle of closure and focus then on the way in which the closure will be carried out.

Careful consideration should be given to when the initial announcement is made and the way in which this is carried out. It is also important to consider who should be the person to make the announcement to the workforce. Announcing a closure is very daunting and not without risks of creating antagonism and conflict. Ideally, the person standing at the front of the workforce needs to be sufficiently senior be able to shoulder the responsibility and take questions, without making commitments beyond the intention to consult. On the other hand, it is better to have someone as close to the workforce as possible to provide reassurance to those who may be affected. In the case of Standard Tools, while US leaders offered to read out announcements, it was felt that this would be unnecessarily inflammatory and the decision was made that the plant manager of the central site should take personal responsibility.

## Press release

If the press picks up on a good story then it will report it and an organization can do little to prevent this. All that an organization can hope to do is to give factually correct information to ensure that what is written in the press is representative of the company's viewpoint. If incorrect information is reported, while court action can be taken to sue the newspaper responsible, this will usually only make the organization look worse and generate negative publicity, as well as incurring significant legal costs. It can also become a distraction to management. Perhaps the best course of action is to prepare a brief press release that is either sent 'proactively' to local newspapers or held as a 'reactive' statement, for release in the event of enquiries.

Public relations (PR) agencies can handle media interest on behalf of the company and this can help it to focus its own attention on managing internal processes, rather than getting embroiled with answering questions from the media. This is often represented in the media as: 'A spokesperson for the company said . . .'. It may also be helpful to nominate one person to deal with queries from outside.

**STUDENT ACTIVITY 15.3**

1. Prepare a written announcement outlining the company's proposals to close the central Northton factory. This would be read out by the factory manager to the workforce as part of the initial announcement of the closure and then distributed to all employees. The document should not exceed 300 words. This might seem to be a relatively simple task but based on the experience of the authors, it is much more challenging and requires careful thought about what is said and the inferences that might be drawn by those the announcement is directed to.
2. Prepare a press release to be sent to local and regional newspapers, with title, presenting the company case for the closure and reorganization. Think of the press release as the actual article that would be published. It should not exceed 250 words.

In completing both of these tasks, give particular regard to the different audiences that each will be communicating to and the objectives associated with each of the two documents.





# The Consultation Process

There is a legal responsibility to consult at the earliest opportunity with individuals affected and, if appropriate, their representatives (ACAS, 2010). There must also be a proposal against which to consult, however, and pulling together these proposals takes time. Herein lies the first dilemma, because there is a degree of contradiction between these requirements. At what point should consultation start for it to be fair and meaningful? Legally, this should be as soon as the possibility of closure is a serious possibility, but in reality, this can only be once the company is prepared and ready to initiate the process. Confidentiality and the careful management of information are of the utmost importance during this early period, prior to the full proposal being formulated.

Employees and their representatives are entitled to receive sufficient information about the management's proposals to be able to take a useful and constructive role in the process of consultation. In law, the purpose of consultation is to try to avoid redundancies or dismissals, or, if this cannot be achieved, to reduce the number of dismissals involved and to mitigate the effects of any dismissals. Consultations need, therefore, to be seen to be genuine and must be undertaken with a view to reaching agreement with the employees' representatives. The expectation is that management and employees, together with representatives, will work to try to find common solutions (Lewis and Sargeant, 2007).

Management teams engaged in reorganizations of the kind in which Standard Tools is involved, are only likely to change their plans fundamentally in exceptional circumstances. This means that, while the details over the number of redundancies and the terms under which these are announced might change as a result of the consultation process, the principal decision itself is unlikely to be rescinded. This is because it is difficult to see how representatives and individuals can put forward alternatives that can deliver the objectives that managers are seeking to achieve. In reality, the process of consultation predominantly serves the purpose of mitigating the consequences, rather than of providing any worthwhile challenge to the strategy—although representatives often feel that this is their role in earlier stages of consultation.

Following on from the previous point, consultation needs to be expressed in terms of responding to a proposal and not to a plan, and herein lies the second dilemma. From a managerial perspective, consultation cannot commence until there is sufficient clarity over management's intentions that it can present at least an outline of what it intends to do. To avoid the criticism of not engaging in meaningful consultation, however, management cannot be seen to be submitting a complete plan. It is difficult to demonstrate that consultation is meaningful unless something has changed as a result of it having taken place. While it is essential for managers to have a plan, it can only be presented as a draft that is sufficiently flexible to allow for meaningful consultation to take place.

**STUDENT ACTIVITY 15.4**

**Devise a detailed communication and consultation strategy, covering the period from the point at which the first announcement is made to the closure of the factory. This task is more strategic than operational and requires groups to think much more deeply than they might otherwise do to develop a strategy. This means agreeing on strategic objectives and then working out what actions need to be taken to achieve them. An interesting way of completing this task is to use no more than three, and it can even be one, PowerPoint slides to capture the essence of the strategy, but don't make the mistake of presenting lots of information—the objective is to communicate to the audience your overall approach and strategy not detail.**

# Collective Redundancy



According to ACAS (www.acas.org.gov), a collective redundancy situation arises if an employer proposes to dismiss as redundant twenty or more employees at one establishment within a ninety-day period. Such a situation might occur if a business or plant closes down, or if an employer no longer needs as many employees to carry out a particular task. It might also occur if dismissals are to take place in a reorganization or reallocation of work. This latter case applies to the situation in which Standard Tools finds itself. Redundancies can also exist if there are job losses in one section, but, because of new recruitment in a different section with different skill requirements, there is no overall reduction in the number of people employed.

If these conditions are met, an employer is required to consult in advance with representatives of the affected employees and to notify the projected redundancies to the Department of Business, Innovation, and Skills. Consultation must be completed before any notices of dismissal are issued to employees. Employees, or their representatives, may bring a complaint to an employment tribunal if they feel that an employer has failed to comply with these requirements. Any complaint must normally be brought within three months of the last of the dismissals.

The obligation to consult may apply even when an employer intends to offer alternative employment on different terms and conditions to some, or all, of the employees, with the result that the number actually dismissed is less than twenty. This will be the case if employees are to be redeployed on such different terms and conditions that accepting the new posts amounts to dismissal and re-engagement.

The obligations apply particularly to situations in which compulsory redundancies are likely, but may, in some circumstances, also apply to 'voluntary' redundancies if an employee has no real choice about whether to stay or to leave. If, in the case of Standard Tools, management believes that twenty or more redundancies may result from the intended changes, but is not sure whether there will be sufficient volunteers for redundancy or whether some of the redundancies can be avoided, the obligation to consult employees and to notify the Department of Trade and Industry still applies.

The management at Standard Tools would not be under any specific legal obligation to consult employee representatives or notify the Department if they were to believe that less than twenty employees would need to be made redundant. They would, however, be at risk of successful unfair dismissal claims if they were to fail to warn and consult individual employees who might be dismissed, fail to apply dispute resolution procedures if required, and fail to adopt a fair basis for selection or to take reasonable steps to redeploy such employees.

The Information and Consultation of Employees Regulations 2004 (ICE), introduced in April 2005, apply to organizations with fifty or more employees (with effect from April 2008). The Regulations give employees the right to:

- be informed about the organization's economic situation;
- be informed and consulted about its future employment prospects;
- be informed and consulted about any decisions it might contemplate making that could lead to significant changes in the way in which work is undertaken, changes in contractual issues, and to redundancies and transfers.

**STUDENT ACTIVITY 15.5**

**Identify and discuss all of the legal implications of the closure and transfer of staff to Bramham, and those arising from any possible redundancies. This task requires students to think carefully about the rights employees have and the duties and responsibilities of the management. But students need to avoid seeing this task as simply one that involves establishing 'what the law says'. Remember, HR often is faced with dilemmas and being pulled in different directions. In this case the senior management expect problems to be overcome and the timetable of the closure and transfers met; on the other hand UK law has to be adhered to. Can both demands be met? If so, how?**

# Managing and Selecting for Redundancy

The majority of HR professionals will, at some stage in their careers, be involved in managing job losses. At the time of writing some 600,000 public sector jobs are planned to be cut, although whether the same number of people lose their jobs is more uncertain and depends on the strategy adopted for managing the job losses. A reduction in the number of jobs does not necessarily mean that the jobholders will have to be made redundant, although this can be the case depending on the numbers involved and the time scale over which the job losses have to be achieved.

Whenever a closure or reorganization announcement is made, the employees directly affected, as well as those whose jobs may be preserved, are likely to experience a range of emotional reactions. According to the CIPD (2007):

> **Redundancy is one of the most traumatic events an employee may experience. Announcement of redundancies will invariably have an adverse impact on morale, motivation and productivity, but the negative effects can be reduced by sensitive handling of redundant employees and those remaining.**

This is the general view on the effects of redundancy on employees, but it fails to reflect the complex and changing reactions that employees go through when faced with the enforced loss of their jobs. To help them to develop the 'right' strategies, HR professionals need to understand the following matters.

- Not all employees will react in the same way, although, initially, all are likely to feel the negative effects identified by the CIPD. The loss of one's job can be perceived as a direct threat to one's self-esteem, self-identity, and standard of living, but while this might be an initial reaction, it is unlikely to be a permanent one for all of those affected.
- Different employees will be in different situations regarding age, length of service, and employability. Those who are relatively young, with limited service and marketable skills, are likely to take control over their own destiny and seek employment elsewhere at an early stage. Those coming towards the

end of their working lives and with many years' service are in a different position. They may well come to view the prospect of redundancy in a more positive light, as they contemplate the attractiveness of what might be a generous, tax-free redundancy payment.

- Employees are unlikely to remain passive in the face of management attempts to keep control of the situation. Even those not affected by the threat of redundancy may well decide that they no longer wish to remain with a company whose future seems unsure and leave. Retaining important employees can often run in parallel with making others redundant!
- Future recruitment requirements can be made more difficult to achieve as a result of the publicity over the closure and uncertainty over the long-term future of the company.

While the experience of redundancies is likely to involve negative emotions, these will vary between people, with many employees moving from one emotional state to another as the situation evolves and as individual positions become clearer. Critically, from a company perspective, these negative emotions and reactions need to be managed, as far as possible, to ensure that they do not undermine the economic well being of the company or its ability to continue to meet customer requirements during the transitional period.

## The key stages of the redundancy process

Most redundancy situations share common features, although all are unique. As was pointed out earlier, a reduction in jobs does not necessarily mean that the same number of employees will have their employment terminated. Some will decide to leave, over time; natural wastage will reduce the number as employees leave who do not need to be replaced; casual or agency staff can bear the brunt of job losses; internal transfers may be possible. Much depends on the timescale of the planned changes and the extent to which management has the ability to reduce the labour force without having to make employees redundant. If a complete closure of a facility is planned, however, it is likely that either voluntary and/or compulsory redundancies will be experienced. Decisions on redundancies need to be based on:



- planning and scoping the numbers likely to be involved;
- agreeing on the financial terms and level of redundancy payments, including statutory rights;
- inviting employees to volunteer for redundancy;
- agreeing on the use of objective selection criteria and the way in which these will be applied;
- identifying and notifying those selected for redundancy;
- creating opportunity for appeals;
- allowing opportunity to seek alternative employment;
- calculating redundancy payment;
- helping redundant employees obtain training or alternative work.

## Selecting for redundancy

Arguably, the task of reaching agreement on the choice and application of criteria for selecting employees for redundancy represents the most challenging part of the whole process. Whatever the choice of criteria, they must be objectively fair and consistently applied. If they are not, then the whole process can be compromised, with the possibility of delays in completing the project (Bradley, 2010).

Selection criteria should also be reasonably applied in the light of individual circumstances. The Disability Discrimination Act 1995, extended by the Discrimination Act of 2005 (from 1 October 2010, the majority of the Equality Act 2010 will have been implemented and will have replaced major parts of the provisions of the Disability Discrimination Act) makes it unlawful for an employer to treat a disabled person less favourably because of a reason relating to their disability that cannot be justified. Reasonable adjustments to working conditions or the workplace, if that would help to accommodate a particular disabled person, may need to be considered. Care also needs to be taken to ensure that the criteria are neither directly nor indirectly discriminatory on grounds of sex, marital status, race, disability, sexual orientation, religion or belief, or age.

Signpost to Chapter 7: Equality and Diversity in Employment

As a result of the Employment Equality (Age) Regulations 2006, which came into force on 1st December 2006, employers now need to take even more care to ensure that their choice of objective criteria for redundancy selection is non-discriminatory. The use of 'last in, first out' (LIFO), one of the more commonly used selection methods in the 1970s and 1980s, was effectively made unlawful in most cases due to the relative advantage it gives to older workers.

**STUDENT ACTIVITY 15.6**

Devise a strategy for handling redundancies at Standard Tools and specifically develop a mechanism for selecting employees for redundancy. This task is about developing a coherent strategy and then designing a mechanism for choosing people for redundancy, either voluntary or compulsory, in a way that reflects legal requirements and employee rights/interests and those of the business.

See the Online Resource Centre for an example of a selection matrix that can be used to help to select employees for redundancy.

# Managing the Transfer of Employees from the Old to the New Location

In addition to managing the factory closure and redundancies, Standard Tools' HR team also has to ensure, together with other members of the project team, that the company experiences minimum disruption to its production targets, despite the many changes associated with the closure. Critical to achieving this is the retention and transfer of designated staff from the Northton to the Bramham site. The company may know what it wants, but it still has to develop practices that ensure that the employees involved become committed to their transfer and trial periods, if these are involved. The following is an account of how this was achieved.

The ninety-day consultation period with the company over the closure of the old factory ended on 2 June 2011. After this date, the company began to serve notice on employees who wished to transfer to the new site and made redundant those employees who had been selected for compulsory redundancy (in addition to those volunteers who had already been released earlier at their own request). Employees transferring to the new site were entitled to a week's notice for every year of service, up to a maximum of twelve weeks, before they transferred.

Because many of those involved in the move had asked that the situation be resolved as quickly as possible and because of the financial benefits that the company would enjoy if people moved earlier, the decision was taken to try to expedite the transfer process. To achieve this, it was decided that, if employees were willing to move early on a date set by the company (which would be no earlier than 29 April and, in most cases, would be in July), the company was prepared to offer the following options:

- £100 per employee payable on the date on which they started working at the new site; free transport for twelve months by bus from, and to, the old site if they worked on the day shift; transport from, and to, the old site at a subsidized cost of £12.50 per week for a further six months. Employees would have to commit to this for at least twelve months; or

- £300 per employee payable on the date on which they started working at the new site; subsidized transport for eighteen months by bus at a cost of £12.50 per week for those ten employees at the old site who had already stated that they wished to transfer, but had no other means of transport to the new site than the company bus. These employees would have to commit to this for at least twelve months; or
- £350 per employee—other than those in engineering, who would get £200 each—payable on the date on which they started working at the new site.

The company also agreed that, if the above were to be accepted, they would extend the trial period to eight weeks (from the statutory four weeks) and gave assurances that, should any employee in the seventh week of their trial period declare a genuine reason why their position at the new site were not suitable, they would be granted redundancy within a further three months of the end of the trial period. This request for redundancy could only then be rescinded at the company's discretion due to recruitment commitments that might subsequently be made. The union supported the company's concern that finding other employment would not count as a genuine reason.

The above is another example of the kinds of creative solution with which the HR team needed to come up to ensure that the project went according to plan and that key workers were not lost to the company.

The final student activity involves looking forward to the six-month period after the closure of the Northton site and the implementation of the planned changes for Bramham.

**STUDENT ACTIVITY 15.7**

Consider all of the other HR issues and requirements that need to be managed during the post-closure phase of the project.

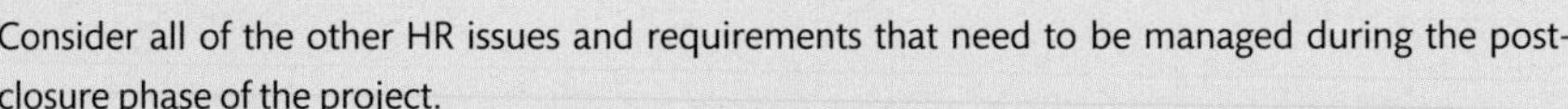

It is important to recognize that the work of HR continues after the formal completion of the project and this task provides an opportunity of 'seeing' what needs to be done in the post-completion phase. We suggest that this task is based on power-point slides or on flip chart paper. The exercise is much more creative if symbols, images. Pictures etc. are used and words kept to a minimum.



# Summary

Handling the closure of a business is a complex challenge facing both line managers and HR. This complexity is often further complicated if another part of the business is to remain operational and if it is necessary to transfer employees from one area of the business to another. The process required is time-consuming and the overriding issue of impending redundancies can affect other HR activity that occurs during this time.

Legal requirements must be met if the business is to avoid the potential of excessive costs of unfair dismissal and other legal claims that may arise as a result of poorly managed redundancies. The legally required consultation process can be an effective framework to help maintain morale and productivity through constructive two-way dialogue with those whose jobs are at risk.

Those who are not made redundant can also be adversely affected either by facing a period of personal uncertainty and evaluation or by working in close proximity to those affected. Businesses need to consider carefully what can be done to support these people to ensure that they remain motivated and feel secure following redundancies elsewhere. Retaining 'survivors' can be critical to future success, and their retention can be encouraged by ensuring a fair and flexible approach is taken from the beginning, and by comprehensively communicating accurate and timely information, and by acting upon feedback throughout the process.

**Visit the Online Resource Centre that accompanies this book for self-test questions, weblinks, and more information on the topics covered in this chapter. www.oxfordtextbooks.co.uk/orc/banfield_kay2e/**

## CASE STUDIES

The final part of this chapter offers students the opportunity to deal with four situations that emerged during the transfer of staff from Northton to Bramham. In these four mini case studies, don't try to guess what the HR team actually did to resolve the situations, but use your own knowledge and judgement to produce 'the best possible solutions'.

### The team leader

A team leader in one of the redundant team leader positions makes the decision to transfer to the new plant in a non-managerial position, on a job with which he is not familiar and in a different department. He has also worked in a supervisory position at Standard Tools.

During his first few weeks, he learns the job quickly but expresses concern to the HR department that he is finding it extremely difficult to adjust to being in a non-supervisory role. He is reluctant to share his feelings with his new supervisor because they used to be colleagues previously and he does not want to appear to be either uncooperative or awkward. At the end of his trial period, he decides to stay and take advantage of the generous red circling arrangements in place. (Essentially, this is an agreement that his old salary will be preserved.) One week later, he approaches the HR department again requesting redundancy. There has been an incident between him and his new supervisor, who has accused him of wandering off the job without permission and who has told him he is not happy with his performance, and he regards this as being the last straw. He does not have a job to go to and is really unhappy about his situation.



#### Questions

1. What is the legal position with regards to the company's obligation to consider this request?
2. What options might be open to the company and the supervisor, and what are the pros and cons associated with each option?
3. What actions should the HR team recommend to best resolve the present situation?

### The warehouse operative

A warehouse operative, whose position is redundant, has requested to be released early and be made redundant before the company had planned to lose his position, because he has another job to go to. He requests to be released at least three weeks prior to the date on which his work ceases. He was to be required to stay beyond the actual date in which manufacturing ceased, to help count stock and ship out remaining stock, and to help to clear the other items on site, such as furniture files and obsolete machinery. He is 59 years old and extremely concerned about his ability to get another job if he is not released.

#### Questions

1. What is the legal and ethical position of the company, given this request?
2. What options are open to the company, given this request, and what pros and cons are associated with each course of action?
3. What steps might the company consider to resolve the situation?

### The key manager who drives

A key manager in the business has requested voluntary redundancy because she does not want to transfer to the new site. She has stated that her childcare arrangements rely on her being able to get to and from work within fifteen minutes. Although she drives and earns a reasonable salary, and can afford the extra cost of transport, she does not wish to alter her existing childcare arrangements. She has critical plant and process knowledge, and the company believes that losing her at the time of transfer of production would be extremely detrimental to the ongoing efficiency of the Bramham factory.

**Questions**

1. What options might the company consider to encourage the manager to transfer to the new plan?
2. Is there any legal argument that might be used to refuse to grant the manager's request for voluntary redundancy?
3. What might the implications be of refusing the request?
4. What options might be available to reach a compromise in this situation?

### The key manager who cycles

Another key manager who lives very close to the site that is closing currently cycles to and from work. His responsibilities cover both plants and, because he can drive, he has begun to use a pool car to get from the old site to the new site to cover these duties. He is not, however, willing to buy a car or to pay the tax on a company vehicle that he would be obliged to pay if he were to be allocated a car in which to travel to the new plant.

**Questions**

1. What options might the company consider, and which would you consider to be 'the best' and why?
2. What implications would the decision have, taking into account the preferred way of dealing with this situation and other people at different levels whose jobs are to be transferred and who do not have *any* means of transport to get to and from the new site?

## REFERENCES

Advisory Conciliation and Arbitration Service (2010) 'Redundancy Handling', www.acas.org.uk.

Bee, F. and Bee, R. (1997) *Project Management*, CIPD.

Bradley, H. (2010) 'Guide to Assessment—how to use assessment for redundancy', *People Management*, 14 October.

Chartered Institute of Personnel and Development (2007) 'Redundancy factsheet', www.cipd.co.uk.

Dix, G. and Oxenbridge, S. (2003) *Information and Challenges at Work: From Challenges to Good Practice*, www.acas.org.uk.

Lewis, D. and Sargeant, M. (2007) *Essentials of Employment Law*, 9th ed. CIPD.

Tuckman, B.W. and Jensen, M.A.C. (1977) 'Stages of small group development revisited', *Group and Organizational Studies*, **2**:4, pp. 419–27.

# Glossary

**Accident** An unplanned event that causes, or may have caused, injury or harm to people, equipment, or property.

**Assessment** The tools and techniques used by an organization to identify and measure, either qualitatively or quantitatively, the skills, knowledge and potential of applicants.

**Assessment centre** A collection of activities designed to assess the suitability of a number of candidates for a job. The assessment typically involves several assessors evaluating the performance of a number of candidates in a series of exercises and tests. Candidates are normally presented with individual or group-based exercises and tests which can extend to two or three days, the results of which determine whether the candidate progresses to the next stage in the selection process or is considered not to be suitable for the specific job in question or for employment by the organization. (CIPD 2010)

**Assessment criteria** Predetermined qualities involving both skill and knowledge against which candidates are scored in a particular assessment activity to assess their suitability and potential for success in a job. The basis of assessment criteria is that the higher the score the stronger the likelihood that a candidate will perform well in the job role. Scoring against assessment criteria can be done subjectively by the assessing team or against pre-determined performance standards. The choice of standards, whether subjective or objective will clearly affect the ease or difficulty applicants will experience in meeting the standards in use.

**Balanced scorecard** A specific model for measuring business outcomes, devised by management theorists Kaplan and Norton, that allows managers to balance the financial perspective with those of the customer, internal processes, and innovation and learning. The model has been adapted and applied for use within the HR function.

**Benefit** Normally contractually agreed 'additions' to the wage or salary, provided by an employer as part of the overall employment package.

**Best practice** This terms implies that in carrying out HR activities there is 'one best way' of doing things, irrespective of the context or circumstances.

**Best fit** This approach decides what should be done and how it should be done based on the unique circumstances that characterize every organization. It links action to specific requirements rather than following an established approach.

**Blended learning** This technique uses several different but complementary learning methods, which, when used together, are considered to be more effective at generating the required learning outcomes than one single method.

**Bonus** An additional, but variable, payment associated with individual, group or organizational performance.

**Bradford absence index** This technique calculates the impact on business of an individual's absence pattern based on the frequency and number of days lost.

**Bullying** The abuse of power, or of physical or mental strength, by someone in a position of authority towards a person (or group of people), resulting in harmful stress and undermined self-confidence.

**Coaching** A process in which a 'coach' supports an individual to develop his or her skills through a series of structured conversations by exploring the nature of challenges faced at work and helping the individual to identify the best approaches to those challenges to achieve the desired outcomes.

**Collective agreement** A written statement defining the arrangements agreed between a union and employer, and the terms that will apply. Such agreements are only legally enforceable if this is expressly stated or if the collective agreement is referred to in individual written terms and conditions of employment.

**Collective bargaining** The process of negotiation between trade union representatives and employers, or employer representatives, to establish by agreement the terms and conditions of employment of a group of employees.

**Collective redundancy** This arises when an organization intends to dismiss, because of redundancy, twenty or more employees at one establishment within a ninety-day period. In such cases, dismissal is not related to individual performance or behaviour, but is for business reasons, such as plant closure, reorganization, or reallocation of work.

**Competence** The combination of skills, knowledge and experience that results in a person's ability to carry out specific tasks and procedures to a required standard. Can be equated to 'know-how' (Gladstone, 2000). A specific competency can also be understood as an underlying characteristic of a person, i.e. a trait, a belief, an ability or an attitude, that distinguishes one person from another and explains differences in job performance (Rothwell, 2004).

**Competency profiles/framework** These are statements of what people need to be able to do in order to perform their job to the required standard.

**Consultation** A process that can be individual and collective, and involves managers and employees, or their representatives, jointly examining and talking about issues of mutual concern. There is also an expectation that the discussions will seek to produce jointly acceptable solutions through a genuine exchange of views and ideas (Dix and Oxenbridge, 2003).

**Contributory negligence** If an injury is partly due to lack of reasonable care on behalf of the individual bringing about the claim, then the damages received may be reduced due to the claimant's own contribution towards the incident.

**Development** A term often used to describe changes in the whole person and what that person is, as well as what they can do. It reflects the belief that all people have the potential to be more and do more, and that this potential needs to be developed as well as utilized. People can develop to a limited degree through training, but development implies the employment of a much wider range of learning experiences and methods, such as coaching and mentoring, not all of which are necessarily connected to the working environment (cf Learning; Training).

**Dialectic** The tension that arises between conflicting ideas, interacting forces or competing interests. The term can also be used to explain the process of reconciling opposing opinions or facts by means of argument and discussion.

**Discipline** The formal measures taken, sanctions applied and outcomes achieved by management in response to perceived acts of misconduct.

**Discrimination** Treating a person or group of people less favourably compared to another person or group of people.

**Diversity** A multifaceted approach to the management of employees, reflecting the changing social and demographic characteristics of the workforce. The approach reflects the belief that maximizing the potential and contribution of all organizational stakeholders is inextricably linked to recognizing and valuing difference, and to treating people with respect.

**Due diligence** Written documentary evidence that all reasonably practicable steps have been taken to ensure the health and safety of an individual or group of individuals.

**Equal opportunity** The process of ensuring that employment practices in an organization are fair and unbiased, and do not breach any of the legislative provisions that are in place to protect workers from unlawful discrimination.

**Ethnocentric** A way of looking at the world primarily from the perspective of one's own culture and experience, which are perceived as being superior or more important than those of others (cf Polycentric).

**Expatriate worker** An employee deployed overseas, usually sourced from his or her country of origin.

**External recruitment** The process of identifying and attracting potential employees to an organization to fill current or future vacancies (cf Internal recruitment).

**Global organization** An organization that employs a workforce in different countries throughout the world, with a view to maximizing performance by sourcing or providing goods and/or services in a globally based market, and in which decisions are driven by markets rather than by geography.

**Grievance** The formalization of a claim that one or more persons, either co-workers or management, have acted wrongly towards another person(s) and, as a consequence, inflicted physical or psychological harm on that person, or others. This may involve an act, or acts, of misconduct.

**Harassment** Any unwelcome attention or behaviour from another that a person finds offensive or unacceptable and which results in the person feeling offended, uncomfortable or threatened, and leads to a loss of dignity or self-worth. Anything that has the potential to cause harm or injury to people, equipment or property.

**Hiring or employing** The overall process of taking on new staff from outside the organization.

**Human Capital** What people are capable of doing, based on the skills and knowledge they posses which is 'owned' by the individual but can grow and increase in value through personal and professional development.

**Human Resource Development** This term came into usage in the late 1980s and early 1990s, and is used by many writers, but fewer practitioners, in preference to training. Its relationship to training is similar to that between Human Resource Management and Personnel Management, in that it represents a more holistic and strategic approach to learning than does training (Walton, 1999; cf Training).

**Human Resource Management (HRM)** A more recent approach to the management of employees, which sees people as a key organizational resource that needs to be developed and utilized to support the organization's operational and strategic objectives (cf Personnel Management).

**Human Resource Planning (HRP)** Originally known as 'manpower planning', this is concerned with planning and controlling the quantity and quality of labour available to an organization.

**Human Resources (HR)** An alternative to 'people' and also the name used by many organizations to describe the specialized department that deals with the administration and management of employees (cf Human Resource Management; Personnel Management).

**Incentive** The prospect or promise of a reward that is conditional upon an agreed outcome being achieved.

**Induction** This needs to be understood as a multistaged process rather than as a single, course-based event. It represents the introduction of new employees into the organization, into the department in which they work and into the job they have to do, although it can also relate to the transfer and promotion of existing employees. It should introduce the employee to the social environment, the technical aspects of work, and the rules and procedures of employment.

**Integration** A preferred relationship between different parts of an organization and 'the whole' and between different functional strategies and the corporate strategy.

**Internal recruitment** The process of identifying current employees who may be suitable for newly created vacancies or for replacing staff who leave (cf External recruitment).

**Learning** A fundamental and natural human process involving growth and change. Learning is about behavioural modification. It cannot be seen, but is inferred from differences in what we know, believe and can do. Learning is the way in which we can improve and be different from that which we were. Learning needs to be understood as both a process and an outcome (cf Training; Development).

**Mediation** A voluntary process where an independent facilitator assists two or more parties to explore options for resolving a dispute, disagreement, or problem situation by attempting to reach a mutually acceptable agreement.

**Mentoring** The development of a relationship between a much more senior person in an organization and more junior person, often as part of a development programme, involving the experienced person using his or her greater knowledge and expertise to accelerate the junior colleague's development.

**Metrics** Relates to what and how something is measured. HR metrics focus on key aspects of the labour force, its behaviours, and its costs and contributions. The use of measures is increasingly associated with important features of the HR function, as part of the process of evaluating its efficiency and effectiveness.

**Misconduct** Behaviour that transgresses contractual arrangements, work rules, established norms of performance or other standards that can be seen as reasonable and necessary for the effective employment and management of people at work; behaviour that is deemed to be unacceptable by reference to formally established norms.

**MNCs** Multinational companies that have a national base, but which operate and trade multinationally.

**National Cultures** A complex system of norms, social values and behaviours, expectations and legal frameworks that gives an identity to a particular country.

**Opportunity cost** This is the cost associated with not choosing to pursue one course of action in favour of another. This is a difficult calculation but is nevertheless an important consideration when deciding which course of action to take.

**Organizational capability** This refers to an organization's ability to create, mobilize and utilize its key resources to maximum effect. The concept is important because it helps to redefine what HR represents; it is seen less as a series of activities and responsibilities, and more in terms of a resource and capability builder.

**Organizational structure** This relates to aspects of the formal organization, particularly the roles and responsibilities that people have, the hierarchy and reporting lines, the different departments and sections within the organization and how they are connected, formal communication channels and the way in which power and authority are distributed. Organizational structure is analogous to the human skeleton or the framework of a new building: it is what gives the organization shape and influences how it operates.

**Pay** Regular and contractually agreed monetary rewards, usually linked to position or job and paid as a wage or salary.

**Performance** Can be interpreted as expressing the relationship between a person's capabilities and what the person actually achieves, usually related to a person's job.

**Performance appraisal** A process for reviewing the past performance of an employee, and agreeing future objectives and development activities. It can be seen as '*the process of evaluating and judging the way in which someone is functioning*', (Coens and Jenkins, 2000).

**Performance management** '*. . . , A broad term that has come to stand for the set of practices through which work is defined and reviewed, capabilities are developed, and rewards are distributed*', (Morhman and Morhman, 1995).

'*A strategic and integrated approach to delivering sustained success to organizations by improving the performance of the people who work in them and by developing the capabilities of team and individual contributions*', (Armstrong and Baron, 1998).

**Personnel Management** The name given to the specialized management function responsible for an organization's employees (cf Human Resource Management).

**Philosophy** An enduring framework of beliefs, values, and ways of doing things that can exist at the individual and organizational levels. A shared philosophy is a powerful way of creating a common purpose and set of expectations as to how people behave.

**Planning** Can be understood as a set of techniques, an approach and a mindset, all of which relate to achieving specified objectives. It should be understood as a process, rather than a time-constrained event.

**Polycentric** A way of looking at the world that recognizes and accepts difference, and the legitimacy of different values and systems (cf Ethnocentric).

**Productive capacity/potential** Productive capacity expresses what employees can currently do and thus conveys their current value to the organization. Productive potential on the other hand represents employees' future value and contribution based on future learning and development.

**Psychological contract** The obligations that an employer and an employee, or group of employees, perceive to exist between each other as part of the employment relationship, comprising both expectations of each other and promises made to each other.

**Reliability** A test with a high level of reliability means that candidates who repeat the test consistently gain similar scores. It is important assessment tests and exercises have a high level of reliability.

**Rewards** Can be both material and symbolic in form, and are outcomes of the employment and psychological contracts.

**Reward system** All of the practices, procedures and methods of rewarding employees either in use by, or potentially available to, management.

**Risk** The likelihood that harm or injury will occur.

**Selection** The process, culminating in the decision to offer employment or fill a vacancy from internal or external applicants, used by the organization to choose the most suitable candidate from a pool of applicants.

**Selection criteria** The overall skills knowledge and abilities that are either essential or desirable from candidates in order for them to be successful in their role against which selection decisions are made. These may include qualifications or specific experience as well as broader skills and abilities. Usually a minimum standard is required against specific selection criteria to be successful. This term is a much broader term than assessment criteria and could include criteria that are used to screen applicants to go forward for further assessment such as minimum qualifications and experience. The application of the selection criteria at the point of the whole process where a final decision is made on which candidate, if any, is offered the job/ position can be based on an aggregate numerical score which reflects how well candidates have met specific selection criteria or through a discussion amongst the panel of selectors, or both. At this point, additional selection criteria may come into play, consciously or subconsciously where the decision-makers attempt to ensure the 'right' applicant is selected.

**Strategy** A way of doing things that is intended to produce required outcomes and results.

**Strategic** A particular mindset and approach defined by a more integrated and holistic view of the world of business and management.

**Trade union** An organization that is independent of an employer and funded by member contributions, the function of which is to represent worker interests in relations between workers and employers.

**Training** Can best be understood as planned, structured and often formalized learning experiences that seek to develop specific skills and knowledge needed for effective job performance. Historically, employees have learnt many of the competences they need to perform effectively by being trained (cf Learning; Development).

**Validity** It is important that any test or assessment used in selection has a high degree of validity. If the scores obtained by a sample group of job holders in a test correlate highly with job performance the test has a high degree of validity and can be regarded as effective in predicting job performance.

**Vicarious liability** An employer can be liable for the acts of an employee towards another. This can arise if there is an employment relationship and if the employee commits a civil wrong during the course of their employment.

# Index

## A

## B

K

## N



## O



## P

## Q



## R

Z